The Applied Psychology of Work Behavior

A Book of Readings

The Applied Psychology of Work Behavior

A Book of Readings

Dennis W. Organ
Indiana University

1987   Third Edition

BUSINESS PUBLICATIONS, INC.
Plano, Texas   75075

© BUSINESS PUBLICATIONS, INC., 1978, 1983, and 1987

ISBN 0-256-03431-1

Library of Congress Catalog Card No. 86-72246

Printed in the United States of America

1 2 3 4 5 6 7 8 9 0 ML 4 3 2 1 0 9 8 7

Preface

I wish I could honestly say that I started out with a well-defined notion of exactly what I wanted this third edition to look like. Unfortunately, the revision of a book of readings never seems to work quite that way. One begins with a portion (usually about half or a little more) of the older pieces that one simply can't bear to part with. One then goes hunting—through what one has recently read, through several years of respected journals and periodicals, through the bibliographic indexes of admired books. Up to the very last minute, it seems, one is deleting something that "just doesn't fit" and returning to the hunt.

Nonetheless, out of this messy, inefficient, seemingly aimless process there does emerge, even if retrospectively, some kind of logic and pattern to what was evolving. Looking at the decisions of inclusion and omission that I have made for this volume, I think I can see something of the drift of my thinking and teaching over the last four years. This edition includes more selections that cross over into what some would call the human resources area—and that certainly coincides with my growing conviction that basic courses in organizational behavior/organizational psychology should provide exposure to such logically related institutional matters as compensation systems and performance appraisal. This version also reflects the influence that recent "management best-sellers" have had on the development of our discipline, with reference to corporate cultures, quality circles, managing in high-tech industries, and the postrecession shakeout of "lean and mean" structures managed in a no-nonsense fashion.

Yet I hope I have retained a hard core of selections that articulate the essential conceptual framework of organizational behavior. It is that conceptual core that provides the continuity and coherence of our discipline, a body of work that will have sustained value regardless of the fads and fashions that come and go. The really important issues in the management of people at work are long-standing, if not eternal. That such issues appear in ever-changing forms and expressions renders them all the more interesting. Thus I have sought to provide a set of materials that takes contemporary themes into account, while placing them in a durable context of theory and perspective.

Again in this edition, I express unrestrained gratitude to the authors who have allowed me to use their works and to colleagues at Indiana University and elsewhere who have alerted me to useful sources I would have otherwise overlooked.

Dennis W. Organ

Contents

* New selection.

section one

Organizational Behavior: Scope and Method

Introduction

In the beginning, there was Management. Those who reflected upon organizational phenomena were bound, however loosely, by one discipline or quasi discipline which could be identified as the study of administration or management. Anyone who sought to design a task more efficiently, to motivate employees to perform more effectively, to clarify lines of authority, or to propose ethical standards for organizations belonged to this quasi discipline.

The loose bonds of this quasi discipline endured through most of the first half of this century. Since then, most of the substantive areas within management have been largely "appropriated" by disciplines outside of management. Economics, mathematics, psychology, sociology, political science, anthropology, and law, to name a few, have staked the claim of their particular expertise upon topics formerly thought to be the exclusive domain of management. Instead of one discipline, we now have several, including organizational behavior, organization theory, operations research, personnel, and administrative (or business) policy. Management, as a discipline, is not so much a distinctive, ongoing enterprise as it is now simply a holding company.[1]

The first selection in this book should help the reader to understand how organizational behavior stands in relation to the larger sphere of what was once management. The article by Organ notes some of the historically significant events that served as catalysts to accelerate the process by which organizational behavior became a

---

[1] For a more complete account of the fractionation of management as a discipline, see Charles Perrow, "The Short and Glorious History of Organizational Theory," *Organizational Dynamics,* Summer 1973, pp. 2–15.

distinctive discipline. A specially prepared "update" notes some of the developments in this discipline within the last decade.

As other disciplines have preempted the concerns of management, they have generally sought to impose upon these concerns the philosophy and methods of science. Armchair theorizing from the basis of informal personal observation gave way to the experiment, the survey, the simulation, the mathematical model, multivariate statistical analysis, and life under the rule of the .05 level of significance. Recently, some within our profession have expressed doubts about the value of an unqualified adherence to the natural science model of studying organizational behavior; they fear that a narrowly construed definition of legitimate approaches will constrain us from addressing the more timely and relevant phenomena in organizations. Behling provides a succinct statement of the essential tenets of a natural science approach, addresses the criticisms and the purported limitations of this approach, and states the case for why the scientific method should nonetheless guide our efforts. The article by Scott provides a more detailed description of how rigorous methods of research bear upon the pursuit of knowledge about behavior in organizations. Lawler, in the selection concluding this part of the book, addresses the question of how we can generate knowledge about organizational behavior that is valid but also useful.

The reader will probably, and rightfully, conclude from the selections in Section One that organizational behavior as a discipline reflects an ongoing state of *tension*. This tension emanates from many different sources: the tension between description versus prescription; between rigor and relevance; between objectivity and humanism; between the status quo and change. Inevitably, this tension means that unanimity is the exception rather than the rule, and only the most daring of our spokesmen will offer the grandiose, unqualified generalizations that the reader might seek. Yet it is precisely this tension that maintains the interest of its practitioners. And, in the final analysis, it is a tension which faithfully reflects its own subject of discourse: behavior in organizations.

1
Organizational Behavior as an Area of Study: Some Questions and Answers—and an Update*

DENNIS W. ORGAN

Q: What is "organizational behavior"?

A: The precise answer depends on which specific textbook or authority you consult. The consensual core of most definitions, however, would run something like this: "Organizational Behavior (OB), as a field of study, represents the application of behavioral science concepts and methods to the study of human behavior in the organizational environment."

Q: Is organizational behavior simply the "human" side of management, or a "behavioral approach" to management?

A: No, although it might be fair to say that OB started out that way.

In the late 1920s and early 1930s, some experiments in illumination, pay systems, work breaks, and other job conditions took place at the Western Electric Hawthorne plant near Chicago. The results made little sense, at first, because productivity in an experimental group of female operators seemed to hold steady at a fairly high level regardless of the particular set of working conditions arranged. Finally the experimenters, after bringing in some outside consultants, realized that they had unwittingly altered supervisory styles (toward being more considerate of the individual workers and allowing them to make more job decisions) and allowed the operators to become a cohesive work group. These findings, plus others that emerged from an intensive interviewing program and close observation of a work group in action, made it clear that traditional management thought up to that time was deficient. Previous approaches to administration had concentrated on the mechanics of getting things coordinated and controlled, without due consideration of the complexity of the human element. After the publication of *Management and the Worker* (which reported the Hawthorne findings and probed their implications) in 1938, the "behavioral" aspects of work organization were elevated to a much more serious status. Management thinking began to accord much greater emphasis to worker feelings, motives, and the social forces in the "informal organization" not covered by the organization chart.

While these developments spurred a new interest in the relevance of

---

* Prepared especially for this volume and updated for this edition.

behavioral sciences for management, they hardly resulted in a new discipline or field of knowledge. It was sometime later, near the end of the 1950s, that OB began to jell as a discipline.

In 1956, the Ford Foundation commissioned two economists, Professors R. A. Gordon and J. E. Howell, to undertake a comprehensive survey and assessment of business education at the college and university level. In their report, published in 1959, Gordon and Howell stated the view that business administration is the "enlightened application" of the behavioral sciences, among other things, to business problems. They felt, however, that business schools at the time were providing too little exposure in their curricula to basic conceptual material in the behavioral sciences.

Gordon and Howell noted approvingly that, at a number of the leading business schools, psychologists, sociologists, and political scientists were finding full-time positions on the faculty, and encouraged other schools to consider this possibility. They urged, too, more cooperation between business schools and departments of psychology and sociology on behavioral research—basic as well as applied—of interest to the business community and aspiring students of management and administration.

The Gordon and Howell report had an enormous impact on the design of business school curricula and recruitment of faculty in the 1960s. The trickle of behavioral scientists, especially psychologists, into business schools became, if not a flood, certainly a sizable stream. As they increased in numbers, they began to share an emerging professional kinship, developing their own national associations and doctoral programs within business schools. They, along with their intellectual offspring, gradually defined a coalescing discipline of OB. The discipline had reached a stage of considerable maturity by the mid-to-late 1960s, although it is of course still evolving, like all fields of knowledge, and not locked into a rigid scheme of development or a fixed set of topics.

Q: Is OB, then, just the *application* of psychology and other behavioral sciences to the study of behavior in organizations?

A: Not exactly. It is certainly more than the mere mechanical process of fitting known facts, laws, findings, and so forth, from psychology to work organizations. We *have* found it useful not to "reinvent the wheel." Where underlying disciplines such as psychology and sociology offer readily available concepts and methods of study that "fit" the organizational context, we do not hesitate to adopt them. Increasingly, however, we sometimes find it worth our while to develop our own constructs, theories, measuring instruments, and so on, when we address problems or issues unique to the organizational setting that have not been attended to by other behavioral sciences.

In any case, OB is not solely concerned with "application" in the narrow sense of the word. True, much of our effort is guided by the hope that we can contribute to pressing, urgent problems in work organizations, such as increasing the productivity and quality of work life in organizations. However, truly valid and lasting contributions will in some instances have to await a thorough testing and "thinking out" stage of our ideas, theories, and findings. Finally, as an intellectual discipline, OB, like any other, prizes knowledge and understanding as a goal in itself. Ultimately, knowledge is a seamless whole piece, and so any advance in our understanding of work behavior is worthwhile as well as intrinsically gratifying.

Q: How do developments in OB reach the practicing manager?

A: It might help, in answering this question, to look at the accompanying diagram of overlapping circles.

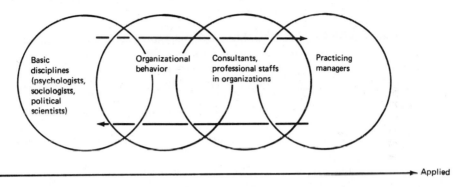

At the far left, we have those behavioral scientists (usually on the faculties of psychology or sociology departments) who teach and do basic research in such areas as human motivation, learning, attitude change, group dynamics, social stratification, and the like. Some of them have particular interests in organizations, most of them do not. Let us say a number of social psychologists conduct research showing that people's attitudes and opinions have little correspondence to their actual behavior. Now, people in OB, most of whom are affiliated with schools of business and administration, find out about this. They find out because many of them keep in touch with what people in the basic disciplines are doing; in fact, since the circles overlap, some of the organizational behavior types may be as much involved in the basic disciplines as anyone else. They ponder the implications of this finding about attitudes not jibing with behavior. Satisfaction with one's job is a type of attitude; productivity is a type of behavior. Maybe job satisfaction and productivity aren't too closely related, then. In any case, it's something to think about and investigate. So research is undertaken by organizational behaviorists, generally confirming that job satisfaction and productivity are not closely correlated. These findings stimulate new thinking about the links between satisfaction and performance (see Section Two-A in this volume). Later it turns up that social psychologists have found that certain factors determine whether attitudes and behavior are related. *If* the attitude is sufficiently specific (not general or vague) and not linked to powerful opposing attitudes, and if the behavior is not constrained by other forces, there may be a reasonably close correspondence between attitudes and behavior. So we may find that certain specific facets of job satisfaction *are* related to certain kinds of performance.

Many of the people who teach, write, and do research in OB also act as consultants to private firms and other organizations. In fact, some of them do part-time work in their own outside consulting firms, and a few do not belong to university faculties, but work full-time on the professional staffs (e.g., in industrial relations, planning, personnel) of corporations. All of these people draw from their expertise and knowledge in teaching students (who later become managers), advising client managers, teaching in management development programs, or writing in popular periodicals, magazines, or trade publications.

Throughout the history of science, lines of influence have sometimes run from the practical problem-solving arena back to basic theory and research, as well as in the other direction. OB is no exception. In the late 1950s, an issue of immediate concern among executives was whether groups made more cautious, conservative decisions than individuals acting alone. A master's thesis (Stoner, 1961) research project by a student in industrial management produced evidence that groups actually make *riskier* decisions. The implications of this finding soon rocked academic social psychology to its foundation and influenced more than a decade of research in social psychology.

Q: Doesn't it take a long time for this communication process to operate?

A: The problem more frequently has been that it operates too quickly. In an address to the Academy of Management in 1974, Professor Lyman Porter reminded the organizational behaviorists that often we have been too quick to offer prescriptions to managers on the basis of premature, tentative, sometimes downright invalid findings. One result is that by promising too much with a hard-sell approach, we have damaged our credibility with practitioners. We have foisted programs upon them that were attractive in package, but weak in substance, and the implied payoffs were not realized.

Part of the problem is that OB, like any science, is a system or collection of "technologies" as well as a field of study. Professor L. L. Cummings (1977) of Wisconsin identifies OB techniques for training leaders, designing tasks, evaluating performance, and designing reward systems. Technologies have their market appeal even when they are based on untested or oversimplified representations of reality.

Q: How can premature prescribing be minimized?

A: Only by the discipline of the scientific method. As Cummings points out, OB is becoming more "influenced by the norms of skepticism, caution, replication of findings, and public exposure of knowledge based on facts."

Q: Doesn't the cold-blooded posture of "scientism" put a damper on the genuine and immediate concern for people?

A: Actually, as Cummings observes, "there is a distinctly humanistic tone within OB." That is, as much as anything else, we want to contribute a knowledge basis for designing organization environments that foster self-development, psychological growth, choice, and fulfillment of individuals—yet do it in a way that also makes organizations more effective in serving the larger society. As Cummings puts it, this is a "humanism without softness." OB is performance-oriented, as well as people-oriented; its orientation toward both is circumscribed by intellectual and scientific honesty, lest we delude ourselves into thinking we have already reached the promised land for which we strive (and will never reach, since it really exists only as a guiding ideal).

Q: What has OB accomplished? What is its track record?

A: To date, our major contribution has been, in a sense, negative. We have been more successful in challenging and overturning previous conceptions about behavior in organizations than we have been creative in providing alternative conceptions. Nowhere is this better illustrated than in the study of leadership. As Professor H. Joseph Reitz (1977) remarks, "the study of leadership is interesting and yet confusing. We seem to have been more proficient at discovering the misconceptions of leadership than the principles of leadership." We realize now that effective leaders cannot be picked on the basis of personality traits, that democratic leadership is not necessarily more effective than autocratic leadership, and leader behavior is as much or more affected by subordinate performance than vice versa.

Q: Isn't this discouraging?

A: It is certainly cause for humility on our part. We realize now that grand theories which will explain any and every thing are not in the offing. If we can't endorse a particular style of leader behavior that is optimal for all situations, maybe we can find a style that at least seems to work reasonably well in a very limited set of situations.

Q: In the final analysis, what does OB have to offer the student?

A: It can help the student become, in the words of Professor R. J. House of the University of Toronto, a "good crap-detector." It can provide a basic framework for evaluating the assertions, conclusions, programs, and slogans that the manager is bombarded with from all sides. It can help the student recognize fallacies in his or her own thinking about work behavior. It can help one avoid painting oneself into a logical corner. It can provide a basis for informal, intelligent observation of behavior in organizations.

UPDATE: JULY 1986

Q: What developments have occurred in the last decade in OB?

A: Probably the most positive development for those of us who teach OB has been a livelier popular interest in the subject. Corporation presidents, business school deans, and public officials have recently been quoted in magazines, newspapers, and business periodicals to the effect that more emphasis should be accorded OB in business education and management development. And it is my impression that undergraduate and MBA students these days are also more receptive to behavioral concepts.

Q: How do you account for this development?

A: I attribute it in part to the suddenly increased awareness people have of Japanese management. In the late 1970s and early 1980s, numerous writers drew attention to the success of Japanese management in global markets, especially the auto industry. Meanwhile our own economy was not performing so well, as productivity lagged and unsold inventories of cars and steel mounted. People wanted to know what the Japanese "secret" was, and scholars responded with an outpouring of books and articles on Japanese management. Most of these publications expounded at length on the effectiveness with which Japanese managers developed team spirit, worker commitment, and constructive participation by all ranks of employees. Of course, perceptive readers learned that numerous other differences exist between their system and ours, that no one could guarantee that their system could be exported to our culture, and that the Japanese had some problems of their own. But out of all this discussion came the idea that American management had much to learn in the areas of worker motivation and group performance.

Q: Can you think of any other reasons for increased popular interest in OB?

A: Well, somewhat related to the interest in Japanese management was the emergence in the early 1980s of what Frank Freeman (1985) called the "management book as best-seller." The most noteworthy example of this was *In Search of Excellence* (Peters & Waterman, 1982). The authors of this book, which sold millions of copies, searched for the common characteristics of large American companies that had consistently competed very well, the Japanese onslaught notwithstanding. Peters and Waterman found the answers not in elaborate financial controls, complex formal structures, or technological advantages, but rather in the type of environment that fosters employee dedication to the customer, pride in product quality, and a pervasive sense of proprietorship in nurturing new ideas and small experiments. Furthermore, the authors were able to relate these findings to a fairly sophisticated discussion of concepts and theories from OB and related fields of study. Other top-selling management books, such as *Theory Z* (Ouchi, 1981), *Megatrends* (Naisbitt, 1982), and *The One Minute Manager* (Blanchard & Johnson, 1982) also contributed to an increased popular interest in OB.

Q: How has the field of OB responded to this popular interest?

A: Ironically, the effect has not been to unify the discipline, but apparently to intensify some of the differences between various camps and perspectives within OB. Cummings (1981), in a fairly accurate prophecy of how OB would develop in the 1980s, noted the differences between "conservatives" and "radicals" within OB. Conservatives push for more and more rigor in our measurement tools, research designs, and statistical analysis. Radicals, on the other hand, are afraid that OB will become sterile and lacking in relevance if it exalts scientific rigor above substance. Conservatives argue that worthwhile contributions to the management of organizations can come only from sound research practices that offer reliable and valid findings; radicals contend that slavish imitation of the physical sciences leads to a widening gap between what is researched in OB and what managers need to know and can usefully apply.

Q: Are you saying that OB has to make a choice between what is rigorous but not relevant and what is relevant but not valid?

A: Actually, I don't think we are locked into quite such a painful dilemma; neither, apparently, does Lawler (see Reading 4 in this section), who continues to hold hope for valid and useful research in OB. One promising role for loose, even downright unscientific methods, is that of sparking bold new theoretical advances. The last 10 years or so have not seen much of that in OB; the advances in research methods have been put to good use in assessing the theories and models that were already around, but did little to provide fresh, reinvigorating perspectives.

Q: Are you expressing dissatisfaction with existing theories in OB?

A: No. Current OB frameworks have made and will continue to make their contributions. Just as early OB research had a contribution that was more negative than positive, in that it worked mainly to question and refute conventional wisdom, so has recent OB research been more impressive in its ability to find the weak spots in the theories first put forth to replace conventional wisdom. We cannot afford to throw out what we have; neither can we in good conscience junk what we know to be proper methods of research. Instead, we may have to be more patient with theories that do not readily yield to rigorous quantitative research. And, undoubtedly, if we in OB wish to influence what happens in the work environment, we need to devote as much ingenuity and care to the selection of *what* we study as we do in regard to *how* we study it.

REFERENCES

Blanchard, K., and Johnson, S.   *The one minute manager.* New York: Morrow, 1982.

Cummings, L. L.   Organizational behavior in the 1980s. *Decision Sciences,* 1981, *12,* 365–377.

Cummings, L. L.   Toward organizational behavior. *Academy of Management Review,* 1977.

Freeman, F. H.   Books that mean business: The management best sellers. *Academy of Management Review,* 1985, *10,* 345–350.

Gordon, R. A., & Howell, J. E.   *Higher education for business.* New York: Columbia University Press, 1959.

Naisbitt, J.   *Megatrends: Ten new directions transforming our lives.* New York: Warner, 1982.

Ouchi, W. G.   *Theory Z: How American business can meet the Japanese challenge.* Reading, Mass.: Addison-Wesley Publishing, 1981.

Peters, T. J., & Waterman, R. H.   *In search of excellence: Lessons from America's best-run companies.* New York: Harper & Row, 1982.

Porter, L. W.   Presidential address, Academy of Management meeting, Seattle, 1974.

Reitz, H. J.   *Behavior in organizations.* Homewood, Ill.: Richard D. Irwin, 1977, p. 535.

Roethlisberger, F. J., & Dickson, W. J.   *Management and the worker.* New York: John Wiley & Sons, Science Editions, 1964.

Stoner, J. A. F.   *A comparison of individual and group decisions including risk.* Unpublished master's thesis, School of Industrial Management, Massachusetts Institute of Technology, 1961.

2

The Case for the Natural Science Model for Research in Organizational Behavior and Organization Theory*

ORLANDO BEHLING

Research methods similar to those used in the natural sciences have long been the norm in organizational behavior and organization theory. However, several writers have recently questioned their appropriateness for the study of organizations and the groups and individuals who make them up. In this paper I examine five major objections to the use of such methods in organizational behavior and organization theory and conclude that, while they may indicate a need for more thoughtful application of the natural science approach, they do not rule it out as the primary research strategy for the study of organizations.

One widely accepted view of the role that science plays in organizational behavior and organization theory is that it functions to:

> establish general laws covering the behavior of empirical events or objects with which the science is concerned, and thereby enable us to connect together our knowledge of separately known events and to make reliable predictions of events yet unknown [Braithwaite, 1973, p. 1].

In the tradition of Campbell and Stanley [1963], Cook and Campbell [1976], and Kerlinger [1973], most advocates of this view hold that good research is characterized by careful sampling, precise measurement, and sophisticated design and analysis in the test of hypotheses derived from tentative general laws. Popper [1964] labels this rigorous search for general laws the *natural science model* because it repre-

---
* From *Academy of Management Review* 5, no. 4, (1980), pp. 483–90. © 1980 by the Academy of Management 0363-7425.

sents a social science approximation of the approach that serves the natural sciences (e.g., physics, chemistry, biology) so well. I will use Popper's label throughout this paper.

Clearly, the authors of mainstream texts in organizational behavior and organization theory accept the natural science model of good research. Those who include research methods chapters [e.g., Bobbitt, Breinholt, Doktor, & McNaul, 1978; Hamner & Organ, 1978; Jackson & Morgan, 1978] clearly follow this approach and generally appear to owe an intellectual debt to Kerlinger, a strong proponent of the natural science model. Some authors are even more definite in their advocacy of the model. First, Luthans quotes Berelson and Steiner [1964]:

> Organizational behavior should strive to attain the following hallmarks of a science:
>
> 1. The procedures are public.
> 2. The definitions are precise.
> 3. The data collecting is objective.
> 4. The findings are replicable.
> 5. The approach is systematic and cumulative.
> 6. The purposes are explanation, understanding, and prediction [1973, p. 77].

While Berelson and Steiner's points 1, 4, and 6 can be encompassed by all but the most radical definitions of good research, it is clear that 2, 3, and to a certain extent 5, call for application of the natural science approach. Second, Filley, House, and Kerr [1975] have discussed research methods in terms of "levels of rigor." Though they point out the dangers of undervaluing less rigorous research methods for exploratory studies, there is a clear implication in their work that the closer a study approximates the natural science ideal, the better it is. They also organize each of their chapters around a series of "propositions" or tentative general laws.

Recently, however, questions have been raised regarding the appropriateness of the natural science approach for organizational behavior and organization theory research. These questions do not arise from the traditional charges that much research on organizational phenomena merely verifies in elaborate and costly ways things that most managers already know [e.g., Gordon, Kleiman, & Hanie, 1978] or that it simply splits hairs to benefit the egos of theoreticians [e.g., Koontz, 1961]. Rather, the questioners hold that organizations and the groups and individuals who make them up differ from phenomena of interest to the natural sciences in ways that make natural science methods inappropriate for their study.

Some of the apparent dissatisfaction is implicit—for example, the increasing interest in models such as functionalism as replacements for or supplements to the currently dominant causal models [Behling, 1979], and the growing use of intuitive participant-observer methods not merely for exploring new areas but also for drawing conclusions. But the dissatisfaction has also been made explicit by Behling and Shapiro [1974], Argyris [1976], Lundberg [1976], and most provocatively by Mitroff and Pondy, who write:

> We are conditioned by our scientific training to associate progress with greater rigor, greater precision, disintegrative analysis, more empirical documentation of a phenomenon, and the progressive exorcism of value-laden questions in favor of a purer pursuit of "truth," that is, a closer and closer fitting of our theories to the one objective reality we presume exists. . . . If you are spinning off ideas, you are allowed to be intuitive and nonrigorous, so long as you get scientific again when you begin testing your ideas empirically. But we believe that . . . increased openness toward imprecision extends *beyond* the hypothesis-generation stage. This is not to say that precise, rigorous, empirically testable descriptions and theories are out. But it does mean that looser, nontestable, nongeneralizable descriptions (e.g., poems) of social facts are equally legitimate forms of representation and, perhaps, . . . even more appropriate forms of inquiry than the normal model of science . . . perhaps "science" is the wrong strategy for understanding social phenomena [1978, pp. 145–146].

I share the frustration of Mitroff and Pondy and the other critics with the nitpicking and repeated "back to the drawing board" retrenchments that accompany natural science methods in some areas of organizational behavior and organization theory. I feel, however, that those who argue against the natural science approach should not go unchallenged, for two reasons. First, they typically present only one side of the question. Second, they usually consider only one or two of the important issues bearing on the usefulness of the natural science approach to research. Sociologists [Popper, 1964], social psychologists [Gergen, 1973; Schlenker, 1974], and those in other applied social sciences [Campbell, 1974] have explored a wide range of issues that deserve discussion in organizational behavior and organization theory.

In the following paragraphs, working from Brown [1965], Gergen [1973], Homans [1967], Kaplan [1964], Nagel [1961], Popper [1964], and Schlenker [1974], I identify five key objections to the use of the natural science model raised in other social and behavioral sciences that have been or could be raised in organizational behavior and organization theory, and I explain why they do not rule out attempts to apply the model to solving riddles in the discipline. These objections have been discussed under many different labels; I refer to them as:

1. *Uniqueness.* Each organization, group, and person differs to some degree from all others; the development of precise general laws in

organizational behavior and organization theory is thus impossible.

2. *Instability.* The phenomena of interest to researchers in organizational behavior and organization theory are transitory. Not only do the "facts" of social events change with time, but the "laws" governing them change as well. Natural science research is poorly equipped to capture these fleeting phenomena.

3. *Sensitivity.* Unlike chemical compounds and other things of interest to natural science researchers, the people who make up organizations, and thus organizations themselves, may behave differently if they become aware of researchers' hypotheses about them.

4. *Lack of Realism.* Manipulating and controlling variables in organizational research changes the phenomena under study. Researchers thus cannot generalize from their studies because the phenomena observed inevitably differ from their real world counterparts.

5. *Epistemological Differences.* Although understanding cause and effect through natural science research is an appropriate way of "knowing" about physical phenomena, a different kind of "knowledge" not tapped by this approach is more important in organizational behavior and organization theory.

These objections are discussed in greater detail in the following sections.

Uniqueness

This objection holds that the phenomena of concern to organizational behavior and organization theory researchers are specific to the organizations, work groups, or individuals in which they occur. If this is indeed the case, then attempts to generalize from a sample, no matter how carefully chosen, will be futile since no organization, group, or individual can represent any other, much less a broad class. If each case is unique, the idea of general laws is meaningless.

The phenomenological premises underlying Weick's concept of the "enacted organization" [1969] and Pondy and Boje's call for "bringing mind back in" to the study of organizations [1976] lead almost inevitably to the idea that what any one organization, group, or individual has in common with any other exists only in the shared perceptions of the people who interact with them. More directly, Newell and Simon's [1972] and Dawes's [1975] work on individualized processes in decision making represents moves in the direction of substituting appreciation of unique entities for the search for general laws.

Much of the apparent uniqueness of phenomena studied in organizational behavior and organization theory is real, but this fact does not limit the field to the description of singular events. To understand why, it is useful to follow Merton [1949] in differentiating between *empiric generalizations* and *scientific laws*. While both are statements of contingencies of the form "If A, then B," a scientific law is stated in more abstract form than an empiric generalization, permitting the insertion of specific objects, events, and the like as variables and allowing the prediction of specific "events yet unknown" from the abstract statement.

The fact that many works published in organizational behavior and organization theory journals report empiric generalizations (e.g., "matrix organizations work well in aerospace firms" or "urban blue-collar workers are less likely to respond to job enrichment than their rural counterparts") rather than scientific laws does not justify the assertion that the field *cannot* yield scientific laws. (Nor should the statement be interpreted as saying that empiric generalizations are valueless; in fact, they serve as bases for practical decisions in specific situations and also serve as a kind of raw material for builders of scientific laws.)

McKelvey [1975, 1978] points out that the key to the development of meaningful generalizations lies in *taxonomy*, a theory of differences among organizations, together with methods of *classification* derived from it. Such an approach leads to two things. First, McKelvey holds, it permits the development of generalizations about important though relatively narrow populations:

> Narrower, more homogeneous populations would limit the generalizability of any single study, but this would be offset by gains in the definitiveness of the findings, the levels of variance explained, and the applicability of the results to the population. In short, solid findings about a narrower population are better than marginal findings of questionable generalizability to a broadly defined population [1978, p. 1438].

Second, generalizations about narrow populations defined systematically rather than casually can be combined into higher order generalizations. Because such laws must encompass diverse organizations, groups, or individuals, they cannot be as exact or explain as large a portion of the total variance as one might hope. Nevertheless, they represent a form of useful general law.

Instability

The opponents of natural science methods in organizational behavior and organization theory hold that phenomena of concern to researchers in the field change frequently, making it extremely difficult to combine data obtained at different times in order to arrive at general laws, as is commonly done in the natural sciences. Mitroff and Pondy, for example, state:

The phenomenon will never be completely described or understood before it vanishes and some new phenomenon supplants it. That is the guts of our conjecture that *science* is the wrong enquiring system for the social "sciences"; it converges too slowly relative to the rate of decay and evolution of social phenomena [1978, p. 147.].

Were this assertion correct, cumulatively developing knowledge about organizations and groups and individuals within them would be well-nigh impossible. Instead, organizational behavior and organization theory would be journalism—the recording and explaining of ephemeral phenomena—rather than science.

But this does not appear to be the case, for two reasons. First, as explained in the discussion of the uniqueness objection, scientific research seeks laws that transcend time and place, not empiric generalizations that often are specific to certain situations. Second, as explained by Gergen [1973] and Schlenker [1974] in their discussions of a "continuum of historic durability," to assume that *all* phenomena of interest to organizational behavior and organization theory are ephemeral is as much an error as to assume that even the most specific aspects of them remain constant over long periods. Clearly, some phenomena change more rapidly than others. Relationships with roots in human physiology and those reflecting performance limits of organizational and group forms probably change more slowly than those that are socially determined or simply "common practice." Thus, careful consideration of the likely durability of the phenomena studied should be a necessary part of decisions each researcher makes regarding the appropriateness of methods characterized by varying levels of natural science rigor.

Sensitivity

Opponents of natural science methods in organizational behavior and organization theory charge that awareness of hypotheses in the social sciences inevitably changes the behaviors of the persons involved. These changes take two forms. First, such awareness may create *self-fulfilling prophecies* whereby participants change their behavior to increase the chances of supporting the hypothesis. Behling and Shapiro [1974], for example, point out how researchers' attempts to gain managerial permission to study "need for A" (which could be anything) in an organization can sensitize the managers to its manifestations. This in turn could lead the managers to reinforce "A-seeking" behavior on the part of their subordinates. The research process would thus create rather than measure the importance of "need for A."

Second, such sensitivity may take the form of what Nagel [1961] calls *suicidal predictions*. Nagel points out that predictions of a depression immediately following World War II induced business to cut certain prices, which led to increased demand, which made the prediction incorrect. Similarly, I have observed a case in which participants successfully sabotaged a part of a study performed by a researcher they disliked.

Although the sensitivity of some behaviors to the act of studying them is indisputable, this does not rule out natural science methods in organizational behavior and organization theory for three reasons. First, the sensitivity objection assumes that natural science research is necessarily transparent—that the individuals participating in the study are always aware that they are under study and of the nature of the hypotheses being tested. The need for informed consent in organizational research does undoubtedly restrict the degree to which researchers can keep participants in the dark, but it does not eliminate the use of unobtrusive measures and other means of increasing the chance that the behavior of participants in research studies represents their real world actions.

Second, the sensitivity objection assumes that research participants control all dependent variables of concern to organizational researchers. Obviously, participants can change some things quite easily—for example, where they put a checkmark on an anonymous questionnaire; but the likelihood that they could and would change others in an attempt to support or reject the researcher's hypotheses is small. Work behavior over substantial periods of time, organizational structures, and informal interaction patterns are all examples of important phenomena that probably do not change in response to knowledge of research hypotheses. It seems reasonable to posit a hypothetical "continuum of discretion and control" to parallel Gergen and Schlenker's continuum of historic durability. I suspect that relatively few key dependent variables are close enough to the "immediately and completely responsive" end of the scale to result in the self-fulfilling prophecies or the suicidal predictions the sensitivity critics fear.

Third, the sensitivity criticism holds only if any suicidal and self-fulfilling effects cannot be identified and separated from the "true" effects of the variables of interest. Even though our abilities to tease out these effects are limited, given reasonably sophisticated experimental designs it is usually possible to do so. Moreover, although a "theory of reactions to theories" [Schlenker, 1974] creates the possibility of a mind-boggling progression of theories of reactions to theories of reactions to theories, even greater ability to predict such phenomena could come with a better understanding of the widely recognized but poorly understood "Hawthorne effect" and related phenomena.

Lack of Realism

Critics of natural science methods in organizational behavior and organization theory sometimes hold that the study of social phenomena necessarily changes them to such an extent that the researcher cannot generalize from such studies to behaviors of organizations, groups, and individuals in the real world. They hold that such studies are, in a word, unrealistic. Stone [1978, pp. 119–20] lists a series of such charges as part of a survey of the pros and cons of various kinds of research methods. Specifically, seven potential threats to realism can be extracted from his list. The first three apply primarily to laboratory experimentation. The remaining four relate to natural science research in the field as well as in the laboratory:

1. The environments in which laboratory studies are performed are often strange and potentially embarrassing. Thus participants may behave differently there than they would in more familiar circumstances.
2. The laboratory environment may be unrealistic because the researcher may not recognize all of the important aspects of the situation under investigation and thus fail to manipulate or control them or to even include them in the research task or situation.
3. Researchers rarely permit participants to show the full range of behaviors open to them in real organizations. Laboratory "employees," for example, are almost never allowed to quit or to form labor unions.
4. It may be practically impossible to control or manipulate some key variables—for example, the economic climate in which the researcher performs the study.
5. It may be ethically unacceptable to manipulate other variables such as emotional stress, even though they may be crucial to the study.
6. For both practical and ethical reasons, research manipulations are rarely as strong as are encountered in actual organizations, even when variables can be manipulated. For example, "pay" is usually a one-shot supplement to the subject's income in research studies, not his or her primary source of support.
7. Dozens of factors may interact in complex patterns to determine the behaviors of individuals, groups, and organizations, but researchers rarely manipulate more than three or four in a single study.

Such criticisms stem in part from a misunderstanding of what a controlled environment for natural science research need be. As Weick points out in regard to laboratory research:

> Because laboratory experimentation is much more flexible than most persons realize, the laboratory can be adapted to exceedingly complex and ambiguous problems. At the same time, many organizational problems are encumbered with extraneous and superfluous details. These details can be removed with little effect on generality [1965, p. 745].

There are, however, two more important reasons why the lack-of-realism criticism is invalid.

First, three of the objections listed above equate the natural science model with the laboratory, when it is in fact possible to do rigorous natural science research in the field as well. Cook and Campbell, building on previous work by Campbell and Stanley [1963], provide a series of research designs capable of minimizing key threats to validity. They point out:

> As the examples in this chapter illustrated again and again, good quasi-experiments and true experiments have been conducted in the field in the past. They have reduced all or most of the threats to internal and statistical conclusion validity, many of the threats to construct validity of effects, and they have even reduced some of the threats to external validity and the construct validity of causes [1976, p. 318].

Second, I believe the criticism is invalid because it assumes that a flawed study—that is, one which does not control all threats to internal and external validity—yields no useful information. In fact, many of the conclusions drawn in the discipline are extracted grudgingly from the weight of evidence from dozens of studies, most of them flawed in one way or another. Campbell has written:

> Too many social scientists expect single experiments to settle issues once and for all. This may be a mistaken generalization from the history of the great crucial experiments in physics and chemistry. . . . Because we social scientists have less ability to achieve "experimental isolation," and because we have good reason to expect our treatment effects to interact significantly with a wide variety of social factors, many of which we have not yet mapped, we have much greater need for replication experiments than do the physical sciences [1969, pp. 427–28].

It is likely to be the weight of evidence, not the crucial study, that defines scientific law in organizational behavior and organization theory. Constructive replications, designed not only to verify the results of specific studies within specific contexts but also to test for and overcome threats to internal and external validity, are necessary to establish general laws in organizational behavior and organization theory.

Epistemological Differences

Some opponents of natural science methods in organizational behavior and organization theory argue that understanding in the social sciences should differ from that in the natural sciences and this, in turn, demands different research methods. Advocates of this position hold that natural science strives to generalize about *why* things happen by identifying causes. Social science, on the other hand, seeks to explain the *significance* or *meaning* of phenomena in terms of their implications for the unique social systems in which they occur and as manifestations of important social trends, forces, and conflicts. Max Weber, for example, wrote:

> The analysis of the historically given individual configurations of . . . "factors" and their *significant* concrete interaction, conditioned by their historical context, and especially the *rendering intelligible* of the basis and type of this significance would be the next task to be achieved. . . . "Laws" are obviously of great value as heuristic means—but only as such. Indeed they are quite indispensible for this purpose. But even in this function their limitations become evident at a decisive point. . . . The *significance* of a configuration of cultural phenomena and the basis of the significance cannot, however, be derived and rendered intelligible by a system of analytical laws (*Gesetzbegriffin*), however perfect it may be [1949, pp. 75–76; emphasis in original].

Thus, for example, the events at Lordstown should be studied not simply as a chance to build a data base for generalizing about sources of worker demands for things beyond pay, good physical working conditions, and the like. They have meaning as a milestone in a major shift in expectations regarding work.

Although it is difficult, of course, to argue over the relative merits of different kinds of goals for organizational research, comment should be made regarding the methods normally advocated by those who see the identification of significance as a primary goal of research on organizations. Advocates of this approach argue that the best way to learn about complex social phenomena is to immerse the researcher in the organization under study and allow time for the development of intuitive appreciation of its workings. Unquestionably, since the studies of Roy [1952] and the Hawthorne researchers [Roethlisberger & Dickson, 1964], such in-depth observations have affected the course of thought about organizations. Nevertheless, such methods have important limitations. First, as Campbell [1974] points out, such research, improperly performed, is nothing more than a naive phenomenology that discards objective verification in favor of uncritical acceptance of the observer's experiences as reality. In the face of all we know about biases in the perception and interpretation of complex stimuli [e.g., Tversky & Kahneman, 1974], it would be foolish to contend that any social research, natural science or not, is totally free of systematic bias. But the natural science approach has built in extensive means for protecting the researcher against personal biases and thus such biases affect the outcomes of natural science research less often than they do those of other methods.

Second, such research generates a highly affective kind of knowledge. Although there are notable exceptions [e.g., Leighton's *The Governing of Men*, 1945], the process of conveying this very personal information, no matter how potent, to others can entail substantial loss of both completeness and richness. Researchers often find themselves resorting to the stand-up comic's cliché, "Ya hadda be there."

Conclusion

Numerous objections have been raised to the use of natural science methods in organizational behavior and organization theory. Yet none of the barriers raised is insurmountable. Admittedly imperfect and in need of more thoughtful application, natural science research methods represent an important means of understanding organizations and the behaviors of individuals and groups making them up. My attitude toward the natural science approach can be captured in a paraphrase of Winston Churchill's famous comment on democracy: It is the worst possible way to study organizations—except for all the others.

REFERENCES

Argyris, C.   Problems and new directions for industrial psychology. In M. D. Dunnette (Ed.), *Handbook of industrial and organizational psychology*. Skokie, Ill.: Rand McNally, 1976.

Behling, O.   Functionalism as a base for midrange theory in organizational behavior and organization theory. In C. C. Pinder & L. Moore (Eds.), *Middle range theory and the study of organization*. Leiden, The Netherlands: Martinus Nijhoff, 1979.

Behling, O., & Shapiro, M.   Motivation theory: Source of the solution or part of the problem? *Business Horizons*, 1974, 7, 59–66.

Berelson, B., & Steiner, G. A.   *Human behavior*. New York: Harcourt Brace Jovanovich, 1964.

Bobbitt, H. R., Breinholt, R. H., Doktor, R. H., & McNaul, J. P.   *Organizational behavior* (2d ed.). Englewood Cliffs, N.J.: Prentice-Hall, 1978.

Braithwaite, R.   *Scientific explanation*. Cambridge: Cambridge University Press, 1973.

Brown, R.   *Social psychology.* New York: Free Press, 1965.

Campbell, D. T.   *Qualitative knowing in action research*. Unpublished manuscript, Society for the Psychological Study of Social Issues, 1974.

Campbell, D. T.   Reforms as experiments. *American Psychologist*, 1969, 24, 409–429.

Campbell, D. T., & Stanley, J. C.   *Experimental and quasi-experimental design for research*. Skokie, Ill.: Rand McNally, 1963.

Cook, T. D., & Campbell, D. T.   The design and conduct of quasi-experiments and true experiments in field settings. In M. D. Dunnette (Ed.), *Handbook of industrial and organizational psychology*. Skokie, Ill.: Rand McNally, 1976.

Dawes, R. M.   The mind, the model, and the task. In H. L. Casellon & F. Restle (Eds.), *Proceedings of the seventh annual Indiana theoretical and cognitive psychology conference,* 1975.

Filley, A. C., House, R. J., & Kerr, S.   *Managerial process and organizational behavior* (2d ed.). Glenview, Ill.: Scott, Foresman, 1975.

Gergen, K. J.   Social psychology as history. *Journal of Personality & Social Psychology,* 1973, *26,* 309–320.

Gordon, M. E., Kleiman, L. S., & Hanie, C. A.   Industrial-organizational psychology: Open thy ears O house of Israel. *American Psychologist,* 1978, *33,* 893–905.

Hamner, W. C., & Organ, D. W. *Organizational behavior: An applied psychological approach.* Plano, Tex.: Business Publications, 1978.

Homans, G. C.   *The nature of social science.* New York: Harcourt Brace Jovanovich, 1967.

Jackson, J. H., & Morgan, C. P.   *Organization theory.* Englewood Cliffs, N.J.: Prentice-Hall, 1978.

Kaplan, A.   *The conduct of inquiry: Methodology for behavioral science.* San Francisco: Chandler, 1964.

Kerlinger, F. N.   *Foundations of behavioral research* (2d ed.). New York: Holt, Rinehart & Winston, 1973.

Koontz, H.   The management theory jungle. *Academy of Management Journal,* 1961, *4,* 174–188.

Leighton, A. H.   *The governing of men.* Princeton, N.J.: Princeton University Press, 1945.

Lundberg, C. C.   Hypothesis creation in organizational behavior research. *Academy of Management Review,* 1976, *1,* 5–12.

Luthans, F.   *Organizational behavior.* New York: McGraw-Hill, 1973.

McKelvey, B.   Guidelines for the empirical classification of organizations. *Administrative Science Quarterly,* 1975, *20,* 509–525.

McKelvey, B.   Organizational systematics: Taxonomic lessons from biology. *Management Science,* 1978, *24,* 1428–1440.

Merton, R. K.   *Social theory and social structure.* New York: Free Press, 1949.

Mitroff, I. I., & Pondy, L. R.   Afterthoughts on the leadership conference. In M. W. McCall & M. M. Lombardo (Eds.), *Leadership: Where else can we go?* Durham, N.C.: Duke University Press, 1978.

Nagel, E.   *The structure of science: Problems in the logic of scientific explanation.* New York: Harcourt Brace Jovanovich, 1961.

Newell, A., & Simon, H.   *Human problem solving.* Englewood Cliffs, N.J.: Prentice-Hall, 1972.

Pondy, L. R., & Boje, D. M.   *Bringing mind back in: Paradigm development as a frontier problem in organization theory.* Unpublished manuscript, Department of Business Administration, University of Illinois, Urbana, 1976.

Popper, K. R.   *The poverty of historicism.* New York: Harper Torchbooks, 1964.

Roethlisberger, F. J., & Dickson, W. J.   *Management and the worker.* New York: Wiley, 1964.

Roy, D.   Quota restriction and goldbricking in a machine shop. *American Journal of Sociology,* 1952, *57,* 430–437.

Schlenker, B. R.   Social psychology and science. *Journal of Personality and Social Psychology*, 1974, *29*, 1–15.

Stone, E.   *Research methods in organizational behavior*. Santa Monica, Calif.: Goodyear, 1978.

Tversky, A., & Kahneman, D.   Judgment under uncertainty: Heuristics and biases. *Science*, 1974, *185*, 1124–1131.

Weber, M.   *On the methodology of the social sciences*. New York: Free Press, 1949.

Weick, K. E.   Laboratory experimentation with organizations. In J. G. March (Ed.), *Handbook of organizations*. Skokie, Ill.: Rand McNally, 1965.

Weick, K. E.   *The social psychology of organizing*. Reading, Mass.: Addison-Wesley, 1969.

3

The Development of Knowledge in Organizational Behavior and Human Performance*

W. E. SCOTT, JR.

Within the past few years, researchers have been able to develop useful knowledge about the behavior of individuals in organizations to replace the human relations saws of an earlier time. It is comprised of a body of theory as well as empirical generalizations which possess sufficient reliability and generality to be worthy of critical study. While our knowledge of organizational behavior is incomplete, it is clear that we are no longer required to rely upon anecdotal evidence and speculation as our primary source of information. Rather, it is empirical knowledge based upon systematic study and experimentation which needs to be emphasized. That being the case, it may prove helpful to consider the nature and function of knowledge and the methods by which it is produced.

A number of practical benefits are gained from a study and development of knowledge of organizational behavior and human performance. First, systematic studies of this subject are being conducted at a rapidly increasing rate. Administrators and educators will soon become outdated unless they equip themselves to read, understand,

* Abridged from *Decision Sciences*, 1975, *6*, 1, 142–165.

and evaluate the reports of these studies. Second, interest in sponsoring research of all kinds of organizations has been increasing. Specialized research units in many large organizations have presented a number of unresolved, difficult organizational problems. Perhaps, an improved understanding of scientific goals and methods would lead to more satisfactory solutions to these problems. Finally, more interaction between researchers and practitioners is needed. The researcher who seeks to establish relationships between organizational variables and behavior under controlled settings also seeks to apply his findings to an expanding set of conditions. Administrators sensitive to the goals and methods of the behavioral scientist can provide feedback to researchers about the generality of these relationships in complex organizations. This feedback often can raise additional questions which are significant from both a practical and scientific viewpoint. While the popular misconceptions that research is simply a way of solving problems or that the so-called scientific method is applicable to all or most of the complex problems facing the administrator must be rejected, a better understanding of empirical knowledge and its development would enhance the administrator's ability to use and to contribute to the systematic study of organizational behavior.

Characteristics of Knowledge

An individual may acquire knowledge about objects and events in his environment through direct encounter or firsthand experience. Nearly all of us have observed the behavior of others in complex organizations. However, knowledge based solely upon direct encounters with natural phenomena is limited. Some insist that these encounters cannot make the individual knowledgeable at all unless he is able to verbally describe or represent that experience to himself and to others. This is a complex psychological issue not to be pursued here, but raising the issue does provide an opportunity to emphasize two points. First, most of our scientific knowledge is received from significant others by means of conversation, lectures, newspapers, books, and other such media. Second, this process is so ubiquitous that we often forget that verbal symbols, concepts, or terms are different from that to which they refer. The term *organizational behavior,* for example, is a verbal stimulus distinguishable from the phenomena which it signifies. Unfortunately, some concepts from the everyday vernacular signify different meanings to different individuals. To avoid confusion and misunderstanding, the researcher is typically forced to develop a specialized vocabulary which employs precise and invariant meanings, but which lacks appeal until the user gains familiarity with it.

This paper focuses on that knowledge which enables an individual to describe objects and events specifically and to state relationships between objects and events. Several advantages accrue to those who possess this knowledge. First, the knowledgeable individual gains a viewpoint by which to examine and assess behavioral events, especially those in which the significance is not obvious. He is also sensitive to antecedent or causal variables which might not otherwise be perceived either because they are embedded in a complex setting or because they are not a part of the current stimulus field. Second, this kind of knowledge provides the individual with a set of expectancies regarding behavioral outcomes, given the occurrence of or variations in certain environmental and individual difference variables. Therefore, when one has possession of empirical propositions reflecting relationships between antecedent events and behavioral outcomes, that person understands and is able to predict organizational behavior, thereby avoiding uncertainty, surprises, and frustration. Finally, if an individual knows propositions stating relationships between behavior and environmental events which can be changed or varied, then he is able to influence behavior.

Beliefs and Operating Assumptions of the Researcher

The researcher believes in reality. Unlike the solipsist,[1] the scientist assumes that the objects and events which he observes do exist apart from himself.

The researcher also believes that organizational behavior, like other natural phenomena, shows certain consistencies which can be anticipated and explained. He believes that organizational behavior is determined, but he does not assume that there is a single determinant or cause. Rather, he believes that there are multiple determinants which act alone and with other determinants to produce behavior. Yet, he posits *finite* causality. He does not believe that *all* events in nature can influence all other events.

The researcher is an empiricist. He believes reliable knowledge of organizational behavior can best be developed by means of firsthand, controlled observations. He would disagree with the philosophical doctrine which advocates that knowledge may be acquired or developed *solely* through reasoning processes and intuition. For the modern empiricist, reasoning is required for purposes of organizing knowledge and is indispensable to the process of inductive generalization, but the emphasis is upon direct observation and experimentation as the source of knowledge.

---

[1] One who subscribes to the philosophical view that nothing exists or is "real" except the self. [Ed. note]

The researcher has learned to be skeptical, for he has learned that man, as an observer, is subject to error. Consequently, he does not readily agree with a propositional statement simply because it was uttered by a person of recognized status or because it appears intuitively to be true. He does not reject such statements as necessarily false since an empirical test may ultimately lead him to conclude otherwise. He merely asks (1) whether or not they are true, and (2) how could one go about demonstrating their truth or falsity (6, p. 9).

The Researcher and His Language

As stated above, the researcher believes that organizational behavior is a reality apart from himself and that reliable knowledge can be developed about it by means of direct encounter. However, he is aware of the sociolinguistic nature of all scientific endeavor. While linguistic symbols can be distinguished from the objects and events they are meant to represent, few observations of any consequence can be communicated to others without the use of symbols. Direct experience is private and of little social value until it is communicated to others.

The researcher, sensitive to the problems of conceptualization and communication, sets about to construct an objective language which will accurately convey his observations. This language will never be totally independent of the vernacular. Nor should it be. Many terms in the common, everyday language are reasonably precise and unambiguous, in which case they are taken over by the researcher without modification. However, there are also terms in the common language which do not always refer to something out there, or if they do, the "something" is so vague and amorphous that confusion and misunderstanding are rampant. In these cases the researcher is confronted with the necessity of either reconstructing the common language or coining new terms. He will often do both by defining his concepts operationally.

To define a concept operationally means to specify precisely the procedures or operations which are associated with its use. In making a concept synonymous with a set of concrete, reproducible operations, the researcher is able to clarify the phenomenon under investigation and to communicate his observations in an unambiguous manner. For example, to test the proposition that democratic leadership results in (is functionally related to, produces, causes) higher productivity than autocratic leadership, the researcher will have to develop a set of operations defining the terms democratic leadership, autocratic leadership, and productivity. How will the researcher do this?

First of all, the terms are taken from the common language and may require some logical explication[2] before operational definitions can be developed. Upon reflection, the researcher might conclude that the terms *autocratic* and *democratic* leadership refer to specific behavioral patterns exhibited by leaders in formal organizations. But what is the nature of these patterns and how do they differ? Further analysis might lead to the conclusion that autocratic leadership can be characterized by an individual who (1) unilaterally decides what tasks are to be performed by each subordinate, (2) directs subordinates to perform those tasks without deviation, and (3) makes punishment or threats of punishment contingent upon not performing those tasks as directed. The researcher may also decide that democratic leadership can be characterized by an individual who (1) consults with and takes into account the suggestions and preferences of his subordinates in deciding what tasks are to be performed, (2) does not specifically direct his subordinates to perform the tasks, or having elicited task performance, permits deviations in the manner in which they are performed, and (3) makes rewards or promises of rewards contingent upon successful task accomplishment.

If the researcher has not become discouraged at this point, he may attempt to develop a set of operations which he hopes will be somewhat reflective of the explicated concepts. For example, he might develop a behavioral questionnaire which requires organizational leaders to describe how they typically behave with regard to task decisions, methods of eliciting task performance, deviations from task performance, and administration of rewards and punishment. Several analyses and refinements of the questionnaire might enable him to set up a continuum and to classify high scorers on the questionnaire as democratic leaders and low scorers as autocratic leaders. This public and repeatable set of operations is synonymous with and defines the two concepts.[3] After analyzing and defining productivity in the same manner, the researcher is able to investigate the relationship between leadership styles and productivity to be operationally defined in a similar way.

Many concepts in the common, everyday language are rendered less vague and ambiguous by the use of the foregoing procedure. New concepts are also introduced by making them equivalent to a set of operations which others can reproduce. However, the operational

---

[2] Mandler and Kessen (3, pp. 98–104) describe logical explication as a process by which terms in the common language are more precisely defined or redefined.

[3] Perhaps the defining operations should be referred to as "ZIZ" and "ZAZ." Democratic and autocratic leadership are common terms which have already acquired a variety of meanings. It is doubtful that the reader will readily dismiss those ingrained meanings in favor of the defining operations described here. It is for this reason that it is often a good idea to coin new terms to represent operational definitions.

analysis of the concepts must not be considered a panacea. Spence (9) points out that the formulation of operational definitions is merely one faltering step in building a body of empirical knowledge. If the operationally defined concept is not subsequently found to be related to other concepts, then, it has no scientific significance and should be discarded. The number of digits on the left foot multiplied by the number of freckles on the face divided by two is a perfectly acceptable set of operations defining a concept we shall label Welles, but it is highly improbable this would be of any interest to the behavioral scientist.

Another consideration of the researcher is the complexity or "size" of a concept. He may choose to work with concepts referring to a complex of empirical events treated as a syndrome, or he may prefer to work with molecular, unidimensional concepts. Yet, more important than the size or complexity of concepts is the continued persistence of the researcher in conducting research which utilizes a variety of conceptual approaches and which establishes systematic relationships between a syndrome of environmental events and behavioral variables. If these relationships are not found to hold up in every instance, the researcher should break up the syndrome in search of the one or a more limited subset of characteristics which may be responsible for the relationship.

Research Variables in Organizational Behavior and Human Performance

Most concepts contained in empirical propositions refer to things which vary or can be varied in amount, degree, or kind. The researcher seeks to establish relationships between *independent* and *dependent* *variables*.

A dependent variable is anything which is changed or modified as a consequence of a change or a modification in something else. The dependent variable is nearly always some observable aspect of behavior or the consequences of behavior. For example, a researcher may be interested in learning why individuals become members of an organization or *do not* become members, why they remain as members for a long period of time or leave the organization. He may be interested in learning why some individuals or groups are more creative than others, or why some individuals appear to be more satisfied with their jobs than others. He may be interested in learning why some individuals cooperate with each other, while others conflict; why some individuals often contribute far more than is prescribed, while others perform their jobs in the prescribed manner but rarely go beyond that;

and, why some individuals engage in behavior that is judged to be organizationally disruptive.

Obviously, there are a number of dependent variables which are interesting and significant not only because they are functionally related to organizational success, but also because they remain as scientific curiosities, not yet fully explained or predictable. The lives of researchers and managers would be considerably less complicated if they could say that dependent variables were all related and that those factors which lead to high productivity also produce satisfaction, cooperation, and creative contributions. Unfortunately, such is not the case. At least, the relationship between satisfaction and productivity is obscure. Moreover, it is possible that under certain circumstances, such behavior variables as individual productivity and interpersonal cooperation are inversely related. The researcher will frequently direct his attention to these complexities in order to investigate the relationships between behavioral variables or to search for more basic dependent variables.

The independent variable is anything which when changed or modified induces a change or a modification in some aspect of organizational behavior. When a person seeks explanations for turnover, variations in productivity, cooperation, satisfaction, and so on, he is really inquiring about those factors (independent variables) which are functionally related to or cause variations in behavior.

Independent variables in organizational behavior may be viewed as falling into one of two broadly defined classes. There are *environmental* variables, such as task design, magnitude or quality of rewards and punishments and the manner in which they are scheduled, the presence and behavior of significant others, temperature, noise, illumination, group size, and variations in organizational structure. The second class of independent variables is known as *subject* or *individual-difference* variables. These are relatively enduring behavioral characteristics of the individual and include intelligence, aptitudes, propensity to take risks, characteristic energy level, motor skills, and motives.

Observational Strategies

Empirical propositions depend upon firsthand observation for their development, but past experience has made it quite clear that all humans are subject to a variety of observational errors. Consequently, researchers have developed strategies for observing phenomena so that such errors are reduced to a minimum.

Observational strategies may be viewed as falling on a continuum between naturalistic observation and experimentation. As a researcher progresses along the continuum, he exerts increasingly greater control over the phenomena which he is observing.

Naturalistic Observation. Utilizing this strategy, the researcher observes the behavior of individuals as it occurs in a natural setting—namely, in formal organizations. He does not control and manipulate independent variables in order to note their effects on behavior. Rather, he attends to behavior as it ordinarily occurs, watching for apparent covariation between environmental events and behavioral episodes. The researcher may attempt to record those events which seem to be relevant, and he emerges from his study with a verbal description of his observations.

Because naturalistic observation has a number of limitations, a researcher should maintain a cautious attitude toward knowledge based solely upon this strategy. Significant behavioral events may not occur frequently, and since the researcher exerts no control over those events, he may not be prepared to observe them when they do occur. More importantly, the observer makes few attempts to reduce the sources of human error that are attributable to his own act of perceiving. He would not worry much about this source of error if he could depend upon the fact that his sense organs furnish the brain with exact replicas of the real world. However, such is not the case. Illusions are common. Unaided perceptions of physical objects rarely correspond exactly with those resulting from a direct encounter with the object by means of various kinds of measurement techniques.

When the events observed are behavioral, and thus more variable and ambiguous than physical objects, the emotions, expectancies, and past experiences of the observer may become as prominent in determining what is perceived as the behavioral events themselves. Similarly, our perceptions of cause and effect relationships are often inaccurate, especially when the cause and the effect do not always occur together or when the effect does not immediately follow the cause in time (2). Temporal contiguity between events *is* a compelling factor in drawing cause and effect conclusions (11). However, there are a number of events occurring concomitantly with behavior when we observe it in a natural setting. Perhaps the observer could logically dismiss the fly unobtrusively crawling along the sill in another building as a determiner of the behavior of an operative employee on a production line. Yet, which of the several events that are present *will be* selectively attended to? The answer to the question is that the observer will usually arrive on the scene with certain preconceived notions or tentative ideas as to what are the relevant and irrelevant factors, and he will direct his attention to those factors which he believes to be relevant. If he observes a relationship between those events he chooses to concentrate upon, does he do so because there is a relationship which could be confirmed by others, or is the observed relationship attributable to the fact that he expected to find one? Suppose, for example, that the observer suspected that group productivity is higher when the supervisor is physically present than when he is physically absent. Let us further assume (1) that group productivity did not invariably change with the presence or absence of the supervisor, (2) that the supervisor was more often present than absent, (3) that there is *no* inherent relationship between the supervisor's presence and group productivity, and (4) that the observer could accurately discriminate between high and low group productivity and between supervisory presence and non-presence.[4]

Figure 1 shows a record of a series of observations that might have been made under these circumstances.

FIGURE 1
A Record of Observations Made in Organization X Group Productivity

		High	Low	
	Present	10 (a)	5 (b)	15
Supervisor				
	Absent	4 (c)	2 (d)	6
		14	7	21

The naturalistic observer in this situation might perceive only a limited set of instances which would tend to verify his expectation. For example, Figure 1 shows that group productivity was high during 10 of the 15 times the supervisor was present and that group productivity was low only 5 of the 15 times he was present. Alternatively, the supervisor was present during 10 of the 14 times that group productivity was observed to be high and was absent only 4 times during which group productivity was observed to be high. In the event the observer was astute enough to look for *all* confirming and disconfirming cases during the observational period, he would note that there was a total of 12 confirming cases (cells a and d) and only 9 disconfirming ones (cells b and c). Again, however, the observer might erroneously conclude that the supervisor's presence enhances group productivity since his expectation is verified more than it is not.

---

[4] Point four is not a very valid assumption. Changes in group productivity are not easily discernible, and in the absence of an objective means of assessing significant variations in group output, the observer may "see" changes in the direction of his expectations. Naturalistic observers attempt to sharpen the definitions of the concepts they use in reporting their observations, but they rarely define their dependent and independent variables in terms of a reproducible set of measurement operations. An attempt to develop operational definitions of the terms "supervisory presence" and "group productivity" could prove to be humorous, if not enlightening for the reader.

Only the observer who has an abstract appreciation of correlation (2, pp. 14–15) would come to the correct conclusion. He would do so by comparing the probability of high group productivity given the supervisor's presence (10/15 or .67) with the probability of high group productivity given his absence (4/6 or .67). Since the probabilities are identical, he would conclude that in this situation variations in group productivity appear to be independent of the presence or absence of the supervisor.

Let us assume that all the conditions described above are the same except that the observations were made in a different organization in which there *is* a relationship between supervisory presence and group productivity. An example of a series of observations made under these circumstances is shown in Figure 2.

FIGURE 2
A Record of Observations Made in Organization Y Group Productivity

		High	Low	
Supervisor	Present	10 (a)	5 (b)	15
	Absent	2 (c)	4 (d)	6
		12	9	21

This set of observations would reinforce the observer's expectations in the same manner as those made in Organization X. In this case, however, the probability of high group productivity when the supervisor is present is .67, while the probability of high group productivity when he is not present is only .33.

Although the conclusion that the supervisor's presence caused higher group productivity seems to be supported by the observations made in Organization Y, we must consider the possibility that *other* events were operating in this situation to cause the changes in group productivity. While repeated observations would rule out some of them on the basis that they were never present or always present (and nonvarying) when changes in group productivity occurred, perhaps not all of them could be so readily dismissed. Several events may occur together so that it is difficult to say which one is the cause of higher productivity. For example, suppose that the supervisor tended to appear only when production pressure was intense. Then, increased productivity could have resulted because of the varying backlog of visible materials, partially completed assemblies, work orders, etc., rather than the supervisor's presence. The above is an example of *confounding*, a situation in which any variable other than the dependent variable changes along with the independent variable of primary concern. Confounding is always a danger no matter what the observational strategy, but it is most likely to occur when the observer exercises little control over the events he observes.

One often hears that knowledge stemming from naturalistic observation is more relevant to real-life behavior, and hence more valuable to the administrator. But the possibility of confounding places limitations on this knowledge. Different supervisors may not show up only during those times when production pressure increases. Therefore, the results of this study would be of limited generality and quite erroneous if it could be established by more rigorous methods that production pressure rather than supervisory presence was the cause of changes in group productivity.

Despite the limitations of naturalistic observation, a researcher should remain open to knowledge that comes from observers utilizing this strategy. A significant portion of what we know or what we think we know about organizational behavior has been generated by astute individuals who have spent their lives observing behavior as it naturally occurs in formal organizations. Oppenheimer, the physicist, (5) has made a plea not to treat too harshly those who tell a story without having established the completeness or the generality of that story. That plea should not go unheard. In many cases, an observation that has been made in the field has been verified in the laboratory where the observer can exercise the necessary controls over the independent variable and other potentially confounding variables.

Systematic Assessment.   In all probability, the individuals in the production departments of organizations X and Y were not responding as one. Some were undoubtedly producing more than others during the presence *and* absence of the supervisors. Furthermore, both the direction and amount of change may have varied from one individual to another as the supervisors were alternately present and absent. Behavioral scientists have grown to expect significant differences in behavior when several individuals are placed in a common environmental setting, and have approached the problem of explaining those differences by postulating that they are attributable to certain enduring characteristics of the individual. This postulate has led to the development of a wide variety of individual-difference measures, the most common of which are standardized tests. Thus, the term "systematic assessment" has come to be applied to that observational strategy in which events existing in varying degrees in nature are operationally defined, and the relationships between events, so defined, are investigated. The observer does not purposefully manipulate the independent variable as in the experimental strategy, but he typically exercises greater control than the naturalistic observer. An example will serve to illustrate the kinds of control that are exercised when the systematic assessment strategy is employed.

Noting that some employees are consistently more productive than others in the same situation, the observer might hypothesize that the differences are due to variations in aptitude.

The first step in testing the hypothesis is to select or construct operational definitions of the aptitudes which are important in determining productivity. In this case, let us assume that a researcher selects rather than constructs a measure of Closure Flexibility.[5] Then, he assembles all the employees in a room in which noise levels, illumination, and other features of the environment are held constant, and administers the test according to the instructions specified by the test manual. Since the observer has controlled environmental stimulation, he assumes that individual scores are representative of the ability which is measured rather than a function of environmental events. If the observer finds reliable differences in scores, he is ready for the next important step. He must now devise an operational definition of productivity so that he might investigate the relationship between the attribute presumably measured by his test and productivity back at the work site. He may decide to define productivity as the number of acceptable units completed by each individual during a specified period of time. He might also choose to introduce some *additional controls* such as having the supervisor always present and holding the quality and quantity of materials constant for each individual during the observing period.

Having observed and recorded the output of each individual, the researcher is now ready to assess the relationship between scores on the Closure Flexibility Test and productivity. A relationship that might have been obtained is depicted by the scatter diagram in Figure 3.

Utilizing the Pearson product-moment correlation coefficient, one of several techniques for assessing relationships between variables, the observer finds a statistically significant correlation of .49. He concludes, therefore, that there is a functional relationship between scores achieved on the Closure Flexibility Test and the level of individual productivity in this situation.

---

[5] The Closure Flexibility Test is a standardized measure of the ability to hold a configuration in mind despite distraction. This aptitude has been found to be related to certain personality traits and has also been found to differentiate among individuals in various occupational groups.

FIGURE 3
The Relationship between Scores on the Closure Flexibility
Test and Individual Productivity

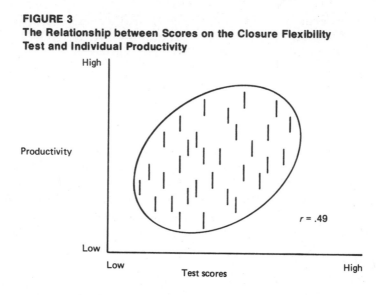

There is a curious mixture of inference and empiricism in this and in all studies utilizing the systematic assessment strategy. It is empirical in the sense that the variables are operationally defined. Since concepts refer to observable events, the observations are capable of being repeated by another individual. Also, the proposition asserting the relationship between Closure Flexibility Test scores and productivity is relatively clear and unambiguous. However, it seems absurd to remain at a strictly empirical level and state that the individual's responses in the test-taking situation caused his subsequent behavior on the production line. Rather, a researcher *infers* some sort of characteristic from the score, and it is that characteristic which is believed to determine the behavioral outcome. In addition to finding that the inferred characteristic is somewhat obscure, a researcher has difficulty specifying and defending the direction of causality. In the above case, it was implicitly assumed that the characteristic measured by the test determined the level of productivity, but variations in task behavior *preceding* the test administration may have determined the score achieved on the test.

The observer utilizing the systematic assessment strategy takes advantage of differences which already exist in nature rather than deliberately creating those differences. As a consequence, the observer does not provide very convincing evidence for causal relationships, whatever the direction. While knowing that individuals differ with regard to closure flexibility, researchers do not know in what other respects the subjects might differ. Perhaps, those who score high on this test also have higher needs for achievement, and the latter characteristic, rather than a high degree of closure flexibility, results in high levels of productivity. The now-familiar problem of confounding is evident here as in every study in which systematic assessment is used.

Nevertheless, functional relationships established by means of systematic assessment can be very useful. Our Closure Flexibility Test, for example, could be used to select from an applicant population those who are most likely to be high producers. However, the possibility of confounding makes it difficult to understand why the relationship exists and places limitations on the generality of the relationship. If the tasks were different and were performed by a different group of individuals in another organization, the same relationship might not hold.

The use of the systematic assessment strategy is not restricted to psychological tests and individual differences. One can also establish operational definitions of organizational characteristics, and then investigate the relationships between differences in those characteristics and behavioral variables. Indik (1), for example, has reviewed a number of studies in which organizational size was found to be related to member satisfaction, absenteeism, and individual output. Size was operationally defined as the number of individuals who are members of the organization, and size was systematically assessed rather than deliberately manipulated as in the experimental strategy. Interestingly enough, Indik offered a set of theoretical postulates to account for the observed relationships between organizational size and behavior (and to account for contradictory findings as well). He speculated that as size increases, communications problems among members tend to increase, task complexity tends to decrease, the need for supervision and coordination increases, and the use of impersonal controls tends to increase. What Indik has done is to ask the reader to consider a variety of *confounding* variables which may be the real causes of dissatisfaction, absenteeism, and productivity. In other words, he seems to be saying that communications problems, task complexity, etc. may often, though not necessarily, vary concomitantly with size to cause the behavior. When they do not vary with size, the relationships will not be observed.

Experimentation. The observer who utilizes the experimental strategy deliberately produces the event he wishes to observe. He systematically varies one event (the independent variable), while controlling the influence of others (potentially confounding variables). Then he notes the effects of the varied event on behavior (the dependent variable). The experimental strategy is by no means a foolproof procedure for producing reliable and generalizable knowledge, but it does provide more convincing evidence for cause-and-effect relationships than other approaches.

Weick (12) prefers to discuss the experimental strategy without reference to a distinction between settings. However, there is some merit in distinguishing between *field experiments* and *laboratory experiments*. The observer may utilize the experimental strategy to study behavior in an ongoing organization, or he may choose to bring behavior into the laboratory where more control can be exercised. Seashore (7) has described the problems which an observer may encounter in conducting a field experiment. They arise primarily because the experiment is incidental to the pursuit of organizational goals and because some loss of control over the appropriate experimental variables is inevitable.

Assume that the observer has decided to conduct a field experiment in order to test the hypothesis that the supervisor's physical presence has a significant effect on group productivity. His first problem is to find an organization which will allow him to conduct the experiment. Having gained entry into an organization, the observer is now faced with a series of experimental design decisions. The experimental strategy, whether employed in the field or in the laboratory, requires at least two different values of the independent variable. Therefore, the observer's first decision is whether to have one group perform the task while the supervisor is present and the other group perform while he is absent (the between-subjects design), or to have *all* employees perform the task under *both* conditions (the within-subjects design). Should the former course of action be chosen, the observer must take care in assigning the subjects to each group so that both groups are approximately equal with respect to confounding variables. He may accomplish this goal by randomly assigning individuals to each group, and then tossing a coin to decide which group will perform with the supervisor present.

A series of observations in which both groups performed the task under identical conditions except the presence and absence of the supervisor may have yielded the data shown in Figure 4.

As the data indicate, the presence of the supervisor seems to affect group productivity. This conclusion assumes that other variables were controlled either by holding them constant or by randomization. If, for example, those who score high on the Closure Flexibility Test are typically the most productive, the random assignment of individuals to the experimental and control groups tends to insure that the average test scores of both groups will be approximately equal before the observations are begun.

The various organizational constraints are likely to prevent the observer from randomly assigning individuals to either the experimental or the control group. Furthermore, it would be nearly impossible to achieve a "pure" condition of supervisory absence for any length of

FIGURE 4
The Relationship between Supervisory Presence and Group Productivity

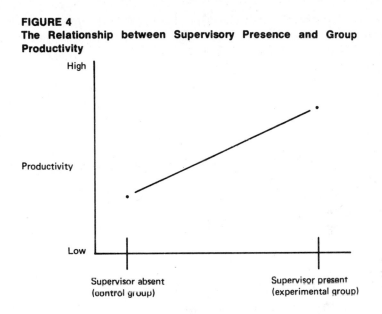

time in a formal organization. A consideration of these and other problems with the implementation of a between-subjects design might have led the observer to adopt the within-subjects design.

The observer is faced with a different kind of problem when he adopts the within-subjects design. He must anticipate the possibility of a progressive error (11, p. 32), a change in behavior that may occur as a function of performing the task over time. In this case, it would not be wise to have the supervisor present during the first four hours of the day and absent during the remaining hours because fatigue effects may confound the results. While there are a number of methods for controlling progressive error, probably the most appropriate one in this experiment would be randomization. The observer would have the supervisor appear at random times throughout the observing period.

The results of the within-subjects experiment may have been quite similar to those obtained from the between-subjects design. However, in both cases, the conclusion that the supervisor's presence enhances group productivity may only hold true in this isolated situation. The observer is dealing with a specific supervisor and a specific work group, and neither is likely to be representative of supervisors and work groups in general. The patterns of interaction between the workers and the relationships between this supervisor and the work group have developed over a period of time. The nature of the interaction history peculiar to this group may be determined by the effects of the supervisor's presence. Moreover, production pressure, which may have affected group productivity and which could not be easily controlled by the observer, may have been significantly higher or lower when the supervisor was present than when he was absent.

The lack of control and the attendant probability of confounding may lead the observer to choose the laboratory as the site for conducting his observations. Here, he might be able to repeat his observations, using different supervisors and different work groups while holding interaction histories, production pressure, and other factors constant. Under these circumstances, the observer is most likely to be able to make a general causal statement about the effect of the supervisor's presence on productivity. However, he is also most likely to be criticized by the laymen on the grounds that the knowledge he has provided is too "theoretical" or has no relevance for the administrator. After all, work groups in organizations have an interaction history. They are not *ad hoc* groups who have never seen each other before, nor are they inexperienced at the task. Furthermore, supervisors come and go at will, and production pressures are variable rather than constant. What the critic really means in this case is that he is not likely to comprehend the influence of the supervisor's presence on behavior in a natural setting because there are other determining factors operating simultaneously there. The effect of the supervisor's physical presence observed in the laboratory may not be observed in the formal organization because that effect is swamped by the effects of other factors which could be controlled in the laboratory. But a researcher will never know whether a supervisor's presence has an effect on behavior until he observes it when the influences of other factors are controlled. If the effect *is* swamped by other variables in a natural setting, then they too need to be observed under controlled conditions.

As we have seen, the observer, suspecting that production pressure has an effect on behavior, could have controlled its influence either by holding it constant at some value or by allowing it to vary randomly. He could just as well have investigated its effects at the same time that he observed the effects of the supervisor's presence. This possibility brings us to a discussion of the *factorial* experiment in which the simultaneous effects of *two* or *more* independent variables are observed.

If production pressure could be defined in a manner that permitted the observer to systematically vary it from a normal value to a high value, the *main* effects of each of the two independent variables could then be examined. The primary influence of the supervisor's presence could be ascertained by contrasting average group productivity when he is present with average group productivity when he is absent, the average being obtained in both cases by summing across both levels of production pressure. This result is shown in Figure 5.

FIGURE 5
The Main Effect of the Supervisor's Presence on Group Productivity

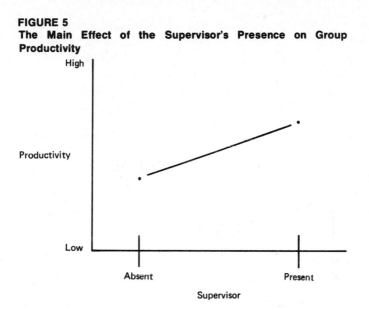

FIGURE 6
The Main Effect of Production Pressure on Group Productivity

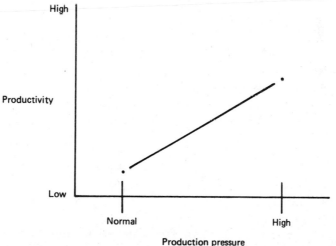

The main effect of variations in production pressure could be examined in a similar fashion, as shown in Figure 6.

The most significant feature of the factorial experiment is that it allows the observer to investigate the *interaction* effects of the independent variables. An interaction effect is said to exist when the relationship between the dependent variable (productivity) and one independent variable (supervisor's presence) varies as a function of the value of another independent variable (production pressure). To clarify the notion of interaction effects, let us assume that the results of the observer's factorial experiment were as illustrated in Figure 7.

FIGURE 7
The Effects of Production Pressure and Supervisor's Presence on Group Productivity

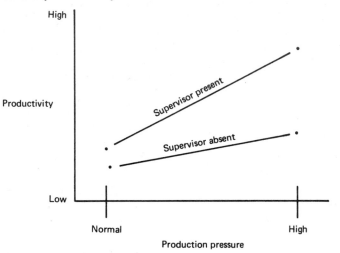

The data suggest[6] that the main effect of production pressure is significant since both lines slope upward. The main effect of the supervisor's presence also appears to be significant since group productivity is generally higher when he is present than when he is absent. However, there appears to be a significant interaction effect as well. That is, the effect of the supervisor's presence on group productivity varies with the value of production pressure. At normal levels of production pressure, the supervisor's presence does not seem to have a large effect on group productivity, but when production pressure is high, his presence has a considerable effect.

One is now able to understand the negative attitude toward knowledge that is produced by the experimental strategy in which the influence of all variables except one is controlled. One observer might have unwittingly or deliberately observed the effects of the supervisor's presence only when production pressure was high, in which case he

---

[6] Needless to say, we cannot discern significant differences in productivity merely by inspection of the data. There are available a number of statistical tests for determining the significance of main and interaction effects.

would have concluded that the physical presence of the supervisor has a very significant effect on group productivity. The response that this bit of knowledge is either irrelevant or theoretical is undoubtedly based upon the subjective feeling that the relationship would only hold under certain conditions which are not typically obtained in nature.

Further observations might support the critic's premise, but such support does not mean that the single factor experiment produced knowledge that is irrelevant or theoretical. That the supervisor's presence has an effect on productivity under certain specifiable circumstances represents a bit of knowledge which we did not possess before the experiment was conducted. Furthermore, researchers seek to extend the generality of their findings by repeating their observations under different conditions. A failure to observe the same relationship under different conditions inevitably stimulates speculation and additional studies until the contradictory findings are resolved. Finally, interaction effects are not always found. If the two productivity lines shown in Figure 7 were parallel or approached that condition, one would have to conclude that the effects of the supervisor's presence were similar whether production pressure was normal or high.

The experimental strategy is most frequently employed by those who seek to establish behavioral propositions which hold for all individuals. Individual differences are deliberately masked or treated as experimental error when changes in behavior, if they occur as a consequence of a change in an environmental event, are shown as changes in group averages. The attempt to establish general behavioral laws is a perfectly legitimate and useful enterprise. However, researchers often observe the behavior of two individuals to be both quantitatively and qualitatively different at the same value of the independent variable. The attempt to explain individual differences in response to constant environmental events and to changes in environmental events has led to the development of a factorial experiment in which at least one of the independent variables is an individual-difference variable systematically assessed (4).

As an example, let us assume that the observer administered the Closure Flexibility Test to his group of subjects and then observed the effects of the supervisor's presence on the productivity of those who scored high and those who scored low on the test. If the observer programmed the supervisor to appear in a randomized sequence, the influence of variations in production pressure would tend to be randomized, and progressive error would similarly be controlled. The results of this hypothetical experiment are shown in Figure 8.

The main effects of both independent variables appear to be significant, but there is also an interaction effect. In this case, the

FIGURE 8
The Effects of Closure Flexibility and the Supervisor's Presence on Productivity

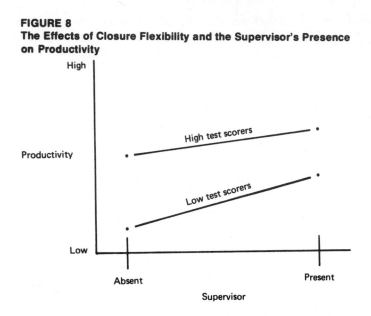

degree to which the supervisor's presence affects productivity depends upon the level of closure flexibility inherent in an individual.

Since behavior is widely held to be a function of the *interaction* between the individual and his environment, the observational approach which combines systematic assessment and experimental manipulation is perhaps the most appropriate one yet devised.

REFERENCES

1. Indik, B. P.   Some effects of organizational size on member attitudes and behavior. *Human Relations*, 1963, *16*, 369–384.

2. Jenkins, H. M., & Ward, W. C.   Judgment of contingency between responses and outcomes. *Psychological Monographs: General and Applied*, 1965, 79, 1–17.

3. Mandler, G., & Kessen, W.   *The language of psychology*. New York: Wiley, 1959.

4. McGuigan, F. J.   *Experimental psychology: A methodological approach* (2d. ed.). Englewood Cliffs, N.J.: Prentice-Hall, 1968.

5. Oppenheimer, R.   Analogy in science. *American Psychologist*, 1956, *11*, 127–135.

6. Scott, W., & Wertheimer, M.   *Introduction to Psychological Research.* New York: Wiley & Sons, 1962.

7. Seashore, S. E.   Field experiments with formal organizations. *Human Organization* 1964, *23*, 164–170.

8. Skinner, B. F. Are theories of learning necessary? *Psychological Review*, 1950, *57*, 193–216.

9. Spence, K. W. The nature of theory constructions in contemporary psychology. *Psychological Review*, 1944, *51*, 47–68.

10. Turner, M. B. *Philosophy and the science of behavior.* New York: Appleton-Century-Crofts, 1967.

11. Underwood, B. J. *Experimental psychology* (2d. ed.). New York: Appleton-Century-Crofts, 1966.

12. Weick, K. E. Laboratory experimentation with organizations. In J. G. March (Ed.), *Handbook of Organizations.* Skokie, Ill.: Rand McNally, 1965.

13. Zajonc, R. B. Social facilitation. *Science,* 1965, *149*, 269–274.

4

Challenging Traditional Research Assumptions*

EDWARD E. LAWLER III

Research on organizations has increased over its 50-year history. Starting in the 1950s, the volume has grown dramatically to the point where, today, we find ourselves overwhelmed with research on organizations. New journals are appearing regularly, books are being produced at an increasing rate, and Ph.D. programs are turning out researchers at a high rate.

As the research on organizational behavior has developed and increased in volume, a relatively well-codified set of principles about what constitutes "good" research has emerged. Indeed, today most people in the field can agree on what constitutes a well-designed research study and what represents a good application of the scientific method to research on organizational behavior. This agreement is clearly exemplified by the increasing use of quantitative methods in the field and by the greater sophistication of recent studies with respect to principles of experimental design. To many, the path toward

* From Edward E. Lawler III, Allan M. Mohrman, Jr., Susan A. Mohrman, Gerald E. Ledford, Jr., and Thomas G. Cummings and Associates, *Doing Research That Is Useful for Theory and Practice,* pp. 1–17. Copyright © 1985 by Jossey-Bass, Inc., Publishers.

further knowledge about organizational behavior is clear. It leads to more rigorous research with better designs, larger samples, and more sophisticated statistical analysis. But is this indeed the best route to lead us toward better understanding of organizations?

Before we can answer this question, we need to ask what constituencies are relevant for research on organizations. Unlike some fields of scientific research, research on organizations has a large, well-defined constituency of practitioners. Indeed, it is this feature of the field, along with a consideration of how data can best be gathered in organizations, that raises the question whether the "traditional" way of doing research is the way most likely to produce useful knowledge about organizations and their management.

This book assumes that research on organizations can serve not only the scientific research community but also those in the society who are generally responsible for and interested in the effectiveness of organizations. In short, it assumes that the research agenda is one that should contribute to both theory and practice. This is an important point because it raises the standard; or perhaps a better way to phrase it is to say that it creates two standards that any research project must meet. The project must help practitioners understand organizations in a way that will improve practice, and it must contribute to a theoretically and scientifically useful body of knowledge about organizations.

USEFULNESS OF RESEARCH FOR THEORY AND PRACTICE

Traditionally, researchers of organizational behavior have not focused on the issue of usefulness. We have assumed that if a research project is methodologically sound, it will contribute to scientific knowledge and ultimately to practice. Indeed, many researchers seem to have found comfort and justification for their basic position in Kurt Lewin's statement that nothing is so practical as a good theory. This comfort has often led to their doing studies that focus only on contributing to theory and justifying research that is far removed from practice.

Perhaps because it is not focused on the goal of usefulness, a considerable amount of the research done in organizational behavior has in fact not had an impact on practice. The belief that good scientific research will ultimately win out often turns out to be naive and misleading. For example, the best-known research on organization effectiveness is contained in the book *In Search of Excellence* (Peters & Waterman, 1983). From a methodological point of view, that book is a disaster (no control group, measures not specified, and so forth).

The suggestion here is that if research is to jointly contribute to theory and practice, it must be designed to accomplish this objective. It cannot simply be taken as a matter of faith that adhering to certain scientific research principles will lead to jointly useful research. Indeed, it may be that adhering to principles that were designed to produce research that contributes to scientific knowledge will make it certain that this research will not contribute to practice.

At this point, I need to expand on my earlier statement about how data can best be gathered. Organizational behavior research has numerous characteristics that make it different from research in the physical and biological sciences. The study of organizations and people in them is a much more complex interactive process than the study of most physical and biological phenomena. People in organizations do not become subjects in the same sense that animals, neutrons, and chemical substances become subjects. They are an active part of the research process, and as such, they influence it very directly. Given this difference, it seems quite possible that what is a good research approach for contributing to theory and scientific knowledge in traditional fields of science may not be a good research approach in dealing with organizations.

Indeed, in the case of organizational behavior research there seems to be a particular danger that we will do research that is more a product of the methodology than of the phenomenon being studied. Taken to its extreme, this tendency could lead to a series of theories and findings that meet the test of traditional scientific validity but that are not useful to the practitioner and, indeed, may not be useful to the theorist either, because they do not describe actual organizational behavior. They may fail to be useful because they do not inform the practitioner or the theorist about the realities of the organizational environment. Instead, they frame the issues in such a way, and report on data so far removed from the realities of the complex, interactive, ever-changing world of organization, that they are not useful as a guide to either theory or practice.

It thus seems possible that a whole series of "scientifically acceptable" findings or theories could be developed that would have little or nothing to say about the realities of organizational behavior. How can this be avoided? The argument here is that it can best be avoided by doing research designed to influence both theory and practice.

Theory and practice are not competing mistresses. Indeed, research that is useless to either the theoretician or the practitioner is suspect. If it is useful to the practitioner but not the theoretician, then one must wonder whether it is a valid finding and whether it has addressed the correct issue. If it is useful to the theoretician but not to the practitioner, then one must wonder whether the research is capturing a critical issue. Indeed, it can be argued that we should always ask two questions about research: Is it useful for practice, and does it contribute to the body of scientific knowledge that is relevant to theory? If it fails either of these tests, then serious questions should be raised. It is a rare research study that can inform practice but not theory, or vice versa.

Research on organizations presents the researcher with a series of dilemmas. Hard choices need to be made and value judgments reached about the best way to design research. At this point I would like to raise some of the critical issues that need to be considered in designing research. I will consider how each of them is traditionally resolved and how each might be resolved if the desire is to be sure that the research produces scientifically and practically useful results.

DOES PRACTICE LAG BEHIND THEORY?

Traditional wisdom in most scientific disciplines says that practice lags behind theory and research, that improvements in practice follow, often by decades, breakthroughs in research and theory. In many areas of organizational behavior the same principle holds. In a number of research and theoretical breakthroughs that have led to changes in practice (for example, the studies on job enrichment and on cafeteria fringe benefit plans), often the lag has been as long as 15 years between research findings and the changes in practice. But it does not necessarily follow that in all or even in most cases theory leads practice.

Virtually everyone is an observer and theorist with respect to organizations. Many people hold organizational positions that call for them to make organizational design decisions, policy decisions, and practice decisions. Quite a few of them are bright, perceptive people, capable of developing insights into practice without the help of theory and empirical research. So in some areas it is quite possible for practice to lead or at least precede theory. Innovative work designs, policies, and procedures can and do exist before there is a theoretical understanding of why they might work and empirical support for their effectiveness. Skill-based pay is an example, as are high-involvement new plants (see, for example, Lawler, 1978, 1981). Instances in which practice is ahead of theory have some important implications for the kind of research that is done. They suggest that unless scholars and researchers are aware of practice, they may miss out on some important breakthroughs that are relevant to theory and research. Indeed, staying in touch with what is happening in the world of practice may be one of the best ways to develop new theory and to discover new research issues.

In short, what is being suggested is that advances in theory and practice are likely to come about not necessarily as a result of theory leading practice or practice leading theory. Either of these can happen and, therefore, research ought to focus not only on developing new theory and findings that will guide practice but also on studying practice that can guide theory and new research.

Researchers are prone to ask, "Why don't managers use what we know?" This is a good question, but so is its reverse, "Why don't researchers use what managers know?"

WHERE IS THE EXPERTISE?

In traditional scientific research the assumption is that expertise about the phenomenon being studied rests with the research scientist, not with the subject of the research. In most cases this is a safe assumption. But is it a safe assumption with respect to organizations and individual behavior in organizations? As already suggested, often managers and organization members are astute observers of the situation they are in, and their innovations in practice often precede theory. The clear implication is that any research targeted at improving both theory and practice needs to be guided by both practitioners and researchers. To ignore theory is to court rejection from the scientific community, and to ignore what managers already know and are doing runs the very definite risk of producing research that lags behind practice and therefore will not be useful to the practitioner.

The view that practitioners have knowledge about organizations has significant implications for research design. It suggests that in many cases members of an organization must be treated as coresearchers; that is, they must have a role in defining the types of research issues that are going to be looked at, and they must be informed of the scientific research issues involved. In short, the argument is that research that is to contribute to both theory and practice needs to be scrutinized by experts in both. Clearly the researcher ought to offer expertise about theory, past research, and methodology, but in many cases he or she has to rely on the members of the organization being studied to provide expertise about practice. For this to happen, the practitioner has to be involved in the study at more than a superficial level and, indeed, has to influence both the kind of topic studied and the methods used.

ROLE OF RESEARCH SUBJECTS

Traditional research design is very clear about defining the role of research subjects. It recommends what might be called an "experimental set" in which the subject, or respondent, is given a minimal amount of information about the study. The subject is told that the data will be used for research purposes only and that there is therefore no need to be concerned about how the data will affect his or her worklife. This research set clearly puts the subject in a dependent passive role with respect to the research study. It has some advantages, but it may not be the one that produces the best data for determining practice or developing research data that lead to valid theory.

The major problem with this approach is that it assumes people will conscientiously provide data simply because they are asked to and that these data will represent the best information that can be gathered about the subject being studied. An alternative view is that with this approach people might not care very much about giving valid data because doing so is not going to affect their lives and that they have other valid and important data that they could contribute to the study if they knew its focus. The latter would be particularly true if, as suggested earlier, people in organizations have expertise on organizations, just as researchers do. This point raises an interesting challenge for the researcher interested in doing theoretically and practically relevant research. It suggests that a researcher may want to rethink the relationship between the subject and the research so that it becomes a more balanced one in which the subject has knowledge of the key research issues. It also suggests, as discussed later, that better data are produced when the subjects know the study will affect practice in their organizations.

USEFULNESS OF COUNTERINTUITIVE FINDINGS

Social science researchers seem to love nothing better than a counterintuitive finding. Proving that "common sense" is wrong seems to produce a great deal of satisfaction and is highly rewarded in the research community. This is hardly surprising. Counterintuitive findings tend to justify the field because they show that social science theory and research can produce things that are otherwise nondiscoverable. There are numerous examples of counterintuitive findings in the organizational behavior literature, and they are often featured in the textbooks of the field. Indeed, they are used to justify study of organizational behavior because they point out clearly that there is something to be learned here that cannot be learned from the everyday experience of practitioners. And to a degree this characteristic has led us to value counterintuitive findings more highly than research findings that support common sense, elaborate on it, or put it in a more comprehensive package.

It is hard to argue against the importance of counterintuitive findings and the theories that support and explain them. They are an important part of scientific research, but it is also possible that our search for respect, esteem, and credibility has led us to overvalue them compared with less spectacular findings and theory. Often the theory or finding that simply confirms common sense, organizes it better, and allows it to be communicated more effectively is the most useful theory. All too often it seems that the counterintuitive theories on which we focus produce long sequences of research projects that explain relatively few of the phenomena that actually occur in the real world. They end up being artifacts of a particular set of conditions that produce the phenomena we studied. In short, they are catchy, but they do not explain many of the situations that occur in the day-to-day operation of organizations. In my own field of research, for example, the work on effects of overpayment and effects of pay on intrinsic motivation produced catchy findings but ones that in fact seem very limited in the situations where they occur (Adams, 1965; Deci, 1975).

What all this suggests is that if we are to do research that is relevant to both theory and practice, we may have to value highly research that does not produce nonobvious findings but that produces confirmation of "common sense." This follows rather directly from the point that managers can be rather astute observers of common sense and, as such, they know something about organizations.

PROJECT SIZE

A great deal of the research in organizational behavior can be characterized as small-scale research. It is usually done on a small budget, involves a few researchers, and covers a short time period. There are a number of reasons for the frequency of such research, including the kind of funding available for organizational behavior research and the career considerations present in most universities. All too often this combination of factors leads to organizational behavior research dealing with issues that can be easily studied and works against investigation of major issues that can be studied only in large-scale research projects.

Reliance on small-scale studies may not have hindered the field so much from a theoretical perspective as it has from a practical one. Organizational behaviorists have been able to study a number of interesting theoretical issues without engaging in large-scale research undertakings. However, many practical questions concerning what works and does not work in influencing productivity, organizational effectiveness, and so on seem to demand large-scale, multivariable, complex research. For example, in order to know how such things as self-managing work teams, quality circles, Scanlon plans, and other new management practices work, when they work, and where they work, large-scale studies seem a necessity. Thus the traditional wisdom that says that a small, "doable" project is better than a large one may need to be changed if research that is relevant to both theory and practice is to be done. Researchers may need to think big, not small, in future research activities.

RESEARCHABLE QUESTIONS

Closely related to the issue of thinking big versus thinking small is the issue of the degree to which available methodology should drive the kind of research question that is addressed. I have often heard the distinction made between interesting questions and researchable questions. As the statement goes, in the field of organizational behavior there are interesting questions and there are researchable questions, and often the two are different.

Often a question is interesting because it is of practical importance. Consequently, to the degree that the field limits its research to researchable questions, it runs the danger of doing research that does not have practical importance. The implication of this point is clear. If we are to do research that is relevant to both theory and practice, we need to have a definition of "acceptable" or "good" methodology that is driven by the type of question being researched as well as by "traditional" scientific standards of what constitutes good research.

This may sound like a radical point of view, but it is not. It merely suggests that different approaches to data gathering, data analysis, and learning need to be used for different kinds of research problems. This follows rather directly from the view that not all problems can be solved with the same research strategy. The research question needs to drive the kind of data collected, and because methods and questions interact in important ways, the kind of data needed to answer certain questions simply cannot be gathered with traditional research methods. Similarly, traditional research methods produce the best kind of data to answer certain kinds of questions.

DO PRACTITIONERS NEED FACTS OR FRAMES?

The field of organizational behavior is perhaps best at producing facts. The justification for this endeavor is that facts are ultimately a useful product because they allow theory testing, theory construction, and, of course, the improvement of practice.

It is quite possible, however, that the best way to improve practice is not by producing facts but by producing frames, or ways of organizing and thinking about the world. A good case can be made that the most important products of the field of organizational behavior are simple, elegant frames, not findings or hugely complex, ugly, inelegant frames.

The problem with saying we need frames is that it is difficult to identify where they come from and to determine the implication of their source for research strategy. However, drawing from some of my earlier points, at least one possibility is that frames come best from interaction between practitioners and researchers in which the researchers learn from the practitioners and vice versa. Frames, however, may come directly from the insights and research data of the researcher. The point here is not that there is one prescribed, clearcut, best way to develop frames. It is merely that if part of the research agenda is to influence practice, frames may be the most important outcome of research.

BROAD-BRUSH VERSUS FINE-GRAINED RESEARCH

A number of the early important studies in organizational behavior were fine-grained research. They looked in depth at a particular interaction or small part of a work organization. The Western Electric studies (Roethlisberger & Dickson, 1939) were of this nature, as was much of the earlier work by William F. Whyte (for example, Whyte, 1955). These studies included dialogue and intensive study of the behavior of small groups and individuals. This type of research has accounted for a smaller and smaller percentage of the total work in the field. Instead we have moved to more and more broad-brush studies that analyze organizations from a distance, either through questionnaires or through secondary data. Organizations are studied by researchers who never see them! The result is rather antiseptic descriptions of organizations and the development of theories from these. To a degree, broad-brush research is the enemy of research that influences practice. Broad-brush research often deals with only a few variables across a large number of people and as a result lacks, in the eyes of many practitioners, a truly comprehensive understanding of the workplace. It tends to lead to simple theories that ignore many of the factors the practitioner must take into account in managing the work organization.

It may be that the most useful research is that which takes a more fine-grained approach to data gathering, but there are problems with this kind of research as well. The challenge with fine-grained research is, of course, to extract from it some general conclusions, insights, and frames that contribute to theory. There is also the problem of gathering data in such a way that it is replicable and meets most people's standards for scientifically valid research.

CERTAINTY VERSUS USEFULNESS

Traditional science places great emphasis on establishing how certain we are of the validity of a particular relationship or finding. Indeed, most of the research in organizational behavior focuses on validating, extending, and establishing the conditions under which a certain finding holds. This focus reflects the high value placed on certainty in scientific research. But to a degree, certainty may be the enemy of usefulness.

The effort to establish certainty almost always leads to large numbers of studies being done on a single small topic and to more and more careful specification of the phenomenon. Once the phenomenon has been subjected to all the tests of certainty, it often ends up so complex that it is no longer useful to the practitioner. Establishing certainty presents a difficult challenge for the researcher who wishes to do research that is useful for both theory and practice. Somehow the researcher has to satisfy the scientific need to establish that the phenomenon is real and, at the same time, not lose sight of the usefulness issue. Often the conflict between these two demands leads the researcher who is concerned with usefulness and theory to stop doing research on a topic before others would say that the necessary level of certainty has been reached. In the researcher's eyes, however, certainty may have been established because of the kind of data that the researcher has gathered. A practice- and theory-oriented researcher, for example, may place more emphasis on observational data, reports by practitioners, and sense-making insights than would a researcher who is concerned with confidence levels, reliability estimates, and research design.

STUDY OF CHANGE

Assessing organizational change is difficult and often creates conditions that violate traditional views of what constitutes good scientific research. It typically requires a long-term involvement with an organization, an adaptive research design in which methods and questions change over time, and a close working relationship with the organization. All these conditions lead many to argue that it is hard to do "good" research on change. However, many of the most interesting practical questions concern change. Managers and practitioners constantly want to know what happens to Y if they do X, and they also want to know the best way to change organizations toward a particular kind of culture or strategy. Hence there is little doubt that if research is going to be practically useful, it needs to deal with the issue of organizational change.

Although there seems to be some reason for believing that doing good research and studying change are mutually exclusive, a good counterargument can be made. If, as stated earlier, good research is often fine-grained and large-scale, the study of change offers an excellent opportunity to do research that meets these conditions. Members of organizations are often very concerned about and interested in research on change, particularly if it can help inform and direct the change in constructive ways. Consequently, in the study of change there is often a natural alliance between the researcher who wants to do long-term, fine-grained research on an important organizational change issue and practitioners who want to understand the change and make it effective. Thus, the study of change may be a particularly good opportunity to do research that is useful both practically and theoretically.

If researchers are to do research on change, they need a set of skills often lacking in organizational behavior researchers. Not only do they need to be familiar with and capable of using a variety of research methods, they need to relate to organizations in a way that allows the research relationship to survive over a long period and, perhaps, even to support the change activities going on in the organization. In short, they need to have both research skills and certain consulting skills. If a researcher has these skills and is able to engage the organization in a study of the change process, the probability of studying significant problems in a comprehensive way is high.

Indeed, the key question may be: Is it possible to do good research *without* studying change? Given that the key issues in understanding organizations are not static and . . . are not the kinds that lend themselves to tightly controlled field experiments, studying change may be the only way.

CONSULTING AND RESEARCH

Many researchers take care to separate consulting and research. The two are seen as competing activities because they demand a different relationship with the organization and its members. This is clearly true in the traditional scientific model of what constitutes good research, but it is not so clear if the research agenda is targeted toward influencing both theory and practice.

It can be argued that testing many important theoretical concepts and developing improved practice depends on having some researchers who can engage in consulting relationships with organizations. It is only through this type of consulting relationship that organizations can actually try new ideas and breakthroughs in practice.

Some new practices and some new theories can be adequately

tested only by putting them in place in an organization. This implies an intervention into an organization's actual operating procedures. Alternatively, one can simply wait for an organization to try something and then capitalize on it as a naturally occurring field experiment or a post hoc study of change. This is often done in the field of organizational behavior, but reliance on this technique places a severe limitation on the development of the field. It requires that new practices be tried by somebody else before the field can progress. A much more attractive alternative is for researchers to help in instituting innovations so that they can study issues that are likely to push the state of theory and practice forward.

SUMMARY

Taken in combination, the points made so far suggest that research that is likely to contribute to both theory and practice can be done but that it may look different from much of the research traditionally done in organizational behavior. To mention just a few points, it is more likely, for example, to involve change, to be large-scale, and to be fine-grained in the depth with which it looks at organizations. This is not to argue that traditional research is to be discontinued or that there is only one right way to do research; rather, there are multiple valid ways to do research on organizations, and the field needs to be eclectic in the approaches it includes. In short, the argument is that there is more than one way of establishing theory and fact. There are multiple ways, and these all need to be used if research that contributes to both theory and practice is to be conducted. . . . The best approach for a particular situation clearly reflects not only the topic to be studied but the skills of the researcher and the strengths and weaknesses of different methods of data gathering.

Figure 1 elaborates on this point by showing a possible relationship

FIGURE 1
Possible Relationship between Data and Confidence

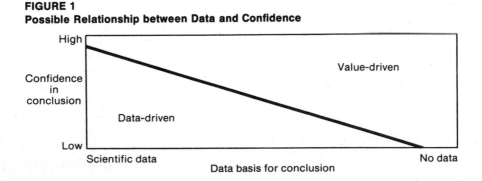

between data and the confidence one has in a finding about how organizations operate. The data gathered may vary from traditional scientific data to no data at all, and confidence can vary from high to low. Where few facts exist but confidence is high, we have entered the arena of value-driven decision making. At the other extreme, when scientific data exist, confidence will be high from a data-based perspective. Yet even where there is a great deal of data, the figure suggests that value contributes to reaching the highest level of confidence. Finally, it suggests that we should have the most "scientific" confidence when we have good traditional data.

Based on the arguments presented in this chapter, it is reasonable to question the nature of the confidence line separating value-driven and data-driven decision making in Figure 1. Figure 1 assumes that the best data are traditionally gathered scientific data. If we assume they are not, then we might draw the line as shown in Figure 2.

FIGURE 2
Alternative Relationship between Data and Confidence

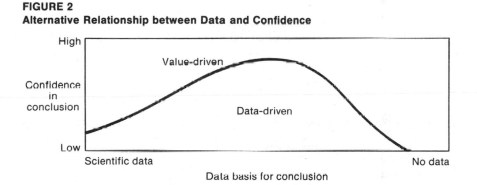

Ultimately, it is up to each researcher to develop his own relationship between data and confidence in the decisions about what findings to believe and how strongly to believe them.

*   *   *   *   *

A Nobel Prize-winning economist has observed that the best current research and theory rarely inform contemporary practice in the field of economics (Stigler, 1976). He argues that the kind of data that economists need and the kind of theories they state are so obscure that they bear almost no relation to practice. At first glance, this might seem to be in contrast to Lewin's statement about the usefulness of theory, but I wonder whether Lewin would consider the theoretical work done in economics today good. In fact, I doubt that he would.

There is an interesting possible variant of Lewin's statement about the usefulness of theory: "Nothing is so useful as research that informs both theory and practice." If, indeed, research informs practice, then it is likely to have something to say about the reality of the workplace and to deal with issues that are relevant to practitioners. If it also informs theory, then it must describe more than just an isolated phenomenon or a nonreplicable phenomenon. It must state something that is generalizable across situations and issues. Unfortunately, much of the research on organizational behavior may be better at informing theory than practice. As a result, we end up with many theories that are not useful to the practitioner. We have many theories, but perhaps we have few good theories.

REFERENCES

Adams, J. S.   Injustice in social exchange. In L. Berkowitz (Ed.), *Advances in experimental social psychology* (Vol. 2). New York: Academic Press, 1965.

Deci, E. L.   *Intrinsic motivation.* New York: Plenum Press, 1975.

Lawler, E. E., III.   The new plant revolution. *Organizational Dynamics,* 1978, *6* (3), 2–12.

Lawler, E. E., III.   *Pay and organization development.* Reading, Mass.: Addison-Wesley Publishing, 1981.

Peters, T., & Waterman, R.   *In search of excellence.* New York: Harper & Row, 1983.

Roethlisberger, F. J., & Dickson, W. J.   *Management and the worker.* Cambridge, Mass.: Harvard University Press, 1939.

Stigler, G. J.   Do economists matter? *Southern Economic Journal,* 1976, *42,* 347–354.

Whyte, W. F.   *Money and motivation: an analysis of incentives in industry.* New York: Harper & Row, 1955.

section two

The Motivational Basis
of Behavior
in Organizations

Except for the infirm and the heirs to family riches, people obviously have to work in order to attain a standard of living and creature comforts beyond mere survival. And most of these people will have to work in organizations. However, these considerations, at best, suffice only to give us a point of departure for understanding behavior at work. We know that other goals and motives become adjoined to the vocational imperative, but what is the nature of these motives? We know that we work harder and better under some conditions than others, but what accounts for this variability in our performance? Would the answers to these questions enable us to design organizational environments which yield both higher member satisfaction and more effective institutions?

These questions raise theoretical and applied issues. The first five articles in Section Two tackle the conceptual problems attendant to the analysis of motivation at work. These are followed by a description and assessment of several approaches to applying work motivation theory.

A. THEORETICAL ISSUES

Introduction

To seek an understanding of the motivation of behavior at work is to ask "what?" and "how?" The question of *what* represents a query as to the *content* or substance of motivation. What are the important goals that people seek to attain through work? What are the rewards, incentives, ends, and driving forces? What do people really want—especially once they can take for granted some reasonable satisfaction of material and security needs?

Aronson argues that we strive to maintain and project some semblance of rationality and consistency in both thought and action. Henry Clay once said that he would rather "be right than be President"; most of us would often rather be consistent than be "right." Unfortunately, otherwise astute administrators underestimate and underappreciate the importance of this motive, both in themselves and others, and therein lies the potential for serious misreading of many acts and utterances.

Kerr turns us from the content to the *process* dimension of motivation. Whatever the stated aims of organizations, people pursue those courses of action that provide paths to the goals they seek. Unfortunately, organizations all too often arrange valued goal objects at the ends of paths that run away from, even opposite to, the paths that would lead to officially espoused objectives. Kerr provides several telling illustrations of this phenomenon and offers some explanations of why it occurs.

Lawler and Porter likewise address primarily the process questions of motivation. In particular, they discuss the issue of how performance becomes part of this process. They argue that the process is *not,* as many would like to believe, one of satisfaction giving rise to subsequent performance. Rather, performance enters into the process only if it is conceived by members as the relevant path to extrinsic rewards (such as greater compensation) or more intangible rewards (such as feelings of achievement and pride in work).

Organ states the case that certain forms of satisfaction *can* lead to certain aspects of performance, provided we take account of yet another motive: the need to bring about what we construe as fairness, equity, or social justice in our relationships with each other. This need affects some people more than others; doubtless we all, from time to time, suppress this need when it conflicts with other, more urgently pressing needs; and, in any case, we can exercise considerable ingenuity in distorting our perceptions of what is really fair. Nonetheless, most of us are conditioned from our earliest ages onward to acquire— either as an internalized ethical prerogative or a socially required rule of conduct—the motive of social justice. Failure to incorporate this motive in our analysis is to blind us to the quintessentially humane aspects of organizations.

Discussions of job motivation nowadays almost invariably touch upon the concept of "intrinsic motivation." Pinder provides an analysis of this concept, its origins and causes, and the intriguing question of how it interacts with the effects of extrinsic incentives.

5

The Rationalizing Animal*

ELLIOT ARONSON

Man likes to think of himself as a rational animal. However, it is more true that man is a *rationalizing* animal, that he attempts to appear reasonable to himself and to others. Albert Camus even said that man is a creature who spends his entire life in an attempt to convince himself that he is not absurd.

Some years ago a woman reported that she was receiving messages from outer space. Word came to her from the planet Clarion that her city would be destroyed by a great flood on December 21. Soon a considerable number of believers shared her deep commitment to the prophecy. Some of them quit their jobs and spent their savings freely in anticipation of the end.

On the evening of December 20, the prophet and her followers met to prepare for the event. They believed that flying saucers would pick them up, thereby sparing them from disaster. Midnight arrived, but no flying saucers. December 21 dawned, but no flood.

What happens when prophecy fails? Social psychologists Leon Festinger, Henry Riecken, and Stanley Schachter infiltrated the little band of believers to see how they would react. They predicted that persons who had expected the disaster, but awaited it alone in their homes, would simply lose faith in the prophecy. But those who awaited the outcome in a group, who had thus admitted their belief publicly, would come to believe even more strongly in the prophecy and turn into active proselytizers.

This is exactly what happened. At first the faithful felt despair and shame because all their predictions had been for naught. Then, after waiting nearly five hours for the saucers, the prophet had a new vision. The city had been spared, she said, because of the trust and faith of her devoted group. This revelation was elegant in its simplicity, and the believers accepted it enthusiastically. They now sought the press that they had previously avoided. They turned from believers into zealots.

Living on the Fault.   In 1957 Leon Festinger proposed his theory of *cognitive dissonance,* which describes and predicts man's rationalizing behavior. Dissonance occurs whenever a person simultaneously holds two inconsistent cognitions (ideas, beliefs, opinions). For example, the belief that the world will end on a certain day is dissonant with the awareness, when the day breaks, that the world has not ended. Festinger maintained that this state of inconsistency is so uncomfortable that people strive to reduce the conflict in the easiest way possible. They will change one or both cognitions so that they will "fit together" better.

Consider what happens when a smoker is confronted with evidence that smoking causes cancer. He will become motivated to change either his attitudes about smoking or his behavior. And as anyone who has tried to quit knows, the former alternative is easier.

The smoker may decide that the studies are lousy. He may point to friends ("If Sam, Jack, and Harry smoke, cigarettes can't be all that dangerous"). He may conclude that filters trap all the cancer-producing materials. Or he may argue that he would rather live a short and happy life with cigarettes than a long and miserable life without them.

The more a person is committed to a course of action, the more resistant he will be to information that threatens that course. Psychologists have reported that the people who are least likely to believe the dangers of smoking are those who tried to quit—and failed. They have become more committed to smoking. Similarly, a person who builds a $100,000 house astride the San Andreas Fault will be less receptive to arguments about imminent earthquakes than would a person who is renting the house for a few months. The new homeowner is committed; he doesn't want to believe that he did an absurd thing.

When a person reduces his dissonance, he defends his ego, and keeps a positive self-image. But self-justification can reach startling extremes; people will ignore danger in order to avoid dissonance, even when that ignorance can cause their deaths. I mean that literally.

Suppose you are Jewish in a country occupied by Hitler's forces. What should you do? You could try to leave the country; you could try to pass as "Aryan"; you could do nothing and hope for the best. The first two choices are dangerous: if you are caught you will be executed. If you decide to sit tight, you will try to convince yourself that you made the best decision. You may reason that while Jews are indeed being treated unfairly, they are not being killed unless they break the law.

Now suppose that a respected man from your town announces that he has seen Jews being butchered mercilessly, including everyone who has recently been deported from your village. If you believe him, you might have a chance to escape. If you don't believe him, you and your family will be slaughtered.

Dissonance theory would predict that you will not listen to the witness, because to do so would be to admit that your judgment and decisions were wrong. You will dismiss his information as untrue, and decide that he was lying or hallucinating. Indeed, Elie Wiesel reported that this happened to the Jews in Sighet, a small town in Hungary, in 1944. Thus people are not passive receptacles for the deposit of information. The manner in which they view and distort the objective world in order to avoid and reduce dissonance is entirely predictable. But one cannot divide the world into rational people on one side and dissonance reducers on the other. While people vary in their ability to tolerate dissonance, we are all capable of rational or irrational behavior, depending on the circumstances—some of which follow.

Dissonance because of Effort. Judson Mills and I found that if people go through a lot of trouble to gain admission to a group, and the group turns out to be dull and dreary, they will experience dissonance. It is a rare person who will accept this situation with an "Oh, pshaw. I worked hard for nothing. Too bad." One way to resolve the dissonance is to decide that the group is worth the effort it took to get admitted.

We told a number of college women that they would have to undergo an initiation to join a group that would discuss the psychology of sex. One third of them had severe initiation: they had to recite a list of obscene words and read some lurid sexual passages from novels in the presence of a male experimenter (in 1959, this really was a "severe" and embarrassing task). One third went through a mild initiation in which they read words that were sexual but not obscene (such as "virgin" and "petting"); and the last third had no initiation at all. Then all of the women listened to an extremely boring taped discussion of the group they had presumably joined. The women in the severe initiation group rated the discussion and its drab participants much more favorably than those in the other groups.

I am not asserting that people enjoy painful experiences, or that they enjoy things that are associated with painful experiences. If you got hit on the head by a brick on the way to a fraternity initiation, you would not like that group any better. But if you volunteered to get hit with a brick *in order to join* the fraternity, you definitely would like the group more than if you had been admitted without fuss.

After a decision—especially a difficult one that involves much time, money, or effort—people almost always experience dissonance. Awareness of defects in the preferred object is dissonant with having chosen it; awareness of positive aspects of the unchosen object is dissonant with having rejected it.

Accordingly, researchers have found that *before* making a decision, people seek as much information as possible about the alternatives. Afterwards, however, they seek reassurance that they did the right thing, and do so by seeking information in support of their choice or by simply changing the information that is already in their heads. In one of the earliest experiments on dissonance theory, Jack Brehm gave a group of women their choice between two appliances, such as a toaster or a blender, that they had previously rated for desirability. When the subjects reevaluated the appliances after choosing one of them, they increased their liking for the one they had chosen and downgraded their evaluation of the rejected appliance. Similarly, Danuta Ehrlich and her associates found that a person about to buy a new car does so carefully, reading all ads and accepting facts openly on various makes and models. But after he buys his Volvo, for instance, he will read advertisements more selectively, and he will tend to avoid ads for Volkswagens, Chevrolets, and so on.

The Decision to Behave Immorally.   Your conscience, let us suppose, tells you that it is wrong to cheat, lie, steal, seduce your neighbor's husband or wife, or whatever. Let us suppose further that you are in a situation in which you are sorely tempted to ignore your conscience. If you give in to temptation, the cognition "I am a decent, moral person" will be dissonant with the cognition "I have committed an immoral act." If you resist, the cognition "I want to get a good grade (have that money, seduce that person)" is dissonant with the cognition "I could have acted so as to get that grade, but I chose not to."

The easiest way to reduce dissonance in either case is to minimize the negative aspects of the action one has chosen, and to change one's attitude about its immorality. If Mr. C. decides to cheat, he will probably decide that cheating isn't really so bad. It hurts no one; everyone does it; it's part of human nature. If Mr. D. decides not to cheat, he will no doubt come to believe that cheating is a sin, and deserves severe punishment.

The point here is that the initial attitudes of these men is virtually the same. Moreover, their decisions could be a hair's breadth apart. But once the action is taken, their attitudes diverge sharply.

Judson Mills confirmed these speculations in an experiment with sixth-grade children. First he measured their attitudes toward cheating, and then put them in a competitive situation. He arranged the test so that it was impossible to win without cheating, and so it was easy for the children to cheat, thinking they would be unwatched. The next day, he asked the children again how they felt about cheating. Those who had cheated on the test had become more lenient in their attitudes; those who had resisted the temptation adopted harsher attitudes.

The data are provocative. They suggest that the most zealous crusaders are not those who are removed from the problem they oppose. I would hazard to say that the people who are most angry about "the sexual promiscuity of the young" are *not* those who have never dreamed of being promiscuous. On the contrary, they would be persons who had been seriously tempted by illicit sex, who came very close to giving in to their desires, but who finally resisted. People who almost live in glass houses are the ones who are most likely to throw stones.

Insufficient Justification.   If I offer George $20 to do a boring task, and offer Richard $1 to do the same thing, which one will decide that the assignment was mildly interesting? If I threaten one child with harsh punishment if he does something forbidden, and threaten another child with mild punishment, which one will transgress?

Dissonance theory predicts that when people find themselves doing something and they have neither been rewarded adequately for doing it nor threatened with dire consequences for not doing it, they will find *internal* reasons for their behavior.

Suppose you dislike Woodrow Wilson and I want you to make a speech in his favor. The most efficient thing I can do is to pay you a lot of money for making the speech, or threaten to kill you if you don't. In either case, you will probably comply with my wish, but you won't change your attitude toward Wilson. If that were my goal, I would have to give you a *minimal* reward or threat. Then, in order not to appear absurd, you would have to seek additional reasons for your speech—this could lead you to find good things about Wilson and hence, to conclude that you really do like Wilson after all. Lying produces great attitude change only when the liar is undercompensated.

Festinger and J. Merrill Carlsmith asked college students to work on boring and repetitive tasks. Then the experimenters persuaded the students to lie about the work, to tell a fellow student that the task would be interesting and enjoyable. They offered half of their subjects $20 for telling the lie, and they offered the others only $1. Later they asked all subjects how much they had really liked the tasks.

The students who earned $20 for their lies rated the work as deadly dull, which it was. They experienced no dissonance: they lied, but they were well paid for that behavior. By contrast, students who got $1 decided that the tasks were rather enjoyable. The dollar was apparently enough to get them to tell the lie, but not enough to keep them from feeling that lying for so paltry a sum was foolish. To reduce dissonance, they decided that they hadn't lied after all; the task was fun.

Similarly, Carlsmith and I found that mild threats are more effective than harsh threats in changing a child's attitude about a forbidden object, in this case a delightful toy. In the severe-threat condition, children refrained from playing with the toys and had a good reason for refraining—the very severity of the threat provided ample justification for not playing with the toy. In the mild-threat condition, however, the children refrained from playing with the toy but when they asked themselves, "How come I'm not playing with the toy?" they did not have a super-abundant justification (because the threat was not terribly severe). Accordingly, they provided additional justification in the form of convincing themselves that the attractive toy was really not very attractive and that they didn't really want to play with it very much in the first place. Jonathan Freedman extended our findings, and showed that severe threats do not have a lasting effect on a child's behavior. Mild threats, by contrast, can change behavior for many months.

Perhaps the most extraordinary example of insufficient justification occurred in India, where Jamuna Prasad analyzed the rumors that were circulated after a terrible earthquake in 1950. Prasad found that people in towns that were *not* in immediate danger were spreading rumors of impending doom from floods, cyclones, or unforeseeable calamities. Certainly the rumors could not help people feel more secure; why then perpetrate them? I believe that dissonance helps explain this phenomenon. The people were terribly frightened—after all, the neighboring villages had been destroyed—but they did not have ample excuse for their fear, since the earthquake had missed them. So they invented their own excuse; if a cyclone is on the way, it is reasonable to be afraid. Later, Durganand Sinha studied rumors in a town that had actually been destroyed. The people were scared, but they had good reason to be; they didn't need to seek additional justification for their terror. And their rumors showed no predictions of impending disaster and no serious exaggerations.

The Decision to Be Cruel.   The need for people to believe that they are kind and decent can lead them to say and do unkind and indecent things. After the National Guard killed four students at Kent State, several rumors quickly spread: the slain girls were pregnant, so their deaths spared their families from shame; the students were filthy and had lice on them. These rumors were totally untrue, but the townspeople were eager to believe them. Why? The local people were conservative, and infuriated at the radical behavior of some of the students. Many had hoped that the students would get their comeuppance. But death is an awfully severe penalty. The severity of this penalty outweighs and is dissonant with the "crimes" of the students. In these circumstances, any information that put the victims in a bad light reduces dissonance by implying, in effect, that it was good that the young people died. One high school teacher even avowed that anyone with "long hair, dirty clothes, or [who goes] barefooted deserves to be shot."

Keith Davis and Edward Jones demonstrated the need to justify cruelty. They persuaded students to help them with an experiment, in the course of which the volunteers had to tell another student that he was a shallow, untrustworthy, and dull person. Volunteers managed to convince themselves that they didn't like the victim of their cruel analysis. They found him less attractive than they did before they had to criticize him.

Similarly, David Glass persuaded a group of subjects to deliver electric shocks to others. The subjects, again, decided that the victim must deserve the cruelty; they rated him as stupid, mean, etc. Then Glass went a step further. He found that a subject with high self-esteem was most likely to derogate the victim. This led Glass to conclude, ironically, that it is precisely because a person thinks he is nice that he decides that the person he has hurt is a rat. "Since nice guys like me don't go around hurting innocent people," Glass's subjects seemed to say, "you must have deserved it." But individuals who have *low* self-esteem do not feel the need to justify their behavior and derogate their victims; it is *consonant* for such persons to believe they have behaved badly. "Worthless people like me do unkind things."

Ellen Berscheid and her colleagues found another factor that limits the need to derogate one's victim: the victim's capacity to retaliate. If the person doing harm feels that the situation is balanced, that his victim will pay him back in coin, he had no need to justify his behavior. In Berscheid's experiment, which involved electric shocks, college students did not derogate or dislike the persons they shocked if they believed the victims could retaliate. Students who were led to believe that the victims would not be able to retaliate *did* derogate them. Her work suggests that soldiers may have a greater need to disparage civilian victims (because they can't retaliate) than military victims. Lt. William L. Calley, who considered the "gooks" at My Lai to be something less than human, would be a case in point.

Dissonance and the Self-Concept.   On the basis of recent experiments, I have reformulated Festinger's original theory in terms of the self-concept. That is, dissonance is most powerful when self-esteem is threatened. Thus the important aspect of dissonance is not, "I said one thing and I believe another," but "I have misled people—and I am a truthful, nice person." Conversely, the cognitions, "I believe the task is dull," and "I told someone the task was interesting," are not dissonant for a psychopathic liar.

David Mettee and I predicted in a recent experiment that persons who had low opinions of themselves would be more likely to cheat than persons with high self-esteem. We assumed that if an average person gets a temporary blow to his self-esteem (by being jilted, say, or not getting a promotion), he will temporarily feel stupid and worthless, and hence do any number of stupid and worthless things—cheat at cards, bungle an assignment, break a valuable vase.

Mettee and I temporarily changed 45 female students' self-esteem. We gave one third of them positive feedback about a personality test they had taken (we said that they were interesting, mature, deep, etc.); we gave one third negative feedback (we said that they were relatively immature, shallow, etc.); and one third of the students got no information at all. Then all the students went on to participate in what they thought was an unrelated experiment, in which they gambled in a competitive game of cards. We arranged the situation so that the students could cheat and thereby win a considerable sum of money, or not cheat, in which case they were sure to lose.

The results showed that the students who had received blows to their self-esteem cheated far more than those who had gotten positive feedback about themselves. It may well be that low self-esteem is a critical antecedent of criminal or cruel behavior.

The theory of cognitive dissonance has proved useful in generating research; it has uncovered a wide range of data. In formal terms, however, it is a very sloppy theory. Its very simplicity provides both its greatest strength and its most serious weakness. That is, while the theory has generated a great deal of data, it has not been easy to define the limits of the theoretical statement, to determine the specific predictions that can be made. All too often researchers have had to resort to the very unscientific rule of thumb, "If you want to be sure, ask Leon."

Logic and Psychologic.   Part of the problem is that the theory does not deal with *logical* inconsistency, but *psychological* inconsistency. Festinger maintains that two cognitions are inconsistent if the opposite of one follows from the other. Strictly speaking, the information that smoking causes cancer does not make it illogical to smoke. But these cognitions produce dissonance because they do not make sense psychologically, assuming that the smoker does not want cancer.

One cannot always predict dissonance with accuracy. A man may admire Franklin Roosevelt enormously and discover that throughout his marriage FDR carried out a clandestine affair. If he places a high value on fidelity and he believes that great men are not exempt from this value, then he will experience dissonance. Then I can predict that he will either change his attitudes about Roosevelt or soften his attitudes about fidelity. But, he may believe that marital infidelity and political greatness are totally unrelated; if this were the case, he might simply shrug off these data without modifying his opinions either about Roosevelt or about fidelity.

Because of the sloppiness in the theory, several commentators have criticized a great many of the findings first uncovered by dissonance theory. These criticisms have served a useful purpose. Often, they have goaded us to perform more precise research, which in turn has led to a clarification of some of the findings which, ironically enough, has eliminated the alternative explanations proposed by the critics themselves.

For example, Alphonse and Natalia Chapanis argued that the "severe initiation" experiment could have completely different causes. It might be that the young women were not embarrassed at having to read sexual words, but rather were aroused, and their arousal in turn led them to rate the dull discussion group as interesting. Or, to the contrary, the women in the severe-initiation condition could have felt much sexual anxiety, followed by relief that the discussion was so banal. They associated relief with the group, and so rated it favorably.

So Harold Gerard and Grover Mathewson replicated our experiment, using electric shocks in the initiation procedure. Our original findings were supported—subjects who underwent severe shocks in order to join a discussion group rated that group more favorably than subjects who had undergone mild shocks. Moreover, Gerard and Mathewson went on to show that merely linking an electric shock with the group discussion (as in a simple conditioning experiment) did not produce greater liking for the group. The increase in liking for the group occurred only when subjects volunteered for the shock *in order* to gain membership in the group—just as dissonance theory would predict.

Routes to Consonance.   In the real world there is usually more than one way to squirm out of inconsistency. Laboratory experiments carefully control a person's alternatives, and the conclusions drawn may be misleading if applied to everyday situations. For example, suppose a prestigious university rejects a young Ph.D. for its one available teaching position. If she feels that she is a good scholar, she will experience dissonance. She can then decide that members of that department are narrow-minded and senile, sexist, and wouldn't recognize talent if it sat on their laps. Or she could decide that if they could reject someone as fine and intelligent as she, they must be extraordinarily brilliant. Both techniques will reduce dissonance, but note that they leave this woman with totally opposite opinions about professors at the university.

This is a serious conceptual problem. One solution is to specify the conditions under which a person will take one route to consonance over another. For example, if a person struggles to reach a goal and fails, he may decide that the goal wasn't worth it (as Aesop's fox did) or that the effort was justified anyway (the fox got a lot of exercise in jumping for the grapes). My own research suggests that a person will take the first means when he has expended relatively little effort. But when he has put in a great deal of effort, dissonance will take the form of justifying the energy.

This line of work is encouraging. I do not think that it is very fruitful to demand to know what *the* mode of dissonance reduction is; it is more instructive to isolate the various modes that occur, and determine the optimum conditions for each.

Ignorance of Absurdity.   No dissonance theorist takes issue with the fact that people frequently work to get rewards. In our experiments, however, small rewards tend to be associated with greater attraction and greater attitude change. Is the reverse ever true?

Jonathan Freedman told college students to work on a dull task after first telling them (a) their results would be of no use to him, since his experiment was basically over, or (b) their results would be of great value to him. Subjects in the first condition were in a state of dissonance, for they had unknowingly agreed to work on a boring chore that apparently had no purpose. They reduced their dissonance by deciding that the task was enjoyable.

Then Freedman ran the same experiment with one change. He waited until the subjects finished the task to tell them whether their work would be important. In this study he found incentive effects: students told that the task was valuable enjoyed it more than those who were told that their work was useless. In short, dissonance theory does not apply when an individual performs an action in good faith without having any way of knowing it was absurd. When we agree to participate in an experiment we naturally assume that it is for a purpose. If we are informed afterward that it *had* no purpose, how were we to have known? In this instance we like the task better if it had an important purpose. But if we agreed to perform it *knowing* that it had no purpose, we try to convince ourselves that it is an attractive task in order to avoid looking absurd.

Man Cannot Live by Consonance Alone.   Dissonance reduction is only one of several motives, and other powerful drives can counteract it. If human beings had a pervasive, all-encompassing need to reduce all forms of dissonance, we would not grow, mature, or admit to our mistakes. We would sweep mistakes under the rug or, worse, turn the mistakes into virtues; in neither case would we profit from error.

But obviously people do learn from experience. They often do tolerate dissonance because the dissonant information has great utility. A person cannot ignore forever a leaky roof, even if that flaw is inconsistent with having spent a fortune on the house. As utility increases, individuals will come to prefer dissonance-arousing but useful information. But as dissonance increases, or when commitment is high, future utility and information tend to be ignored.

It is clear that people will go to extraordinary lengths to justify their actions. They will lie, cheat, live on the San Andreas Fault, accuse innocent bystanders of being vicious provocateurs, ignore information that might save their lives, and generally engage in all manner of absurd postures. Before we write off such behavior as bizarre, crazy, or evil, we would be wise to examine the situations that set up the need to reduce dissonance. Perhaps our awareness of the mechanism that makes us so often irrational will help turn Camus' observation on absurdity into a philosophic curiosity.

6

On the Folly of Rewarding A, while Hoping for B*

STEVEN KERR

Whether dealing with monkeys, rats, or human beings, it is hardly controversial to state that most organisms seek information concerning what activities are rewarded, and then seek to do (or at least pretend to do) those things, often to the virtual exclusion of activities not rewarded. The extent to which this occurs of course will depend on the perceived attractiveness of the rewards offered, but neither operant nor expectancy theorists would quarrel with the essence of this notion.

Nevertheless, numerous examples exist of reward systems that are fouled up in that behaviors which are rewarded are those which the rewarder is trying to *discourage*, while the behavior he desires is not being rewarded at all.

In an effort to understand and explain this phenomenon, this paper presents examples from society, from organizations in general, and from profit-making firms in particular. Data from a manufacturing company and information from an insurance firm are examined to demonstrate the consequences of such reward systems for the organizations involved, and possible reasons why such reward systems continue to exist are considered.

* Reprinted from *Academy of Management Journal*, 1975, *18*, 769–783.

SOCIETAL EXAMPLES

Politics

Official goals are "purposely vague and general and do not indicate . . . the host of decisions that must be made among alternative ways of achieving official goals and the priority of multiple goals . . ." (8, p. 66). They usually may be relied on to offend absolutely no one, and in this sense can be considered high-acceptance, low-quality goals. An example might be "build better schools." Operative goals are higher in quality but lower in acceptance, since they specify where the money will come from, what alternative goals will be ignored, etc.

The American citizenry supposedly wants its candidates for public office to set forth operative goals, making their proposed programs "perfectly clear," specifying sources and uses of funds, etc. However, since operative goals are lower in acceptance, and since aspirants to public office need acceptance (from at least 50.1 percent of the people), most politicians prefer to speak only of official goals, at least until after the election. They of course would agree to speak at the operative level if "punished" for not doing so. The electorate could do this by refusing to support candidates who do not speak at the operative level.

Instead, however, the American voter typically punishes (withholds support from) candidates who frankly discuss where the money will come from, rewards politicians who speak only of official goals, but hopes that candidates (despite the reward system) will discuss the issues operatively. It is academic whether it was moral for Nixon, for example, to refuse to discuss his 1968 "secret plan" to end the Vietnam War, his 1972 operative goals concerning the lifting of price controls, the reshuffling of his cabinet, etc. The point is that the reward system made such refusal rational.

It seems worth mentioning that no manuscript can adequately define what is "moral" and what is not. However, examination of costs and benefits, combined with knowledge of what motivates a particular individual, often will suffice to determine what for him is "rational."[1] If the reward system is so designed that it is irrational to be moral, this does not necessarily mean that immorality will result. But is this not asking for trouble?

---

[1] In Simon's (10, pp. 76–77) terms, a decision is "subjectively rational" if it maximizes an individual's valued outcomes so far as his knowledge permits. A decision is "personally rational" if it is oriented toward the individual's goals.

War

If some oversimplification may be permitted, let it be assumed that the primary goal of the organization (Pentagon, Luftwaffe, or whatever) is to win. Let it be assumed further that the primary goal of most individuals on the front lines is to get home alive. Then there appears to be an important conflict in goals—personally rational behavior by those at the bottom will endanger goal attainment by those at the top.

But not necessarily! It depends on how the reward system is set up. The Vietnam War was indeed a study of disobedience and rebellion, with terms such as "fragging" (killing one's own commanding officer) and "search and evade" becoming part of the military vocabulary. The difference in subordinates' acceptance of authority between World War II and Vietnam is reported to be considerable, and veterans of the Second World War often have been quoted as being outraged at the mutinous actions of many American soldiers in Vietnam.

Consider, however, some critical differences in the reward system in use during the two conflicts. What did the GI in World War II want? To go home. And when did he get to go home? When the war was won! If he disobeyed the orders to clean out the trenches and take the hills, the war would not be won and he would not go home. Furthermore, what were his chances of attaining his goal (getting home alive) if he obeyed the orders compared to his chances if he did not? What is being suggested is that the rational soldier in World War II, *whether patriotic or not*, probably found it expedient to obey.

Consider the reward system in use in Vietnam. What did the man at the bottom want? To go home. And when did he get to go home? When his tour of duty was over! This was the case *whether or not* the war was won. Furthermore, concerning the relative chance of getting home alive by obeying orders compared to the chance if they were disobeyed, it is worth noting that a mutineer in Vietnam was far more likely to be assigned rest and rehabilitation (on the assumption that fatigue was the cause) than he was to suffer any negative consequence.

In his description of the "zone of indifference," Barnard stated that "a person can and will accept a communication as authoritative only when . . . at the time of his decision, he believes it to be compatible with his personal interests as a whole" (1, p. 165). In light of the reward system used in Vietnam, would it not have been personally irrational for some orders to have been obeyed? Was not the military implementing a system which *rewarded* disobedience, while *hoping* that soldiers (despite the reward system) would obey orders?

Medicine

Theoretically, a physician can make either of two types of error, and intuitively one seems as bad as the other. A doctor can pronounce a patient sick when he is actually well, thus causing him needless anxiety and expense, curtailment of enjoyable foods and activities, and even physical danger by subjecting him to needless medication and surgery. Alternately, a doctor can label a sick person well, and thus avoid treating what may be a serious, even fatal ailment. It might be natural to conclude that physicians seek to minimize both types of error.

Such a conclusion would be wrong.[2] It is estimated that numerous Americans are presently afflicted with iatrogenic (physician-*caused*) illnesses (9). This occurs when the doctor is approached by someone complaining of a few stray symptoms. The doctor classifies and organizes these symptoms, gives them a name, and obligingly tells the patient what further symptoms may be expected. This information often acts as a self-fulfilling prophecy, with the result that from that day on the patient for all practical purposes is sick.

Why does this happen? Why are physicians so reluctant to sustain a type 2 error (pronouncing a sick person well) that they will tolerate many type 1 errors? Again, a look at the reward system is needed. The punishments for a type 2 error are real: guilt, embarrassment, and the threat of lawsuit and scandal. On the other hand, a type 1 error (labeling a well person sick) "is sometimes seen as sound clinical practice, indicating a healthy conservative approach to medicine" (9, p. 69). Type 1 errors also are likely to generate increased income and a stream of steady customers who, being well in a limited physiological sense, will not embarrass the doctor by dying abruptly.

Fellow physicians and the general public therefore are really *rewarding* type 1 errors and at the same time *hoping* fervently that doctors will try not to make them.

GENERAL ORGANIZATIONAL EXAMPLES

Rehabilitation Centers and Orphanages

In terms of the prime beneficiary classification (2, p. 42) organizations such as these are supposed to exist for the "public-in-contact,"

---

[2] In one study (4) of 14,867 films for signs of tuberculosis, 1,216 positive readings turned out to be clinically negative; only 24 negative readings proved clinically active, a ratio of 50 to 1.

that is, clients. The orphanage therefore theoretically is interested in placing as many children as possible in good homes. However, often orphanages surround themselves with so many rules concerning adoption that it is nearly impossible to pry a child out of the place. Orphanages may deny adoption unless the applicants are a married couple, both of the same religion as the child, without history of emotional or vocational instability, with a specified minimum income and a private room for the child, etc.

If the primary goal is to place children in good homes, then the rules ought to constitute means toward that goal. Goal displacement results when these "means become ends-in-themselves that displace the original goals" (2, p. 229).

To some extent these rules are required by law. But the influence of the reward system on the orphanage's management should not be ignored. Consider, for example, that the:

1. Number of children enrolled often is the most important determinant of the size of the allocated budget.
2. Number of children under the director's care also will affect the size of his staff.
3. Total organizational size will determine largely the director's prestige at the annual conventions, in the community, etc.

Therefore, to the extent that staff size, total budget, and personal prestige are valued by the orphanage's executive personnel, it becomes rational for them to make it difficult for children to be adopted. After all, who wants to be the director of the smallest orphanage in the state?

If the reward system errs in the opposite direction, paying off only for placements, extensive goal displacement again is likely to result. A common example of vocational rehabilitation in many states, for example, consists of placing someone in a job for which he has little interest and few qualifications, for two months or so, and then "rehabilitating" him again in another position. Such behavior is quite consistent with the prevailing reward system, which pays off for the number of individuals placed in any position for 60 days or more. Rehabilitation counselors also confess to competing with one another to place relatively skilled clients, sometimes ignoring persons with few skills who would be harder to place. Extensively disabled clients find that counselors often prefer to work with those whose disabilities are less severe.[3]

---

[3] Personal interviews conducted during 1972–73.

Universities

Society *hopes* that teachers will not neglect their teaching responsibilities but *rewards* them almost entirely for research and publications. This is most true at the large and prestigious universities. Clichés such as "good research and good teaching go together" notwithstanding, professors often find that they must choose between teaching and research-oriented activities when allocating their time. Rewards for good teaching usually are limited to outstanding teacher awards, which are given to only a small percentage of good teachers and which usually bestow little money and fleeting prestige. Punishments for poor teaching also are rare.

Rewards for research and publications, on the other hand, and punishments for failure to accomplish these, are commonly administered by universities at which teachers are employed. Furthermore, publication-oriented resumés usually will be well received at other universities, whereas teaching credentials, harder to document and quantify, are much less transferable. Consequently it is rational for university teachers to concentrate on research, even if to the detriment of teaching and at the expense of their students.

By the same token, it is rational for students to act based upon the goal displacement which has occurred within universities concerning what they are rewarded for. If it is assumed that a primary goal of a university is to transfer knowledge from teacher to student, then grades become identifiable as a means toward that goal, serving as motivational, control, and feedback devices to expedite the knowledge transfer. Instead, however, the grades themselves have become much more important for entrance to graduate school, successful employment, tuition refunds, parental respect, etc., than the knowledge or lack of knowledge they are supposed to signify.

It therefore should come as no surprise that information has surfaced in recent years concerning fraternity files for examinations, term-paper writing services, organized cheating at the service academies, and the like. Such activities constitute a personally rational response to a reward system which pays off for grades rather than knowledge.

BUSINESS-RELATED EXAMPLES

Ecology

Assume that the president of XYZ Corporation is confronted with the following alternatives:

1. Spend $11 million for antipollution equipment to keep from

poisoning fish in the river adjacent to the plant; or

2. Do nothing, in violation of the law, and assume a one in ten chance of being caught, with a resultant $1 million fine plus the necessity of buying the equipment.

Under this not unrealistic set of choices it requires no linear program to determine that XYZ Corporation can maximize its probabilities by flouting the law. Add the fact that XYZ's president is probably being rewarded (by creditors, stockholders, and other salient parts of his task environment) according to criteria totally unrelated to the number of fish poisoned, and his probable course of action becomes clear.

Evaluation of Training

It is axiomatic that those who care about a firm's well-being should insist that the organization get fair value for its expenditures. Yet it is commonly known that firms seldom bother to evaluate a new GRID, MBO, job enrichment program, or whatever, to see if the company is getting its money's worth. Why? Certainly it is not because people have not pointed out that this situation exists; numerous practitioner-oriented articles are written each year to just this point.

The individuals (whether in personnel, manpower planning, or wherever) who normally would be responsible for conducting such evaluations are the same ones often charged with introducing the change effort in the first place. Having convinced top management to spend the money, they usually are quite animated afterwards in collecting arigorous vignettes and anecdotes about how successful the program was. The last thing many desire is a formal, systematic, and revealing evaluation. Although members of top management may actually *hope* for such systematic evaluation, their reward systems continue to *reward* ignorance in this area. And if the personnel department abdicates its responsibility, who is to step into the breach? The change agent himself? Hardly! He is likely to be too busy collecting anecdotal "evidence" of his own, for use with his next client.

Miscellaneous

Many additional examples could be cited of systems which in fact are rewarding behaviors other than those supposedly desired by the rewarder. A few of these are described briefly below.

Most coaches disdain to discuss individual accomplishments, preferring to speak of teamwork, proper attitude, and a one-for-all spirit. Usually, however, rewards are distributed according to individual performance. The college basketball player who feeds his teammates instead of shooting will not compile impressive scoring statistics and is less likely to be drafted by the pros. The ballplayer who hits to right field to advance the runners will win neither the batting nor home run titles, and will be offered smaller raises. It therefore is rational for players to think of themselves first, and the team second.

In business organizations where rewards are dispensed for unit performance or for individual goals achieved, without regard for overall effectiveness, similar attitudes often are observed. Under most Management by Objectives (MBO) systems, goals in areas where quantification is difficult often go unspecified. The organization therefore often is in a position where it *hopes* for employee effort in the areas of team building, interpersonal relations, creativity, etc., but it formally *rewards* none of these. In cases where promotions and raises are formally tied to MBO, the system itself contains a paradox in that it "asks employees to set challenging, risky goals, only to face smaller paychecks and possibly damaged careers if these goals are not accomplished" (5, p. 40).

It is *hoped* that administrators will pay attention to long-run costs and opportunities and will institute programs which will bear fruit later on. However, many organizational reward systems pay off for short-run sales and earnings only. Under such circumstances it is personally rational for officials to sacrifice long-term growth and profit (by selling off equipment and property, or by stifling research and development) for short-term advantages. This probably is most pertinent in the public sector, with the result that many public officials are unwilling to implement programs which will not show benefits by election time.

As a final, clear-cut example of a fouled-up reward system, consider the cost-plus contract or its next of kin, the allocation of next year's budget as a direct function of this year's expenditures. It probably is conceivable that those who award such budgets and contracts really hope for economy and prudence in spending. It is obvious, however, that adopting the proverb "to him who spends shall more be given," rewards not economy, but spending itself.

TWO COMPANIES' EXPERIENCES

A Manufacturing Organization

A midwest manufacturer of industrial goods had been troubled for some time by aspects of its organizational climate it believed dysfunctional. For research purposes, interviews were conducted with many employees and a questionnaire was administered on a company-wide basis, including plants and offices in several American and Canadian locations. The company strongly encouraged employee participation in the survey, and made available time and space during the workday for completion of the instrument. All employees in attendance during the day of the survey completed the questionnaire. All instruments were collected directly by the researcher, who personally administered each session. Since no one employed by the firm handled the questionnaires, and since respondent names were not asked for, it seems likely that the pledge of anonymity given was believed.

A modified version of the Expect Approval scale (7) was included as part of the questionnaire. The instrument asked respondents to indicate the degree of approval or disapproval they could expect if they performed each of the described actions. A seven-point Likert scale was used, with 1 indicating that the action would probably bring strong disapproval and 7 signifying likely strong approval.

Although normative data for this scale from studies of other organizations are unavailable, it is possible to examine fruitfully the data obtained from this survey in several ways. First, it may be worth noting that the questionnaire data corresponded closely to information gathered through interviews. Furthermore, as can be seen from the results summarized in Table 1, sizable differences between various work units, and between employees at different job levels within the same work unit, were obtained. This suggests that response bias effects (social desirability in particular loomed as a potential concern) are not likely to be severe.

Most importantly, comparisons between scores obtained on the Expect Approval scale and a statement of problems which were the reason for the survey revealed that the same behaviors which managers in each division thought dysfunctional were those which lower level employees claimed were rewarded. As compared to job levels 1 to 8 in Division B (see Table 1), those in Division A claimed a much higher acceptance by management of "conforming" activities. Between 31 and 37 percent of Division A employees at levels 1–8 stated that going along with the majority, agreeing with the boss, and staying on everyone's good side brought approval; only once (level 5–8 responses to one of the three items) did a majority suggest that such actions would generate disapproval.

Furthermore, responses from Division A workers at levels 1–4 indicate that behaviors geared toward risk avoidance were as likely to be rewarded as to be punished. Only at job levels 9 and above was it apparent that the reward system was positively reinforcing behaviors desired by top management. Overall, the same "tendencies toward conservatism and apple-polishing at the lower levels" which divisional management had complained about during the interviews were

TABLE 1
Summary of Two Divisions' Data Relevant to Conforming and Risk-Avoidance Behaviors (extent to which subjects expect approval)

Dimension	Item	Division and Sample	Total Responses	*Percentage of Workers Responding*		
				1, 2, or 3 (Disapproval)	4	5, 6, or 7 (Approval)
Risk avoidance	Making a risky decision based on the best information available at the time, but which turns out wrong.	A, levels 1-4 (lowest)	127	61	25	14
		A, levels 5-8	172	46	31	23
		A, levels 9 and above	17	41	30	30
		B, levels 1-4 (lowest)	31	58	26	16
		B, levels 5-8	19	42	42	16
		B, levels 9 and above	10	50	20	30
Risk	Setting extremely high and challenging standards and goals, and then narrowly failing to make them.	A, levels 1-4	122	47	28	25
		A, levels 5-8	168	33	26	41

	A, levels 9+	17	24	6	70

Description	Level				
	A, levels 9+	17	24	6	70
	B, levels 1-4	31	48	23	29
	B, levels 5-8	18	17	33	50
	B, levels 9+	10	30	0	70
Setting goals which are extremely easy to make and then making them.	A, levels 1-4	124	35	30	35
	A, levels 5-8	171	47	27	26
	A, levels 9+	17	70	24	6
	B, levels 1-4	31	58	26	16
	B, levels 5-8	19	63	16	21
	B, levels 9+	10	80	0	20
Being a "yes man" and always agreeing with the boss.	A, levels 1-4	126	46	17	37
	A, levels 5-8	180	54	14	31
	A, levels 9+	17	88	12	0
	B, levels 1-4	32	53	28	19
	B, levels 5-8	19	68	21	11
	B, levels 9+	10	80	10	10

TABLE 1 (*concluded*)

Dimension	Item	Division and Sample	Total Responses	1, 2, or 3 (Disapproval)	4	5, 6, or 7 (Approval)
				Percentage of Workers Responding		
	Always going along with the majority.	A, levels 1-4	125	40	25	35
		A, levels 5-8	173	47	21	32
		A, levels 9+	17	70	12	18
		B, levels 1-4	31	61	23	16
		B, levels 5-8	19	68	11	21
		B, levels 9+	10	80	10	10
	Being careful to stay on the good side of everyone, so that everyone agrees that you are a great guy.	A, levels 1-4	124	45	18	37
		A, levels 5-8	173	45	22	33
		A, levels 9+	17	64	6	30
		B, levels 1-4	31	54	23	23
		B, levels 5-8	19	73	11	16
		B, levels 9+	10	80	10	10

those claimed by subordinates to be the most rational course of action in light of the existing reward system. Management apparently was not getting the behaviors it was *hoping* for, but it certainly was getting the behaviors it was perceived by subordinates to be *rewarding*.

An Insurance Firm

The Group Health Claims Division of a large eastern insurance company provides another rich illustration of a reward system which reinforces behaviors not desired by top management.

Attempting to measure and reward accuracy in paying surgical claims, the firm systematically keeps track of the number of returned checks and letters of complaint received from policyholders. However, underpayments are likely to provoke cries of outrage from the insured, while overpayments often are accepted in courteous silence. Since it often is impossible to tell from the physician's statement which of two surgical procedures, with different allowable benefits, was performed, and since writing for clarifications will interfere with other standards used by the firm concerning "percentage of claims paid within two days of receipt," the new hire in more than one claims section is soon acquainted with the informal norm: "When in doubt, pay it out!"

The situation would be even worse were it not for the fact that other features of the firm's reward system tend to neutralize those described. For example, annual "merit" increases are given to all employees, in one of the following three amounts:

1. If the worker is "outstanding" (a select category, into which no more than two employees per section may be placed): 5 percent.
2. If the worker is "above average" (normally all workers not "outstanding" are so rated): 4 percent.
3. If the worker commits gross acts of negligence and irresponsibility for which he might be discharged in many other companies: 3 percent.

Now, since (a) the difference between the 5 percent theoretically attainable through hard work and the 4 percent attainable merely by living until the review data is small and (b) since insurance firms seldom dispense much of a salary increase in cash (rather, the worker's insurance benefits increase, causing him to be further overinsured), many employees are rather indifferent to the possibility of obtaining the extra one percent reward and therefore tend to ignore the norm concerning indiscriminant payments.

However, most employees are not indifferent to the rule which states that, should absences or latenesses total three or more in any six-month period, the entire 4 or 5 percent due at the next "merit" review must be forfeited. In this sense the firm may be described as *hoping* for performance, while *rewarding* attendance. What it gets, of course, is attendance. (If the absence-lateness rule appears to the reader to be stringent, it really is not. The company counts "times" rather than "days" absent, and a ten-day absence therefore counts the same as one lasting two days. A worker in danger of accumulating a third absence within six months merely has to remain ill [away from work] during his second absence until his first absence is more than six months old. The limiting factor is that at some point his salary ceases, and his sickness benefits take over. This usually is sufficient to get the younger workers to return, but for those with 20 or more years' service, the company provides sickness benefits of 90 percent of normal salary, tax-free! Therefore . . . .)

CAUSES

Extremely diverse instances of systems which reward behavior A although the rewarder apparently hopes for behavior B have been given. These are useful to illustrate the breadth and magnitude of the phenomenon, but the diversity increases the difficulty of determining commonalities and establishing causes. However, four general factors may be pertinent to an explanation of why fouled-up reward systems seem to be so prevelant.

Fascination with an "Objective" Criterion

It has been mentioned elsewhere that:

> Most "objective" measures of productivity are objective only in that their subjective elements are (a) determined in advance, rather than coming into play at the time of the formal evaluation, and (b) well concealed on the rating instrument itself. Thus industrial firms seeking to devise objective rating systems first decide, in an arbitrary manner, what dimensions are to be rated, . . . usually including some items having little to do with organizational effectiveness while excluding others that do. Only then does Personnel Division churn out official-looking documents on which all dimensions chosen to be rated are assigned point values, categories, or whatever (6, p. 92).

Nonetheless, many individuals seek to establish simple, quantifiable standards against which to measure and reward performance. Such efforts may be successful in highly predictable areas within an organization, but are likely to cause goal displacement when applied anywhere else. Overconcern with attendance and lateness in the insurance firm and with number of people placed in the vocational rehabilitation division may have been largely responsible for the problems described in those organizations.

Overemphasis on Highly Visible Behaviors

Difficulties often stem from the fact that some parts of the task are highly visible while other parts are not. For example, publications are easier to demonstrate than teaching, and scoring baskets and hitting home runs are more readily observable than feeding teammates and advancing base runners. Similarly, the adverse consequences of pronouncing a sick person well are more visible than those sustained by labeling a well person sick. Team-building and creativity are other examples of behaviors which may not be rewarded simply because they are hard to observe.

Hypocrisy

In some of the instances described the rewarder may have been getting the desired behavior, notwithstanding claims that the behavior was not desired. This may be true, for example, of management's attitude toward apple-polishing in the manufacturing firm (a behavior which subordinates felt was rewarded, despite management's avowed dislike of the practice). This also may explain politicians' unwillingness to revise the penalties for disobedience of ecology laws, and the failure of top management to devise reward systems which would cause systematic evaluation of training and development programs.

Emphasis on Morality or Equity Rather than Efficiency

Some consideration of other factors prevents the establishment of a system which rewards behaviors desired by the rewarder. The felt obligation of many Americans to vote for one candidate or another, for example, may impair their ability to withhold support from politicians who refuse to discuss the issues. Similarly, the concern for spreading the risks and costs of wartime military service may outweigh the advantage to be obtained by committing personnel to combat until the war is over.

It should be noted that only with respect to the first two causes are reward systems really paying off for other than desired behaviors. In the case of the third and fourth causes the system *is* rewarding behaviors desired by the rewarder, and the systems are fouled up only from the standpoints of those who believe the rewarder's public statements (cause 3), or those who seek to maximize efficiency rather than other outcomes (cause 4).

CONCLUSIONS

Modern organization theory requires a recognition that the members of organizations and society possess divergent goals and motives. It therefore is unlikely that managers and their subordinates will seek the same outcomes. Three possible remedies for this potential problem are suggested.

Selection

It is theoretically possible for organizations to employ only those individuals whose goals and motives are wholly consonant with those of management. In such cases the same behaviors judged by subordinates to be rational would be perceived by management as desirable. State-of-the-art reviews of selection techniques, however, provide scant grounds for hope that such an approach would be successful (for example, see 12).

Training

Another theoretical alternative is for the organization to admit those employees whose goals are not consonant with those of management and then, through training, socialization, or whatever, alter employee goals to make them consonant. However, research on the effectiveness of such training programs, though limited, provides further grounds for pessimism (for example, see 3).

Altering the Reward System

What would have been the result if:

1. Nixon had been assured by his advisors that he could not win reelection except by discussing the issues in detail?
2. Physicians' conduct was subjected to regular examination by review boards for type 1 errors (calling healthy people ill) and to penalties (fines, censure, etc.) for errors of either type?
3. The President of XYZ Corporation had to choose between (a) spending $11 million for antipollution equipment, and (b) incurring a 50-50 chance of going to jail for five years?

Managers who complain that their workers are not motivated might do well to consider the possibility that they have installed reward systems which are paying off for behaviors other than those they are seeking. This, in part, is what happened in Vietnam, and this is what regularly frustrates societal efforts to bring about honest politicians, civic-minded managers, etc. This certainly is what happened in both the manufacturing and the insurance companies.

A first step for such managers might be to find out what behaviors currently are being rewarded. Perhaps an instrument similar to that used in the manufacturing firm could be useful for this purpose. Chances are excellent that these managers will be surprised by what they find—that their firms are not rewarding what they assume they are. In fact, such undesirable behavior by organizational members as they have observed may be explained largely by the reward systems in use.

This is not to say that all organizational behavior is determined by formal rewards and punishments. Certainly it is true that in the absence of formal reinforcement some soldiers will be patriotic, some presidents will be ecology-minded, and some orphanage directors will care about children. The point, however, is that in such cases the rewarder is not *causing* the behaviors desired but is only a fortunate bystander. For an organization to *act* upon its members, the formal reward system should positively reinforce desired behaviors, not constitute an obstacle to be overcome.

It might be wise to underscore the obvious fact that there is nothing really new in what has been said. In both theory and practice these matters have been mentioned before. Thus in many states Good Samaritan laws have been installed to protect doctors who stop to assist a stricken motorist. In states without such laws it is commonplace for doctors to refuse to stop, for fear of involvement in a subsequent lawsuit. In college basketball additional penalties have been instituted against players who foul their opponents deliberately. It has long been argued by Milton Friedman and others that penalties should be altered so as to make it irrational to disobey the ecology laws, and so on.

By altering the reward system the organization escapes the necessity of selecting only desirable people or of trying to alter undesirable ones. In Skinnerian terms (as described in 11, p. 704), "As for responsibility and goodness—as commonly defined—no one . . . would want or need them. They refer to a man's behaving well despite the absence of positive reinforcement that is obviously sufficient to explain it. Where such reinforcement exists, 'no one needs goodness.' "

REFERENCES

1. Barnard, Chester I. *The functions of the executive*. Cambridge, Mass.: Harvard University Press, 1964.

2. Blau, Peter M., & Scott, W. Richard. *Formal organizations*. San Francisco: Chandler, 1962.

3. Fiedler, Fred E. Predicting the effects of leadership training and experience from the contingency model. *Journal of Applied Psychology*, 1972, *56*, 114–119.

4. Garland, L. H. Studies of the accuracy of diagnostic procedures. *American Journal of Roentgenological, Radium Therapy and Nuclear Medicine*, 1959, 82, 25–38.

5. Kerr, Steven. Some modifications in MBO as an OD strategy. *Academy of Management Proceedings*, 1973, pp. 39–42.

6. Kerr, Steven. What price objectivity? *American Sociologist*, 1973, 8, 92–93.

7. Litwin, G. H., & Stringer, R. A., Jr. *Motivation and organizational climate*. Boston: Harvard University Press, 1968.

8. Perrow, Charles. The analysis of goals in complex organizations. In A. Etzioni (Ed.), *Readings on modern organizations*. Englewood Cliffs, N.J.: Prentice-Hall, 1969.

9. Scheff, Thomas J. Decision rules, types of error, and their consequences in medical diagnosis. In F. Massarik & P. Ratoosh (Eds.), *Mathematical explorations in behavioral science*. Homewood, Ill.: Irwin, 1965.

10. Simon, Herbert A. *Administrative behavior*. New York: Free Press, 1957.

11. Swanson, G. E. Review symposium: Beyond freedom and dignity. *American Journal of Sociology*, 1972, 78, 702–705.

12. Webster, E. *Decision making in the employment interview*. Montreal: Industrial Relations Center, McGill University, 1964.

7

The Effect of Performance on Job Satisfaction*

EDWARD E. LAWLER III and LYMAN W. PORTER

The human relations movement with its emphasis on good interpersonal relations, job satisfaction, and the importance of informal groups provided an important initial stimulant for the study of job attitudes and their relationship to human behavior in organizations. Through the thirties and forties, many studies were carried out to determine the correlates of high and low job satisfaction. Such studies related job satisfaction to seniority, age, sex, education, occupation, and income, to mention a few. Why this great interest in job satisfaction? Undoubtedly some of it stemmed from a simple desire on the

* Reprinted from *Industrial Relations, a Journal of Economy and Society*, vol. 7, no. 1 (October 1967), pp. 20–28.

part of scientists to learn more about job satisfaction, but much of the interest in job satisfaction seems to have come about because of its presumed relationship to job performance. As Brayfield and Crockett have pointed out, a common assumption that employee satisfaction directly affects performance permeates most of the writings about the topic that appeared during this period of two decades.[1] Statements such as the following characterized the literature: "Morale is not an abstraction; rather it is concrete in the sense that it directly affects the quality and quantity of an individual's output," and "Employee morale—reduces turnover—cuts down absenteeism and tardiness; lifts production."[2]

It is not hard to see how the assumption that high job satisfaction leads to high performance came to be popularly accepted. Not only did it fit into the value system of the human relations movement but there also appeared to be some research data to support this point. In the Western Electric studies, the evidence from the Relay Assembly Test Room showed a dramatic tendency for increased employee productivity to be associated with an increase in job satisfaction. Also, who could deny that in the Bank Wiring Room there was both production restriction and mediocre employee morale. With this background it is easy to see why both social scientists and managers believed that if job dissatisfaction could be reduced, the human brake on production could be removed and turned into a force that would increase performance.

Previous Research

But does the available evidence support the belief that high satisfaction will lead to high performance? Since an initial study, in 1932, by Kornhauser and Sharp, more than 30 studies have considered the relationship between these two variables.[3] Many of the earlier studies seemed to have assumed implicitly that a positive relationship existed and that it was important to demonstrate that it in fact did exist. Little attention was given to trying to understand *why* job satisfaction should lead to higher performance; instead, researchers contented themselves with routinely studying the relationship between satisfaction and performance in a number of industrial situations.

---

[1] Arthur H. Brayfield and Walter H. Crockett, "Employee Attitudes and Employee Performance," *Psychological Bulletin,* vol. 52 (September 1955), pp. 396–424.

[2] Ibid.

[3] Arthur Kornhauser and A. Sharp, "Employee Attitudes: Suggestions from a Study in a Factory." *Personnel Journal,* vol. 10 (1932), 393–401.

The typical reader of the literature in the early fifties was probably aware of the fact that some studies had failed to find a significant satisfaction-performance relationship. Indeed, the very first study of the problem obtained an insignificant relationship.[4] However, judging from the impact of the first review of the literature on the topic, by Brayfield and Crockett, many social scientists, let alone practicing managers, were unaware that the evidence indicated how little relationship exists between satisfaction and performance.[5] The key conclusion that emerged from the review was that "there is little evidence in the available literature that employee attitudes bear any simple— or, for that matter, appreciable—relationship to performance on the job." (The review, however, pointed out that job satisfaction did seem to be positively related, as expected, to two other kinds of employee behavior, absenteeism and turnover.)

The review had a major impact on the field of industrial psychology and helped shatter the kind of naïve thinking that characterized the earlier years of the human relations movement. Perhaps it also discouraged additional research, since few post-1955 studies of the relationship between satisfaction and performance have been reported in scientific journals.

Another review, covering much of the same literature, was completed about the same time.[6] This review took a more optimistic view of the evidence: ". . . there is frequent evidence for the often suggested opinion that positive job attitudes are favorable to increased productivity. The relationship is not absolute, but there are enough data to justify attention to attitudes as a factor in improving the worker's output. However, the correlations obtained in many of the positive studies were low."[7] This review also pointed out, as did Brayfield and Crockett, that there was a definite trend for attitudes to be related to absenteeism and turnover. Perhaps the chief reasons for the somewhat divergent conclusions reached by the two reviews were that they did not cover exactly the same literature and that Brayfield and Crockett were less influenced by suggestive findings that did reach statistical significance. In any event, the one conclusion that was obvious from both reviews was that there was not the *strong, persuasive* relationship between job satisfaction and productivity that had been suggested by many of the early proponents of the human relations movement and so casually accepted by personnel specialists.

---

[4] Ibid.

[5] Brayfield and Crocket, "Employee Attitudes and Employee Performance," pp. 396–424.

[6] Frederick Herzberg, Bernard Mausner, R. O. Peterson, and Dora F. Capwell. *Job Attitudes: Review of Research and Opinion* (Pittsburgh: Psychological Service, 1957).

[7] Ibid., p. 103.

A more recent review of the literature by Vroom has received less attention than did the two earlier reviews,[8] perhaps because it is now rather generally accepted that satisfaction is not related to performance. However, before we too glibly accept the view that satisfaction and performance are unrelated, let us look carefully at the data from studies reviewed by Vroom. These studies show a median correlation of +.14 between satisfaction and performance. Although this correlation is not large, the consistency of the direction of the correlation is quite impressive. Twenty of the 23 correlations cited by Vroom are positive. By a statistical test such consistency would occur by chance less than once in a hundred times.

In summary, the evidence indicates that a low but consistent relationship exists between satisfaction and performance, but it is not at all clear *why* this relationship exists. The questions that need to be answered at this time, therefore, concern the place of job satisfaction both in theories of employee motivation and in everyday organizational practice. For example, should an organization systematically measure the level of employee satisfaction? Is it important for an organization to try to improve employee job satisfaction? Is there theoretical reason for believing that job satisfaction should be related to job behavior and if so, can it explain why this relationship exists?

Why Study Job Satisfaction?

There are really two bases upon which to argue that job satisfaction is important. Interestingly, both are different from the original reason for studying job satisfaction, that is, the assumed ability of satisfaction to influence performance. The first, and undoubtedly the most straightforward reason, rests on the fact that strong correlations between absenteeism and satisfaction, as well as between turnover and satisfaction, appear in the previous studies. Accordingly, job satisfaction would seem to be an important focus of organizations which wish to reduce absenteeism and turnover.

Perhaps the best explanation of the fact that satisfaction is related to absenteeism and turnover comes from the kind of path-goal theory of motivation that has been stated by Georgopoulos, Mahoney, and Jones; Vroom; and Lawler and Porter.[9] According to this view, people

---

[8] Victor H. Vroom, *Work and Motivation* (New York: Wiley, 1964).

[9] Basil S. Georgopoulos, G. M. Mahoney, and N. W. Jones, "A Path-Goal Approach to Productivity," *Journal of Applied Psychology,* vol. 41 (1957), 345–53; Vroom, *Work and Motivations;* Edward E. Lawler and Lyman W. Porter, "Antecedent Attitudes of Effective Managerial Performance," *Organizational Behavior and Human Performance,* vol. 2 (May 1967), 122–143. See also Lyman W. Porter and Edward E. Lawler, *Managerial Attitudes and Performance* (Homewood, Ill.: Irwin-Dorsey, 1968).

are motivated to do things which they feel have a high probability of leading to rewards which they value. When a worker says he is satisfied with his job, he is in effect saying that his needs are satisfied as a result of having his job. Thus, path-goal theory would predict that high satisfaction will lead to low turnover and absenteeism because the satisfied individual is motivated to go to work where his important needs are satisfied.

A second reason for interest in job satisfaction stems from its low but consistent *association* with job performance. Let us speculate for a moment on why this association exists. One possibility is that, as assumed by many, the satisfaction *caused* the performance. However, there is little theoretical reason for believing that satisfaction can cause performance. Vroom, using a path-goal theory of motivation, has pointed out that job satisfaction and job performance are caused by quite different things: ". . . job satisfaction is closely affected by the amounts of rewards that people derive from their jobs and . . . level of performance is closely affected by the basis of attainment of rewards. Individuals are satisfied with their jobs to the extent to which their jobs provide them with what they desire, and they perform effectively in them to the extent that effective performance leads to the attainment of what they desire."[10]

Relationship between Satisfaction and Performance

Vroom's statement contains a hint of why, despite the fact that satisfaction and performance are caused by different things, they do bear some relationship to each other. If we assume, as seems to be reasonable in terms of motivation theory, that rewards cause satisfaction, and that in some cases performance produces rewards, then it is possible that the relationship found between satisfaction and performance comes about through the action of a third variable—rewards. Briefly stated, good performance may lead to rewards, which in turn lead to satisfaction; this formulation then would say that satisfaction, rather than causing performance, as was previously assumed, is caused by it. Figure 1 presents this thinking in a diagrammatic form.

This model first shows that performance leads to rewards, and it distinguishes between two kinds of rewards and their connection to performance. A wavy line between performance and extrinsic rewards indicates that such rewards are likely to be imperfectly related to performance. By extrinsic rewards is meant such organizationally controlled rewards as pay, promotion, status, and security—rewards that

[10] Vroom, *Work and Motivation*, p. 246.

are often referred to as satisfying mainly lower level needs.[11] The connection is relatively weak because of the difficulty of tying extrinsic rewards directly to performance. Even though an organization may have a policy of rewarding merit, performance is difficult to measure, and in dispensing rewards like pay, many other factors are frequently taken into consideration. Lawler, for example, found a low correlation between amount of salary and superiors' evaluation for a number of middle and lower level managers.[12]

FIGURE 1
The Theoretical Model

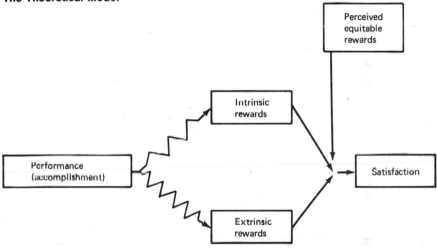

Quite the opposite is likely to be true for intrinsic rewards, however, since they are given to the individual by himself for good performance. Intrinsic or internally mediated rewards are subject to fewer disturbing influences and thus are likely to be more directly related to good performance. This connection is indicated in the model by a semiwavy line. Probably the best example of an intrinsic reward is the feeling of having accomplished something worthwhile. For that matter, any of the rewards that satisfy self-actualization needs or higher order growth needs are good examples of intrinsic rewards.

The model also shows that intrinsic and extrinsic rewards are not directly related to job satisfaction since the relationship is moderated

[11] Abraham H. Maslow, *Motivation and Personality* (New York: Harper, 1954). According to Maslow, needs are arranged in a hierarchy with physiological and security needs being the lowest level needs, social and esteem needs next, and autonomy and self-actualization needs the highest level.

[12] Edward E. Lawler, "Managers' Attitudes toward How Their Pay Is and Should Be Determined." *Journal of Applied Psychology*, vol. 50 (August 1966), 273–279.

by expected equitable rewards. This variable refers to the level or amount of rewards that an individual feels he *should* receive as the result of his job performance. Thus, an individual's satisfaction is a function both of the number and amount of the rewards he receives as well as what he considers to be a fair level of reward. An individual can be satisfied with a small amount of reward if he feels that it is a fair amount of reward for his job.[13]

This model would seem to predict that because of the imperfect relationship between performance and rewards and the importance of expected equitable rewards there would be a low but positive relationship between job satisfaction and job performance. The model also leads to a number of other predictions about the relationship between satisfaction and performance. If it turns out that, as this model predicts, satisfaction is dependent on performance, then it can be argued that satisfaction is an important variable from both a theoretical and a practical point of view despite its low relationship to performance. However, when satisfaction is viewed in this way, the reasons for considering it to be important are quite different from those that are proposed when satisfaction is considered to cause performance. But first, let us look at some of the predictions that are derivable from the model and at some data that were collected in order to test the predictions.

Research Data

Usable data were collected from 148 middle and lower level managers in five organizations. One of the organizations was a large manufacturing company; the others were small social service and welfare agencies. As determined from the demographic data collected from each manager, the sample was typical of other samples of middle and lower level managers, with one exception—31 of the managers were female.

Two kinds of data were collected for each manager. Superior and peer rankings were obtained on two factors: (1) how hard the manager worked, and (2) how well the manager performed his job. Since a number of peers ranked each manager, the average peer's rankings were used for data analysis purposes. The rankings by the superiors and peers were in general agreement with each other, so the rankings met the requirements for convergent and discriminant validity. In addition to the superior and peer rankings each manager filled out an attitude questionnaire designed to measure his degree of satisfaction

---

[13] Lyman W. Porter, "A Study of Perceived Need Satisfaction in Bottom and Middle Management Jobs," *Journal of Applied Psychology*, vol. 45 (January 1961), 1–10.

in five needed areas. This part of the questionnaire was identical to the one used in earlier studies by Porter.[14] It consists of 13 items in the following form:

The opportunity for independent thought and action in my management position:

(*a*) How much is there now?
>   (min) 1 2 3 4 5 6 7 (max)

(*b*) How much should there be?
>   (min) 1 2 3 4 5 6 7 (max)

The answers to the first of these questions (*a*) for each of the 13 items was taken as the measure of need fulfillment or rewards received. The answer to the second of the questions (*b*) was taken as a measure of the individual's expected equitable level of rewards. The difference in answers between the second and first of these questions was taken as the operational measure of need satisfaction. That is, the larger the difference between "should" and "is now" in our findings, the greater the *dis*satisfaction.[15]

The 13 items, though presented in random order in the questionnaire, had been preclassified into five types of needs that have been described by Maslow: security, social, esteem, autonomy, and self-actualization.

Predictions and Research Results

Let us now consider two specific predictions that our model suggests. The first is that an individual's degree of need satisfaction is related to his job performance as rated by his peers and by his superior. A second prediction is that this relationship is stronger for managers than for nonmanagers.

The basis for this second prediction can be found in the assumed connection between rewards and performance. It seems apparent that most organizations have considerably more freedom to reward their managers differentially than they do their often unionized rank-and-file employees (unless the latter are on incentive pay plans). Even in a nonunionized organization (such as a governmental unit), management jobs generally offer the possibility of greater flexibility in differential rewards, especially in terms of prestige and autonomy in deci-

---

[14] Ibid.

[15] A third question about the importance of the various types of needs was also included, but the results based on it are not reported in the findings presented in this article.

sion making. Management jobs also typically provide greater opportunities to satisfy higher order intrinsic needs. As the model shows, satisfaction of these higher order needs is more closely tied to performance.

Satisfaction and Performance.   Data collected from our sample of managers generally support the first two predictions. Job satisfaction (the sum of the difference scores for all 13 items) correlates significantly with both the superiors' rankings ($r = 0.32$, $p < 0.01$) and peers' rankings ($r = 0.30$, $p < 0.01$) of performance. Although the correlations are not large, they are substantially larger than the median correlation between satisfaction and performance at the level of rank-and-file workers ($r = 0.14$ as given in Vroom's review). It is possible that this higher relationship came about because we used a different measure of need satisfaction than has been typically used before or because we used a better performance measure. However, our belief is that it came about because the study was done at the management level in contrast to the previous studies which mainly involved nonmanagement employees. Neither our measure of job performance nor our measure of satisfaction would seem to be so unique that either could account for the higher relationship found between satisfaction and performance. However, future studies that use the same measure for both managers and nonmanagers are needed if this point is to be firmly established.

Satisfaction and Effort.   An additional prediction from the model is that satisfaction should be more closely related to the rankings obtained on performance than to the rankings obtained on effort. The prediction is an important one for the model and stems from the fact that satisfaction is seen as a variable that is more directly dependent on performance than on effort. Others have pointed out that effort is only one of the factors that determines how effective an individual's performance will be. Ability factors and situational constraints are other obviously relevant determinants. It is also important to note that if we assume, as many previous writers have, that satisfaction causes performance then it would seem logical that satisfaction should be more closely related to effort than to performance. Satisfaction should influence an individual's performance by affecting his motivation to perform effectively, and this presumably is better reflected by effort than by job performance.

The results of the present study show, in fact, a stronger relationship between the superiors' rankings of performance and satisfaction ($r = 0.32$), than between the superiors' rankings of effort and satisfaction ($r = 0.23$). Similarly, for the peer rankings there is a stronger relationship between performance and satisfaction ($r = 0.30$), than between effort and satisfaction ($r = 0.20$).

Intrinsic and Extrinsic Rewards. The model suggests that intrinsic rewards that satisfy needs such as self-actualization are more likely to be related to performance than are extrinsic rewards, which have to be given by someone else and therefore have a weaker relationship between their reception and performance. Thus, the satisfaction should be more closely related to performance for higher than for lower order needs. Table 1 presents the data relevant to this point. There is a slight tendency for satisfaction of the higher order needs to show higher correlations with performance than does satisfaction with lower order needs. In particular, the highest correlations appear for self-actualization, which is, of course, the highest order need in the Maslow need hierarchy.

Overall, the data from the present study are in general agreement with the predictions based on the model. Significant relationships did appear between performance and job satisfaction. Perhaps even more important for our point of view, the relationship between satisfaction and performance was stronger than that typically found among blue-collar employees. Also in agreement with our model was the finding that satisfaction was more closely related to performance than to effort. The final prediction, which was supported by the data, was that the satisfaction of higher order needs would be the most closely related to performance. Taken together then, the data offer encouraging support for our model and in particular for the assertion of the model that satisfaction can best be thought of as depending on performance rather than causing it.

Implications of the Findings

At this point we can ask the following question: what does the strength of the satisfaction-performance relationship tell us about an organization? For example, if a strong positive relationship exists we would assume that the organization is effectively distributing differential extrinsic rewards based on performance. In addition, it is providing jobs that allow for the satisfaction of higher order needs. Finally, the poorer performers rather than the better ones are quitting and showing high absenteeism, since, as we know, satisfaction, turnover, and absenteeism are closely related.

Now let us consider an organization where no relationship exists between satisfaction and performance. In this organization, presumably, rewards are not being effectively related to performance, and absenteeism and turnover in the organization are likely to be equally distributed among both the good and poor performers. Finally, let us consider the organization where satisfaction and performance bear a negative relationship to each other. Here absenteeism and turnover

TABLE 1
Pearson Correlations between Performance and
Satisfaction in Five Need Areas

	Rankings by	
Needs	*Superiors*	*Peers*
Security	0.21*	0.17†
Social	0.23*	0.26*
Esteem	0.24*	0.16†
Autonomy	0.18†	0.23*
Self-actualization	0.30*	0.28*

* $p < 0.01$
† $p < 0.05$

will be greatest among the best performers. Furthermore, the poor performers would be getting more rewards than the good performers.

Clearly, most organization theorists would feel that organizational effectiveness is encouraged by rewarding good performers and by restricting turnover to poorer performers. Thus, it may be desirable for organizations to develop a strong relationship between satisfaction and performance. In effect, the argument is that the less positive relationship between satisfaction and performance in an organization, the less effective the organization will be *(ceteris paribus)*. If this hypothesis were shown to be true, it would mean that a measure of the relationship between satisfaction and performance would be a helpful diagnostic tool for examining organizations. It is hardly necessary to note that this approach is quite different from the usual human relations one of trying to maximize satisfaction, since here we are suggesting trying to maximize the relationship between satisfaction and performance, rather than satisfaction itself.

One further implication of the model appears to warrant comment. It well may be that a high general level of satisfaction of needs like self-actualization may be a sign of organization effectiveness. Such a level of satisfaction would indicate, for instance, that most employees have interesting and involving jobs and that they probably are performing them well. One of the obvious advantages of providing employees with intrinsically interesting jobs is that good performance is rewarding in and of itself. Furthermore, being rewarded for good performance is likely to encourage further good performance. Thus, measures of higher order need satisfaction may provide good evidence of how effective organizations have been in creating interesting and rewarding jobs, and therefore, indirect evidence of how motivating the jobs themselves are. This discussion of the role of intrinsic rewards and satisfaction serves to highlight the importance of including measures of higher order need satisfaction in attitude surveys. Too often attitude surveys have focused only on satisfaction with extrinsic rewards, such as pay and promotion, and on the social relations which were originally stressed by the human relations movement.

In summary, we have argued that it is important to consider the satisfaction level that exists in organizations. For one thing, satisfaction is important because it has the power to influence both absenteeism and turnover. In addition, in the area of job performance we have emphasized that rather than being a cause of performance, satisfaction is caused by it. If this is true, and we have presented some evidence to support the view that it is, then it becomes appropriate to be more concerned about which people and what kind of needs are satisfied in the organization, rather than about how to maximize satisfaction generally. In short, we suggest new ways of interpreting job satisfaction data.

8

A Reappraisal and Reinterpretation of the Satisfaction-Causes-Performance Hypothesis*

DENNIS W. ORGAN

It would appear that the last nail has been driven into the coffin of the "Human Relations" notion that satisfaction causes performance, insofar as its respectability among theorists and researchers in organizational psychology is concerned. Some impatient critics might remark, as did Charles II of his own imminent surcease, that the beast was "an unconscionable time adying." Nevertheless, after 40 years of empirical studies and reviews (e.g., 4, 7, 12, 16, 17, 19, 20, 28) addressed to the proposition, the notion appears intellectually bankrupt. A newer, tough-minded generation of teachers in organizational behavior seeks to disabuse its charges of the idea that making people happy will make them more productive. One suspects that this task is

* Abridged from *Academy of Management Review*, 1977, 2, no. 1, 46–53.

undertaken with gusto, for there is nothing dearer to the behavioral scientist's heart than to demolish with hard evidence a tenet of conventional wisdom; no other activity, it seems, does so much to justify the existence of the occupation.

But it does seem worthwhile to take the widespread *belief* (9) in the satisfaction-causes-performance hypothesis as a datum itself worthy of analysis. What is the unarticulated logic from which the proposition emerged? Perhaps a reconstruction of that logic might show it to be compatible with more current and viable theories, with the satisfaction-causes-performance notion being merely a hasty and imprecise deduction. If the latter could be examined in the context of the intuitive framework which gave birth to it; if, interpreted in terms of current social psychological concepts, that framework could also account post hoc for some reliable empirical generalizations not generally associated with the satisfaction-productivity question; and if the framework, amended by qualifications brought to light in its new context, could specify the boundaries of its own predictive powers (i.e., explain those cases in which satisfaction and performance are more or less unrelated); then the satisfaction-causes-performance position might be seen in a more respectable light.

Unfortunately, explication of the mute logic in question is not found in the literature presumably comprising the "Human Relations" school (e.g., 10, 23, 24); those sources lack any unambiguous declaration that increased satisfaction leads to increased performance. Schwab and Cummings (27) did unearth a 1951 statement: "improve the morale of a company and you improve production." Whether "morale" can be interpreted to mean satisfaction is a moot point, and whether the statement is implied to hold true at the individual level is debatable. In any case, the Human Relations writers as a group have not staked their case on the proposition that happy people consistently outproduce unhappy people. The framework which prompts the lay person to believe in the proposition must be sought in a somewhat speculative fashion.

Reconstructing the Logic behind the Satisfaction-Causes-Performance Hypothesis

The framework in question represents a primitive, vaguely cognized version of the theory of equity in social exchange as articulated by Gouldner (11), Homans (15), Blau (3), Adams (1), and recent contributions by Walster, Berscheid, and Walster (29). A unifying theme to this stream of thought is the assumption that most people expect social justice or equity to prevail in interpersonal transactions. An individual who regards himself or herself as inequitably short-changed will experience resentment and, if the additional costs are not prohibitive, will take aggressive action designed to restore equity (even if the costs *are* prohibitive, the individual may still do so in order to "save face"; e.g., Brown, 6). But an individual accorded some manner of social gift— inequitably in excess of what is anticipated—will experience gratitude and a felt obligation to reciprocate the benefactor. Both Adams' presentation of equity theory (1) and elaborations by Walster et al. (29) recognize alternatives to reciprocation as a means of restoring equity; they include perceptual distortions of the exchange or the parties to the exchange. Nevertheless, their treatment suggests that persons who are inequitably over-rewarded will prefer reciprocation, if possible, as a mode of restoring equity, and research appears to bear this out.

Reciprocal Behavior of Benefactees and the Hypothesis. The underlying premise that individuals seek to reciprocate their benefactors represents a conceptual core from which one might deduce the satisfaction-causes-performance hypothesis. But the deduction rests on two implicit qualifying assumptions: first, that satisfaction results from social gifts which can be personalized in their association with the voluntary actions of official organization representatives; and second, that increased productivity or performance is perceived as a viable and appropriate form of reciprocation to those organizational benefactors. While neither assumption is unreasonable, not all satisfaction results from interpersonal rewards, nor is increased performance the only avenue of reciprocation. Even recognizing these limitations, the proposition that satisfaction causes performance is clearly consonant with the underlying premise. Does the empirical literature justify this extrapolation?

Brayfield and Crockett (4) reviewed studies correlating job satisfaction with performance, concluding that:

> there is little evidence that employee attitudes of the type usually measured in morale surveys bear any simple—or, for that matter, appreciable—relationship to performance on the job.

Vroom's (28) review of 23 studies found a median correlation of .14, echoing the same conclusion. Taken together, these two reviews were thought to have pretty well settled the issue. Nevertheless, several points might temper one's conclusion from those reviews:

1. Of the 23 studies reviewed by Vroom, only three yielded negative correlations, one of which was −.03. In the absence of any functional relationship between satisfaction and performance (ignoring for the moment the direction of causality), the probability of ob-

taining 20 positive correlations by chance out of 23 studies would be only .0002.

2. Correlations in the range of .10–.30, which characterize the majority of the studies reviewed by Brayfield and Crockett and Vroom, are dismissed as insufficient evidence to warrant continued consideration of the satisfaction-performance caused link. Yet anyone who follows the empirical literature knows that correlations of such magnitude dot the landscape of the behavioral sciences. Especially when statistically significant, correlations greater than .20 usually signal the continued exploration and analysis of relationships measured at that level (and, of course, boundary conditions within which the relationship holds). Rarely can researchers account for more than 10 percent of the variance in a criterion by a single variable, except in the testing of propositions that verge on the tautological or that are hopelessly confounded by method variance (e.g., by response set when two or more variables are measured by responses from the same source).

Even if the consistent, albeit small, positive correlations between satisfaction and performance are taken as evidence of a relationship, they do not constitute support for any particular causal interpretation. Lawler and Porter (20) find a more plausible and convincing causal model in a scheme in which satisfaction follows from rewards, which in turn are preceded by performance with varying degrees of fit, depending on how closely rewards are tied to level of performance. Thus, a number of crosslagged correlational studies—taking measures of performance, satisfaction, and rewards at two different points in time—have been conducted in an attempt to sort out the magnitudes of the various causal relationships that might contribute to a single static correlation between satisfaction and performance.

The guiding spirit behind these and similar studies seems to have been to pit competing theories (i.e., satisfaction-causes-performance versus performance-rewards-satisfaction) against one another, to find which one received the more support, and declare a winner. If one must pick a single theory, a reasonable assessment of the evidence probably tilts more toward the performance-rewards-satisfaction model. But the contention here is that one need not view these contrasting approaches as running a horse race; there is no reason why attraction to either one excludes the other from consideration. *Both* relationships may exist, in varying degrees of mix from one situation to another. And the reference here is not simply to the feedback mechanism by which satisfaction from previously attained performance-contingent rewards increases the likelihood of future performance, but also the situation in which rewards first granted on a "noncontingent"[1] basis evoke desired behavior in the future as a reciprocal exchange for such rewards.

The Exchange Model and the Environment. If a primitive equity-in-social exchange model contains the logic for an assertion that degree of satisfaction (from interpersonal rewards) may cause level of performance (as measured by objective criteria or supervisory ratings), and if a modicum of evidence supports this position, can that same intuitive model account for other consistent findings in the work environment? It is consistent with the finding that satisfaction generally correlates negatively with unexcused absences; regular attendance may represent an aspect of performance which individuals deem an appropriate reciprocal exchange for rewards previously received. Organizational psychologists have been more willing to admit a causal connection between satisfaction and absenteeism than between satisfaction and performance, even though the correlations obtained in testing the former relationship are neither much greater nor markedly more consistent than those found in researching the latter relationship (cf. Vroom, 28, 178–186).

The social exchange framework could also account for the historic findings by Fleishman (8) that consideration in supervisory behavior reliably predicted the number of grievances processed by subordinates. It explains why Patchen (22) found that, on important decisions, participants tend to defer to those *most affected* by the decision—in order to receive similar deference on future decisions with whose consequences *they* must live.

As Herman (13) pointed out in a cogent analysis of job attitude-behavior relationships, measures of satisfaction or other job attitudes are constructed to maximize the amount of variance they permit, while "situational contingencies may restrict the possible variance on the performance measure." In other words, the design of many tasks in organizations reflects an objective of constraining the variability of task performance among individuals. Technology often tends to exert a leveling effect such that the amount of work to be done per unit time and per person holds roughly constant or varies only within a narrow range. When this is the case, performance—in the objective or quantitative sense—is limited in the opportunity it affords participants to reciprocate rewards from organizational officials; participants, to the extent they actually do wish to reciprocate, must choose other types of work behavior.

---

[1] It is doubtful that anyone ever dispenses a reward on a purely "noncontingent" basis; the reward is presumably contingent on some response by the recipient, if nothing other than physical presence. The word "noncontingent" here signifies rewards given in advance of the behavior which they might evoke.

In numerous situations, outstanding performance or productivity, beyond some minimally acceptable level, is of relatively little interest to organizational officials. They may be more desirous of such things as regular attendance, predictability, following the rules, "not making waves," avoidance of hassles, cooperation, and generalized tendencies toward compliance. Certainly such behaviors represent the glue which holds collective endeavors together, and they are the behaviors about which Roethlisberger and Dickson (23) and Gardner (10) seemed more concerned as a function of "sentiments." In short, whoever first voiced agreement with the proposition that satisfaction affects performance might not have been limiting the concept of performance to a narrow definition of the sort usually measured by industrial psychologists.

Social Exchange and Reciprocity. Contemporary theoretical and empirical study of social exchange has identified some limiting conditions under which reward-produced satisfaction generates reciprocity or equity-striving behavior by recipients. If Human Relations thinking is to be faulted it would be for failing to take these boundaries into account. One such boundary condition, identified by Brehm (5), is the perception by recipients that their behavioral freedom has been unreasonably threatened by obligations foisted upon them. In such a case, their response is likely to be psychological reactance— deliberately avoiding, or even behaving contrary to, reciprocity effecting responses. For example, the perception by recipients of benefactors' manipulative intent is likely to evoke psychological reactance. Organ (21) has shown that the degree of surveillance accompanying conferral of social gifts is one determinant of whether reciprocity or reactance characterizes subordinate responses.

Another boundary condition is the recipient's attribution of volition to the giver. Only social gifts which the benefactor is seen as capable of withholding are deemed as mandating reciprocity. Thus, one would expect that in unionized organizations, satisfaction produced by extrinsic rewards would not produce the same degree of reciprocity in behavior as in non-union organizations. Similarly, social rewards under the personal control of superiors would likely effect more reciprocity than those administered by company policy on an impersonal basis.

Furthermore, as Blau (3) notes:

> regular rewards create expectations that redefine the baseline in terms of which positive sanctions are distinguished from negative ones.

That is, rewards which once exerted obligatory holds on persons may do so decreasingly as they begin to be perceived as "rights." A corollary derivable from this principle is that organizational participants may show greater degrees of reciprocity for prior rewards in the early stages of their tenure than in later stages. A study reviewed by Brayfield and Crockett (4) found a significant positive correlation between satisfaction and performance for inexperienced and untrained women, but an insignificant correlation for women with longer tenure. Wanous's (30) finding that extrinsic rewards significantly predicted later performance came from a sample of newly hired telephone operators, and Schiemann's (26) similar findings drew from a sample of management trainees. Schein (25) argued that one mechanism for securing commitment from new organization members is to shower them with such lavish gifts of time and perquisites that they feel guilty if they do not reciprocate with loyalty and hard work.

Ultimately equity in social exchange is a perceptual matter, defined by private and idiosyncratic evaluations of the individual. This consideration complicates formulation of precise behavioral predictions from a social exchange conceptual framework. Individuals differ in what they regard as appropriate repayment of social gifts, in the time horizon appropriate for achieving equity, in their capacity for perceptual distortion of the intents and attributions of the benefactor, and, perhaps even more generally, in sensitivity to social exchange morality. Identification of the personality dimensions which subsume such differences should lend greater predictive power to a social exchange-equity framework and enhance its viability as a general theory of organizational behavior.

Reconsideration of Reciprocity in the Context of the Hypothesis. The satisfaction-causes-performance hypothesis, then, merits reconsideration in the perspective which views reciprocity as a normative determinant of much behavior in organizations. This perspective is not fully developed, either theoretically or empirically. It requires conceptual development and systematic research along several dimensions.

There is a need to know what types of satisfiers evoke feelings of obligation and how these vary as a function of different kinds of organizational environments. In addition, there is a need to identify which behaviors organization officials perceive as appropriate and desirable forms of reciprocation, and how such perceptions are affected by contextual factors—e.g., the range of individual production that is possible due to technological or job design constraints, the costs of absenteeism or turnover, threats posed by powerful unions, the types of pressures exerted on the immediate superior, and so on. Subordinate perceptions of what behaviors qualify as reciprocation are also important; these may not conform to the expectations of superiors due to contextual variables such as group norms, the history of labor-management politics and relationships, the physical or psychological costs of such behaviors, or conflicts with professional credo.

Finally, there is a need to explore the alternatives to reciprocation, especially in the case where a salient mode of reciprocation is not viable. Blau (3) identifies status-enhancement of the benefactor as the most probable consequence. But the aversion of indebtedness may prompt other coping techniques, such as derogation of the value of the benefaction, minimizing the cost to the benefactor of supplying the benefaction, or avoiding as far as possible any future interaction with the benefactor.

Conclusion

The skeptic may contend that any conceptual approach which predicts desired behavior as following from noncontingent rewards is bankrupt from the start, because it flies in the face of known operant principles. But this objection would rest on an unnecessarily narrow and short-sighted application of reinforcement processes. From childhood persons are rewarded by socializing agents for demonstrating equity in interpersonal relationships and often punished (e.g., by withholding of approval) for not so doing. That such conditioning occurs on an aperiodic rather than perfectly consistent basis only strengthens the tendency for such behavior to occur long after it has ceased to generate explicit social rewards. Intermittent schedules of reinforcement produce a resistance to extinction which, even in lower organisms, may endure for years. Of course, individuals differ in the nature of their prior reinforcement histories in this regard.

In summary, the argument here is that the satisfaction-causes-performance notion and the "Human Relations" syndrome which it connotes deserve more judicious consideration than recently accorded it. Results of empirical research, while hardly lending a ringing confirmation, are sufficiently equivocal to justify an open mind on the issue. The proposition can be deduced, with some qualifications, from a respectable and tractable conceptual framework, a crude layman's version of which probably gave birth to the idea. Rather than prematurely burying this idea, one should set it in proper perspective and glimpse whatever truths it might imperfectly reflect.

Scientific inquiry has traditionally been governed, at least in lip service, by the heuristic of conservatism. This principle is interpreted to mean, among other things, that the null hypothesis is given the benefit of a doubt and that we err on the cautious side in endorsing the validity of propositions. In the behavioral sciences, the principle of conservatism might also be taken as putting the burden of proof on the behavioral scientists in their repudiation of folk-style psychology. This is not to say that folk-style psychology itself constitutes scientific knowledge, but rather that it arises from some kind of mute logic and phenomenology. The full understanding of this logic and phenomenology is itself a task of the behavioral sciences.

REFERENCES

1. Adams, J. S.   Inequity in social exchange. In L. Berkowitz (Ed), *Advances in experimental social psychology*, vol. 2. New York: Academic Press, 1965.
2. Alwin, D. F.   Making inferences from attitude-behavior correlations. *Sociometry*, 1973, *36*, 253–278.
3. Blau, P. M.   *Exchange and power in social life*. New York: Wiley, 1967.
4. Brayfield, A. H., & Crockett, W. II.   Employee attitudes and employee performance. *Psychological Bulletin*, 1955, *52*, 396–424.
5. Brehm, J. W.   *A theory of psychological reactance*. New York: Academic Press, 1966.
6. Brown, B. R.   The effects of effort to maintain face on interpersonal bargaining. *Journal of Experimental Social Psychology*, 1968, *4*, 107–122.
7. Cherrington, D. L., Reitz, H. J., & Scott, W. E., Jr.   Effects of contingent and noncontingent reward on the relationship between satisfaction and task performance. *Journal of Applied Psychology*, 1971, *55*, 531–537.
8. Fleishman, E. A.   Twenty years of consideration and structure. In E. A. Fleishman & J. G. Hunt (Eds.), *Current developments in the study of leadership*. Carbondale, Ill.: Southern Illinois University Press, 1973.
9. Gannon, M. J., & Noon, J. P.   Management's critical deficiency. *Business Horizons*, 1971, *14*, 49–56.
10. Gardner, B. B.   *Human relations in industry*. Chicago: Richard D. Irwin, Inc., 1945.
11. Gouldner, A. W.   The norm of reciprocity: A preliminary statement. *American Sociological Review*, 1960, *25*, 161–178.
12. Green, C. N.   Causal connections among managers' merit pay, job satisfaction, and performance. *Journal of Applied Psychology*, 1973, *58*, 95–100.
13. Herman, J. B.   Are situational contingencies limiting job attitude-job performance relationships? *Organizational Behavior and Human Performance*, 1973, *10*, 208–224.
14. Herzberg, F. (Ed.).   *Job attitudes: review of research and opinion*. Pittsburgh, Pa.: Psychological Service of Pittsburgh, 1955.
15. Homans, G. C.   *Social behavior: Its elementary forms*. New York: Harcourt, Brace and World, 1961.

16. Katz, D., Maccoby, N., Gurin, G., & Floor, L. G. *Productivity, supervision and morale among railroad workers.* Ann Arbor: University of Michigan Survey Research Center, 1951.

17. Katz, D., Maccoby, N., & Morse, N. *Productivity, supervision and morale in an office situation.* Ann Arbor: University of Michigan Survey Research Center, 1950.

18. Kesselman, G. A., Wood, M. T., & Hagen, E. L. Relationships between performance and satisfaction under contingent and noncontingent reward systems. *Journal of Applied Psychology,* 1974, 59, 374–376.

19. Kornhauser, A., & Sharp, A. Employee attitudes: Suggestions from a study in a factory. *Personnel Journal,* 1932, *10,* 393–404.

20. Lawler, E. E., III, & Porter, L. W. The effect of performance on job satisfaction. *Industrial Relations,* 1967, 7, 20–28.

21. Organ, D. W. Social exchange and psychological reactance in a simulated superior-subordinate relationship. *Organizational Behavior and Human Performance,* 1974, *12,* 132–142.

22. Patchen, M. The locus and basis of influence on organizational decisions. *Organizational Behavior and Human Performance,* 1974, *11,* 195–221.

23. Roethlisberger, F. J., & Dickson, W. J. *Management and the worker.* New York: Wiley, Science Editions, 1964.

24. Saltonstall, R. *Human relations in administration.* New York: McGraw-Hill, 1959.

25. Schein, E. H. Organizational socialization and the profession of management. *Industrial Management Review,* 1968. Reprinted in H. L. Tosi & W. C. Hamner (Eds.), *Organizational behavior and management.* Chicago: St. Clair Press, 1974.

26. Schiemann, W. A. Satisfaction-rewards-performance: Review of the literature and a causal analysis. Paper presented at the meeting of the Midwestern Psychological Association, Chicago, April 1975.

27. Schwab, D. P., & Cummings, L. L. Theories of performance and satisfaction: A review. *Industrial Relations,* 1970, 9, 408–430.

28. Vroom, V. H. *Work and motivation.* New York: Wiley, 1964.

29. Walster, E., Berscheid, E., & Walster, G. W. New directions in equity research. *Journal of Personality and Social Psychology,* 1973, *25,* 151–176.

30. Wanous, J. P. A causal-correlational analysis of the job satisfaction and performance relationship. *Journal of Applied Psychology,* 1974, 59, 139–144.

9

Growth Needs and Intrinsic Work Motivation*

CRAIG C. PINDER

Imagine you are walking with a friend through your neighborhood on a warm summer evening. As you walk, you notice a nine-year-old boy pushing a lawn mower in erratic circles and strips around the grass on his parents' front yard. The boy has his head lowered between his straight, extended arms, and he is bent over at the waist as he runs and pushes the mower. Upon getting closer, you hear him making sounds like an engine—an airplane engine. You stop and ask the young man what he is doing, and learn that he is pretending to be a pilot flying an airplane. The sounds he was emitting, of course, were those made by the plane's motor. The young pilot seems friendly enough so you stop to chat for a while. The conversation reveals that the boy is having fun with his fantasy Beechcraft and that he did not consider his activity to be work. Further probing on your part informs you that the boy receives no pay or other form of direct compensation from his parents for cutting the grass (or flying his airplane). You part company, wishing him a safe flight.

Is the boy in this example working (cutting the lawn) or playing (flying his aircraft)? Or, does it matter at all what you call or how you classify his behavior? For the boy, the behavior clearly was playing. On the other hand, the boy's father would view it as work—a chore that he would now not have to perform himself. It may simply be a matter of one's perspective, as seemed to be the case when Tom Sawyer managed to lure his friends into whitewashing his Aunt Polly's fence.

We can look a bit deeper behind the reasons for our young pilot's behavior, asking, for example, what motivated him to behave the way he did. We can probably rule out existence and relatedness needs as

* From Craig C. Pinder, *Work Motivation: Theories, Issues, and Applications* (Glenview, Ill.: Scott, Foresman, 1984), pp. 57–70.

explanations for the boy's action, because it did not seem that he was deriving any monetary rewards for his play, nor did he seem to be seeking any social interaction from it. If we assume that the boy's behavior was, in fact, motivated (as opposed to being simply random or compulsive), we are left with the conclusion that the boy must have been motivated largely by growth needs. What, you may ask, has *growth* got to do with the erratic flight of a low altitude lawn mower?

*   *   *   *   *

WHAT IS INTRINSIC MOTIVATION?

Current thinking in work motivation would view the boy's behavior as being *intrinsically* motivated. Or, we might say the boy was intrinsically motivated to do what he was doing. Intrinsically motivated behavior can be defined, loosely, as behavior that is performed for its own sake, rather than for the purpose of acquiring any material or social rewards. One scholar who has extensively investigated intrinsically motivated behaviors defines them as those "which a person engages in to feel competent and self determining" (Deci, 1975, p. 61). Consistent with this view, Wexley and Yukl (1977, p. 89) define intrinsic motivation in work settings as "a term used to describe effort that is expended in an employee's job to fulfill growth needs such as achievement, competence, and self-actualization." In short, these various definitions imply a motivational force that originates in what Maslow (1954) would call the higher order needs, or what Alderfer (1972) would classify as growth needs—a force directed toward behavior that is its own incentive.

The distinction between internal and external work motivation originated with Herzberg, Mausner, and Snyderman's (1959) study of the determinants of job satisfaction. And although the concepts of intrinsic and extrinsic motives, rewards, and outcomes have not always been consistently understood and used in recent years (Dyer & Parker, 1975), the distinction is important, and intrinsic motivation is a major factor in explaining much of the work behavior of many employees. In fact, it may be that intrinsic motivation (and hence the intrinsic rewards required to satisfy it) will become increasingly more important as the work force becomes more highly educated and less threatened by challenging jobs (Cooper, Morgan, Foley, & Kaplan, 1979).

Intrinsic and Extrinsic Outcomes

Insofar as we can distinguish between intrinsic and extrinsic motivation, we can also distinguish between intrinsic and extrinsic job outcomes (Lawler, 1969). Intrinsic outcomes relate to either the satisfaction or frustration of the higher level, or growth needs. Examples of intrinsic outcomes would include positive feelings of accomplishment or a sense of diminished self-esteem. Intrinsic outcomes occur, when they occur, immediately upon the performance of the acts that produce them. They are, in a sense, self-administered by the individual, rather than distributed by others.

Extrinsic outcomes tend to relate more to the gratification and frustration of the existence and relatedness needs. They include things such as pay, promotions, and social interaction with one's colleagues. Moreover, they tend to be mediated by outsiders, such as one's supervisor or peers.

There is some dispute about the precise dividing line between intrinsic and extrinsic outcomes (Dyer & Parker, 1975), so some writers discourage continued use of the distinction (e.g., Guzzo 1979). This author's view is that some job outcomes can often appeal to both higher and lower level needs (e.g., pay increases can enhance one's feelings of self-esteem), and although there may be some disagreement concerning where one draws the boundary, it is useful to refer to intrinsic outcomes as those job-related consequences that, at least in part, function either to gratify or frustrate a person's growth needs.

The Origins and Nature of Intrinsic Motivation

According to Deci (1975), there have been at least three general approaches taken by psychologists to understand intrinsically motivated behavior. One of these, represented by the work of Hebb (1955), posits that human beings seek preferred or *optimum* levels of arousal (where arousal is seen as the stimulation of the brain and central nervous system). Arousal levels result primarily from the stimulation that is found in the individual's environment. If the arousal level is too low in comparison with a person's desired level, the person will be motivated to behave in such a way as to increase it. For example, an employee who is used to a fairly hectic work pace, but who finds things slower than usual on a particular day, will be motivated to seek out other people for conversation, set new tasks to be accomplished, or do something, simply to "stir things up." On the other hand, if the person's level of arousal is sufficiently greater than the preferred level, the individual will attempt either to withdraw from the highly arousing circumstances, or take steps to slow things down toward the desired level (for example, by turning off a noisy radio or moving into a job that is less demanding). In this view then, intrinsically motivated behavior is behavior intended to increase or decrease the physiological stimulation a person experiences, in order to bring it into line with desired levels.

A second approach (which is similar to the first), posits that people desire and behave to achieve an optimum level of uncertainty or *incongruity*, where incongruities consist of psychological inconsistencies in a person's beliefs, thoughts, perceptions, values, or behaviors (Zajonc, 1960). Unlike Festinger (1957) who posited that people find *cognitive dissonance* aversive, and that they are motivated to minimize the number of inconsistent cognitions they hold, this approach claims that individuals vary in the number and intensity of disparate beliefs, acts, and perceptions they prefer in their lives. When a person is experiencing either too little consistency ("Things just don't add up!") or too much consistency ("The world is in total harmony with itself"), behavior is instigated either to reduce or increase the level of congruity in the person's mind. Whereas the optimum arousal approach described above is physiological in orientation, the optimal congruity approach stresses the level of psychic comfort or discomfort a person experiences as a consequence of his or her acts and perceptions. The work of Hunt (1965) and Berlyne (1973) represents this second approach to explaining the origins of intrinsically motivated behavior.

The third approach to intrinsic motivation identified by Deci (1975) is best represented by White's (1959) concept of competence (or *effectance*) motivation, and de Charm's (1968) notion of personal causation.

According to White (1959), competence refers to a person's capacity to master and deal effectively with the surroundings—to be in charge of them. The exploratory behavior of children characterizes a desire to be competent, as do adult behaviors that are intended to enquire, to manipulate, and to learn about things. Competence motivation represents a need that is always available to instigate and direct behavior, although this need is less urgent (or prepotent to use Maslow's term) than are the types of existence needs we have examined in a previous chapter. When it is aroused, however, competence motivation causes people to seek out challenging situations in their environments, and then to conquer those situations, leading to feelings of competence and efficacy.

Likewise, according to de Charms (1968), people desire to be the *origin* of their own behavior, rather than the *pawns* of circumstances beyond their control. People strive for personal causation, to be in charge of their own lives, and for the outcomes that accrue to them.

In short then, Deci (1975) sees intrinsically motivated behaviors as those behaviors a person engages in to feel competent and self-determining. These behaviors consist of two general types—those intended to find or create challenge and those intended to conquer it. Hence, the adult who deliberately takes a clock apart merely to see how it works, or who learns a foreign language simply for the sake of learning it, are two other examples of intrinsically motivated behavior from this third perspective.

In summary then, there have been at least three conceptual interpretations of intrinsic motivation, each of them predicated on a different fundamental assumption regarding human nature: the first one is primarily biological/physiological; the second is cognitive/perceptual; and the third is based on a need fulfillment model of human functioning. Does this mean that there is no similarity or overlap among the three approaches?

Similarities among the Three Approaches. Notice that the *challenge* associated with any of the exploratory behaviors mentioned in connection with the third approach (above) might serve to increase or decrease a person's level of arousal, and/or the level of consistency he experiences, suggesting that the three general approaches to understanding intrinsic motivation are somewhat compatible with one another.

For example, the man who disassembles a machine that does not need repair opens (literally) a great deal of new arousal as he perceives and manipulates the delicate internal mechanisms. Further, there is a strong chance that he may either confirm or disconfirm his prior beliefs about what he would find inside the machine, thereby either reducing or increasing the net level of congruity he holds in his mind about the way things operate. Finally, if he were successful at reassembling the machine, he is likely to experience feelings of mastery and competence. The point is that the three concepts of intrinsic motivation cited by Deci (1975) are compatible (or at least reconcilable) with one another, so one might conclude that, in a sense, a process of increasing incongruity, arousal, and challenge followed by attempts to reduce this incongruity, arousal, and challenge constitute the psychological mechanisms behind behaviors we refer to as intrinsically motivated behavior. Thus, Deci (1975, pp. 61–62) states:

> Only when a person is able to reduce incongruity . . . and only when a person is able to conquer the challenges which he encounters or creates will he feel competent and self-determining. He will feel satisfied when he is able to seek out pleasurable stimulation and deal effectively with overstimulation. In short, people seem to be engaged in the general process of seeking and conquering challenges which are optimal.

According to Deci (1975), the need to be competent and self-determining is innate among humans, although the specific types of behaviors required of an individual to satisfy it varies from one person to the next. Deci considers self-actualization to be one common manifestation of the need for competence and self-determination; he sees achievement motivation as another. In fact, achievement motivation has been one of the most thoroughly researched needs in psychology and is one that has special relevance to work behavior. Therefore, let's take a close look at this particular human need.

Achievement Motivation

Henry Murray generated numerous lists of human needs. One of these needs is referred to as the *need for achievement*, which he defined as a need to:

> accomplish something difficult. To master, manipulate, or organize physical objects, human beings, or ideas. To do this as rapidly and as independently as possible. To overcome obstacles and attain a high standard. To excel oneself. To rival and surpass others. To increase self-regard by the successful exercise of talent (Murray, 1938, p. 164).

The overlap between this need and the notion of self-actualization from Maslow is apparent, although not complete. The essence of achievement motivation might be seen as a struggle against one's *own* standards of excellence, which clearly is consistent with the idea of becoming all that one is capable of becoming. But the element of achievement motivation having to do with mastering objects and overcoming obstacles and challenges is not necessarily part of self-actualization, although the two can, in practice, go hand in hand. Further, the aspects of the need for achievement pertaining to mastering and organizing the environment are clearly consistent with White's (1959) concept of competence motivation, and de Charms's (1968) notion that people prefer to be responsible for their outcomes rather than merely being pawns.

In short, these various growth needs are not identical, in large measure because they have been identified and studied by scholars working more or less independently of one another. But they do converge considerably in terms of the types of behaviors they instigate.

David McClelland, a student of Henry Murray, has devoted much of his career to developing our understanding of achievement motivation and to the role it plays in entrepreneurial behavior and the economic prosperity of nations (Stewart, 1982). His work is far too extensive to be summarized completely here, so the reader is referred to some of the original sources (e.g., McClelland, 1961, 1962, 1965; McClelland & Winter, 1969). But a number of features of this work of particular relevance to our understanding of employee work motivation will be discussed here.

The Origins of Achievement Motivation. First, McClelland believes that all motives are learned from experiences in which certain cues in the environment are paired with positive or negative consequences. Accordingly, the need for achievement is learned when opportunities for competing with standards of excellence become associated with positive outcomes. Hence, childhood rearing practices that encourage youngsters to independently tackle challenges and to do well against them are critical. In fact, McClelland holds that child rearing practices are the most important determinants of the level of a person's achievement motivation (McClelland, 1961, pp. 340–50). However, McClelland has also shown that deliberate programs of training that involve the development of an achievement-oriented mentality can induce entrepreneurial behavior among adults where it did not previously exist (McClelland, 1965; McClelland & Winter, 1969). In other words, adults can be trained, it seems, to create and respond to opportunities to strive against challenges, and to behave in the ways described in the definition above. It is important to recognize that most of McClelland's research evidence pertains to boys and men, so his theory is limited to males. Attempts to generalize it to females have not yet been successful (Stein & Bailey, 1973).

Characteristics of Achievement-Motivated Behavior. It was stated in an earlier chapter that we can sometimes detect the existence of many particular needs in an individual by observing the person's behavior and drawing inferences from it. Accordingly, the behavior of achievement-motivated individuals is commonly characterized by three features. First, achievement-motivated people prefer tasks of *moderate* levels of difficulty. Second, achievement-motivated people prefer tasks for which successful performance depends upon their own efforts, rather than upon luck. Finally, achievement-motivated people demand feedback and knowledge about their successes and failures to a far greater degree than do people who are low in achievement motivation.

The preference for tasks of moderate levels of difficulty deserves special attention. According to Atkinson (1964), the total *achievement-oriented force* impacting a person who confronts a task is determined by three variables. Further, the three combine multiplicatively, so that if one of them is inactive, or "zero," there is no psychological force to engage in the task.

The first factor is the strength of the person's underlying need for achievement. This remains constant from one day to the next, although, as suggested above, it can be developed among male adults using focused training procedures.

The second factor is the level of difficulty of the task, as the person perceives it. Whether a particular task will be viewed as easy or difficult depends on a host of variables, such as the individual's perception of his ability to perform the task, for example.

The third factor which determines the strength of achievement-oriented motivation is the degree of intrinsic reward (or feelings of accomplishment) the individual expects he will experience if he manages to accomplish the task. Naturally, achieving a difficult challenge will bring the person greater feelings of accomplishment than will achieving a task that is perceived as simple. Therefore, the value of this third factor is inversely related to the second factor—the perceived level of difficulty of the task. Symbolically:

$$\text{T.A.F.} = \text{nACh} \times \text{P.S.} \times \text{I.S.}$$
$$\text{I.S.} = (1 - \text{P.S.})$$

where:

> T.A.F. = Total achievement-motivated force
> nAch = Strength of the person's underlying need for achievement
> P.S. = The perceived probability of task success
> I.S. = Intrinsic feeling of accomplishment

To illustrate how this formula works, consider the net force operating on an employee if (*a*) he has a very low level of the need for achievement, or (*b*) if he perceives the task to be too difficult for him to succeed, or (*c*) he perceives the task as very easy. In all three cases, we would not expect much achievement motivation in the person contemplating the task. His level of effort toward performing the task would be determined by the strength of other needs and incentives he believed would result from task success (such as the recognition of a female he might be trying to impress.)

The Importance of Perceived Task Difficulty. Notice that insofar as a person's level of underlying need strength is constant in the short run, the net level of achievement-related force acting on him to engage in a particular task will be determined by his perception of the level of difficulty of that task. The implication of this for the design of jobs and for the assignment of people to jobs is clear: In order to arouse motivational force associated with achievement needs, a supervisor must structure jobs and assign people to them so that employees see their chances of job performance as "50–50": not too low, but not too high. There must be a moderate level of challenge perceived. In practice, application of this principle can be difficult, because it requires that a supervisor be capable of accurately perceiving the difficulty level of a task as the employee sees it. So, a supervisor who overestimates or underestimates an employee's ability vis-à-vis a task will probably fail to arouse and take advantage of a certain amount of the natural achievement motivation of that worker. In theory, the principle is relatively simple; effectively applying it can be another matter.

COMBINING INTRINSIC AND EXTRINSIC MOTIVATION

Return for a moment to the hypothetical case of the boy and the lawn mower that opened this chapter. Consider what would happen if the boy's father elected to compensate him for cutting the lawn, using pay or some other form of extrinsic reward. Further, assume his father agreed to pay the boy some amount of money for cutting the grass each time he did it, thereby making the receipt of the money contingent upon his cutting the lawn. What would happen to the boy's net level of motivation to cut the lawn, and what would happen to the amount of fun the boy would have in cutting the grass/flying his imaginary airplane?

Both common sense and considerable research evidence (Lawler, 1971) support the proposition that compensation systems that tie pay and other rewards to the performance of an activity increase the level and rate of performance of that task. It would stand to reason, therefore, that paying the boy to fly his lawn mower would add considerable extrinsic motivation to the level of intrinsic motivation the boy already had for that task. In other words, the net level of motivation in the lad to cut the lawn should now be greater than before, because the extrinsic motivation provided by the money will somehow combine with his prior level of intrinsic motivation, resulting in a greater overall level of motivation than the boy had before he started to receive the pay. Again, common sense would support this reasoning, as do some formal theories of work motivation (e.g., Galbraith & Cummings, 1967; Porter & Lawler, 1968).

A series of experiments by Deci (e.g., 1971, 1972) and others (e.g., Condry, 1975; Greene & Lepper, 1974; Pritchard, Campbell & Campbell, 1977) has generated sufficient cause to believe, however, that intrinsic and extrinsic motivation may not always "add up" (in a psychological sense) the way common sense suggests. Instead, it may be that in some circumstances, the addition of an extrinsic, contingently paid incentive (such as money) to a work context in which the employee is intrinsically motivated to do the work, may result in a loss of some (or all) of the employee's prior level of intrinsic motivation toward that task, and maybe toward other tasks perceived as similar.

The possibility that intrinsic and extrinsic incentives may not be additive has generated considerable research (see Notz, 1975; and Guzzo, 1979, for two reviews), although the evidence on the issue is mixed (e.g., Arnold, 1976; Hamner & Foster, 1975; Pinder, 1976). Sometimes extrinsic rewards have been shown to reduce intrinsic motivation; other times the opposite effect occurs—the contingent reward enhances intrinsic motivation. How can we explain the inconsistent results of studies into the matter?

Among others, Staw (1976) has reviewed the evidence on this so-called *overjustification hypothesis*, and has suggested that whether extrinsic rewards enhance or reduce intrinsic motivation depends on at least five factors:

1. The degree of saliency of the reward.
2. The prevailing norm regarding the appropriateness of payment for the activity in question.
3. The prior level of commitment of the person to the task.
4. The degree of choice the individual has to perform, or not to perform, the task.
5. The existence of potential adverse consequences.

So, according to Staw, extrinsic rewards are more likely to reduce subsequent levels of intrinsic motivation if the reward is highly salient, meaning that it is obvious to those who are to receive it and that it is understood that the reward will be received upon the performance of the act. The more salient the reward, the more likely it is to have an adverse impact on intrinsic motivation (Ross, 1975).

Second, Staw suggests that rewards that are normally provided for a behavior in our culture are less likely to reduce a person's intrinsic motivation to engage in that behavior. He notes that in many of the studies in which rewards have been observed to reduce intrinsic motivation, those rewards were provided for the performance of acts that are not usually followed by reward (such as participating in games and puzzles in a laboratory setting). On the other hand, behaviors that are normally compensated in our culture (and that we might be inclined to classify as work) are less likely to be influenced by the provision of extrinsic outcomes. Hence, rewards may be more damaging to play behavior and learning behaviors than they are to work behavior.

Third, if the person is initially *very* committed to the task being rewarded, according to Staw, extrinsic rewards are less likely to dampen intrinsic motivation. Those studies that have demonstrated an adverse impact of extrinsic rewards have tended to involve tasks of only moderate prior levels of intrinsic motivation (cf. Arnold, 1976, with Pinder, 1976).

A fourth factor is the level of choice or compulsion a person feels with regard to performing the task. If the individual feels a high level of external pressure to engage in a task, she is more likely to believe that she is extrinsically motivated to behave in that manner, so little intrinsic rationale is available, and little damage can be done by the provision of extrinsic rewards. Finally, the perception that failure to perform the task might result in adverse consequences also contributes to the chances that the person will not attribute her own behavior to internal causes.

The point here is this: it is believed that people observe and rationalize their own behavior in a manner similar to that by which they observe the behavior of others and make attributions about the causes of that behavior. When an act is conducted in the context of a highly salient, highly compelling set of extrinsic circumstances (such as the fear of threats or the inducement of rewards), individuals are more likely to attribute their own behavior to these external causes. Otherwise, when there are few apparent external forces to which their behavior can be attributed, the individuals are more likely to assume that they are behaving in a certain manner because they want to—they like doing so. It seems that the presence or absence of such external factors largely determines whether people make intrinsic or extrinsic attributions about their own acts, as well as the cultural appropriateness of those external factors (such as money). While research on this issue is far from conclusive, one thing is clear: money is an interesting incentive and reward for a number of reasons, and it may not have the simple psychological effects on human motivation that appear at first glance.

Cognitive Evaluation Theory

Deci (1975; Deci & Porac, 1978) has developed a *Cognitive Evaluation Theory* in an attempt to reconcile the contradictory evidence pertaining to the relationship between intrinsic and extrinsic motivation. According to the theory, rewards can bear at least two fundamental features for the individual receiving them. The first of these is referred to as feedback, meaning that rewards given for performance of a task can convey information to the individual concerning how well she is doing at the task. A second feature of rewards can be the messages, if any, they have for the individual about why she is performing the task. Deci refers to these as *control* perceptions (i.e., "Why am I doing this job? For the reward, of course!").

Depending upon which of these two features of a reward system is more salient for an individual, it can serve either to enhance or reduce the person's intrinsic motivation toward it. If control perceptions are more salient, they may cause a shift in the person's perceived *locus of causality*, such that she attributes her reasons for engaging in the task to the external inducements surrounding it, rather than to any internal satisfaction provided by the task itself.

This notion draws on self-perception theory (Bem, 1967), which states that people examine their own behavior, much as they do the behavior of other people, and make attributions about their own motives for behaving as they do. In Deci's theory, control perceptions arising from a reward are said to shift from self-perceptions of intrinsic motivation ("I am cutting the lawn because it is fun") to extrinsic self-attributions ("I am doing it for the money"). As the perceived locus of causality shifts, the person's intrinsic motivation to do the task diminishes. Highly contingent rewards (such as in a piece rate or commission payment system) seem more likely to imply control perceptions, and thereby reduce intrinsic motivation, than less contingent pay systems (such as monthly salaries or hourly wages), largely because they are salient and undeniably connected with the behavior.

According to Deci, feedback perceptions may either enhance or reduce intrinsic motivation. If the feedback indicates to the person that he is doing well at a task, his feelings of competence are enhanced, and his intrinsic motivation for the task is increased (because, for Deci, competence and self-determination are the essence of intrinsic motivation). But if the person perceives that he is doing poorly as a result of the feedback implied by the rewards (or lack of rewards), his feelings of competence will be diminished, as will his intrinsic motivation, and the person will be less likely to engage in the task in the future without some form of extrinsic incentive.

A major shortcoming of Cognitive Evaluation Theory is that it fails to specify the conditions under which either of the two facets of reward (feedback or control) will be more salient for a particular individual in a given situation (Guzzo, 1979). In a recent statement of the theory, Deci and Porac (1978) state only that "'individual differences and situational factors' are related to the way people interpret the meaning of the rewards they receive" (pp. 163–164). Arnold's (1976) work suggests that when an individual's prior level of intrinsic motivation for a task is very high, feedback perceptions may be more salient, although one experiment failed to confirm this hypothesis (Pinder, Nord, & Ramirez, 1984).

In sum, the relationship between intrinsic and extrinsic motivation is not as simple as originally assumed (Lepper & Green, 1978), and further study is needed before final conclusions are warranted. At present, however, there is some cause to believe that paying people, especially children, for performing voluntary activities is probably detrimental to their continued intrinsic motivation to engage in these activities.

A major implication of the "Deci effect" for industrial work settings (if and when it occurs) is that contingent payment systems may offset or undermine the intrinsic motivation generated by managerial programs, such as job enrichment (Deci, 1975). At present, however, there seems to be little empirical evidence that this occurs in practice (Staw, 1977), in spite of our common, everyday encounters with surly employees who refuse to perform duties that are not strictly within the formal definitions of their jobs ("I'm not paid to do that!"). More research is needed to determine whether this phenomenon bears the same applied importance in work settings as it does in educational settings.

SUMMARY AND CONCLUSION

In brief, human needs for growth can exhibit themselves through a variety of behaviors for different individuals. It would seem that as our society continues to enjoy relative economic abundance and high levels of education, growth needs will continue to account for a significant proportion of our overall motivation to work, and to behave on the job as we do. Members of the older generation are often critical of younger employees, whom they perceive as irresponsible, or as lacking in the *work ethic*, when they observe them leaving jobs for no apparent reason, or complaining about not receiving enough challenge from their work. The point is that older employees in today's work force had their views about work and the value of holding a job formed during tougher economic times than have been experienced by most employees who are less than 40 years of age today. This generation gap in work values is understandable, although at times it contributes to considerable intergeneration conflict and intolerance.

* * * * *

B. INTERVENTIONS

Introduction

Theoretical models of job motivation have inspired a variety of formal programs aimed at increasing the effectiveness and productivity of employee performance. Of these programs those centered around behavior modification, job redesign, and goal-setting have found widespread application. They have also aroused spirited debates among managers and behavioral scientists who represent competing philosophical and ideological perspectives upon worker motivation.

Lawrence Miller, a consultant who helps organizations design programs of employee behavior modification, provides a brief sketch of the essential steps in such programs. Behavior modification represents a practical application of operant concepts and methods, as found in the writings of B. F. Skinner and the work of other "neo-behaviorist" psychologists influenced by Skinner. The techniques of behavior modification do not presuppose any particular classes of "motives" or other internal psychological states. Rather, they provide a straightforward self-correcting method of arranging the immediate antecedents and consequences of specific behaviors so as to strengthen those behaviors.

The article from *Organizational Dynamics* reports the experience of Emery Air Freight with a behavior modification program. As of the date of this report, the company had a very positive experience using this approach. However, not all instances of behavior modification in work organizations have met with resounding success. Some attempts have proved abortive, not because of any flaw inherent in operant precepts, but due to naive or shortsighted use of these techniques without taking the larger context into analysis.

Programs of job redesign—variously termed "job enlargement" and "job enrichment"—seek to increase the role of "intrinsic" rewards from work. These programs restructure jobs so as to permit greater scope for worker autonomy, responsibility, and sense of achievement. Another selection from *Organizational Dynamics* assesses the practical gains from such approaches, with particular reference to some European firms that have experimented on a large scale with them.

For most organizations, wage and salary programs continue to serve—for better or worse—as the primary source of member motivation. Those organizations that emphasize merit pay in their compensation systems must, however, have a means of identifying the varying levels at which people perform. Typically, this requirement dictates some method of performance appraisal. Berkeley Rice reviews the problems often associated with appraisal methods, some efforts to develop methods for eliminating those problems, and a sampling of expert opinion on the state of the art of performance appraisal.

Recent years have witnessed some imaginative variations in compensation programs. Feldman and Arnold note five of these, describing their rationale and some promising early results where they have been tried. Corey Rosen discusses what appears to be a rapidly growing development in worker compensation: employee stock ownership plans (ESOPs). Rosen describes the legal and financial basis of such plans and cites preliminary evidence suggesting that they can exert a powerful, pervasive motivational force on participants.

10

Behavior Management*

LAWRENCE M. MILLER

The advantage of the behavior management approach to changing performance is well illustrated by an incident that occurred on an airplane a few years back. One of our consultants sat next to the president of a medium-sized corporation. They began talking, and the consultant described the type of service he performed. The president responded by noting that he could really use some help with his senior vice president. He described this vice president as having a very bad attitude, which had persisted for several months. Our consultant asked "What does this vice president do that causes you to feel that he has a bad attitude?" The president thought for a while and then responded, "Well, whenever I give him a report to read, I never hear back from him. And when I do, he's always so critical." It was agreed that there was nothing else that this vice president did to manifest his bad attitude and that if these behaviors were to change it would indicate an improvement in attitude. Our consultant then made some specific recommendations involving measurement and techniques of feedback that would be likely to alter the rates of the problem behaviors.

The president was able to understand and implement a few relatively quick and simple procedures to alter these specific behaviors. The problem of his vice president's "bad attitude" had become a simple and relatively easy matter to improve. This is the essence of the direct approach to behavior change in the workplace.

DIRECT, EXTERNAL APPROACH TO BEHAVIOR

The direct or external approach to changing behavior has gained increasing acceptance and adherence over the past 10 to 20 years. This direct approach is also referred to as the behavioral model, behaviorism, behavior modification, or behavior management. All these terms refer to the behavior change techniques based on the effects of envi-

---

* From Lawrence M. Miller, *Behavior Management* (New York: Wiley-Interscience, 1978), pp. 52–66. Copyright © 1978. John Wiley & Sons, Inc. Reprinted by permission.

ronmental events, stimuli, without reference to explanations of mental conditions, states, motivations, needs, or drives. Behavior management does not deny that internal states exist. Whether internal states exist or not is irrelevant. The question is can behavior be changed and predicted from changes in the external environment? The research overwhelmingly demonstrates that the answer is affirmative (*Journal of Applied Behavior Analysis*, 1967–1977).

The differences between the direct and indirect approaches to improving human performance in organizations can be summarized in the following four points:

1.   The *change in behavior is explained as a direct function of the changes* in the environment, rather than as a change in an internal motivation or need that in turn causes a change in behavior. Behavior management studies the specific conditions that exist in the individual's environment, alters those conditions, and measures the subsequent change in behavior.

2.   *Evaluation of the effort to improve performance is based on the direct measurement of behavior and its results.* The indirect approaches have relied heavily on measures of attitude and satisfaction.

These internal conditions are generally assessed by the use of attitude questionnaires. Behavior management does not consider the responses to questionnaires significant when the goal behaviors of concern, such as rates of work, attendance, and on-time arrivals to work, can be measured directly.

Goals for behavior management are stated in terms of increasing or decreasing rates of behavior or the product of behavior. The ongoing measurement of behavior is an essential element of every behavior management effort. Because of this direct measurement and because goals are stated in terms of increasing or decreasing behavior, the evaluation mechanism is built into every project. Economic evaluation of these projects becomes relatively simple and direct.

3.   *Behavior management is a technique of management.* Behavior management is not a theory to which managers should attempt to conform because it is a correct theory of human nature. It is a technique designed to assist the manager in achieving his goals and should be applied to aid the organization in accomplishing the specific goals that define its productivity. It may be applied to improve the quality of products, reduce absenteeism or turnover and increase output measures, sales, new business development, and increase other specific contributions of managers and employees. The manager should have specific, measurable objectives in mind before implementing a behavior change effort.

4.   *The direct approach is more acceptable and receives a more favorable response from the manager because it is focused on his*

objectives, for it provides him with a procedure for directly affecting the achievement of his objectives and demonstrates observable results in a relatively short period of time. Because of these factors and the compatibility of the direct approach with the "business of managing," the manager is more favorably disposed toward performance improvement efforts.

Behavior management is a nontheory of behavior (Skinner, 1950). It is the study and application of what works. Its development is based on empirical research. It did not start with a grand theory of human nature. Simple questions were asked and tested. Why does one specific behavior increase or decrease? How is a behavior acquired, or why does a behavior decrease? Highly controlled laboratory studies were conducted to answer these questions. As these questions have been answered through data collection and analysis, a set of principles has developed. The goal of behavior management is to discover lawful relationships. Investigation has determined that some lawful relationships between environmental events and behavior do exist, much as the study of physics has determined that larger bodies tend to attract smaller bodies.

Whereas the historical evolution of behavior management is undoubtedly of secondary interest to most managers, a brief review of its development may help in understanding its principles.

The development of the science of behavior involved dozens of individual researchers; however, the work of the following men represents the most essential contributions: John B. Watson, Edward L. Thorndike, and B. F. Skinner.

John B. Watson

John B. Watson, more than any other single individual, is responsible for the initiation of behaviorism and for its first applications to business. Watson believed that all behavior was explainable as a function of stimuli that preceded the behavior. The so-called Stimulus-Response (S–R) model is the result of Watson's work. Watson described the purpose of his work in the following passage:

> Behaviorism, as I tried to develop it in my lectures at Columbia in 1912 and in my earliest writings, was an attempt to do one thing—apply to the experimental study of man the same kind of procedure and the same language of description that many research men had found useful for so many years in the study of animals lower than man. We believed then, as we do now, that man is an animal different from other animals only in the types of behavior he displays (Watson, 1920).

Before Watson psychology had been dominated by the internal ap-

proach, and he challenged its advocates to demonstrate the effects of
their work and to apply the methods of empirical science. Watson
demonstrated that human behavior could be studied scientifically and
that it occurred in predictable patterns relative to conditions in the
environment.

Perhaps Watson's most famous experiment, the one that led him to
some of his conclusions, involved Little Albert, an 11-month-old boy
who had become friendly with a white rat (Watson, 1920). Although
this experiment was highly questionable from an ethical point of view,
it did demonstrate some important principles of behavior. Watson decided that he would try to condition the response of fear in poor Little
Albert. He attempted to pair a number of different stimuli with the
white rat to condition a fear of the rat. He tried scaring Little Albert
with a mask, a dog, a monkey, burning newspapers and other stimuli
that might elicit the fear response. Albert was not impressed by any of
these. Finally, Watson created a loud noise by hitting an iron bar with
a hammer behind Little Albert's head. This succeeded in sending
Albert into a screaming fit. Watson then paired the frightening stimulus of the loud noise with the white rat. Every time Albert was permitted to see his little white friend, he was startled by the loud noise.
Eventually the sight of the white rat, by itself, created the fear and
caused poor Little Albert to cry.

In addition to showing that fears may be caused by conditions of the
environment, this experiment demonstrated the principle of generalization. The newly acquired fear of the white rat generalized to other
furry objects. Albert was now afraid of a dog, a rabbit, and even a Santa
Claus mask. At Albert's expense some of the most basic forms of emotional learning had been demonstrated. (In Watson's defense it must
be reported that he demonstrated that Albert could be deconditioned
or unlearn these same fears.)

Watson limited his investigation to the relationship between preceding stimuli and subsequent behavior. For this reason the relationship he described is referred to as the Stimulus–Response (S–R)
model. He believed that all behavior could be explained in terms of
eliciting stimuli that occurred some time before the behavior. Although this explanation is no longer considered sufficient to explain all
forms of learning, it did lay the foundation for the empirical investigation of human learning.

Watson defined the "behaviorists' platform":

> The behaviorist asks why don't we make what we can observe the real
> field of psychology? Let us limit ourselves to things that can be ob-
> served, and formulate laws concerning only those things. Now what can
> we observe? We can observe behavior—what the organism does or says.

And let us point out at once: that saying is doing—that is behaving. Speaking overtly or to ourselves (thinking) is just as objective a type of behavior as baseball (Watson, 1924).

Edward L. Thorndike

While Watson was pursuing the study of the effect of preceding stimuli on behavior, E. L. Thorndike was developing his Law of Effect (Thorndike, 1913). He placed small animals such as cats, dogs, and chickens in "puzzle boxes" from which they learned to escape. There was an exit door to the box that could be opened by manipulating a lever. The animals were deprived of food until they managed to open the door. They obtained food, their reinforcer, after they managed to manipulate the lever and open the door. Thorndike found that the animal's speed of opening the door increased following experience. The animals were learning. From these experiments Thorndike formulated his Law of Effect:

> When a modifiable connection between a situation and a response is made and is accompanied or followed by a satisfying state of affairs, that connection's strength is increased; when made and accompanied or followed by an annoying state of affairs, its strength is decreased.

Thorndike accepted Watson's stimulus–response relationship but added that these relationships are strengthened as a function of the consequences that follow the behavior. Thorndike also argued that the effects or consequences of a behavior are direct and do not need to be explained in terms of mediating processes such as thought. The behavior is increased or decreased as a direct effect of the consequence.

B. F. Skinner

B. F. Skinner has been acclaimed by the American Psychological Association as the most influential living psychologist, and he is without a doubt the most controversial. Skinner's contributions to the development of psychology as a science and as a means of improving human behavior are tremendous but difficult to categorize. Many cannot be as clearly defined as his own science would require. Four of the more significant are (1) his development and articulation of a technology of empirical investigation of behavior, (2) his distinction between operant and respondent behavior, (3) his development of the concept of "contingencies of reinforcement," and (4) his advocacy of behavior change and cultural design based on the empirical analysis of behavior.

Empirical Investigation.   Skinner is the antitheorist. Whereas the results of his research may be termed a theory of behavior, he opposed the formulation of theories of human behavior. Skinner (1950) argues that the empirical data from the direct observation of behavior and its environment are a sufficient source of knowledge and that no interpretative theories are necessary. Skinner defined terms empirically. For example, reinforcement is defined as the presentation or removal of a stimulus, resulting in an increase in the rate of a response. It is defined by its effect on the behavior; reinforcement increases the rate of behavior. It is impossible, therefore, to say that an event is reinforcing unless an increase in the rate of a behavior can be demonstrated.

Skinner developed the language of the empirical investigation of behavior. All sciences require clear definition of terms to enable investigation to proceed in an orderly fashion. The definition of the language of behaviorism is one of Skinner's most significant contributions.

Skinner also provided a framework for behavioral research. He divided his observations into those concerned with independent variables (factors that affect a behavior and that can be managed in such a way as to cause a change in behavior) and the dependent variables (the behaviors affected by the independent variable). Skinner is concerned with discovering the specific relationships or "functional relationships" between the dependent and independent variables.

The essential elements of Skinner's system are summarized in the following table:

Independent Variables

Type of reinforcement or punishment
Schedule of reinforcement or punishment

Dependent Variables

Rate of responding
Rate of acquiring a new response
Rate of extinction

At least as great as any technical innovations Skinner may have contributed is the general approach toward his subject that he promoted. This "attitude of science" is the single most distinguishing feature of the direct approach to behavior change.

> Science is first of all a set of attitudes. It is a disposition to deal with the facts rather than with what someone has said about them. . . . Science is a willingness to accept facts even when they are opposed to wishes. . . . The opposite of wishful thinking is intellectual honesty. . . . Scientists

have simply found that being honest—with oneself as much as with others—is essential to progress. Experiments do not always come out as one expects, but the facts must stand and the expectations fall. The subject matter, not the scientist, knows best (Skinner, 1953).

Operant and Respondent Behavior.   Skinner defined types of behavior according to the manner in which they are acquired and maintained. Respondent behaviors are those *elicited* by a stimulus and are acquired through the procedures of "classical conditioning," the pairing of an unconditioned stimulus with a conditioned stimulus. Operant behaviors are those that are *emitted* by the organism and that act on the environment. They result in reinforcement. In other words, in respondent behavior, the organism reacts to the environment, while in operant behavior the response acts on the environment.

Skinner defined and studied operant behavior. He argued that most of the behaviors performed by any organism, human or animal, are operant behaviors and may be explained by an analysis of the reinforcements that have resulted from the operant behavior's acting on the environment. For example, the behavior of coming to work results in social approval, payment of money, and other reinforcers that maintain the performance of this behavior. If the behavior of coming to work did not act on the environment, if there were no consequences resulting from it, the operant of coming to work would extinguish; that is, it would cease to occur.

The "Contingencies of Reinforcement."   The relationships between the behavior of an individual and the environment are described by Skinner as the contingencies of reinforcement:

> An adequate formulation of the interaction between an organism and its environment must always specify three things: (1) the occasion upon which a response occurs, (2) the response itself, and (3) the reinforcing consequences. The interrelationships among them are the "contingencies of reinforcement" (Skinner, 1969).

The contingencies between behavior and environment are often stated in terms of an if–then relationship. If A occurs, then B will follow. If I finish this chapter on time, I can go to the beach this weekend. If you increase the number of customers on whom you call, then you will increase your commissions. If Johnny finishes his homework by eight o'clock, he may watch television for one hour.

Our world is composed of our behavior and the reaction of the environment to our behavior. These contingencies of reinforcement are the structure within which we live, the relationships that may explain our slow rate of learning, our feelings of depression, or our overeating. Skinner laid the foundation for the analysis of the contingencies of reinforcement.

FIGURE 1
The Contingencies of Reinforcement

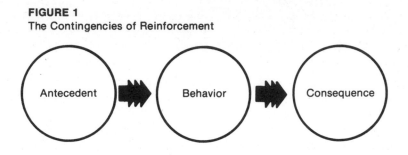

Advocacy of Behavior Change and Cultural Design.   Many of Skinner's writings are not scientific. Most notably his well-known novel *Walden II* and his more recent *Beyond Freedom and Dignity* have gone beyond his data to propose applications of the science of behavior to social problems. Unfortunately, this advocacy has led to serious misunderstandings of the science of behavior and of his own positions in regard to this science. Skinner has devoted the greatest portion of his most recent book *About Behaviorism* to answering these criticisms and misunderstandings.

Skinner desired to create public debate on the social and cultural application of behavior change, and he has undoubtedly succeeded. If, however, the degree to which his recent writings have been misunderstood is an indication of his success at communicating his ideas, he has not been entirely successful. Perhaps the greatest controversy followed his publication of *Beyond Freedom and Dignity.* Contrary to the misinterpretation of many, Skinner does not argue against freedom. He is very much in favor of freedom and increasing individual freedom. He does, however, argue that the popular comprehension and the literature of freedom have hindered the progress of our culture. Skinner argues that mankind is not free in the sense of being autonomous and free from influence. On the contrary, Skinner argues that mankind's behavior is controlled by his environmental conditioning, and freedom must, therefore, be viewed in the context of this environmental control. He believes that mankind reacts negatively to aversive or negative control such as would be imposed by a dictator. These forms of control characterized by the threat of punishment are the ones we fear. Forms of control based on positive reinforcement are the ones that we least notice and that are most desirable. Skinner argues that these forms, already present in our environment, should be carefully studied and used to create a society that results in the greatest benefit.

Skinner's outspoken advocacy of the application of his techniques to cultural design has created considerable debate because these techniques contradict the popular view and require a reexamination of accepted beliefs and habits. As has been the case at previous periods in human history, positions that contradict popular understandings of the human condition and that are supported by empirically gathered data have resulted in significant changes in the course of human history. The work of Galileo and Darwin resulted in similar controversy, change of traditional views, and eventual progress. Only future generations will be able to assess Skinner's final contribution to the understanding of the human condition.

DOES BEHAVIOR MANAGEMENT WORK IN ORGANIZATIONS?

Behavior management is the result of the trial-and-error applications of operant conditioning principles in the work setting. Does it work? This is the question that Skinner would hope we would ask. Behavior management has been systematically applied in the business and industrial settings only during the past few years. The contingencies of reinforcement have, however, been operating since the first person began working. All work behavior, regardless of the system or philosophy of management in effect, is explainable by analyzing the contingencies of reinforcement and may be changed by altering these contingencies.

The argument is often made that changing behavior in the work setting is not as simple as in the laboratory, classroom, or mental hospital. This is certainly true, and the complexity of the contingencies operating in the workplace is one of the primary reasons why application to organizations has not been more extensive. But behavior management has demonstrated its ability to change behavior, both in the workplace and other settings. It is the task of this book to present some of the results, as well as the principles and techniques of behavior management.

Behavior management systems are currently in use in more than fifty major corporations that I know of, and probably many more. Among the corporations now using these programs are the 3M Corporation, Western Electric, Westinghouse, Airco Alloys, Inc., Milliken & Company, General Mills, AT&T, Dart Industries, Inc., Pennwalt Corporation, Emery Air Freight, Questor Corporation, Ford Motor Company, American Can, Connecticut General Life Insurance Company, General Electric, Weyerhaeuser Company, and numerous others.

The application of behavior management to industrial organizations may be the best kept secret in management today. Most companies have no desire to advertise the techniques they are using or the results they have received. Nonetheless, a sampling of results leaves one wondering why there is not more discussion of these techniques in management publications and why more systematic research has not been conducted. The following are a few of the documented results witnessed during the past few years:

- One of the largest textile firms in the country has reported savings or earnings of approximately $20 million that can be directly attributed to behavior management programs.
- A midwestern plant of one of the major corporations listed in the preceding paragraph has reported that their cost accountants have attributed $600,000 in annual cost reductions to a behavior management effort that cost approximately $70,000 to implement.
- A textile-finishing plant that had been having a number of serious personnel problems implemented a six-month behavior management training program, and a year later the plant set a record for attendance—down to 0.9 percent absenteeism for eight weeks running. This same plant boosted quality savings to $25,000 per week over the same eight-week period.
- The City of Detroit garbage collectors instituted a behavior management program in which efficiency was reinforced with bonuses to the garbage collectors. The city saved $1,654,000 during the first year, after bonuses of $307,000 were paid to the collectors.
- ACDC Electronics Division of Emerson Electronics, instituting a program to improve attendance, met engineering specifications and production objectives. Profits increased 25 percent over forecast; costs were reduced by $550,000, and they received a return on investment, including consultant fees, of 1,900 percent.
- B. F. Goodrich Chemical Company started a program to meet production schedules and increased production by 300 percent.
- Emery Air Freight has instituted numerous programs since 1969 and attributes direct savings of more than $3 million to behavior management.
- Waste in the spinning department of a carpet mill was identified as an area in need of improvement. By posting feedback data and providing verbal reinforcement and small tangible reinforcements, waste variance was reduced from $1,153 per week to $437 per week—an annualized savings of $37,232.
- A thorough analysis of the cost benefit of one behavior management program in one textile plant demonstrated improvements in plant turnover ($102,000 savings); finishing department efficiency ($32,895 savings); attendance ($26,457 savings); quality ($29,725 savings); sewing department efficiency ($15,158 savings); attendance in the sewing department ($27,333 savings); for a total plant-wide annual savings of $233,369.

- A major textile firm began several programs with their trucking operations. One involved reducing the average time that loaded trailers wait for a tractor. The time was reduced from an average 67 minutes to between 35 to 40 minutes. This program is in operation in 42 plants and has reported savings in excess of $1 million.

The results here are only a small sample of those obtained. Each of these programs specified behaviors to be changed, altered specific environmental contingencies, and measured the changes in behavior and corresponding outcomes in terms of productivity, and so forth. In each of these programs environmental contingencies were complex, though the ones changed were relatively simple. While there may be a dozen consequences to our behavior (such as quitting a job or remaining on a job), one consequence may change the course of our actions (such as a raise or a compliment by our boss). It is not necessary to understand all the complexities of environmental influence to put the technology of behavior management to work. It is necessary only to identify clearly the behavior to be changed, the consequence to be altered, and measure the rate of the behavior before and after the consequence is changed. The result, in terms of an increase or decrease in the rate of behavior, indicates whether or not the procedure is working.

More than 20,000 managers and supervisors have been trained in the application of behavior management during the past five years by just one consulting firm specializing in it. All of these managers or supervisors have used behavior change projects as a routine part of their job. Most of these projects have followed a four-step process that has become known as the "cookbook" method of behavior management. This method, while deceptively simple, contains the basic ingredients of operant conditioning as applied to the work situation. These four steps are *pinpoint, record, consequate, evaluate* (Miller, 1974) and include the following:

- *Pinpoint:* The manager must identify and define the specific behavior or behaviors he wishes to change. A behavior is pinpointed when it may be accurately and reliably observed and recorded. For example, "working slowly" is not pinpointed. Completing "43 work units per eight-hour day" is. Similarly, "having a good attitude" is not pinpointed; "smiling at least once during each conversation with another person" is. The ability to specify behavior in pinpointed terms is both a necessary first skill for the manager who wishes to increase his ability to manage his employee's (or his own) behavior and a skill that requires a major change in the behavior pattern of most industrial supervisors.

- *Record:* The manager is asked to count the occurrence of the pinpointed behavior or some result of it. The frequency is to be recorded before any effort is made to change the behavior. This is for
  establishing baseline data. These data serve as the means of evaluating the behavior change strategy to be implemented after their
  establishment. The manager generally graphs these data to determine whether the frequency of the behavior is increasing, decreasing, or remaining the same. The establishment of baseline data
  before the initiation of a change procedure is a fundamental practice of the scientist that has been adopted with no great difficulty by
  the line manager and supervisor, who often have less than a high
  school education. The value of knowing where you have been,
  where you want to get to, and when you have arrived is understood
  by most individuals of good sense.
- *Consequate:* To consequate a behavior is to arrange for a consequence to follow it. The manager is encouraged to arrange a "reinforcing consequence," one that results in an increase in the rate of
  the desired performance. The reinforcing consequence most commonly used in behavior management is visualized feedback or
  knowledge of results. Managers often use the graph of the baseline
  data they have plotted to illustrate a goal level of performance and
  either post the graph in a visible location in the work area or personally show it to the worker whose performance is being recorded.
  The supervisor pairs verbal praise and approval with the visual
  feedback. This simple procedure has been used literally thousands
  of times to increase individual workers' productivity. Other reinforcers are raffle tickets, time off, job changes, letters of recognition,
  or anything else that may prove meaningful to the employee. A
  consequence may also include a "punisher," an event that results
  in the decreased rate of behavior. Managers have been taught the
  empirical meaning and effective use of punishment as a management procedure. Punishment, which is used only when reinforcement does not work, usually involves the least drastic punishing
  consequence available. A consequence may also involve the removal of a reinforcer that may be maintaining the performance of an
  undesirable behavior. The emphasis in most behavior management
  programs is on the use of "social" reinforcement. This includes the
  recognition by the manager of a job well done. When social reinforcement can be instituted in an organization on an ongoing basis,
  the organization is most likely to maintain high levels of performance. The use of tangible reinforcement, unless it becomes an
  institutionalized part of the compensation system, is not likely to be
  maintained over a long time, and performance is likely to drop as
  the procedure is discontinued.

• *Evaluate:* Every behavior management project, whether conducted by a consulting psychologist, an inhouse change agent, or the line manager, must include an evaluation procedure if it is to qualify as behavior management. The evaluation of most behavior management projects simply involves the continuation of the counting and recording initiated before the change procedure. Most managers continue to graph the data on the performance with which they are concerned. Behavior management teaches the manager to measure performance on an ongoing basis, even when it is good, so that the conditions affecting it can be studied and managed. One of the primary effects of this evaluation is to provide built-in, or intrinsic, reinforcement for the manager. The manager or supervisor can obtain a great deal of satisfaction from observing the line on a graph go upward or downward as he alters the conditions that he believes affects that performance.

Behavior management is much more than these four simple steps. These steps are one method used to initiate behavior management at the level of the individual supervisor. Behavior management may also involve the alteration of a company-wide system of compensation, objective setting, or information flow. When the principles of behavior management are fully understood by the manager, they become, not a technique to be called upon on difficult occasions, but a "way of life."

REFERENCES

Miller, Lawrence M. *Behavior Management: New Skills for Business and Industry.* Atlanta: Behavioral Systems, 1974.

Skinner, B. F. "Are Theories of Learning Necessary?" *Psychological Review* 57 (1950), pp. 193–216.

Skinner, B. F. *Science and Human Behavior.* New York: Free Press, 1953, pp. 12–13.

Skinner, B. F. *Contingencies of Reinforcement: A Theoretical Analysis.* New York: Appleton-Century-Crofts, 1969, p. 7.

Thorndike, E. L. *The Psychology of Learning.* New York: Columbia University Teachers College, 1913.

Watson, John B. *Behaviorism.* New York: W. W. Norton, 1924, p. ix.

Watson, J. B., & R. Raynor, "Conditioning Emotional Reactions." *Journal of Experimental Psychology* 3 (February 1920), pp. 1–14.

11

At Emery Air Freight:
Positive Reinforcement
Boosts Performance*

At Emery these days, P.R. stands for *positive reinforcement*, not public relations, and the payoffs from applying Skinner's ideas to the motivation of employees exceed the wildest claims ever made by public relations practitioners for the results of their art. One example: Small shipments intended for the same destination fly at lower rates when shipped together in containers rather than separately. By encouraging employees to increase their use of containers (from 45 percent to 95 percent of all possible shipments), Emery has realized an annual saving of $650,000.

"With savings this large we can't afford to worry about charges that we're manipulating our employees," says Edward J. Feeney, Vice-President—System Performance, the man primarily responsible for introducing P.R. at Emery. Continues Feeney: "Actually, the charge that you're manipulating people when you use positive reinforcement—I prefer myself to say that you're shaping their behavior—is a hollow one to start with. People in business manipulate their employees all the time—otherwise they would go bankrupt. The only questions are, how effective are you as a manipulator and what ends do you further with your manipulation? Our end is improved performance, and we've been damned effective in getting it." Feeney emphasizes that his approach and that of Emery's management generally is pragmatic, not doctrinaire. They're sold on the merits of Skinner's ideas, not because of their internal logic or the eloquence with which they are frequently proposed, but because so far at least they paid off handsomely in each area Emery has seen fit to apply them.

Importance of Performance Audit

Emery has been selective in its application of P.R.; it's a powerful tool that should be employed where it's most needed and where the potential for improvement is the greatest. These are things that

* Reprinted by permission of the publisher from *Organizational Dynamics*, Winter 1973 © 1973 by AMACOM, a division of American Management Associations.

Feeney feels strongly can't be left to intuition or guesswork—hence the necessity for a performance audit before you institute P.R. in a given area. Emery doesn't want to be in the position of the corporation that targeted tardiness reduction as the object of a major effort. Before the drive, tardiness averaged ½ of 1 percent; after the drive ¼ of 1 percent. Big deal! Emery has a different magnitude of payoff in mind.

Take the example of container utilization that we mentioned. Executives at Emery were convinced that containers were being used about 90 percent of the times they could be used. Measurement of the actual usage—a measurement made by the same managers whose guesses had averaged 90 percent—showed that the actual figure was 45 percent, or half the estimate. Feeney saw no reason, given the proper motivational climate, why employees couldn't consistently meet a standard of 95 percent and save Emery $650,000 annually— which, of course, subsequently happened.

The performance audit fulfills two primary purposes. First, it indicates the areas in which the biggest potential profit payoffs exist—the areas in which Emery should focus its attention; second, it convinces previously skeptical managers on quantitative grounds that no words can contravene that there is need for substantial improvement.

The performance audit would be justified for the second effect alone—convincing managers that improvement is needed and persuading them to cooperate with a program designed to bring about the improvement. "Most managers genuinely think that operations in their bailiwick are doing well; a performance audit that proves they're not comes as a real and unpleasant surprise," says Feeney.

We also suspect that an unpleasant surprise of some magnitude is necessary to secure the cooperation of a goodly number of managers in implementing a program that, with its concentration on praise and recognition as motivators and the elimination of censure, runs contrary to the beliefs and practices of a working lifetime.

On the other hand, Feeney emphasizes the importance of cushioning the blow if you want to enlist their cooperation. "We structure the performance audit so that the managers are heroes for making the audits, and we reassure them that irrespective of the current level, they will look good if they can improve."

What about the performance standards set as a part of each performance audit? How are they set? What do they signify? Sometimes, as in the case of the customer service department with its goal of customer call-backs within 90 minutes of the initial telephone query, the department had set the goal in advance of the audit study. On study, it appeared reasonable and it was left unchanged. Sometimes there is no standard, and one has to be set on the basis of observation and common sense.

The latter usually indicates the impracticality of setting perfection or 100 percent performance as your standard. For example, the ideal in answering phone calls from customers would be for the customer never to get a busy signal that might lead him to call one of Emery's competitors. The problem is that studies have shown that in any given hour, five minutes, although not the same five minutes, is always going to account for 35 percent of the calls during the hour. Hence, it's much too costly to staff a switchboard with the number of operators necessary to prevent busy signals during those peak five minutes.

Emery has experimented, with a measure of success, with having employees set the standards for their own jobs. It was done in the customer service office in Chicago. The employees set a higher standard: not just giving customers a progress report within 90 minutes, but having *all* the requested answers to customer queries within that time—and they have presently reached this standard, although they fall short of the 90 to 95 percent achieved on progress reports. The problem, as Feeney sees it, is in giving the employees all the data they need to hit on a reasonable standard—a very time-consuming process. Otherwise, employee-set standards either will be unrealistically high or unacceptably low. Either way, both the company and the employee lose out. The standard that is too low deprives the employee of self-satisfaction and the company of work that it is paying for; the standard that is too high, achievable only once in a while by virtue of extraordinary effort or luck, will leave the employee frustrated and embittered. Sooner or later—and it's usually sooner—his performance will revert to a lower level than before he participated in setting the unattainable standard.

Providing Praise and Recognition—Avoiding Censure

In those areas in which Emery uses P.R. as a motivational tool, nothing is left to chance. Each manager receives two elaborate programmed instruction workbooks prepared in-house and geared to the specific work situation at Emery. One deals with recognition and rewards, the other with feedback. Under recognition and rewards, the workbook enumerates no less than 150 kinds, ranging from a smile and a nod of encouragement, to "Let me buy you a coffee," to detailed praise for a job well done.

Of all forms of praise, the most effective, according to Feeney, is praise for the job well done—expressed in quantitative terms. Not "Keep up the fair work, Murray," as shown on TV, or even "Great going, Joe—keep it up," but "Joe, I liked the ingenuity you showed just now getting those crates into that container. You're running pretty consistently at 98 percent of standard. And after watching you, I can understand why."

In bestowing praise and recognition, Emery follows Skinner pretty closely. There is the same emphasis on reinforcing specific behavior; the same insistence that the behavior be reinforced as soon as possible after it has taken place; the same assertion that you reinforce frequently in the beginning to shape the desired behavior, but that as time goes on, maintaining the desired behavior requires progressively less frequent and unpredictable reinforcement. As Skinner wrote, in reference to Emery's application of his ideas, "You don't need to maintain a system of contrived reinforcers indefinitely. People get the impression that I believe we should all get reinforcers indefinitely. People get the impression that I believe we should all get gumdrops whenever we do anything of value. There are many ways of attenuating a system of reinforcement. . . . But the main thing is to let non-contrived reinforcers take over."

At the gumdrop stage of P.R., Feeney urges supervisors to supply praise and recognition at least twice a week during the early weeks or months of behavior shaping. It's impractical to require them to provide P.R. more frequently—they are too busy, they would forget, etc. Once the desired behavior has been established, managers have more discretion—the key point being the unpredictability of the reinforcement, not the frequency. Keep P.R. coming on a descending scale of frequency—but keep the employee guessing as to when or whether he's going to be praised or recognized.

At least in the early days of shaping behavior, it's difficult to determine which deserves the most credit for the improvement in performance—providing praise and recognition or withholding censure and criticism. Particularly in those cases where the manager seldom praised before—even when he had good reason—the switchover from censure to praise produces instant, almost miraculous results. Performance improves dramatically, and along with it, employee morale and superior-subordinate relations.

What do you do with the employee when praise, recognition, and feedback don't work? Do you contrive to refrain from criticising his or her work? At what point do you throw in the sponge?

Feeney's general answer was that P.R. worked with nine employees out of ten. On those occasions where it appeared not to be working, investigation usually revealed that below-standard performance was not the employee's fault—factors such as the wrong tools or work overload were responsible. And once they were corrected, the employee responded as positively to praise and recognition as anyone else. He cited several instances, not among the rank-and-file, where a custom-tailored program of P.R. salvaged men who were 30 days short of being fired.

Even with the below-par employee, the manager takes the positive note. He would probably ignore a day or a week in which no improvement took place, preferring to wait for a period of even slight improvement—say from 70 to 75 percent. Then he might follow up his praise of the improvement by asking the man what he thought could be done to improve further. Everything he said from there on would be an attempt to solve the problem and provide the manager with additional opportunities for reinforcement.

All in all, we got the impression of a program that failed, on the few occasions when it did, not because of employee resistance, but because of supervisory intransigence—the boss was unable or unwilling to apply it, especially with the so-called problem employee—and a few supervisors have left Emery in consequence.

Feedback is easier to institutionalize than praise and rewards. A written report is a tangible artifact that you can see. But even with feedback you have occasional lapses, Feeney cautions, in any areas where it isn't mandatory. Some managers loathe paperwork; others are too busy to extend the measure of praise and recognition indicated by the feedback or they don't recognize behavior that deserves positive reinforcement. "The biggest problem with the program occurs," adds Feeney "when managers stop asking for feedback and stop offering recognition and rewards because there's been no recognition of their efforts from above—their boss hasn't asked, 'Why didn't I see your performance report?' or extended any reward or recognition himself. In other words, the program breaks down whenever there are no consequences and no positive reinforcement for the manager who is supposed to implement it."

Beyond Gumdrops—Continuous Feedback

Skinner talks about the necessity of letting the noncontrived reinforcers take over in any program of P.R.—which, in our view, explains the crucial importance at Emery, and probably in any industrial setting, of continuous feedback. Emery, in each area where it has utilized P.R., has required each employee to keep a record himself of what he or she has accomplished each and every day. In customer service, for example, each representative ticked off daily on a sheet how long it had taken to reply to each call. It took no special skill to compare this with the standard of 90 minutes. Similar sheets, all relatively simple and all recorded by the employees themselves, were instituted in all departments covered by P.R.

Noncontrived reinforcers they were not. Emery provided the sheets, gave no option on filling them out, and defined the terms and frequency. But we think this is an example of a contrived reinforcer laying the essential groundwork—providing the time framework for noncontrived reinforcers to mature and take over. Let's postulate three basic stages of development: (1) a period in which frequent P.R. by the supervisor plus continuous feedback leads to rapid progress towards the desired behavior; (2) a period in which infrequent P.R. by the boss is accompanied by continuous feedback—itself, of course, a species of P.R.; (3) a period in which the supervisor is only a very occasional source of P.R. and feedback is overwhelmingly the principal source of contrived reinforcement.

Feeney emphasizes the effect of feedback on improved performance. "We found that when we provided daily feedback only one week out of four or one out of five, performance in the periods without feedback reverted to the previous level or was almost as bad." There's no question that feedback is the critical variable in explaining the success of the program, he adds.

What is continuous feedback, and what is its relation to Skinner's requirement that, in any program of P.R., "The main thing is to let noncontrived reinforcers take over"? The noncontrived reinforcer clearly is the conviction on the employees' part that they are doing a good job, a fair day's work. But how are they to know? Part of the answer is observable—they've been busy, the customers have seemed satisfied, maybe the boss has extended P.R. More conclusive, if they're in doubt, they can look at the sheets and see at a glance exactly how they stand in reference to the standard. In other words, the internal or natural reinforcer—the conviction and satisfaction of a job well done—is corroborated and itself powerfully reinforced by the evidence of a sheet on which the work accomplished is compared daily with the standard for the job.

Feeney tells a story that illustrates both the necessity for continuous feedback and the way in which previous consequences determine present behavior. Emery requires any employee who receives a package damaged during shipment from an airline to fill out a fairly time-consuming form. At a certain installation, he pointed out to the boss that without feedback and P.R. the employees wouldn't bother—the reinforcements they got from filling out the form were all negative. The paperwork was time-consuming and boring, they were likely to get some flack from airline representatives who would in their own good time find ways of hitting back, they were taking time from their number one priority—getting the shipment delivered on time. A check revealed that no damage forms were turned in. However, a physical check of cartons received showed several damaged, one with a hole punched in the side, another that looked as if a hand had reached into the top and taken something out, etc. Feeney feels that his colleague, at this point, got the message. The only way around the problem of getting the damage slips filled out was to (1) specify the desired behavior—i.e., set the standard; (2) require the employee to provide continuous feedback—keep daily records on how many cartons were damaged and submit them to his supervisor; and (3) whenever feasible, positively reinforce the behavior—when the feedback showed that it was justified.

Money and Positive Reinforcement

Skinner includes money in his list of positive reinforcers, as long as it is linked to specific behavior. The weekly paycheck doesn't positively reinforce; it's a negative reinforcer. You work to avoid the loss of the standard of living supported by the paycheck. On the other hand, piece-rate payments geared to specific on-the-job behavior are positive reinforcers; so are commissions paid to salesmen. Just as effective, Skinner argues, would be to take a leaf from gambling and introduce a lottery into industry, with each employee getting a weekly lottery ticket that might pay off in a weekly drawing. Here it's paying off unpredictably but in the long run on a determined schedule that provides the positive reinforcement.

Emery does not use money as a positive reinforcer. Several reasons seem to underly the choice. First, Emery has no employees on incentive payments, not even salesmen; there is therefore no built-in necessity to link dollar payments to improved performance. Second, management holds the belief that performing up to standard is what it has a right to expect from each employee in return for his paycheck. The savings achieved through the program have helped to make it possible for Emery to pay as much or more than its competitors, and offer equal or bigger benefits—facts not lost on its employees. Finally, Emery's experience suggests that praise and recognition, especially self-recognition through feedback, are enough. In some areas, employees have consistently performed up to standard for more than three years. The savings for Emery in consequence have been substantial, despite the omission of money as a positive reinforcer.

At first blush this seems surprising. Interestingly, AT&T had a similar experience with a job-enrichment program that also substantially increased employee productivity and performance. In an AT&T experiment with 120 women answering stockholder inquiries, various measures were taken to give employees more responsibility and control over their jobs. The response was uniformly positive, with one exception—a girl who quit because she wasn't getting more money for a more responsible job. She felt that she was worth more to the company and should be paid more. That only one employee out of 120 expected to get paid more as the consequence of a program that improved the value of their services calls for a little explaining. So does the continuing success of P.R. at Emery.

There are several possible explanations. People know a good thing when they see it. The programs at both AT&T and Emery have improved the intrinsic nature of the job as seen by the employees themselves—that's sufficient reward.

Also, many studies have shown that employees have a crude but keen sense of distributive justice on the job. They may do less than what they themselves consider a fair day's work for a large number of reasons, even though they frequently feel guilty about it. On the other hand, they resent and resist any attempt to exact more than their perception of a fair day's work in return for what they are paid. Improve the job—in Emery's case, provide via praise, recognition, and continuous feedback the evidence of a job well done—and eventually you will develop what Skinner would call the natural reinforcer of job satisfaction. This, in turn, guarantees that the employee will want to live up to his own standard of a fair day's work. In other words, part of the success of P.R. at Emery is that the standards set for employees were seen by them as reasonable to begin with. The missing element was any positive incentive to reach them. The weekly paycheck was ineffective—Skinner is correct—it took praise, recognition, and feedback to do the job. Similarly, at AT&T, job enlargement and job enrichment provided the incentives to improved performance that hitherto were lacking.

A story that Feeney tells illuminates the problem. A Harvard Business School student on a summer assignment with Emery was helping with a performance audit on one of the loading docks. In the process he managed to gain the confidence of a union steward, who told him in so many words that any problems Emery had with the workers were not due to money—they were well paid. The one thing they weren't getting paid was attention. Many of them worked at night with a minimum of supervision and recognition. A situation in which employees feel fairly paid in relation to the work expected of them but in which money is almost the sole recognition received is ripe for improvement via positive reinforcement.

Proof of the Pudding

At present, P.R. is fully operative in three areas at Emery—in sales and sales training, operations, and containerized shipments. The benefits in all three are impressive, and they have been sustained for periods of from three to four years. We can forget about the Hawthorne effect in explaining the success of P.R. at Emery.

In sales training, each salesman completes a programmed instruction course on his own, with plenty of feedback structured into the course to let him know how he is doing. In addition, sales managers apply P.R. in their day-to-day relations with salesmen, and sales reports provide the indispensable feedback. Sales have gained at a more rapid rate since P.R. entered the sales picture, and Feeney feels that it deserves some of the credit for the increased rate.

The relationship between P.R. and improved customer service, part of operations, is undeniable. Before P.R., standards were met only 30 to 40 percent of the time; after P.R., the figure was 90 to 95 percent. Most impressive is the rapidity of the improvement and its staying power. In the first test office, for example, performance skyrocketed from 30 percent of standard to 95 percent in a single day. Staying power? After almost four years, performance in the vast majority of Emery customer service offices still averages 90 to 95 percent.

In containerized shipping operations the story is the same: With P.R., container use jumped from 45 percent to 95 percent—with the increase in 70 percent of the offices coming in a single day.

There were a few cases in which feedback was temporarily interrupted because of managerial changes and other reasons. Whenever this occurred, performance slumped quickly by more than 50 percent, only to return rapidly to the 95 percent level once the feedback was resumed.

All in all, Emery has saved over $3 million in the past three years. No doubt about it: Positive reinforcement pays.

On the basis of this kind of success, Emery has big plans to expand the use of P.R. It's already been extended to overall dock operations. Emery's route drivers are covered and measured on items such as stops per hour and sometimes on shipments brought back versus shipments dispatched. Eventually P.R. will be introduced wherever it's possible to measure work and set quantifiable standards. Feeney and his group will set their priorities, of course, on the basis of what performance audits tell them about the potential for improvement and savings.

When you have scored the kind of success that Emery has you're not quick to innovate. However, thought is being given to the introduction in certain areas of different rewards and schedules, including having the computer acknowledge behavior and even using some kind of financial reward as a positive reinforcer.

What Does Emery Prove?

More precisely, what does Emery prove about the feasibility of behavior modification through positive reinforcement? The question must be asked and answered at several levels. At the first and most apparent level, the answer is easy: In those areas in which Emery has used P.R., behavior modification has been instant, dramatic, sustained, and uniformly in the desired direction. There also seems little doubt that P.R. deserves most of the credit for the dramatic improvement in performance.

A few qualifiers are in order. Positive reinforcement so far has been used selectively at Emery in areas where work could be measured and quantifiable standards set if they didn't already exist, and areas where observation showed that the existing level of performance was far below the standard. This last point applies equally to the customer-service representatives and the dock loaders, but is less true for the salesmen—their performance was lower than Emery felt it should be, but not in the same category as the other two employee groups.

Also Emery has yet to arrive at the point where the natural reinforcers—in this case an internally generated sense of job satisfaction—have taken over. After three to four years of P.R., praise and recognition from the boss is applied infrequently and unpredictably, but the other contrived reinforcer, continuous feedback, is still administered daily. In fact, Emery's past experience has been that whenever it stopped providing continuous feedback, performance rapidly reverted to the previous low levels. On the other hand, this experience occurred during the early days of supplying positive reinforcement. Perhaps now Emery could stop providing continuous feedback and maintain the current high levels of performance. We can only guess.

At another level we have to take into account the context in which P.R. has been used at Emery. We have to consider whether or not special conditions exist at Emery that favor the successful application of positive reinforcement. How far are we justified in claiming that what has worked at Emery will work equally well in a different organization with a different product, a different climate, and different problems?

On the basis of the available evidence, we can't go overboard in generalizing from Emery's undeniable success in applying positive reinforcement to solve its performance problems. That Emery has no incentive programs and is therefore spared the complexity and the conflict habitually generated in manufacturing situations where standards, performance, and earning are inextricably linked; that Emery has so far restricted P.R. to areas in which it has been possible to positively reinforce one employee without producing adverse consequences for any other employee; and that Emery, during the period it has applied P.R., has been a rapid growth organization, able to offer far more than the usual opportunities for growth and promotion are factors that provide a partial measure of the conditions, by no means common in organizations, that have fostered an atmosphere conducive to the application of positive reinforcement.

The second condition we mentioned is something Emery has worked at. Feeney emphasized that Emery was careful not to set individuals or groups competing against each other to see which came closest to meeting the standard. Instead, managers were coached to urge employees to think in terms of what they were doing now compared to what they had done in the past. Comments Feeney, "If you set individuals or teams competing against each other, there's only room for one first—but lots of losers. If you want to know the effect of this kind of competition on performance, all you need is to look at what happens at the end of the baseball season to the performance of the team that's 32 games behind."

Whether the conditions we have described are indispensable to the successful application of P.R. or merely helpful we have no way of determining. The problem is lack of evidence. Emery is the only company to date to have applied P.R. on a fairly broad scale over a fairly long period of time. Even with Emery, neither this report nor a previous article in *Business Week* (December 28, 1971) can claim to be the kind of objective in-depth study that's called for. A few other organizations—among them Cole National in Cleveland, Michigan Bell Telephone, and Ford Motor Co.—are in the early stages of experimenting with positive reinforcement, and more organizations are giving serious thought to using positive reinforcement. More than 200 have contacted Feeney since Emery's work with P.R. received public recognition.

Will positive reinforcement work? Feeney believes that the question has already been answered with a resounding affirmative. He cites upwards of 1,000 case studies involving mental patients, delinquent children, and problem pupils in which P.R. resulted in dramatic improvement in behavior. The only questions remaining, as he sees it, are questions of methodology and application.

Of course, none of these episodes took place in an industrial setting. Until we have a lot more evidence—both from Emery and from other sources—any conclusions about the use of P.R. in industry have to be tentative.

One last level of consideration. Positive reinforcement as the answer to organizational problems of productivity and performance has a plethora of rivals. A generation of theorists and practitioners has systematically overturned stones in the search for a formula or method for converting low-producing groups or individuals into high-producing ones. A partial enumeration would include job enrichment and job enlargement, organization development in all its varied guises. Theory Y, participative management, team development, the Scanlon Plan, autonomous leadership. We could go on—but we won't. How does

P.R. stack up against these other and we think competing approaches to improving productivity and performance?

At this point it's impossible to give a conclusive answer. We have seen the problems with the evidence on the results of positive reinforcement. Similar problems exist with the results of every other technique for improving productivity and performance. There's little objective evidence available, and what evidence there is abounds in caveats—the technique will work under the proper circumstances, the parameters of which are usually not easily apparent.

Take the entire field of organization development. An exhaustive search of the literature on the subject by Professor George Strauss of the University of California Business School at Berkeley turned up exactly three research studies worthy of the name. What did they prove? That under the proper circumstances OD can increase productivity, though perhaps not as much as conventional techniques such as purchasing new equipment, job simplification, and "weeding out" inefficient operators. So far, the search for a sure-fire all-purpose formula for turning low-producing groups into high-producing ones appears to be almost as elusive as the search for the philosopher's stone that would turn everything it touched into gold.

Which leads us to what conclusion as to the merits of positive reinforcement relative to its rivals? With the customary caveats, we feel that P.R. has much to recommend it. As an approach, it deserves more recognition and application than it has hitherto received. It suffers from its sponsorship: Positive reinforcement has a bad name with businessmen and with the general public because of its association with Skinner, his alleged totalitarian leanings, his denial of free will, and the inescapable fact that his theory of human behavior is rooted in his experiments with pigeons. People instinctively resent a theory that seems to suggest that they're not much brighter than pigeons and can be controlled in similar ways.

We understand the problem, but it's unfortunate that it has prevented the more extensive application of positive reinforcement. On the basis of what little we can observe, P.R. is easier, less complex, and less expensive to introduce than most of its rivals, while the results are at least as impressive as those achieved by any of them.

Feeney is probably correct: A lot of managers practice positive reinforcement without knowing it. He cites, for example, Vince Lombardi, who provided endless feedback on performance to his players and who after a really bad defeat never uttered a word of criticism in the locker room. True, but until more organizations consciously and systematically apply positive reinforcement, it will never get the recognition that it appears to deserve.

SELECTED BIBLIOGRAPHY

To anyone who wants to review the evidence that positive reinforcement works, Feeney recommends the following books and articles: Schafer and Martin, *Behavioral Therapy* (McGraw-Hill, 1969); Tharp and Wetzel, *Behavior Modifications of the Natural Environment* (Academic Press, 1969), describe in readable prose how positive reinforcement was used with 150 delinquent children to bring about a remarkable behavior change in 135; Ulrich et al., *Control of Human Behavior* (Scott Foresman), a book described by Feeney as important but highly technical and difficult to read. Finally, the June 1969 issue of *Psychology Today* contains an article, "Smiles, Praise, and a Food Basket," that describes the remarkable improvement positive reinforcement induced in a schizophrenic mental patient.

12

Job Redesign on the Assembly Line: Farewell to Blue-Collar Blues?*

EDITOR, *ORGANIZATIONAL DYNAMICS*

The authors of the much-quoted, much-praised, and much-criticized HEW report *Work in America* wound up their study with a rhetorical bang: "Albert Camus wrote that 'without work life goes rotten. But when work is soulless, life stifles and dies.' Our analysis of work in America leads to much the same conclusion: Because work is central to the lives of so many Americans, either the absence of work or employment in meaningless work is creating an increasingly intolerable situation."

Most who argue that the rhetoric in the report is exaggerated and the thesis overstated would exempt the assembly line, particularly the auto assembly line, from their dissent. The auto assembly line epitomizes the conditions that contribute to employee dissatisfaction: fractionation of work into meaningless activities, with each activity repeated several hundred times each workday, and with the em-

* From *Organizational Dynamics*, 1973, 2(2), 51–67. Copyright 1973 by AMACOM, a division of American Management Associations. Reprinted by permission.

ployees having little or no control over work pace or any other aspect of working conditions.

Two generations of social scientists have documented the discontent of auto workers with their jobs. Yet the basic production process hasn't changed since Ford's first Highland Park assembly plant in 1913. We read a lot about the accelerating pace of technology: Here's a technology that's stood still for 60 years despite the discontent.

The social explanations are easy. The automakers—when they thought about the problem at all—dismissed it. The economic advantages of the assembly line seemingly outweighed any possible social costs—including the high wages, part of which might properly be considered discontentment pay. In short, the cash register rang more clearly than the gripes.

Recently, the situation has changed. The advent of an adversary youth culture in the United States, the rising educational levels, with a concomitant increase in employee expectations of the job, the expansion of job opportunities for all but the least skilled and the most disaffected, have raised the level of discontent. One of the big three automakers, for example, now has an annual turnover rate of close to 40 percent. G.M.'s famous Lordstown Vega plant, the latest triumph of production engineering—with the average time per job activity pared to 36 seconds and workers facing a new Vega component 800 times in each eight-hour shift—has been plagued with strikes, official and wildcat, slowdowns, and sabotage. At times, the line has shut down during the second half of the day to remedy the defects that emerged from the line during the first half.

IS JOB REDESIGN THE ANSWER?

Much has been written about the two automobile plants in Sweden, Volvo and Saab-Scania, that have practiced job redesign of the assembly line on a large scale. The results, variously reported, have appeared in the world press. Also receiving wide press coverage have been the efforts of Philips N.V. in the Netherlands to redesign jobs on the lines assembling black-and-white and color TV sets. So much for instant history!

We visited the three companies during a recent trip to Europe and shall attempt to evaluate and compare them. But first a caveat: We eschew chic terms, such as job enrichment, autonomy, job rotation, and employee participation, in favor of the drabber *job redesign* for several reasons. First, the other terms have taken on emotional connotations; they've become the rallying ground for true believers who view them as a partial answer or panacea to the problem of employee alienation in an industrial society. The term *job redesign,* by contrast, has no glamor and no followers. Second, most efforts at job redesign, certainly the three we're going to write about, include elements of job enrichment, autonomy, job rotation, and employee participation in varying degrees at different times, but none of the competing terms affords a sufficiently large umbrella to cover what's happened and what's planned in the three organizations. Last, true believers passionately define their faiths differently; using any of the other terms as central would involve us in tiresome and trivial questions of definition. Hence, our choice of job redesign. It's comprehensive, and noncontroversial.

"Job redesign—the answer to what?" might have been a more descriptive subhead than one implying that our sole concern would be the question of employee discontent and its converse, employee satisfaction. Ours is a wider net. We're going to ask and answer (the answers, of course, being partial and tentative) these questions:

1. What conditions on the assembly line are economically favorable to which forms of job redesign?
2. Do many employees resent and resist job redesign? Do they prefer monotonous, repetitious work?
3. Are the "best" results from job redesign obtained when it's at its most thorough (job rotation plus job enrichment plus autonomy plus employee participation)?
4. Is there any single element in job redesign that seems to account for the biggest increase in employee satisfaction?
5. What are the benefits of job redesign—both those we can measure and monetize and those that can only be described?
6. On balance, does management gain as much from job redesign as the employee whose job is redesigned?
7. Last, what's the impact of the overall culture and political system on job redesign? What's the evidence, pro or con, that the success of job redesign at Volvo, Saab-Scania, or Philips—or the lack of it—would be replicated on similar assembly lines in the United States?

A tall order, but remember that we promised only tentative and partial answers to the seven questions.

JOB REDESIGN AT PHILIPS

First Generation, 1960–1965

We start with Philips because, of our three companies, Philips is the pioneer; its experience with job redesign goes back to 1960. We use the terms *first generation, second generation,* and so on to mark the stages of the Philips program because this is Philips's terminology—obviously appropriated from computer lingo.

In the first experiment, concern was more with the deficiencies of long assembly lines than it was with improving job satisfaction. Breaking up the existing line of 104 workers into five shorter assembly lines, installing buffer stocks of components between groups, and placing inspectors at the end of each group instead of the whole assembly line reduced waiting times by 55 percent, improved feedback, and improved the balance of the system—various short chains being stronger than one long chain because the line can never travel faster than the worker with the longest average time per operation.

Almost incidentally, morale also improved: Only 29 percent of the workers on the assembly line responded positively to the survey question "I like doing my job," versus a 51 percent positive response from the test line. Furthermore, when the test line was restructured with half the number of workers, so that each one performed twice the original cycle and workplaces alternated with empty seats, production flowed more smoothly and quality improved. Dr. H. G. Van Beek, a psychologist on the original study team, drew a dual lesson from the experiment: "From the point of view of production, the long line is very vulnerable; from the point of view of morale—in the sense of job satisfaction—downright bad."

Subsequent experiments in several plants involved rotating workers between different jobs on the assembly line, enriching jobs by having employees set their own pace within overall production standards, and enlarging them by making employees responsible for inspecting their own work. Most of the gains from the experiments Philips entered under the heading of "social profit." In other words, morale and job satisfaction improved but bread-and-butter items such as productivity and scrap showed little improvement.

Second Generation, 1965–1968

The key feature of the second phase, a program that involved a few thousand employees scattered over 30 different locations, was the abolition of foremen. With supervisors' enlarged span of control, the men on the assembly line acquired autonomy and more control over their jobs. Even an authoritarian supervisor would find that he was spread too thin to exercise the same amount of control as the previous foreman had.

Once again, the bulk of the profits were social. The bill for waste and repairs dropped slightly, and, of course, Philips pocketed the money that had been paid to the foremen. Otherwise, the gains to Philips were nonmonetary.

Third Phase, 1968

This phase, one that is ongoing, has focused on giving various groups of seven or eight employees total responsibility for assembling either black-and-white TV sets or color selectors for color TV sets, a task equivalent in complexity to assembling a black-and-white set from scratch.

We want to emphasize the word *total:* The group responsible for assembling the black-and-white sets, for example, not only performs the entire assembling task but also deals directly with staff groups such as procurement, quality, and stores, with no supervisor or foreman to act as intermediary or expediter. If something is needed from another department or something goes wrong that requires the services of another department, it's the group's responsibility to deal with the department.

"This third phase has had its problems," concedes Den Hertog, staff psychologist. "Typically, it's taken about six months for the groups to shake down—adjust to the increased pressures and responsibilities." Establishing effective relationships with unfamiliar higher-status employees in staff departments has proved the biggest single problem. On the other hand, anyone in an experimental group can opt out at any time—an option that has yet to be taken up. Of course, it may be the satisfaction of being a member of a select group, even physically separated from other work groups by a wall of green shrubbery, that accounts for no employee's having made a switch. Hertog, however, believes that the increase in intrinsic job satisfactions has more than compensated for any pains of adjustments and accounts for the lack of turnover.

What about results? What's the measurable impact of the program? There have been additional costs, such as increased training costs; more important, small, autonomous groups require new and smaller machines to perform traditional assembly line tasks. On the other hand, there have been measurable benefits. Overall, production costs in manhours have dropped 10 percent, while waiting times have decreased and quality levels have increased by smaller but still significant amounts.

To restructure work and redesign jobs in ways that increase employee job satisfaction at no net cost to the company over the long run is all that Philips, as a matter of policy, requires of such programs. Short-term deficits caused by purchases of new equipment are something it's prepared to live with.

Where is Philips going from here? Obviously, the potential for effective job redesign is large. With 90,000 workers in 60 plants, Philips has barely scratched the surface. Part of the answer would seem to lie in the future strength of the movement for employee participation and power equalization that is particularly strong in Norway and Sweden and is gaining adherents in the Netherlands.

At Philips the primary response has been the establishment of worker consultation in some 20 different departments. Worker consultation is just what it sounds like: Employees meet with first- and second-level supervision to discuss problems of joint interest. Worker consultation exists at different levels in different departments, stresses Hertog, who attributes the difference to the level of maturity of the group itself: "In some groups we're still at the flower pot phase, talking about what should be done to improve meals in the cafeteria, while at other extremes we have departments where we have left the selection of a new supervisor for the group up to the workers."

It's significant that those groups who have considered the question of job redesign consistently have criticized Philips for not doing more of it. The expansion of job redesign, in part, would seem to depend on the expansion of work consultation and the pressures exerted by the workers themselves to get job redesign extended.

JOB REDESIGN AT SAAB-SCANIA

To claim that Saab-Scania has abolished the auto assembly line would misrepresent the facts. Saab-Scania, or to speak more precisely, the Scania Division, has instituted small-group assembly of auto engines—not the whole car—in its new engine plant. Even so, this effort is limited to 50 employees in a plant with a work force of approximately 300, most of whom monitor automatic transfer machines that perform various machining tasks. (See Figure 1.) There's only one manual loading operation in the entire machining process.

More important, the humanization of the auto assembly line is the most dramatic single instance in a series starting in 1969 that Palle Berggen, the head of the industrial engineering department, characterized as "one phase in the development of enhanced industrial democracy."

We won't quarrel with his description, although we think he succumbed to the rhetoric of public relations. Scania, in its actions from 1969 on, has responded to some problems for which the best word is *horrendous*. Employee turnover was running around 45 percent annually, and in the auto assembly plant, 70 percent. Under such conditions, the maintenance of an even flow of production, something crucial in an integrated work system like Scania's, presented insuperable problems. Also, it was increasingly difficult to fill jobs on the shop floor at all. A survey taken in 1969 indicates what Scania was up against:

FIGURE 1
Diagram of Engine Plant, Saab-Scania

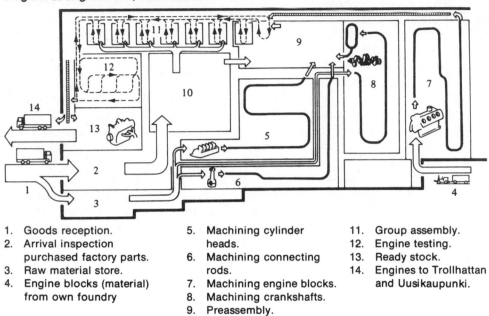

1. Goods reception.
2. Arrival inspection purchased factory parts.
3. Raw material store.
4. Engine blocks (material) from own foundry
5. Machining cylinder heads.
6. Machining connecting rods.
7. Machining engine blocks.
8. Machining crankshafts.
9. Preassembly.
10. Parts store.
11. Group assembly.
12. Engine testing.
13. Ready stock.
14. Engines to Trollhattan and Uusikaupunki.

Only four out of 100 students graduating from high school in Sweden indicated their willingness to take a rank-and-file factory job. In consequence, Scania became heavily dependent on foreign workers—58 percent of the current work force are non-Swedes. This in turn created problems, both expected and otherwise—among the former, problems of training and communications, among the latter, an epidemic of wildcat strikes, previously unknown in Sweden, that largely resulted from the manipulation by extreme left elements of foreign workers ignorant of the tradition among Swedish employees of almost total reliance upon the strong trade union organization to protect their interests.

Any response to these conditions *had* to have as its number-one objective the maintenance of productivity. To assert anything else is window dressing—unconvincing as well as unnecessary. No one can fault an industrial organization for undertaking a program whose primary goal is the maintenance of productivity.

This is not to deny that one by-product of the program has been "enhanced industrial democracy." What happened is that the pursuit of productivity led to an examination of the conditions that created job satisfactions; these, in turn, suggested the series of actions "that enhance industrial democracy"—a term subject to almost as many definitions as there are interpreters.

Production Groups and Development Groups

Employee representation is nothing new at Scania. Like every company in Sweden with more than 50 employees, it's had an employee-elected Works Council since 1949. However, these bodies have no decision-making function; their role is limited to receiving and responding to information from top management, and their effectiveness depends on the willingness of top management to seriously consider suggestions from the Works Council. David Jenkins, in his recent book *Job Power*, tells of asking a company president if he had ever been influenced by worker suggestions. His reply: "Well, yes. We were going to build a new plant and we showed the workers the plans at one of the meetings. They objected very much to the fact that the plant would have no windows. So we changed the plans and had some windows put in. It doesn't cost much more and, actually, the building looks better. And the workers feel better."

The production and development groups initiated in the truck chassis assembly plant in 1969, by contrast, have real decision-making power. Production groups of five to 12 workers with related job duties decide among themselves how they will do their jobs, within the quality and production standards defined by higher management; they can rotate job assignments—do a smaller or larger part of the overall task. At the same time, the jobs of all members of the production group were enlarged by making them jointly responsible for simple service and maintenance activities, housekeeping, and quality control in their work area, duties formerly performed by staff personnel.

Development groups, a parallel innovation, consist of foremen, industrial engineers, and two representatives of one or more production groups whose function is to consider ideas for improving work methods and working conditions. Representatives of the production groups are rotated in a way that guarantees that every member of a production group will serve each year on a development group.

Employee reception of the production group has been mixed but largely positive. The results appear to be favorable, although Scania has done little or nothing to measure them quantitatively. However, impressions have been sufficiently favorable so that within four years production and development groups have expanded to include 2,200 out of the 3,600 employees in the main plant at Södertälje, and within the year they will be extended throughout the company.

Work Design in the Engine Plant

The four machine lines for the components in the engine factory—the cylinder block, the cylinder head, the connecting rod, and the crankshaft—mainly consist of transfer machines manned or monitored by individual operations. Group assembly is restricted to the seven final assembly stations, each of which contains a team of fitters that assemble an entire engine.

Team members divide the work among themselves; they may decide to do one third of the assembly on each engine—a ten-minute chore—or follow the engine around the bay and assemble the entire engine—a 30-minute undertaking. In fact, only a minority prefer to do the total assembly job. (Using traditional assembly line methods, each operation would have taken 1.8 minutes.) The team also decides its own work pace, and the number and duration of work breaks within the overall requirement of assembling 470 engines in each ten-day period, a specification that allows them a good deal of flexibility in their pacing. Incidentally, over half the employees in the engine plant are women, while the assembly teams are over 80 percent female. We personally saw four assembly teams with only a single man in the lot.

Benefits and Costs

Kaj Holmelius, who is responsible for planning and coordination of the production engineering staff, ticked off the principal credits and debits, along with a few gray areas in which it would be premature to estimate results. On the plus side, he cited the following:

1. Group assembly has increased the flexibility of the plant, making it easier to adjust to heavy absenteeism.
2. The group assembly concept is responsible for a lower balancing loss due to a longer station time.
3. Less money is invested in assembly tools. Even allowing for the fact that you have to buy six or seven times as many tools, the simpler tools make for a smaller overall cost.
4. Quality has definitely improved, although by how much it's hard to estimate.
5. Productivity is higher than it would have been with the conventional assembly line—although once more, there is no proof. Lower production speed per engine, because it's not economical to use some very expensive automatic tools, is outweighed by higher quality and reduced turnover.
6. Employee attitudes have improved, although there have been no elaborate surveys taken. To Holmelius the best indication of job

satisfaction is that it's impossible to fill all the requests to transfer from other parts of the plant to the assembly teams.

On the negative side, in addition to the reduced production speed, group assembly takes up considerably more space than the conventional assembly line.

In the neutral corner is the impact on absenteeism and turnover. Absenteeism is actually higher in the engine plant—18 percent versus 15 percent for overall plant operations at Södertälje. However, Holmelius attributes the difference to the fact that the engine plant employs a heavier percentage of women. As for turnover, with the plant in operation for a little more than a year, it's too early to tell. Because of an economic slowdown, turnover generally is down from the 45 percent crisis level of 1969 to 20 percent, and it's Holmelius' belief that turnover in the assembly teams will prove significantly lower than average.

What's the Future of Group Assembly?

It's easier to point out the directions in which Scania does *not* plan to extend group assembly. An experiment with having employees assemble an entire truck diesel engine—a six-hour undertaking involving 1,500 parts—was abandoned at the employees' request; they couldn't keep track of all the parts. Similarly, group assembly wouldn't work with the body of the trucks—truck bodies are too complex, and group assembly would require twice the space currently needed. The moot question at the moment is car assembly. So far, group assembly has been applied only to assembling doors. We suspect that in any decision, economic calculations will predominate, including, of course, the inherently fuzzy calculation about the economic value of job satisfaction.

JOB REDESIGN AT VOLVO

Job redesign at Volvo began, almost accidentally, in the upholstery shop of the car assembly plant during the mid-1960s, but a company-wide effort had to wait until 1969, when Volvo faced the same problems that plagued Scania—wildcat strikes, absenteeism, and turnover that were getting out of hand and an increasing dependence on foreign workers. Turnover was over 40 percent annually; absenteeism was running 20 to 25 percent, and close to 45 percent of the employees of the car assembly plant were non-Swedes. One other event in 1971 made a difference: Volvo acquired a young, hard-driving, new managing director, Pehr Gyllenhammar, who developed a keen interest in the new methods of work organization.

Ingvar Barrby, head of the upholstery department, started job redesign by persuading production management to experiment with job rotation along the lines he had read about in Norway. The overwhelmingly female work force complained frequently about the inequity of the various jobs involved in assembling car seats; some jobs were easier than others, while still others were more comfortable and less strenuous, and so on. To equalize the tasks, Barrby divided the job into 13 different operations and rotated the employees among tasks that were relatively arduous and those that were relatively comfortable. Jealousy and bickering among employees disappeared: First, jobs were no longer inequitable; second, employees perceived that they had exaggerated the differences between jobs anyway—the grass-is-greener syndrome. More important, turnover that had been running 35 percent quickly fell to 15 percent, a gain that has been maintained over the years.

Job Alternation and "Multiple Balances"

Volvo uses these phrases instead of the more commonly used *job rotation* and *job enrichment,* but the concepts are the same. In job alternation or job rotation, the employee changes jobs once or several times daily, depending on the nature of the work in his group. Take Line IV A, for example, whose function is to do the external and internal sealing and insulation of car bodies. Because internal sealing is such uncomfortable work—employees work in cramped positions inside the car body—the work is alternated every other hour. The remaining jobs are rotated daily.

"Multiple balances" is our old friend, job enrichment, under another name. One example involves the overhead line where the group follows the same body for seven or eight stations along the line for a total period of 20 minutes—seven or eight times the length of the average job cycle.

Not all employees have had their jobs rotated or enriched—only 1,500 out of 7,000 in the car assembly at Torslanda are affected by the program. Because participation is strictly voluntary, the figures at first glance seem to indicate a massive show of disinterest on the part of Volvo employees. Not so. True, some employees prefer their jobs the way they are. The bigger problem is that Volvo has, to date, lacked the technical resources to closely scrutinize many jobs to determine whether and how they can be enlarged or enriched, or it has scrutinized them and determined that it isn't economically feasible to enlarge or enrich them. A company spokesman gave the job of coating under the car body to prevent rust as an example of a thoroughly unpleasant job that so far has defied redesign.

Production Teams at Volvo Lundbyverken

In the truck assembly plant at Lundbyverken, Volvo has carried job redesign several steps further, with production teams who, in form and function, roughly duplicate the production groups previously described at Scania. The production team, a group of 5 to 12 men with a common work assignment, elects its own "chargehand," schedules its own output within the standards set by higher management, distributes work among its members, and is responsible for its own quality control. In these teams, group piecework replaces individual piecework and everyone earns the same amount, with the exception of the chargehand. Currently, there are 23 production teams involving 100 out of the plant's 1,200 employees. Plans call for the gradual extension of the production team approach to cover most, if not all, of the factory work force.

The Box Score at Volvo

Have the various forms of job redesign, job rotation, job enrichment, and production teams paid off for Volvo? If so, what forms have the payoff taken? Anything we can measure or monetize? Or are we reduced to subjective impressions and interesting although iffy conjectures about the relationship between factors such as increased job satisfaction and reduced turnover?

The two plants deserve separate consideration: Absenteeism and turnover traditionally have been lower at the truck assembly plant than at the car assembly plant. The jobs are inherently more complex and interesting—even before job enrichment, some individual jobs took up to half an hour. The workers, in turn, are more highly skilled and tend to regard themselves as apart from and above the rank-and-file auto worker. They see themselves more as junior engineers. Within this context, it's still true that the introduction of production teams has led to further improvement: less labor turnover, less absenteeism, an improvement in quality, and fewer final adjustments.

At the auto assembly plant the picture isn't clear. Turnover is down from 40 to 25 percent. However, an economic slowdown undoubtedly accounts for some of the decline, while other actions unrelated to job redesign may account for part of the remainder. When Volvo surveyed its employees to probe for the causes of turnover and absenteeism, most of the causes revealed were external—problems with housing, child care, long distances traveling to the plant, and so on. Volvo responded with a series of actions to alleviate these causes, such as extending the bus fleet, together with the community, to transport employees; loaning money to employees to purchase apartments at very favorable rates of interest; putting pressure on the community to expand day-care centers, and so on. Such measures presumably contributed to the decline of turnover. Nevertheless, Gyllenhammar is convinced that "we can see a correlation between increased motivation, increased satisfaction on the job, and a decrease in the turnover of labor." Absenteeism is a sadly different picture: It's double what it was five years ago, a condition that Gyllenhammar attributes to legislation enabling workers to stay off the job at practically no cost to themselves.

As for output in that part of the auto assembly plant covered by job enrichment or job enlargement, there was no measurable improvement. Quality, on balance, has improved, and the feeling is that improved quality and decreased turnover had more than covered the costs of installing the program.

The Future of Job Redesign at Volvo

Despite the relatively ambiguous success of Volvo's job redesign efforts, whatever Volvo has done in the past is a pale prologue to its future plans. In about nine months, Volvo's new auto assembly plant at Kalmar will go on stream. And, for once, that overworked term *revolutionary* would seem justified.

Physically, the plant is remarkable. Gyllenhammar describes it as "shaped like a star and on each point of the star you have a work group finishing a big share of the whole automobile—for example, the electrical system or the safety system, or the interior." Assembly work takes place along the outer walls, while component parts are stored in the center of the building. Architecturally, the building has been designed to preserve the atmosphere of a small workshop in a large factory, with each work team having its own entrance, dressing room, rest room, and so on. Each team is even physically shielded from a view of the other teams. (See Figure 2.)

Each work team, of 15 to 25 men, will distribute the work among themselves and determine their own work rhythm, subject to the requirement of meeting production standards. If the team decides to drive hard in the morning and loaf in the afternoon, the decision is theirs to make. As with production teams in the truck assembly plant, the team will choose its own boss, and deselect him if he turns out poorly.

The new plant will cost about 10 percent more—some 10 million Swedish kroner—than a comparable conventional auto assembly plant. Time alone will tell whether the extra investment will be justified by

FIGURE 2
Diagram of Small Workshop at Volvo Assembly Plant at Kalmar

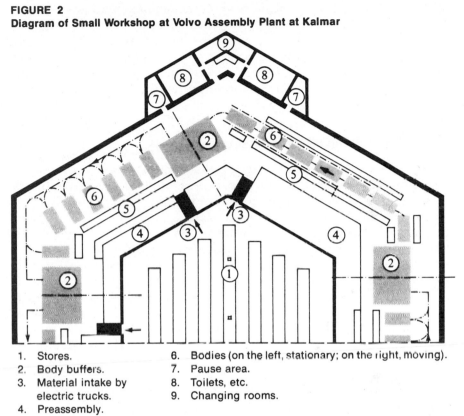

1. Stores.
2. Body buffers.
3. Material intake by electric trucks.
4. Preassembly.
5. Materials.

6. Bodies (on the left, stationary; on the right, moving).
7. Pause area.
8. Toilets, etc.
9. Changing rooms.

the decreased turnover, improved quality, and even reduced absenteeism that its designers confidently expect at the new facility. In announcing the plan for the new factory, Gyllenhammar's economic objectives were modest enough, his social objectives more ambitious. "A way must be found to create a workplace that meets the needs of the modern working man for a sense of purpose and satisfaction in his daily work. A way must be found of attaining this goal without an adverse effect on productivity." With luck, he may achieve both.

WHAT DOES IT ADD UP TO?

On the basis of what we learned at Philips, Saab-Scania, and Volvo, what answers—tentative and partial—do we have to the seven questions that we raised earlier in the article? Or are the results of the programs so ambiguous and inconclusive that, as long as we restrict ourselves to the context of these three companies, we must beg off attempting to answer some of the questions at all? That none of the companies answered all of the questions, and that many of the answers rely on subjective impressions haphazardly assembled, rather than on quantitative data systematically collected, of necessity, limit our answers, but they don't prevent us from presenting them—with the appropriate caveats.

1. *What conditions on the assembly line are economically favorable to which forms of job redesign?*

The basic question here is under what conditions can a man-paced assembly line replace a machine-paced assembly line? Unless this is economically feasible, no form of job redesign is likely to be adopted. Even allowing for rhetoric, none of our three companies—and no other organization of which we are aware—has indicated a willingness to suffer economic losses in order to increase the satisfactions employees might feel if they switched over from machine-paced to man-paced assembly lines. Take the case of manufacturing a pair of man's pants in a garment factory. Give the job to one man and he will take half a day; divide the work among many people on a line with each one using advanced technical equipment, and it takes one man-hour to produce a pair of trousers. The future of job redesign is not bright in a pants factory.

The man-paced assembly line, however, has a couple of widely recognized advantages over the machine-paced line: First, it's much less sensitive to disruption; the whole line doesn't have to stop because of one breakdown—human or technical; second, extensive and costly rebalancing need not be undertaken every time production is increased or decreased. You simply add more people or groups. Of course, there are advantages to machine-paced production, the outstanding one being speed of production, which depends, in turn, on an even flow of production.

There's the rub—and there's the number one cause for job redesign, certainly at Volvo and Saab-Scania. Absenteeism and turnover had risen to the point where they canceled out the economic advantages of machine-paced production. At the same time, evidence had accumulated that job redesign organized around a man-paced assembly line might strike at the root causes of inordinate turnover and absenteeism.

If you look at the design of the new engine plant at Scania, it incorporates Drucker's insight that "the worker is put to use to use a poorly designed one-purpose machine tool, but repetition and uniformity are two qualities in which human beings are weakest. In everything but the ability to judge and coordinate, machines can perform better than man." In the new engine plant, everything that can be automated economically has been—probably 90 percent of the total task—with the final assembly paced by teams on the assumption that the relatively slight increases in production time will be more than compensated for by better balancing and decreased disruption— improvements inherent in the technical change—and improvements in quality, turnover, and absenteeism, the anticipated by-products of job satisfaction.

The results, as you have seen, are sketchy. However, we can affirm that none of the three organizations, by their own testimony, has lost economically by the changeover from a machine-paced to a man-paced assembly line. How much they have gained is decidedly a more iffy question.

2. *Do many employees resent and resist job redesign? Do they prefer monotonous, repetitious work?*

A flip answer might be "God only knows—and he isn't talking." Any answer, at best, is based largely on conjecture. Joseph E. Godfrey asserts that "workers may complain about monotony, but years spent in the factories lead me to believe that they like to do their jobs automatically. If you interject new things you spoil the rhythm of the job and work gets fouled up." As head of the General Motors Assembly Line Division he is qualified, but biased. But even Fred Herzberg, whose bias is obviously in the other direction, concedes that "individual reaction to job enrichment is as difficult to forecast in terms of attitudes as it is in terms of performance. Not all persons welcome having their job enriched." The Survey Research Center at The University of Michigan in a 1969 study concluded that factors such as having a "nutrient supervisor, receiving adequate help, having few labor standard problems all seem to relate at least as closely to job satisfaction as having a challenging job with 'enriching demands.'" One thing does seem clear: Assuming the job level is held constant, education is inversely related to satisfaction. And when Pehr Gyllenhammar foresaw a near future in which 90 percent of the Swedish population would at least have graduated from high school, he was realistically anticipating a situation in which Volvo would become almost entirely dependent on foreign employees unless it found ways of enriching the auto assembly jobs.

3. *Are the "best" results from job redesign obtained when it's at its most thorough (job rotation plus job enrichment plus autonomy plus employee participation)?*

Work in America flatly endorses the thesis that "it is imperative that employers be made aware of the fact that thorough efforts to redesign work, not simply 'job enrichment' or 'job rotation,' have resulted in increases of productivity from 5 to 40 percent. In no instance of which we have evidence has a major effort to increase employee participation resulted in a long-term decline in productivity." Obviously, in this context "best" results means increased productivity.

Before we can answer the question and respond to the claims asserted in *Work in America* a few definitions are necessary. Most descriptions of the elements that enter into a satisfying job concentrate on three: (1) variety, (2) responsibility, and (3) autonomy. Variety defines itself. Responsibility is more complex; it involves both working on a sufficiently large part of the total job to feel that it is a meaningful experience and having a sufficient amount of control over what you are doing to feel personally responsible.

Companies responding to this need for more responsibility may add set-up and inspection to the employee's duties or ask him to assemble one third of an engine instead of a single component—both examples of horizontal job enrichment; and the employee may be permitted to control the pace at which he works—an example of vertical job enrichment. Everything that is subsumed under vertical job enrichment is included in autonomy but it also means something else and something more—giving to the employee himself some control over how his job should be enlarged or enriched—a clear demarcation point between almost all American approaches to job enrichment and some European.

We're describing a circular process; the worker in Sweden and the Netherlands places a higher value on autonomy than the worker in the United States. Therefore, job redesign that incorporates increased autonomy for the employee will be more appreciated and lead to more job satisfaction than comparable efforts would in the United States. Here, Huey Long's concept of a satisfying job, with allowances for the regional overtones, and the hyperbole, still makes sense: "There shall be a real job, not a little old sowbelly black-eyed pea job, but a real spending money beefsteak, and gray Chevrolet Ford in the garage, new suit, Thomas Jefferson, Jesus Christ, red, white, and blue job for every man." The employee did then and still does define, although to a progressively decreasing degree, a satisfying job in terms of how much it pays. For a measure of the difference, take the definition of a dissatisfying job by Malin Lofgren, a 12-year-old Swedish schoolboy: "A bad job is one where others make all the decisions, and you have to do what others say."

Now that the tedious, although necessary, business of definition is out of the way, how do we answer the question with reference to our three companies? Inconclusively. If we define "best" results in terms of gains in productivity, the only certifiable gain occurred with the Philips production groups that scored high on both horizontal and vertical job enrichment, and in which employees were consulted in advance about the ways in which their job should be enriched. In the body of the article, we didn't go into their institutional arrangements, but suffice it to say that both Saab-Scania and Volvo have comparable consultative institutions. Thus, the autonomy factor assumes less significance. The only significant differences would appear to be: (1) The increased status caused by making the production groups at Philips wholly responsible for liaison with other departments, (2) the Hawthorne, or, as the Philips personnel call it, the "Princess" effect—the groups having been visited and complimented by such dignitaries as Queen Juliana and Marshal Tito. On the other hand, the groups at Volvo that chose their own supervisors—certainly a measure of autonomy—have not increased their productivity. Quality, turnover, attendance had improved. But with productivity, there was no measurable impact.

4. *Is there any single element in job redesign that seems to account for the biggest increase in employee satisfaction?*

In a word—no. But that requires an explanation. Our failure to respond principally reflects lack of evidence; none of the organizations concerned asked themselves the question. None tried on any systematic basis to relate what they were doing in redesigning jobs to what they were accomplishing in increased job satisfaction. Word-of-mouth testimony and more cheerful figures—as in the case of Volvo and Saab-Scania with turnover—seemed sufficient to confirm the efficacy of past efforts and sanction future ones, on similar although expanded lines.

5. *What are the benefits of job redesign—both those we can measure and monetize and those that can only be described?*

We begin with a proposition shared by a generation of social scientists who have studied the problem and attempted to answer the question: Employee attitudes and job satisfaction are correlated much more clearly with factors such as absenteeism, turnover, and quality than they are with productivity.

The three companies reinforce this finding. Only one experiment at Philips establishes a positive correlation between job satisfaction and productivity, while several—Philips with productivity groups in Phase III, Saab-Scania in the engine plant and the truck assembly plant, and Volvo in its truck plant—all report improvements in quality, the problem in each case being the absence of quantifiable data. Turnover is another area in which the responses are positive, but suggestive rather than conclusive—"probably lower" in the Scania engine plant; lower in the truck assembly plant; down in both the truck assembly and auto assembly plant at Volvo—but there are no firm figures at the Volvo truck assembly line, while the decrease in turnover at the auto assembly plant is partly attributed to causes unrelated to job redesign. Philips offers no comparisons of absenteeism or turnover before and after job redesign. All we know is that so far no one in the production groups has decided to quit. In short, the evidence—what there is of it—is positive, but fragmented and based more on impressions than on data.

6. *On balance, does management gain as much from job redesign as the employee whose job is redesigned?*

A two-headed question that logically requires both extensive employee attitude surveys before and after job redesign, along with firm measurements that demonstrate the impact of job redesign on factors such as quality, output, absenteeism, and turnover. As we have seen, we have very little of either. The only attitude surveys were, first, the one conducted at the Volvo auto assembly plant to determine the causes of excessive absenteeism and turnover—most of which had nothing to do with job satisfaction and where the subsequent substantial drop in turnover at best could only partially be ascribed to job redesign—and the survey at Philips, where the switchover from machine-paced to man-paced assembly line improved employees' satisfaction with their jobs.

On the balance, as previously stated, management has achieved at least an economic draw from its efforts at job redesign, along with a measure of insurance against a fretful future in which employee expectations will become increasingly difficult to fulfill. The job redesign carried out or contemplated will, it is hoped, help to meet those expectations.

As for the satisfactions the employees have gained from the collective efforts at enlarging and enriching their jobs, we can only guess. We have a few pieces of anecdotal evidence, such as the flood of applications to work in the final assembly at Scania's engine plant, or the absence of turnover among the production groups at Philips. In short, we know too little to generalize.

7. *Last, what's the impact of the overall culture and political system on job redesign? What's the evidence, pro or con, that the success of job redesign at Volvo, Saab-Scania, or Philips—or lack of it— would be replicated in similar assembly lines in the United States?*

Technologically, there are no convincing reasons why assembly lines in new automobile factories or television plants in the United States couldn't be redesigned along lines similar to what has been done at Philips, Saab-Scania, and Volvo. It might prove prohibitively expensive in existing plants—after all, job redesign at Volvo's auto assembly plant was largely restricted, on economic grounds, to job rotation. However, new plants in the United States should present no more inherent problems of job redesign than new plants in Sweden. Yet auto executives in the United States have gone on record as feeling that the situation is hopeless. A 1970 report of the Ford Foundation found that none of the corporation executives interviewed "really believe that assembly line tasks can be significantly restructured," and "no one really believes that much can be done to make the assembly jobs more attractive."

Not that all the features of job redesign at Philips, Saab-Scania, and Volvo are equally exportable. The three companies exist in a different political and social ethos, one in which both management and the workers have gone much further in accepting the idea of employee participation in decision making than all but a handful of managers and a small minority of workers in the United States. A survey of Swedish managers in 1970, for example, showed that 75 percent favored more employee decision making in all departments. Even the idea of replacing the decision of the supervisor with collective employee decisions elicited a favorable response from 11 percent of the managers. Given this different ethos, it is not surprising that all three companies have experimented with what would be in the United States the radical step of either dispensing with first-level supervision or leaving it up to the employees to choose their own supervisor. It is a form of autonomy that few managements in the United States would consider for an instant, and one in which few employees would take much interest.

But why not consider it, as long as management continues to set overall standards of production and quality and to hold the group responsible for meeting them? The experiment of having employees choose their own bosses with the experimental groups in the truck assembly plant at Volvo works so well that it has been incorporated as one of the basic design features in the new auto assembly plant. Employees demonstrated that, given the opportunity, they would choose as leaders men who could organize the work and maintain order and discipline.

Let's indulge in speculation. The single quality that most clearly distinguishes between the efforts at job enrichment here and in the three companies we visited is the emphasis abroad on letting the employees have a part—and sometimes a decisive part—in deciding how their jobs should be enriched. By contrast, most exponents of job enrichment in the United States take the "papa knows best" approach. Fred Herzberg, the best-known work psychologist, asserts that when people took part in deciding how to change their own jobs, "the results were disappointing." We suspect that Herzberg's real objection is not to the results themselves, but to the difficulty of selling most managements on the idea that employee participation should be an integral part of any process of job enrichment. The experiences at Volvo, Saab-Scania, and Philips suggest that the objection to the employee's participating in how his own job should be enriched or redesigned has its roots in symbolism, rather than substance, in the irrational preoccupation with management prerogatives, rather than in any real or potential threat to productivity or profits.

What about the future? Technologically, there seem to be no compelling reasons why Ford, GM, and Chrysler cannot take a lead from Volvo and Saab-Scania. Whether they will is another question. The combination of inertia, custom, and commitment is a formidable one. So far the automakers have chosen to move in the opposite direction: shorter work cycles, smaller jobs, more rapidly moving lines. We should recall that it took a crisis—nothing less than the probability that most people would refuse to work at all or only for uneconomic periods on the jobs the organization had to offer them—to "break the cake of custom" at Volvo and Saab-Scania. Even today, it is clear that there are limits to which auto assembly jobs can be enriched, a limitation obvious in Gyllenhammar's bitter observation that " 'absenteeism with pay' is based on the very utopian hypothesis that people love to work, and no matter what happens they will strive to go to their job every morning." Still, the situation he is in is preferable to the situation he faced. And some of the difference is due to job redesign.

We suspect that it will take a crisis of similar magnitude, together with the belief that they have no choice, to unfreeze the attitudes of automakers in the United States and get them moving in the direction of man-paced assembly lines and the forms of job redesign they facilitate. That such a development, over the long run, is in the cards we strongly believe, but how long it will take for the cards to show up, we leave to the astrologers.

SELECTED BIBLIOGRAPHY

On the general subject of job redesign we strongly recommend three books: The HEW *Work in America* (MIT Press, Cambridge, Mass., 1971) is scarcely unbiased but it pulls together much material in the whole area of employee discontent—what causes it and what can be done about it. David Jenkins' *Job Power: Blue and White Collar Democracy* (Doubleday, New York, 1973) is remarkable for the number of case studies of job redesign both here and in Europe—all based on personal visits to the organizations described. Jenkins, like the various authors of *Work in America*, is convinced of the need for wholesale job redesign as the prime means of alleviating growing employee discontent. Last, *Design of Jobs* (Penguin Books Ltd., Harmondsworth, England, 1972) is a first-rate collection of papers on different aspects of job design. All are worth reading, but of special interest are J. Richard Hackman and Edward E. Lawler III, "Conditions Under Which Jobs Will Facilitate Internal Motivation" (pp. 141–154) and James C. Taylor, "Some Effects of Technology in Organizational Change" (pp. 391–414).

On Philips, there is a suggestive article on the first phase of job redesign that shows clearly that Philips's interest in getting away from the machine-paced assembly line arose mainly from technical and economic dissatisfactions with the line—H. G. Van Beek, "The Influence of Assembly Line Organization on Output, Quality and Morale," *Occupational Psychology*, vol. 38, pp. 161–172. On Scania, there's a section on the company—but not identified by name—in Hans Lindestad and Jan-Peter Norstedt, *Autonomous Groups and Payment by Result* (Swedish Employers Confederation, Stockholm, 1973). The Employers Confederation also has published a detailed account of job redesign at Saab-Scania that is being translated into English but that, unfortunately, was not available at the time this article was written.

13

Performance Review: The Job Nobody Likes*

BERKELEY RICE

A common criticism is that it creates a kind of parent-child relationship between boss and employee. *Industry Week* calls it "a periodic agony thrust on both bosses and subordinates." A personnel administration expert laments, "Probably fewer than 10 percent of the nation's companies have systems that are reasonably good." The focus of all this concern is the methods used to assess how well workers do their jobs. Personnel experts aren't the only ones dissatisfied with such procedures, known as performance review, evaluation, appraisal, or rating. Supervisors and workers are unhappy too.

One reason for the general dissatisfaction with such systems is a lack of agreement on their purpose. Should they merely evaluate performance, or critique and improve it as well? Should they be used primarily to determine salaries and prospects for promotion, or as a means of training and career development? Should they focus on how

* Reprinted from *Psychology Today*, September 1985, pp. 30–36. Copyright © 1985 by the American Psychological Association.

an employee does the job or the results achieved? Just who are they supposed to help, the employee or the supervisor? No performance-review system can accomplish all these goals, but confusion about conflicting purposes often undermines attempts at effective evaluation.

Many employees complain that the forms and procedures used invite unfair evaluations. They are often based on personality traits or vague qualities such as reliability, initiative, or leadership—factors difficult to measure objectively. Many standardized appraisal forms also use criteria that are not relevant to the job under review. Others provide a quick and superficial checklist that leaves no room for individual evaluation. Too often, one-sided performance reviews put employees on the defensive, particularly when they turn into lectures or harangues that end with the boss commenting on "how great it's been to have this open exchange of views."

It might surprise employees who feel threatened by performance reviews to learn that many bosses find them equally burdensome. They, too, grumble about the irrelevance of standardized review forms and the vague criteria. They complain that reviews require piles of paperwork, don't leave room for individual judgment, and don't lead to improved performance.

Many managers feel they need more training in how to conduct reviews, but few companies offer any help. Robert Lefton, president of Psychological Associates, a firm that conducts such training sessions, describes performance review as a tough job, "the equivalent of walking up to a person and saying, 'Here's what I think of your baby.' It requires knowing how to handle fear and anger and a gamut of other emotions which a lot of managers aren't comfortable with."

If you wonder why evaluating an employee's performance can be so difficult, consider a simpler appraisal: one made by the barroom fan who concludes that his team's quarterback is a bum because several of his passes have been intercepted. An objective appraisal would raise the following questions: Were the passes really that bad or did the receivers run the wrong patterns? Did the offensive line give the quarterback adequate protection? Did he call those plays himself, or were they sent in by the coach? Was the quarterback recovering from an injury?

And what about the fan? Has he ever played football himself? How good is his vision? Did he have a good view of the TV set through the barroom's smoky haze? Was he talking to his friends at the bar during the game? How many beers did he down during the game?

Compared with barroom appraisals, evaluating performance at work is far more complex. Because evaluation is both difficult and important, it has grown into one of the busiest fields in industrial psychology. Since 1950, more than 300 studies have appeared in academic and management journals. Most of them, until quite recently, focused on the rating format used and on the biasing effect of various nonperformance factors such as race and sex. These latter concerns were spurred by the federal government's Equal Employment Opportunity guidelines, issued in 1969 and 1970.

No consistent pattern of sexual bias has emerged from the research. For example, Michigan State University psychologist Kenneth N. Wexley and a colleague studied nearly 300 manager-subordinate pairs in several companies and uncovered no evidence of sexual bias in the ratings. Research by psychologist Laurence H. Peters of Southern Illinois University found a similar lack of sexual bias in supervisors' reviews of retail-store managers. When psychologist William H. Mobley studied more than 1,000 employees at another company, he found that women generally received higher ratings than did men, regardless of the supervisors' sex.

Occupational sex stereotypes are a different story. Laboratory studies of women working at traditionally masculine jobs show that they usually receive lower ratings than do men of comparable ability in the same jobs. (This effect may lessen as more women enter managerial and other "male" domains.) On the other hand, women in traditionally feminine occupations, such as clerical work, don't seem to benefit from a compensating bias in their favor.

Studies of racial bias have revealed a consistent pattern: White supervisors tend to give higher ratings to white subordinates, while black supervisors favor blacks. A study of psychologist W. C. Hamner and three colleagues found evidence of another, more subtle form of discrimination: White supervisors were more likely to differentiate between high and low levels of performance among individual whites than they did among individual blacks, whom they generally rated close to average on a performance scale.

Some critics of performance reviews suggest that ratings by supervisors may be less accurate than those by fellow workers or subordinates or even self-appraisals by the employees themselves. Several studies have shown that supervisors tend to give tougher evaluations than do fellow workers, while the fellow workers' ratings generally show greater consistency among several raters.

In a study of self-evaluation among job applicants, psychologist Cathy D. Anderson and others at the Colorado State Department of Personnel asked 350 men and women to rate their ability on a variety of job-related tasks. The list included several bogus skills, such as "matrixing solvency files," "planning basic entropy programs," and "resolving disputes by isometric analysis." Nearly half the applicants for what were mostly clerical jobs claimed they had experience with one or more of the nonexistent tasks. Among those who took a typing test, few achieved the speed they claimed, leading researchers to conclude that "inflation bias" in the self-appraisals was "prevalent and pervasive."

Several studies of actual and simulated work conditions have indicated that an employee's attitude and experience can affect the validity of a supervisor's ratings. In a field study, psychologists Ronald Grey and David Kipnis found that supervisors gave "compliant" workers higher ratings when the workers were surrounded by "noncompliant" peers and lower ratings when co-workers were more amenable. An early review by psychologists Rutledge Jay and James Copes of 47 studies showed that employees who had held their jobs longer, particularly in managerial jobs, usually got higher ratings than did peers of equal ability.

The appraisal method itself has received considerable attention from researchers. By far the most widely used format is still the traditional numerical or graphic rating scale. For each trait or skill being evaluated, the scale may be marked simply by numbers, say from 1 to 10, or by such vague adjectives as "unsatisfactory, below average, average, above average, outstanding."

In an attempt to improve the reliability of ratings, several researchers have experimented with varying the number of rating categories. The results indicate that consistency among raters drops significantly when there are less than 4 or more than 10 categories. Five to nine categories seem to produce the most consistent ratings.

Whether these ratings represent accurate measures of performance is another matter. According to industrial psychologist Robert Guion, editor of the *Journal of Applied Psychology*, "You get fairly valid ratings when you look mainly for the extremes of outstanding or very poor performance. But when you look closely at the middle or average range, distinctions among people are less accurate and valid."

That middle range, of course, is where most ratings fall, for several reasons. One is a manager's natural reluctance to cause pain by giving low ratings to poor performers. When supervisors know their subordinates will see the ratings, as they do in most systems, or that they will have to confront them with the ratings in a feedback session, they tend to be more lenient. This is perfectly human, but it doesn't lead to valid appraisals. Another factor may be what psychologists call "central tendency error," the fact that we tend to avoid the extremes when we rate almost anything. Then there's the problem of personal standards that lead tenderhearted managers to give consistently high ratings while "tough guys" rate consistently low. Both tendencies cause inequities when the reviews determine salary increases or promotions.

Some companies try to head off these errors with forced distribution systems that set minimums or maximums for the percentage of ratings in each category; for example, no more than 10 percent of one's subordinates can be rated outstanding, no more than 50 percent rated average. Many supervisors and psychologists object to such arbitrary limits, arguing that no one really knows what the distribution curve for such ratings should be.

Another common source of rating error is the "halo effect" whereby people who are generally well liked get favorable ratings on all categories. Bad chemistry between a subordinate and supervisor can have the opposite effect and produce unfairly low ratings. In both cases, ratings end up based on general impressions of the employee as a person rather than on specific aspects of performance.

Because of growing dissatisfaction with traditional rating scales, and the search for more objective appraisal methods, many companies have adopted some form of "behaviorally anchored" rating scales (BARS). This development is based on the work of psychologists Patricia Cain Smith and Lorne Kendall, using John Flanagan's theory of critical incidents.

To create a BARS scale, companies first conduct a formal job analysis to determine what kinds of behavior constitute degrees of adequate performance for specific tasks in each job. They then use these behavioral descriptions to define or "anchor" the ratings on the scale. For example, for an item such as "perseverance," a BARS scale might offer choices ranging from "Keeps working on difficult tasks until job is completed" to "Likely to stop work on a hard job at the first sign of difficulty."

While the job analyses used to develop BARS scales are often conducted by outside consultants, many industrial psychologists feel that participation by the employees and their supervisors leads to more realistic performance expectations. Their involvement in the process should increase their awareness of what good work behavior is and thereby improve their performance.

While advocates of BARS, particularly the consultants who do a thriving business with it, claim it's a great leap forward, critics point to several drawbacks. The lengthy job analyses and complex scale construction require a major investment of a company's time and money. A scale designed for use in one department may not apply in another. In fact, separate scales may be necessary for each job category within the same department, since the requirements for good performance may differ markedly.

Comparative studies have found that the BARS method, because of its behavioral specificity, results in greater reliability than do traditional rating scales, and that it may reduce leniency, halo effects, and central tendency error. But the improvements may be too slight to justify the time and money required. In addition, while BARS scales are suitable for jobs such as production or clerical work, they are harder to devise for managerial positions in which performance cannot easily be reduced to specific kinds of observable behavior. In such jobs, complex judgment, not easily reduced to a six-point scale, may be more important than measurable behavior.

For managerial and supervisory jobs, many companies have adopted another form of evaluation, "management by objectives" (MBO), which focuses on results rather than behavior. MBO was proposed in the 1950s by psychologist Douglas McGregor. As customarily practiced today, supervisors and their subordinates sit down at the beginning of each year, or every six months, and agree (often in writing) on specific goals to be accomplished. At the end of the period, the supervisors evaluate their subordinates in terms of how well they have met those objectives.

MBO became popular because, in theory, it can be tailored to each individual job and because it lets subordinates know how their performance will be measured and gives them specific, mutually agreed-on goals.

In practice, however, MBO appraisals are just as open to claims of unfairness as other systems of performance review are. One major weakness is the difficulty of setting reasonable goals well in advance, when they may be vulnerable to factors outside the employee's control, such as economic conditions, labor problems, and price increases. Beyond that, the method's very individuality makes it difficult to compare one subordinate's performance with another's—one ostensible purpose of performance review. For these reasons, use of MBO has declined in recent years.

Frank J. Landy, a psychologist at Pennsylvania State University, reviews performance appraisal studies for the *Journal of Applied Psychology*. He has grown discouraged by the numerous attempts to build a better mousetrap by experimenting with rating scales or sources of bias. Even when those attempts reduce error, he says, the improvements are often so small that they're merely cosmetic.

"After more than 30 years of serious research," Landy wrote, "it seems that little progress has been made in developing an efficient and psychometrically sound alternative to the traditional graphic rating scale. . . . One major conclusion to be drawn from this research is that there is no 'easy way' to get accurate and informative performance data. Methods that aim toward easing the pain for managers who are busy will pay a price in terms of accuracy and value of the information obtained."

Faced with generally meager results from earlier studies, some researchers are turning to cognitive psychology in the hope of better understanding the processes of observation, information storage, retrieval, classification, and communication that supervisors use, or should use, in performance evaluation. They suspect that perceptual and cognitive differences among raters may affect their ratings as much as or more than the nature of the rating scale itself and may be impervious to any changes in the evaluation system or the structure of the rating scale.

Many cognitive researchers point to the work of University of Washington psychologist Elizabeth Loftus and others who have demonstrated the fallibility of human observation and memory in studies of eyewitness testimony. Using videotapes of accidents and other incidents, those studies reveal the unconscious tendency of witnesses to "reconstruct" events based on cognitive biases, stereotypes, and other unrelated information. If witnesses make all these mistakes on the comparatively simple task of recalling a few details about something that might have happened only a few hours or days before, imagine how difficult it is for a manager to evaluate the work of many subordinates over a period of six months or a year. Like witnesses at a busy intersection, managers often must base their judgments on only fragmentary evidence. It's understandable that unconscious mental habits play a vital part in their evaluations.

In his review of research on the cognitive processes involved in performance appraisal, Jack Feldman, a professor of management at the University of Texas at Arlington, showed that once a rater puts someone in a category, the category filters and colors the rater's observation and recall of that person's behavior. Supervisors thus attend chiefly to behavior that confirms the stereotype they have developed and ignore or forget behavior that conflicts with it. An admired employee whose performance declines may still receive excellent evaluations while another employee, who makes a serious effort to improve, may be condemned by a previous reputation.

When the time comes for evaluation, if the supervisor cannot recall any specific information relevant to a category on the rating form, he or she may unconsciously invent imaginary examples of "appropriate" behavior based on the stereotype. According to Feldman, these false memories are particularly likely when a supervisor has many subordinates to evaluate and little time or opportunity to observe them on the job.

This kind of categorical information processing is influenced not only by such obvious factors as age, sex, race, and attractiveness but also by stereotypes about jobs. Thus some managers may evaluate the performance of all salespeople by how well they fit the traditional image of the fast-talking, aggressive go-getter and all bookkeepers by the image of the cautious, meticulous grind, whether or not these qualities apply to the particular job.

Advice for Managers

However imperfect, performance reviews will continue to be required of most managers. Fortunately, along with all the criticism and research, there is also plenty of advice around on how to conduct them. The current edition of *Books in Print* lists more than 50 titles devoted to performance review or appraisal, and journals frequently publish articles on the subject. While not all of the advice is useful for every manager, much of it can be adapted to individual needs:

- Know precisely what you want to achieve (and what company policy says you should achieve) with your performance reviews, such as determining raises, evaluation, criticism, training, or morale-building.
- Don't wait until the review itself to let your staff know what you expect. Let them know early on exactly what the job requires, what specific goals, standards and deadlines you expect them to meet, and how you plan to evaluate and reward their performance.
- Keep a record of subordinates' performance so that you can cite specific examples to back up any criticisms or comments.
- Listen. Numerous surveys of employee attitudes reveal the feeling that "management doesn't care what we think." The review is your chance to get valuable feedback from your own subordinates about their jobs or company policy.
- Ask fact-finding questions to get employees to recall instances in which they performed well or poorly. See if they have a realistic estimate of their abilities.
- Go over your written evaluation with each employee. Find out if they feel your ratings are fair. They don't have to agree with you completely, but strong disagreements will lessen their motivation to improve.
- Focus steadily on each individual's performance. Show that you care about that person's career. Otherwise it looks like you're just going through the motions, and employees will get the message that the review, and perhaps their performance, doesn't really matter.

- When critiquing an employee's performance, do some stroking: Reinforce the good habits with praise.
- Be specific and constructive in your criticism. Don't just tell employees they're not "aggressive enough." Point out how they can improve, with specific examples.
- Critique the behavior, not the employee. Keep the discussion on a professional level.
- Be fair, but don't be afraid to give honest criticism when necessary. Most employees don't want a meaningless pat on the back. They want to know where they stand and how they can improve.
- Don't play the role of therapist. If personal problems are affecting an employee's performance, be supportive, but be careful about getting involved. Suggest outside professional help if necessary.
- Explain how the employee's performance in meeting goals contributes to department or corporate objectives. In this way, the review can help build morale and loyalty.
- Don't wait until the next performance review to follow up. Use informal progress reports or mini-reviews to help spot problems before they become serious.
- Use the occasion to get an informal review of your own performance. Encourage your staff to tell you about any of your habits that make their work difficult or to suggest changes you could make that would help them do their jobs better.

Personality or cultural conflicts can also create problems. Feldman cites the example of employees who act in what they feel is a friendly manner toward their boss, only to find that the boss considers it disrespectful. When review time rolls around, such employees may be shocked to find they have been labeled "insubordinate."

According to H. John Bernardin, professor of management at Florida Atlantic University, another type of error in performance reviews can be explained by attribution theory, which deals with the inferences people make as to why they and others act as they do. Bernardin has found that workers doing poorly on a job will attempt to justify their performance by attributing it to such situational factors as lack of supplies, unpredictable or excessive workload, difficult co-workers, and ambiguous assignments. A worker's supervisor, however, is likely to blame personal factors such as lack of ability or motivation.

In one study of middle-level managers, Bernardin found that most of them cited low ability or motivation for their employees' unsatisfactory performance. But when asked to explain poor reviews of their own work, only 20 percent saw such personal factors as the cause. Most cited factors "beyond their control."

While many cognitive researchers are excited about the prospect of applying their findings to performance review, others remain dubious, particularly about using the work to improve rater training. In a recent research review, Bernardin points out that of the 34 rater-training studies he examined, only 3 involved data from real evaluations of real work. "It is a sad commentary on our discipline," he writes, "that an obvious applied area like rater training should be studied almost exclusively with student raters in an experimental context. . . . There appears to be an increasing emphasis on methodologically sound, internally valid laboratory research, the results of which have added little to our understanding of performance appraisal beyond what we already know."

According to a survey Bernardin did of personnel administrators and supervisors, inaccuracy in performance ratings stems more from intentional distortion than from rating error. Inflated ratings are one example. In tough times, managers may inflate ratings to make sure their subordinates qualify for raises, to keep their departments from being cut or to keep valuable employees from seeking transfers. Central tendency error is another example. It may make good administrative sense to lump most of one's subordinates in the middle range, thereby avoiding invidious comparisons and perhaps heading off arguments with or between employees.

Kevin Murphy, a psychologist at Colorado State University who has done considerable cognitive research on performance evaluation, also questions its relevance in training managers to be better raters. "The real problem is not how well managers can evaluate performance, but how willing they are," he says. "The problem is one of motivation, not ability."

In addition, he says, companies should stop trying vainly to improve rating forms and instead train managers in skills that would make them better observers: gathering and recording supporting evidence; discriminating between relevant and irrelevant information; doing selective work sampling when direct observation is infrequent; and deciding which aspects of performance are really measurable.

The discovery of how cognitive processes affect performance review, Landy says, has shaken the world of management psychology. "Eight years ago we would have given plenty of prescriptive advice about how to do an accurate review," he says, "but most of it would have been wrong. The bad news is that there's simply no easy way to do performance review. As appealing as the notion of a precise method of appraisal is, it's never going to be possible to measure such complex behavior in any absolute way."

"The good news," Landy adds, "is that we've discovered that a lot of that stuff about rating scales and evaluation formats is really trivial. The particular format doesn't make much difference. There is no one 'right' way to do it. There are dozens of ways. You just use whichever method feels right for your company. It may not be very accurate, but the degree of error won't make much difference."

"There's no one system that works," says management psychologist David DeVries, who conducts research and teaches courses on performance appraisal to corporate executives at the Center for Creative Leadership in Greensboro, North Carolina. "What we try to do here," he explains, "is show what the options are and how the companies' own managers can generally design a system most appropriate for them."

DeVries believes strongly that most managers "are much more sophisticated than the researchers realize. I think they understand the appraisal process pretty well because they are the ones who have to live with the results.

"Take traits like integrity, initiative, optimism, energy, and intelligence. Researchers today feel such traits shouldn't be used in performance reviews because they're highly subjective, and therefore psychometrically suspect. But in business, those traits are very important, subjective or not. Executives make personnel decisions based on them all the time. If they do, then those traits should be evaluated, and we researchers can't afford to ignore them."

DeVries argues that companies can try to control the level of subjectivity in an appraisal system even though they can't make it go away. Despite the drawbacks of performance appraisal, he insists, "it's important to reward your top performers, and to make it clear to the others why they're being rewarded. . . . A good performance-appraisal system can help managers do this. It must be taken seriously by the managers, by the employees and by the company. It must be the basis for deciding who gets ahead and who doesn't."

14

Recent Innovations in Reward Systems*

DANIEL C. FELDMAN and HUGH J. ARNOLD

There has been increased interest recently in the design of organizational reward systems. As a result, a number of innovative approaches have been developed to the administration of pay and other rewards for effective performance. This increased interest has largely arisen from recognition of the fact that pay, far from being an almost irrelevant factor in modern organizations, as suggested by theorists such as Maslow and Herzberg, is in fact an important determinant of the satisfaction and motivation of organization members. Edward Lawler has been a leading proponent of the importance of pay in organizations and has been in the forefront of the development and study of innovative approaches to pay. Lawler (1976) recently discussed five new approaches to the administration of pay in organizations which have been shown to be effective. These innovations are discussed below and their strengths and weaknesses are summarized in Table 1.

CAFETERIA FRINGE BENEFITS

Almost every organization rewards its members with some combination of pay and fringe benefits such as life insurance, health insurance, and pension plans. Quite commonly an organization has one standard fringe benefit package for nonsalaried employees, another for salaried employees, and a third for senior managers. The weakness of such approaches to fringe benefits is that they fail to take into account differences among individuals in the value and importance they place upon the different benefits available. Research consistently indicates that factors such as age, marital status, and number of chil-

---

* From Daniel C. Feldman and Hugh J. Arnold, *Managing Individual and Group Behavior in Organizations* (New York: McGraw-Hill, 1983), pp. 178–87, 189–90. Copyright © 1983 by McGraw-Hill, Inc.

TABLE 1
Overview of Innovative Approaches to Pay

	Major Advantages	*Major Disadvantages*	*Favorable Situational Factors*
Cafeteria fringe benefits	Increased pay satisfaction	Cost of administration	Well-educated, heterogeneous work force
Lump-sum salary increases	Increased pay satisfaction; greater visibility of pay increases	Cost of administration	Fair pay rates
Skill-based evaluation	More flexible and skilled work force; increased satisfaction	Cost of training; higher salaries	Employees who want to develop themselves; jobs that are interdependent
Open salary information	Increased pay satisfaction, trust, and motivation; better salary administration	Pressure to pay all the same; complaints about pay rates	Open climate; fair pay rates; pay based on performance
Participative pay decisions	Better pay decisions; increased satisfaction, motivation, and trust	Time-consuming	Democratic management climate; work force that wants to participate and that is concerned about organizational goals

Source: Reprinted, by permission of the publisher, from E. E. Lawler III, "New Approaches to Pay: Innovations that Work," *Personnel 53* (1976), 11–23. Copyright © 1976 by AMACOM, a division of American Management Associations. All rights reserved.

dren influence the extent to which individuals value different types of benefits (Glueck, 1978). For example, young, single members tend to value higher salaries and more vacations, and to be less concerned regarding things like insurance and pensions. Middle-aged members with young families value salaries and bonuses but tend to be less concerned with vacation time and more concerned with various types of insurance. Older members are concerned less with current salaries and more with pensions and retirement benefits.

A fringe benefit program that ignores these differences among people and treats all organization members identically fails to obtain the maximum payoff from the considerable monetary investment involved in such fringe benefit programs. If fringe benefit plans are to assist the organization by increasing the levels of satisfaction and motivation of their members, the plans must be capable of responding to the significant differences among individuals in the value they place on the benefits available.

An innovative approach to the resolution of this problem is known as a cafeteria-style fringe benefit program. The term *cafeteria* is employed as an analogy, since under such a plan the organization presents its employees with a whole range of alternative benefits and permits the employees to pick and choose those that they individually value most up to some set maximum value (the employee's total compensation level). At one extreme an individual could take his or her compensation entirely in the form of salary with no other benefits, while at the other extreme an individual could in any given year opt for a reduction in salary and an increase in other benefits, such as insurance or pension contributions. A variant of the cafeteria-style plan requires all employees to accept a minimal level of certain benefits such as health and life insurance and then permits free choice in allocation of compensation beyond these minimal levels.

The advantages of cafeteria-style benefit plans are twofold. First, they increase employees' perceptions of the value of their total compensation package. Second, they increase the likelihood that employees will be satisfied with their pay and benefits package. This increased satisfaction is associated with lower levels of turnover and absenteeism and greater ease in attracting new members.

Although cafeteria fringe benefits have significant advantages, they are obviously not without their drawbacks. First, they tend to create bookkeeping difficulties for the organization, which must keep track of exactly who has chosen which benefits and insure that the benefits are properly administered and dispensed. Fortunately, the use of computer systems greatly alleviates the difficulties encountered and brings the problems down to quite manageable proportions. Second, the uncertainty regarding exactly how many people will choose each benefit can make it difficult for the organization to price certain benefits such as insurance, for which the cost to the organization is partially dependent upon the number of people choosing the benefit. This difficulty is particularly salient for smaller organizations and may result in some short-term costs to the organization in the early stages of a program until the numbers of employees choosing various options have stabilized and accurate pricing can be employed. Cafeteria-style fringe benefit programs have been successfully implemented and maintained in both large organizations (e.g., the Systems Division of the TRW Corporation, with 12,000 employees) and small organizations (e.g., the Educational Testing Service, with 3,000 employees).

SKILL-EVALUATION PAY PLANS

Basing a person's salary upon the job-related skills which he or she possesses was previously mentioned briefly under our discussion of alternative methods of pay administration. The most common approach to pay administration in the past has been to base an employee's pay upon what the job requires the individual to do (this is referred to as the job-requirement or job-evaluation approach to pay administration). Skill-evaluation pay plans, on the other hand, base the amount of pay not on what the current job requires of the employee, but upon what that employee is capable of doing, as indicated by the range of job-related skills that the employee has demonstrated that he or she possesses. The wider the range of skills possessed, and hence the more jobs that a person is capable of performing, the higher the salary.

Skill-evaluation pay plans have been successfully implemented in organizations in Europe as well as in a number of North American plants operated by Procter & Gamble and General Foods. The plans have frequently been employed in plants organized and designed around work groups. In such situations group members are generally highly dependent upon one another for the effective performance of their group and a high level of rotation among jobs is common. A skill-evaluation pay plan is particularly well suited to such a situation since it increases the flexibility of the work force and encourages individuals to develop a broad perspective on the operation and effectiveness of the plant.

Where skill-evaluation pay plans are in effect, new organization members typically start at a basic pay rate and move up in salary as they demonstrate the skill to perform more and more jobs. Once all of the production jobs have been mastered the individual achieves the top or "plant" rate. Further salary increases can only be obtained by acquiring a specialty rate based upon the development of expertise in a skilled trade such as electricity or plumbing.

Skill-based pay plans are successful in developing a highly skilled and flexible work force and have also been found to lead to feelings of personal growth and development among the individuals participating in them. They are also perceived to be a fair method of administering pay. On the negative side, such plans can be costly to the organization in two respects. First, they require that the organization provide individuals with formal training and other opportunities to learn, such as on-the-job practice. These training costs can frequently become quite high. Second, as the majority of employees develop a wide variety of skills they must be paid accordingly, resulting in a highly paid work force. A final potential problem that needs to be noted can arise when individuals who have been encouraged to grow and develop their skills reach the top level and have nowhere further to go. Such individuals may become frustrated and unhappy if new avenues for development such as interplant transfers or special assignments are not identified.

LUMP-SUM SALARY INCREASES

Almost all organizations review the salaries of their members once a year to determine the amount by which the annual salary of each of their members will be increased. The amount of increase decided upon is then averaged over the number of pay periods in a year (e.g., 12 if members are paid monthly), and then each regular paycheck is incremented accordingly. Thus, it usually takes an employee an entire year actually to collect the full amount of the annual increase, and the increase is received in small installments. The advantages of this system from the organization's viewpoint are that the organization does not have to part with large amounts of cash at any one time and, further, the organization does not put itself in a position of having paid for services prior to their being rendered by the employee. At the same time, however, the practice of integrating annual increments into regular paychecks suffers both from the fact that it is an inflexible method of administering pay as a reward and from the fact that it serves to make even quite large annual salary increases relatively unnoticeable to the employee when they are averaged over many pay periods.

An alternative that a number of organizations have begun to experiment with is the administration of annual salary increases in a single lump sum. Under such a system the individual is informed of the amount of his or her annual salary increase and is then given the choice of how and when to receive the increase. The individual may choose to take the full amount immediately, to have the increment integrated into each regular paycheck, or to receive the increment in any combination of lump-sum payments and regular increments that may be convenient. Such a system has a number of advantages. First, it is an innovative approach to pay administration and can serve to encourage innovation and experimentation throughout the organization. Second, it makes the organization's pay system much more flexible and permits it to meet the unique needs of individual members rather than treating everyone in an identical fashion. Finally, it serves to make pay increments much more visible as an organizational reward, and hence increases the likelihood that individuals will perceive a link between effective performance and the receipt of rewards. Naturally, the greater visibility afforded by lump-sum increases will only be viewed as desirable by organizations that have in place an equitable pay system that effectively links pay to performance. If an organization's pay system is inequitable or does not tie pay to performance, then the greater visibility afforded by lump-sum increases will be more likely to create than eliminate problems.

Like all innovative approaches to pay, lump-sum increases are not without their drawbacks. They clearly create bookkeeping and record-keeping difficulties of keeping track of who has chosen which specific mode of receiving salary increases. Again, computerization has made such problems eminently manageable. A more serious problem has to do with the cost to the organization of providing individuals with the full amount of their increase at a single time, prior to the individual actually having earned it. Most organizations that employ lump-sum increases deal with this problem by treating a lump-sum increase as a loan on which the employee is charged a low rate of interest until the work has been done to earn the increase. Individuals who quit prior to the end of the year for which they have received a lump-sum increment are expected to repay that portion they have not earned (e.g., one third of the total if they were to quit eight months after receiving the lump sum and hence four months or one third of a year prior to "earning" the full increment). There will naturally be some losses associated with such a program from employees who leave without repaying the unearned amount of their lump-sum increases.

Overall, the advantages of lump-sum increases in terms of increased flexibility and visibility of the reward system appear to outweigh quite clearly the potential disadvantages.

OPEN SALARY INFORMATION

Pay secrecy is standard practice in most organizations. The precise amount of money being earned by individual members is treated as confidential information. The most common rationale for maintaining secrecy is that members of the organization prefer a secrecy policy and would not like others to know how much they are making. However, such a justification is almost always an assumption or fabrication on the part of managers when they are asked to explain why pay is kept secret. It is extremely rare that an organization has systematically polled its members and discovered that they do indeed prefer pay secrecy. An alternative explanation for the prevalence of pay secrecy is that it permits managers to avoid having to explain and justify their pay decisions to their subordinates.

Although pay secrecy does have this advantage of making life easier and less demanding for the manager making pay decisions, it also has a number of disadvantages for the organization. Research indicates that when pay is secret individuals consistently and significantly overestimate the amount of pay being received by others at the same level in the organization. The research further shows that the degree to which people overestimate the pay of others at the same level is directly related to levels of dissatisfaction. The more a person overestimates the pay of others, the more dissatisfied that person becomes. When pay rates are kept secret, the organization is incapable of correcting such false impressions since the organization's policy is to withhold precisely that information necessary to correct the erroneous impressions.

A further disadvantage of pay secrecy is that it reduces the potential of pay to serve as a positive motivating force. As we pointed out earlier, if pay is to motivate effective performance, two factors must be present. First, individuals must perceive that pay is related to performance, and second, an adequate level of trust must exist such that individuals trust that the organization will in the future reward them with more pay if they work hard now in order to perform effectively. Pay secrecy effectively undermines both of these essential factors. First, since pay is secret it is extremely difficult for the individual to determine whether or not the organization does or does not relate pay to performance. The individual has only his or her own personal experience to go on and is denied access to information regarding how the organization treats all the rest of its members. Second, a policy of pay secrecy is itself a manifestation of a low level of trust between the organization and its members. This low level of trust again impedes the capacity of the pay system to motivate effective performance.

The obvious alternative to pay secrecy is a policy of openness regarding pay. By sharing pay information openly, the organization can contribute to the creation of a climate of greater trust and can help clarify for employees the relationship between pay and performance. Both these factors can lead to increased motivation if it is in fact the case that the organization's pay system does relate pay to performance. If the pay system does not successfully tie pay to performance, then sharing pay information will make the inequities more obvious and clearly would not be expected to increase motivation.

A further potential advantage of an open pay system lies in the fact that it may encourage members to make better and more equitable pay decisions. When pay is secret there may be little motivation for the manager to give a lot of attention to pay decisions since he or she knows that there is little if any chance that those decisions will be challenged or questioned. On the negative side, however, an organization implementing an open pay policy must take care that managers do not respond by paying all of their subordinates equally in order to avoid having to explain and justify their decisions. Such a practice would obviously undermine any potential benefits to be gained from open pay information.

A decision to switch from a policy of pay secrecy to one of open salary information must obviously be handled with care. If an organization is characterized by a long history of pay secrecy and low levels of trust, an abrupt switch to open pay information may be neither feasible nor desirable. A gradual opening of pay information may be more effective in such situations, beginning, for example, with publication of salary ranges and averages for various positions and moving gradually over time to full, open salary information. An organization must also attend to difficulties in measuring performance when implementing open salary information. As jobs become more complex, the criteria for evaluating performance effectiveness frequently become more ambiguous. In such situations, a policy of full salary openness may not be desirable, since individuals may disagree about the quality of performance of different individuals.

What is critical for all types of jobs at all levels is for managers to rethink their policies regarding pay information. Keeping pay information secret because "we've always done it that way" or because it makes life easier for the managers who don't have to justify their decisions is scant justification for a policy that clearly undermines the potential of pay to serve as a positive motivator of effective performance.

PARTICIPATIVE PAY DECISIONS

A relatively recent innovation that has been tried by some organizations is to involve individuals in the process of setting salaries by permitting all members of the organization to participate directly in pay decisions. Several organizations that have permitted employees to participate directly in the design of salary or bonus systems found that the participatively designed systems resulted in improved attendance, reduced turnover, and higher levels of satisfaction (Lawler, 1976; Jenkins & Lawler, 1981). Other organizations that have permitted decisions regarding annual pay increments to be made by work peers have found that peer groups tend to make such decisions in a highly responsible manner and that such a system results in a high degree of satisfaction with pay and a high level of commitment to the organization.

Naturally, a participative approach to pay decisions is not without its potential difficulties, particularly in situations in which pay decisions are made by work peers and no clear-cut standards of performance (such as number of items produced and sales volume) are available. When the organization places no restriction on the total amount of money available for salary increases, peer groups frequently find it hard to say no to a raise for each member. On the other hand, when the organization does put a limit on total raises available and performance standards aren't clear-cut, there is a tendency for a peer group to decide on equal raises for everyone in order to avoid conflict and disagreement. Such an approach undermines the capacity of the pay system to motivate effective performance since all receive an equal increment regardless of their performance. Finally, as is the case with all types of participative management, the participative process itself is time-consuming and results in a reduction in the total time available for individuals to devote to their primary work responsibilities.

REFERENCES

Glueck, W. F. *Personnel: A diagnostic approach* (Rev. ed.). Dallas: Business Publications, 1978.

Jenkins, G. D., Jr., & Lawler, E. E., III.   Impact of employee participation in pay plan development. *Organizational Behavior and Human Performance*, 1981, *28*, 111–128.

Lawler, E. E., III. New approaches to pay: Innovations that work. *Personnel*, 1976, *53*(5), 11–23.

15
Employee Stock Ownership Plans: A New Way to Work*

COREY ROSEN

Since the Industrial Revolution, it has always been assumed that a few people would actually own the means of production and everyone else would work for them. Any other alternative, it seemed, was socialistic—or worse. In the last 10 years, however, more and more American businesses are taking a new approach—they're making their workers owners.

About 5,000 companies now have employee ownership plans, and a majority of the stock of at least 500 of these is owned by employees. These companies range from small businesses to industrial giants. A hypothetical executive might in any one day use several products made by employee-owned companies. He might, for instance, get up in the morning and have a glass of Juice Bowl orange juice, Starflower granola, Celestial Seasonings tea, and Rath bacon while perusing his *Milwaukee Journal*. Later, he might scan *U.S. News & World Report*

---

* From *Business Horizons*, 1983, *26*, pp. 48–54. Copyright © 1983 by the Foundation for the School of Business, Indiana University.

and the *Daily Tax Report* from the Bureau of National Affairs. When he returns home, he might don his running shoes made out of Gore-Tex and go to sleep under his George Washington bedspread made by Bates Fabric. All of those products would be produced by companies substantially owned by their employees.

The perhaps surprising fact is that employee ownership has moved into the mainstream of American business. It has received the blessings of Congress through a whole series of tax breaks, and has been endorsed by such disparate figures as Russell Long (its most active proponent), Ted Kennedy, Ronald Reagan, and even Pope John Paul. Some companies are interested in employee ownership simply because it provides tax breaks, but most are attracted to the possibility of creating a new, and more productive, way to work. By making employees owners, the argument goes, everyone becomes a capitalist, with the result that everyone works harder and more effectively. So far, the evidence seems to bear this theory out, but it also raises some very distinct warnings. Employee ownership can work very well indeed, it seems to be saying, but it is not magic, and only well-designed plans will live up to expectations.

HOW EMPLOYEE OWNERSHIP PLANS WORK

There are lots of ways to make employees owners, but a vehicle created by Congress in 1974 called an ESOP (employee stock ownership plan) is overwhelmingly the ownership plan of choice.

An ESOP works by creating an employee stock ownership trust (ESOT). The rules of the ESOP are drawn to meet all the requirements of ERISA (the Employee Retirement Income Security Act), which governs employee benefit plans generally. Plans meeting these rules are called "qualified," meaning that companies can take tax deductions or, in some cases, credits, for contributions to them, at least within certain limits.[1]

Companies contribute either stock or cash to buy stock for the trust, where it is allocated to employee accounts and held until the employee leaves the company or retires. Under the law, allocations can be made according to relative compensation or some more egalitarian formula, but they cannot be made in a way that would favor higher paid employees proportionately more than lower paid employees. The amount of stock allocated to employees is not yet theirs, however. In order to encourage employees to stay with the company, most plans

---

[1] For more detailed information, see "ESOPs: An Employer Handbook," U.S. Senate Committee on Finance, Washington, D.C.: 1979; "Employee Ownership: A Handbook," National Center for Employee Ownership, Arlington, Va.: 1982.

use a gradual vesting schedule under which employees acquire an increasing right to the shares as the years go by. Typically, employees are not vested for the first 3 years, then vested 30 percent after the third year, 40 percent after the fourth, and so on up to 10. Generally, vesting must be completed by the 10th year (but it can sometimes be the 15th), though it can be completed as fast as a company wants.

In most cases, all full-time employees who have worked at least 1,000 hours in one year must be eligible to participate in the ESOP. It is possible, although generally not a good idea (as we shall see later), to limit the ESOP to just one class of employees, such as office workers, but only if such a limitation is not a way to reward more highly compensated employees. Employees covered by a collective bargaining agreement can also be excluded, but they must have the right to negotiate in.

The stock in the trust must have full voting rights in companies whose stock is publicly traded. In other companies, employees must be able to vote their allocated shares only on those issues which by state law or corporate charter require more than a majority vote. Companies can pass through full voting rights, however, and about 15 percent of them do.[2] Companies that do not have a ready market for their stock must also agree to buy the stock back from their departing employees within a reasonable period of time (generally five years), and with interest if the payment is not immediate. The company can, however, also exercise a right of first refusal on the stock to make sure it stays in friendly hands. In order to determine how much the stock being contributed or purchased is worth, closely held companies must have a regular outside valuation done.

Stock contributed to the trust is not taxable to the employee until it is distributed, at which time it can be rolled over into an IRA (in which case no taxes are paid until withdrawals are made), or can be treated according to capital gains or 10-year averaging for most of the amount.

ESOPs also are governed by two very special rules concerning how the company may use them. First, ESOPs are required to invest primarily in the stock of the employer. Second, ESOPs may borrow money. The first rule makes it practical to use an ESOP as a device to make employees owners. Other plans can invest in employer stock too, but generally cannot hold more than 10 percent of their assets in such stock. If they do, they must be able to show that that decision is fiduciarily sound, which can be hard to do considering all the other

---

[2] Thomas Marsh and Dale McAllister, "ESOPs Tables: A Survey of Companies with Employee Stock Ownership Plans," *Journal of Corporation Law*, Spring 1981, pp. 593–94.

investment possibilities. Yet if an employee benefit plan owns only a little employer stock and many other things, it will be hard to convince employees that they are really owners.

The second rule allows companies to use the ESOP to raise capital in a manner that can save tax dollars. Say the Modern Baking Company wants to borrow money for new pie-making machinery. Normally, it would go to the bank, borrow the dollars, and then deduct the interest when it repaid them. If Modern Baking were to use an ESOP, however, it would have the ESOT go to the bank (Modern Baker executives actually, acting for the ESOT) and borrow the money. The ESOT would then use the cash to buy new issues of company stock, meaning the company would get the cash it needs and the ESOT would provide ownership for employees. To repay the loan, the company would make *deductible* cash contributions to the trust. What that means is that the company is deducting, in effect, both the principal and the interest from the loan repayment. Moreover, with the same dollars it uses to finance growth, it is creating an employee benefit plan that (you've guessed it by now) provides the employees not just with a piece of the pie, but the pie-making machinery.

SOME SPECIFIC USES OF THE ESOP

For most companies, an ESOP is basically an employee benefit plan. Since companies can contribute new issues of stock to the ESOP, it provides a way to provide a benefit without paying any cash up front. Even better, the company can take a tax deduction for the value of the stock it contributes. The company is betting, of course, that the extra productivity the plan generates will create enough growth so that when employees start to leave the company, there will be cash to pay them off. Good plans anticipate this by making periodic cash contributions to the ESOP to enable it to buy the stock itself.

Another common use of ESOPs is creating a market for the stock of an owner in a closely held firm. Many smaller companies are closed or liquidated even though they are profitable simply because no one can be found who is willing to take all the risks that buying them would entail. Even where buyers can be found, owners often prefer to see their employees keep their business tradition going. ESOPs provide a mechanism for addressing this problem. The owner can make deductible cash contributions out of company earnings to allow the ESOP to purchase his or her stock. Alternatively, the ESOP can borrow the cash needed to buy out the owner. In either case, the sale is treated as a capital gain, even though normally a gradual sale of stock by an owner back to the company is treated as dividend income and taxed as ordinary income would be.

A third common use of an ESOP is in cases where employees want to buy a company outright, either because it is failing or because the parent firm wants to divest that operation. Employee buyouts have become increasingly common in recent years although, contrary to popular impression, they are only a small part of the employee ownership movement. To accomplish a buyout, the employees form a new shell corporation, which sets up an ESOP. The ESOP borrows money to buy the assets of the old company. It then trades the assets for all the stock in the new firm and, presto, the employees own the company. As in any leveraged ESOP, the new company makes tax-deductible contributions to the trust to enable it to repay the loan. In some cases, employees may agree to wage concessions to help assure that their new firm will have the cash flow needed for repayment.

In a related use, ongoing, but distressed, companies are now beginning to trade stock for wage concessions. Pan Am, Conrail, McClouth Steel, and a number of other firms have used this approach. Essentially, the workers are saying that if they make concessions, they are investing in the company and should, like any investor, get an ownership share.

ESOPs can also be used to acquire companies (the trust takes out a loan to acquire the assets of the target firm), to divest subsidiaries, to go private, or, as in the leveraging model described earlier, to raise capital. One special kind of ESOP, the so-called PAYSOP (payroll-based ESOP) also deserves mention. Starting this year [1983], employers can take a tax credit equal to 0.5 percent of payroll (0.75 percent in 1985–1987) for contributions to a specially regulated ESOP. The plan, which generally must be separate from a conventional ESOP, must provide immediate vesting, must not distribute benefits for seven years, and must ignore compensation in excess of $100,000 when allocating stock. According to a recent survey, 70 percent of all major companies either have a PAYSOP or plan to install one.[3] These plans provide such a small amount of stock, however, that, in themselves, they really do not create what would normally be understood as employee ownership.

FINANCIAL DISADVANTAGES OF ESOPs

Despite their much-touted benefits, ESOPs have some significant financial limitations. First, the tax benefits are, obviously, of use only if a firm is making a profit or expects to make one soon. Unused deductions or credits can be carried forward 15 years, but, practically, the real dollar value of deductions used so far in the future is minimal.

---

[3] *Bureau of National Affairs Tax Report,* October 21, 1982, #204: G-1.

Second, any of the ESOP tax benefits are up-front. Down the road, as employees start to leave, the company has a new liability. That means that if the company has not put aside the cash needed to repurchase this stock, it could be in trouble. The ability to put this cash aside will, of course, depend on the company's profitability. For this and the above reason, most ESOP consultants contend that ESOPs are appropriate only for financially healthy firms, and are best for ones with growth prospects.

Third, ESOPs cause a dilution in the equity of other owners where new treasury stock is issued to the trust. Whether this dilution causes a decline in shareholder values depends on whether the ESOP itself creates at least an equivalent amount of value. In a leveraged plan, for instance, the ESOP is being used to acquire new capital, meaning the shareholders now own a smaller percentage of a larger pie. In any ESOP, the extra productivity the ESOP can create can offset or more than offset the dilution effect. Whenever the ESOP passes through voting rights on the stock, however, there is necessarily a dilution in voting control. Whether or not that is an issue, of course, depends on the company.

Finally, ESOP legal fees are high, although model plans developed by the National Center for Employee Ownership and others may help keep costs down. Normally, an ESOP costs a minimum of $10,000 to $15,000 to install, with costs rising with the size of the company. Yearly valuations and administrative costs can add a few thousand dollars every year. Although some very small companies do have ESOPs, and are happy with them, firms with fewer than ten employees need to consider the costs and benefits very carefully.

HOW ESOPs HAVE WORKED

All these financial considerations are of little consequence, though, if employee ownership fails its real test—improving employee performance. So far, the idea is still too new to have received the thorough testing needed to produce a definitive answer. The initial evidence, however, has been very striking.

A 1978 study by the Institute for Social Research at the University of Michigan, for instance, found that companies with employee ownership plans were 150 percent as profitable as comparable companies without them, and that the ratio was directly related to the amount of equity employees owned (the more they owned, the higher was the ratio).[4] A survey of more than 200 ESOP companies reported in the

[4] Michael Conte and Arnold Tannenbaum, *Employee Ownership*, Ann Arbor: University of Michigan Survey Research Center, 1981.

Journal of Corporation Law found that the ESOP firms had an average annual productivity growth rate of 1.52 percent greater than comparable conventional firms.[5] When one considers that average annual U.S. productivity for the period studied grew at only 0.2 percent per year (in the 1960s it was around 3 percent), the magnitude of the difference becomes apparent. Perhaps most impressive are data gathered at Cornell University, where William Whyte and his colleagues have been tracking the approximately 60 employee buyouts of distressed firms that have occurred since 1971. All but four of these are still in business, and most have become profitable.[6] Chicago and Northwestern Railroad, the first major buyout, saw its stock value go up over 100 times. Its first owner, Ben Heilman of Northwest Industries, had complained that the rate of return on the line was "disgusting."

A wide variety of case studies bear these data out, and no methodologically reliable study has yet been done which, on a case or survey basis, suggests that ownership does not contribute to productivity. Still, two major surveys and a handful of case studies cannot prove the point, although they certainly are suggestive.

FOUR ESOP FABLES

Four companies—W. L. Gore and Associates, Allied Plywood, the Lowe's Companies, and Saratoga Knitting Mills—typify the positive uses of employee-ownership plans.

W. L. Gore is a high-technology manufacturer of a variety of products, including Gore-Tex, a fabric coating that is commonly used in outdoor products. The company is 95 percent owned by employees, or, to be more precise, associates. According to Gore, there are no employees, since everyone owns stock and everyone participates in company affairs. In fact, the company uses what it calls a "lattice" organization in which anyone can communicate with anyone else, without having to go up and down the traditional corporate hierarchies. Employees vote all their stock and elect the board.

The high level of employee involvement may seem to some a recipe for chaos, but Gore has grown at an annual compound rate of 40 percent for the last several years, and now employs 2,000 employees. It is currently building another seven plants around the world.

Allied Plywood, by contrast, is a small plywood distributor in Northern Virginia. Ed Sanders, the company's founder, had built the

---

[5] Marsh and McAllister, "ESOPs Tables," pp. 612–15.
[6] Correspondence with William F. Whyte, Cornell University School of Industrial and Labor Relations, 1981–82.

company in the course of his business career. In the mid-1970s he began to think about cashing in his stock and retiring. At first, he simply had the company redeem his stock, but, to his dismay, found that the IRS asked for 70 percent of the price (the top rate at the time). Fortunately, he chanced on a letter to the editor of the *Washington Post* which described how a company could be sold to its employees through an ESOP. Since he had always considered his 20 employees almost part of the family, this seemed like an ideal approach. Sanders proceeded to set up the ESOP and make annual cash contributions to it. The ESOP took the contributions and bought his shares, with Sanders now paying just capital gains. In 1982, the ESOP took out a loan to buy the remaining 45 percent of the stock Sanders then owned, and the company became 100 percent employee-owned.

Since the ESOP was established, only one employee has left, and that was for personal reasons. Sales have increased, but the number of employees hasn't—a testimony to the fact that as owners the employees want to maximize company earning. Job satisfaction, according to a National Center for Employee Ownership survey, is very high. Perhaps most importantly, the company has been consistently profitable even in the midst of the construction industry depression.

The Lowe's Companies are a notable example of using an ESOP as an employee benefit plan. Lowe's set up an employee ownership plan in 1957. Although technically not an ESOP, the plan operated much like the ESOPs now in use. In 1978, in fact, the plan was formally converted to an ESOP. Lowe's employs 7,000 people in a chain of home improvement and building supply stores throughout the Southeast. Under its ESOP, employees own 25 percent of the company—a figure Lowe's President Bob Strickland hopes will grow.

When the Lowe's employee ownership plan was started, the company had six stores. Today it has 205. When the plan started, there were five competitors. Three have since sold out, one is only one fourth the size of Lowe's, and the other has just started an ESOP. Lowe's success has filtered down to its employee owners. The company made news in 1975, for instance, when an 18-year employee who never made more than $125 per week cashed in his ESOP shares for $660,000. Six- and even a few seven-figure checks are a regular part of the ESOP program now.

Lowe's plan is not charity, however. Former President Carl Buchan started the plan because he wanted to "give employees a direct, personal self-interest in improving the company's earnings." Strickland says the concept has worked. Sales per employee are three times those of the big three retailers, while profits per employee are twice as high. Shrinkage is less than 0.5 percent. According to Strickland, Lowe's success is a direct function of its employee ownership plan.

Saratoga Knitting Mills, a manufacturer of tricot fabric for women's intimate apparel, presents a very different picture. The company had been a subsidiary of Cluett-Peabody, but in 1975 that conglomerate decided to shut down the mill, claiming its profit potential was inadequate. Together with some outside investors, the employees arranged for a buyout. The ESOP now owns 51 percent of the stock.

In 1975, the company had 64 employees. Today, its stock value has tripled and it employs 134. An ESOP-based acquisition is possible. Productivity is up, waste is down. Scrap loss, for instance, was cut from 1.5 percent to 0.28 percent.

AND SOME FOIBLES

These four cases illustrate the potential of employee ownership, but it should be understood that it would be equally easy to give examples of companies that either fail to realize that potential or simply abuse the idea. Of course, these companies are not eager to have their names in print, but their general characteristics can be identified.

At one company we have studied, for instance, employees own about 9 percent of the stock, but there are no voting or other participation rights associated with the stock. Employees do not think of themselves as owners; if anything, the ESOP has made them somewhat skeptical of management. When employees own so little stock, there simply is no reason to believe that there will be any change in their behavior. The typical ESOP in a closely held firm owns at least 20 percent of the company's stock. Our initial research is indicating that the threshold level at which ownership becomes real to employees is probably around this number in smaller firms. In larger companies, where a smaller percentage means more in terms of control and dollar values, a smaller percentage will probably do the trick. The typical Fortune 500 PAYSOP, however, where employees own less than 1 percent of the stock, will have no significant impact.[7]

Another company made its employees 100 percent owners, and constantly reminded them of this fact, but did not provide any ownership rights. One consultant has suggested that these plans be called "ESAPs"—employee stock appreciation plans—since that is what they really provide. The result was that employees became skeptical about management's motives. Although they appreciated the extra benefit the ESOP represented, they really did not feel like owners, and there was little evidence that they acted that way either. An even

---

[7] Corey Rosen, "Employee Ownership in the Fortune 500," *Employee Benefit Plan Review Research Report No. 208*, May 1982, pp. 1–5.

more dramatic case is South Bend Lathe, where employees bought the company through an ESOP, but did not acquire voting rights for the stock. That was handled by a trust committee appointed by the management. A few years ago, workers at South Bend Lathe, upset about wages and other policies, went on strike.

The essential lesson these companies are teaching is that "ownership" is a very connotative word. Companies that want their employees to act like owners need to treat them like owners. If they simply want to provide an employee benefit plan, with the hopes that it will improve motivation in much the same way a profit-sharing plan might, then they should not call their employees owners. The term may be technically correct, but it is bound to cause confusion and even cynicism.

Treating employees like owners will mean different things in different companies. Voting rights may or may not be crucial, but a clear sense among employees that they have some control over what they do, and that their ideas are treated with respect, is crucial indeed. Companies that provide full participating rights, in our experience, are uniformly pleased with their decision, reporting that employees are responsible shareholders and that employee motivation is very high.

In fact, the joining of employee ownership and participation seems to provide a very effective combination. Although data on this point are scarce, our own experience, and that of consultants in the field, suggests that employee owners are much more ready to participate effectively at the job and company level. Since an overwhelming literature now confirms the productivity gains that can be made from worker participation, this is a very important connection.[8]

A third company had its stock valued at $10 per share. The owner then wanted to get a bank loan for the ESOP to buy his shares at $70 per share, claiming that this is what he could get on the open market. The bank turned him down. He was lucky they did, for the transaction would have been illegal. These kinds of manipulations of share values, as well as a variety of other practices, violate the basic principle of ESOP law—that the plan operate for "the exclusive benefit of the employees." "Exclusive" does not mean that other people cannot benefit, but whenever there is a conflict between the interests of the employees and some other party, however, the employees come first. Companies that set up plans solely for their tax benefits run a good risk of violating this principle.

Finally, there is the company that had installed an ESOP, but most

---

[8] Carl Frieden, *Workplace Democracy and Productivity*, Washington, D.C.: Center for Economic Alternatives, 1980.

of whose employees didn't know it. As this article suggests, ESOPs are complicated. An effective and ongoing communications program is essential to making an ownership plan work.

The real question a company must ask itself in considering an ESOP, then, is, "Do we really want to share ownership with employees?" If the answer is yes, research and experience indicate that everyone can benefit. By sharing ownership (and, it appears, control as well), the company actually grows, making both management and workers better off.

THE FUTURE OF EMPLOYEE OWNERSHIP

For all its rapid growth, and for all the recent attention it has garnered, employee ownership is still just a footnote to the American economic system. For it to become a basic part of the way we do business, a number of things need to happen.

First, businesses need to be convinced that employee ownership contributes to the bottom line. The data so far are enticing, but not yet decisive. Moreover, most businesspeople still have only a vague familiarity with the concept. It will take, then, more positive results, more publicity, and, mostly, more word of mouth, before the idea really settles into the consciousness of American entrepreneurs and managers. Whether or not this will happen is still uncertain.

Second, business must feel pressure to change and innovate. It has only been recently that American businesses have had to reexamine some of their basic conceptions about management styles and employee relations. Whether the current openness to change remains will presumably depend upon the continued existence of external competitive threats. That, alas, seems likely.

Third, labor unions need to take a more positive approach. Until recently, most unions opposed employee ownership plans, contending that they clouded the union role, were too often used in desperate situations (an inaccurate perception, but a powerful one), and were a threat to pension plans. In the last year or two, however, some national unions, such as the UAW and the Communications Workers, have endorsed the idea and many others are reexamining their position. As unions look for a new relationship to management, it is conceivable that employee ownership could become part of their bargaining agenda. At this time, however, that still seems far off.

The final determinant of the future of employee ownership is whether employees will seek it. As far back as 1975, a Peter Hart opinion poll indicated that Americans would rather work for an employee-owned firm by a three to one margin. As the American worker becomes more educated, moreover, it seems reasonable to assume, as work psychologists have, that more will be demanded from work than just a salary. This trend might well be juxtaposed against an increasing interest in the workplace as a community, one to replace the communities a mobile America is losing. Since people desire to have some control over their communities, they might begin to demand more control over their workplace.

Whatever may come of these trends, employee ownership does seem to represent a very practical alternative for the American economy, one that deserves careful consideration.

section three

Organizations and People: Patterns of Conflict and Accommodation

Introduction

So far as is known, no work organization to date has provided a means of completely reconciling its goals and operations with the needs and interests of all its members. In part, this statement reflects the inevitable condition that participants have discordant preference orderings among themselves, giving rise to political processes (examined in Section Four) in which trade-offs are made and viable goals are established. Furthermore, the structural devices that create the very condition of organization place constraints upon behavior. And since these devices are both designed and administered by human beings, with all of the limitations and temptations that implies, we know that instances of abuse to some members will occur, whether by accident or plan.

Increasingly, one hears these days of the "stress" suffered by people at work. Organ examines the varying interpretations of what is meant by this term and the implications for health, emotions, performance, and adaptation.

Sims and Gioia examine an organizational phenomenon that is familiar to all of us, but seldom analyzed: disagreement about the causes of poor performance. This form of dispute stems from fundamental perceptual processes in the actor (or subordinate) and observer (boss). Rosen and Jerdee then provide evidence of still another problem area originating in the perceptual process: the influence of widespread, uncritically accepted stereotypes on managerial decisions about people—in this case, the older employee.

A continued cause of dismay to many observers of American business is the earnings gap between men and women. Some analysts contend that the differential follows from impersonal market forces; others say the cause is discrimination and argue for compensation based on the inherent "comparable worth" of the jobs people perform. Mahoney examines the economic, philosophical, and administrative dimensions of this issue and assesses the prospects for its amicable resolution.

Some individuals, whether by temperament or prior conditioning, are predisposed to accept without quarrel the constraints and discipline of work; others are not. Merrens and Garrett empirically assess the notion of the "Protestant ethic" as a trait which accounts for these differences.

In the reckoning of some students of organization, turnover of personnel represents the ultimate index of poor management. Yet, ironically, while turnover may indicate unresolved points of conflict between people and organizations, Dalton and Todor provide a strong case for turnover itself as a constructive means of improving the fortunes of the individual as well as the organization. They view a certain degree of turnover as a sign of a healthy labor market, a mechanism for the diffusion of innovation across firms, a benefit for careers, and a necessary condition for social progress.

16

The Meanings of Stress*

DENNIS W. ORGAN

> Stress has become a modern watchword with a variety of meanings, both popular and scientific. Recent studies in the physiology of stress have important implications for executive behavior.

Everybody knows about it, everyone talks about it, and—judging by the number of paperback books and magazine articles currently devoted to the subject—everyone seems to be interested in it. People complain about the stress of work and the stress of retirement; the stress of poverty and the stress created by fame and riches; the stress of crowding and the stress of isolation; the stress of adolescence and the stress of the midlife crisis. To describe someone as "working under enormous stress" is at once to offer sympathy and to accord a measure of respect. To fail at a task *because* of stress is no shame; to succeed *in spite of* stress renders success all the more glorious. Any behavior, no matter how bizarre, cruel, or apparently irrational, is suddenly understandable if we imagine the behaver as operating under stress. Any act of love or benevolence is somehow tarnished if it did not create stress for the actor or was not born out of the very crucible of stress.

Stress, in sum, has become a watchword of the time, a sibilant one-syllable utterance that comes as close as any one word to expressing the subjective tone of a world view. But the term has developed an elasticity of meaning. The word functions more and more to express rather than to denote. Thus the term becomes more susceptible to usage when it can be neither proved nor disproved, and when it is therefore neither meaningful nor helpful. This would not be cause for concern if stress were merely a vernacular term like *love, anger, ambition,* or *luck*. Certain words are useful precisely because they are preserved for signifying what is, after all, ineffable. *Stress*, however, is also a scientific term. Now there would be no problem if the scientific use of stress were strictly divorced from its vernacular usage; after all, one seldom experiences any problem distinguishing between the ten-

* From *Business Horizons* 22, no. 3 (1979), pp. 32–40. Copyright, 1979, by the Foundation for the School of Business at Indiana University. Reprinted by permission.

sion of a wire and the tension of studying for an exam, or between the pressure exerted by a liquid in a container and the pressure experienced when one is working on a tight schedule. In both cases the technical terms are precise, and the nontechnical meanings are vague and inchoate. One will at times belabor the analogies for literary or rhetorical effect, but no one seriously tries to apply the laws of physics to studying for an exam or working under a deadline. Unfortunately, the vernacular and technical meanings of "stress" have become thoroughly confused, possibly because they do overlap to some degree. The confusion has occasioned some serious misunderstanding about the relationships between stress and illness, stress and adaptation, stress and performance, and even stress and life.

VERNACULAR MEANINGS

In everyday discourse, "stress" has a pejorative connotation. If used in reference to something outside us, it generally means something to be avoided or, at best, a necessary evil: a critical, hard-driving boss; congested urban traffic; a final exam; preparing an income tax return on the night of April 14; enduring Howard Cosell's commentary while you watch the Cowboys and the Vikings. If used to describe a subjective feeling, the term is roughly synonymous with tension, dread, anxiety, or worry. Occasionally we do, of course, dilute the pejorative color of the term by associating it with achievements of one sort or another, as when a speaker welcomes the "edge" of stress (tension) before taking the podium, or the stress (pain) of training and preparing for the Boston Marathon. Yet even then the term is used in what is essentially as intrinsically negative sense, "good" only because it is inextricably linked to an eventual outcome (success, victory) which is sought. In brief, we use the term in everyday parlance to mean either a source or cause of discomfort, or the feelings of discomfort itself—that is, "distress."

Now there is nothing wrong or incorrect in using the word in this manner. In fact, the dictionary will confirm that this is a perfectly acceptable form of usage. It is wrong only when one substitutes this definition of stress for the precise technical meaning of stress in statements about relationships between stress and illness, performance, and adaptation. As a technical term in medical science, stress is not something "out there," nor is it a state of mind. Both external circumstances and internal emotional states can be *stressors*, or sources of stress (although neither the circumstances nor the emotion need be unpleasant, undesired, or negative in order to qualify as stressors). But stress itself, as a technical term, refers to a pattern of complex, albeit well-defined physiological reactions.

STRESS AS A PHYSIOLOGICAL STATE

Stress became a scientific construct when it was defined and elaborated in the research and writing of Professor Hans Selye. As a young medical student at the University of Prague in 1925, Selye was struck by the observation that certain symptoms seemed to correlate with illness of all types. A physician could not complete a diagnosis for a patient based on the evidence that he was suffering from headaches, loss of appetite, nausea, and weakness in the muscles; the doctor would need something more "specific" in order to determine what the underlying problem was. Selye wondered if there might not be something of significance to this observation, namely that the body has a stereotyped, nonspecific reaction to any demand placed upon it. He later discovered in experiments with laboratory animals that whether one subjected rats to extreme cold, injected chemical irritants into their tissue, or simply forcefully immobilized them, there were certain common reactions in the animal's physiological processes. Of course, there were specific effects associated with each particular treatment, but Selye was interested in the common denominators—the invariant response of the organism's body to any demand placed upon it. The common features constituted what Selye labeled the general adaptation syndrome, or G.A.S.—the symptoms by which a state of stress is manifested.

Selye's *The Stress of Life*, published in 1956 and written for nontechnically trained audiences, makes it clear that one of the conspicuous agents in this syndrome is the pituitary, a cherry-sized organ resting at the base of the brain. When some external force (a germ, overload on a muscle group, extreme cold) threatens the body, the pituitary signals the alarm stage, the first of the three-stage G.A.S., by sending ACTH (the adrenocorticotrophic hormone) to the endocrine glands, including the adrenals. The adrenals, in response, secrete their hormones (adrenalin and noradrenalin, collectively called the catecholamines) into the bloodstream, and eventually these in collaboration with the sympathetic nervous system trigger a succession of changes in the body chemistry, including changes in the digestive organs, metabolism, and the level of fatty acids and clotting elements in the blood. These effects triggered by the adrenals constitute the second stage of Selye's G.A.S., the stage of resistance, during which the organism seemingly adapts to the demand placed upon it, enabling it to neutralize, isolate, or minimize the damage to the integrity of the organism as a whole. Given sufficiently long exposure to any of the noxious elements (severe cold, chemical irritant, electric shock), the third stage, exhaustion, follows as the adaptive energies of the organism are depleted.

For Selye, then, stress means the common denominator of all adaptive reactions by the body to stressors placed upon it. While Selye means demands of any kind, his interest is clearly in those demands which are clearly physical in nature. Psychologists have, on the other hand, been more interested in demands which are more subtle—demands originating from the social environment, demands cued by symbols, or demands exerted by the emotions and the psyche. Such demands are quite relevant to the concept of stress as defined by Selye because of the mediating role played by the hypothalamus, one of the lower centers of the brain. The hypothalamus regulates many functions of the body, including hunger and temperature; it regulates emotions; and, under conditions of emotional arousal (fear, anger, even ecstasy), sends messages to the pituitary which trigger the sequence of events described in Selye's endocrine studies. It is important, however, to note that any strong emotional response—whether interpreted as "good" or "bad," or even whether a person is consciously aware of or attending to the emotion—results in stress as defined by Selye.

But the emotion is the stressor, not the stress itself; the emotion is the source of the demand which triggers the stress response. The demand need not be emotional in nature to evoke the stress response. So when we speak of *psychological stress* in a way which is at all faithful to the technical meaning of stress, we mean demands or sources of stress that are psychological in nature—for example, anxiety, frustration, or approach-avoidance conflict. There are other demands on the body which evoke the stress response yet arouse no strong feelings at all, and we find that many instances of emotional arousal not ordinarily thought of as "stressful" (in the vernacular) do in fact lead to stress as defined by Selye.

STRESS AND FEELINGS

Consider the results of an experiment conducted by Dr. Lennart Levi of the Karolinska Institute in Stockholm.[1] On successive evenings he arranged for 20 female clerical workers to see four films. The first of these was a bland movie about the Swedish countryside. The other movies were selected for their presumed ability to arouse some strong emotion: "Paths of Glory," a movie about the arbitrary execution of three men as scapegoats following a breakdown of a French army unit in World War I, was considered to be anger-provoking; "Charley's Aunt," a comedy, was expected to induce a pleasant emotional arousal; and "The Mask of Satan," a horror film, was selected to

---

[1] Lennart Levi, *Stress and Distress in Response to Psychosocial Stimuli* (New York: Pergamon Press, 1972), pp. 55–73.

arouse fear and anxiety. The films had their intended effects, as shown by the subjects' ratings and descriptions of the movies as well as their reports of their own reactions. The natural scenery film they judged to be rather boring; they felt aggressive and angry watching "Paths of Glory"; amused, happy, and laughing at "Charley's Aunt"; and frightened by "Mask of Satan." In other words, subjects "felt" different emotions for the different movies. Levi found, however, in an analysis of subjects' urine samples following each movie, that except for the dull scenery film the movies were equally stressful, regardless of whether the film provoked a "pleasant" or "unpleasant" emotion. All three of the movies inducing emotional arousal were associated with increased levels of adrenalin and noradrenalin in the urine, a tell-tale indicator of the stress syndrome defined by Selye.

STRESS AND ILLNESS

The accompanying table shows a list of changes or events that can occur in a person's life. With each event a number is associated that serves as a rough index of the relative degree of adjustment demanded by the event. The weighting scheme was derived through studies by Professors T. H. Holmes and R. H. Rahe and their colleagues at the University of Washington.[2] Their studies asked people of varying ages and from several different cultures to compare each event with each other in terms of the degree of adjustment required. It seems to be universally agreed that the death of a spouse requires more adjustment on the part of the surviving spouse than any other single event. The table provides a rough measure of the degree of adjustment required of a person by totaling the number of points associated with each change in a given period.

Holmes and his co-workers find that once a person "earns" 200 or more points in a single year, there is at least a 50–50 chance of experiencing a fairly serious breakdown in health in the following year. One who totals up 300 or more points in a year runs that risk factor up to a 75–80 percent chance. The illness brought on by such demands for adjustment can appear in almost every specific form: digestive ailments, respiratory problems, back trouble, kidney malfunction, injuries to the bones or muscles, almost any breakdown in the body's economy. What is the explanation for this relationship? Significant changes in one's immediate life environment trigger a rapid succession of new situations with which one has to cope. The endocrine system—the intricate collaborative workings of the pituitary, the adre-

[2] T. H. Holmes and R. H. Rahe, "The Social Readjustment Rating Scale," *Journal of Psychosomatic Research*, November 1968, pp. 213–218.

Social Readjustment Rating Scale

Life Event	Scale Value
Death of spouse	100
Divorce	73
Marital separation	65
Jail term	63
Death of a close family member	63
Major personal injury or illness	53
Marriage	50
Fired from work	47
Marital reconciliation	45
Retirement	45
Major change in health of family member	44
Pregnancy	40
Sex difficulties	39
Gain of a new family member	39
Business readjustment	39
Change in financial state	38
Death of a close friend	37
Change to a different line of work	36
Change in number of arguments with spouse	35
Mortgage over $10,000	31
Foreclosure of mortgage or loan	30
Change in responsibilities at work	29
Son or daughter leaving home	29
Trouble with in-laws	29
Outstanding personal achievement	28
Wife begins or stops work	26
Begin or end school	26
Change in living conditions	25
Revision of personal habits	24
Trouble with boss	23
Change in work hours or conditions	20
Change in residence	20
Change in schools	20
Change in recreation	19
Change in church activities	19
Change in social activities	18
Mortgage or loan less than $10,000	17
Change in sleeping habits	16
Change in number of family get-togethers	15
Change in eating habits	15
Vacation	13
Christmas	12
Minor violations of the law	11

Source: L. O. Ruch and T. H. Holmes, "Scaling of Life Change: Comparison of Direct and Indirect Methods," *Journal of Psychosomatic Research,* June 1971, p. 224.

nals, the extra doses of hormones—provides the means for borrowing from the long-term store of adaptation energy in order to provide the sustained arousal and vigilance needed to cope with the novelty, uncertainty, or conflict occasioned by the new situations. But remember it is this encodrine system which provides the basis for resistance to any agent which threatens the body. We are constantly exposed to, even constantly transporting within us, microbes that can do damage to body tissues. Usually a healthy immune system defends against such bacteria. But if the endocrine system is constantly marshaling the body's energy for adjustment, the capacity for resisting those lurking microbes will be exhausted. Thus wherever the body is most vulnerable, a breakdown can occur after a period of sufficiently great demands for social or psychological adjustment.[3]

One should take note of the fact that a number of events in the table are "positive"; one ordinarily thinks of them as occasions for pleasure or celebration. The layman's definition of "stress" as something to be avoided, something not preferred, hardly seems to apply to events such as marriage, birth of a child, promotion, outstanding personal achievement, sudden drastic improvement in financial position, moving to a bigger home in a better neighborhood, or graduation from college. Yet, to the extent that these events pose demands for adjustment, they are stressful in Selye's sense; and, if enough of these changes are bunched together, they can produce health problems.

One can also see in the "Type A" coronary-prone behavior pattern, described by Meyer Friedman and Ray H. Rosenman, how the linkage between stress, technically defined, and illness is somewhat different from the relationship involving the vernacular meaning of stress as distress. The Type A pattern is one of struggle against the limitations of time; of poised, combative, even hostile striving to compete against other people; of stretching one's self incessantly against self-imposed goals in leisure as well as work.[4]

In *The Hurricane Years*, Cameron Hawley has given us a personification of the Type A executive in the character of Judd Wilder. In the opening pages of the novel, Wilder, an advertising and promotion executive for a carpet company, is leaving the Pennsylvania turnpike and trying to return from New York with the proofs of the stockholders' report before 8:30 that evening. There is no particular urgency in getting the report back by that time; it is simply a goal Wilder has set for himself. Behind the wheel, he experiences a massive heart attack and is rushed to a county hospital. There he comes under the care of

---

[3] For a readable account of the effect of life changes on illness, see Alvin Toffler, *Future Shock* (New York: Random House, 1970), pp. 289–304.

[4] Meyer Friedman and Ray H. Rosenman, *Type A Behavior and Your Heart* (New York: Alfred A. Knopf, 1974).

Dr. Aaron Kharr, who soon recognizes the behavior pattern characteristic of men like Wilder: ". . . inherently aggressive, competitive, energetic, and ambitious . . . naturally geared to operate at a high
adrenaline level."

The incessant process of struggle provokes a chronically fast-paced
tempo of the endocrine system with consequent chronically high levels of adrenal hormones in the blood. These hormones, which cannot
be metabolized in the overt fight-or-flight response for which they
were designed by evolution, cause clotting elements in the blood
which speed up the formation of plaques in the arterial walls. Thus
Type As have a much higher than average risk of premature coronary
artery disease, even when other risk factors (such as high blood pressure, cigarette smoking, high-fat diet) are held constant.

Curiously, though, the Type A does not think of himself as "nervous," "under stress," or in any sense crippled by anxiety. Indeed,
according to Friedman and Rosenman, anxiety is an unfamiliar state of
mind to the extreme Type A. Also, Type As seldom experience the
subjective sense of fatigue.[5] The stress which is the bane of Type As is
not conscious discomfort or distress on an emotional dimension, but
rather the response of the endocrine system to the unreasonable succession of demands they place upon themselves as they, like Judd
Wilder, become "hooked on adrenaline."

STRESS AND PERFORMANCE

An issue long of interest to layman and scientist alike concerns the
effect of stress on job performance. Some people believe that a lapse in
performance is itself evidence of unusual stress experienced by the
performer; others believe that stress is a direct contributor to improved, more effortful work on a job. Certainly stress, in the vernacular
sense, is likely to impair performance of a complex task because of the
distractions produced by worry or fear or other connotations inherent
in the layman's definition of stress. However, if we define stress in the
more precise, scientific manner as intended by Selye, we can discern
no general relationship in the empirical data between stress and quality of performance. The reason for this is that the stress syndrome is in
response to the total demand from all sources placed on the person.
Part of that demand may be the very effort to maintain performance in
the presence of simultaneously competing demands from the environment, such as unpredictable noise, information overload, fatigue from
illness, or even distractions by sexually arousing stimuli.

---

[5] See David C. Glass, *Behavior Patterns, Stress, and Coronary Disease* (Hillsdale,
N.J.: Lawrence Erlbaum Associates, 1977), pp. 42–50.

Studies by Professor David Glass and his colleagues at Rockefeller University show that subjects working on a clerical task under conditions of randomly intermittent, irritating noise were able to stabilize at a performance level equivalent to subjects working under less adverse conditions.[6] The evidence of stress induced by the noise came not in any differences in quantity or quality of work between groups, but later, *after* the noise ended. Subjects who had coped with the simultaneous demands of performing as well as coping with the noise later showed less tolerance for the frustration of trying to solve what was (unbeknownst to them) actually an insoluble puzzle. Glass was not willing to go so far as to say that the stress of adaptation had *caused* the subsequent decline in frustration tolerance, but the link certainly suggests that stress is more often behaviorally reflected in situations temporally and spatially removed from the original sources of demand than it is shown directly or immediately in "performance." The adaptation energy extracted by a higher than normal level of endocrine activity must be replenished sooner or later, and the involuntary "let-down" which seems to be necessary for such replenishment may show up in such trivial, apparently unrelated symptoms as forgetting to lock the garage door, injuring oneself with a power saw, or inadvertently dumping cigarette ashes into one's full cup of coffee.

STRESS AND ADAPTATION

Actually, the replenishment of adaptation energy referred to above is illusory, according to Selye. Selye believes that each person has a fixed, finite reservoir of adaptation energy to feed the endocrine system. One cannot increase this amount; all one can do is occasionally transfer some from long-term reserves to a smaller but more immediately available status—much like depositing some of your life's savings into current withdrawal accounts. That transfer, it appears, does require some temporary lapse in the form of rest or even "depression." But it is nonetheless a borrowing which can never be repaid.

Thus "adaptation" is costly. To the layman, someone adapting to a stressful condition is functioning in the condition so that it is no longer stressful; one "is getting used to it so it doesn't bother him anymore." For Selye, however, adaptation is the very stuff of which stress is made. It is precisely the process of getting used to it—whether "it" be cold temperatures, muscular strain, or a critical boss—which uses up some of the fixed store of adaptation energy.

[6] David C. Glass and Jerome E. Singer, *Urban Stress: Experiments in Noise and Social Stressors* (New York: Academic Press, 1972).

IMPLICATIONS FOR MANAGERS

To eliminate stress means to eliminate all things which require adaptation, and that virtually means to eliminate life itself. Even to reduce stress to minimal practical levels means never to visit a stimulating city, never to gaze at an attractive woman, never to take up new activities, never to pursue one's dreams—if possible, even never to dream. Surely, such a life is hardly worth living, whatever it might promise in the form of longevity. As Selye puts it,

> Vitality is like a special kind of bank account which you can use up by withdrawals but cannot increase by deposits. Your only control over this most precious fortune is the rate at which you make your withdrawals. . . . The intelligent thing to do is to withdraw generously but never expend wastefully.

Selye concedes that there are probably vast differences among individuals in the amount of adaptation energy given to them to draw upon. And even his basic premise, that the amount of adaptation energy available to a person is a genetically predetermined constant, is a theoretical supposition not shared by all other experts. Nevertheless, his point of view is worth pondering, for it poses some serious philosophical implications.

Consider, for example, the adage that "anything worth doing at all is worth doing well." Quite a few people, many successful managers among them, seem to live and work implicitly by this principle. Yet managers often seem to agree with another notion that "80 percent of your success is determined by 20 percent of what you do." Selye's position would be that the crucially important 20 percent may be well worth the extravagant stores of endocrine-derived adaptation energy necessary to meet the demands posed by that 20 percent. For the remaining 80 percent, however, it would be wasteful, uneconomical, and downright inefficient to place the same demands upon one's self or upon others. The 80 percent is worth doing, and perhaps has to be done in some fashion in order for the other 20 percent to mean anything; but it does not necessarily have to be done immediately, perfectly, or even well. Yet it is curious that many managers who seem to be so judiciously and expertly selective in the expenditure of money and other finite physical resources can be so indiscriminate in disbursing the most precious finite resource of all—vitality.

17

Performance Failure: Executive Response to Self-Serving Bias*

HENRY P. SIMS, JR., and DENNIS A. GIOIA

Joe is in a quandary. He is the division general manager for Chemtek Corporation's Electrolytic Products Division. This last quarter, his division has failed to meet either the total shipments target or the cash flow target. Today his stomach is really in knots. He has to explain the division's performance to the corporate operating committee, which includes the chairman, who is not in the habit of viewing subpar performance leniently. As he waits in the corporate conference room, he ponders last quarter's efforts: "I'm really not a bad executive after all," he thinks. "Most of the time in the past, I've achieved my targets. Why, last year my division was even 4 percent ahead of target on cash flow. This quarter, I've done a heck of a job in bringing in our new photographic products plant. We were really in danger of losing that one, and I salvaged the start-up schedule. Where the division missed the boat was on our old chemical plating products business. I was so preoccupied with the new plant, I just didn't see the effect of the new Japanese competitor in that business. Our volume in that business was really down, which was the major cause of our division's overall shortfall. I just wish I had more time, or a more dependable marketing manager of the plating products business. And I still think our competitor is dumping at below cost prices. I know I could have handled that business if . . ." At that, the door of the conference room opens, and Joe is greeted by the grim voice of the chairman.

When Joe begins to explain his poor performance, he will not be aware that his perceptions are colored by a "self-serving bias," the tendency for individuals to take personal responsibility for their successes, but to attribute failures to external or situational causes. This phenomenon also has been called "attributional egotism." Whatever

* From *Business Horizons*, 1984, 27, pp. 64–71. Copyright © 1984 by the Foundation for the School of Business, Indiana University.

the name, managers often intuitively recognize its symptoms and struggle to deal with it. It is only recently, however, that social scientists have begun to investigate the self-serving bias on a systematic basis. Some interesting insights have emerged from this line of research and from our own specific studies in performance appraisal situations, which have useful implications for managers who must deal with self-serving bias in day-to-day situations or in formal performance reviews. Thus, we address four basic questions: What is self-serving bias? How and why does it occur? What are the consequences of this bias? What can managers do to deal with it?

WHAT IS SELF-SERVING BIAS?

Self-serving bias occurs when an employee (yourself included) makes attributions about the causes of performance in achievement-related tasks. Each of us acts as an amateur psychologist. When we achieve success or experience failure on a task, we typically search for and assign a cause for that success or failure. This process, called making an attribution, is a retrospective mental causal explanation of why past events occurred as they did.

However, employees typically have different patterns of causal attributions depending on whether they succeed or fail. Credit for success is considered to be an internal attribution: "The success was due to myself." But blame for failure is considered to be an external attribution: "What happened was beyond my control." In short, people tend to accept responsibility for good performance but to deny responsibility for poor performance. This is the specific phenomenon known as self-serving bias.

Within the categories of internal and external attributions, several specific reasons for good performance have been identified. Among the likely internal attributions are

- Personal ability: "I succeeded and will probably continue to succeed in the future because I am good at this task."
- Typical effort: "I succeeded because I always try very hard."
- Effort on this task: "I succeeded because I tried very hard on this project."
- Mood: "I succeeded this time because I was in a particularly good mood and felt like doing it right."

Interestingly, mood is a flexible attribution. Ability and effort are typically used to explain success but are avoided as explanations for failure, while mood often can be used to explain either: "I failed this time because I just wasn't in a good mood."

An employee is more likely to use external factors to explain failure. Some of these external attributions are

- Task difficulty: "This job was just impossible."
- Luck: "That's the way the ball bounces. It'll bounce my way next time."
- Supervision: "I could have gotten it done if he had just let me do it my way."
- Co-workers/competition: "It would have been done if production had just gotten the materials out on time," or "My competitor is cutting prices to suicide levels."

In our own research, self-serving bias shows up as significant and strong in manager/subordinate relations. In more than 100 performance appraisal situations, we have seen subordinates tend to blame failure on any factor other than themselves. Typical excuses were "the other department," "the changing economy," and "I don't have enough control." Conversely, subordinates were quite comfortable with the notion that their successes were due to their own efforts and ability. There is no question that self-serving bias does occur in performance appraisals, and it is indeed troublesome for both managers and subordinates. But why does it occur?

WHY SELF-SERVING BIAS?

Most of the early explanations for self-serving bias focused on the notion that individuals are motivated to protect and enhance their own self-esteem. This is called the *motivational* explanation. Other explanations are the *information-processing* and the *self-presentational* ones.

The first explanation, the motivational effect, is based on private concepts of self-esteem, or how an individual regards him- or herself. Most of us have a significant need to maintain and enhance our internal self-esteem in order to maintain our psychological health. We like to feel good about ourselves and what we are. Consequently, we tend to defend ourselves from anything that has negative implications for our self-esteem. We are likely to observe events through egocentric perception: We perceive events so that they contribute to self-image, but we tend to avoid or misperceive events that threaten self-image. Obviously, task failure might be construed as a threat to self-esteem. If we can place the blame for such an event on external factors, our self-esteem remains intact. Task success is likely to enhance self-esteem, so we are much more likely to assume credit for such a success.

According to the information-processing explanation, self-serving bias occurs because of an imbalance in the logical processing of available information. Subordinates are fully aware of their own history. From their viewpoints, the major difference in any task-oriented situation is the *situation*. If something is different this time—if there has been a failure—then, from the employee's viewpoint, the major factors that have changed are the circumstances surrounding the task. Attention is focused on these contextual circumstances. To the employee these circumstances are most salient. Not surprisingly, the attention focused on the external circumstances is transformed into an external attribution of cause: "I failed because of external factors."

Notice that each of these two explanations for self-serving bias entails unconscious, unwitting distortions of reality. It is actual perceptual bias; these are sincere, true, private perceptions. However, the third explanation, self-presentation, entails a conscious, intentional distortion of causality.

In self-presentation, individuals carry out strategies for managing the impressions they make on others. The premise is that individuals are highly concerned with winning approval and avoiding disapproval of significant others. Employees, in particular, might spend considerable energy thinking about which factors are likely to influence the impression they make on their superiors or influential peers. Self-serving bias arises when individuals act to manage the impression they make on others by taking public credit for successes and denying personal responsibility for blameworthy acts. These three explanations are not mutually exclusive. For example, the self-presentation effect might be viewed as a second stage to the motivational effect. Individuals might originally experience self-serving bias because of an internal motivation to preserve their own self-esteem, an internal and private stage. Then, in order to enhance esteem in the eyes of others, the self-presentation effect will come into play as a second, now public, stage.

ACTOR/OBSERVER COMPLICATIONS

In manager/subordinate interactions, this problem of bias is further compounded by a related psychological phenomenon known as the "actor/observer" difference. In a performance appraisal context, the actor is the subordinate, the one who acts out the performance-related tasks. The manager is the observer, the one who watches the subordinate employee acting out the task.

Research has clearly shown that actors and observers often perceive the same events quite differently, and the manager/subordinate, actor/observer relationship is certainly no exception. An actor's judgment of the causes of behavior is likely to be markedly different from the observer's judgment of the causes of the same behavior; furthermore, these two judgments are likely to be directly contradictory. That is, while the subordinate (actor) is likely to make external attributions under conditions of failure, the manager (observer) is likely to make internal attributions.

One explanation of this difference is related to the information-processing explanation for the self-serving bias. Managers are apt to process performance information differently from subordinates. Stated most simply, the subordinate (actor) bases judgments on differences in the situation. Most employees view themselves as sensitive information processors, responding to subtle differences between task situations, so causes for performance failure are attributed to the external situational factors. The manager (observer), however, typically sees employees as having skills, abilities, and personality characteristics that are essentially the same from situation to situation, so the manager finds the causes for failure in factors internal to the subordinate.

Needless to say, this difference in perceptions causes problems. Is serious conflict inevitable? What are some of the consequences of self-serving bias, and its first cousin, actor/observer differences?

CONSEQUENCES OF SELF-SERVING BIAS

Interpersonal conflict is the consequence of both these phenomena, especially as they affect perceptions about performance failures. The manager and the subordinate view the same set of events, but perceive them differently. The special difficulty of this issue is that the difference is usually sincere. Neither the subordinate nor the manager are overtly attempting to "pull the wool over the other's eye." Intellectually and emotionally, each believes that his or her viewpoint is correct and that the other misunderstands. Each believes that his or her picture of the situation is rational, while the other's is irrational or emotional.

Obviously, this difference in perception interferes with constructive problem solving. From the manager's viewpoint, the major purpose of any performance appraisal should be to improve the *future* performance of the subordinate employee. If problems exist, the role of the manager is to help the employee identify the problem, generate alternatives, and help select constructive courses of future action. But when self-serving bias is significant, the capability to be constructive is substantially limited. Furthermore, self-serving bias is not strictly a phenomenon associated with subordinates. Managers are human too, and would like to receive some credit for success, but their own self-serving biases make them want to dissociate themselves from performance failures too. As a result, when self-serving bias and actor/observer differences come together concerning a performance failure, the tendency is even stronger for a manager to attribute the cause for failure to something internal to the subordinate, and the tendency is just as strong for the subordinate to attribute the cause to something external to him or herself (perhaps even to poor supervision!).

The performance appraisal interaction then degenerates into a reciprocal blame-placing sequence, with frustration the typical emotional response of both. The manager's capability to motivate is severely diminished. The subordinate's motivation for future tasks declines. Sometimes, the natural result is a downward spiral in which the emotions and negative attitudes intensify and escalate over a period of time, becoming progressively more and more frustrating and nonproductive. Frequently, the only end result is escape: either the manager leaves, or the employee terminates, is terminated, or transfers. In its most severe form, self-serving bias serves as a starting point for damage to the employee's self-esteem and also to the manager's self-esteem about his or her capability to manage.

There are various behavioral manifestations of self-serving bias. First, the employee may *deny it*. Remember, more often than not, this denial is not a deliberate attempt to deceive, but is a sincere representation of the way the situation exists according to the way the subordinate sees it. Denial is a logical defense mechanism that is intended to preserve self-esteem and to minimize and contain damage due to the failure. As a second stage, the employee may attempt to *hide the failure*. This hiding behavior, of course, is part of a self-presentational strategy, where one presents positive or flattering information, but attempts to remove, minimize, or shield negative information. It is part of a subordinate's attempt to look good in the eyes of authority figures.

Another phase occurs when the subordinate attempts to *justify the failure*. If it can't be denied or hidden, what can be done to enhance self-presentation? An attempt to rationalize or justify the failure is a frequent response. This behavior includes attempts to minimize the importance of the failure: "It's just not a very high-priority item!"

In the last phase, the employee may attempt to *allocate the failure;* that is, the subordinate may try to spread the blame. Usually, this involves further external attributions, with the failure laid to outside factors such as unfair competition, unreliable co-workers, or an erratic economy. This coping strategy is a last-ditch defensive effort to convince the manager that the fault lies elsewhere. By this phase, emotions are running high and typically entail aggressive blame-placing. The manager, in turn, is extremely frustrated because the employee will not face reality.

But this escalating spiral of negativism is not inevitable. Managers can and do find ways to overcome and diminish the effects of self-serving bias.

HOW CAN MANAGERS HANDLE SELF-SERVING BIAS?

The fact that self-serving bias is common does no mean that managers are powerless to deal with it. Much of the art of effective managerial leadership is wrapped around this specific challenge. Effective managers are capable of coping with self-serving bias when it does occur, and can minimize the probability of occurrence through preventive measures. A substantial amount of research has shown the effectiveness of specific managerial behaviors. In our research, we have observed (and video-recorded) these behaviors on numerous occasions. Our findings, in Figure 1, are put in the form of tips on how managers can effectively respond to, and prevent, self-serving bias. Our emphasis, of course, is on what a manager can do to deal with less than effective subordinate employees—employees who fail. The specific context for our prescriptions is a typical manager/subordinate performance appraisal situation. However, these tips are perhaps even more appropriate in day-to-day, less formal personal interaction.

Recognize and Expect Self-Serving Bias. The effective manager should not be surprised when the self-serving bias does occur. He or she should be able to recognize it, confront it, and move beyond it to more constructive interaction. Most of all, the effective manager should recognize that self-serving bias is a natural human reaction, that it is likely to be sincere rather than a lie. The self-serving bias is fairly common when employees evaluate their own job performances.

FIGURE 1
Ten Tips: Dealing with Self-Serving Bias

1. Recognize and expect self-serving bias.
2. Verbally reinforce owning up; verbally reprimand covering up.
3. Probe for true causes; use active listening.
4. Distinguish between circumstances and employee effort as possible causes.
5. Probe for consistency, distinctiveness, and consensus of performance-related behavior.
6. Train yourself to define effective performance for subordinates.
7. Set specific goals for/with employees.
8. Focus on behavior: avoid emphasis on attitude and personality traits.
9. Use critical incidents.
10. Use contingent rewarding consequences for accomplishments.

Furthermore, the effect is heightened when subordinates are faced with a relatively formalized periodic performance appraisal, in which they are expected to account directly to their superiors for past successes and failures.

It is clear that the prudent manager should expect the subordinate to describe success as the result of above-average motivation, ability, or effort. Failure, however, typically might be described as peculiar to some past situation only, and now that these peculiar events have passed, the subordinate may well claim that the problem will essentially correct itself. Clearly, if the manager is alert to this perceptual bias at the onset, he or she is in a far better position to evaluate critically the subordinate's explanations rather than becoming disturbed at flimsy excuses for failure. The effective manager should realize that the subordinate may well be relating events honestly as they appear to him or her, and any effort to change the subordinate's mind is likely only to entrench a defensive position.

Verbally Reinforce Owning Up; Verbally Reprimand Covering Up. Over the long run, the manager wants to get the employee into the practice of self-recognition and self-disclosure concerning performance failure. To encourage this, the manager must be supportive whenever a subordinate has the courage and forthrightness to identify and talk about performance problems. The manager should directly reinforce the recognition of a performance deficiency. It is important to distinguish between reinforcing self-recognition and disclosure and reinforcing the failure itself. A useful approach might be: "I'm disappointed that Task A didn't get done, but I'm pleased to see that you recognize the problem, and especially the importance of the problem. It makes it easier for us to deal with whatever needs to be done to prevent it from happening again."

Conversely, confronting the subordinate who manifests self-serving behavior with a mild expression of disappointment would also be appropriate: "Frankly, you and I perceive the reasons behind this failure differently. I would feel better if you would consider the possibility that you might be responsible, in part, for the problem. It would make it easier for us to work together to reduce the likelihood of its happening again. But let's move on to see what we can do anyway, even if we do see the picture differently. At this point, it's more important that we are together about where we go from here."

Probe for True Causes; Use Active Listening. One of the most important things for the manager to realize is that the subordinate might, in fact, be right when he assigns cause to some external factor. Just as the subordinate has the natural tendency to assign causes for failure externally, the natural tendency of the manager is to assign causes for failure internally. The effective manager should recognize this personal tendency and refrain from making preemptory judgments without seeking full information. Often, the best technique for pursuing information is to ask brief questions, and then to listen, listen, listen. A useful opening question might be, "Tell me how that happened."

The concept of active listening is especially appropriate when circumstances surrounding a failure are in doubt or under dispute. In active listening, the manager repeats back, in summary form, the information given to him by the subordinate: "Let me make sure I understand you correctly. You say that (repeat subordinate information here). Is that correct?" Active listening is a very effective mechanism for opening up a reluctant subordinate employee and for probing to remove uncertainties from the situation. In addition to increasing the store of the manager's available information, it has a positive motivational effect on the subordinate, because it stimulates a feeling of involvement and participation.

Distinguish between Circumstances and Employee Effort as Possible Causes.   This tip is an extension of the previous one, but perhaps more direct. Most managers attempt to make this distinction intuitively. We suggest, however, that a more deliberate overt strategy to tease out the facts surrounding an employee's performance failure is best guided by attempts to distinguish whether the true cause for failure is lack of effort or some unusual circumstances surrounding the performance incident.

Probe for Consistency, Distinctiveness, and Consensus of Performance-Related Behavior.   Research has shown the importance of these factors in determining attributions of cause. The greater the knowledge of a manager about the consistency, distinctiveness, and consensus of a subordinate's performance, the less likely the manager is to make an error in attributing cause for performance. Sometimes this information is not always immediately available to a manager, and must therefore be sought from the employee or from other sources. Sometimes, significant homework is required to complete this information. It is useful to have some idea about what to search for.

Consistency refers to the subordinate's performance on a particular task in comparison to his or her performance in similar situations at other times. If performance failure on a particular task in question is consistent with other performance failures in other circumstances, then an internal attribution is more likely to be warranted. Conversely, if performance failure on this particular task is different from performance under other circumstances, then an external attribution is more likely to be warranted.

Distinctiveness refers to whether the employee's behavior is different (distinctive) in different situations. Does the employee also fail at projects that are quite different from this particular project? If the answer is yes, then an internal attribution would seem to be more appropriate. However, if the employee fails only in a given type of situation, but is successful in other types of situations, the appropriate attribution is more likely to be external, or, at least, some unique interaction between the person and the situation.

Consensus deals with the question of how this particular employee responds in comparison to how other employees typically respond. If other employees would be reasonably expected to be able to succeed where this employee has failed, then an internal attribution is more likely to be warranted. On the other hand, if other employees would be expected to be similar to the employee in question, then an external attribution would more likely be warranted.

These questions can thus help to guide the manager as he or she seeks to determine the cause for an employee's failure. Does the employee show similar performance in similar situations at different times (consistency)? Does the employee show similar performance in different situations (distinctiveness)? Does the employee show performance similar to other employees in similar situations (consensus)? Probing for answers to these questions will assist a manager to establish more valid attributions about a specific performance failure.

Train Yourself to Define Effective Performance for Subordinates. In addition to dealing with self-serving bias as it occurs, the effective manager can take several steps to reduce the likelihood of self-serving bias in the future. Most of these practices revolve around the concept of establishing clear expectations for employees about the future. But, of course, clear expectations are impossible if a manager is unable to recognize and, more importantly, to articulate just what effective performance is. It is indeed ineffective for a manager to say, "I can't tell you what effective performance is, but I know it when I see it!" Knowing is not enough. One must be able to articulate performance expectations to subordinates. In the case of the employee whose performance has been below par, this aspect of managerial behavior takes on critical importance because it is the first step in reducing uncertainty and ambiguity. Establishing clear expectations about performance is one way of reducing the sticky problem of the employee who failed at a task because, "I didn't know what you wanted!"

Set Specific Goals for/with Employees. Goal setting is the logical extension of establishing clear expectations about employee future performance. Despite the well-known problems of system-wide management by objectives programs, research has clearly shown that individual goal setting remains one of the most effective achievement-oriented strategies available to the manager. Through goal setting, an employee is much more likely to accept the notion that whether performance is achieved or not is within his or her own control.

Of course, several aspects of goal setting help the process. First, goal setting trends to be more effective when goals are as specific as possible. Quantitative standards are preferred; at the very least, when goals consist of clusters of activities, a firm deadline serves as an intermediate goal. Second, goals of moderate difficulty are likely to result in higher performance levels. Easy goals lead to low performance because employees stop when the goal has been achieved. Extremely difficult goals lead to low performance because employees give up if they see that the attainment of a goal is beyond their capabilities; attainable but difficult goals generally do lead to higher performance.

Finally, participation in goal setting has been linked theoretically to high performance, because improved psychological commitment is thought to stem from participation. Participation can elicit a sense of ownership about an achievement-related task. However, several studies have also shown that assigned goals are as effective as participatively set goals. The issue of participation remains somewhat controversial. We believe that participatively set goals are particularly useful when employees are experienced, mature, and capable, and where the task is more likely to involve innovation and creativity. In cases where the employee is less capable, which is more likely the situation with a failed employee, assigned goals may be appropriate to get an employee back on the track. Whatever the form or process, goal setting is an extremely useful technique for reducing the probability of self-serving bias.

Over the long run, it is best for managers to focus on end-result types of goals for experienced and successful employees. A manager should work with the employee to establish a desired end state, but should leave room for a great deal of creativity and self-control over how that end state is likely to be achieved. For employees who are having problems, it may be more useful to focus on more short-term, behaviorally oriented goals. For a problem employee, it may be better to focus on the means rather than the ends, with attention directed toward behavior-specific aspects of performance.

Focus on Behavior: Avoid Emphasis on Attitude and Personality Traits. This recommendation might be difficult to implement where managers must contend with a performance appraisal system that utilizes personality traits. Yet, even within these trait-oriented systems, managers can strengthen their personal leadership by focusing conversations with subordinates on behavior-specific aspects of performance and by downplaying personality and attitude aspects. Managers may know that bad attitudes play an important part in performance failures, but correcting a bad attitude is all but impossible, while correcting a bad behavior has some hope of success. Moreover, attitudes improve remarkably as a by-product of improvements in performance-oriented behaviors.

Use Critical Incidents. The technique is especially useful in formal performance appraisal situations, and is an effective way of providing behavior-specific feedback. Be sure to label each critical incident as an example of behavior that is desired or effective versus an example of ineffective behavior. Even if the formal appraisal system does not utilize a critical incident approach, the manager can informally use critical incidents in the verbal feedback to the employee.

Use Contingent Rewarding Consequences for Accomplishments. By contingent we mean that rewarding consequences should be used only when performance merits them. (Some rewarding consequences are task-oriented praise, favored job assignments, or additional control over the job.) Also, an effective manager should avoid placing overall labels on an employee. Each employee's performance is some mixture of success and failure. The feedback and consequences for each incident should reflect the nature of that specific incident. For example, even for an employee whose overall performance is lacking, a manager should reward specific task accomplishments when they do occur, even if only rarely. It is only through this kind of reward for desirable behavior and achievements that an employee learns that the manager will differentiate between poor performance and good performance.

Self-serving bias is a natural psychological phenomenon which frequently occurs in performance appraisal situations. Employees tend to take credit for task successes, but to place blame for task failure on external sources. The problems caused by this tendency are further compounded by an actor/observer difference effect, especially in attributing cause for performance failures. The manager typically holds the subordinate responsible for poor performance, but the subordinate generally feels that external factors are to blame. These biases and differences in perception occur because of processing, motivational, and self-presentational reasons.

Dysfunctional consequences are typically the result of self-serving bias and actor/observer differences in attributions of cause of performance. Emotions often run high, and sometimes interfere with constructive problem-solving. However, the manager has several strategies that can be used to cope with and reduce the probability of self-serving bias. Among others, these include recognizing the existence of self-serving bias, encouraging "owning up" to failures, knowing how to probe for the "true" causes of a failure, defining effective performance, setting specific goals and clear expectations, and focusing on behavior as opposed to attitudes or personality.

Sooner or later, every manager encounters self-serving bias from a subordinate. It happens in both formal performance appraisal and in everyday manager/subordinate interactions. An important part of overall success as a manager depends on how well the manager can deal with this bias.

18

The Influence of Age Stereotypes on Managerial Decisions*

BENSON ROSEN and THOMAS H. JERDEE

Until recently the problem of age discrimination in employment practices has been overshadowed by the problems of race and sex discrimination. However, there are now several indications that government agencies intend to enforce vigorously the 1967 Age Discrimination in Employment Act. For example, in 1974 the U.S. Department of Labor won an agreement from Standard Oil of California to pay $2 million in back wages to 160 employees over the age of 40 who had been victimized by discriminatory managerial practices. In a recent interview, a Labor Department official stated that over 400 cases involving alleged age discrimination were in preparation ("Age Discrimination Moves into the Limelight," 1974).

In many instances of age discrimination, it is quite likely that managerial bias against older workers is based on age stereotypes, that is, widely held beliefs regarding the characteristics of people in various age categories. Research by Aaronson (1966) suggests that increasingly negative stereotypes are associated with increasing age. However, a Louis Harris poll indicated that public expectations concerning the problems of old age were exaggerated compared to the actual experiences reported by the elderly (Harris, 1975).

* From *Journal of Applied Psychology* 1976, vol. 61, no. 4, 428–432. Copyright 1976 by the American Psychological Association. Reprinted by permission.

In a recent study (see Rosen & Jerdee, 1976) we examined differences in evaluations of the average younger and the average older person on 65 job-related traits. We found that respondents viewed older persons, compared to younger persons, to be deficient in on-the-job performance, potential for development, certain interpersonal skills, vitality, and propensity for risk taking. Older persons were rated higher than younger persons on integrity. These perceptions of age differences in job-related characteristics were held by respondents of all ages.

The effects of these age stereotypes on managerial decision making were studied in the present investigation. Participants were presented with a series of six hypothetical administrative incidents in which an employee's age might be expected to have an influence on a managerial decision. We then compared the administrative evaluations and actions recommended for use with younger and older employees in identical circumstances. For each of the incidents, we hypothesized differential administrative evaluations reflecting the aforementioned age stereotypes. We also hypothesized administrative actions indicating less organizational concern and support for the older employee.

THE STUDY

Method

Subjects. The subjects were 142 undergraduate business students (115 males and 27 females) attending the University of North Carolina; 99 percent of the participants were between the ages of 21 and 29.

Procedure. Experimental materials were embedded in an in-basket exercise. Participants were asked to assume the role of a division manager and to react to a series of six in-basket items presented in memo or letter form, each dealing with a different incident. Each incident depicted a different type of managerial problem and was presented in two versions, so as to manipulate the age of the focal person depicted in the memo or letter.

In each of the incidents, age was manipulated by specifying the focal employee's age or describing the focal employee as an "older" or "younger" person. In addition, to enhance the realism of the experimental task and to strengthen the age manipulation, four of the memos included personnel forms with pictures of the focal employees. The pictures were of younger or older men dressed in business attire and were preselected and matched by a three-judge panel to ensure uniformity of physical attractiveness. To control for a possible "specific picture" effect (in which age might be confounded with non-age-related qualities), three different pictures of older men and three different pictures of younger men were used in each of these four incidents. This also permitted separate estimation of the specific picture effect for each of the four incidents.

For each item, participants indicated on fixed response scales their evaluations and the extent to which they would find certain administrative actions appropriate for dealing with the managerial problem. Since each participant received only one version of each of the experimental items, manipulation of the age variable was unobtrusive. The design can best be conceptualized as a series of six separate experiments with random assignment of treatments to participants within each experiment.

The six incidents were as follows:

1. *Resistance to change.* The first incident was concerned with the stereotype that older workers are rigid in their work attitudes and resistant to change. This incident was in the form of a memo from a foreman about a shipping room employee who appeared unresponsive to customer calls for service. The employee was described as either a younger or an older employee, in either case with only 3 months' experience in his present position. Participants indicated the difficulty anticipated in getting the employee to change his behavior and selected one of five possible alternatives for resolving the problem.

2. *Lack of creativity.* In this incident, participants evaluated a candidate for promotion to a marketing position that required "fresh solutions to challenging problems" and "a high degree of creative and innovative behavior." Participants made a promotion decision for a 61-year-old or a 32-year-old candidate with identical qualifications.

3. *Cautiousness and slowness of judgment.* This position was described as requiring a person "who not only knows the field of finance, but who is capable of making quick judgments under high risk." Subjects evaluated either a 29-year-old or a 58-year-old applicant with identical backgrounds and experience.

4. *Lower physical capacity.* The next incident examined stereotypes reflecting diminished physical capacities of older workers. This item was written in letter form and depicted a request from a clerical employee to be reassigned to a higher paying, but physically demanding, truck loader position. The employee was described as either 52 years old or 23 years old, slender, and in good condition. Participants evaluated the desirability of rejecting the request.

5. *Disinterest in technological change.* The next case concerned perceptions about older employees' desire and ability to keep up with technical change. Participants evaluated a request from a production staff employee asking permission and financial support to attend a conference devoted to "new theories and research relevant to produc-

tion systems." The employee was described as either 62 years old or 34 years old with 10 years of production experience. Participants evaluated the employee's motives and the desirability of approving the request.

6. *Untrainability.* This item depicted a computer programmer whose technical skills had become obsolete as a result of changes in computer operations. The programmer was described as either 30 years old or 60 years old and of average ability. Participants evaluated the desirability of terminating the programmer and the desirability of retraining him.

Results

Two preliminary analyses were made prior to testing for age effects. The first analysis tested for specific picture effects within the three pictures of older persons and within the three pictures of younger persons, for each of the in-basket incidents that included photographs as part of the age manipulation. Picture effects were not significant for any of the cases. Therefore, data from the specific picture subgroups within older and younger age categories were pooled.

In the second preliminary analysis, comparisons were made between male and female subjects for each of the incidents. Sex effects were not significant. Accordingly, the major analyses are based on responses from both male and female participants.

Resistance to Change.   The first incident tested the hypothesis that older employees are seen as more resistant to change. We also hypothesized that people are less likely to decide on positive corrective action when confronted with an older "problem" employee. Age stereotype effects were found on the question "How much difficulty would you anticipate in getting the shipping employee to change his behavior?" The mean difficulty rating for the older worker was 3.13 compared to a mean rating of 2.76 for the younger worker ($t = 2.41$, $p < .05$). Participants also recommended different ways of dealing with the older and younger employee. A positive corrective strategy, "a talk in which the employee is encouraged to change his behavior," was recommended by 65 percent of the participants who read the younger version, but this alternative was recommended by only 42 percent of the participants who read the older version. On the other hand, the alternative, "find someone else to handle customer complaints," was endorsed by 55 percent of the respondents to the older version, compared to only 32 percent of the respondents to the younger version ($\chi^2 = 9.84$, $p < .05$).

Clearly, the older employee was seen as more resistant to managerial influences. Thus, rather than attempt to encourage an older worker to improve his performance, a majority of participants recommended avoiding a confrontation and reassigning the older employee.

Lack of Creativity. We hypothesized that older employees are seen as less promotable to a position requiring creativity and innovative thinking. Among participants who reviewed the record of the older candidate, 25 percent recommended promotion, compared to 54 percent of participants who reviewed the identical qualifications, but for a younger candidate ($\chi^2 = 9.75$, $p < .01$).

Cautiousness. We hypothesized that there is a bias against older applicants for positions requiring financial risk taking. Findings supported the hypothesis. The mean rating on "suitability for the job" was 3.46 for the young applicant compared to a mean rating of 2.97 for the older applicant ($t = 2.91$, $p < .01$). Among participants who reviewed the qualifications of the younger applicant, 25 percent recommended selection, compared to 13 percent of respondents who reviewed an identically qualified older applicant ($\chi^2 = 3.48$, $p < .06$).

Results of these two selection and promotion incidents clearly reflect discrimination against older employees. It appears that when job demands such as innovative thinking, creativity, and risk taking are inconsistent with widely held stereotypes about the characteristics of older people, the potential for discriminatory managerial decisions is quite high.

Lower Physical Capacity. This incident tested the hypothesis that people are less likely to approve an older employee's request for a transfer to a job requiring strenuous physical activity. Again, findings strongly supported the hypothesis. Participants rated the administrative action "persuade the employee to withdraw the transfer request" significantly higher for the older worker ($M = 4.38$), compared to the younger worker ($M = 3.46$; $t = 3.42$, $p < .01$). In addition, a decision to reject the transfer request was evaluated significantly higher for the older worker compared to the younger worker (M older $= 3.35$, M younger $= 2.57$; $t = 2.95$, $p < .01$). In this instance, it appears that general stereotypes about the decline of physical strength with age had more influence on managerial judgments than our statement that the 52-year-old employee was in "good physical condition." We now turn to results concerning the influence of age stereotypes on training and development decisions.

Disinterest in Technological Change. This incident tested the hypothesis that older workers are seen as less interested in learning about new technical developments relevant to the job, and the hypothesis that people are less likely to recommend financial support for the development of an older worker. Both hypotheses were strongly supported.

Participants perceived that an older employee was significantly less motivated to keep up to date compared to a younger employee (*M* older = 4.35, *M* younger = 4.97; *t* = 3.79, *p* < .01). The decision to allocate funds so that the employee could attend a training seminar was also influenced by the requester's age. A decision to deny the request for company sponsorship of additional training was more strongly recommended for an older employee compared to a younger employee (*M* older = 3.49, *M* younger = 2.38; *t* = 5.01, *p* < .01).

Untrainability. With the final incident, we tested the hypothesis that older employees whose skills have become obsolete are viewed as less suitable for retraining and are considered expendable. Participants evaluated the desirability of a company-sponsored refresher course significantly lower for a 60-year-old computer programmer compared to a 30-year-old programmer. Mean desirability of organizational support for retraining was 2.95 for the older employee compared to 3.63 for the younger employee (*t* = 2.52, *p* < .05).

The administrative action "terminate the employee whose skills have become obsolete and hire a fully qualified replacement" was evaluated more favorably for an older employee (*M* = 3.21) compared to a younger employee (*M* = 2.53; *t* = 2.40, *p* < .05).

When considered together, findings from the last two incidents suggest that people are less likely to recommend organizational support to maintain and develop the skills of older employees, and are also strongly opposed to providing retraining opportunities for older employees who no longer possess the job knowledge to carry out their job assignments effectively. In these instances, older workers become the double victims of age stereotypes.

Discussion

At a time when increased organizational attention is focused on the career progress of women and minority employees, the plight of older workers has been relatively ignored. Despite legislation prohibiting age discrimination, there is evidence that older workers may be even more subject to unjust treatment than other clases of employees (Palmore & Manton, 1973).

In a previous study, we found that negative job-related characteristics are attributed to older workers (see Rosen & Jerdee, 1976). We hypothesized that when these negative stereotypes are relevant to a work situation, older workers are potential victims of discriminatory managerial decisions. Our findings consistently support this hypothesis. Participants' assumptions about the physical, cognitive, and emotional characteristics of older employees accompanied a series of administrative actions that were clearly damaging to the well-being and career progress of older workers.

In several incidents, assumptions about the decline in mental and physical capacities of older workers were associated with bias against older employees in personnel decisions. However, denying selection, promotion, and training opportunities on the basis of an employee's age is prohibited by the Age Discrimination in Employment Act (Lundquist, 1968).

In another incident, age stereotypes that depict older workers as rigid and resistant to change accompanied a decision to avoid efforts to correct an older employee's performance. The managerial decision to reassign an older employee who is unresponsive to customer complaints deprives that employee of an opportunity to improve his performance. In instances such as this, managerial actions based on age stereotypes are extremely resistant to change. By transferring the older employee, the manager avoids a direct test of his assumptions about the worker's rigidity and resistance to change and, in so doing, precludes the possibility of learning that the age stereotype is not valid.

In other incidents, assumptions about the decline among older workers of the interest, motivation, and ability to improve their job-related skills were reflected in decisions to avoid investments in the continued development of older employees. However, when the older employee's skills become outdated, as depicted in the final incident, the decision to terminate the employee rather than invest in his retraining is favored.

The present study demonstrates the influence of work-related age stereotypes on managerial decisions. These findings are based on the perceptions of undergraduate business students, and generalizations about potential age bias among older respondents must be made with caution. Whether similar biases would be found among personnel administrators and executives remains to be demonstrated.

It should also be noted that an older worker's opportunity for career advancement and job satisfaction is further affected by mandatory retirement policies. In instances where mandatory retirement restricts the potential tenure of older employees, administrators may view investments in the development or promotion of older employees as yielding less organization benefit, compared to similar expenditure for the development or promotion of younger employees. Whether these administrative assumptions are valid depends to some extent on factors such as the turnover rates among younger and older employees. Nevertheless, mandatory retirement tends to work against the career progress of the older worker.

When taken together, our results provide insights about another age stereotype, the commonly accepted belief that older employees reach a time in their careers when motivation significantly declines and they merely "go through the motions" until retirement. The implicit assumption in this belief seems to be that aging produces a decline in motivation. An alternative explanation for the relationship between age and motivation can be deduced from our findings. It is possible that a pattern of discriminatory managerial decisions based on age stereotypes may significantly influence the motivation of older workers during the last 10–15 years of employment. To the extent that an older employee perceives that his actions are no longer instrumental for career advancement because of managerial biases against older workers, his motivation may gradually be lowered. Limited opportunities for development and lack of feedback for ineffective performance further reduce the older employee's work motivation. Thus, it is quite likely that lowered motivation is not a direct result of aging, but a result of changes in managerial attitudes and treatment of older employees.

REFERENCES

Aaronson, B. S. Personality stereotypes of aging. *Journal of Gerontology,* 1966, *21,* 458–462.

Age discrimination moves into the limelight. *Business Week,* June 15, 1974, p. 101.

Harris, L.   *The myth and reality of aging in America.* New York: The National Council on Aging, 1975.

Lundquist, T.   The Age Discrimination in Employment Act. *Monthly Labor Review,* 1968, *91,* 48–50.

Palmore, E. B., & Manton, K.   Ageism compared to racism and sexism. *Journal of Gerontology,* 1973, *28,* 363–369.

Rosen, B., & Jerdee, T. H.   The nature of job-related age stereotypes. *Journal of Applied Psychology,* 1976, *61,* 180–183.

19

Approaches to the Definition of Comparable Worth*

THOMAS A. MAHONEY

Despite the flurry of current attention to the topic, comparable pay for jobs of comparable worth is not a new social or economic issue. Biblical discussion of the comparable worth and pay for harvesters working different amounts of time in the vineyard testifies to the continuing vitality of the issue for thousands of years. Comparable worth, then and now, is conceived as a measure of individuals and/or work, a criterion measure that in some sense "ought" to dictate actual income or compensation. As illustrated in the Biblical parable, the criterion of comparable worth applied by the employer conflicted with that applied by employees, and the compensation provided appeared unjustified to them. Search for a generally accepted criterion of worth continues today in the effort to achieve "comparable pay for jobs of comparable worth." (This phrase is chosen in preference to the more popular phrase of "equal pay for jobs of comparable worth" which, taken literally, would imply equal pay for all jobs whose worth can be compared.)

Judgments about the distribution of income and wealth are made in every society, and policies are formulated to achieve some desired distribution. These policies appear in statutes regarding taxation, welfare payments, other forms of transfer payments, and in social norms regarding individual charity. Various social criteria of justice regarding income and wealth distribution are incorporated in provisions for inheritance, minimal social welfare, and the variation of benefit levels with size of family, age, and other variables. These norms, expressed in custom and statute, vary over time and from one society to another. Social philosophy regarding the distribution of wealth and income in the United States is a continuing concern in political debates.

* From *Academy of Management Review*, 1983, 8, pp. 14–22. Reactions and comments by Sara Rynes were most helpful. A version of this paper was presented at the Academy of Management meeting, San Diego, 1981.

Social concerns for income distribution cannot be differentiated from considerations of employment compensation because fully four fifths of personal income in the United States is derived from employment earnings. Nevertheless, with certain exceptions, the determination of employment compensation has been accomplished independently of the political process. Social norms regarding income distribution have been expressed primarily in statutes concerning income taxation and transfer payments rather than direct regulation of compensation. This is not the case in all societies and need not continue in this country. Concerns for comparable worth, for example, are based in broad social concerns for income distribution and seek changes in income distribution through changes in the distribution of employment compensation.

Comparable worth issues of today derive in part from concern about the economic status of different groups in society, specifically the lower economic status of females compared with that of males (Grune, 1980). This differential in status appears particularly in what has been termed the "earnings gap" between men and women. Female earnings persistently average about 60 percent of male earnings. The male-female earnings gap has been subjected to various analyses seeking to identify causes of the gap and, where appropriate, policies that would eliminate that gap (England & McLaughlin, 1979; Ferber & Lowry, 1976; Fuchs, 1971; Mincer & Polachek, 1978; Oaxaca, 1973; Sawhill, 1973). Implicitly, the earnings gap has been judged socially undesirable. Analyses of the earnings gap attempt to apportion causal influence to different policies and actions in order to give a better understanding of the reasons for the gap and the likely consequences of policy changes.

One significant influence of the male-female earnings gap lies in the occupational distributions of male and female employment (Sanborn, 1964; Treiman & Terrell, 1975). Males and females are not represented equally in the various occupations, and male-dominated occupations are compensated at higher rates than are female-dominated occupations. Causes (and thus potential remedies) of these male-female occupational wage differentials are unclear. The "crowding hypothesis" illustrates one line of reasoning about male-female occupational distributions and wage differentials (England & McLaughlin, 1979). Occupational and industrial labor markets are segmented by sex, according to the crowding hypothesis, with the result that females are discouraged and restricted from entry to male dominated occupations and are crowded into lower paid, female dominated occupations. The consequence of this segmentation and crowding is that restricted supplies in male dominated occupations permit upward wage pressure, and the competition of relative oversupply in female occupations holds down wages there. Correction of the earnings gap, according to proponents of the crowding hypothesis, will occur as barriers to occupational mobility are removed, thus permitting redistribution of occupational employment of males and females with the consequent narrowing of wage differentials.

Another line of reasoning attributes the wage differentials between male- and female-dominated occupations to discrimination in the setting of wage rates (Treiman, 1979). Probably because of custom and social tradition, women's work is undervalued in social attitudes. Social attitudes of the past condoned the payment of lower wages to women than to men regardless of the similarity of work assignments.

More critically, it is argued that social attitudes toward the evaluation of men's and women's work are generalized to the occupations typically performed by each sex. These attitudes are incorporated in existing wage structures and in systems of job evaluation that perpetuate bias in the evaluation of tasks performed in female-dominated occupations. Correction of the earnings gap, then, requires revaluation and realignment of the occupational wage structure, raising the rates of compensation for female-dominated occupations relative to male dominated occupations. Concern for comparable worth derives from this line of reasoning. Some criterion of occupational worth other than traditional wage criteria is sought as the basis for realignment of the wage structure.

Although current concern for comparable worth arises in the context of relative compensation for male- and female-dominated occupations, comparable worth in truth is a more general issue pervading social and economic analysis. Assessments of comparable worth in male- and female-dominated occupations cannot fail to affect assessments of relative worth among any occupations regardless of sex composition. Thus, considerations of criteria of comparable worth naturally extend beyond the more limited range of concern for the male-female earnings gap.

CONCEPTS OF COMPARABLE WORTH

Three major streams of thought can be identified as contributing to the development of concepts of comparable worth. These are arbitrarily labeled (1) social philosophy, (2) economics, and (3) administrative theory. These traditions share many similar concerns and concepts, but they offer different approaches to the development of concepts of comparable worth.

Social Philosophy

This approach to the definition of worth derives from concepts of social comparison, reference groups, and distributive justice (Homans, 1961; Runciman, 1966). Basically, persons and groups that are equal in some critical sense ought to be treated equally, and persons and groups that are different ought to be treated proportionally differently. More specifically, different reward treatments (e.g., earnings) that are not proportional to differences in a critical comparison variable (e.g., skill) are violations of the norms of justice. As applied to the concept of comparable worth, the social philosophy tradition suggests that earnings from employment ought to be proportional to the contributions made through employment.

Although the general norm of proportionality enjoys widespread acceptance, there is less consensus on the operational definition of contributions. In general, the social philosophy tradition tends to emphasize aspects of work inputs, the labor service capabilities brought to and expended in work, and aspects of personal characteristics such as education, skill, and experience. Thus, generalizing, persons or groups expending equal work capabilities ought to be paid equally, and pay differentials should be proportional to the expenditure of work capabilities.

Economics

Two streams of thought in economics are differentiated in terms of approach to the concept of comparable worth, the neoclassical and radical economics approaches. Neoclassical economics approaches the definition of worth in terms of individual valuations expressed in market exchanges. First, each individual buyer and seller assesses the worth of an exchange in terms of its opportunity costs and typically assigns different valuations to the exchange. (Indeed, without these different valuations of worth, no exchange would occur!) A more general concept of worth emerges as market price, the rate at which marginal exchanges occur at general equilibrium in a system of competitive markets. These rates of exchange directly express comparable worth to marginal buyers and sellers. Applied in the context of work and wages, comparable worth is defined as market wage rates realized in a system of competitive markets. The neoclassical tradition thus defines comparable worth as the outcome of a specified system of market exchanges, and it does not specify any particular wage structure or measure of work contributions in the definition (Hicks, 1966).

The tradition of radical economics takes issue with and modifies this approach to the definition of comparable worth (Edwards, Reich, & Gordon, 1975). Briefly, the tradition of radical economics challenges the assumptions of neoclassical economics and views that tradition as an apology for a capitalistic society (Bronfenbrenner, 1970). Considerable emphasis is placed on assertions that the process assumptions of general equilibrium and competitive markets are unrealizable in our society, and that there exist numerous sociopolitical barriers to mobility, competition, and freedom of access and exchange. Various social groups (e.g., females) may be denied entry to selected occupations for employment, thus restricting competition in those occupations and intensifying competition in other occupations (e.g., the crowding hypothesis). Significant wage differentials thus may be maintained between occupations that otherwise would disappear. The tradition of radical economics might accept the ideal definition of comparable worth from the neoclassical tradition, but it stresses the unworkability of this definition in society. Given the realities of sociopolitical structuring of economic opportunities in society, the radical economics tradition would be more inclined to align with the comparable worth concepts of the social philosophy tradition and to specify those contribution characteristics critical in assessing comparable worth.

Administrative Practice

Administrative practice in the establishment of wage rates typically addresses issues of worth within the context of a single employer or work group. Although most administrative practice developed pragmatically, various criteria of worth are evidenced in this practice and employed in the rationalization of practice.

Job evaluation is a major component of administrative practice and is the primary method of determining relative worth of different jobs in a single employing organization (Belcher, 1974; Lytle, 1954). The unit of analysis is the job, and the intent is to evaluate jobs in terms of relative worth to the employer. Evaluations typically are based on arbitrarily specified criteria of comparison that often reflect aspects of work inputs rather than work outputs. Typical criteria for comparison include measures of skill requirements, level of responsibility, and physical and mental demands of the job rather than direct measures of output. The specific criteria for job evaluation often vary from one employer and/or work group to another and, because they are arbitrarily specified, may conflict with normative criteria suggested in the tradition of social philosophy. The approaches of job evaluation and the tradition of social philosophy to assessment of worth are similar in many respects. Both are normative and prescriptive in approach, both employ arbitrary criteria of worth, and both often apply measures of occupational inputs, rationalized in job evaluation as proxies for outputs and in the tradition of social philosophy as direct measures of exchange. The two approaches differ critically, however, in defining the scope of the relevant social population, job evaluation often focusing on a subset of jobs within a single organization (e.g., clerical, production, or managerial) and the tradition of social philosophy tending to include all occupations of society as the relevant population.

A second criterion of worth employed in administrative practice is the concept of market wage derived from the tradition of economics. Some organizations employ surveys of market wages directly in the establishment of wage rates, but others employ market surveys in the validation of job evaluation systems. Job evaluation factors and factor weights must yield relative job evaluations consistent with relative wage rates observed in market surveys (Schwab, 1980). Administrative practice thus tends to employ both a normative criterion of job worth (job evaluation) and an empirical criterion (market surveys). The distinction between these two criteria appears most starkly when the results of job evaluation conflict with wage survey information. No consistent approach to resolving this conflict is apparent either in current practice or in rationalizations of practice.

COMMON DIMENSIONS

Although the various approaches to the definition of comparable worth appear to be quite different, several dimensions of comparison can be identified. Admittedly, the dimensions of comparisons are rather fuzzy, but they nevertheless are useful in highlighting similarities and differences in the broad, analytical approaches to comparable worth and thus in focusing the debate among advocates of each. These dimensions are displayed in Figure 1, which presents an overall summary of the different approaches.

FIGURE 1
Comparisons of Alternative Concepts of Comparable Worth

Comparative Dimensions	Traditions			
	Social Philosophy	Neoclassical Economics	Radical Economics	Administrative
Process/outcome focus	Outcome	Process	Outcome	Process/outcome
Level of analysis	Societal	Market	Societal/market	Firm/market
Person/job focus	Person	Job/person	Person	Job

Process—Outcome

Both the process and outcome of wage determination obviously are closely related. Approaches to the definition of comparable worth differ, however, in terms of relative emphasis on process and outcome in the judgment of job worth. Briefly, worth may be defined as (1) whatever outcomes result from a specified *process* of wage determination (process focus), without regard to the nature of those outcomes; or (2) in terms of comparison of the wage determination *outcomes* with some exogenous criterion of worth (outcome focus) without regard to the process producing those outcomes. Neoclassical economics, for example, defines occupational worth in terms of the process of market exchange. Assuming a system of competitive market exchanges, the resulting market wages are direct expressions of worth independent of any exogenous criteria of worth. Market determined wage rates reflect consumer valuations of the products and services of labor as realized by employers, the comparative productivities of labor in satisfying consumer demands, and employee tastes and preferences for alternative jobs. Relative wages are presumed to change over time as influenced by market demand and supply, and, assuming a competitive market process, they will indicate change in job worth. Market wage surveys employed in wage determination employ this same definition of job worth, and survey results are treated as direct expressions of worth.

Alternatively, the approaches of social philosophy and radical economics tend to emphasize exogenous criteria of worth rather than the process of wage determination. Thus, for example, relative education may be specified as an appropriate criterion for reward differentiation and may be imposed on the assessment of worth; similarly, sex may be rejected as inappropriate. Job evaluation approaches to wage determination also impose externally derived criteria of worth on the system of wage determination, criteria specified by an employer or negotiated through collective bargaining.

Level of Analysis

Three levels of analysis appear in the different approaches to determination of worth—a firm or micro level, a market level, and a societal or macro level. Although wage and earnings relationships at all three levels are interrelated, analytical approaches differ in terms of relative emphasis on the different levels. Also, the application of a single approach to determination of worth at one level of analysis may be inconsistent with application of that same approach at another level of analysis.

The approach of social philosophy, for example, considers macro or societal comparisons of worth to be of greatest significance as evidenced by continuing reference to the male-female earnings gap. The issue of comparable worth is important as it relates to this earnings gap. Although an earnings gap also might be evidenced at market and establishment levels of analysis, the broader societal earnings gap is of primary interest.

The principal level of analysis in the neoclassical approach is the labor market, and comparisons of worth at both firm (micro) and societal (macro) levels of analysis are derived from these market comparisons. The primary focus of radical economics is less clear; both labor market and societal concerns are considered. Societal influences are evidenced in the structuring of labor markets and market processes. Barriers to entry, mobility, and information in both capital and labor markets, for example, contribute to market segmentation and the channeling of competitive forces. Market rates are a joint influence of societal structuring of markets and competitive behaviors within markets. The primary concern, however, is with achieving appropriate societal wage outcomes.

Administrative approaches to wage determination are concerned, of course, with wage setting at the establishment level. They employ concepts reflective of both firm (micro) and market levels of analysis. The primary focus of job evaluation is on relative job comparisons within work groups and establishments, almost regardless of market and societal considerations except as reflected in judgments of worth and equity by employees of the organization. Acceptance by the affected work group is a critical requirement in a system of job evaluation. At the same time, comparability of the job evaluation results with surveys of market wages also figures as an alternative criterion of validity of the system. Thus, alternative levels of analysis are employed in administrative approaches to wage determination, and the relative concern for each varies from one organization to another.

Person—Job

A fundamental differentiation among conceptual approaches is the relative emphasis on person or job as the appropriate basis for determinations of worth. In its extreme form, this distinction appears in assertions that people equal in some critical respect ought to be paid equally and in contradictory assertions that jobs equal in some critical respect ought to be paid equally. In terms of economic analyses, this distinction can be related to the distinction between characteristics of labor supply and labor demand, a distinction that has plagued wage theory for years. Labor demand is conceptualized as demand for the output of labor services (marginal revenue product), yet labor supply is characterized in terms of input characteristics (skill and hours). Neoclassical economics equates demand and supply characteristics in the abstract as "standardized unit of labor," a concept that is virtually impossible to operationalize. Also, because market wage rates reflect marginal decisions in which demand and supply evaluations of worth are presumed to be equal, there is no necessity to differentiate between supply and demand characteristics at the margin.

Concepts of human capital developed and applied in economic analysis illustrate the distinction between job and person characteristics in terms of the concepts of labor demand and supply (Mincer, 1970). Worth based on demand for labor is expressed in characteristics of job performance. Worth thus is assumed to be associated with labor supply or personal characteristics associated with job performance. Certain labor supply characteristics such as education, skill, and experience are assumed to be more productive of desired job performances and deserving of relatively higher wages. Because these labor supply characteristics both command higher wage rates and are considered more productive, they are viewed as measures of human capital. Employees invest in human capital (e.g., education) as justified by the rates of return (wages) for such investments. Human capital concepts thus might be applied to comparable worth judgments in rationalizing personal characteristics of labor supply as the basis for judgments of worth. However, human capital concepts developed from empirical observation of wage differentials associated with personal characteristics also require rationalization or justification on grounds other than labor market wage determination. They require some rationalization of productivity assumptions external to the process of wage determination. Otherwise, all correlations of personal variables (e.g., sex) with wage differentials might be treated as evidence of human capital relationships. Human capital theory, although reliant on market concepts, is equally reliant on independent assumptions about imputations of productivity to personal characteristics of labor supply.

The traditions of social philosophy and radical economics tend to focus on labor supply or personal characteristics—a consequence, in part, of their concern for social group comparisons. Groups equal in terms of relevant personal input characteristics such as education ought to be paid equally. Part of the rationale for this focus is drawn from human capital concepts, but the rationale also is based on social comparison norms of cost, investment, and contribution. Persons making equal investments and contributions to work should be equally compensated.

The administrative approach of job evaluation focuses on the job as the basis of worth, and it considers personal characteristics only as required by the job. Although job evaluation measures tend to reflect measures of contribution and personal input to the job, the intent is to base assessments of worth on the job without differentiating among persons in the same job. One major exception to this approach occurs in the use of maturity curves in the payment of scientific and technical employees; the job in this instance is characterized in terms of qualifications of the incumbent, discipline, and years since graduation (Fuller, 1972). The use of wage survey data in wage determination also is intended to focus on job characteristics rather than personal characteristics.

APPLICATIONS OF CONCEPTS

Applications of conceptual approaches to comparable worth have been varied, ranging from direct applications in wage determination and the formulation of public policy to less direct applications of the concepts in analyses attempting to explain wage phenomena. Direct applications of the concepts in wage determination are observed in job evaluation, wage negotiations, and arbitrators' rulings on wages, all of which employ concepts of comparability. They also figure prominently in recent court decisions and in efforts by the EEOC to develop guidelines for assessing wage discrimination and nondiscrimination under Title VII of the Civil Rights Act (Treiman & Hartmann, 1981).

The dimensions employed in assessing comparability in wage determination vary from one decision to another. Job evaluation, for example, specifies arbitrary, weighted criteria for use in the assessment of relative worth of jobs, and both criteria and weights may vary from one administrative unit to another. Although certain approaches, such as the Hay System, generally are standardized in all settings, other approaches based on empirical factor analyses and policy-capturing analyses may be unique to each application (Robinson, Wahlstrom, & Mecham, 1974). Typically the criteria employed in job evaluation concern dimensions of task requirements rationalized as measures of work contribution. These criteria are assumed to be reflective of both input and output valuations of worth; more onerous tasks both demand greater input contributions and are more productive of valued outputs.

Judgments of the validity of any system of job evaluation employ validity criteria drawn from one or another of the different conceptual approaches. One such criterion is derived from economics. It involves comparison of relative job evaluations with relative wage rates observed in market surveys (Fox, 1972). The job evaluation system is judged valid to the extent that relative market rates are duplicated for key jobs. Several approaches to statistical job evaluation, in fact, are derived from multivariate analysis of wage survey data, with both factors and weights identified empirically (Edwards, 1948). Predictably, this approach to validity assessment of job evaluation is criticized from the traditions of social philosophy and radical economics as merely perpetuating wage inequities established and maintained through discriminatory market institutions. Rather, comparable worth advocates seek an alternative criterion of worth (Treiman & Hartmann, 1981).

Another approach to assessment of the validity of job evaluation rests on its acceptance by those affected by the system—acceptance as demonstrated in terms of attitude surveys, recruiting and turnover experience, grievances, and collective wage negotiations. Acceptability of job evaluation presumably reflects acceptance of both criteria used to assess worth and the assessment of relative value resulting from the evaluation process (Livernash, 1957). Consistent with the tradition of social philosophy, the source of this criterion is found in the social norms and values of groups affected by the system. The scope of the relevant society is relatively confined, however, and norms of acceptability likely vary considerably from one group to another, thus accounting for the many variants of job evaluation observed in practice (Kerr & Fisher, 1950). The application of social norms of acceptability in job evaluation provides the potential for yielding consensus norms of comparable worth assessments in relatively confined societies that are contradictory when aggregated in a larger social setting.

The criteria of job worth expressed in public policy are derived from various influences. The Equal Pay Act of 1963, for example, requires that men and women be paid equally for doing equal work, and it defines equal work as requiring equal skill, effort, and responsibility performed under similar working conditions. Differential payments reflecting seniority, merit, quantity or quality of production, or any factor other than sex are permitted, however. The Equal Pay Act is applicable at the firm or employer level of analysis. It is concerned primarily with wage outcomes rather than wage determination processes, and it tends to focus on job rather than personal characteristics, characteristics similar to those often specified in job evaluation systems.

Most concern for comparable worth issues is derived from Title VII of the 1964 Civil Rights Act, which prohibits discrimination because of race, color, religion, sex, or national origin in all employment practices including compensation (Williams & McDowell, 1980). What constitutes discrimination in compensation is not specified, however. The current debate over comparable worth concepts reflects attempts to establish definitions and guidelines for nondiscriminatory compensation. A committee of the National Academy of Sciences (NAS), under contract with the EEOC, recently completed an investigation of the validity of compensation systems and methods for determining the relative worth of jobs (Treiman & Hartmann, 1981). The committee investigation analyzed male-female wage differentials in light of several of the criteria reviewed here and concluded that (1) market wages cannot be used as the sole standard for judging the relative worth of jobs, and (2) policy interventions to alter market outcomes may be required in order to end discrimination. The committee recommended that some form of job evaluation might be developed for the determination of comparable worth, but it did not recommend any specific criteria for job evaluation. (The NAS committee also considered potential discrimination and bias in job description and job rating, issues not examined here as relevant to the definition of comparable worth.)

The NAS committee recommended a process for determining job worth that reflects several of the approaches to the determination of worth reviewed above. Briefly, the committee recommended that wage differentials paid to white males be accepted as market rates reflecting relative job worth. The same market influences cannot be expected to operate in the determination of wages for females, however. A form of job evaluation was recommended as a means of generalizing market influences to female wages. A method of job evaluation that reproduces relative wage differentials among jobs held by white males might be developed and then applied in the determination of worth of female jobs. Such a norm of comparable worth based solely on the earnings treatment of white males is not likely to satisfy comparable worth advocates of the social philosophy tradition. In fact, it is this norm that is challenged when it is argued that job characteristics common in female occupations are less common and undervalued in male occupations.

CONCLUDING OBSERVATION

One feature that appears in all of the approaches to the definition of worth and that has not been noted explicitly is the role of subjective taste, preference, and norms. Subjective social norms of justice figure prominently in the traditions of both social philosophy and radical economics. These norms dictate the criteria appropriate in the justification of relative earnings. Taste and preference also figure in the labor supply behaviors critical in determining worth in the neoclassical tradition and are expressed in marginal decisions. Although viewed as individual tastes, these preferences undoubtedly are influenced also by social norms and traditions. Further, the ultimate test of job evaluation lies in acceptance of the process by those affected and the compatability of results with their subjective norms of comparability. Judgments of worth ultimately are based on subjective norms, regardless of the tradition employed, and will vary with the subjective norms applied.

The scope of consensus of tastes or norms of relative worth is likely to vary inversely with the specificity of comparisons made. Although broad social consensus regarding the relative worth of male and female mail carriers is conceivable, it is unlikely that consensus regarding the relative worth of secretaries and welders or of two different secretarial positions can be achieved beyond the confines of a single firm or work group.

Finally, note the paradox of aggregation of judgments of relative worth. Judgments of relative worth of different jobs that are acceptable within small social settings may aggregate into measures of earnings at another level of analysis that conflict with broad social norms of worth. Analogously, it would appear unlikely that any specific norms or criteria of comparable worth applied uniformly across society would be accepted consensually within all industries, firms, and work groups. The search for consensual norms of job worth is most likely to be successful if confined to individual firms, regardless of implications for male-female earnings differentials throughout society. The current concern over comparable worth may be rooted in the male-female earnings gap in society, but comparable worth is a more general issue than merely male-female comparisons. It is an issue based on subjective judgments, an issue most likely to be resolved within relatively small groups of employees. Realizations of consensus on comparable worth thus are most likely within small employee groups. "Comparable pay for jobs of comparable worth" within these groups is not likely to impact significantly on the male-female earnings gap in society.

REFERENCES

Belcher, D. W. *Compensation administration.* Englewood Cliffs, N.J.: Prentice-Hall, 1974.

Bronfenbrenner, M. Radical economics in America, 1970. *Journal of Economic Literature,* 1970, *8,* 747–766.

Edwards, P. M. Statistical methods in job evaluation. *Advanced Management,* 1948, *13* (4), 155–163.

Edwards, R. C., Reich, M., & Gordon, D. M. (Eds.). *Labor market segmentation.* Lexington, Mass.: D. C. Heath, 1975.

England, P., & McLaughlin, S. D. Sex segregation of jobs and male-female income differentials. In R. Alvarez, K. Lutterman, & Associates (Eds.), *Discrimination in organizations.* San Francisco: Jossey-Bass, 1979, 189–213.

Ferber, M. A., & Lowry, H. M. The sex differential in earnings: A reappraisal. *Industrial and Labor Relations Review,* 1976, *29,* 377–387.

Fox, W. M. Purpose and validity in job evaluation. *Personnel Journal,* 1972, *51* (10), 432–437.

Fuchs, V. R. Differences in hourly earnings between men and women. *Monthly Labor Review,* 1971, *94,* 9–15.

Fuller, L. E.   Designing compensation programs for scientists and professionals in business. In M. L. Rock (Ed.), *Handbook of wage and salary administration.* New York: McGraw-Hill, 1972, 824–835.

Grune, J. A.   *Manual on pay equity: Raising wages for women's work.* Washington, D.C.: Conference on Alternative State and Local Policies, 1980.

Hicks, J. R.   *The theory of wages.* New York: St. Martin's Press, 1966.

Homans, G.   *Social behavior: Its elementary forms.* New York: Harcourt Brace Jovanovich, 1961.

Kerr, C., & Fisher, L. H.   Effect of environment and administration on job evaluation. *Harvard Business Review,* 1950, *28* (3), 77–96.

Livernash, E. R.   The internal wage structure. In G. W. Taylor & F. C. Pierson (Eds.), *New concepts in wage determination.* New York: McGraw-Hill, 1957, 140–172.

Lytle, C. W.   *Job evaluation methods.* New York: Ronald Press, 1954.

Mincer, J.   The distribution of labor incomes: A survey with special reference to the human capital approach. *Journal of Economic Literature,* 1970, *8,* 1–26.

Mincer, J., & Polachek, S.   Women's earnings reexamined. *Journal of Human Resources,* 1978, *13,* 119–135.

Oaxaca, R.   Male-female wage differentials in urban labor markets. *International Economic Review,* 1973, *14,* 693–709.

Robinson, D. D., Wahlstrom, O. W., & Mecham, R. C.   Comparison of job evaluation methods: A "policy capturing" approach using the position analysis questionnaire. *Journal of Applied Psychology,* 1974, *59,* 633–637.

Runciman, W. G.   *Relative deprivation and social justice.* London: Routledge & Kegan Paul, 1966.

Sanborn, H.   Pay differences between men and women. *Industrial and Labor Relations Review,* 1964, *17,* 534–550.

Sawhill, I. V.   The economics of discrimination against women. *Journal of Human Resources,* 1973, *8* (3), 383–395.

Schwab, D. P.   Job evaluation and pay setting: Concepts and practices. In E. R. Livernash (Ed.), *Comparable worth: Issues and alternatives.* Washington, D.C.: Equal Employment Advisory Council, 1980, 49–78.

Treiman, D. J.   *Job evaluations: An analytical review.* Interim Report of the Committee on Occupational Classification and Analysis to the Equal Employment Opportunity Commission, National Research Council. Washington, D.C.: National Academy of Sciences, 1979.

Treiman, D. J., & Hartman, H. I. (Eds.).   *Women, work, and wages: Equal pay for jobs of equal value.* Washington, D.C.: National Academy Press, 1981.

Treiman, D. J., & Terrell, K.   Women, work and wages—trends in the female occupational structure since 1940. In K. Land & S. Spilerman (Eds.), *Social indicator models.* New York: Russell Sage Foundation, 1975, 157–200.

Williams, R. E., & McDowell, D. S.   The legal framework. In E. R. Livernash (Ed.), *Comparable worth: Issues and alternatives,* Washington, D.C.: Equal Employment Advisory Council, 1980, 197–250.

20

The Protestant Ethic Scale as a Predictor of Repetitive Work Performance*

MATTHEW R. MERRENS and
JAMES B. GARRETT

The influence of the Protestant ethic in relation to the development of capitalism and western society has been widely discussed (Fullerton, 1959; Weber, 1958). However, until recently the Protestant ethic has not been conceptualized as a personality variable. Through efforts of Mirels and Garrett (1971) a scale was constructed to assess the Protestant ethic as a major personality construct. Their initial investigation firmly established the internal consistency of the Protestant Ethic Scale and also reported a number of relevant correlations with other established measures. Significant positive correlations were found with the Mosher Sex Guilt ($r = .29, p < .01$) and Morality Conscience Guilt Scales ($r = .30, p < .01$), as well as with the California F Scale ($r = .51, p < .001$). A significant negative correlation was obtained in relation to Rotter's Internal-External Scale ($r = .30, p < .01$). Nonsignificant correlations were found in relation to the Marlowe-Crowne Social Desirability Scale ($r = -.10$) and the Sensation Seeking Scale ($r = -.06$). In two later investigations by MacDonald (1971, 1972), further correlational exploration of the Protestant ethic was undertaken. In his investigations high Protestant ethic scores were significantly related to negative attitudes toward the poor and opposition to a guaranteed minimum annual income. In addition, MacDonald reported that values such as comfortable life, equality, exciting life, and pleasure were negatively related, while ambition, self-control, salvation, and social responsibility were positively related to Protestant ethic endorsement. As the brief review above indicates, the research to date used a correlational strategy and disclosed several interesting relationships with more established scales and variables.

* From *Journal of Applied Psychology*, 1975, *60*, 125–127. Copyright 1975 by the American Psychological Association. Reprinted by permission.

One of the most basic elements of the original conception of the Protestant ethic concerned work behavior (Weber, 1958). The quote "He who will not work, neither shall he eat" summarizes the essential point that hard and steady work is valued, while unwillingness to work is a symptom of absence of grace and a great sin. Since the work component was an important element in Weber's conception of the Protestant ethic/capitalism relationship, the same component may be an important element of the Protestant ethic now conceived as a personality variable. Therefore, the purpose of this study was to experimentally determine the work styles of high and low Protestant ethic individuals in a task designed to provide low motivation and interest levels. In this investigation a departure from previous studies was the use of an experimental strategy in which the Protestant ethic is related to independently measured nontest behavior. A similar approach was taken by Crowne and Marlowe (1964) in exploring the social desirability variable.

METHOD

Subjects

The Protestant Ethic Scale was administered as part of a large test battery to 333 introductory psychology students with a resultant mean of 86.57 and a standard deviation of 13.55. The 40 male and female subjects in this study were drawn from that population. The high Protestant ethic group was composed of 20 subjects scoring at least one standard deviation above the mean of the Protestant Ethic Scale, and the low Protestant ethic group was composed of 20 subjects scoring at least one standard deviation below the mean on the Protestant Ethic Scale.

Procedure

To eliminate the possible influence of any demand characteristics for specific work performance resulting from the administration of the Protestant Ethic Scale:

1. The Protestant Ethic Scale (19 items) was administered as a small segment of the total test battery.
2. The assessment of work behavior occurred at least seven weeks after the Protestant ethic assessment.
3. The Protestant Ethic Scale and the assessment of work behavior were administered by different experimenters.
4. The 40 subjects chosen for the work behavior task were told that

their names were selected *at random* to participate in a psychology experiment for which they would receive extra credit.

Subjects were seated alone at a table in a small room. Neatly stacked on a table in front of each subject were 100 sheets of 8 × 10-inch paper. On each sheet were printed 25 rows of 10 circles, a total of 250 circles. The subject was given the following directions:

> This is an experiment testing eye-hand coordination. I would like you to draw an "X" in the circles on the sheets in front of you with your non-preferred hand. If you are right-handed, use your left hand. Complete as many as you are able until you become tired. When you are finished, open the door and I will collect your completed sheets.

For each subject the time spent in the room and the number of circles marked served as the dependent measures of work behavior. If the subject did not leave the room after 30 minutes, the experimenter entered the room and told the subject the experiment was over. For such subjects a time of 30 minutes was recorded. All subjects were debriefed upon completing the experimental task.

RESULTS AND DISCUSSION

Table 1 presents the means and standard deviations for both high and low Protestant ethic groups on the two dependent measures. On both dependent measures a significant difference was found between

TABLE 1
Work Behavior of High and Low Protestant Ethic Groups

Protestant Ethic Group	M	SD	df	t
Time spent (in minutes)				
High	23.00	6.25	38	3.49*
Low	16.85	4.80		
Sheets completed				
High	4.10	.72	38	4.98†
Low	2.55	1.19		

Note: For each group, n = 20.
* p < .01.
† p < .001.

the Protestant ethic groups, with high Protestant ethic subjects spending more time working and also producing more output.

The results provide support for the contention that type of work behavior is clearly a component of the Protestant ethic personality variable as measured by the Protestant Ethic Scale. A replication of these findings was obtained with a different population of students ($N = 20$) at another institution with similar results, thus providing additional support of generality and reliability.[1] Since work behavior is a very important and relevant aspect of many human experiences (e.g., academic achievement and occupational success), a paper-and-pencil predictive measure should have wide utility for applied as well as research purposes.

The authors are presently investigating various types of work activities with various interest and motivational levels in relation to the Protestant ethic personality variable.

REFERENCES

Crowne, D. P., & Marlowe, D.   *The approval motive.* New York: Wiley, 1964.

Fullerton, K.   Calvinism and capitalism: An explanation of the Weber thesis. In R. W. Green (Ed.), *Protestantism and capitalism: The Weber thesis and its critics.* Boston: Heath, 1959.

MacDonald, A. P., Jr.   Correlates of the ethics of personal conscience and the ethics of social responsibility. *Journal of Consulting and Clinical Psychology,* 1971, *37,* 443.

MacDonald, A. P., Jr.   More on the Protestant ethic. *Journal of Consulting and Clinical Psychology,* 1972, *39,* 116–122.

Mirels, H. L., & Garrett, J. B.   The Protestant ethic as a personality variable. *Journal of Consulting and Clinical Psychology,* 1971, *36,* 40–44.

Weber, M.   *The Protestant ethic and the spirit of capitalism* (Trans. by Talcott Parsons). New York: Scribner's, 1958.

---

[1] Matthew R. Merrens, "The Protestant Ethic Scale and Work Behavior: A Replication." Unpublished paper, 1974. The findings were replicated at the State University of New York, Plattsburgh, with 10 high and 10 low Protestant Ethic Scale subjects.

21

Turnover Turned Over: An Expanded and Positive Perspective*

DAN R. DALTON and WILLIAM D. TODOR

The references to turnover in the organizational literature began to appear around the year 1900 (104). Soon an emphasis emerged which considered both the costs of turnover and how these costs might be reduced (5, 6, 7, 24, 33, 83, 116). Nonorganizational scholars, notably economists, have also shared a concern with turnover (117). These early studies have much in common with current views of organizational turnover and its implications. Recent reviews of turnover (19, 51, 53, 102, 104, 115, 133) continue to emphasize the dysfunctional aspects of turnover on the organization.

These negative connotations have become axiomatic. In its most visible form turnover tends to be associated with short-term disturbances imposed on the organization: interruptions of normal operations, retraining, scheduling difficulties, etc. This lack of stability fosters responses which range from managerial irritation to organizational arrest.

However, before concluding that turnover is invariably undesirable, it should be placed into a larger perspective. How does turnover fit into the individual and societal context in which it is found?

Porter and Steers (102) suggest that turnover represents an interesting and important phenomenon to those concerned with studying the behavior of individuals in organizations. Turnover is referred to as a "relatively clear-cut act of behavior that has potentially critical consequences for both the person and the organization" (102, p. 151). However, these "critical consequences" need not be, and often are not, undesirable to the individual, the organization, or society. It is sug-

* From *Academy of Management Review*, 1979, 4, pp. 225–235. The authors wish to express their appreciation to Robert Dubin, Newton Margulies, Joseph W. McGuire, and Lyman W. Porter for their comments on this manuscript.

gested here that turnover is a *positive* phenomenon. It is with this focus that turnover will be examined.

This investigation will be conducted from four perspectives: *(a)* organizational, *(b)* economic, *(c)* sociological, and *(d)* psychological/social psychological.

ORGANIZATIONAL PERSPECTIVE OF TURNOVER

Most organizational theorists have focused on the negative aspects of turnover. This view is related to an alleged inverse relationship between turnover and organizational effectiveness (104). Establishing empirical support for this view is problematic. Often the research is biased because it fails to consider the possible benefits of turnover.

For instance, there is evidence that describes the costs of turnover to the organization (39, 66, 86, 87, 132). These costs are generally for recruitment, replacement, and training of personnel. In a recent article, Mirvis and Lawler (86) measured the financial impact of employee attitudes. Among dimensions measured was the cost of turnover to the organization. An essential qualification can be made to these analyses as they do not consider both sides of the balance sheet. Investigations of this nature may mislead the reader because only the costs are reported. In order to accurately evaluate the consequences of turnover on organizational effectiveness, both the costs and the benefits should be assessed.

Accounting procedures aside, there is evidence that turnover does not decrease organizational effectiveness. Available research does not indicate a consistent relationship between measures of production and turnover (80, 89, 100).

Turnover Can Increase Effectiveness

There is evidence that turnover *increases,* not decreases, organizational effectiveness (47, 60, 131, 135, 140). Innovation has clear implications for organizational effectiveness. Mobility has been cited by many as a force by which innovation is moved from firm to firm (25, 46, 65). Grusky (46) has indicated that the process of mobility brings "new blood" and new ideas into the organization. This process vitalizes the organization and enables it to adapt more adequately to internal demand and ever-changing environmental pressures. Dubin (25) says one of the important consequences of the immobile work career is that which Thorstein Veblen has referred to as "trained incapacity." Dubin suggested that "trained incapacity" is the inability to conceive of, or utilize, new ideas. Immobility, then, is dysfunctional to innovation and may reduce organizational effectiveness.

Recent work in the area of institutional management (4, 98) has also posited the importance of personnel movement from firm to firm as a mechanism for the transfer of innovation. These movements are also essential to the development of interfirm organization, which is believed to be a critical element of institutional management (97).

Another key dimension in organizational effectiveness is the capacity and ease by which technological changes can be incorporated (26, 37, 38). Flexibility and adaptability are critical elements of organizational effectiveness (13, 29, 40, 88, 93, 114, 125, 126, 134). The influx of trained personnel is vital. Work force mobility may be fundamental to achieving this goal.

Lawler (66) has suggested that organizations should adopt a policy to reduce turnover. This position may be subject to several exceptions. In the case of seasonal industries and seasonal employment the costs of stability are enormous. For example, the expense of maintaining a year-round labor force in the fruit picking and canning industry would be prohibitive.

Variables Affecting Turnover

There are several variables which purportedly affect the level of turnover. The following illustrate some of the relationships which are common in the literature:

a. The level of pay is inversely related to turnover (11, 16, 18, 36, 58, 66, 77, 102).
b. Routinization is positively related to turnover (9, 44, 56, 102).
c. Accurate communication about the nature of the job is inversely related to turnover (44, 66, 102).
d. Centralization is inversely related to turnover (10, 44, 66, 80, 96, 102).
e. Integration is inversely related to turnover (66, 96, 102, 115).

These relationships suggest that an organization could reduce turnover by reviewing practices and procedures, and by modifying pay scales and structure. But at what cost? Mechanisms may be available to reduce turnover but organizations may be hesitant to utilize them. Perhaps the cost incurred to reduce turnover might exceed the cost of turnover itself. There is, for example, a characteristically high rate of turnover among waitresses. Perhaps by raising wages, the organizations could reduce the incidence of turnover. But is this strategy cost effective? It may be far less expensive to cope with turnover than to prevent it.

There are other areas in which organizations benefit from turnover. Private pension funds are based on nonturnover employees. Recent managerial opposition to the vesting of pension funds may have reflected a view that employee turnover would substantially reduce the future payout from such funds.

ECONOMIC PERSPECTIVE OF TURNOVER

Turnover is not an issue for the classical economist. In the analysis of the competitive firm, wages must equal marginal product. Since wages and marginal product are assumed to be equal in most firms, no one person nor firm should suffer from turnover (12). Unless the managers of a firm believed that the marginal productivity of a prospective employee was at least equal to the wage which would be paid, the employee would not be hired.

The assumptions which lead to this analysis are not entirely self-evident. It is not clear that all employees are rational nor all firms competitive in the classical sense. Also, firms or individuals may not have sufficient knowledge about marginal products or relative wages to operationalize this simple model.

There is evidence to support the marginal productivity theory. According to this theory, there is a close relationship between wage differentials and the allocation of labor to various employments. Wage differentials reflect present variations in the supply-demand proportions of labor for different types and/or locations of work. Being rational and income-maximizing, labor will respond to existing structure of wages (and nonmonetary incentives) by moving away from employments of less net attractiveness and toward employment of relatively greater attractiveness (41).

This assertion is subject to criticism. Individual rationality and the propensity to maximize income are questionable. Nonetheless, the Office of Research and Statistics of the U.S. Social Security Administration (90) concluded that there is a meaningful amount of purposive mobility in the economy. Moreover, it is possible for the labor market to make marginal adjustments that are envisaged in conventional economic theory of the labor market.

Gallaway (37) suggests empirical evidence concerning geographic mobility argues that behavior is reasonably consistent with the premises of conventional economic theory. Differential economic advantage may not be the only factor, but it is clearly an important one.

Wertheimer (136) supports this view. In his book, *The Monetary Rewards of Migration within the United States,* he says the income difference attributable to migration is positive for all categories of employment investigated. Furthermore, there is evidence that individuals do not leave an organization without having assessed the market (57, 82, 93). A large percentage of individuals have made arrangements for new employment before leaving (82).

The existence of opportunity knowledge suggests an important implication of turnover for the economy. Given that mobility results in net positive income to the migrators, it may be concluded that mobility increases net national product (35, 69) and contributes to the long-term growth rate of the economy (37, 38).

For a variety of economic, ethical, and social reasons, many people favor mitigation of income differences, and therefore find equalizing measures desirable. Again, horizontal and vertical mobility is a mechanism for decreasing income differences (35, 69).

Nonmobility in the labor force may result in "stickiness" in local labor markets. This tendency is especially problematic in declining labor markets. Rather than moving to more viable markets, some employees prefer to remain until such time as employment is finally terminated. This has two important consequences. *First,* this persistence increases short-run costs to employers in wages and benefits. *Second,* this lack of migration may generate a long-run cost to the community in terms of unemployment compensation and related support programs.

Two Labor Market Theories

Economics offers two theories closely aligned with turnover: the dual labor market and the theory of labor market segmentation. Virtually all labor market studies have shown that the labor force is segmented in some sense (91, 106). Segmentation separates labor into primary and secondary markets. Piore (99) discusses the character of these markets.

The *primary* market offers jobs which possess several of the following traits: *(a)* high wages, *(b)* good working conditions, *(c)* employment stability, *(d)* job security, *(e)* equity, *(f)* due process in the administration of work rules, and *(g)* chances for advancement.

The *secondary* market is decidedly different. Secondary jobs are less attractive with *(a)* lower wages, *(b)* poorer working conditions, *(c)* considerable variation in employment stability, *(d)* harsh and often arbitrary discipline, and *(e)* little opportunity for advancement.

This segmentation may have very important implications for turnover in organizations and society. Typically, the primary market is not characterized by ease of entry. Kerr (63) points out that many jobs in the primary market are distinguished by limited ports of entry and various sorting procedures. They require preparation and ritual. Proper educational and/or social levels must be attained in order to enter the primary labor market.

The relevance to turnover is clear. Individuals, by and large, begin their employment in the secondary market. Vertical mobility from the secondary market to the primary is difficult. Orderlies do not ordinarily become doctors and mail room clerks do not become accountants through vertical mobility. More often individuals must quit their jobs in the secondary market, attain the necessary educational and social prerequisites, and then enter the primary market. In order to bridge these labor market levels one must become a turnover "statistic." What are the implications of reducing this secondary-to-primary labor market turnover? Osterman (91) has suggested that movements between segments are important matters of public concern. Each of us could consider our employment history and cite many instances of turnover in the secondary market while striving to train for and enter the primary market.

The findings that turnover increases concomitantly with the educational level of the worker (14, 44, 96) may be partially explained by the dual market phenomenon. Education may ease entry into the primary market. If so, horizontal turnover may be necessary since it is not usually possible to enter the primary market vertically within the subject organization. The individual must leave the secondary, acquire the requisite education, and reenter the labor market in the primary sector.

To summarize from the economic perspective, turnover increases net national product, may reduce inequitable distribution of income, contributes to the long-term growth rate of the economy, and reduces market "stickiness" with its resultant dysfunctions. Additionally, turnover, in an economic context, becomes a necessary behavior for those who would aspire to enter the primary market.

SOCIOLOGICAL PERSPECTIVE OF TURNOVER

With respect to turnover, there may be a Smithian "invisible hand" prejudice operating. Increasing the satisfaction of an individual, and thereby preventing turnover, does not necessarily enhance the satisfaction of society. Adam Smith, writing in *An Inquiry into the Nature and Causes of the Wealth of Nations* (118), popularized the notion of the "invisible hand." Simply, this concept suggests that individual decisions are "led by an invisible hand to promote . . . the public interest." Adam Smith did *not* state that this was invariably true. However, he and his followers have contributed to a dominant tendency of thought, that is, a propensity to assume that decisions reached individually will, in fact, be in the best interests of an entire society.

This illustrates the fallacy of composition wherein premises assert something about the parts of the whole and the conclusion asserts what is true of the parts is necessarily true of the whole (79). Examples of this fallacy are clearly seen in the "paradox of thrift" (120) and the "tragedy of the commons" (74).

Society does not necessarily gain by the reduction of turnover in the organization. The reduction may, in fact, involve important dysfunctions to society. Society has a stake in the advancement, both social and economic, of its citizenry. One way this growth can be accomplished is through vertical mobility within the organization. Fortunately, vertical and horizontal mobility are not contradictory or mutually exclusive concepts (127). Hall (49) suggests horizontal and spatial mobility are generally closely related to vertical mobility. Job changes are important components of the vertical mobility process. This movement provides a legitimating mechanism for individuals to move toward those positions best suited to their abilities (109). Indeed, horizontal migration has become increasingly effective as a selection process by which individuals are channeled to places where their potential can be realized more fully (17).

Mobility is of importance, not only to the individual, but to the efficiency and well-being of society (71). Progress comes through movements to new jobs involving more skill, responsibility, and independence (107). Very often the firm does not have the growth potential or the positions available wherein the individual can prosper. Turnover may be an expected consequence of the limited opportunity for vertical mobility within an organization.

Notions of success and achievement are central to the study of mobility. When occupational achievement and open class ideology are present, mobility becomes a primary mechanism for distributing the labor force and providing progressive career stages (85, 94). Other studies have shown similar relations between levels of aspiration and turnover (23, 105). Also, individuals tend to change jobs as their perception of opportunity increases (18, 21, 36, 81, 96).

In fact, it may be that turnover in these cases does not arise merely as a reaction to lack of opportunity in the organization. Individuals may seek mobility as a proactive strategy. Increasingly, people seem to be planning, and actually having, careers involving multiple organizations and even multiple occupations (101). The "stepping stone" job strategy appears to be operational in some individuals (42, 60, 119).

In a survey of executives (reported in the *Los Angeles Times*, October 31, 1977), mobility was cited as essential for success in the business world. Two thirds of the respondents had worked for three or more organizations and only 14 percent had held their present positions for five or more years. Greater potential for advancement and increased scope of responsibility were identified as the primary motives for horizontal mobility.

It has been estimated that one third of the work force may be employed in career-type occupations and professions (137). Evidence supports the generalization that upward occupational achievement is more probable when one has high aspirations and a willingness to be horizontally as well as vertically mobile (127). It is no surprise that people with a high "career anchor" (129) commonly turn over. It may well be a sound strategy for advancement.

Mobility Reduces Inequality

Mobility may also serve to reduce inequality or inequity in social exchange (2, 3, 15, 54, 111, 130). Indeed the exchange approach in sociology might be described as the economic analysis of noneconomic social situations (31). From the perspective of any approach, perceived inequity and inequality may be reduced by mobility of the actors.

Society may be served by diverting migration away from large cities to less crowded areas. This amounts to a reduction in ecological pressure (136). In all probability, any such migration results in turnover for some firm, somewhere.

Given turnover could be substantially reduced, what are the consequences and costs to society? Assume individuals are convinced (co-opted) to remain at their first job. What are the social costs of not advancing beyond that point in their career development; not having become a turnover "statistic"?

From a sociological perspective, the positive aspects of turnover are impressive. Horizontal mobility may be the means by which the social and economic growth of the citizenry may be accomplished. Occupational achievement, beneficial to society, is facilitated by those who are horizontally as well as vertically mobile. Mobility may reduce inequity in social exchange. Finally, turnover may be a mechanism to reduce ecological pressure.

PSYCHOLOGICAL/SOCIAL PSYCHOLOGICAL PERSPECTIVES OF TURNOVER

As living organisms, individuals are endowed with the ability to respond to both benign and noxious environmental stimuli (28, 56). Systems possessing the ability to react to their environments in a manner favorable to the viability of the organism have a quality referred to as "adaptability" (48). Coping and response to organizational stress have been addressed in the organizational literature (61). An individual's decision to initiate a particular movement (turnover) can be defined as an adjustment process in an adaptive system maintaining its homeostatic level (43). The literature is replete with references to the notion of movement as a response to stress (20, 43, 56, 67, 68, 70,

92, 121, 138, 139). Ritchey's (108) analysis adequately summarizes the view: When the stress threshold is exceeded, it produces the decision to move.

Organizations may not benefit from reducing turnover caused by environmental stress. Kurt Lewin's (72, 73) concept of force field analysis illustrates this point. Movement from a quasi-stationary equilibrium may be accomplished by increasing forces to move or by reducing resisting forces. The former *increases* while the latter *decreases* pressure on the individual. Organizations attempting to reduce turnover create forces resisting the decision to move. The original quasi-stationary equilibrium may be maintained but the total pressure on the individual will have increased. The individual may take other, perhaps counterproductive, actions to reduce the pressure. Turnover would have been a positive action in this case for the individual involved and the organization as well.

For the extreme case there is evidence that turnover may be the end product of the somatic conversion to stress (32, 61, 62, 124, 128). The organization should not deter turnover by employees inflicted with physical manifestations of stress. The health of the individual and the organization are clearly enhanced by withdrawal in these cases.

In the less extreme case, the process of adjustment to employment by the individual may be dysfunctional to the organization (9, 75). Individuals may not leave the organization for a variety of reasons, including the fact that they may have been co-opted by the organization. The organization may succeed in reducing turnover. This, however, does not suggest that individuals will not display coping mechanisms and withdrawal behavior. The employee may resort to temporary withdrawals. As a response to role conflict or stress the employee may answer with alcoholism, drug abuse, accidents, or other nonproductive behaviors (52, 78). Chung (22) suggests that dissatisfied performers who do not leave the organization may express dissatisfaction with apathy, sabotage, absenteeism, and other counterproductive behaviors. It would be far better for the organization if these individuals would leave.

A Judgmental Error

Turnover may be a response to judgmental error by the employee. Proactive mobility excepted, some aspirants, while theoretically free to choose an occupation, have no means to ascertain occupational opportunities or have their occupational aptitudes evaluated (127). Individuals have little market information and few resources to sustain themselves while job searching (37, 108). An individual's choice of occupation may be influenced more by social space than by knowledge, experience, or a rational approach to the labor market (127). Dubin (26) points out that for the bulk of the population, the decision about type of work is made when the choice becomes necessary, namely, when the labor market is initially entered. This strategy leads to error. Individuals enter the labor market with little information and have a large degree of ignorance about future outcomes (30). Under these circumstances, turnover as a response to error in judgment is an inevitable and expected consequence of such work-search behavior.

This tendency may exist later in individuals' careers as well. Pavalko (95) refers to this phenomenon as the "career crunch," suggesting that expectations about present and future occupational activities are often inconsistent with the reality. When an alternative employment opportunity arises, an increase in turnover may be expected (8, 36, 66).

Too much commitment can be disadvantageous to an organization's flexibility (112). This can be true on several dimensions. Commitment can lead to an inviolate trust of past policies (112), or to the affirmation of past mistakes (64, 122, 123). It may be partially responsible for the phenomenon which Janis (59) has referred to as "groupthink." The infusion of new personnel may mitigate these tendencies. The cosmopolitan (45, 84) whose commitment is more focused on professional ability and not on the organization, might be a more valuable asset to the organization's flexibility and innovation than the individual not likely to turn over.

Turnover may be seen as a reaction to stress which may be far less destructive than its alternatives, a strategy by which initial job-entry errors are rectified, and a possible amelioration of the dysfunctions associated with overcommitment to an organization.

CONCLUSION

The emphasis has been on turnover with a positive focus from the perspective of several disciplines: (a) organizational, (b) economic, (c) sociological, and (d) psychological/social psychological. Any substantial reduction in the amount of turnover may have short-run positive consequences for the firm. However, the long-run implications may be dysfunctional to the individual, the organization, and to society.

From the organizational standpoint, turnover costs may be misrepresented because of a failure to account for the benefits as well as the costs of turnover. There is evidence that turnover increases organizational effectiveness and innovation, assists the development of institutional management and interfirm cooperation, and augments technological change. Furthermore, the costs of reducing turnover may exceed the actual cost of turnover.

From an economic viewpoint, it has been suggested that mobility and migration are essential. In general, mobility increases net national product and contributes to the long-term growth rate of the economy. It serves to reduce the income disparity of individuals. Turnover may also be the main process by which individuals progress from the *secondary* to the *primary* job market.

Sociologically, mobility aids both the social and economic development of the individual. Mobility may provide a means to promote progression through career stages and a selective process whereby individuals are channeled to areas in which their potential can be more fully realized. Mobility may serve to reduce inequity and inequality in social exchange. Also, migration may be a strategy for reducing ecological pressure.

Finally, turnover may be a coping mechanism for the individual under stress. Blocking this process may invite absenteeism, apathy, sabotage, and other nonproductive or counterproductive behaviors. Turnover allows for the rectification of errors that occur in the job search process. In addition, the organization must be aware of the consequence of little or no turnover coupled with overcommitment to the organization.

To view turnover as a strictly positive or negative phenomenon seems somewhat shortsighted. Certainly, turnover has both positive and negative ramifications for the organization. What, then, is the appropriate level of turnover? Several factors should be considered.

First, the amount of turnover is most often expressed in terms of a percentage. This measure is difficult to interpret and may be misleading. For instance, an unusually high percentage of turnover would not be meaningful in a seasonal industry and/or seasonal employment. Also, high rates of turnover can be anticipated in industries in which the cost of preventing turnover exceeds the cost of turnover itself. Therefore, for those working as bank tellers, waitresses, and other, similar jobs, this tendency would be expected.

Second, raw turnover percentages are difficult to evaluate without considering the individual component. A relatively low percentage of turnover of 1 or 2 percent could have critical consequences for an organization if the individuals who have chosen to leave had essential or exclusive skills or information. Similarly, a rather large percentage turnover rate would have little impact if the individuals who leave are perceived to have little of such information. To compare one organization's 20 percent turnover rate with another's 35 percent rate on the basis of the raw percentage alone would be hazardous.

Third, in order to assess turnover accurately, both the costs and the benefits of turnover should be appraised. Estimating the impact of turnover on the organization by summing the costs of recruitment, training, etc. only reflects one side of the equation. It ignores the possibility that turnover has positive consequences for the organization, some of which have been the subject of preceding sections.

Fourth, turnover, to be evaluated accurately, should include a perspective broader than that of a single individual or even the single firm because it has consequences that transcend the organization or any of its members.

REFERENCES

1. Abbott, L. D. *Masterworks of economics.* New York: McGraw-Hill, 1973.
2. Adams, J. S. Toward an understanding of inequity. *Journal of Abnormal Social Psychology,* 1963, 67, 422–436.
3. Adams, J. S. Inequality in social exchange. In L. Berkowitz (Ed.), *Advances in experimental social psychology.* New York: Academic Press, 1966.
4. Aldrich, H. E. & Pfeffer, J. Environments of organizations. In Alex Inkeles, James Coleman, and Neil Smelser (Eds.), *The annual review of sociology.* Palo Alto, Calif.: Annual Reviews, Inc., 1976, 79–116.
5. Alexander, M. Cost of hiring and firing men. *Engineering Magazine,* 1915a, *48,* 733–736.
6. Alexander, M. Waste in hiring and discharging employees. *Scientific American,* 1915b, 79, 102–103.
7. Alexander, M. Hiring and firing: Its economic waste and how to avoid it. *Annals of the American Academy of Political and Social Science,* 1916, 65, 128–144.
8. Anderson, B. W. Empirical generalizations on labor turnover. In R. Pegnetter (Ed.), *Labor and manpower.* Iowa City: University of Iowa Press, 1974.
9. Argyris, C. *Understanding organizational behavior.* Homewood, Ill.: Dorsey, 1960.
10. Argyris, C. Personality and organization theory revisited. *Administrative Science Quarterly,* 1973, *18,* 141–167.
11. Armknecht, P. A. & Early, J. F. Quits in manufacturing: A study of their cause. *Monthly Labor Review,* 1972, 95, 31–37.
12. Becker, G. S. *Human capital.* New York: National Bureau of Economic Research, 1975.
13. Bennis, W. G. Toward a truly scientific management: The concept of organizational health. *General Systems Yearbook,* 1962, 7, 269–282.
14. Berg, I. *Education and jobs.* New York: Praeger, 1970.
15. Blau, P. M. *Exchange and power in social life.* New York: Wiley, 1964.
16. Blau, P. M. *The organization of academic work.* New York: Wiley, 1973.
17. Blau, P. M., & Duncan, O. D. *The American occupational structure.* New York: Wiley, 1967.
18. Bowey, A. M. *A guide to manpower planning.* London: MacMillan, 1974.

19. Brayfield, A. H., & Crockett, W. H. Employee attitudes and employee performance. *Psychological Bulletin*, 1955, 52, 396–424.
20. Brown, L. A., & Moore, E. G. The intraurban migration process: A perspective. *General Systems Yearbook*, 1970, 15, 109–122.
21. Burton, B. R., & Parker, J. E. Interindustry variations in voluntary labor mobility. *Industrial Labor Relations Review*, 1969, 22, 199–216.
22. Chung, K. H. *Motivational theories and practices.* Columbus, Ohio: Grid, 1977.
23. Crockett, H. J. The achievement motive and differential occupational mobility in the United States. *American Sociological Review*, 1962, 27, 191–204.
24. Dennison, H. S. Methods of reducing the labor turnover. *U.S. Bureau of Labor Statistics Bulletin No. 202.* Washington, D.C.: U.S. Government Printing Office, 1916, 56–59.
25. Dubin, R. Management in Britain—impressions of a visiting professor. *Journal of Management Studies*, 1970, 7, 183–198.
26. Dubin, R. Work in modern society. In R. Dubin (Ed.), *Handbook of work, organization, and society.* Chicago: Rand McNally, 1976, 5–36.
27. Dubin, R., Hedley, R. A., & Taveggia, T. C. Attachment to work. In R. Dubin (Ed.), *Handbook of work, organization, and society.* Chicago: Rand McNally, 1976, 281–341.
28. Dubos, R. *Man adapting.* New Haven, Conn.: Yale University Press, 1965.
29. Duncan, R. B. Multiple decision making structures in adapting to environmental uncertainty: The impact on organizational effectiveness. *Human Relations*, 1973, 26, 273–291.
30. Dunkerley, D. *Occupations and society.* London: Routledge & Kegan Paul, 1975.
31. Emerson, R. M. Social exchange theory. In A. Inkeles, J. Coleman, & N. Smelser (Eds.), *The annual review of sociology.* Palo Alto, Calif.: Annual Reviews, Inc., 1976, 335–362.
32. Ferguson, D. A study of neurosis and occupation. *British Journal of Industrial Medicine*, 1973, 30, 187–198.
33. Fisher, B. Methods of reducing the labor turnover. *Annals of the American Academy of Political and Social Sciences*, 1916, 65.
34. Fraser, R. The incidence of neurosis among factory workers. *Industrial Health Research Board Report No. 90*, 1947.
35. Friedman, M. *Capitalism and freedom.* Chicago: University of Chicago Press, 1962.
36. Fry, F. L. A behavioral analysis of economic variables affecting turnover. *Journal of Behavioral Economics*, 1973, 2, 247–295.
37. Gallaway, L. E. *Manpower economics.* Homewood, Ill.: Irwin, 1971.
38. Gallaway, L. E. The significance of the labor market. In R. L. Rowan (Ed.), *Readings in labor economics and labor relations.* Homewood, Ill.: Irwin, 1977.
39. Gaudet, F. J. *The literature on labor turnover.* New York: Industrial Relations Press, 1960.
40. Georgopoulos, B. S., & Tannenbaum, A. S. The study of organizational effectiveness. *American Sociological Review*, 1957, 22, 534–540.

41. Gitlow, A. L. *Labor and manpower economics.* Homewood, Ill.: Irwin, 1971.
42. Glickman, A. S., Hahn, C. P., Fleishman, E. A., Baxter, B. *Top management development and succession.* New York: MacMillan, 1968.
43. Golant, S. M. Adjustment process in a system: A behavioral model of human movement. *Geographical Analysis,* 1971, *3,* 203–220.
44. Goodman, P. S., Salipante, P., & Paransky, H. Hiring, training, and retraining the hard core unemployed: A selected review, *Journal of Applied Psychology,* 1973, *58,* 23–33.
45. Gouldner, A. W. Cosmopolitans and locals: Towards an analysis of latent social role. *Administrative Science Quarterly,* 1957, *12,* 281–306.
46. Grusky, O. Administrative succession in formal organizations. *Social Forces,* 1960, *39,* 105–115.
47. Guest, R. H. Managerial succession in complex organizations. *American Journal of Sociology,* 1962, *68,* 47–56.
48. Hall, A. D., & Fagen, R. E. Definition of a system. In W. R. Buckley (Ed.), *Modern systems research for the behavioral scientist.* Chicago: Aldine Publishing, 1968, 81–92.
49. Hall, R. H. *Occupations and the social structure.* Englewood Cliffs, N.J.: Prentice-Hall, 1969.
50. Hardin, G. The tragedy of the commons. *Science,* 1968, *162* (2), 1243–1248.
51. Herzberg, F., Mausner, B. Peterson, R. O., Capwell, D. G. *Job attitudes: Review of research and opinion.* Pittsburgh: Psychological Service of Pittsburgh, 1957.
52. Hill, J. M. The representation of labour turnover as a social process. In B. O. Pettman (Ed.), *Labour turnover and retention.* Epping, Eng.: Gower, 1975, 77–98.
53. Hinrichs, J. R. Psychology of men at work. In P. H. Mussen & M. R. Rosenzweig (Eds.), *Annual Review of Psychology.* Palo Alto, Calif.: Annual Reviews, Inc., 1970.
54. Homans, G. C. Social behavior as exchange. *American Journal of Sociology,* 1958, *62,* 597–606.
55. Homans, G. C. *Social behavior: Its elementary forms.* New York: Harcourt, Brace & World, 1961.
56. Howard, A., & Scott, R. A. A proposed framework for the analysis of stress in the human organism. *Behavioral Science,* 1965, *10,* 141–160.
57. Hyman, R. Economic motivation and labor stability. *British Journal of Industrial Relations,* 1970, *8,* 159–178.
58. Ingham, G. K. *Size of industrial organization and worker behavior.* Cambridge: Cambridge University Press, 1970.
59. Janis, I. L. *Victims of groupthink.* Boston: Houghton Mifflin, 1972.
60. Jennings, E. E. *The mobile manager.* Lansing: University of Michigan Press, 1967.
61. Kahn, R. L., Wolfe, D. M., Quinn, R. P., Snoek, J. D., & Rosenthal, R. A. *Organizational stress: Studies in role conflict and ambiguity.* New York: Wiley, 1964.
62. Kasl, S. V., & Cobb, S. Some psychological factors associated with ill-

ness behavior and selected illnesses. *Journal of Chronic Disease.* 1964, *17*, 325–345.

63. Kerr, C. The balkanization of labor markets. In E. Bakke (Ed.), *Labor mobility and economic opportunity.* Cambridge, Mass.: MIT Press, 1954, 92–110.

64. Kiesler, C. A., & R. Mathog. Resistance to influence as a function of number of prior consonant acts. In C. A. Kiesler (Ed.), *The psychology of commitment,* New York: Academic Press, 1971, 66–73.

65. Kirshenbaum, A. B., & Goldberg, A. Organization behavior, career orientations, and propensity to move among professionals. *Sociology of Work and Occupations,* 1976, *3* (3), 357–372.

66. Lawler, E. E. *Motivation in work organizations.* Monterey, Calif.: Brooks/Cole, 1973.

67. Lazarus, R. S., Deese, J., & Oster, S. F. The effects of psychological stress upon performance. In I. G. Sarason (Ed.), *Contemporary research in personality.* Princeton: D. Van Nostrand, 1962, 288–302.

68. Lee, D. H. The role of attitude in response to environmental stress. *Journal of Social Issues,* 1966, *22*, 83–91.

69. Leftwich, R. *The price system and resource allocation.* New York: Holt, Rinehart & Winston, 1966.

70. Leslie, G. R., & Richardson, A. H. Life cycle, career pattern, and the decision to move. *American Sociological Review,* 1961, *26*, 894–902.

71. Levitan, S. A., Mangum, G. L., & Marshall, S. *Human resources and labor markets.* New York: Harper & Row, 1976.

72. Lewin, K. *The conceptual representation and the measurement of psychological forces.* Durham, N.C.: Duke University Press, 1938.

73. Lewin, K. *Field theory in social science.* New York: Harper & Row, 1951.

74. Lloyd, W. F. Two lectures on the checks of population, (pamphlet). Oxford: University of Oxford Press, 1833. In G. Hardin, The tragedy of the commons. *Science,* 1966, *162* (2), 1243–1248.

75. Lundquist, A. Absenteeism and job turnover as a consequence of unfavorable job adjustment. *Acta Sociologica,* 1959, *3* (2), 119–131.

76. Lyons, T. F. *Nursing attitudes and turnover.* Ames: Industrial Relations Center, Iowa State University, 1968.

77. MacKay, D. I., Boddy, D., Brack, J., Diack, J. A., & Jones, N. *Labor markets.* London: George Allen, 1971.

78. Mangione, T. W., & Quinn, R. P. Job satisfaction, counterproductive behavior, and drug use at work. *Journal of Applied Psychology,* 1975, *60* (1), 114–116.

79. Manicas, T., & Kruger, A. N. *Logic: The essentials.* New York: McGraw-Hill, 1976.

80. March, J. G., & Simon, H. A. *Organizations.* New York: Wiley, 1958.

81. Marsh, R. M., & Mannari, H. Lifetime commitment in Japan: Roles, norms and values. *American Journal of Sociology,* 1971, *76*, 796–812.

82. Mattila, J. P. Job quitting and frictional unemployment. *American Economic Review,* 1974, *64*, 235–239.

83. Mayo, E. Revery and industrial fatigue. *Personnel Journal*, 1924, *8*, 273–281.
84. Merton, R. K. Patterns of influence: Local and cosmopolitan influentials. In R. K. Merton (Ed.), *Social theory and social structure*. Glencoe, Ill.: Free Press, 1957.
85. Mills, C. W. *White collar*. New York: Oxford University Press, 1951.
86. Mirvis, P. M., & Lawler, E. E. Measuring the financial impact of employee attitudes. *Journal of Applied Psychology*, 1977, *62* (1), 1–8.
87. Moffatt, G. W., & Hill, K. Labor turnover in Australia: A review of research. *Personnel Practice Bulletin*, 1970, *26*, 142–149.
88. Mott, P. E. *The characteristics of effective organizations* (New York: Harper & Row, 1972).
89. Mueller, E. H. *The relationship between teacher turnover and student achievement*. Unpublished Ph.D. Dissertation, School of Education, University of Virginia. In J. Price. *A study of turnover*. Ames: Iowa State University Press, 1977.
90. Office of Research and Statistics, Social Security Administration. Interindustry Mobility in the United States, 1957–1960. *Research Report No. 18*. Washington, D.C.: U.S. Government Printing Office, 1967.
91. Osterman, P. An empirical study of labor market segmentation. *Industrial and Labor Relations Review*, 1975, *28* (4), 508–523.
92. Parnes, H. S., & Spitz, R. S. A conceptual framework for studying labor mobility. *Monthly Labor Review*, 1969, *92*, 55–58.
93. Parsons, D. O. Quit rates over time: A search and information approach. *American Economic Review*, 1973, *63*, 390–401.
94. Parsons, T. The professional and social structure. *Social Forces*, 1939, *17*, 457–467.
95. Pavalko, R. M. *Sociology of occupations and professions*. Itasca, Ill.: F. E. Peacock, 1971.
96. Pettman, B. O. Some factors influencing labor turnover: A review of research literature. *Industrial Relations*, 1973, *4*, 43–61.
97. Pfeffer, J., & Leblebici, H. Executive recruitment and the development of interfirm organizations. *Administrative Science Quarterly* 1973, *17*, 218–228.
98. Pfeffer, J. Beyond management and the worker: The institutional function of management. *Academy of Management Review*, 1976, *1* (2), 36–46.
99. Piore, M. J. Notes for a theory of labor market stratification. Department of Economics Working Paper No. 95, MIT, 1972. In P. Osterman, An empirical study of labor market segmentation. *Industrial Relations Review*, 1975, *28*, 508–523.
100. Pomeroy, R., & Yahr, H. *Studies in public welfare*. New York: Center for the Study of Urban Problems, Graduate Division, Bernard Baruch College, City University, 1967. In James Price. *The study of turnover*. Ames: Iowa State University Press, 1977.
101. Porter, L. W., Lawler, E. E., & Hackman, J. R. *Behavior in organizations*. New York: McGraw-Hill, 1975.

102. Porter, L. W., & Steers, R. M. Organizational, work, and personal factors in employee turnover and absenteeism. *Psychological Bulletin,* 1973, *80,* 151–176.
103. Price, J. L. *Organizational effectiveness: An inventory of propositions.* Homewood, Ill.: Irwin, 1968.
104. Price, J. L. *The study of turnover.* Ames: Iowa State University Press, 1977.
105. Reismann, L. Levels of aspiration and social class. *American Sociological Review,* 1953, *18,* 233–242.
106. Reynolds, L. G. *The structure of labor markets.* New York: Harper & Row, 1951.
107. Reynolds, L. G. *Labor economics and labor relations.* Englewood Cliffs, N.J.: Prentice-Hall, 1964.
108. Ritchey, P. N. Explanations of migration. In A. Inkeles, J. Coleman, and N. Smelser (Eds.), *The annual review of sociology.* Palo Alto, Calif.: Annual Reviews, Inc., 1976, 363–404.
109. Ritti, R. R. Underemployment of engineers. *Industrial Relations,* 1970, *9,* 437–452.
110. Rowan, R. L. (Ed.), *Readings in labor economics and labor relations.* Homewood, Ill.: Irwin, 1977.
111. Runciman, W. G. *Relative deprivation and social justice.* Berkeley: University of California Press, 1967.
112. Salancik, G. R. Commitment and the control of organizational behavior and belief. In B. M. Staw and G. R. Salancik (Eds.), *New directions in organizational behavior.* Chicago: St. Clair, 1977, 1–54.
113. Sales, S. M., & House, J. Job dissatisfaction as a possible contributor to risk of death from coronary disease. *Proceedings of the Annual Convention of the American Psychological Association,* 1970, 593–594.
114. Schein, E. A. *Organizational psychology.* Englewood Cliffs, N.J.: Prentice-Hall, 1970.
115. Schuh, A. The predictability of employee tenure: A review of the literature. *Personnel Psychology,* 1967, *20,* 133–152.
116. Sheridan, J. E. Reducing labor turnover. *100%,* 1916, *6,* 92–96.
117. Slichter, S. H. *The turnover of factory labor.* New York: Appleton, 1919.
118. Smith, A. *[An inquiry into the nature and causes of the wealth of nations].* In L. D. Abbott, *Masterworks of economics.* New York: McGraw-Hill, 1973. (Originally published, 1776.)
119. Sofer, C. *Men in mid-career: A study of British managers and technical specialists.* Cambridge: Cambridge University Press, 1970.
120. Solman, L. C. *Macroeconomics.* Reading, Mass.: Addison-Wesley, 1977.
121. Speare, A. Residential satisfaction as an intervening variable in residential mobility. *Demography,* 1974, *11,* 173–188.
122. Staw, B. M. Knee-deep in the big muddy: A study of escalating commitment to a chosen course of action. *Organizational Behavior and Human Performance,* 1976, *16,* 27–44.

123. Staw, B. M., & Fox, F. V. Escalation: The determinants of commitment to a previously chosen course of action. *Human Relations*, 1977, *30*, 431–450.

124. Staw, B. M., & Salancik, G. R. *New directions in organizational behavior.* Chicago: St. Clair, 1977.

125. Steers, R. M. Problems in the measurement of organizational effectiveness. *Administrative Science Quarterly*, 1975, *20*, 546–558.

126. Steers, R. M. When is an organization effective?: A process approach to understanding effectiveness. *Organizational Dynamics*, Autumn 1976, 50–63.

127. Taylor, L. *Occupational sociology.* New York: Oxford Press, 1968.

128. Taylor, P. J. Sickness and absence resistance. *Transactions of the Society of Occupational Medicine*, 1968, *18*, 96–100.

129. Tausky, C., & Dubin, R. Career anchorage: Managerial mobility motivations. *American Sociological Review*, 1965, *30*, 725–735.

130. Thibaut, J., & Kelley, H. *The social psychology of groups.* New York: Wiley, 1959.

131. Torrence, P. Some consequences of power differences on decision making in permanent and temporary three man groups. In A. P. Hare, E. F. Borgatta, and R. F. Bales (Eds.), *Small groups.* New York: Knopf, 1966, 600–609.

132. Tuchi, B. J., & Carr, B. E. Labor turnover. *Hospitals*, 1971, *45*, 88–92.

133. Vroom, V. *Work and motivation.* New York: Wiley, 1964.

134. Webb, R. J. Organizational effectiveness and the voluntary organization. *Academy of Management Journal*, 1974, *17*, 663–677.

135. Wells, W. P., & Pelz, D. C. *Scientists in organization.* New York: Wiley, 1966.

136. Wertheimer, R. F. *The monetary rewards of migration within the United States.* Washington, D.C.: The Urban Institute, 1970.

137. Wilensky, H. L. Work, careers, and social integration. *International Social Science Journal*, 1960, *12*, 533–560.

138. Wolpert, J. Behavioral aspects of the decision to migrate. *Regional Science Association*, 1965, *15*, 159–169.

139. Wolpert, J. Migration as an adjustment to environmental stress. *Journal of Social Issues*, 1966, *22*, 92–102.

140. Ziller, R. C., Behringer, R. D., & Goodchilds, J. D. Group creativity under conditions of failure and variations in group stability. *Journal of Applied Psychology*, 1962, *46*, 43–49.

section four

Groups and Social Influence Processes in Organizations

Introduction

Very little of significance occurs in organizations on a purely individual basis. The respective participants, whatever their rank, almost always confront the fact of their dependence upon others.

Kanter, in a selection from her book *Men and Women of the Corporation,* discusses the meaning of power for those whom she observed in a large industrial firm. Their conception of power had little to do with formal authority over a group of subordinates; rather, power inhered in the ability to influence people and events *outside* of one's formally designated responsibilities. Kanter notes how the successful carcerists acquire this ability and comments on the counterproductive behavior syndrome of those who lack external clout.

Groups in organizations not only seldom make optimal decisions; occasionally they make very bad decisions that no one individual would have made or wanted to make. Harvey terms this the "Abilene Paradox" (so named after one of his personal experiences used to illustrate the phenomenon). The forces unleashed by group dynamics may, ironically, prevent a group from expressing and managing the areas of agreement which the parties actually share. Harvey recounts some of the corporate and government fiascos attributable to the Abilene Paradox and offers suggestions for how to prevent it.

Whatever the potential risks in group decision making, the fact remains that often there is no real alternative. Groups provide the necessary pool of expertise for considering the many dimensions of complex problems. Also, group-generated decisions are more likely than individual decisions to be accorded credibility and legitimacy, and hence to be supported by others. Andrew Grove, president of Intel Corporation (which he helped found, after a career as a scientist), reflects upon these and other considerations about groups in "Decisions, Decisions," a chapter taken from his book *High Output Management*.

One of the alleged superiorities of Japanese management is the involvement of the rank-and-file in "quality circles," groups of workers who discuss methods of improving operations. Numerous U.S. businesses have adopted this practice in recent years. Mitchell Lee Marks examines the evidence in support of claims that "quality circles" lead to significant gains by both company and employees and confronts the charge by skeptics that "QCs" are just the latest fad promoted by snake oil salesmen.

22

Power*

ROSABETH MOSS KANTER

> The level of decision-making is way up. The level of accountability is
> way down. That's a problem.
> > —First line manager at Industrial Supply Corporation
>
> Powerlessness corrupts. Absolute powerlessness corrupts absolutely.
> > —Variation on Lord Acton's comment

Organizational politics was an endlessly fascinating topic of conversation for the people who carried out the day-to-day administration of
Industrial Supply Corporation. They watched for the signs of favor and
inclusion. They talked over the interesting new people. They speculated about the effects of changes in senior management. They chuck-
led over the real story behind certain decisions (but were never sure of
the truth). A young manager amused himself by starting a rumor about
the name of the replacement for a fired vice president, and then heard
the word come back to him "on substantial authority." One day, a
fairly new sales worker from the field went into the cafeteria at headquarters, and, because all the other tables were filled, he sat down at
one where an older man was eating alone. He introduced himself, but
the other's name did not register. It was the corporate president. All
heads turned. The talk started: "Who's that young guy with Peter
Farrell?"

Somewhere behind the formal organization chart at Indsco was another, shadow structure in which dramas of power were played out.
An interest in corporate politics was a key to survival for the people
who worked at Indsco. This had both a narrower, more personal meaning (how individuals would do in the striving for hierarchical success)
and an important job-related meaning (how much people could get
done and how satisfying they cold make their conditions of work).
First, individual careers rose and fell, and people found the "top"
more or less open to them, through dealings in power. Sometimes,
crossing the wrong person could be dangerous. There was the story of

___

* From Rosabeth Moss Kanter, *Men and Women of the Corporation,* copyright ©
1977 by Rosabeth Moss Kanter. Reprinted by permission of Basic Books, Inc.,
Publishers, New York.

the powerful executive who was angry at the president of a supplier and wanted to make it difficult for that supplier to sell to Indsco, even though its products were an important manufacturing component. A slightly junior manager—let's call him X—created an arrangement for buying from the supplier that was acceptable to the executive, and that firm's dealings were processed separately. Then another manager—Y—looked over the figures with his subordinate and asked why things were done differently. The subordinate replied, "It's always been like that. That's how it comes down from X." Y said he didn't understand it and asked the subordinate to check into it. The subordinate came back with the story and the word that the arrangement could not be changed, but Y had the manufacturing area in his business plan and wanted to change the situation. He elected to fight, against the advice of his subordinate. Y lost. The situation stayed the same, and he was pushed out of the line of ascent. For the next four or five years, he remained in limbo in a dead-end job. As an observer commented, "He blew it with one move."

However, it was not only individual competition and jockeying for position that made power dynamics important. Sometimes, people could only do their work effectively and exercise whatever competence gave them personal satisfaction if they knew how to make their way through the more cumbersome and plodding official structure via the shadow political structure underneath. Since the labyrinthine complexities of the large, fairly centralized organization reduced everyone's autonomy of action and made every function dependent on every other, politics was automatically necessitated by the system in order for people to gain some control over the machine. Politics was a way of reducing something too large, incomprehensible, and unmanageable to something smaller, more human, and more familiar. For some people, certainly, the concern with power represented individualistic striving for competitive advantage and a lion's share of scarce resources. For others, however, power was a necessary tool for living or surviving in the system at all, and they cared primarily about having a share (a sphere of autonomy and a right to call on resources) rather than monopolizing it.

For the people called "leaders," power was supposedly an automatic part of their functioning. They were given the formal titles of leadership (director, manager, supervisor), and they were expected to aid the mobilization of others toward the attainment of objectives. They had responsibility for results, and they were accountable for what got done; but as everyone knew, power did not necessarily come automatically with the designation of leaders, with the delegation of formal authority. People often had to get it not from the official structure but from the more hidden political processes.

A DEFINITION OF POWER

Power is a loaded term. Its connotations tend to be more negative than positive, and it has multiple meanings. Much has been written in the attempt to distinguish power from related concepts: authority, influence, force, dominance, and others. William Gamson has differentiated the forms of power that contribute something to another person in exchange for compliance (inducements) from those that only remove a threat (constraints).[1] There have been many debates about whether power exists in fixed quantities, in a zero-sum sense, so that one person's amount of power inherently limits another person's, or whether power refers to expansible capacities that could grow, synergistically, in two people simultaneously. Because the hierarchical form of large organizations tends to concentrate and monopolize official decision-making prerogatives and the majority of workers are subject to "commands" from those above, it would be natural to assume that any use of the term *power* must refer to this sort of scarce, finite resource behind hierarchical domination.

However, I am using power in a sense that distinguishes it from hierarchical domination. As defined here, power is the ability to get things done, to mobilize resources, to get and use whatever it is that a person needs for the goals he or she is attempting to meet. In this way, a monopoly on power means that only very few have this capacity, and they prevent the majority of others from being able to act effectively. Thus, the *total* amount of power—and total system effectiveness—is restricted, even though some people seem to have a great deal of it. However, when more people are empowered—that is, allowed to have control over the conditions that make their actions possible— then more is accomplished, more gets done. Thus, the meaning of power here is closer to "mastery" or "autonomy" than to domination or control over others. Power does refer to interpersonal transactions, the ability to mobilize other people; but if those others are powerless, their own capacities, even when mobilized, are limited. Power is the ability to *do*, in the classic physical usage of power as energy, and thus it means having access to whatever is needed for the doing. The problems with absolute power, a total monopoly on power, lie in the fact that it renders everyone else powerless. On the other hand, empowering more people through generating more autonomy, more participation in decisions, and more access to resources increases the total capacity for effective action rather than increases domination. The powerful are the ones who have access to tools for action.

---

[1] William A. Gamson, *Power and Discontent* (Homewood, Illinois: Dorsey Press, 1968).

THE IMPORTANCE OF POWER FOR LEADERSHIP FUNCTIONS

What makes leaders effective in an organization? What transforms people into effective bosses, managers, supervisors, team leaders? Trying to answer these questions has, of course, long engaged the energies of a large number of social scientists, especially psychologists, and their answers have filled volumes. After an early emphasis on leader "traits," stemming from characteristics of individuals, a more social perspective took hold, one that saw leadership as consisting of transactions between leaders and followers. The leader was presented as a kind of "super-follower," serving through follower designation and follower consent, and able to inspire because first able to respond to the needs, concerns, wishes, and desires of the group. Attention shifted away from the cataloging of individual attributes to the cataloging of behaviors and resources: a series of functions needed by a group that could be called *leadership,* a series of resources useful in interpersonal exchanges. Tuning in to other people was considered very important. For a time in the 1960s, in fact, the belief that sensitive human relations skills held the key to success as a leader achieved almost cult-like proportions in American organizations, and Industrial Supply Corporation was no exception in instituting sensitivity training for managers—made acceptable under such bland labels as "organizational skills" or "management awareness."

Yet research attempts to distinguish more effective and less effective leadership styles based on a human relations emphasis have generally failed, in part because there are trade-offs associated with one or another form of supervision. As early studies comparing authoritarian, democratic, and laissez-faire leaders showed, there were advantages and disadvantages in group productivity and morale associated with each emphasis. Although most theorists today would conclude that human relations skills are important if coupled with a production emphasis, the evidence is mixed enough to permit few conclusions about leader behaviors alone.[2] Two researchers tried to differentiate instrumental and expressive exchanges between superiors and subordinates in several Michigan businesses as a way to predict interactions and group process. The distinction was ultimately not very useful. Subor-

---

[2] See Arnold S. Tannenbaum, *Social Psychology of the Work Organization* (Belmont, Calif.: Wadsworth, 1966), pp. 78–79. After a computerized review of a large number of studies, Suresh Srivastva and colleagues concluded that different ways of supervising do affect subordinates' performance and internal states but that the results seem context-determined; in other words, no conclusions can be drawn about style in the absence of situation. Srivastva, et al., *Job Satisfaction and Productivity* (Cleveland: Department of Organizational Behavior, Case Western Reserve University, 1975), p. 44.

dinates reported getting about equally as much job-related information, whether the leaders emphasized task or human relations matters, and the researchers found very little relationship between style of leadership behavior and subordinate group process.[3] This is one of a number of studies demonstrating that choices about how to relate to other people (listen to their problems? offer praise?) fail to make much, if any, difference in effective management—at least by themselves.

What does make a difference is *power*—power outward and upward in the system: the ability to get for the group, for subordinates or followers, a favorable share of the resources, opportunities, and rewards possible through the organization. This has less to do with how leaders relate to followers than with how they relate to other parts of the organization. It has less to do with the quality of the manager-subordinate relationship than with the structure of power in the wider system. Early theory in organizational behavior assumed a direct relation between leader behavior and group satisfaction and morale, as if each organizational subgroup existed in a vacuum. However, Donald Pelz, in a study at Detroit Edison in the early 1950s, discovered that perceived influence *outside* the work group and upward in the organization was a significant intervening variable. He compared high- and low-morale work groups to test the hypothesis that the supervisor in high-morale groups would be better at communicating, more supportive, and more likely to recommend promotion. Yet when he analyzed the data, the association seemed to be nonexistent or even reversed. In some cases, supervisors who frequently recommended people for promotion and offered sincere praise for a job well done had *lower* morale scores. The differentiating variable that Pelz finally hit upon was whether or not the leaders had power outside and upward: influence on their own superiors and influence over how decisions were made in the department as a whole. The combination of good human relations *and* power produced high morale. Human relations skills coupled with low power sometimes had negative effects on morale.[4] What good is praise or a promise if the leader can't deliver? As other research discovered, both women and men attach more importance to having a competent, rather than a nice, boss—someone who gets things done. A classic study of first-line supervisors showed that more secure (and hence effective) foremen were those who had closer relationships up-

---

[3] Philip M. Marcus and James S. House, "Exchange Between Superiors and Subordinates in Large Organizations," *Administrative Science Quarterly* 18 (1973), pp. 209–22.

[4] Donald C. Pelz, "Influence: A Key to Effective Leadership in the First-Line Supervisor," *Personnel* 29 (1952), pp. 3–11.

ward in the hierarchy; they had the most frequent exchanges with superiors.[5]

Power begets power. People who are thought to have power already and to be well placed in hierarchies of prestige and status may also be more influential and more effective in getting the people around them to do things and feel satisfied about it. In a laboratory experiment, subordinates were more likely to cooperate with and to inhibit aggression and negativity toward leaders of higher rather than lower status. In a field study of professionals, people who came into a group with higher external status tended to be better liked, talked more often, and received more communications. The less powerful, who usually talked less, were often accused of talking *too much*. There was a real consensus in such groups about who was powerful, and people were more likely to accept direct attempts to influence them from people they defined as among the powerful. Average group members, whether men or women, tended to engage in deferential, approval-seeking behavior toward those seen as higher in power.[6] Thus, people who look like they can command more of the organization's resources, who look like they can bring something that is valued from outside into the group, who seem to have access to the inner circles that make the decisions affecting the fate of individuals in organizations, may also be more effective as leaders of those around them—and be better liked in the process.

Twenty Indsco executives in a sample of managers reached the same conclusion when asked to define the characteristics of effective managers. The question of the relative importance of "people sensitivity," as they put it, provoked considerable debate. Finally, they agreed that credibility was more important than anything else. *Credibility* was their term for competence plus power—the known ability to get results. People with credibility were listened to, their phone calls were answered first, because they were assumed to have something important to say. People with credibility had room to make more mistakes and could take greater risks because it was believed that they would produce. They were known to be going somewhere in the orga-

---

[5] Joan E. Crowley, Teresa E. Levitan, and Robert P. Quinn, "Seven Deadly Half-Truths About Women," *Psychology Today* 7 (March 1973); William F. Whyte and Burleigh Gardner, "The Man in the Middle," *Applied Anthropology* 4 (Spring 1945), pp. 1–28.

[6] The study of negativity: John W. Thibaut and Henry W. Riecken, "Authoritarianism, Status, and the Communication of Aggression," *Human Relations* 8 (1955), pp. 95–120. The study of professionals: Jacob I. Hurwitz, Alvin F. Zander, and Bernard Hymovitch, "Some Effects of Power on the Relations among Group Members," in *Group Dynamics*, ed. D. Cartwright and A. Zander (New York: Harper & Row, 1968). See also R. Lippit, N. Polansky, and S. Rosen, "The Dynamics of Power," *Human Relations* 5 (1952), pp. 44–50; this is a classic study.

nization and to have the ability to place their people in good jobs. They could back up their words with actions. Thus, the ultimate in credibility in the corporate bureaucracy was "the guy who doesn't have to make recommendations; he comes out with a *decision* and all supporting material. Everyone else just says yes or no. . . ."

Credibility upward rather than downward—that is, wider-system power—rendered managers effective, they thought. To have it downward, with subordinates, they must first have it upward, with their own superiors and the people with whom their tasks were interwoven in the matrix. Credibility downward was based on subordinates' belief in their managers' importance, which in turn was based on their political position. People-sensitivity could be an added bonus, but it was considered much less important than power. "Some managers are very successful and very tough," an executive commented. "John Fredericks is as tough as they come but also sensitive to people. His people have gone far, but is that because he's sensitive or because he has clout? It's impossible to untangle." "You can get people to do nearly anything for you if they think you have their interest at heart and will fight for them. They must see that you can produce for them, that the fighting will pay off." And lack of system power could undermine the best of human relations: "Fred Burke came in as an outsider to manage his department, so he didn't know the business and he didn't have the right connections in the company. When he tried to get things from headquarters, he had no clout. Headquarters wanted to talk to the people *under* him because they knew the answers. But sensitive, yes! Christ, I don't know anyone more sensitive than Fred Burke. You've never seen a more sensitive guy; but his people turned against him anyway. They had no respect for him." "What we're saying, I guess," someone tried to summarize the discussion, "is that you need a combination of both—people-skills and credibility." "No," others disagreed. "It's the need to take action that distinguishes effective managers. Having some results at the end of all that people-sensitivity. What good is it if you can't get anything done in Indsco?"

The preference for association with the powerful and the degree to which this preference motivates members of organizations is a function of the degree of dependency built into the organization itself. Where people can do their work rather independently, where they can easily get the things they need to carry out their tasks, where they have a great deal of latitude in decision making, and where rewards are not so contingent on career mobility, then there need not be the same concern with appropriate political alliances. However, the large, complex hierarchical corporation fosters dependency. Emile Durkheim, in *The Division of Labor in Society*, called this "interdependence": the way specialization had created bonds of "organic solidarity" between people who needed each other for the completion of complex tasks. However, an uncomfortable feeling of *dependency* is often the psychological result when the problems of getting approval, being recognized, or moving resources through multiple checkpoints make people see one another as threats, roadblocks, or hindrances rather than as collaborators. A manager known as highly competent made these revealing comments about himself: "I had psychological tests a few years ago. They showed that the weakest point I had was lack of independence, inability to make independent decisions. I bet it would be true of a lot of people in this company. We don't make a decision alone; we are always consulting other people. Because we are not allowed to make decisions without going through too many channels. And that's the other problem as a manager in this company. You don't really have a lot of authority when you come right down to it." In the context of such organizationally fostered dependency, people seem willing to work very hard to reduce it. One way to do this is by allying themselves with the powerful, with people who can make them more independent by creating more certainty in their lives.

Power in an organization rests, in part, on the ability to solve dependency problems and to control relevant sources of uncertainty.[7] This can be true with respect to the system as a whole as well as around individuals. For the system, the most power goes to those people in those functions that provide greater control over what the organization finds currently problematic: sales and marketing people when markets are competitive; production experts when materials are scarce and demand is high; personnel or labor relations specialists when labor is scarce; lawyers, lobbyists, and external relations specialists when government regulations impinge; finance and accounting types when business is bad and money tight.[8] There is a turning to those elements of the system that seem to have the power to create more certainty in the face of dependency, to generate a more advantageous position for the organization.

There is a wide range of dependencies faced by individuals in large corporations, varying in kind and degree with specific organizational location. Weber considered a virtue of rationalized bureaucracies that they rendered power impersonal through the development of rules,

---

[7] Michel Crozier, *The Bureaucratic Phenomenon* (Chicago: University of Chicago Press, 1964), p. 164.

[8] Charles Perrow has also analyzed the ways in which changing technical requirements affect organizational authority structures in his studies of hospitals. See Perrow, "Hospitals: Technology, Structures, and Goals," in *Handbook of Organizations,* ed. J. G. March (Skokie, Ill.: McNally, 1965), and Perrow, "The Analysis of Goals in Complex Organizations," *American Sociological Review* 26 (1961), pp. 854–66. James Thompson made a similar point with respect to businesses in *Organizations in Action* (New York: McGraw-Hill, 1967).

thereby reducing one sort of uncomfortable dependency: the need to be subject to the arbitrary and unpredictable whim of rulers. Michel Crozier echoed the Weberian proposition: bureaucracies are built because people are "trying to evade face-to-face relationships and situations of personal dependency whose authoritarian tone they cannot bear."[9] However, ironically, as one source of dependency on other people is reduced, others spring up. People become dependent on those who can help them make their way through the system or who provide the means to bypass rules that are behaviorally constraining or inappropriately applied. They become dependent on those with discretion over necessary resources; and to the extent that the system cannot be perfectly rationalized, with pockets of uncertainty remaining, those who control important contingencies retain a strong basis for personal power.

The uncertainty inherent in managerial roles has already been discussed. This uncertainty makes pre-selection and automatic movement in careers, or reduced discretion in performance, highly unlikely. It means that people who can influence promotion and placement decisions have a source of power to the extent that people feel dependent because of the uncertainties in their careers. Other sources of dependency derive from the size of giant corporations like Indsco. Beyond the people in the most routine of functions, no one has within a small domain all of the things he or she needs to carry out his or her job. Everyone must get things done through others who are not part of the same face-to-face group in which personal agreements and informal understandings develop. There must be power tools to use in bargaining with those others who are not bound with the person in any form of communal solidarity, or else those others can keep the person in a state of dependency that renders both planning and autonomous action impossible. What makes this more bearable is that others are in the same situation, equally dependent. So as long as dependencies are relatively symmetrical, people can agree to cooperate rather than trade on each other's vulnerabilities. Problems arise as asymmetry grows.

James Thompson developed a set of propositions about the kinds of political processes that develop when organizations contain interdependencies among discretionary jobs; that is, positions that are not completely routinized, where decisions are possible and can affect outcomes: (1) Individuals in highly discretionary jobs seek to maintain power equal to or greater than their dependence on others in the organization. (2) When power is less than dependency, people seek a coalition. Depending on the function, the coalition may be formed

---

[9] Crozier, *Bureaucratic Phenomenon*, p. 54.

inside or outside of the organization. Coalitions with people in the external environment that is relevant for the organization's success may increase power. (3) The more sources of uncertainty or contingency for the organization, the more bases there are for power and the larger the number of political positions in the organization.[10] Thus, more complicated organizations have more politics than less complicated ones, and power is a much more relevant concern for the people who must function within large, complex, hierarchical systems.

To see power as a dominant issue around people in leadership positions in organizations, then, is not the same as positing individual motives such as "needs for power" or "achievement motivation." It is not a characterological but a social structural issue. Critics sometimes assume that a defect in the American character makes people (such as followers or subordinates) prefer winners to losers, or that some excessive striving for status makes people seek vicarious identification with success. However, this should also be seen as a survival mechanism for people who live in the typically American organizational worlds created in the 20th century: to know that one is better off, less dependent and uncertain, when in league with people who are powerful in the dependency-creating systems that one must somehow make one's way through. There are real as well as symbolic payoffs in working for someone who is powerful in systems where resources are scarce and there is constant scrambling for advantage. Powerful authorities can get more for their subordinates. They can more effectively back up both promises and threats; they can more easily make changes in the situation of subordinates. They offer the possibility of taking subordinates with them when they move, so that the manager's future mobility may help others' prospects. Subordinates as well as peers may indeed capitalize on the success of a "comer" in the organization, as Barry Stein has pointed out.[11]

That is not all. There can also be something more immediately empowering about working under a powerful person. Opportunity and power both have structural impact on managers' authority styles. Bernard Levenson suggested that the fact of promotability itself shapes style of supervision. Mobile managers are likely to behave like "good" leaders *because* of their opportunity, whereas nonmobile managers behave in the rigid, authoritarian way characteristic of the powerless, as I show later. *Promotable* supervisors, he argued, are more likely to adopt a participatory style in which they share information, delegate authority, train subordinates for more responsibility, and al-

---

[10] Thompson, *Organizations in Action*, pp. 125–29.

[11] Barry A. Stein, "Getting There: Patterns in Managerial Success," working paper, Center for Research on Women, Wellesley College, 1975. Available through Center for Social and Evaluation Research, University of Massachusetts, Boston.

low latitude and autonomy. They do this, first, to show that they are not indispensable in their current jobs—to show that someone else could indeed take over when they advance. They also find it in their political interest to delegate control as a method of training a replacement, so that the vacancy created by their promotion will be filled with someone on their team. Unpromotable supervisors, on the other hand, may try to retain control and restrict the opportunities for their subordinates' learning and autonomy. The current job is their only arena for power, and they anticipate no growth or improvement for themselves. Moreover, they have to keep control for themselves, so that it will be clear that no one else could do their job. Subordinates must be forced to exercise their skills as narrowly as possible, for a capable subordinate represents a serious replacement threat.[12]

For people at Indsco, having a powerful boss was considered an important element in career progress and the development of competence, just as lack of success was seen as a function of working under a dead-ender. People wanted to work for someone on the move who had something to teach and enough power to take others along. A secretary recalled, "I came in looking for a place to stake out my career. I was first assigned to work for a man who was a dowdy dresser and never cleaned his shoes. (I have a thing about men and shoes. How they take care of their shoes is a good sign of other things.) The whole atmosphere in the group made it clear that people were going nowhere. It was not businesslike. So I said to myself, 'He's going nowhere. I'd better change.' And he did go nowhere." One of Indsco's highest ranking women said, "I had to learn everything myself. So did men. Lots of people go into managerial jobs without any training. I had to model myself after my boss. If the boss is good, okay. If not, that can be terrible. It's better to get a boss who is successful in the organization's terms." In response to a question about what is "helpful" in a manager, a sales worker wrote, "He sees a subordinate's growth as in his interest. He is confident, capable, and conveys a sense that he will be promoted. Clichés like 'being on a winner's team' have taken on new meaning for me. . . . Unhelpful managers are uncertain of themselves, their abilities, present position, or future." An older executive commented, "It's a stroke of luck to get an opportunity to work for someone who's a mover and demonstrate performance to him because astute managers look for good workers and develop them." There was much agreement among managers that people were more likely to emerge with "manager quality" if they worked for the right boss. "Right" meant high credibility. Credibility meant power.

---

[12] Bernard Levenson, "Bureaucratic Succession," in *Complex Organizations: A Sociological Reader*, ed. Amitai Etzioni (New York: Holt, Rinehart & Winston, 1961), pp. 362–75.

ORGANIZATIONAL POLITICS AND THE SOURCES OF POWER

There have been a number of useful classifications of the bases of social power. John R. P. French and Bertram Raven proposed five: reward power (controlling resources that could reward), coercive power (controlling resources that could be used to punish), expert power (controlling necessary knowledge or information), reference power (being personally attractive to other people, so that they are likely to identify or seek a relationship), and legitimate power (authority vested in a position or role and accepted by others as appropriate).[13] Each of these certainly plays a part in determining who becomes powerful in an organization; personal characteristics and background combine with the way an organization distributes scarce resources through positions to give people differential opportunities to become influential.

However, there are also a number of bases of power that are specifically organizational. The French and Raven typology and others of its kind are most useful for understanding one-on-one exchanges or the exercise of influence in rather small-scale interpersonal situations. The politics of a large-scale system are more complex and often do not seem reducible to such simple elements, even though the actual wielding of influence in any one instance may seem to rest on one or another of those five bases of power. This is the familiar problem of system levels in social science. Whereas there are many ways in which human systems are similar, regardless of level, more complex systems also add elements and problems not characteristic of simpler systems. However, social psychology has often treated power as though its operation in the small group were directly analogous to its operation in the large organization, thereby missing some of the more important dynamics of the latter.

The accumulation of power in a corporation is closely tied to the overall state of the system. At Indsco, formal position in the hierarchy was very important, and competence within the position was also a major factor. (Competence, indeed, is often a neglected side of power.) However, rank and decision-making authority alone were sometimes no more than a formal confirmation of already accumulated power; and getting into such a position was not enough to keep a person there, even though the position often provided the means for the consolidation of power. The size of the system and the complexity of its prob-

---

[13] John R. P. French, Jr., and Bertram H. Raven, "The Bases of Social Power," in *Studies in Social Power*, ed. D. Cartwright (Ann Arbor, Michigan: Institute for Social Research, 1959), pp. 150–67.

lems meant that even those with advantageous formal positions had to work with and through many others who had similar bases for power—what Thompson signified when he proposed that the number of power bases in an organization increase with the number of uncertainties or contingencies it faces. Finally, as I have already argued, the relative importance of functions reflected in formal positions shifted with shifting organizational problems and priorities. Though up-the-ladder managerial jobs supposedly became less tied to function, in reality, identification in terms of functional specialties remained. This was even truer lower down the management hierarchy, where people often promoted their function in order to promote themselves and could get trapped when their function was suddenly seen as less critical to financial success or other goals than some other one. A changing business climate was known to shift the relative position of functions with respect to one another and to account for the balance of power between people who depended on each other across functions. The relative centralization or decentralization of decision making within each function and product area accounted for the relative power that lower-level representatives of an area brought to their task interactions with each other. In addition, whether a person was one of few or one of many in a position to bring pressure on a worker in a related function also affected relative amounts of power.

These abstractions came to life at Indsco in the relationships of field sales managers to product line managers in headquarters. Field sales managers directed the activities of sales workers over a number of product lines in a specific geographic territory; they were concerned with the performance of their people and the kinds of deals that could be made with customers. They responded to the exigencies of a competitive market situation and wanted to be in a favorable position on such things as price, quantity (especially during a time of material shortages), and shipping arrangements. Product line managers had a different set of priorities; they were the "business types" with responsibility, responsible for the profitability of their products across all geographic areas. They controlled price and allocation of product lines. The arrangements actually offered to customers were derived from the negotiations of sales people and line managers. There could be a great deal of tension between the people in these two positions. They had few face-to-face contacts, relating primarily by telephone or by telegram and mail, and their views from their locations differed. Field sales managers would insist that the product people were out of touch with the market, that they had no idea of the competitive scene out there, that they didn't know the customers. Product line managers, on the other hand, complained that the sales force was parochial and lacked knowledge of the overall business picture, that salespeople became too involved with their own special customers and forgot about the fate of Indsco as a whole.

The relative power of the people in these two jobs was determined by a number of system issues. In a growing economy several years earlier, when the corporation was also more decentralized, field managers were considered very powerful, running their "own little business." As the recession emerged and business fell off, and as the corporation began to centralize more and more decisions, the importance of the product line managers grew. Hierarchical position and departmental organization also had an effect. Depending on the department, many of the product managers held grade 16 positions; field managers were more typically at grade 12 or 14. Where this discrepancy in rank occurred, the field managers felt more dependent on the evaluations of product managers for their own career progress, and winning credibility with product managers was more important than the reverse ("They have the power to make or break our careers"), creating an asymmetry in power when the time for negotiations occurred. This asymmetry was reinforced by the typical form of interactions: field managers requested, product managers responded. If a product manager could not be reached by phone, field managers often could not act because they lacked important information. This infuriated them, but often there was nothing they could do without jeopardizing their relationship with the product manager. (A field manager once became so frustrated when he called a product manager several times one day, only to be told that he was in a meeting, then at lunch, then at another meeting, that he finally called the other's boss to say that he was needed right away. "He'll return my messages faster next time." However, he knew that this "kamikaze move" was risky. "With credibility you can get away with it. It depends on your relative position.") So field managers were generally much more concerned with winning favor with product managers, since they were functionally often more dependent, and they were much more effective managers of their own people when they had credibility with headquarters people. Finally, the relative numbers of field managers or product managers interfacing with each other could also affect the balance of power. Dealing with many made it easier for a person to retain some independence and to play them off against one another. One field sales manager related to seven different product line managers, and "with that many, there's no way I'm going to see them as my boss. If one isn't responsive, we'll just work harder on the other products, that's all."

There was thus a formal organizational component of power that was often out the hands of individuals to determine. However, there were also a number of ways in which people could use the organization or operate through it that could increase the power available to them. These involved both activities and alliances.

ACTIVITIES AS A ROUTE TO POWER

Power could be accumulated as a result of performance—the job-related activities people engaged in. The organization itself could be used as a source of power. (This is a side of power that political scientists consider more often with respect to the public arena than do social psychologists and sociologists of organizations.) However, for activities to increase the power of the persons engaging in them, they have to meet three criteria: (1) they are extraordinary, (2) they are visible, and (3) they are relevant—identified with the solution to a pressing organizational problem.

Extraordinary Activities

Not everyone in an organization is in a position to accumulate power through competent performance because most people are just carrying out the ordinary and the expected—even if they do it very well. The extent to which a job is routinized fails to give an advantage to anyone doing it because "success" is seen as inherent in the very establishment of the position and the organization surrounding it. Neither persons nor organizations get "credit" for doing the mandatory or the expected. Excellent performance on tasks where behavior is more or less predictable may be valued, but it will not necessarily add to power. Most factory workers and lower participants in organizations have been rendered powerless not only by the managerial monopoly on decision making but also by the routinization of tasks that reduces, if not eliminates, the opportunity to show enterprise or creativity, or ever do anything out of the ordinary or larger than life. This is a stronger and obverse version of Thompson's proposition that performance requiring discretion is more likely to be noticeable, and noticeability increases power. Crozier, too, theorized that the edge in a bargaining relationship is held by the person whose behavior is not predictable.[14]

There were several ways people at Indsco did something extraordinary: by being the first in a new position, by making organizational changes, or by taking major risks and succeeding. The rewards go to

---

[14] Thompson, *Organizations in Action,* pp. 107–9; Crozier, *Bureaucratic Phenomenon,* p. 158. Thompson also proposed that since highly routinized jobs are protected from the environment and employ skills commonly available, they cannot easily become visible outside the organization.

innovators, not to the second ones to do something; "the first to volunteer for extra work exhibits 'leadership,' " a quality anyone after that seems to lack.[15] A cycle could be observed around new functions and new positions in the corporation. The first time certain jobs were filled, fast track people were attracted. One of the inducements was the chance to step out of the ordinary and to participate in the development of a new function. The second cycle of people started to get trapped, and in one case a job that had been given a high grade when it was new (and required a person with sophisticated skills) was downgraded on the five-year reviews, so that it was seen to require a less senior manager. It became more and more difficult to fill the job as the function became more and more established. It was almost paradoxical: the success of the function as a whole made it less and less possible for the people running it to seem successful as individuals.

It becomes clear why some organizations seem to be continually changing, why new proposals and procedures are always under development. New managers must make changes or handle crises to demonstrate their abilities. If everything was running smoothly before and continues to run smoothly along the same track, what has the leader done? The "builder's complex" may emerge. Each leader needs his or her monument, which can be a physical structure or a redesigned organization chart. Crozier wrote about the plant directors whose ability to initiate action was curtailed by routinization of their functions—except in the case of planning and guiding the construction of new buildings or new physical layouts for shops. So people had a stake in finding reasons to undertake construction.[16] Very top executives at Indsco similarly became identified with the building of new field offices or proposed corporate moves. They would look for businesses to acquire or businesses to divest. They would have pet projects with which they were heavily identified, especially sweeping proposals such as taking the entire sales force off for a week-long meeting. There were definite costs if such plans did not work well—such single events were behind a number of firings—but enhanced power if they did.

Reorganizations were a common way to manipulate the structure to increase power. One new top executive at Indsco quickly established his position by making two power plays: firing the person in a key position under him and bringing in someone from outside the organization to fill the post, and creating a new division from a subgroup of the largest division, putting in someone he had worked with as its

[15] Wilbert Moore, The Conduct of the Corporation (New York: Random House, 1962), Vintage Books, p. 115.

[16] Crozier, Bureaucratic Phenomenon, pp. 155–56.

general manager. Another head of a function removed levels of the hierarchy; when he was promoted, his replacement put it back in. On a smaller scale, the manager of a personnel staff unit created two new levels of hierarchy in his nine-person group, putting in an assistant and developing two levels of the remaining people by upgrading some. (The people left on the lowest rung maintained their former position in the organization, retaining their "downward anchoring" and distance from the bottom, but they suddenly felt less powerful because when they looked up, they felt more junior.) Reorganizations were a frequent and important power move, for they served several functions at once. They ensured leaders that their own teams were well placed; opposition could be removed or rendered less effective. They provided leaders with rewards to dole out in the form of new opportunities and job changes. They enhanced the leader's power by creating new uncertainties in a situation that had been relatively routinized, making people more dependent on central authorities while they learned the new system. They were highly visible and difficult not to notice. In addition, because the question of the "best way to organize" was always relevant at Industrial Supply Corporation, reorganizations could always be presented as a problem-solving innovation.

Pulling off extraordinary risks was also power-enhancing—a classic source of the awe inspired by charismatic leaders. Very few people dared, but those who did became very powerful, for both organizational and social reasons. Organizationally, they had indicated their task-related value: they could perform in the most difficult of circumstances. Socially, they developed charisma in the eyes of the less daring. This was true of Indsco's most noted charismatic leader, an executive who had died prematurely, in Kennedy-like fashion. I heard about the devotion he inspired at many different levels of the organization and from many different kinds of people: "If we had him still with us, he'd shoot from the hip and say, 'Do it.' We'd all fall all over ourselves to do it, no matter whether it was logical or not. Unfortunately, he's gone; but where this thing might be were he still here! . . ." It was assumed that he could do anything, that no problem would be as bad if he were in charge. His rise to the top and the power he consolidated once he got there, was based almost entirely on one extraordinary risk: he took over a very unproductive plant and turned it around, staking his career on the outcome. When he finally became a division president, he continued to assume personal responsibility for events, to seek relationships and information far down the line, and to make himself available for criticism or blame if employees were unhappy with company decisions.

Visibility

For activities to enhance power, they have to be visible, to attract the notice of other people. Jobs that straddle the boundaries between organizational units or between the organization and its environment tend to have more noticeable activities, for example, than those that are well within a unit. These often become "power positions" because of their visibility. The chance to be noticed is differentially distributed in organizations, especially one that is so large that personal knowledge of everyone in even one's own function is impossible. It was also possible to gain visibility through participation on task forces or committees.

People who looked like "comers" seemed to have an instinct for doing the visible. A new marketing manager found that there was a communications gap around his function; no one seemed to know what was going on in other relevant corners of the unit, so he put out a report every other week. He netted a great deal of appreciation—and visibility. However, in other cases the things that were done for the sake of visibility seemed less beneficial. There were numerous complaints about certain managers who were more interested in choosing those programs that would be visible than those that represented high priorities to other people for reasons of organizational effectiveness or social value.

There were also some games played around "risks" because of the high costs of failure in an organization not set up to reward innovation: "Here when someone takes a chance, he strikes out on his own. If that sucker fails, he's got no place back at home. Nobody's got a string on my ass that's going to pull me back into this thing if I take a chance and try something new. Even the vice president of the new business department says, 'If you come into this department, I can't give you a string to get back with. I don't have that much authority yet.' So we're saying to that guy that it's a total-risk, no-win situation. It's safer to be part of a group. The whole group can't fail. You learn to take a calculated risk, to be 90 percent sure. That's the game to play. The thing to do is to make it *look* like a risk but have it in your back pocket. You need the attention that comes from taking a risk but the security of knowing you can't fail." In short, public appearance was more important than substance.

Relevance

Finally, even extraordinary and visible activities would not necessarily build power if they failed the relevance test: whether or not they could be identified with the solution to pressing organizational problems. Relevance is similar to what other theorists have termed *immediacy*.[17] As I have indicated, reorganizations can always demonstrate some relevance in systems where there can be no such thing as the "perfect" way to organize, but the relevance of other kinds of activities will be dependent on larger system issues, such as a current set of pressures upon the organization, and on how the actor presents his or her activities. Activities could not be engaged in for their own sake, even if brilliantly performed; wider system goals and ideology always had to be honored.

The importance of relevance in organizational politics was made very clear at Indsco in the case of a highly talented and very promising executive who became involved with the design of some new programs for employee relations. He was personally charismatic, and the people under him were highly devoted. He was also highly innovative; the programs he developed were very successfully received, and the organizational model he built represented a highly effective use of resources. His strategy for extending the applicability of his programs ran from the bottom up: first junior people would be involved, then they would pass the word on to their bosses, who would get a personal invitation to attend "briefing sessions" to learn what their subordinates were getting. All of this fit the organization development textbook picture of how to develop a new program. However, the manager became trapped in his own over-investment in his territory; his primary interest was in "drumming up business" so that he could create an even larger and more widespread set of programs. He was such a zealous advocate of his programs and his function that at a time when the company was having financial trouble, he began to be seen as "out to lunch." Questions were raised about his business sense, if he was still pushing development of people when the company might have to lay off people. Those who were against such activities in the first place found their excuse for criticism in declaring them irrelevant or saying that they might be a good thing but that the timing was off. Then the manager also had problems with his own alliances. The people who usually backed him were no longer in positions of power. He had one strong supporter at a high corporate level who saw that his next job was at least a lateral move, but developing the new function did not produce the career advance the manager had originally anticipated and seemed to decrease rather than increase his power.

Another staff unit was more aware of the relevance problem, if less

[17] One group which used the concept of immediacy proposed that activities generate power when their consequences are close to, rather than remote from, goals. C. R. Hinings, D. J. Hickson, D. M. Pennings, and R. E. Schneck, "Structural Conditions of Intraorganizational Power," *Administrative Science Quarterly* 19 (March 1974), pp. 22–44.

creative in its programs. There the major strategy was to "sell things by finding an already acceptable label and an organization need to hang it on."

ALLIANCES: POWER THROUGH OTHERS

The informal social network that pervades organizations can be very important, as many theorists have pointed out. In a large, complex system, it is almost a necessity for power to come from social connections, especially those outside of the immediate work group. Such connections need to be long-term and stable and include "sponsors" (mentors and advocates upward in the organization), peers, and subordinates.

Sponsors

Sponsors have been found to be important in the careers of managers and professionals in many settings. In the corporation, "sponsored mobility" (controlled selection by elites) seems to determine who gets the most desirable jobs, rather than "contest mobility" (an open game), to use Ralph Turner's concepts.[18] At Indsco, high-level sponsors were known as "rabbis" or "godfathers," two colorful labels for these unofficial bestowers of power.

Sponsors are often thought of as teachers or coaches whose functions are primarily to make introductions or to train a young person to move effectively through the system. However, there are three other important functions besides advice that generate power for the people sponsored. First, sponsors are often in a position to *fight* for the person in question, to stand up for him or her in meetings if controversy is raised, to promote that person for promising opportunities. When there are large numbers of personnel distributed across wide territories, as in Industrial Supply Corporation, there was much advantage to being the favorite of a powerful person who could help distinguish a person from the crowd and argue his or her virtues against those of other people. ("They say the rabbi system is dead," commented a young manager, "but I can't believe we make promotion decisions without it.") Despite a rating system that tried to make the system more open and equitable at lower levels, sponsors could still make a difference. Indeed, one of the problems with not having a powerful manager, Indsco workers thought, was that the manager would not be strong

---

[18] In a system of sponsored mobility, elites or their agents choose recruits early and then carefully induct them into elite status. Ralph H. Turner, "Sponsored and Contest Mobility in the School System," *American Sociological Review* 25 (December 1960), pp. 855–67.

enough to stand up and fight for subordinates in places where they could not fight for themselves.

Second, sponsors often provided the occasion for lower-level organization members to *bypass the hierarchy:* to get inside information, to short-circuit cumbersome procedures, or to cut red tape. People develop a social relationship with a powerful person which allows them to go directly to that person, even though there is no formal interface, and once there, a social interchange can often produce formal results. This could be very important to formal job success in Indsco, to the ability to get things done, in a system where people could easily get bogged down if they had to honor official protocol. One salesman with a problem he wanted to solve for a customer described Indsco as "like the Army, Air Force, and Navy—we have a formal chain of command." The person who could make the decision on his problem was four steps removed from him, not in hierarchical rank but according to operating procedure. Ordinarily, he would not be able to go directly to him, but they had developed a relationship over a series of sales meetings, during which the more powerful person had said, "Please drop by anytime you're at headquarters." So the salesman found an occasion to "drop by," and in the course of the casual conversation mentioned his situation. It was solved immediately. A woman manager used her powerful sponsors in a similar way. Whenever her boss was away, she had lunch with her friends among the corporate officers. This provided an important source of information, such as "secret" salary information from a vice president. In fact, the manager revealed, "much of what I get done across groups is based on informal personal relations through the years, when there is no formal way to do it."

Third, sponsors also provide an important signal to other people, a form of *reflected power*. Sponsorship indicates to others that the person in question has the backing of an influential person, that the sponsor's resources are somewhere behind the individual. Much of the power of relatively junior people comes not from their own resources but from the "credit" extended to them because there appears to be a more powerful set of resources in the distance. This was an important source of the power of "comers" at Indsco, the "water walkers" and "high fliers" who were on fast tracks because they were high performers with powerful backing. A manager in that position described it this way: "A variety of people become impressed with you. You see the support at several levels; someone seems comfortable with you although he's a vice president, and he looks you in the eye. You get offered special jobs by powerful people. You're pulled aside and don't have to go through channels. If you can sustain that impression for three to four years, your sphere of influence will increase to the point where you have a clear path for a few miles. You can have anything you want up to a certain level, where the power of the kingpins changes. Here's how it happens. A manager who is given a water walker, knowing that the person is seen as such from above and from below, is put in a no-win situation. If the person does well, everyone knew it anyway. If the person doesn't do well, it is considered the manager's fault. So the manager can only try to get the star promoted, move him or her out as fast as possible; and the manager wants to help accelerate the growth of water walkers because someday the manager might be working for them. All of this promotes the star's image." Another rising executive commented, "Everyone attempts to get on the heels of a flier. Everyone who does well has a sponsor, someone to take you on their heels. In my case, I had three managers. All of them have moved but continue to help me. A vice president likes me. I can count on getting any job up a level as long as he remains in favor."

Those seen as moving accumulated real power because of their connections with sponsors, but they also had to be careful about the way they used the reflected power of the sponsor: "It's an embryonic, gossamer-type thing because four levels up is *far* away, and the connection is very tenuous. It's only a promise of things to come. You can't use it with your own manager, or you get in trouble. The rabbis are not making commitments right now. One guy tried to use his connections with his manager, to cash in his chips too early. The axe fell. He had to go back to zero." Handling relationships with sponsors could be tricky, too. "It's scary because you have to live up to others' expectations. There is great danger if you go up against a godfather. It becomes a father/son issue as well as business. God help you if you are not grateful for the favors given." And, of course, fast trackers can also fall when their sponsors fall if they have not developed their own power base in the interim.

If sponsors are important for the success of men in organizations, they seem absolutely essential for women. If men function more effectively as leaders when they appear to have influence upward and outward in the organization, women need even more the signs of such influence and the access to real power provided by sponsors. Margaret Cussler's and Margaret Hennig's studies of those few women in top management positions in U.S. corporations showed dramatically the importance of sponsorship. A British study concluded that "office uncles" were important in the careers of women in organizations because they offered behavioral advice and fought for the women to be promoted.[19] Ella Grasso, the first woman elected to a state governorship

---

[19] Margaret Cussler, *The Woman Executive* (New York: Harcourt Brace Jovanovich, 1958); Margaret Hennig, *Career Development for Women Executives*. unpublished doctoral dissertation, Harvard Business School, 1970; Michael Fogarty, A. I. Allen, Isobel Allen, and Patricia Walters, *Women in Top Jobs: Four Studies in Achievement* (London: George Allen and Unwin, 1971).

on her own, had a sponsor in John Bailey, who was chairman of the
Democratic National Committee from 1961 to 1968. He first spotted
her as a political "comer" in the 1950s. Since then he has provided
advice, campaign help, and introductions to certain circles.[20] At Indsco the same pattern emerged. One woman was brought into her
management position at Indsco by a sponsor, a vice president for
whom she had worked as an executive secretary. Her relation to him
and the connections she had already made through him made her
reception into management quite different from that of other former
secretaries. Another secretary who was promoted without sponsorship
felt ignored, isolated, and resented after her move, but the first woman's experience was different. Male peers immediately made her one
of the gang. During her first week in the new position, she remem-
bered, she was deluged with phone calls from men letting her know
they were there if she had any questions, making sure she had a lunch
date, and inviting her to meetings.

If sponsors are more important for women, they can also be harder
to come by. Sponsorship is sometimes generated by good performance, but it can also come, as one of Indsco's fast trackers put it,
"because you have the right social background or know some of the
officers from outside the corporation or look good in a suit." Some
people thought that higher-ups decided to sponsor particular individuals because of identification and that this process almost automatically eliminated women. (There is, indeed, much research evidence
that leaders choose to promote the careers of socially similar subordinates.)[21] Men could not identify with women, and very few women
currently held top positions. Identification was the issue in these remarks: "Boy wonders rise under certain power structures. They're
recognized by a powerful person because they are very much like him.
He sees himself, a younger version, in that person. . . . Who can look
at a woman and see themselves?" This was a good question. When
women acquired sponsors, the reasons were often different from the
male sponsor-protégé situation. In one case, officers were looking for a
high-performing woman they could make into a showpiece to demon-

---

[20] Paul Cowan, "Connecticut's Governor Grasso Remembers How She Made It,"
New York Times, May 4, 1975.

[21] The evidence that social similarity and compatibility affects a leader's evaluation
of followers or subordinates comes from a variety of situations. Borgatta found that high
acceptability to a supervisor at the social level was associated with receiving high
ratings from him, in an all-male sample. Edgar Borgatta, "Analysis of Social Interaction
and Socio-metric Perception," *Sociometry* 17 (February 1954), pp. 7–32. A study of staff
nurses and their supervisors in three hospitals discovered that friendship with supervisors was a greater determinant of high evaluations than shared work attitudes and
values. Ronald Corwin, Marvin J. Taves, and J. Eugene Haas, "Social Requirements for
Occupational Success: Internalized Norms and Friendships," *Social Forces* 39 (1961),
pp. 135–40. The cause-effect relationship is not clear in these studies, of course.

strate the organization's openness to good women. In another instance, an executive was thought to have "hung his hat on a woman" (decided to sponsor her) to demonstrate that he could handle a "tricky" management situation and solve a problem for the corporation.

Peers

More often neglected in the study of the accumulation of organizational power is the importance of strong peer alliances, although Barry Stein has written about the ways groups can capitalize on the success of a "comer."[22] At Indsco high "peer acceptance," as managers put it, was necessary to any power base or career success. "Individual performers" found their immediate accomplishments rewarded, but their careers stuck . . . because they had not built, nor were seen as capable of building, the kinds of connections necessary for success in ever more interdependent higher-level jobs. "The group needs each other," a sales manager remarked. "To become powerful, people must first be successful and receive recognition, but they must wear the respect with a lack of arrogance. They must not be me-oriented. Instead of protecting their secrets in order to stand taller than the crowd, they are willing to share successes. They help their peers. . . . This is 'leader quality.' "

Strong alliances among peers could advance the group as a whole, as Stein noted in commenting on the fact that certain cohorts sometimes seem to produce all of the leaders in an organization.[23] However, a highly competitive situation could also imbue peer relations with politics and pitfalls. A star performer just promoted to his first management position told me quite proudly how he had just handled his first political battle with a counterpart in his position. One reason he was telling me at such length, he explained, was because he had no one he could tell within the organization. He had decided to take care of the issue by going directly to the other man and working it out with him, then promising him it would go no further. My informant had been the one who was wronged, and he could have gone to his boss or the other person's boss, but he decided that in the long run he was wiser to try to honor peer solidarity and try to build an ally out of the person who had hurt him. "I didn't want to create enemies," he commented. "Some peers look to you for help, to work with you for mutual gain, but others wait for you to stumble so they can bad-mouth you: 'Yeah, he's a sharp guy, but he drinks a lot.' If I had gone against the other guy now, even if I had won, he would have had a knife out for me sometime. Better to do him a favor by keeping quiet, and then he'll be grateful later."

---

[22] Stein, "Getting There: Patterns in Managerial Success."
[23] Ibid.

Peer alliances often worked through direct exchange of favors. On lower levels information was traded; on higher levels bargaining and trade often took place around good performers and job openings. In a senior executive's view, it worked like this: "A good job becomes available. A list of candidates is generated. That's refined down to three or four. That is circulated to a select group that has an opportunity to look it over. Then they can make bargains among themselves." A manager commented, "There's lots of 'I owe you one.' If you can accumulate enough chits, that helps you get what you need; but then, of course, people have to be in a position to cash them in."

Subordinates

The accumulation of power through alliances was not always upward oriented. For one thing, differential rates of hierarchical progress could mean that juniors or peers one day could become a person's boss the next. So it could be to a person's advantage to make alliances downward in the hierarchy with people who looked like they might be on the way up. There was a preference for "powerful" subordinates as well as powerful bosses. Just in the way Bernard Levenson proposed, a manager on the move would try to develop subordinates who could take over, keeping a member of "his team" in place. Professionals and executives needed more junior people loyal to them as much as they needed the backing of higher-level people. Especially higher up, the successful implementation of plans and policies depended heavily upon the activities of those people lower down in the hierarchy who were responsible for the carrying out of day-to-day operations or the translation into specifics of general guidelines. So alliances with subordinates often developed early in careers, anticipating the time when managers would need the support of "their team." There was often a scrambling by managers to upgrade the jobs reporting to them so that they could attract more powerful subordinates. Also, as I have indicated, managers could benefit from speeding up the career of a person already on a fast track.

However, if power was something that not everyone could accumulate, what happened to the powerless?

ACCOUNTABILITY WITHOUT POWER: SOURCES OF BUREAUCRATIC POWERLESSNESS

People who have authority without system power are powerless. People held accountable for the results produced by others, whose formal role gives them the right to command but who lack informal political influence, access to resources, outside status, sponsorship, or mobility prospects, are rendered powerless in the organization. They lack control over their own fate and are dependent on others above them—others whom they cannot easily influence—while they are expected by virtue of position to be influential over those parallel or below. Their sense of lack of control above is heightened by its contrast with the demands of an accountable authority position: that they mobilize others in the interests of a task they may have had little part in shaping, to produce results they may have had little part in defining.

First-line supervisors in highly routinized functions often are functionally powerless. Their situation—caught between the demands of a management hierarchy they are unlikely to enter because of low opportunity and the resistance of workers who resent their own circumstances—led classic writers on organizations to describe them as "men in the middle."[24] (However, they are also often "women in the middle.") They have little chance to gain power through activities, since their functions do not lend themselves to the demonstration of the extraordinary, nor do they generate high visibility or solutions to organizational problems. They have few rewards to distribute, since rewards are automatically given by the organization; and their need for reliable performance from workers in order to keep their own job secure limits the exercise of other forms of power. "I'm afraid to confront the employees because they have the power to slack, to slouch, to take too much time," a supervisor of clerical workers said, "and I need them for results. I'm measured on *results*—quantitative output, certain attendance levels, number of reports filed. They have to do it for me." Another one said, "When I ask for help, I get punished because my manager will say, 'But it's your job. If you can't do it, you shouldn't be in that job.' So what's *their* job? Sending me notes telling me it's unacceptable? They're like teachers sending me a report card." First-line supervisors also felt powerless because their jobs were vulnerable during times of recession, while people farther up in the hierarchy seemed secure. They resented the fact that their peers were let go, while higher managers were not. "Why us? Aren't they running the show? Shouldn't they be the ones to suffer if business isn't going well?" And supervisors of secretaries . . . were also rendered powerless by the secretary's allegiance to a boss with more status and clout in the organization.

Occupants of certain staff jobs were similarly organizationally powerless.[25] They had no line authority and were dependent on managers

---

[24] Whyte and Gardner, "Man in the Middle." See also Donald R. Wray, "Marginal Men of Industry, the Foremen," *American Journal of Sociology* 54 (January 1949), pp. 298–301.

[25] See Melville Dalton, "Conflicts between Staff and Line Managerial Officers," *American Sociological Review*, 21 (June 1950), pp. 342–51.

to implement their decisions and carry out their recommendations. Staff programs that managers saw as irrelevant to their primary responsibilities would be ignored. Affirmative action and equal employment opportunity officers often found themselves in this position. Their demands were seen by line people as an intrusion, a distraction from more important business, and the extra paperwork that EEO entailed was annoying. Personnel staff who tried to introduce more rational, universalistic, and equitable systems for job placement for nonexempts also had difficulty selling their programs. These staff activities were seen as destroying a managerial prerogative and interfering with something managers preferred to do for themselves. The aims of personnel people in sending out certain candidates for jobs could conflict with the desires of the manager who would be using the candidate and when battles resulted, it was often the more prestigious line manager who prevailed.

Regardless of function, people could also be rendered powerless if their own management did not extend opportunities for power downward—if their situations did not permit them to take risks, if their authority was undercut, or if their sphere of autonomous decision making was limited. There seemed to be a consensus at Indsco that superiors who solved problems themselves or tried to do the job themselves disempowered the managers or professionals under them. Considered ideal, by contrast, was the manager who "never gave anyone an answer; but when you walked out of his office, you had it because he asked you the questions that made you think of it." Many women thus objected to the "protectiveness" that they perceived in their managers, protection that "encased them in a plastic bubble," as one put it, and rendered them ineffectual. Anyone who is protected loses power, for successes are then attributed to the helpful actions of others, rather than the person's own actions. Women complained about the "people who want to move walls for me instead of saying, 'Hey, here's a wall. Let's strategize working through it.' " Another said, "You need a lot of exposure to get ahead, a broad base of experience. I don't want to be protected, given the easy management situations, the easy customers, the sure-fire position." And being in a position where decisions were reviewed and authority could be undercut also created powerlessness. A customer service representative faced a situation where she had to tell a customer that she couldn't ship to him because the materials were not available; this was an order that had come down to her. The customer said he would call the immediate manager. The manager backed up the representative, indicating that he would call headquarters but that the rep was right and had the information. So the customer went one step higher in the hierarchy, calling headquarters himself. This time he managed to get a change. Everyone lost credibility, but especially the woman. Nothing diminishes leaders' power more than subordinates' knowledge that they can always go over their heads, or that what they promise has no real clout. A management recruiter advised companies that wanted to ensure the success of new women managers not to inadvertently encourage resistance to the new manager; even seemingly innocuous requests, such as a higher manager asking to be kept informed, could encourage subordinates to bypass the woman and do their reporting higher up.[26]

Powerlessness, finally, was the general condition of those people who could not make the kinds of powerful alliances that helped to manage the bureaucracy. People without sponsors, without peer connections, or without promising subordinates remained in the situation of bureaucratic dependency on formal procedures, routine allocations of rewards, communication that flowed through a multi-layered chain of command, and decisions that must penetrate, as Robert Presthus put it, "innumerable veto barriers."[27] People who reached dead ends in their careers also rapidly lost power, since they could no longer promise gains to those who followed them and no longer had the security of future movement. Powerlessness was also the psychological state of people who, for whatever reason, felt insecure in their functioning as leaders and anticipated resistance rather than cooperation from those whom they were to lead. Indeed, the structural characteristics of modern organizational life tend to produce the symptoms of powerlessness in more and more lower-to-middle managers, supervisors, bureaucrats, and professionals. The chance to engage in the nonroutine, to show discretion, to take risks, or to become known, are all less available in the large bureaucracy.

BEHAVIORAL RESPONSES TO POWERLESSNESS

Controlling Behavior and Close Supervision

Psychoanalyst Karen Horney, in *The Neurotic Personality of Our Time*, described people's neurotic attempt to dominate when they feel anxious or helpless, inferior or insignificant. As a protection and a defense, the psychologically powerless turn to control over others. They want to be right all the time and are irritated at being proven wrong. They cannot tolerate disagreement.[28] In short, they become critical,

---

[26] Sidney Reynolds, "Women on the Line," *MBA* 9 (February 1975), pp. 27–30.

[27] Robert Presthus, *The Organizational Society* (New York: Alfred A. Knopf, 1962), p. 35.

[28] Karen Horney, *The Neurotic Personality of Our Time* (New York: W. W. Norton, 1937), pp. 163–70.

bossy, and controlling. Some degree of power, in the sense of mastery and control over one's fate, is necessary for feelings of self-esteem and well-being, as Rollo May has indicated.[29] When a person's exercise of power is thwarted or blocked, when people are rendered powerless in the larger arena, they may tend to concentrate their power needs on those over whom they have even a modicum of authority. There is a displacement of control downward paralleling displacement of aggression. In other words, people respond to the restrictiveness of their own situation by behaving restrictively toward others. People will "boss" those they can, as in the image of the nagging housewife or old-maid schoolteacher or authoritarian boss, if they cannot flex their power muscles more constructively and if, moreover, they are afraid they really are powerless.

One example of this syndrome comes from research on the leadership style of low-power male Air Force officers. Officers of lower status and advancement potential favored more directive, rigid, and authoritarian techniques of leadership, seeking control over subordinates. Subordinates were their primary frame of reference for their own status assessment and enhancement, and so they found it important to "lord it over" group members. They also did not help talented members of the group get ahead (perhaps finding them too threatening) and selected immediate assistants of mediocre rather than outstanding talent.[30] Similarly, in a French bureaucracy technical engineers in an isolated position with low mobility and low power with respect to directors were, in turn, extremely authoritarian and paternalistic with *their* subordinates.[31]

When people expect to be successful in their influence attempts, in contrast, they can afford to use milder forms of power, such as personal persuasion. Even a little bit of influence is likely to work, and it is so much more pleasant to avoid conflict and struggle. But when people anticipate resistance, they tend to use the strongest kind of weapon they can muster. As Frantz Fanon proposed in *The Wretched of the Earth*, the powerless may come to rely on force, first and foremost.[32] In a series of laboratory studies simulating supervision of three production workers, male subjects who lacked confidence in their own abilities to control the world or who thought they encountered resistance from the mock subordinates used more coercive than persuasive power, especially when resistance stemmed from "poor attitude" (a

[29] Rollo May, *Power and Innocence* (New York: W. W. Norton, 1972).

[30] Stanley H. Hetzler, "Variations in Role-Playing Patterns among Different Echelons of Bureaucratic Leaders," *American Sociological Review* 20 (December 1955), pp. 700–706.

[31] Crozier, *Bureaucratic Phenomenon*, pp. 122–23.

[32] Franz Fanon, *The Wretched of the Earth* (New York: Grove Press, 1965).

direct threat to their power) rather than ineptness.[33] We know from other laboratory studies that people are more automatically obedient toward the organizationally powerful than the powerless, regardless of formal position. Subordinates inhibit aggression in the face of power, but they direct more intense aggression to the relatively powerless. Indeed, it can be argued, as a number of other theorists have also done, that a controlling leadership style is a *result* rather than a *cause* of hostile, resistant, or noncompliant behavior on the part of subordinates.[34]

Thus, the relatively powerless in positions of organizational authority also have reason to be more controlling and coercive. If they have less call on the organization's resources, less backup and support from sponsors and managers, less cooperative subordinates, and less influence in the informal power structure, people can only use the strongest tools at their disposal: discipline or threats or maintaintaining tight control over all of the activities in their jurisdiction. If managers or supervisors who encounter resistance from those they are trying to direct tend to become more coercive in their power tactics, it is a vicious cycle: powerless authority figures who use coercive tactics provoke resistance and aggression, which prompts them to become even more coercive, controlling, and behaviorally restrictive.

At Indsco relatively powerless managers who were insecure about their organizational status tended to give the least freedom to subordinates and to personally control their department's activities much more tightly. (I used formal job characteristics, other people's perceptions, and my own observations to decide who was relatively powerless.) These managers made all of the decisions, did an amount of operating work themselves that others in the organization would consider "excessive," and did not let subordinates represent them at meetings or on task forces. They tried to control the communication flow in and out of their department, so that all messages had to pass through them. One manager in a low-power situation, who was consid-

---

[33] B. Goodstadt and D. Kipnis, "Situational Influences on the Use of Power," *Journal of Applied Psychology* 54 (1970), pp. 201–7; B. Goodstadt and L. Hjelle, "Power to the Powerless: Locus of Control and the Use of Power," *Journal of Personality and Social Psychology* 27 (July 1973), pp. 190–96.

[34] Thibaut and Riecken, "Authoritarianism, Status, and the Communicaton of Aggression." Chow and Grusky, in a laboratory simulation with complicated results, found that worker compliance (the degree of productivity and the degree of aggressiveness) shaped supervisory style, especially closeness of supervision and adoption of a punitive style; there were complex interaction phenomena in the data. Esther Chow and Oscar Grusky, "Worker Compliance and Supervisory Style: An Experimental Study of Female Superior-Subordinate Relationships," paper presented at the 1973 meeting of the American Sociological Association. Blau and Scott also pointed out that a group's low productivity may be a cause of supervisory style, as well as a result. Peter M. Blau and W. Richard Scott, *Formal Organizations* (San Francisco: Chandler, 1962), p. 50.

ered "tough to work for—too tight," jumped on a subordinate for calling a vice president directly to ask a question, saying "*I'm* the one who represents this function to v.p.'s." Another manager with good people working for him wanted to see that all the credit went to him. He wrote a report of his unit's activities that made it seem as though he, and not the salespeople involved, had generated an increase in sales: "By negotiating with the profit center, I saw to it that. . . ."

Sometimes low-power managers and supervisors took over the task and tried to do or direct closely the work of subordinates instead of giving them a free hand, because technical mastery of job content was one of the few arenas in which they *did* feel powerful. Often people get to first-line managerial jobs, for example, because they are good at the operating tasks. Trying to do the job themselves or watching over subordinates' shoulders to correct the slightest deviation from how the supervisors themselves would do it represents a comfortable retreat into expertise from the frustrations of trying to administer when organizational power is low. People can still feel good knowing that they could do the job well—or better than their subordinates. Thus, they are tempted to control their subordinates, keep them from learning or developing their own styles, jump in too quickly to solve problems, and "nitpick" over small things subordinates do differently. All of these things were considered characteristics of ineffective managers at Indsco. However, the temptation to take over the work of the next level down instead of engaging in more general leadership—a temptation that always existed, even for people at the very top, as one of them told me—was succumbed to especially by the powerless.

Conditions of work could intersect with low organizational power to reinforce a tendency toward closeness of supervision. Departments of women clerical workers run by powerless women managers were a case in point. The supervisors were, in turn, managed by men, who gave them detailed orders and little discretion, and the supervisors tended to be in a terminal job and poorly connected to informal power alliances. At the same time, the office setup encouraged a restrictive, controlled atmosphere. The clerical workers were confined to banks of desks in large offices virtually under the nose of the supervisor. These departments were considered among the most tightly run in the corporation. They had the least absenteeism and a decided "schoolroom" atmosphere. In contrast, the conditions of work in sales made it more difficult for even the most control-prone manager to supervise as tightly, since salespeople under one manager were often scattered throughout several field offices, and sales workers were legitimately out of the office a great deal of the time. Field sales managers, similarly, operated away from the direct view of their own managers. So the greater freedom of the sales function was empowering all down the line. However, the setting for clerical workers and their bosses made it easier for them to remain powerless.

Rules-Mindedness

The powerless inside an authority structure often become rules-minded in response to the limited options for power in their situation, turning to "the rules" as a power tool. Rules are made in the first place to try to control the uncontrollable; invoking organization rules and insisting on careful adherence to them is a characteristic response of the powerless in authority positions. For one thing, "the rules" represent their only safe and sure legitimate authority, the place where higher-ups are guaranteed to give them backing, because higher-ups wrote or represent the rules. They have few other means to use in bargaining with subordinates for cooperation. As Crozier wrote, "If no difference can be introduced in the treatment given to subordinates, either in the present definition of the job or in the fulfillment of their career expectations, hierarchical superiors cannot keep the power over them. Superiors' roles will be limited to controlling the application of rules."[35]

Second, powerlessness coupled with accountability, with responsibility for results dependent on the actions of others, provokes a cautious, low-risk, play-it-safe attitude. Getting everything right is the response of those who lack other ways to impress those above them or to secure their position; and in turn they demand this kind of ritualistic conformity from subordinates, like schoolteachers more concerned about neatness of a paper than its ideas. Secretarial supervisors at Indsco tended to be known for these traits: a concern with proper form rather than a good outcome. Or, as someone else said, "You don't give freedom or experiment with procedure when you're a first liner. You try to cover your ass and not make a mistake they can catch you on."

Overconformity to the rules and ritual concern with formalities are characteristics of the "bureaucratic personality" identified in Robert Merton's classic essay. Bureaucratic organizations, by their very structures, exert constant pressures on employees to perform reliably within prescribed and predictable behavioral limits. At the same time, routinization of careers within a bureaucracy—the provision of planned, graded, incremental promotions and salary increases—offers incentives for disciplined action and conformity to official regulations. These features taken together, Merton concluded, produced the bureaucrat's substitution of means (the rules, the forms, the procedures) for ends (goals, purposes, underlying rationales).[36]

---

[35] Crozier, *Bureaucratic Phenomenon*, p. 188.

[36] Robert K. Merton, "Bureaucratic Structure and Personality," in *Social Theory and Social Structure*, rev. ed. (Glencoe, Ill.: Free Press, 1957).

Melville Dalton also recognized that the powerless hang on to rules, contrasting the "strong" and the "weak" as models of managerial tendencies.

> The weak are fearful in conflict situations and absorb aggressions to avoid trouble. . . . They hesitate to act without consulting superiors and take refuge in clearly formulated rules, whether adequate or not for their footing at the moment. Following their fairy-tale image of the organization as a fixed thing, they suffer from their experience that it is not. This, of course, aggravates their difficulty in grasping the tacit expectations that associations do not want to spell out, when events are troublesome. . . . As they seek to escape dilemmas, their unfitness to act outside the haven of understood rules invites aggression from the strong who are searching for shortcuts in the network of official routes.[37]

Thus, it is those lower in power who become rules-minded, but it is a bit too simple to attribute the concern with rules only to a reactive stance—a general bureaucratic world view. For those with relatively little organizational power but who must lead or influence others, *their control of "the rules" can represent one of their few areas of personal discretion.* They can exchange a bending of the rules for compliance; they can reward their favorites with a lighter application of the rules. However, first the rules must be experienced and honored. Subordinates or clients or workers must know what the formalities are like before they can be grateful for a bit of special treatment. They must see that the manager or supervisor or official has the right to invoke the full measure of the rule. So the persons who concern themselves with the rules both have something that *must* command obedience and have the basis for a form of power through differential application of those same rules. Staff officials without the power or credibility to persuade people in other departments to carry out the *spirit* of new programs (like affirmative action or centralized secretarial hiring) could fall back on their *letter,* burying uncooperative departments in mounds of paperwork.

One Indsco manager who was particularly concerned about protocol, formalities, and proper procedure had come up the ranks the hard way and was still not in a very influential position. He was upset that perquisites and privileges that had taken him long to earn were now automatically given out to younger people. He felt that they took liberties and behaved much too casually. One time, a young person introduced himself to the manager at a company function and then called to make a lunch date. The manager turned him down and then phoned his boss to complain that the young person was trying to get into the executive dining room. However, there were hints of the true

---

[37] Melville Dalton, *Men Who Manage* (New York: John Wiley & Sons, 1959), p. 247.

feelings behind the manager's complaints. The manager was someone whose only source of power and respect came through the organizational formalities. He counted on being able to control his subordinates by carefully doling out privileges or offering small deviations from the formal rules. If the rules did not mean much anymore, what did he have left?

Territoriality and Domain Control

Merton went on to argue that bureaucrats adopt a domineering manner because whenever they use the authority of their office with clients or subordinates, they are acting as representatives of the power and prestige of the entire structure.[38] Vicarious power—power through identification—Merton seemed to say, breeds bossiness. However, if we look more closely at the organizational structures he described, we can see that this aspect of the "bureaucratic personality" reflects a response to *powerlessness* rather than to power, delegated or otherwise. The organization's concern with regulations reduces administrators' spheres of autonomy, limits their influence and decision-making power. The very provision of graded careers stressing seniority, in which incremental advances are relatively small and all must wait their turn, fosters dependency on the organization, which always holds back some rewards until the next advance. It removes incentives for assertion and reduces people to a common denominator—one in which they did not participate in defining. Unless people can accumulate power through activities or alliances, they face a sense of helplessness and insignificance.

In response to organizational insignificance, officials turn to their own small territory, their own little piece of the system—their subordinates, their function, their expertise. They guard their domain jealously. They narrow their interests to focus exclusively on it. They try to insulate and protect it and to prevent anyone else from engaging in similar activities without their approval or participation as "the experts." Another organizational cycle is set in motion. As each manager protects his or her own domain, the sense of helplessness and powerlessness of other administrators in intersecting units increases. They, in turn, may respond by redoubling their domination over their territory and their workers. The result can be "suboptimization": each subgroup optimizing only its own goals and forgetting about wider system interests. For example, a worker in Crozier's clerical agency described this territoriality of supervisors. Supervisors were squeezed by higher management, which blamed them for poor morale and deliv-

---

[38] Merton, "Bureaucratic Structure and Personality."

ered speeches and written instructions advising them to pay more attention to leadership. In the worker's view, "They worry too much about their career and the possibility of promotion. They are jealous and awfully competitive. They are also sectarian. Often there is a lot of hostility between sections. . . . Each one of them wants to have his little kingdom."[39]

At Indsco, territoriality seemed more often a response of relatively powerless staff than of line officials. Line officials could turn to close supervision or rules application, but staff had only whatever advantage they could gain through specialized knowledge and jurisdiction over an area of expertise. This was especially clear around personnel functions. The organization was so large that personnel training, management development, and organization development responsibilities were divided up among many different units, some attached to divisions, some attached to the corporation, and some attached to specific functions. Such units often prevented each other from acting by claiming territorial encroachments. The result was that nearly all of them remained narrowly specialized and highly conservative. It was enough to kill a proposal with which other units would have to cooperate if the idea originated in one that was looking temporarily more powerful. There was a parallel problem on the wider system level, where one division was much larger and more powerful than others. Organizational and personnel innovations developed by the major division were rarely adopted by any of the others, even if they proved highly effective, because the other units were trying to protect their own territory as an independent domain.

There were also reflections of territoriality among low-power staff people on the individual level. The tendency was to hang on to a territory that provided legitimacy, even when inappropriate. One staff woman, hired to run affirmative action programs, tended to bring up the women's issue wherever she was, as though she would have no right to participate unless she dragged in her "expertise." Yet, on one occasion she had been invited to join a group of managers because of what she might contribute to general discussions of organizational issues. But she could not let go of her domain, and the managers were sorry they had included her. Similarly, sometimes staff people clung to whatever might help solve their future power issues, regardless of its relevance to present tasks. One manager asked a personnel staff official to send him an older, experienced woman for a position as his administrative assistant. Instead, the man in the personnel department insisted on sending him three ambitious, rather inexperienced younger women, making it clear that personnel matters, such as the deci-

[39] Crozier, *Bureaucratic Phenomenon*, pp. 40–42.

sion about which candidates were appropriate, were his domain. However, perhaps there was something else underneath. The three women were ambitious and on the move. If he placed them fast, they owed him a favor, and because they were going to seek to move, they would have to keep coming back to him. Therefore, they were "his" candidates and represented possible future alliances.

Territorial control and domain concerns were also behind much of the treatment of secretaries at Indsco; but now it also becomes clear that relatively powerless bosses are likelier to be the ones who try to keep strong personal control over secretaries. Those secretaries who were encouraged by their bosses to seek promotions out of the secretarial ranks tended to work for the more powerful bosses.

The behavioral responses of powerless "leaders" to their situations, then, in controlling behavior, rules-mindedness, and territoriality, could make the conditions of work less satisfying for subordinates. To seek a more powerful leader could also be a way of seeking a more empowering, freedom-enhancing environment.

CYCLES OF POWER AND POWERLESSNESS

Power rises and falls on the basis of complex exigencies: the organizational situation, environmental pressures, the simultaneous actions of others. However, in terms of individual behavior at least, power is likely to bring more power, in ascending cycles, and powerlessness to generate powerlessness, in a descending cycle. The powerful have "credibility" behind their actions, so they have the capacity to get things done. Their alliances help them circumvent the more restricting aspects of the bureaucracy. They are able to be less coercive or rules-bound in their exercise of leadership, so their subordinates and clients are more likely to cooperate. They have the security of power, so they can be more generous in allowing subordinates power of their own, freedom of action. We come full circle. The powerful are not only given material and symbolic advantage but they are also provided with circumstances that can make them more effective mobilizers of other people. Thus they can accomplish and, through their accomplishments, generate more power. This means they can build alliances, with other people as colleagues rather than threats, and through their alliances generate more power.

The powerless are caught in a downward spiral. The coping mechanisms of low power are also those most likely to provoke resistance and further restriction of power. The attitudes of powerlessness get translated downward, so that those under a low-power leader can also become ineffective. There was this vicious circle at Indsco: A young trainee was assigned to a "chronic complainer" of a manager, who had

had organizational problems and had fallen well below the level of peers in his cohort. The trainee was talented but needed to be channeled. The manager's negativism began to transfer down to the trainee, and the young man started to lose his motivation. Nothing was done to correct the atmosphere. He became less motivated and more critical of the organization. He vented his hostility in nonconformist ways (long hair, torn clothes, general disrespect for people and things). Then people began to reinforce his negativity by focusing on what they observed: he's a "wise guy." They observed the symptoms but never looked at the real problem: the manager's situation. Finally, the trainee resigned just before he would have been terminated. Everyone breathed a sign of relief that the "problem" was gone. The manager lost even more credibility. This just reinforced his negativity and his coerciveness.

Since the behavioral responses of the powerless tend to be so ineffective as leadership styles, it would be the last rather than the first solution of most organizations to give such ineffective people more power or more responsibility. Yet all the indicators point to the negative effects of behavior that come from too little power, such as rules-mindedness and close supervision. Chris Argyris has noted that alienation and low morale accompany management's praise for the reliable (rules-obedient) rather than the enterprising (risk-taking) worker. Studies have shown that turnover varies with the degree to which supervisors structure tasks in advance and demand compliance, absenteeism with the tendency of supervisors to be "directive" and maintain close and detailed control. Yet when supervisors at Sears Roebuck had responsibility for so many people that they could not watch any one person closely, employees responded to this greater latitude with greater job satisfaction.[40] So perhaps it is meaningful to suggest interrupting the cycle of powerlessness: to empower those in low-power situations by increasing their opportunities and their latitude rather than to continue to punish them for their ineffectiveness, reinforcing their powerless state of mind.

Power in organizations, as I am using the term, is synonymous with autonomy and freedom of action. The powerful can afford to risk more, and they can afford to allow others their freedom. The bureaucratic machinery of modern organizations means that there are rather few

[40] Chris Argyris, *Integrating the Individual and the Organization* (New York: John Wiley & Sons, 1964); M. Argyle, G. Gardner, and I. Cioffi, "Supervisory Methods Related to Productivity, Absenteeism, and Labor Turnover," *Human Relations* 11 (1958), pp. 23–40; study by E. Fleishman and E. Harris cited in Charles Hampden-Turner, "The Factory as an Oppressive Environment," in *Worker's Control: A Reader on Labor and Social Change,* ed. G. Hunnius, G. D. Garson, and J. Case, (New York: Vintage, 1973), pp. 30–44. The Sears study was James Worthy, "Organizational Structure and Employee Morale," *American Sociological Review* 15 (1950), pp. 169–79.

people who are really powerful. Power has become a scarce resource that most people feel they lack. Although the scramble for political advantage still distinguishes relative degress of power, the organization places severe limits on everyone's freedom of action. The powerful get more, but they still share some of the mentality of powerlessness.

23

The Abilene Paradox: The Management of Agreement*

JERRY B. HARVEY

The July afternoon in Coleman, Texas (population 5,607) was particularly hot—104 degrees as measured by the Walgreen's Rexall Ex-Lax temperature gauge. In addition, the wind was blowing fine-grained West Texas topsoil through the house. But the afternoon was still tolerable—even potentially enjoyable. There was a fan going on the back porch; there was cold lemonade; and finally, there was entertainment. Dominoes. Perfect for the conditions. The game required little more physical exertion than an occasional mumbled comment, "Shuffle 'em," and an unhurried movement of the arm to place the spots in the appropriate perspective on the table. All in all, it had the makings of an agreeable Sunday afternoon in Coleman—that is, it was until my father-in-law suddenly said, "Let's get in the car and go to Abilene and have dinner at the cafeteria."

I thought, "What, go to Abilene? Fifty-three miles? In this dust storm and heat? And in an unairconditioned 1958 Buick?"

But my wife chimed in with, "Sounds like a great idea. I'd like to go. How about you, Jerry?" Since my own preferences were obviously out of step with the rest I replied, "Sounds good to me," and added, "I just hope your mother wants to go."

"Of course I want to go," said my mother-in-law. "I haven't been to Abilene in a long time."

---

* Reprinted by permission of the publisher from *Organizational Dynamics* (Summer 1974). Copyright © by AMACOM, a division of American Management Associations.

So into the car and off to Abilene we went. My predictions were fulfilled. The heat was brutal. We were coated with a fine layer of dust that was cemented with perspiration by the time we arrived. The food at the cafeteria provided first-rate testimonial material for antacid commercials.

Some four hours and 106 miles later we returned to Coleman, hot and exhausted. We sat in front of the fan for a long time in silence. Then, both to be sociable and to break the silence, I said, "It was a great trip, wasn't it?"

No one spoke.

Finally my mother-in-law said, with some irritation, "Well, to tell the truth, I really didn't enjoy it much and would rather have stayed here. I just went along because the three of you were so enthusiastic about going. I wouldn't have gone if you all hadn't pressured me into it."

I couldn't believe it. "What do you mean 'you all'?" I said. "Don't put me in the 'you all' group. I was delighted to be doing what we were doing. I didn't want to go. I only went to satisfy the rest of you. You're the culprits."

My wife looked shocked. "Don't call me a culprit. You and Daddy and Mama were the ones who wanted to go. I just went along to be sociable and to keep you happy. I would have had to be crazy to want to go out in heat like that."

Her father entered the conversation abruptly. "Hell!" he said.

He proceeded to expand on what was already absolutely clear. "Listen, I never wanted to go to Abilene. I just thought you might be bored. You visit so seldom I wanted to be sure you enjoyed it. I would have preferred to play another game of dominoes and eat the leftovers in the icebox."

After the outburst of recrimination we all sat back in silence. Here we were, four reasonably sensible people who, of our own volition, had just taken a 106-mile trip across a godforsaken desert in a furnace-like temperature through a cloud-like dust storm to eat unpalatable food at a hole-in-the-wall cafeteria in Abilene, when none of us had really wanted to go. In fact, to be more accurate, we'd done just the opposite of what we wanted to do. The whole situation simply didn't make sense.

At least it didn't make sense at the time. But since that day in Coleman, I have observed, consulted with, and been a part of more than one organization that has been caught in the same situation. As a result, they have either taken a side-trip, or, occasionally, a terminal journey to Abilene, when Dallas or Houston or Tokyo was where they really wanted to go. And for most of those organizations, the negative consequences of such trips, measured in terms of both human misery and economic loss, have been much greater than for our little Abilene group.

This article is concerned with that paradox—the Abilene Paradox. Stated simply, it is as follows: Organizations frequently take actions in contradiction to what they really want to do and therefore defeat the very purposes they are trying to achieve. It also deals with a major corollary of the paradox, which is that *the inability to manage agreement is a major source of organization dysfunction*. Last, the article is designed to help members of organizations cope more effectively with the paradox's pernicious influence.

As a means of accomplishing the above, I shall: (1) describe the symptoms exhibited by organizations caught in the paradox; (2) describe, in summarized case-study examples, how they occur in a variety of organizations; (3) discuss the underlying causal dynamics; (4) indicate some of the implications of accepting this model for describing organizational behavior; (5) make recommendations for coping with the paradox; and, in conclusion, (6) relate the paradox to a broader existential issue.

Symptoms of the Paradox

The inability to manage agreement, not the inability to manage conflict, is the essential symptom that defines organizations caught in the web of the Abilene Paradox. That inability effectively to manage agreement is expressed by six specific subsymptoms, all of which were present in our family Abilene group.

1.   Organization members agree privately, as individuals, as to the nature of the situation or problem facing the organization. For example, members of the Abilene group agreed that they were enjoying themselves sitting in front of the fan, sipping lemonade, and playing dominoes.

2.   Organization members agree privately, as individuals, as to the steps that would be required to cope with the situation or problem they face. For members of the Abilene group "more of the same" was a solution that would have adequately satisfied their individual and collective desires.

3.   Organization members fail to accurately communicate their desires and/or beliefs to one another. In fact, they do just the opposite and thereby lead one another into misperceiving the collective reality. Each member of the Abilene group, for example, communicated inaccurate data to other members of the organization. The data, in effect, said, "Yeah, it's a great idea. Let's go to Abilene," when in reality members of the organization individually and collectively preferred to stay in Coleman.

4. With such invalid and inaccurate information, organization members make collective decisions that lead them to take actions contrary to what they want to do, and thereby arrive at results that are counterproductive to the organization's intent and purposes. Thus, the Abilene group went to Abilene when it preferred to do something else.

5. As a result of taking actions that are counterproductive, organization members experience frustration, anger, irritation, and dissatisfaction with their organization. Consequently, they form subgroups with trusted acquaintances and blame other subgroups for the organization's dilemma. Frequently, they also blame authority figures and one another. Such phenomena were illustrated in the Abilene group by the "culprit" argument that occurred when we had returned to the comfort of the fan.

6. Finally, if organization members do not deal with the generic issue—the inability to manage agreement—the cycle repeats itself with greater intensity. The Abilene group, for a variety of reasons, the most important of which was that it became conscious of the process, did not reach that point.

To repeat, the Abilene Paradox reflects a failure to manage agreement. In fact, it is my contention that the inability to cope with (manage) agreement, rather than the inability to cope with (manage) conflict is the single most pressing issue of modern organizations.

Other Trips to Abilene

The Abilene Paradox is no respecter of individuals, organizations, or institutions. Following are descriptions of two other trips to Abilene that illustrate both the pervasiveness of the paradox and its underlying dynamics.

Case 1: The Boardroom. The Ozyx Corporation is a relatively small industrial company that has embarked on a trip to Abilene. The president of Ozyx has hired a consultant to help discover the reasons for the poor profit picture of the company in general and the low morale and productivity of the R&D division in particular. During the process of investigation, the consultant becomes interested in a research project in which the company has invested a sizable proportion of its R&D budget.

When asked about the project by the consultant in the privacy of their offices, the president, the vice president for research, and the research manager each describes it as an idea that looked great on paper but will ultimately fail because of the unavailability of the technology required to make it work. Each of them also acknowledges that continued support of the project will create cash flow problems that will jeopardize the very existence of the total organization.

Furthermore, each individual indicates he has not told the others about his reservations. When asked why, the president says he can't reveal his "true" feelings because abandoning the project, which has been widely publicized, would make the company look bad in the press and, in addition, would probably cause his vice president's ulcer to kick up or perhaps even cause him to quit, "because he has staked his professional reputation on the project's success."

Similarly, the vice president for research says he can't let the president or the research manager know his reservations because the president is so committed to it that "I would probably get fired for insubordination if I questioned the project."

Finally, the research manager says he can't let the president or vice president know of his doubts about the project because of their extreme commitment to the project's success.

All indicate that, in meetings with one another, they try to maintain an optimistic façade so the others won't worry unduly about the project. The research director, in particular, admits to writing ambiguous progress reports so the president and the vice president can "interpret them to suit themselves." In fact, he says he tends to slant them to the "positive" side, "given how committed the brass are."

The scent of the Abilene trail wafts from a paneled conference room where the project research budget is being considered for the following fiscal year. In the meeting itself, praises are heaped on the questionable project and a unanimous decision is made to continue it for yet another year. Symbolically, the organization has boarded a bus to Abilene.

In fact, although the real issue of agreement was confronted approximately eight months after the bus departed, it was nearly too late. The organization failed to meet a payroll and underwent a two-year period of personnel cutbacks, retrenchments, and austerity. Morale suffered, the most competent technical personnel resigned, and the organization's prestige in the industry declined.

Case 2: The Watergate.

> Apart from the grave question of who did what, Watergate presents America with the profound puzzle of why. What is it that led such a wide assortment of men, many of them high public officials, possibly including the President himself, either to instigate or to go along with and later try to hide a pattern of behavior that by now appears not only reprehensible, but stupid? (*The Washington Star and Daily News,* editorial, May 27, 1973.)

One possible answer to the editorial writer's question can be found by probing into the dynamics of the Abilene paradox. I shall let the reader reach his own conclusions, though, on the basis of the following excerpts from testimony before the Senate investigating committee on "The Watergate Affair."

In one exchange, Senator Howard Baker asked Herbert Porter, then a member of the White House staff, why he (Porter) found himself "in charge of or deeply involved in a dirty tricks operation of the campaign." In response, Porter indicated that he had had qualms about what he was doing, but that he ". . . was not one to stand up in a meeting and say that this should be stopped. . . . I kind of drifted along."

And when asked by Baker why he had "drifted along," Porter replied, "In all honesty, because of the fear of the group pressure that would ensue, of not being a team player," and ". . . I felt a deep sense of loyalty to him [the President] or was appealed to on that basis." (the *Washington Post*, June 8, 1973, p. 20.)

Jeb Magruder gave a similar response to a question posed by committee counsel Dash. Specifically, when asked about his, Mr. Dean's, and Mr. Mitchell's reactions to Mr. Liddy's proposal, which included bugging the Watergate, Mr. Magruder replied, "I think all three of us were appalled. The scope and size of the project were something that at least in my mind were not envisioned. I do not think it was in Mr. Mitchell's mind or Mr. Dean's, although I can't comment on their states of mind at that time."

Mr. Mitchell, in an understated way, which was his way of dealing with difficult problems like this, indicated that this was not an "acceptable project." (the *Washington Post*, June 15, 1973, p. A14.)

Later in his testimony Mr. Magruder said, ". . . I think I can honestly say that no one was particularly overwhelmed with the project. But I think we felt that this information could be useful, and Mr. Mitchell agreed to approve the project, and I then notified the parties of Mr. Mitchell's approval." (the *Washington Post*, June 15, 1973, p. A14.)

Although I obviously was not privy to the private conversations of the principal characters, the data seem to reflect the essential elements of the Abilene Paradox. First, they indicate agreement. Evidently, Mitchell, Porter, Dean, and Magruder agreed that the plan was inappropriate. ("I think I can honestly say that no one was particularly overwhelmed with the project.") Second, the data indicate that the principal figures then proceeded to implement the plan in contradiction to their shared agreement. Third, the data surrounding the case clearly indicate that the plan multiplied the organization's problems rather than solved them. And finally, the organization broke into subgroups with the various principals, such as the President, Mitchell, Porter, Dean, and Magruder, blaming one another for the dilemma in which they found themselves, and internecine warfare ensued.

In summary, it is possible that because of the inability of White House staff members to cope with the fact that they agreed, the organization took a trip to Abilene.

Analyzing the Paradox

The Abilene Paradox can be stated succinctly as follows: Organizations frequently take actions in contradiction to the data they have for dealing with problems and, as a result, compound their problems rather than solve them. Like all paradoxes, the Abilene Paradox deals with absurdity. On the surface, it makes little sense for organizations, whether they are couples or companies, bureaucracies or governments, to take actions that are diametrically opposed to the data they possess for solving crucial organizational problems. Such actions are particularly absurd since they tend to compound the very problems they are designed to solve and thereby defeat the purposes the organization is trying to achieve. However, as Robert Rapaport and others have so cogently expressed it, paradoxes are generally paradoxes only because they are based on a logic or rationale different from what we understand or expect.

Discovering that different logic not only destroys the paradoxical quality but also offers alternative ways for coping with similar situations. Therefore, part of the dilemma facing an Abilene-bound organization may be the lack of a map—a theory or model—that provides rationality to the paradox. The purpose of the following discussion is to provide such a map.

The map will be developed by examining the underlying psychological themes of the profit-making organization and the bureaucracy and it will include the following landmarks: (1) Action Anxiety; (2) Negative Fantasies; (3) Real Risk; (4) Separation Anxiety; and (5) the Psychological Reversal of Risk and Certainty. I hope that the discussion of such landmarks will provide harried organizations' travelers with a new map that will assist them in arriving at where they really want to go and, in addition, will help them in assessing the risks that are an inevitable part of the journey.

Action Anxiety

Action anxiety provides the first landmark for locating roadways that bypass Abilene. The concept of action anxiety says that the reason organization members take actions in contradiction to their understanding of the organization's problems lies in the intense anxiety that is created as they think about acting in accordance with what they believe needs to be done. As a result, they opt to endure the professional and economic degradation of pursuing an unworkable research project or the consequences of participating in an illegal activity rather than act in a manner congruent with their beliefs. It is not that organization members do not know what needs to be done—they do know. For example, the various principals in the research organization cited *knew* they were working on a research project that had no real possibility of succeeding. And the central figures of the Watergate episode apparently *knew* that, for a variety of reasons, the plan to bug the Watergate did not make sense.

Such action anxiety experienced by the various protagonists may not make sense, but the dilemma is not a new one. In fact, it is very similar to the anxiety experienced by Hamlet, who expressed it most eloquently in the opening lines of his famous soliloquy:

> To be or not to be; that is the question:
> Whether 'tis nobler in the mind to suffer
> The slings and arrows of outrageous fortune
> Or to take arms against a sea of troubles
> And by opposing, end them? . . . (*Hamlet,* Act III, Scene II)

It is easy to translate Hamlet's anxious lament into that of the research manager of our R&D organization as he contemplates his report to the meeting of the budget committee. It might go something like this:

> To maintain my sense of integrity and self-worth or compromise it, that is the question. Whether 'tis nobler in the mind to suffer the ignominy that comes from managing a nonsensical research project, or the fear and anxiety that come from making a report the president and V.P. may not like to hear.

So, the anguish, procrastination, and counterproductive behavior of the research manager or members of the White House staff are not much different from those of Hamlet; all might ask with equal justification Hamlet's subsequent searching question of what it is that

> makes us rather bear those ills we have than fly to others we know not of. (*Hamlet,* Act III, Scene II)

In short, like the various Abilene protagonists, we are faced with a deeper question: Why does action anxiety occur?

Negative Fantasies

Part of the answer to that question may be found in the negative fantasies organization members have about acting in congruence with what they believe should be done.

Hamlet experienced such fantasies. Specifically, Hamlet's fantasies of the alternatives to current evils were more evils, and he didn't entertain the possibility that any action he might take could lead to an improvement in the situation. Hamlet's was not an unusual case, though. In fact, the "Hamlet syndrome" clearly occurred in both organizations previously described. All of the organization protagonists had negative fantasies about what would happen if they acted in accordance with what they believed needed to be done.

The various managers in the R&D organization foresaw loss of face, prestige, position, and even health as the outcome of confronting the issues about which they believed, incorrectly, that they disagreed. Similarly, members of the White House staff feared being made scapegoats, branded as disloyal, or ostracized as nonteam players if they acted in accordance with their understanding of reality.

To sum up, action anxiety is supported by the negative fantasies that organization members have about what will happen as a consequence of their acting in accordance with their understanding of what is sensible. The negative fantasies, in turn, serve an important function for the persons who have them. Specifically, they provide the individual with an excuse that releases him psychologically, both in his own eyes and frequently in the eyes of others, from the responsibility of having to act to solve organization problems.

It is not sufficient, though, to stop with the explanation of negative fantasies as the basis for the inability of organizations to cope with agreement. We must look deeper and ask still other questions: What is the source of the negative fantasies? Why do they occur?

Real Risk

Risk is a reality of life, a condition of existence. John Kennedy articulated it in another way when he said at a news conference, "Life is unfair." By that I believe he meant we do not know, nor can we predict or control with certainty, either the events that impinge upon us or the outcomes of actions we undertake in response to those events.

Consequently, in the business environment, the research manager might find that confronting the president and the vice president with the fact that the project was a "turkey" might result in his being fired. And Mr. Porter's saying that an illegal plan of surveillance should not be carried out could have caused his ostracism as a nonteam player. There are too many cases when confrontation of this sort has resulted in such consequences. The real question, though, is not, Are such fantasized consequences possible? but, Are such fantasized consequences likely?

Thus, real risk is an existential condition, and all actions do have consequences that, to paraphrase Hamlet, may be worse than the evils of the present. As a result of their unwillingness to accept existential risk as one of life's givens, however, people may opt to take their organizations to Abilene rather than run the risk, no matter how small, of ending up somewhere worse.

Again, though, one must ask, What is the real risk that underlies the decision to opt for Abilene? What is at the core of the paradox?

Fear of Separation

One is tempted to say that the core of the paradox lies in the individual's fear of the unknown. Actually, we do not fear what is unknown, but we are afraid of things we do know about. What do we know about that frightens us into such apparently inexplicable organizational behavior?

Separation, alienation, and loneliness are things we do know about—and fear. Both research and experience indicate that ostracism is one of the most powerful punishments that can be devised. Solitary confinement does not draw its coercive strength from physical deprivation. The evidence is overwhelming that we have a fundamental need to be connected, engaged, and related and a reciprocal need not to be separated or alone. Every one of us, though, has experienced aloneness. From the time the umbilical cord was cut, we have experienced the real anguish of separation—broken friendships, divorces, deaths, and exclusions. C. P. Snow vividly described the tragic interplay between loneliness and connection:

> Each of us is alone; sometimes we escape from our solitariness, through love and affection or perhaps creative moments, but these triumphs of life are pools of light we make for ourselves while the edge of the road is black. Each of us dies alone.

That fear of taking risks that may result in our separation from others is at the core of the paradox. It finds expression in ways of which we may be unaware, and it is ultimately the cause of the self-defeating, collective deception that leads to self-destructive decisions within organizations.

Concretely, such fear of separation leads research committees to fund projects that none of its members want and, perhaps, White House staff members to engage in illegal activities that they don't really support.

The Psychological Reversal of Risk and Certainty

One piece of the map is still missing. It relates to the peculiar reversal that occurs in our thought processes as we try to cope with the Abilene Paradox. For example, we frequently fail to take action in an organizational setting because we fear that the actions we take may result in our separation from others, or, in the language of Mr. Porter, we are afraid of being tabbed as "disloyal" or are afraid of being ostracized as "nonteam players." But therein lies a paradox within a paradox, because our very unwillingness to take such risks virtually ensures the separation and aloneness we so fear. In effect, we reverse "real existential risk" and "fantasied risk" and by doing so transform what is a probability statement into what, for all practical purposes, becomes a certainty.

Take the R&D organization described earlier. When the project fails, some people will get fired, demoted, or sentenced to the purgatory of a make-work job in an out-of-the-way office. For those who remain, the atmosphere of blame, distrust, suspicion, and backbiting that accompanies such failure will serve only to further alienate and separate those who remain.

The Watergate situation is similar. The principals evidently feared being ostracized as disloyal nonteam players. When the illegality of the act surfaced, however, it was nearly inevitable that blaming, self-protective actions, and scapegoating would result in the very emotional separation from both the President and one another that the principals feared. Thus, by reversing real and fantasied risk, they had taken effective action to ensure the outcome they least desired.

One final question remains: Why do we make this peculiar reversal? I support the general thesis of Alvin Toffler and Philip Slater, who contend that our cultural emphasis on technology, competition, individualism, temporariness, and mobility has resulted in a population that has frequently experienced the terror of loneliness and seldom the satisfaction of engagement. Consequently, though we have learned of the reality of separation, we have not had the opportunity to learn the reciprocal skills of connection, with the result that, like the ancient dinosaurs, we are breeding organizations with self-destructive decision-making proclivities.

A Possible Abilene Bypass

Existential risk is inherent in living, so it is impossible to provide a map that meets the no-risk criterion, but it may be possible to describe the route in terms that make the landmarks understandable and that will clarify the risks involved. In order to do that, however, some commonly used terms such as victim, victimizer, collusion, responsibility, conflict, conformity, courage, confrontation, reality, and knowledge have to be redefined. In addition, we need to explore the relevance of the redefined concepts for bypassing or getting out of Abilene.

Victim and Victimizer. Blaming and fault-finding behavior is one of the basic symptoms of organizations that have found their way to Abilene, and the target of blame generally doesn't include the one who criticizes. Stated in different terms, executives begin to assign one another to roles of victims and victimizers. Ironic as it may seem, however, this assignment of roles is both irrelevant and dysfunctional, because once a business or a government fails to manage its agreement and arrives in Abilene, all its members are victims. Thus, arguments and accusations that identify victims and victimizers at best become symptoms of the paradox, and, at worst, drain energy from the problem-solving efforts required to redirect the organization along the route it really wants to take.

Collusion. A basic implication of the Abilene Paradox is that human problems of organization are reciprocal in nature. As Robert Tannenbaum has pointed out, you can't have an autocratic boss unless subordinates are willing to collude with his autocracy, and you can't have obsequious subordinates unless the boss is willing to collude with their obsequiousness.

Thus, in plain terms, each person in a self-defeating, Abilene-bound organization *colludes* with others, including peers, superiors, and subordinates, sometimes consciously and sometimes subconsciously, to create the dilemma in which the organization finds itself. To adopt a cliché of modern organization, "It takes a real team effort to go to Abilene." In that sense each person, in his own collusive manner, shares responsibility for the trip, so searching for a locus of blame outside oneself serves no useful purpose for either the organization or the individual. It neither helps the organization handle its dilemma of unrecognized agreement nor does it provide psychological relief for the individual, because focusing on conflict when agreement is the issue is devoid of reality. In fact, it does just the opposite, for it causes the organization to focus on managing conflict when it should be focusing on managing agreement.

Responsibility for Problem-Solving Action. A second question is, Who is responsible for getting us out of this place? To that question is frequently appended a third one, generally rhetorical in nature, with "should" overtones, such as, Isn't it the boss (or the ranking government official) who is responsible for doing something about the situation?

The answer to that question is no.

The key to understanding the functionality of the no answer is the knowledge that, when the dynamics of the paradox are in operation, the authority figure—and others—are in unknowing agreement with one another concerning the organization's problems and the steps necessary to solve them. Consequently, the power to destroy the paradox's pernicious influence comes from confronting and speaking to the underlying reality of the situation, and not from one's hierarchical position within the organization. Therefore, any organization member who chooses to risk confronting that reality possesses the necessary leverage to release the organization from the paradox's grip.

In one situation, it may be a research director's saying, "I don't think this project can succeed." In another, it may be Jeb Magruder's response to this question by Senator Baker:

> If you were concerned because the action was known to you to be illegal, because you thought it improper or unethical, you thought the prospects for success were very meager, and you doubted the reliability of Mr. Liddy, what on earth would it have taken to decide against the plan?

Magruder's reply was brief and to the point:

> Not very much, sir. I am sure that if I had fought vigorously against it, I think any of us could have had the plan cancelled. (*Time*, June 25, 1973, p. 12.)

Reality, Knowledge, Confrontation. Accepting the paradox as a model describing certain kinds of organizational dilemmas also requires rethinking the nature of reality and knowledge, as they are generally described in organizations. In brief, the underlying dynamics of the paradox clearly indicate that organization members generally know more about issues confronting the organization than they don't know. The various principals attending the research budget meeting, for example, knew the research project was doomed to failure. And Jeb Magruder spoke as a true Abilener when he said, "We knew it was illegal, probably, inappropriate." (the *Washington Post*, June 15, 1973, p. A16.)

Given this concept of reality and its relationship to knowledge, confrontation becomes the process of facing issues squarely, openly, and directly in an effort to discover whether the nature of the underlying collective reality is agreement or conflict. Accepting such a definition of confrontation has an important implication for change agents interested in making organizations more effective. That is, organization change and effectiveness may be facilitated as much by confronting the organization with what it knows and agrees upon as by confronting it with what it doesn't know or disagrees about.

Real Conflict and Phony Conflict

Conflict is a part of any organization. Couples, R&D divisions, and White House staffs all engage in it. However, analysis of the Abilene Paradox opens up the possibility of two kinds of conflict—real and phony. On the surface, they look alike, but, like headaches, have different causes and therefore require different treatment.

Real conflict occurs when people have real differences. ("My reading of the research printouts says that we can make the project profitable." "I come to the opposite conclusion.") ("I suggest we 'bug' the Watergate." "I'm not in favor of it.")

Phony conflict, on the other hand, occurs when people agree on the actions they want to take, and then do the opposite. The resulting anger, frustration, and blaming behavior generally termed "conflict" are not based on real differences. Rather, they stem from the protective reactions that occur when a decision that no one believed in or was committed to in the first place goes sour. In fact, as a paradox within a paradox, such conflict is symptomatic of agreement!

Group Tyranny and Conformity

Understanding the dynamics of the Abilene Paradox also requires a "reorientation" in thinking about concepts such as "group tyranny"— the loss of the individual's distinctiveness in a group, and the impact of conformity pressures on individual behavior in organizations.

Group tyranny and its result, individual conformity, generally refer to the coercive effect of group pressures on individual behavior. Sometimes referred to as Group-think, it has been damned as the cause for everything from the lack of creativity in organizations ("A camel is a horse designed by a committee") to antisocial behavior in juveniles ("My Johnny is a good boy. He was just pressured into shoplifting by the kids he runs around with").

However, analysis of the dynamics underlying the Abilene Paradox opens up the possibility that individuals frequently perceive and feel as if they are experiencing the coercive organization conformity pressures when, in actuality, they are responding to the dynamics of mismanaged agreement. Conceptualizing, experiencing, and responding to such experiences as reflecting the tyrannical pressures of a group again serves an important psychological use for the individual: As was previously said, it releases him from the responsibility of taking action and thus becomes a defense against action. Thus, much behavior within an organization that heretofore has been conceptualized as reflecting the tyranny of conformity pressures is really an expression of collective anxiety and therefore must be reconceptualized as a defense against acting.

A well-known example of such faulty conceptualization comes to mind. It involves the heroic sheriff in the classic Western movies who stands alone in the jailhouse door and singlehandedly protects a suspected (and usually innocent) horsethief or murderer from the irrational, tyrannical forces of group behavior—that is, an armed lynch mob. Generally, as a part of the ritual, he threatens to blow off the head of anyone who takes a step toward the door. Few ever take the challenge, and the reason is not the sheriff's six-shooter. What good would one pistol be against an armed mob of several hundred people who *really* want to hang somebody? Thus, the gun in fact serves as a face-saving measure for people who don't wish to participate in a hanging anyway. ("We had to back off. The sheriff threatened to blow our heads off.")

The situation is one involving agreement management, for a careful investigator canvassing the crowd under conditions in which the anonymity of the interviewees' responses could be guaranteed would probably find: (1) that few of the individuals in the crowd really wanted to take part in the hanging; (2) that each person's participation came about because he perceived, falsely, that others wanted to do so; and (3) that each person was afraid that others in the crowd would ostracize or in some other way punish him if he did not go along.

Diagnosing the Paradox

Most individuals like quick solutions, "clean" solutions, "no risk" solutions to organization problems. Furthermore, they tend to prefer solutions based on mechanics and technology, rather than on attitudes of "being." Unfortunately, the underlying reality of the paradox makes it impossible to provide either no-risk solutions or action technologies divorced from existential attitudes and realities. I do, however, have two sets of suggestions for dealing with these situations. One set of suggestions relates to diagnosing the situation, the other to confronting it.

When faced with the possibility that the paradox is operating, one must first make a diagnosis of the situation, and the key to diagnosis is an answer to the question, Is the organization involved in a conflict-management or an agreement-management situation? As an organization member, I have found it relatively easy to make a preliminary diagnosis as to whether an organization is on the way to Abilene or is involved in legitimate, substantive conflict by responding to the Diagnostic Survey shown in the accompanying figure. If the answer to the first question is "not characteristic," the organization is probably not in Abilene or conflict. If the answer is "characteristic," the organization has a problem of either real or phony conflict, and the answers to the succeeding questions help to determine which it is.

In brief, for reasons that should be apparent from the theory discussed here, the more times "characteristic" is checked, the more likely the organization is on its way to Abilene. In practical terms, a process for managing agreement is called for. And finally, if the answer to the first question falls into the "characteristic" category and most of the other answers fall into the category "not characteristic," one may be relatively sure the organization is in a real conflict situation and some sort of conflict management intervention is in order.

ORGANIZATION DIAGNOSTIC SURVEY

Instructions: For each of the following statements please indicate whether it *is* or *is not* characteristic of your organization.

---

1. There is conflict in the organization.
2. Organization members feel frustrated, impotent, and unhappy when trying to deal with it. Many are looking for ways to escape. They may avoid meetings at which the conflict is discussed, they may be looking for other jobs, or they may spend as much time away from the office as possible by taking unneeded trips or vacation or sick leave.
3. Organization members place much of the blame for the dilemma on the boss or other groups. In "back room" conversations among friends the boss is termed incompetent, ineffective, "out of touch," or a candidate for early retirement. To his face, nothing is said, or at best, only oblique references are made concerning his role in the organization's problems. If the boss isn't blamed, some other group, division, or unit is seen as the cause of the trouble: "We would do fine if it were not for the damn fools in Division X."
4. Small subgroups of trusted friends and associates meet informally over coffee, lunch, and so on to discuss organizational problems. There is a lot of agreement among the members of these subgroups as to the cause of the troubles and the solutions that would be effective in solving them. Such conversations are frequently punctuated with statements beginning with, "We should do . . ."
5. In meetings where those same people meet with members from other subgroups to discuss the problem they "soften their positions," state them in ambiguous language, or even reverse them to suit the apparent positions taken by others.
6. After such meetings, members complain to trusted associates that they really didn't say what they wanted to say, but also provide a list of convincing reasons why the comments, suggestions, and reactions they wanted to make would have been impossible. Trusted associates commiserate and say the same was true for them.
7. Attempts to solve the problem do not seem to work. In fact, such attempts seem to add to the problem or make it worse.
8. Outside the organization individuals seem to get along better, be happier, and operate more effectively than they do within it.

Coping with the Paradox

Assuming a preliminary diagnosis leads one to believe he and/or his organization is on the way to Abilene, the individual may choose to actively confront the situation to determine directly whether the underlying reality is one of agreement or conflict. Although there are, perhaps, a number of ways to do it, I have found one way in particular to be effective—confrontation in a group setting. The basic approach involves gathering organization members who are key figures in the problem and its solution into a group setting. Working within the context of a group is important, because the dynamics of the Abilene Paradox involve collusion among group members; therefore, to try to solve the dilemma by working with individuals and small subgroups would involve further collusion with the dynamics leading up to the paradox.

The first step in the meeting is for the individual who "calls" it (that is, the confronter) to own up to his position first and be open to the feedback he gets. The owning up process lets the others know that he is concerned lest the organization may be making a decision contrary to the desires of any of its members. A statement like this demonstrates the beginning of such an approach:

> I want to talk with you about the research project. Although I have previously said things to the contrary, I frankly don't think it will work, and I am very anxious about it. I suspect others may feel the same, but I don't know. Anyway, I am concerned that I may end up misleading you and that we may end up misleading one another, and if we aren't careful, we may continue to work on a problem that none of us wants and that might even bankrupt us. That's why I need to know where the rest of you stand. I would appreciate any of your thoughts about the project. Do you think it can succeed?

What kinds of results can one expect if he decides to undertake the process of confrontation? I have found that the results can be divided into *two* categories, at the technical level and at the level of existential experience. Of the two, I have found that for the person who undertakes to initiate the process of confrontation, the existential experience takes precedence in his ultimate evaluation of the outcome of the action he takes.

The Technical Level.   If one is correct in diagnosing the presence of the paradox, I have found the solution to the technical problem may be almost absurdly quick and simple, nearly on the order of this:

"Do you mean that you and I and the rest of us have been dragging along with a research project that none of us has thought would work? It's crazy. I can't believe we would do it, but we did. Let's figure out how we can cancel it and get to doing something productive." In fact, the simplicity and quickness of the solution frequently don't seem possible to most of us, since we have been trained to believe that the solution to conflict requires a long, arduous process of debilitating problem solving.

Also, since existential risk is always present, it is possible that one's diagnosis is incorrect, and the process of confrontation lifts to the level of public examination real, substantive conflict, which may result in heated debate about technology, personalities, and/or administrative approaches. There is evidence that such debates, properly managed, can be the basis for creativity in organizational problem solving. There is also the possibility, however, that such debates cannot be managed, and, substantiating the concept of existential risk, the person who initiates the risk may get fired or ostracized. But that again leads to the necessity of evaluating the results of such confrontation at the existential level.

Existential Results. Evaluating the outcome of confrontation from an existential framework is quite different from evaluating it from a set of technical criteria. How do I reach this conclusion? Simply from interviewing a variety of people who have chosen to confront the paradox and listening to their responses. In short, for them, psychological success and failure apparently are divorced from what is traditionally accepted in organizations as criteria for success and failure.

For instance, some examples of success are described when people are asked, "What happened when you confronted the issue?" They may answer this way:

> I was told we had enough boat rockers in the organization, and I got fired. It hurt at first, but in retrospect it was the greatest day of my life. I've got another job and I'm delighted. I'm a free man.

Another description of success might be this:

> I said I don't think the research project can succeed and the others looked shocked and quickly agreed. The upshot of the whole deal is that I got a promotion and am now known as a "rising star." It was the high point of my career.

Similarly, those who fail to confront the paradox describe failure in terms divorced from technical results. For example, one may report:

> I didn't say anything and we rocked along until the whole thing exploded and Joe got fired. There is still a lot of tension in the organization, and we are still in trouble, but I got a good performance review last time. I still feel lousy about the whole thing, though.

From a different viewpoint, an individual may describe his sense of failure in these words.

> I knew I should have said something and I didn't. When the project failed, I was a convenient whipping boy. I got demoted; I still have a job, but my future here is definitely limited. In a way I deserve what I got, but it doesn't make it any easier to accept because of that.

Most important, the act of confrontation apparently provides intrinsic psychological satisfaction, regardless of the technological outcomes for those who attempt it. The real meaning of that existential experience, and its relevance to a wide variety of organizations, may lie, therefore, not in the scientific analysis of decision making but in the plight of Sisyphus. That is something the reader will have to decide for himself.

The Abilene Paradox and the Myth of Sisyphus

In essence, this paper proposes that there is an underlying organizational reality that includes both agreement and disagreement, cooperation and conflict. However, the decision to confront the possibility of organization agreement is all too difficult and rare, and its opposite, the decision to accept the evils of the present, is all too common. Yet those two decisions may reflect the essence of both our human potential and our human imperfectibility. Consequently, the choice to confront reality in the family, the church, the business, or the bureaucracy, though made only occasionally, may reflect those "peak experiences" that provide meaning to the valleys.

In many ways, they may reflect the experience of Sisyphus. As you may remember, Sisyphus was condemned by Pluto to a perpetuity of pushing a large stone to the top of a mountain, only to see it return to its original position when he released it. As Camus suggested in his revision of the myth, Sisyphus' task was absurd and totally devoid of meaning. For most of us, though, the lives we lead pushing papers or hubcaps are no less absurd, and in many ways we probably spend about as much time pushing rocks in our organizations as Sisyphus did in his.

Camus also points out, though, that on occasion as Sisyphus released his rock and watched it return to its resting place at the bottom of the hill, he was able to recognize the absurdity of his lot, and for brief periods of time, transcend it.

So it may be with confronting the Abilene Paradox. Confronting the absurd paradox of agreement may provide, through activity, what Sisyphus gained from his passive but conscious acceptance of his fate. Thus, through the process of active confrontation with reality, we may take respite from pushing our rocks on their endless journeys and, for brief moments, experience what C. P. Snow termed "the triumphs of life we make for ourselves" within those absurdities we call organizations.

SELECTED BIBLIOGRAPHY

Chris Argyris in *Intervention Theory and Method: A Behavioral Science View* (Addison-Wesley, 1970) gives an excellent description of the process of "owning up" and being "open," both of which are major skills required if one is to assist his organization in avoiding or leaving Abilene.

Albert Camus in *The Myth of Sisyphus and Other Essays* (Vintage Books, Random House, 1955) provides an existential viewpoint for coping with absurdity, of which the Abilene Paradox is a clear example.

Jerry B. Harvey and R. Albertson in "Neurotic Organizations: Symptoms, Causes and Treatment," Parts I and II, *Personnel Journal* (September and October 1971) provide a detailed example of a third-party intervention into an organization caught in a variety of agreement-management dilemmas.

Irving Janis in *Victims of Groupthink* (Houghton-Mifflin Co., 1972) offers an alternative viewpoint for understanding and dealing with many of the dilemmas described in "The Abilene Paradox." Specifically, many of the events that Janis describes as examples of conformity pressures (that is, group tyranny) I would conceptualize as mismanaged agreement.

In his *The Pursuit of Loneliness* (Beacon Press, 1970), Philip Slater contributes an in-depth description of the impact of the role of alienation, separation, and loneliness (a major contribution to the Abilene Paradox) in our culture.

Richard Walton in *Interpersonal Peacemaking: Confrontation and Third Party Consultation* (Addison-Wesley, 1969) describes a variety of approaches for dealing with conflict when it is real, rather than phony.

24

Decisions, Decisions*

ANDREW S. GROVE

Making decisions—or more properly, participating in the process by which they are made—is an important and essential part of every manager's work from one day to the next. Decisions range from the profound to the trivial, from the complex to the very simple: Should we buy a building or should we lease it? Issue debt or equity? Should we hire this person or that one? Should we give someone a 7 percent or a 12 percent raise? Can we deposit a phosphosilicate glass with 9 percent phosphorus content without jeopardizing its stability in a plastic package? Can we appeal this case on the basis of Regulation 939 of the Internal Revenue Code? Should we serve free drinks at our departmental Christmas party?

In traditional industries, where the management chain of command was precisely defined, a person making a certain kind of decision was a person occupying a particular position in the organization chart. As the saying went, authority (to make decisions) went with responsibility (position in the management hierarchy). However, in businesses that mostly deal with information and know-how, a manager has to cope with a new phenomenon. Here a rapid divergence develops between power based on position and power based on knowledge, which occurs because the base of knowledge that constitutes the foundation of the business changes rapidly.

What do I mean? When someone graduates from college with a technical education, at that time and for the next several years, that young person will be fully up-to-date in the technology of the time. Hence, he possesses a good deal of knowledge-based power in the organization that hired him. If he does well, he will be promoted to higher and higher positions, and as the years pass, his position power will grow but his intimate famliarity with current technology will fade. Put another way, even if today's veteran manager was once an

---

* From Andrew S. Grove, *High Output Management* (New York: Vintage Books, 1985), pp. 88–101. Copyright © 1983 by Andrew S. Grove.

outstanding engineer, he is not now the technical expert he was when he joined the company. At Intel, anyway, we managers get a little more obsolete every day.

So a business like ours has to employ a decision-making process unlike those used in more conventional industries. If Intel used people holding old-fashioned position power to make all its decisions, decisions would be made by people unfamiliar with the technology of the day. And in general, the faster the change in the know-how on which the business depends or the faster the change in customer preferences, the greater the divergence between knowledge and position power is likely to be. If your business depends on what it *knows* to survive and prosper, what decision-making mechanism should you use? The key to success is again the middle manager, who not only is a link in the chain of command but also can see to it that the holders of the two types of power mesh smoothly.

IDEAL MODEL

Illustrated [in Figure 1] is an ideal model of decision making in a know-how business. The first stage should be *free discussion,* in which all points of view and all aspects of an issue are openly welcomed and debated. The greater the disagreement and controversy,

FIGURE 1
The Ideal Decision-Making Process

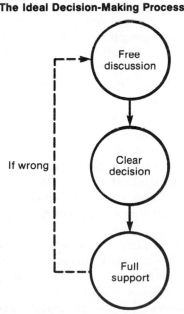

the more important becomes the word *free*. This sounds obvious, but it's not often the practice. Usually when a meeting gets heated, participants hang back, trying to sense the direction of things, saying nothing until they see what view is likely to prevail. They then throw their support behind that view to avoid being associated with a losing position. Bizarre as it may seem, some organizations actually encourage such behavior. Let me quote from a news account relating to the woes of a certain American automobile company: "In the meeting in which I was informed that I was released, I was told, 'Bill, in general, people who do well in this company wait until they hear their superiors express their view and then contribute something in support of that view.'" This is a terrible way to manage. All it produces is bad decisions, because if knowledgeable people withhold opinions, whatever is decided will be based on information and insight less complete than it could have been otherwise.

The next stage is reaching a *clear decision*. Again, the greater the disagreement about the issue, the more important becomes the word *clear*. In fact, particular pains should be taken to frame the terms of the decision with utter clarity. Again, our tendency is to do just the opposite: when we know a decision is controversial we want to obscure matters to avoid an argument. But the argument is not avoided by our being mealy-mouthed, merely postponed. People who don't like a decision will be a lot madder if they don't get a prompt and straight story about it.

Finally, everyone involved must give the decision reached by the group *full support*. This does not necessarily mean agreement: so long as the participants commit to back the decision, that is a satisfactory outcome. Many people have trouble supporting a decision with which they do not agree, but that they need to do so is simply inevitable. Even when we all have the same facts and we all have the interests of an organization in mind, we tend to have honest, strongly felt, real differences of opinion. No matter how much time we may spend trying to forge agreement, we just won't be able to get it on many issues. But an organization does not live by its members agreeing with one another at all times about everything. It lives instead by people committing to support the decisions and the moves of the business. All a manager can expect is that the commitment to support is honestly present, and this is something he can and must get from everyone.

The ideal decision-making model seems an easy one to follow. Yet I have found that it comes easily to only two classes of professional employees—senior managers who have been in the company for a long time, who feel at home with the way things are done, and who identify with the values of the organization; and the new graduates that we hire, because they used the model as students doing college work. This is the way a team of students working on a laboratory experiment will resolve its differences, so for the young engineer the Intel model is a continuation of what he was used to. But for middle managers, the decision-making model is easier to accept intellectually than it is to practice. Why? Because they often have trouble expressing their views forcefully, a hard time making unpleasant or difficult decisions, and an even harder time with the idea that they are expected to support a decision with which they don't agree. It may take a while, but the logic of the ideal scheme will eventually win everyone over.

Another desirable and important feature of the model is that any decision be worked out and reached at the *lowest competent level*. The reason is that this is where it will be made by people who are closest to the situation and know the most about it. And by "know" I don't just mean "understand technically." That kind of expertise must be tempered with judgment, which is developed through experience and learning from the many errors one has made in one's career. Thus, ideally, decision making should occur in the middle ground, between reliance on technical knowledge on the one hand, and on the bruises one has received from having tried to implement and apply such knowledge on the other. To make a decision, if you can't find people with both qualities, you should aim to get the best possible mix of participants available. For experience, we at Intel are likely to ask a person in management senior to the other members of the group to come to the meeting. But it is very important that everybody there voice opinions and beliefs as *equals* throughout the free discussion stage, forgetting or ignoring status differentials.

A journalist puzzled by our management style once asked me, "Mr. Grove, isn't your company's emphasis on visible signs of egalitarianism such as informal dress, partitions instead of offices, and the absence of other obvious perks like reserved parking spaces, just so much affectation?" My answer was that this is not affectation but a matter of survival. In our business we have to mix knowledge-power people with position-power people daily, and together they make decisions that could affect us for years to come. If we don't link our engineers with our managers in such a way as to get good decisions, we can't succeed in our industry. Now, status symbols most certainly do not promote the flow of ideas, facts, and points of view. What appears to be a matter of style really is a matter of necessity.

THE PEER-GROUP SYNDROME

The model is also hard to implement because anybody who makes a business decision also possesses emotions such as pride, ambition, fear, and insecurity. These tend to come to the surface quickly when people who are not used to working with one another are asked to make a decision. This means we need to think about what keeps decision making from happening smoothly along the lines we've advocated.

The most common problem is something we call the *peer-group syndrome.* A number of years ago, at Intel's very first management training session, we tried some role-playing to show people what can occur when a group of peers meets to solve a problem or make a decision. We sat the people around a table to tackle what was then a live issue for them in their real jobs. Everyone was an organizational equal. The chairman of the meeting was one level higher, but was purposely sent out of the room so he couldn't hear what was to happen. Observers in the audience couldn't believe their eyes and ears as the mock meeting proceeded. The managers working on the problem did nothing but go around in circles for some 15 minutes, and none of them noticed they weren't getting anywhere. When the chairman was brought back in, he sat down and listened for a while and couldn't believe things either. We watched him lean forward as if he were trying to glean more from the conversation. We then saw a black cloud form over his head; finally he slapped the table and exclaimed, "What's going on here? You people are talking in circles and getting nowhere." After the chairman intervened, the problem was resolved in very short order. We named this the *peer-plus-one* approach, and have used it since then to aid decision making where we must. Peers tend to look for a more senior manager, even if he is not the most competent or knowledgeable person involved, to take over and shape a meeting.

Why? Because most people are afraid to stick their necks out. This is how John, an Intel software engineer, sees things:

> One of the reasons why people are reluctant to come out with an opinion in the presence of their peers is the fear of going against the group by stating an opinion that is different from that of the group. Consequently, the group as a whole wanders around for a while, feeling each other out, waiting for a consensus to develop before anyone risks taking a position. If and when a group consensus emerges, one of the members will state it *as a group opinion* ("I think *our* position seems to be . . ."), not as a personal position. After a weak statement of the group position, if the rest of the mob buys in, the position becomes more solid and is restated more forcefully.

Note the difference between the situation described earlier by the auto executive and the one John describes. In the former instance, the people were expected to wait for their supervisor to state his opinion first. In the latter, members of the group were waiting for a consensus to develop. The dynamics are different, but the bottom line in both is that people didn't really speak their minds freely. That certainly makes it harder for a manager to make the right decisions.

You can overcome the peer-group syndrome if each of the members has self-confidence, which stems in part from being familiar with the issue under consideration and from experience. But in the end self-confidence mostly comes from a gut-level realization that nobody has ever died from making a wrong business decision, or taking inappropriate action, or being overruled. And everyone in your operation should be made to understand this.

If the peer-group syndrome manifests itself, and the meeting has no formal chairman, the person who has the most at stake should take charge. If that doesn't work, one can always ask the senior person present to assume control. He is likely to be no more expert in the issues at hand than other members of the group—perhaps less expert—but he is likely to act as a godfather, a repository of knowledge about how decisions should be made, and give the group the confidence needed to make a decision.

One thing that paralyzes both knowledge and position power possessors is the fear of simply *sounding dumb*. For the senior person, this is likely to keep him from asking the question he should ask. The same fear will make other participants merely think their thoughts privately rather than articulate them for all to hear; at best they will whisper what they have to say to a neighbor. As a manager, you should remind yourself that each time an insight or fact is withheld and an appropriate question is suppressed, the decision-making process is less good than it might have been.

A related phenomenon influences lower-level people present in the meeting. This group has to overcome the fear of being *overruled*, which might mean embarrassment: if the rest of the group or a senior-level manager vetoed a junior person or opposed a position he was advocating, the junior manager might lose face in front of his peers. This, even more than fear of sanctions or even of the loss of job, makes junior people hang back and let the more senior people set the likely direction of decision making.

But some issues are so complex that those called on to make a decision honestly aren't really sure how they feel. When knowledge and position power are separated, the sense of uncertainty can become especially acute, because the knowledge people are often not comfortable with the purely business-related factors that might influence a decision. What is often heard is, "We don't know what the company [or division or department] wants of us." Similarly, managers holding position power don't know what to do because they realize they don't know enough about the technical details to arrive at the correct decision. We must strive not to be done in by such obstacles. We are all human beings endowed with intelligence and blessed with willpower. Both can be drawn upon to help us overcome our fear of sounding dumb or of being overruled, and lead us to initiate discussion and come out front with a stand.

STRIVING FOR THE OUTPUT

Sometimes no amount of discussion will produce a consensus, yet the time for a decision has clearly arrived. When this happens, the senior person (or "peer-plus-one") who until now has guided, coached, and prodded the group along has no choice but to make a decision himself. If the decision-making process has proceeded correctly up to this point, the senior manager will be making the decision having had the full benefit of free discussion wherein all points of view, facts, opinions, and judgments were aired without position-power prejudice. In other words, it is legitimate—in fact, sometimes unavoidable—for the senior person to wield position-power authority if the clear decision stage is reached and no consensus has developed. It is not legitimate—in fact, it is destructive—for him to wield that authority any earlier. This is often not easy. We Americans tend to be reluctant to exercise position power deliberately and explicitly—it is just "not nice" to give orders. Such reluctance on the part of the senior manager can prolong the first phase of the decision-making process— the time of free discussion—past the optimum point, and the decision will be put off.

If you either enter the decision-making stage too early or wait too long, you won't derive the full benefit of open discussion. The criterion to follow is this: don't push for a decision prematurely. Make sure you have heard and considered the real issues rather than the superficial comments that often dominate the early part of a meeting. But if you feel that you have already heard everything, that all sides of the issue have been raised, it is time to push for a consensus—and failing that, to step in and make a decision. Sometimes free discussion goes on in an unending search for consensus. But, if that happens, people can drift away from the near consensus when they are close to being right, diminishing the chances of reaching the correct decision. So moving on to make the decision at the right time is crucial.

Basically, like other things managers do, decision making has an *output* associated with it, which in this case is the decision itself. Like other managerial processes, decision making is likelier to generate high-quality output in a timely fashion if we say clearly at the outset that we expect exactly that. In other words, one of the manager's key tasks is to settle six important questions in advance:

- What decision needs to be made?
- When does it have to be made?
- Who will decide?
- Who will need to be consulted prior to making the decision?
- Who will ratify or veto the decision?
- Who will need to be informed of the decision?

Let me illustrate how these six questions came into play in a recent decision I was involved in. Intel had already decided to expand its Philippine manufacturing plant, roughly doubling its capacity. The next question was where. Only limited space was available next to the existing plant. But, other things being equal, building there was the most desirable thing to do because overhead and communications could be shared, transportation costs between the two plants would amount to virtually nothing, and our employees could be transferred from one plant to the other very easily. The alternative consisted of buying a less expensive plot of land quite some distance away. The land would be not only cheaper but more plentiful, which would allow us to build a relatively inexpensive one- or two-story building. Buying the lot near the existing plant meant that we would have had to build a high-rise to get the amount of floor space we needed, and a high-rise semiconductor manufacturing plant would not be the most efficient. That made us hesitate. But it would be nice to have a second building next to the one we already own. Back and forth and so on and so forth went the discussion.

Let's apply our six questions here. It is clear *what* decision needed to be made: we either build a multistory building next to our existing plant, or we build a one- or two-story building at a new outlying location. As for the question *when:* according to our long-range plans, we needed the new plant in two to two and a half years; if we apply time offsets, we must make the decision within a month. This answers the *when.*

Who will decide? Our facilities/construction people or the Intel group that manages the manufacturing plants? The answer is not easy. The first organization is more sensitive to matters pertaining to the costs and difficulties of construction, and will probably lean toward the new location. The plant management group, knowing that operational benefits will come from having the two plants side by side, will probably opt for the high-rise. So the decision-making body is composed of our construction manager for our Far East locations; his supervisor, the construction manager for the corporation; the manager of the Far East manufacturing plant network; and his supervisor, the senior manufacturing manager. The meeting gave us parallel levels of managers from the two organizations. The sensitivities of two interest groups coming to bear on a single decision is quite common in real corporate life. In such meetings, it is important to give to the two sides roughly equal representation, because only from such balance will an even-handed decision emerge. All of these individuals have consulted their staffs prior to the decision and gathered all relevant knowledge and views on the subject.

Who will ratify or veto the decision? The first common person to whom the senior managers of both organizations report is myself. Also, this was a big enough deal that the president of the company should be involved. Moreover, I was somewhat familiar with the locations in the Philippines and how a plant like the one we have there operates. So I was chosen as the person to veto or ratify the decision of the meeting.

Who will need to be informed of this decision? I chose Gordon Moore, our chairman of the board. He's not directly involved with manufacturing plants like the one contemplated, but we don't build a new one in the Far East every day, so he should know about what happened.

This is how the decision was made. After studying maps, construction plans and costs, land costs, and traffic patterns, and considering several times everything we thought was important, the group decided to build next to our existing plant but to accept only as much manufacturing area as four stories would yield. The cost would have escalated had we exceeded that. This, with all relevant background, was presented to me at the meeting described on the agenda shown in the previous chapter. I listened to the presentation of the alternatives the group considered and to the reasons why they preferred their choice to these, and after asking a series of questions and probing both the group's information and its thinking process, I ratified the decision. Subsequently I informed Gordon Moore of the outcome, and as you are reading this, the plant is either under construction or already operating.

Employing consistent ways by which decisions are to be made has value beyond simply expediting the decision making itself. People invest a great deal of energy and emotion in coming up with a decision. Then somebody who has an important say-so or the right to veto it may come across the decision later. If he does veto it, he can be regarded as a Johnny-come-lately who upsets the decision-making applecart. This, of course, will frustrate and demoralize the people who may have been working on it for a long time. If the veto comes as a surprise, however legitimate it may have been on its merits, an impression of political maneuvering is inevitably created. Politics and manipulation or even their appearance should be avoided at all costs. And I can think of no better way to make the decision-making process straightforward than to apply *before the fact* the structure imposed by our six questions.

One last thing: If the final word has to be dramatically different from the expectations of the people who participated in the decision-making process (had I chosen, for example, to cancel the Philippine plant project altogether), make your announcement but don't just walk away from the issue. People need time to adjust, rationalize, and in general put their heads back together. Adjourn, reconvene the meeting after people have had a chance to recover, and solicit their views of the decision at that time. This will help everybody accept and learn to live with the unexpected.

If good decision making appears complicated, that's because it is and has been for a long time. Let me quote from Alfred Sloan, who spent a lifetime preoccupied with decision making: "Group decisions do not always come easily. There is a strong temptation for the leading officers to make decisions themselves without the sometimes onerous process of discussion." Because the process is indeed onerous, people sometimes try to run away from it. A middle manager I once knew came straight from one of the better business schools and possessed what we might call a "John Wayne" mentality. Having become frustrated with the way Intel made decisions, he quit. He joined a company where his employers assured him during the interview that people were encouraged to make individual decisions which they were then free to implement. Four months later, he came back to Intel. He explained that if he could make decisions without consulting anybody, so could everybody else.

25

The Question of Quality Circles*

MITCHELL LEE MARKS

Blue Cross of Washington and Alaska reports that more efficient employee procedures have saved $430,000 in less than three years, improved service to customers, and increased communication between departments. A better method for checking coating thickness of floppy disks has saved $100,000 for the Verbatim Corporation in Sunnyvale, California. Sales agents at Hertz Rent a Car in Oklahoma City now get information about car availability 27 seconds faster using computers rather than microfiche.

Neither industrial engineers nor human factors analysts developed these innovations. Rather, they came directly from the workers themselves—sales agents, clerks, and factory workers participating in quality circles (QCs, as they are often called), an employee-participation technique popularized in Japan and now widely applied in the United States.

Many businesspeople, management experts, and organizational psychologists dispute the savings claimed by QC adherents and say that QCs fail more often than they work. These critics describe the technique as management snake oil, a quick fix too often aimed at generating short-term profits rather than addressing the real problems underlying poor productivity, quality, and employee morale.

A major reason for these sharp differences of opinion is that until recently the benefits of QCs have been studied and touted chiefly by people with a vested interest in QC success: managers whose bonuses and career advancement are at stake and consultants looking for ways to impress and sell new clients. There have been few rigorously collected data on how QCs affect the attitudes and productivity of employees and the effectiveness and financial performance of their organizations.

Several such evaluations have been made in the last few years. Before examining what they found, it will be useful to look at how

QCs work and the reasons—aside from any accomplishments—for their tremendous growth in popularity.

Although QC programs vary from site to site, most share a basic format: Small groups of people who perform similar work meet voluntarily on a regular basis, usually once a week, to analyze work-related problems and propose solutions to them. QCs are usually led by the supervisor or manager of the work unit in which they are located. Members receive training in problem solving, quality control, and group dynamics to help them function well.

Discussions are limited to issues directly related to the quantity or quality of work, such as paperwork and material waste, machine maintenance, cooperation between departments, and productivity. Pay, benefits, hiring or promotion decisions, and factors restricted by labor-relations contracts are out of bounds. Members of QCs have no power to implement ideas directly. Instead, they present them to the person in charge of the operation involved, usually a middle-level manager, who is free to accept or reject the recommendations.

The QC process draws substantially upon psychological theory and research for its rationale. The technique, consistent with the work of theorists such as Abraham Maslow, assumes that employees become more motivated if jobs meet their need for growth. Proponents claim that QCs accomplish this by giving workers opportunities to identify and solve real problems, make presentations to company management, and operate successfully in groups. They also contend that QCs offer the advantages of group decision making—advantages that include, according to psychologist Norman R. F. Maier of the University of Michigan, higher-quality decisions and increased commitment to implementing them.

QCs are a major part of a broader current movement toward greater employee participation in decision making. Robert E. Cole, a sociologist at the University of Michigan and former director of that school's Center for Japanese Studies, notes, "In the early 1970s there were extensive discussions in America . . . about the need to 'humanize work' and raise the quality of work life. By increasing employee participation in workplace decisions, increasing job variety, and making more effective use of worker potential, it was argued, not only would the quality of work life be enhanced, but organizational efficiency and worker productivity would be improved."

Cole recalls, "Japan scared the pants off U.S. business in the 1970s. People were desperately looking for something to try." The media, as well as many academics, attributed Japan's success in the late 1970s to its superior approach to management, and QCs were seen as the easiest part of the Japanese approach to implement. QC programs were accessible, well packaged, and aggressively marketed by management consultants. Additionally, American business leaders saw them as a low-risk method for increasing worker involvement without changing the organization. Finally, QC usage also became a fad. Many managers jumped on the bandwagon simply because the technique symbolized modern management.

QC proponents argue that their technique is much more than a fad, that it is part of a trend that is permanently changing managerial assumptions and practices in the United States. Donald Dewar, president of Quality Circle Institute, the largest QC consulting firm in the United States, insists, "You don't have quality control without quality circles. Of all the participative management techniques, this is the first time it went below supervisory levels and down to the people who actually do the work. Many managers have been surprised that people could learn the problem-solving techniques. It is changing not only the quality of work, but also how managers regard their people."

Many American management scholars and practitioners, including executives who refuse to use QCs in their organizations, view these claims with caution. They contend that the technique is a poor fit with American management styles. Tai K. Oh, a management professor at California State University at Fullerton and a consultant to businesses in the United States on Japanese management techniques, says that QC programs have failed in more than 60 percent of the American organizations in which they have been tried.

At the core of these failures are the very reasons that QC programs are so popular in this country: their availability as easy-to-implement packages and the perception by many managers that the technique is a simple way to solve a firm's personnel problems. Oh likens the effects of QCs to those of aspirin or Valium: They treat symptoms and provide some immediate relief but don't touch the underlying issues of management-employee tensions, lack of respect, and underutilization of workers that cause the problems in the first place.

Three recent studies provide some light to supplement the heat of the debate over the value of QCs. In one of them, psychologists Philip H. Mirvis and James F. Grady, sociologist Edward J. Hackett, and I examined the claims that QCs improve participants' quality of work life and job performance. Specifically, we studied whether QCs actually increase decision-making opportunities, change employees' attitudes toward their work by convincing them that their jobs are challenging and satisfy their needs for growth. We also examined whether participating in a QC program improves productivity and lessens absenteeism.

We conducted our study in the manufacturing department of a decentralized manufacturing firm that was about to start a QC program. About half of the machine operators eligible for the program chose to participate. Working independently of the program, we developed an employee-attitude survey and administered it twice to all the machine operators, immediately before the program started and 20 months later. We also collected raw data directly from company records to assess any changes in employee behavior during the QC program. We used these data to compare rates of productivity and attendance for a 30-month period, starting 6 months before the QC program began.

Looking first at employee attitudes, we found that participation in the QC had a strong impact only in work-life areas directly related to QC activity—decision-making opportunities, group communication, and opportunities and skills needed for advancement. Participation did not, however, contrary to the usual claims of QC proponents, affect worker attitudes toward communication through the entire organization, job challenge, personal responsibility for getting work done, and overall job satisfaction.

We also found, unexpectedly, that being in a QC did not make machine operators more satisfied with any facets of their work situation, even those directly related to their QC work. Their ratings of the quality of their work life didn't change during the 30-month period. I suspect that this was due to factors separate from the QC program. During the 20 months between the two surveys, the division we studied was merged with a much larger division and the local economy experienced a severe recession. Rumors abounded about cutbacks and layoffs; these, combined with the poor economic news, could well have depressed the operators' outlook on work and life in general.

This interpretation is strengthened by the fact that the work satisfaction of machine operators who did not participate in the QC program decreased during the same 20-month period. Perhaps taking part in QCs provided satisfaction and social support that lessened some of the stress and negative feelings produced by the rumors and the bad economic news.

Unlike the mixed nature of these attitudinal findings, our analysis of the behavioral data is quite positive: Participation in QCs raised machine operators' productivity and reduced absenteeism. Before the program started, the participants and nonparticipants had similar records of productivity, percentage of paid hours actually spent on production, quality, efficiency, and monthly attendance. Over the course of the QC program, participants showed steady increases in each of these areas while nonparticipants stayed about the same.

In another study, a professor of organizational behavior, James W. Dean, Jr., of Pennsylvania State University, examined why employees chose to join QC programs in the electronic equipment division of a large manufacturing corporation and how their participation affected job satisfaction. He interviewed and administered questionnaires to members of 15 QCs in both the engineering and assembly functions and to a group of similar employees who were not QC members. The QC program had been in place for two years when he did his research.

Dean found several factors that distinguish QC participants from nonparticipants. Those who join QCs want greater involvement at work and believe that a QC will address this need. They also believe that the QC process can really change things by improving their jobs and the overall organization. Factors such as age, tenure, and wanting a break from work did not affect the decision to participate.

Dean concluded that employees who join a QC see it as a way to accomplish real change at work and usually choose problems that are likely to be successfully solved and implemented. Workers are satisfied by the experience if they see a direct link between QC activities and organizational change and if their QC has capable and productive people.

Commenting on this last point, Dean suggests that QC successes, both in terms of employee satisfaction and effective problem solving, can be increased through appropriate training. In his observations of QC programs, however, he finds that "training is largely pro forma in most applications and not taken very seriously. Most people who go through training are bored to death because much of what is covered does not relate to their personal work situation. Training should be differentiated for engineers, blue-collar or clerical workers, and others."

Dean attributes the training problem to the fact that most QCs use the very detailed problem-solving model originally adopted by Lockheed in the early 1970s (see "Quality Circles" box). Unfortunately, as

---

Quality Circles: From America to Japan and Back Again

The QC technique began in the late 1940s with H. Edwards Deming, an American who lectured in post–World War II Japan about statistical methods for quality control. He stressed that production quality must involve both workers and management; the Japanese combined these ideas with a philosophy of bringing workers together in groups to solve problems. At the heart of the Japanese program was the assumption that the person who performs a job is the one who best knows how to identify and correct its problems.

This was a radical departure from the traditional American approach to management, in which quality was the responsibility of special departments called quality assurance or quality control. All workers had to do was work. This task specialization reflected a managerial attitude that workers were incapable of performing more than a few well-defined tasks, motivated exclusively by economic rewards and indifferent to organizational needs. With this attitude prevailing in the United States, it is not surprising that QCs were ignored here.

In post–World War II Japan, QCs quickly became an integral part of a collaborative effort by government and industry leaders to improve the quality of the country's manufactured goods. By the late 1970s, "made in Japan," once a stigma, had come to represent the epitome of product quality and technological advancement to consumers worldwide. Simultaneously, American productivity stagnated. A new generation of workers, better educated and more financially secure than their older colleagues, began demanding jobs that were more psychologically rewarding and a greater say in decisions that affected their work.

In November 1973, the Lockheed Corporation sent six employees to Japan to study QCs. They were impressed by how the QC technique led to major improvements and by the excitement and involvement of Japanese workers in QC meetings and in their jobs. The visiting Americans were especially taken with the thoroughness of the problem-solving process: a nearly invariable sequence of problem generation and selection, causal analysis, solution generation and analysis, presentation to management, trial implementation, monitoring and feedback and, ultimately, full implementation.

The Lockheed people brought the Japanese technique back to the United States and, with very few changes, established the first QCs in this country one year later. The technique spread slowly at first, starting with other aerospace firms that had noticed Lockheed's success. By 1977, only five companies had QC programs. Then, as the recession forced business leaders to find new ways to increase employee productivity and as companies lost sales to high-quality Japanese products, QCs took off. The most recent national survey, conducted by the New York Stock Exchange in 1982, reported that 44 percent of all companies with more than 500 employees had QC programs. Three out of every four had been started within the previous two years.

The International Association of Quality Circles—composed of QC members, managers, and consultants—has grown in membership from 100 in 1978 to more than 7,000 in 1985. QCs are now found in virtually every sector, from transportation, entertainment, and finance to the military and government, and involve workers of all types and shades of collar.

Dean sees it, most problems addressed by QCs do not require that approach. "It is like using a tank to kill a fly," he says.

In a third study, a team from the University of Southern California (USC) Center for Effective Organizations focused on the factors that influence QC success. Organizational behaviorist Susan A. Mohrman and psychologists Edward E. Lawler III and Gerald E. Ledford, Jr., studied QCs in nine separate units of a large conglomerate, using interviews, questionnaires, and company data such as internal reports, newsletters, and training material. The nine units varied greatly in the amount of training provided, membership criteria, and use of rewards.

The researchers found that most QCs that succeed in changing the organization share several characteristics. They include sufficient training of members and direct efforts to improve group process dynamics; access to useful information inside and outside the organization; accurate record-keeping, including the establishment of measurable goals for the QC; and creation of QCs from intact work teams. However, while such QCs usually prompt some technical changes in an organization, the researchers found little evidence that they change corporate culture or improve individual work satisfaction and productivity.

The USC team also found reason to doubt the extent of the financial savings claimed for QCs. Mohrman cautions that while changes proposed by QCs often seem likely to save a great deal of money, "In many cases, the change is not implemented well, is not implemented at all, or is implemented and just does not save the money projected."

This is largely because the people who propose the changes are usually not the ones who actually implement them. The workers who do may resist the change because they do not understand the need for it or because they give priority to their regular work responsibilities. Moreover, since recognition and rewards are given only to people who develop the ideas, those who must implement them have little incentive to do so.

The USC team identified several other problems that limit QC success. One is resistance by middle-level managers, who have no direct involvement until they are called upon to approve or implement a QC suggestion. Many are uncomfortable with getting ideas from subordinates and either reject them out of hand or respond slowly and unenthusiastically.

Either response may discourage QC participants; they may feel that the program is a waste of time or a management trick and eventually stop meeting. Other QCs become victims of their own success. Having successfully dealt with key issues, they have no major problems left to solve and disband. Sometimes, as QCs become less productive, the company scales down the resources provided for their activities. Participants become less enthusiastic, begin to meet less often, and finally stop completely.

Despite these problems, Mohrman, Lawler, and Ledford conclude that QCs can be valuable under the right conditions. They recommend three effective ways to use them. First, QCs may operate as group suggestion programs to improve communications and raise employee consciousness about quality and productivity. Second, QCs may be used for special projects when organizations must deal with temporary or critical issues, such as introducing a new technology, retooling for a new product line, or solving a major quality problem. Third, QCs may help in making the transition toward more participative management systems. This can take place when a company, recognizing limitations of the QC approach, moves on to make the basic managerial and organizational changes needed to create a more participative organization.

Taken together, the three studies verify that QCs may have a positive impact on organizations and employees. But they do not support the larger claims of some QC proponents that the technique routinely improves employee productivity, morale, and growth as well as overall organizational effectiveness. QCs can improve employee productivity and have a limited impact on morale and work satisfaction, but only when programs are backed by sufficient training and genuine management commitment to them.

As Mohrman points out, the QC technique "does not take the huge financial commitment of some other programs and does rally people, but it clearly is not the stable long-term organizational change that some people make it out to be. The technique does not go far enough, it is not strong enough to promote real organizational change. For that, you need to go further and rethink the design of jobs, decision-making processes, and organizational structures."

Clearly, much more research is needed to evaluate QCs accurately. We should compare, for example, how well they work in various kinds of organizations and why they work better in some than in others. In Japan, a government-sponsored association oversees QC activity. A similar industry-sponsored organization in the United States could support the necessary studies and at the same time promote a national commitment to quality and to participative management.

Bill Courtright, a corporate manager of QCs for Hughes Aircraft, has no doubts about why QCs have grown so rapidly: "It is a spiritual reason—people want to work together. They are more effective as a team. It increases their knowledge. It increases their communication. It increases their security. It increases their dignity. If handled properly, with a serious commitment on the part of management, then quality circles can do nothing but succeed."

However, as the many failed QC programs show, that's an awfully big "if." Implementing some of the suggestions made by the researchers mentioned in this article, as changed and supplemented by future research, could help QCs remove the "fad" label and more fully live up to the claims made by their advocates. They might then clearly improve the design and management of organizations, help make American companies more competitive, and enhance the quality of their employees' work life.

section five

Leadership

Introduction

Upon leaders falls the not always enviable task of fusing organizational purpose with the drives of individuals and groups. Until about the middle of this century, the study of how leaders do this concerned itself almost totally with a search for personality traits that somehow combined to produce leadership. The meager and inconsistent findings from this approach gave way to an emphasis on leader behavior. A series of studies at The Ohio State University identified two broad dimensions of leader behavior, *consideration* (relationship-oriented behavior by the leader) and *initiating structure* (task-oriented behavior). Researchers and theorists then groped for the discovery of some optimal blend of these dimensions that would generally characterize effective leaders.

Alas, no such simple formula could be unearthed. The effects of consideration on performance, and the effects of initiating structure on both satisfaction and performance, were not at all consistent. Furthermore, no consistent effects could be ascribed to the manner or degree in which leaders involved subordinates in decision making.

Kerr and Jermier find considerable heuristic value in the concept "substitutes for leadership." They view effective leadership as that which complements other sources of structure and rewards in the work situation. Where substitutes for these functions abound, much of leader behavior will be either redundant, neutralized, or resisted.

Miles notes that different motives may underlie what superficially seems to be the same leader style. Thus, leaders who involve subordinates in decision making may do so for the purpose of dissolving subordinate resistance or because the leaders feel the need to use their expertise. Miles' discussion suggests that the inner purpose of the leader will determine whether the outward style has significance.

In some quarters, "managing by the numbers" has fallen out of fashion. Harold Geneen, reporting from his career as an executive in varied industries, argues that managerial leadership is unavoidably a

349

"numbers game." A properly managed, properly read set of numbers registers not only the extent or lack of progress, but also the reasons and the indicated courses for subsequent actions.

Muczyk and Hastings would discourage corporate leaders from seizing upon faddish concepts and methods, whether imported from Japan or home grown. They argue instead for an enlightened form of "hardball" management that faces up to real problems and makes the tough, often unpopular decisions necessary for correcting those problems.

Pfeffer urges us to consider a much more disturbing question: do we give leaders too much credit, as well as too much blame, for what happens to organizations? Pfeffer argues, on the one hand, that the latitude of action by leaders is limited by constraints. On the other hand, external forces neither controlled nor understood by leaders account for most of the variance in a firm's performance. Is leader effectiveness little more than a distortion of our perceptual process?

26

Substitutes for Leadership: Their Meaning and Measurement*

STEVEN KERR and JOHN M. JERMIER

Current theories and models of leadership seek to explain the influence of the hierarchical superior upon the satisfaction and performance of subordinates. While disagreeing with one another in important respects, these theories and models share an implicit assumption that while the style of leadership likely to be effective may vary according to the situation, *some* leadership style will be effective *regardless* of the situation. It has been found, however, that certain individual, task, and organizational variables act as "substitutes for leadership," negating the hierarchical superior's ability to exert either positive or negative influence over subordinate attitudes and effectiveness. This paper identifies a number of such substitutes for leadership, presents scales of questionnaire items for their measurement, and reports some preliminary tests.

A number of theories and models of leadership exist, each seeking to most clearly identify and best explain the presumedly powerful effects of leader behavior or personality attributes upon the satisfaction and performance of hierarchical subordinates. These theories and models fail to agree in many respects, but have in common the fact that none of them systematically accounts for very much criterion variance. It is certainly true that data indicating strong superior-subordinate relationships have sometimes been reported. In numerous studies, however, conclusions have had to be based on statistical rather than practical significance, and hypothesis support has rested upon the researcher's ability to show that the trivially low correlations obtained were not the result of chance.

Current theories and models of leadership have something else in common: a conviction that hierarchical leadership is always important. Even situational approaches to leadership share the assumption that while the *style* of leadership likely to be effective will vary ac-

---

* From *Organizational Behavior and Human Performance* 22, (1978), pp. 375–403.

cording to the situation, *some* leadership style will *always* be effective *regardless* of the situation. Of course, the extent to which this assumption is explicated varies greatly, as does the degree to which each theory is dependent upon the assumption. Fairly explicit is the Vertical Dyad Linkage model developed by Graen and his associates (Graen, Dansereau, & Minami, 1972; Dansereau, Cashman, & Graen, 1973), which attributes importance to hierarchical leadership without concern for the situation. The Fiedler (1964, 1967) Contingency Model also makes the general assumption that hierarchical leadership is important in situations of low, medium, and high favorableness, though predictions about relationships between LPC and performance in Octants VI and VII are qualified (Fiedler & Chemers, 1974, p. 82). Most models of decision-centralization (e.g., Tannenbaum & Schmidt, 1958; Heller & Yukl, 1969; Vroom & Yetton, 1973; Bass & Valenzi, 1974) include among their leader decision-style alternatives one whereby subordinates attempt a solution by themselves, with minimal participation by the hierarchical superior. Even in such cases, however, the leader is responsible for initiating the method through delegation of the problem, and is usually described as providing (structuring) information.

The approach to leadership which is least dependent upon the assumption articulated above, and which comes closest to the conceptualization to be proposed in this paper, is the Path-Goal Theory (House, 1971; House & Mitchell, 1974). Under circumstances when both goals and paths to goals may be clear, House and Mitchell (1974) point out that "attempts by the leader to clarify paths and goals will be both redundant and seen by subordinates as imposing unnecessary, close control." They go on to predict that "although such control may increase performance by preventing soldiering or malingering, it will also result in decreased satisfaction."

This prediction is supported in part by conclusions drawn by Kerr, Schriesheim, Murphy, and Stogdill (1974) from their review of the consideration-initiating structure literature, and is at least somewhat consistent with results from a few recent studies. A most interesting and pertinent premise of the theory, however, is that even unnecessary and redundant leader behaviors will have an impact upon subordinate satisfaction, morale, motivation, performance, and acceptance of the leader (House & Mitchell, 1974; House & Dessler, 1974). While leader attempts to clarify paths and goals are therefore recognized by Path-Goal Theory to be unnecessary and redundant in certain situations, in no situation are they explicitly hypothesized by Path-Goal (or any other leadership theory) to be irrelevant.

This lack of recognition is unfortunate. As has already been mentioned, data from numerous studies collectively demonstrate that in many situations these leader behaviors *are* irrelevant, and hierarchical leadership (as operationalized in these studies) per se does not seem to matter. In fact, leadership variables so often account for very little criterion variance that a few writers have begun to argue that the leadership construct is sterile altogether, that "the concept of leadership itself has outlived its usefulness" (Miner, 1975, p. 200). This view is also unfortunate, however, and fails to take note of accurate predictions by leadership theorists even as such theorists fail to conceptually reconcile their inaccurate predictions.

What is clearly needed to resolve this dilemma is a conceptualization adequate to explain both the occasional successes and frequent failures of the various theories and models of leadership.

SUBSTITUTES FOR LEADERSHIP

A wide variety of individual, task, and organizational characteristics have been found to influence relationships between leader behavior and subordinate satisfaction, morale, and performance. Some of these variables (for example, job pressure and subordinate expectations of leader behavior) act primarily to influence which leadership style will best permit the hierarchical superior to motivate, direct, and control subordinates. The effect of others, however, is to act as "substitutes for leadership," tending to negate the leader's ability to either improve or impair subordinate satisfaction and performance.

Substitutes for leadership are apparently prominent in many different organizational settings, but their existence is not explicated in any of the dominant leadership theories. As a result, data describing formal superior-subordinate relationships are often obtained in situations where important substitutes exist. These data logically ought to be, and usually are, insignificant, and are useful primarily as a reminder that when leadership styles are studied in circumstances where the choice of style is irrelevant, the effect is to replace the potential power of the leadership construct with the unintentional comedy of the "Law of the instrument."[1]

What is needed, then, is a taxonomy of situations where we should not be studying "leadership" (in the formal hierarchical sense) at all. Development of such a taxonomy is still at an early stage, but Woodward (1973) and Miner (1975) have laid important groundwork through their classifications of control, and some effects of nonleader sources of clarity have been considered by Hunt (Note 2) and Hunt and Osborn (1975). Reviews of the leadership literature by House and

---

[1] Abraham Kaplan (1964, p. 28) has observed: "Give a small boy a hammer, and he will find that everything he encounters needs pounding."

Mitchell (1974) and Kerr et al. (1974) have also proved pertinent in this regard, and suggest that individual, task, and organizational characteristics of the kind outlined in Table 1 will help to determine whether or not hierarchical leadership is likely to matter.

Conceptual Domain of Substitutes for Leadership. Since Table 1 is derived from previously conducted studies, substitutes are only suggested for the two leader behavior styles which dominate the research literature. The substitutes construct probably has much wider applicability, however, perhaps to hierarchical leadership in general.

It is probably useful to clarify some of the characteristics listed in Table 1. "Professional orientation" is considered a potential substitute

TABLE 1
Substitutes for Leadership

	Will Tend to Neutralize	
Characteristic	Relationship-Oriented, Supportive, People-Centered Leadership: Consideration, Support, and Interaction Facilitation	Task-Oriented, Instrumental, Job-Centered Leadership: Initiating Structure, Goal Emphasis, and Work Facilitation
Of the subordinate		
1. Ability, experience, training, knowledge		X
2. Need for independence	X	X
3. "Professional" orientation	X	X
4. Indifference toward organizational rewards	X	X
Of the task		
5. Unambiguous and routine		X
6. Methodologically invariant		X
7. Provides its own feedback concerning accomplishment		X
8. Intrinsically satisfying	X	
Of the organization		
9. Formalization (explicit plans, goals, and areas of responsibility)		X
10. Inflexibility (rigid, unbending rules and procedures)		X
11. Highly specified and active advisory and staff functions		X
12. Closely knit, cohesive work groups	X	X
13. Organizational rewards not within the leader's control	X	X
14. Spatial distance between superior and subordinates	X	X

for leadership because employees with such an orientation typically cultivate horizontal rather than vertical relationships, give greater credence to peer review processes, however informal, than to hierarchical evaluations, and tend to develop important referents external to the employing organization (Filley, House, & Kerr, 1976). Clearly, such attitudes and behaviors can sharply reduce the influence of the hierarchical superior.

"Methodologically invariant" tasks may result from serial interdependence, from machine-paced operations, or from work methods which are highly standardized. In one study (House, Filley, & Kerr, 1971, p. 26), invariance was found to derive from a network of government contracts which "specified not only the performance requirements of the end product, but also many of the management practices and control techniques that the company must follow in carrying out the contract."

Invariant methodology relates to what Miner (1975) describes as the "push" of work. Tasks which are "intrinsically satisfying" (another potential substitute listed in Table 1) contribute in turn to the "pull" of work. Miner believes that for "task control" to be effective, a force comprised of both the push and pull of work must be developed. At least in theory, however, either type alone may act as a substitute for hierarchical leadership.

Performance feedback provided by the work itself is another characteristic of the task which potentially functions in place of the formal leader. It has been reported that employees with high growth-need strength in particular derive beneficial psychological states (internal motivation, general satisfaction, work effectiveness) from clear and direct knowledge of the results of performance (Hackman & Oldham, 1976; Oldham, 1976). Task-provided feedback is often: (1) the most immediate source of feedback given the infrequency of performance appraisal sessions (Hall & Lawler, 1969); (2) the most accurate source of feedback given the problems of measuring the performance of others (Campbell, Dunnette, Lawler, & Weick, 1970); and (3) the most self-evaluation evoking and intrinsically motivating source of feedback given the controlling and informational aspects of feedback from others (DeCharms, 1968; Deci, 1972, 1975; Greller & Herold, 1975). For these reasons, the formal leader's function as a provider of role structure through performance feedback may be insignificant by comparison.

Cohesive, interdependent work groups and active advisory and staff personnel also have the ability to render the formal leader's performance feedback function inconsequential. Inherent in mature group structures are stable performance norms and positional differentiation (Bales & Strodtbeck, 1951; Borgatta & Bales, 1953; Stogdill, 1959; Lott

& Lott, 1965; Zander, 1968). Task-relevant guidance and feedback from others may be provided directly by the formal leader, indirectly by the formal leader through the primary work group members, directly by the primary work group members, by staff personnel, or by the client. If the latter four instances prevail, the formal leader's role may be quite trivial. Cohesive work groups are, of course, important sources of affiliative need satisfaction.

Programming through impersonal modes has been reported to be the most frequent type of coordination strategy employed under conditions of low-to-medium task uncertainty and low task interdependence (Van de Ven, Delbecq, & Koenig, 1976). Thus, the existence of written work goals, guidelines, and ground rules (organizational formalization) and rigid rules and procedures (organizational inflexibility) may serve as substitutes for leader-provided coordination under certain conditions. Personal and group coordination modes involving the formal leader may become important only when less costly impersonal strategies are not suitable.

ELABORATION OF THE CONSTRUCT

Table 1 was designed to capsulize our present knowledge with respect to possible substitutes for hierarchical leadership. Since present knowledge is the product of past research, and since past research was primarily unconcerned with the topic, the table is probably oversimplified and incomplete in a number of respects. Rigorous elaboration of the substitutes construct must necessarily await additional research, but we would speculate that such research would show the following refinements to be important.

Distinguishing between "Substitutes" and "Neutralizers." A *neutralizer* is defined by Webster's as something which is able to "paralyze, destroy, or counteract the effectiveness of" something else. In the context of leadership, this term may be applied to characteristics which make it effectively *impossible* for relationship and/or task-oriented leadership to make a difference. Neutralizers are a type of moderator variable when uncorrelated with both predictors and the criterion, and act as suppressor variables when correlated with predictors but not the criterion (Zedeck, 1971; Wherry, 1946).

A *substitute* is defined to be "a person or thing acting or used in place of another." In context, this term may be used to describe characteristics which render relationship and/or task-oriented leadership not only impossible but also *unnecessary*.[2] Substitutes may be corre-

---

[2] This potentially important distinction was first pointed out by M. A. Von Glinow in a doctoral seminar.

lated with both predictors and the criterion, but tend to improve the validity coefficient when included in the predictor set. That is, they will not only tend to affect which leader behaviors (if any) are influential, but will also tend to impact upon the criterion variable.

The consequences of neutralizers and substitutes for previous research have probably been similar, since both act to reduce the impact of leader behaviors upon subordinate attitudes and performance. For this reason it is not too important that such summaries of previous research as Table 1 distinguish between them. Nevertheless, an important theoretical distinction does exist. It is that substitutes do, but neutralizers do not, provide a "person or thing acting or used in place of" the formal leader's negated influence. The effect of neutralizers is therefore to create an "influence vacuum," from which a variety of dysfunctions may emerge.

As an illustration of this point, look again at the characteristics outlined in Table 1. Since each characteristic has the capacity to counteract leader influence, all 14 may clearly be termed neutralizers. It is *not* clear, however, that all 14 are substitutes. For example, subordinates' perceived "ability, experience, training, and knowledge" tend to impair the leader's influence, but may or may not act as substitutes for leadership. It is known that individuals who are high in task-related self-esteem place high value upon nonhierarchical control systems which are consistent with a belief in the competence of people (Korman, 1970). The problem is that subordinate perceptions concerning ability and knowledge may not be accurate. Actual ability and knowledge may therefore act as a substitute, while false perceptions of competence and unfounded self-esteem may produce simply a neutralizing effect.

"Spatial distance," "subordinate indifference toward organizational rewards," and "organizational rewards not within the leader's control" are other examples of characteristics which do not render formal leadership unnecessary, but merely create circumstances in which effective leadership may be impossible. If rewards are clearly within the control of some other person this other person can probably act as a substitute for the formal leader, and no adverse consequences (except probably to the leader's morale) need result. When no one knows where control over rewards lies, however, or when rewards are linked rigidly to seniority or to other factors beyond anyone's control, or when rewards are perceived to be unattractive altogether, the resulting influence vacuum would almost inevitably be dysfunctional.

Distinguishing between Direct and Indirect Leader Behavior Effects. It is possible to conceptualize a *direct effect* of leadership as one which occurs when a subordinate is influenced by some leader behavior *in and of itself*. An *indirect effect* may be said to result when the subordinate is influenced by the *implications* of the behavior for some future consequence. Attempts by the leader to influence subordinates must always produce direct and/or indirect effects or, when strong substitutes for leadership exist, no effect.

This distinction between direct and indirect effects of leader behavior has received very little attention, but its importance to any discussion of leadership substitutes is considerable. For example, in their review of path-goal theory, House and Dessler (1974, p. 31) state that "subordinates with high needs for affiliation and social approval would see friendly, considerate leader behavior as an immediate source of satisfaction" (direct effect). As Table 1 suggests, it is conceivable that fellow group members could supply such subordinates with enough affiliation and social approval to eliminate dependence on the leader. With other subordinates, however, the key "may be not so much in terms of what the leader does but may be in terms of how it is *interpreted* by his members" (Graen et al., 1972, p. 235). Graen et al. concluded from their data that "consideration is interpreted as the leader's evaluation of the member's role behavior. . ." (p. 233). For these subordinates, therefore, consideration seems to have been influential primarily because of its perceived implications for the likelihood of receiving future rewards. In this case the effect is an indirect one, for which group member approval and affiliation probably cannot substitute.

In the same vein, we are told by House and Dessler (1974, pp. 31–32) that:

> Subordinates with high needs for achievement would be predicted to view leader behavior that clarifies path-goal relationships and provides goal-oriented feedback as satisfying. Subordinates with high needs for extrinsic rewards would be predicted to see leader directiveness or coaching behavior as instrumental to their satisfaction if such behavior helped them perform in such a manner as to gain recognition, promotion, security, or pay increases.

It is apparent from House and Dessler's remarks that the distinction between direct and indirect effects need not be limited to relationship-oriented behaviors. Such characteristics of the task as the fact that it "provides its own feedback" (listed in Table 1 as a potential substitute for task-oriented behavior) may provide achievement-oriented subordinates with immediate satisfaction (direct effect), but fail to negate the superior's ability to help subordinates perform so as to obtain future rewards (indirect effect). Conversely, subordinate experience and training may act as substitutes for the indirect effects of task-oriented leadership, by preventing the leader from improving subordinate performance, but may not offset the direct effects.

Identifying Other Characteristics and Other Leader Behaviors. Any elaboration of the substitutes construct must necessarily include the specification of other leader behaviors, and other characteristics which may act as substitutes for leader behaviors. As was mentioned earlier, most previous studies of leadership were concerned with only two of its dimensions. This approach is intuitively indefensible. Richer conceptualizations of the leadership process already exist, and almost inevitably underscore the importance of additional leader activities. As these activities are delineated in future research, it is likely that substitutes for them will also be identified.

Table 2 is offered as a guide to research. It portrays a state of increased sophistication of the substitutes construct, assuming future development along lines suggested in this section. Substitutes would be differentiated from neutralizers, and direct effects of leadership empirically distinguished from indirect effects. The columns on the right are intended to represent as-yet-unexplored leader behaviors, and the dotted lines on the bottom indicate the presence of additional characteristics which may act either as neutralizers, or as true substitutes for leadership.

Distinguishing between Cause and Effect in Leader Behavior. Another area where the substitutes construct appears to have implications for leadership research concerns the question of causality. It is now evident from a variety of laboratory experiments and longitudinal field studies that leader behavior may result from as well as cause subordinate attitudes and performance. It is possible to speculate upon the effect that leadership substitutes would have on the relative causal strength of superior- and subordinate-related variables. This paper has tried to show that such substitutes act to reduce changes in subordinates' attitudes and performance which are *caused* by leader behaviors. On the other hand, there seems no reason why leadership substitutes should prevent changes in leader behavior which *result* from different levels of subordinate performance, satisfaction, and morale. The substitutes for leadership construct may therefore help to explain why the direction of causality is sometimes predominantly from leader behavior to subordinate outcomes, while at other times the reverse is true.

Specification of Interaction Effects among Substitutes and Neutralizers. From the limited data obtained thus far, it is not possible to differentiate at all among leadership substitutes and neutralizers in terms of relative strength and predictive capability. We have received some indication that the strength of a substitute, as measured by its mean level, is not strongly related to its predictive power. Substitutes for leadership as theoretically important as intrinsic satisfaction, for example, apparently need only be present in moderate amounts.

TABLE 2
Substitutes for Leadership: A Theoretical Extension

	Will Act as a Substitute for					
	Relationship-Oriented, Supportive, People-Centered Leadership (Consideration, Support, and Interaction Facilitation):		Task-Oriented, Instrumental, Job-Centered Leadership (Initiating Structure, Goal Emphasis, and Work Facilitation):		(Other Leader Behaviors . . .)	
Characteristic	Directly	Indirectly	Directly	Indirectly	Directly	Indirectly
Substitutes						
Of the subordinate						
1. Ability	X			X	?	?
3. "Professional" orientation		X		X	?	?
Of the task						
5. Unambiguous and routine			X	X	?	?
7. Provides its own feedback concerning accomplishment			X		?	?
8. Intrinsically satisfying	X				?	?
Of the organization						
12. Closely knit, cohesive work groups	X		X	X	?	?
Neutralizers						
4. Indifference toward organizational rewards		X		X	?	?
13. Organizational rewards not within the leader's control		X		X	?	?

Other, less important substitutes and neutralizers, might have to be present to a tremendous degree before their effects might be felt. Clearly, the data reported in this study are insufficient to determine at what point a particular substitute becomes important, or at what point several substitutes, each fairly weak by itself, might combine to collectively impair hierarchical leader influence. Multiplicative functions involving information on the strength and predictive power of substitutes for leadership should be able to be specified as evidence accumulates.

CONCLUSIONS

The research literature provides abundant evidence that for organization members to maximize organizational and personal outcomes, they must be able to obtain both guidance and good feelings from their work settings. Guidance is usually offered in the form of role or task structuring, while good feelings may stem from "stroking" behaviors,[3] or may be derived from intrinsic satisfaction associated with the task itself.

The research literature does *not* suggest that guidance and good feelings must be provided by the hierarchical superior; it is only necessary that they somehow be provided. Certainly the formal leader represents a potential source of structuring and stroking behaviors, but many other organization members do too, and impersonal equivalents also exist. To the extent that other potential sources are deficient, the hierarchical superior is clearly in a position to play a dominant role. In these situations the opportunity for leader downward influence is great, and formal leadership ought to be important. To the extent that other sources provide structure and stroking in abundance, the hierarchical leader will have little chance to exert downward influence. In such cases it is of small value to gain entree to the organization, distribute leader behavior questionnaires to anything that moves, and later debate about which leadership theory best accounts for the pitifully small percentage of variance explained, while remaining uncurious about the large percentage unexplained.

Of course, few organizations would be expected to have leadership substitutes so strong as to totally overwhelm the leader, or so weak as to require subordinates to rely entirely on him. In most organizations it is likely that, as was true here, substitutes exist for some leader activities but not for others. Effective leadership might therefore be described as the ability to supply subordinates with needed guidance

---

[3] *Stroking* is used here, as in transactional analysis, to describe "any type of physical, oral, or visual recognition of one person by another" (Huse, 1975, p. 288).

and good feelings which are not being supplied by other sources. From this viewpoint it is inaccurate to inform leaders (say, in management development programs) that they are incompetent if they do not personally provide these things regardless of the situation. While it may (or may not) be necessary that the organization as a whole function in a "9–9" manner (Blake & Mouton, 1964), it clearly is unnecessary for the manager to behave in such a manner unless no substitutes for leader-provided guidance and good feelings exist.

Dubin (1976, p. 33) draws a nice distinction between "proving" and "improving" a theory, and points out that "if the purpose is to prove the adequacy of the theoretical model . . . data are likely to be collected for values on only those units incorporated in the theoretical model. This usually means that, either experimentally or by discarding data, attention in the empirical research is focused solely upon values measured on units incorporated in the theory."

In Dubin's terms, if we are really interested in improving rather than proving our various theories and models of leadership, a logical first step is that we stop assuming what really needs to be demonstrated empirically. The criticality of the leader's role in supplying necessary structure and stroking should be evaluated in the broader organizational context. Data pertaining to both leadership and possible substitutes for leadership (Table 1) should be obtained, and both main and interaction effects examined. A somewhat different use of information about substitutes for leadership would be as a "prescreen," to assess the appropriateness of a potential sample for a hierarchical leadership study.

What this all adds up to is that, if we really want to know more about the sources and consequences of guidance and good feelings in organizations, we should be prepared to study these things *whether or not* they happen to be provided through hierarchical leadership. For those not so catholic, whose interest lies in the derivation and refinement of theories of formal leadership, a commitment should be made to the importance of developing and operationalizing a *true* situational theory of leadership, one which will explicitly limit its propositions and restrict its predictions *to those situations* where hierarchical leadership theoretically ought to make a difference.

REFERENCES

Bales, R., & Strodtbeck, F.   Phases in group problem solving. *Journal of Abnormal and Social Psychology*, 1951, **46**, 485–495.

Bass, B., & Valenzi, E.   Contingent aspects of effective management styles. In J. G. Hunt & L. L. Larson (Eds.), *Contingency approaches to leadership*. Carbondale: Southern Illinois University Press, 1974.

Blake, R., & Mouton, J. *The managerial grid.* Houston: Gulf, 1964.

Borgatta, E., & Bales, R. Task and accumulation of experience as factors in the interaction of small groups. *Sociometry,* 1953, **16,** 239–252.

Campbell, J., Dunnette, E., Lawler, E., & Weick, K. *Managerial behavior, performance and effectiveness.* New York: McGraw-Hill, 1970.

Dansereau, F., Cashman, J., & Graen, G. Instrumentality theory and equity theory as complementary approaches in predicting the relationship of leadership and turnover among managers. *Organizational Behavior and Human Performance,* 1973, **10,** 184–200.

DeCharms, R. *Personal causation.* New York: Academic Press, 1968.

Deci, E. Intrinsic motivation, extrinsic reinforcement, and inequity. *Journal of Personality and Social Psychology,* 1972, **22,** 113–120.

Deci, E. *Intrinsic motivation.* New York: Plenum, 1975.

Dubin, R. Theory building in applied areas. In M. Dunnette (Ed.), *Handbook of industrial and organizational psychology.* Skokie, Ill.: Rand McNally,1976.

Fiedler, F. E. A contingency model of leadership effectiveness. In L. Berkowitz (Ed.), *Advances in experimental social psychology.* New York: Academic Press, 1964.

Fiedler, F. E. *A theory of leadership effectiveness.* New York: McGraw-Hill, 1967.

Fiedler, F. E., & Chemers, M. M. *Leadership and effective management.* Glenview, Ill.: Scott, Foresman, 1974.

Filley, A. C., House, R. J., & Kerr, S. *Managerial process and organizational behavior* (2nd ed.). Glenview, Ill.: Scott, Foresman, 1976.

Graen, C., Dansereau, F., Jr., & Minami, T. Dysfunctional leadership styles. *Organizational Behavior and Human Performance,* 1972, **7,** 216–236.

Greller, M., & Herold, D. Sources of feedback: A preliminary investigation. *Organizational Behavior and Human Performance,* 1975, **13,** 244–256.

Hackman, R., & Oldham, G. Motivation through the design of work: Test of a theory. *Organizational Behavior and Human Performance,* 1976, **16,** 250–279.

Hall, D., & Lawler, E. Unused potential in R and D labs. *Research Management,* 1969, **12,** 339–354.

Heller, F. A., & Yukl, G. Participation, managerial decision making, and situational variables. *Organizational Behavior and Human Performance,* 1969, **4,** 227–234.

House, R. J. A path-goal theory of leader effectiveness. *Administrative Science Quarterly,* 1971, **16,** 321–338.

House, R. J., & Dessler, G. The path-goal theory of leadership: Some post hoc and a priori tests. In J. G. Hunt & L. L. Larson (Eds.), *Contingency approaches to leadership.* Carbondale: Southern Illinois University Press, 1974.

House, R. J., Filley, A. C., & Kerr, S. Relation of leader consideration and initiating structure to R and D subordinates' satisfaction. *Administrative Science Quarterly,* 1971, **16,** 19–30.

House, R. J., & Mitchell, T. R. Path-goal theory of leadership. *Journal of Contemporary Business,* 1974, 3, 81–97.

Hunt, J. G., & Osborn, R. N.   An adaptive-reactive theory of leadership: The role of macro variables in leadership research. In J. G. Hunt & L. L. Larson (Eds.), *Leadership frontiers*. Carbondale: Southern Illinois University Press, 1975.

Huse, E. F.   *Organization development and change*. St. Paul: West, 1975.

Kaplan, Abraham.   *The conduct of inquiry*. San Francisco: Chandler, 1964.

Kerr, S., Schriesheim, C., Murphy, C. J., & Stogdill, R. M.   Toward a contingency theory of leadership based upon the consideration and initiating structure literature. *Organizational Behavior and Human Performance*, 1974, **12**, 62–82.

Korman, A.   Toward a hypothesis of work behavior. *Journal of Applied Psychology*, 1970, **54**, 31–41.

Lott, A., & Lott, B.   Group cohesiveness as interpersonal attraction: A review of relationships with antecedent and consequent variables. *Psychological Bulletin*, 1965, **64**, 259–302.

Miner, J.   The uncertain future of the leadership concept: An overview. In J. G. Hunt & L. L. Larson (Eds.), *Leadership frontiers*. Carbondale: Southern Illinois University Press, 1975.

Oldham, G.   Job characteristics and internal motivation: The moderating effect of interpersonal and individual variables. *Human Relations* 1976, **29**, 559–570.

Stogdill, R.   *Individual behavior and group achievement*. New York: Oxford University Press, 1959.

Tannenbaum, R., & Schmidt, W.   How to choose a leadership pattern. *Harvard Business Review*, 1958, **36**, 95–101.

Van de Ven, A., Delbecq, A., & Koenig, R.   Determinants of coordination modes within organizations. *American Sociological Review*, 1976, **41**, 322–338.

Vroom, V., & Yetton, P.   *Leadership and decision making*. Pittsburgh: University of Pittsburgh Press, 1973.

Wherry, R.   Test selection and suppressor variables. *Psychometrika*, 1946, **11**, 239–247.

Woodward, J.   Technology, material control, and organizational behavior. In A. Negandhi (Ed.), *Modern organization theory*. Kent: Kent State University, 1973.

Zander, A.   Group aspirations. In D. Cartwright & A. Zander (Eds.), *Group dynamics: Research and theory* (3d ed.), New York: Harper & Row, 1968.

Zedeck, S.   Problems with the use of "moderator" variables. *Psychological Bulletin*, 1971, **76**, 295–310.

REFERENCE NOTES

1.   Bish, J., & Schriesheim, C.   *An exploratory analysis of Form XII of The Ohio State Leadership Scales*. Paper presented at the National Academy of Management Conference, 1974.

2.   Hunt, J.   *Different nonleader clarity sources as alternatives to leadership*. Paper presented at the Eastern Academy of Management Conference, 1975.

3. Schriesheim, C. *The development and validation of instrumental and supportive leadership scales and their application to some tests of path-goal theory of leadership hypotheses.* Unpublished doctoral dissertation. The Ohio State University, 1978.
4. Wigdor, L. *Effectiveness of various management and organizational characteristics on employee satisfaction and performance as a function of the employee's need for job independence.* Unpublished doctoral dissertation, City University of New York, 1969.

27

Human Relations or Human Resources?*

RAYMOND E. MILES

The proselyting efforts of the advocates of participative management appear to have paid off. The typical modern manager, on paper at least, broadly endorses participation and rejects traditional, autocratic concepts of leadership and control as no longer acceptable or, perhaps, no longer legitimate.

However, while participation has apparently been well merchandised and widely purchased, there seems to be a great deal of confusion about what has been sold and what has been bought. Managers do not appear to have accepted a single, logically consistent concept of participation. In fact, there is reason to believe that managers have adopted two different theories or models of participation—one for themselves and one for their subordinates.

These statements reflect both my analysis of the development of the theory of participative management and my interpretation of managers' attitudes toward these concepts.

My views are based in part on a number of recent surveys of managers' beliefs and opinions. The most recent of these studies, which I

* Reprinted from *Harvard Business Review*, July–August 1965. © 1965 by the President and Fellows of Harvard College; all rights reserved.

conducted, was begun with a group of 215 middle and upper level managers in West Coast companies, and has been continued with a sample of over 300 administrators from public agencies.[1] This study was designed to clarify further certain aspects of managers' attitudes uncovered by earlier research under the direction of Dale Yoder of Stanford[2] and Profs. Mason Haire, Edwin Ghiselli, and Lyman Porter of the University of California, Berkeley.[3]

This series of studies involved the collection of questionnaire data on managers' opinions about people and on their attitudes toward various leadership policies and practices. Several thousand managers in all, both here and abroad, have participated.

This article is not intended to summarize all of the findings on managers' leadership attitudes available from these studies. Rather, my primary purpose is to construct a theoretical framework that may explain some of the principal dimensions of managers' views and some of the implications of their beliefs and opinions, drawing on the research simply to illustrate my views.

Participative Theories

While the suggestion that managers have accepted a two-sided approach to participation may be disturbing, it should not be too surprising. Management theorists have frequently failed to deal with participation in a thorough and consistent manner. Indeed, from an examination of their somewhat ambivalent treatment of this concept, it is possible to conclude that they have been selling two significantly different models of participative management.

One of the scholars' models, which we will designate the *human relations* model, closely resembles the concept of participation which managers appear to accept for use with their own subordinates.

The second, and not yet fully developed, theory, which I have labeled the *human resources* model, prescribes the sort of participative policies that managers would apparently like their superiors to follow.

---

[1] See Raymond E. Miles, "Conflicting Elements in Managerial Ideologies," *Industrial Relations*, October 1964, pp. 77–91. The subsequent research with public administrators is still being conducted, and reports have not yet been published.

[2] See Dale Yoder, "Management Theories as Managers See Them," *Personnel*, July–August 1962, pp. 25–30; "Management Policies for the Future," *Personnel Administration*, September–October 1962, pp. 11–14 ff.; Dale Yoder et al., "Managers' Theories of Management," *Journal of the Academy of Management*, September 1963, pp. 204–211.

[3] See Mason Haire, Edwin Ghiselli, and Lyman W. Porter, "Cultural Patterns in the Role of the Manager," *Industrial Relations*, February 1963, pp. 95–117, for a report on the Berkeley studies.

I shall develop and examine these two models, compare them with managers' expressed beliefs, and consider some of the implications of managers' dual allegiance to them.

Both the *human relations* and the *human resources* models have three basic components:

1. A set of assumptions about people's values and capabilities.
2. Certain prescriptions as to the amount and kind of participative policies and practices that managers should follow, in keeping with their assumptions about people.
3. A set of expectations with respect to the effects of participation on subordinate morale and performance.

This third component contains the model's explanation of how and why participation works—that is, the purpose of participation and how it accomplishes this purpose. In outline form, the models may be summarized as shown in Exhibit 1.

Human Relations Model

This approach is not new. As early as the 1920s, business spokesmen began to challenge the classical autocratic philosophy of man-

EXHIBIT 1
Two Models of Participative Leadership

Human Relations	*Human Resources*
Attitudes toward People	
1. People in our culture share a common set of needs—to belong, to be liked, to be respected.	1. In addition to sharing common needs for belonging and respect, most people in our culture desire to contribute effectively and creatively to the accomplishment of worthwhile objectives.
2. They desire individual recognition but, more than this, they want to feel a useful part of the company and their own work group or department.	2. The majority of our work force is capable of exercising far more initiative, responsibility, and creativity than their present jobs require or allow.
3. They will tend to cooperate willingly and comply with organizational goals if these important needs are fulfilled.	3. These capabilities represent untapped resources which are presently being wasted.
Kind and Amount of Participation	
1. The manager's basic task is to make each worker believe that he is a useful and important part of the department "team."	1. The manager's basic task is to create an environment in which his subordinates can contribute their full range of talents to the accomplishment of organizational goals. He must attempt to uncover and tap the creative resources of his subordinates.

EXHIBIT 1 *(concluded)*

Human Relations	*Human Resources*
2. The manager should be willing to explain his decisions and to discuss his subordinates' objections to his plans. On routine matters, he should encourage his subordinates to participate in planning and choosing among alternative solutions to problems.	2. The manager should allow, and encourage, his subordinates to participate not only in routine decisions but in important matters as well. In fact, the more important a decision is to the manager's department, the greater should be his effort to tap the department's resources.
3. Within narrow limits, the work group or individual subordinates should be allowed to exercise self-direction and self-control in carrying out plans.	3. The manager should attempt to continually expand the areas over which his subordinates exercise self-direction and self-control as they develop and demonstrate greater insight and ability.

Expectations

1. Sharing information with subordinates and involving them in departmental decision making will help satisfy their basic needs for belonging and for individual recognition.	1. The overall quality of decision making and performance will improve as the manager makes use of the full range of experience, insight, and creative ability in his department.
2. Satisfying these needs will improve subordinate morale and reduce resistance to formal authority.	2. Subordinates will exercise responsible self-direction and self-control in the accomplishment of worthwhile objectives that they understand and have helped establish.
3. High employee morale and reduced resistance to formal authority may lead to improved departmental performance. It should at least reduce intradepartment friction and thus make the manager's job easier.	3. Subordinate satisfaction will increase as a by-product of improved performance and the opportunity to contribute creatively to this improvement.

Note: It may fairly be argued that what I call the *human relations* model is actually the product of popularization and misunderstanding of the work of pioneers in this field. Moreover, it is true that some of the early research and writings of the human relationists contain concepts which seem to fall within the framework of what I call the *human resources* model. Nevertheless, it is my opinion that while the early writers did not advocate the *human relations* model as presented here, their failure to emphasize certain of the *human resources* concepts left their work open to the misinterpretations which have occurred.

agement. The employee was no longer pictured as merely an appendage to a machine, seeking only economic rewards from his work. Managers were instructed to consider him as a "whole man" rather than as merely a bundle of skills and aptitudes.[4] They were urged to create a "sense of satisfaction" among their subordinates by showing interest in the employees' personal success and welfare. As Bendix notes, the "failure to treat workers as human beings came to be re-

---

[4] See Reinhard Bendix, *Work and Authority in Industry* (New York: John Wiley & Sons, 1956), pp. 287–340.

garded as the cause of low morale, poor craftsmanship, unresponsive-ness, and confusion."[5]

The key element in the *human relations* approach is its basic objec-tive of making organizational members *feel* a useful and important part of the overall effort. This process is viewed as the means of ac-complishing the ultimate goal of building a cooperative and compliant work force. Participation, in this model, is a lubricant which oils away resistance to formal authority. By discussing problems with his subor-dinates and acknowledging their individual needs and desires, the manager hopes to build a cohesive work team that is willing and anx-ious to tangle with organizational problems.

One further clue to the way in which participation is viewed in this approach is provided in Dubin's concept of "privilege pay."[6] The manager "buys" cooperation by letting his subordinates in on de-partmental information and allowing them to discuss and state their opinions on various departmental problems. He "pays a price" for allowing his subordinates the privilege of participating in certain de-cisions and exercising some self-direction. In return he hopes to obtain their cooperation in carrying out these and other decisions for the accomplishment of departmental objectives.

Implicit in this model is the idea that it might actually be easier and more efficient if the manager could merely make departmental deci-sions without bothering to involve his subordinates. However, as the advocates of this model point out, there are two parts to any decision—(1) the making of the decision and (2) the activities required to carry it out. In many instances, this model suggests, the manager might do better to "waste time" in discussing the problem with his subordinates, and perhaps even to accept suggestions that he believes may be less efficient, in order to get the decision carried out.

In sum, the *human relations* approach does not bring out the fact that participation may be useful for its own sake. The possibility that subordinates will, in fact, bring to light points which the manager may have overlooked, if considered at all, tends to be mentioned only in passing. This is treated as a potential side benefit which, while not normally expected, may occasionally occur. Instead, the manager is urged to adopt participative leadership policies as the least-cost method of obtaining cooperation and getting his decisions accepted.

In many ways the *human relations* model represents only a slight departure from traditional autocratic models of management. The

---

[5] Ibid., p. 294.

[6] Robert Dubin, *The World of Work* (Englewood Cliffs: N.J., Prentice-Hall, 1958), pp. 243–244. It should be noted that Dubin treats the concept of privilege pay within a framework which goes beyond the *human relations* approach and, in some respects, is close to the *human resources* model.

method of achieving results is different, and employees are viewed in more humanistic terms, but the basic roles of the manager and his subordinates remain essentially the same. The ultimate goal sought in both the traditional and the *human relations* model is compliance with managerial authority.

Human Resources Model

This approach represents a dramatic departure from traditional concepts of management. Though not yet fully developed, it is emerging from the writings of McGregor, Likert, Haire, and others as a new and significant contribution to management thought.[7] The magnitude of its departure from previous models is illustrated first of all in its basic assumptions concerning people's values and abilities, which focus attention on all organization members as reservoirs of untapped resources. These resources include not only physical skills and energy, but also creative ability and the capacity for responsible, self-directed, self-controlled behavior. Given these assumptions about people, the manager's job cannot be viewed merely as one of giving direction and obtaining cooperation. Instead, his primary task becomes that of creating an environment in which the total resources of his department can be utilized.

The second point at which the *human resources* model differs dramatically from previous models is in its views on the purpose and goal of participation. In this model the manager does not share information, discuss departmental decisions, or encourage self-direction and self-control merely to improve subordinate satisfaction and morale. Rather, the purpose of these practices is to improve the decision making and total performance efficiency of the organization. The *human resources* model suggests that many decisions may actually be made more efficiently by those directly involved in and affected by the decisions.

Similarly, this model implies that control is often most efficiently exercised by those directly involved in the work in process, rather than by someone or some group removed from the actual point of operation. Moreover, the *human resources* model does not suggest that the manager allow participation only in routine decisions. Instead, it implies that the more important the decision, the greater is his *obligation* to encourage ideas and suggestions from his subordinates.

In the same vein, this model does not suggest that the manager

---

[7] See particularly Douglas McGregor, *The Human Side of Enterprise* (New York: McGraw-Hill, 1960); Rensis Likert, *New Patterns of Management* (New York: McGraw-Hill, 1961); and Mason Haire, "The Concept of Power and the Concept of Man," in *Social Science Approaches to Business Behavior*, ed. George Strother (Homewood, Ill.: The Dorsey Press, Inc., 1962), pp. 163–183.

allow his subordinates to exercise self-direction and self-control only when they are carrying out relatively unimportant assignments. In fact, it suggests that the area over which subordinates exercise self-direction and control should be continually broadened in keeping with their growing experience and ability.

The crucial point at which this model differs dramatically from other models is in its explanation of the causal relationship between satisfaction and performance. In the *human relations* approach improvement in subordinate satisfaction is viewed as an intervening variable which is the ultimate cause of improved performance. Diagrammatically, the causal relationship can be illustrated as in Exhibit 2.

In the *human resources* model the causal relationship between satisfaction and performance is viewed quite differently. Increased

EXHIBIT 2
Human Relations Model

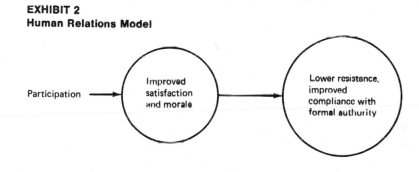

subordinate satisfaction is not pictured as the primary cause of improved performance; improvement results directly from creative contributions which subordinates make to departmental decision making, direction, and control. Subordinates' satisfaction is viewed instead as a by-product of the process—the result of their having made significant contributions to organizational success. In diagram form the *human resources* model can be illustrated as in Exhibit 3.

The *human resources* model does not deny a relationship between participation and morale. It suggests that subordinates' satisfaction may well increase as they play more and more meaningful roles in decision making and control. Moreover, the model recognizes that improvements in morale may not only set the stage for expanded participation, but create an atmosphere which supports creative problem solving. Nevertheless, this model rejects as unsupported the concept that the improvement of morale is a necessary or sufficient cause of improved decision making and control. Those improvements come directly from the full utilization of the organization's resources.

EXHIBIT 3
Human Resources Model

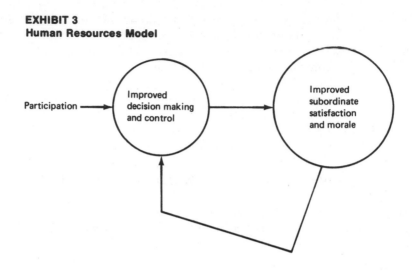

Managers' Own Views

Which approach to participative management do managers actually follow? It was suggested earlier that managers' views appear to reflect both models. When they talk about the kind and amount of participation appropriate for their subordinates, they express concepts that appear to be similar to those in the *human relations* model. On the other hand, when they consider their own relationships with their superiors, their views seem to flow from the *human resources* model. A brief review of the relevant findings suggests some of the bases for this interpretation.

Participation for Subordinates. When we look at managers' views on the use of participative policies and practices with the subordinates who report to them, two points seem clear:

1. Managers generally accept and endorse the use of participative concepts.
2. However, they frequently doubt their subordinates' capacity for self-direction and self-control, and their ability to contribute creatively to departmental decision making.

In the Stanford studies, an overwhelming majority of managers indicated their agreement with statements emphasizing the desirability of subordinate participation in decision making.[8] In the Berkeley studies, a majority of the managers in each of 11 countries, including the United States, indicated their agreement with such concepts as sharing information with subordinates and increasing subordinate in-

---

[8] Yoder et al., "Managers' Theories of Management," pp. 204–211.

fluence and self-control.[9] Similarly, in my recent studies, managers overwhelmingly endorsed participative leadership policies.

On the other hand, while managers appear to have great faith in participative policies, they do not indicate such strong belief in their subordinates' capabilities. For example, the Berkeley group in their international study found that managers tended to have a "basic lack of confidence in others" and typically did not believe that capacity for leadership and initiative was widely distributed among subordinates.[10] In my own study, managers in every group to date have rated their subordinates and rank-and-file employees well below themselves, particularly on such important managerial traits as *responsibility, judgment,* and *initiative.*

But if managers do not expect creative, meaningful contributions from their subordinates, why do they advocate participative management? A reasonable answer seems to be that they advocate participative concepts as a means of improving subordinate morale and satisfaction. This interpretation gains support from my recent studies. Here, managers were asked to indicate their agreement or disagreement with statements predicting improved morale and satisfaction and statements predicting improved performance as the result of following various participative leadership policies. In connection with each of these policies, managers indicated consistently greater agreement with the predictions of improved morale than with the predictions of improved performance.

The fact that managers appear to have serious doubts about the values and capabilities of those reporting to them seems to rule out their acceptance of the *human resources* model for use with their subordinates. On the other hand, the fact that they do endorse participation and seem quite certain about its positive impact on morale suggests a close relationship between their views and those expressed in the *human relations* model. Moreover, the types of participative policies which managers most strongly advocate seem to support this interpretation.

In my research, managers indicate strongest agreement with policies that advocate sharing information and discussing objectives with subordinates. However, they tend to be somewhat less enamored with the policies which suggest increasing subordinate self-direction and self-control. This pattern of participation seems much closer to that of the *human relations* approach than to the pattern advocated in the *human resources* model.

Participation for Themselves.   When I examined managers' views

---

[9] Haire, Ghiselli, and Porter, "Cultural Patterns," pp. 95–117.
[10] Ibid.

toward their relationships with their own superiors, a much different pattern of responses became evident:

1. Managers in my studies tend to see little, if any, difference between their own capabilities and those of their superiors. In fact, they tend to rate themselves equal to, if not higher than, their superiors on such traits as *creativity, ingenuity, flexibility,* and *willingness to change.*
2. When asked to indicate at which levels in their organizations they feel each of the participative policies would be most appropriate, managers invariably feel most strongly that the full range of participative policies should be used by their own superiors.

More importantly, they also tend to be most certain that these participative policies will result in improved organizational performance *at their own level.*

Thus, when managers discuss the type of participative policies which their superiors should follow with managers at their own level, they appear to espouse the *human resources* model. They see themselves as reservoirs of creative resources. Moreover, the fact that they frequently view themselves as more flexible and willing to change than their superiors suggests that they feel their resources are frequently wasted. Correspondingly, they expect improvement in organizational performance to result from greater freedom for self-direction and self-control on their part.

Reasons behind Views

If the evidence of the current survey does represent managers' attitudes toward participative leadership, one serious question immediately comes to mind. How can managers desire one type of authority and control relationship with their superiors and at the same time advocate another type with their subordinates? A general answer, of course, is that this pattern of attitudes is just human nature. We tend not only to think more highly of ourselves than we do of others, but also to want more than we are willing to give. There are, however, other logical, more specific explanations for managers' reluctance to accept the *human resources* model for use with their subordinates.

In the first place, the *human relations* model has been around much longer, and an exceptionally good selling job has been done in its behalf. The causal relationship among participation, satisfaction, and performance, despite a lack of empirical validation, has become common wisdom. The *human resources* model, on the other hand, has not been as fully or systematically developed, and has not been the subject of as hard a sell. Managers may "feel" some of the concepts expressed in the *human resources* model and intuitively grasp some of their implications for their relationships with their superiors, but little pressure has been put on them to translate their attitudes into a systematic model for use with their subordinates.

A second explanation for managers' failure to accept the *human resources* model for use with their subordinates is that they are simply reluctant to "buy" a theory that challenges concepts to which they are deeply and emotionally attached. There is no question that the *human resources* model does attack a number of traditional management concepts. Two of the bedrock concepts that are directly challenged deal with: (1) the origins and applicability of management prerogatives, and (2) the source and limits of control.

The *human resources* model recognizes no definable, immutable set of management prerogatives. It does not accept the classical division between those who think and command and those who obey and perform. Instead, it argues that the solution to any given problem may arise from a variety of sources, and that to think of management (or any other group) as sufficient in and of itself to make all decisions is misleading and wasteful.

This approach does not directly challenge the "legal" right of management to command. It suggests, however, that there is a higher "law of the situation" that thoughtful managers will usually observe, deferring to expertise wherever it may be found. In this model the manager's basic obligation is not to the "management team" but to the accomplishment of departmental and organizational objectives. The criterion of success, therefore, is not the extent to which orders are carried out but the results obtained.

Admitting that he may not have all the answers is as difficult for the manager as for any of the rest of us. He has been taught to hide his deficiencies, not to advertise them. Holding on to information, maintaining close control, and reserving the right to make all decisions are ways by which the manager can ensure his importance. Further, many organizations have reinforced this type of behavior either (*a*) by failing to emphasize the manager's obligation to develop and utilize his human resources or (*b*) by failing to reward him when he does make this effort.

In the area of control the *human resources* model challenges the traditional concept that control is a scarce resource. In traditional theory there is presumed to be a virtually fixed amount of control. This fixed amount can be distributed in a variety of ways, but control given to one group must eventually be taken away from another. Given this concept, the manager is reluctant to allow his subordinates any real degree of self-control—what he gives up to them, he loses himself. In fact, it is frequently this basic fear of losing control which limits the amount of participation that managers are willing to allow.

The *human resources* model does not accept this lump-of-control theory. Instead, it argues that the manager increases his total control over the accomplishment of departmental objectives by encouraging self-control on the part of his subordinates. Control is thus an additive and an expanding phenomenon. Where subordinates are concerned with accomplishing goals and exercising self-direction and self-control, their combined efforts will far outweigh the results of the exercise of any amount of control by the manager.

Moreover, the fact that subordinates desire to exercise greater self-control does not mean that they reject the manager's legitimate concern for goal accomplishment. Rather, there is evidence that they in fact seek a partnership that will allow them to play a larger role, yet also will allow for a corresponding increase in management's control activity.[11]

In all, the fact that managers are reluctant to adopt a model which forces them to rethink, and perhaps restructure, their perceptions of their own roles and functions is not surprising. It is also not surprising that some writers in this field have hesitated to advocate a model which challenges such deeply held concepts. The *human relations* approach is easy to "buy," since it does not challenge the manager's basic role or status. It is correspondingly easy to sell, since it promises much and actually demands little. The *human resources* model, on the other hand, promises much but also demands a great deal from the manager. It requires that he undertake the responsibility of utilizing all the resources available to him—his own and those of his subordinates. It does not suggest that it will make his job easier; it only acknowledges his obligation to do a much better job.

Logical Implications

The nature of the evidence to date does not warrant any firm or sweeping conclusions. Nevertheless, it does suggest enough support for the interpretations made here to make it worthwhile, and perhaps imperative, to draw some logical implications from the fact that managers seem to have adopted two apparently conflicting attitudes regarding participative management.

The first implication, and the easiest one to draw, is that, given managers' present attitudes, the *human resources* model has little chance of ever gaining real acceptance as a guide to managers' relationships with their subordinates. Managers at every level view them-

---

[11] See Clagget C. Smith and Arnold Tannenbaum. "Organizational Control Structure: A Comparative Analysis," *Human Relations,* November 1963, pp. 299–316.

selves as capable of greater self-direction and self-control, but apparently do not attribute such abilities to their subordinates. As long as managers throughout the organizational hierarchy remain unaware that the kind of participation *they* want and believe *they* are capable of handling is also the kind their subordinates want and feel they deserve, there would seem to be little hope for the *human resources* approach being actually put into practice.

A second, and somewhat more complex, implication of managers' current views is that real participation will seldom be found in modern organizations. Participation, in the *human relations* model, is viewed as an "ought" rather than a "must." The manager is under no basic obligation to seek out and develop talent, or to encourage and allow participation; it is something which he "probably should do" but not something for which he is made to feel truly responsible. Viewing participation in this fashion, the manager often junks it when problems arise or pressure builds up from above—the very times when it might be expected to produce the greatest gains.

A third implication, closely related to the second, is that the benefits which the *human resources* approach predicts from participative management will not accrue as long as managers cling to the *human relations* view. From the *human relations* model, a manager may draw a rule for decision making which says that he should allow only as much participation, self-direction, and self-control as is required to obtain cooperation and reduce resistance to formal authority. In the area of job enlargement, for example, the manager following the *human relations* model would be tempted to enlarge his subordinates' jobs just enough to improve morale and satisfaction, with little real concern for making full use of their abilities. This limited approach borders on pseudoparticipation and may be interpreted by subordinates as just another manipulative technique.

The *human resources* model, on the other hand, does not hold the manager to so limited a decision rule. In fact, it affirms that he is obligated to develop and encourage a continually expanding degree of responsible participation, self-direction, and self-control. The only limiting factors legitimate in this approach are the basic requirements of capacity to perform and the need for coordination. The manager following the *human resources* model would therefore continually expand subordinates' responsibility and self-direction up to the limits of their abilities, and/or to the point at which further expansion would produce a wasteful overlap among the responsibilities of members of his department. Even these limits, however, are far from absolute. The *human resources* model suggests that with subordinates' broadened abilities and expanded information, voluntary cooperation can erase much of the need for specific job boundaries.

A fourth and final implication can be drawn from managers' confused and conflicting attitudes toward participative management. Managers' attitudes, as suggested earlier, in part reflect the ambivalent and inconsistent treatment which scholars have given to participative leadership concepts, and are not likely to change until theorists firm up their own thinking.

Some Final Comments

It must be clear at this point that I feel that management scholars should focus their attention on developing and promoting the application of the *human resources* approach. While I cannot, at this stage, base my preference for the *human resources* model on solid empirical evidence, there is one strong argument for its potential usefulness. It is the fact that managers up and down the organizational hierarchy believe their superiors should follow this model.

Critics of the *human resources* approach have argued that (1) its costs outweigh its benefits because in its final form the *human resources* model prescribes management by committee at every level, which results in wasted effort and the inability to act in crisis situations; and (2) this approach is unsuitable for organizations or organizational groups whose members have neither the desire nor the ability to meet its challenge.

In answer to the first charge, this approach does imply a need for additional information flow to subordinates at all levels, and I admit that collecting and disseminating information increases costs.

However, information collected and *used* at lower levels may be less costly than information collected for use at upper levels that is subsequently ignored or misused. Further, and more important, the application of the *human resources* model does not require—in fact, would make unnecessary—committee-type sharing of routine departmental tasks.

This model would suggest that subordinates are generally willing to go along with their superiors' decisions on more or less routine matters, particularly when they are well informed and feel free to call important points to their bosses' attention. Moreover, this approach implies that many matters are to be delegated directly to one or more subordinates who, in most instances, will coordinate their own activities. At the same time, this model emphasizes that full and extended discussion by the whole department will be utilized where it can do the most good—on complex and important problems that demand the full talent and complete concern of the group. One could argue that under these circumstances crises should arise less often and consensus should be more quickly reached when they do arise.

There is no quick and easy answer to the second charge that the *human resources* model is more adaptable to and more easily applied with some groups than with others. Note, however, that it is the *human relations* approach, and not the *human resources* model, which promises quick and easy application. The latter cannot be put into full-blown practice overnight in any situation, particularly where subordinates have been conditioned by years of traditional or pseudoparticipative techniques of leadership. It involves a step-by-step procedure wherein the manager expands subordinates' responsibilities and participation in keeping with their developing abilities and concerns. High expectations and full support, coupled with an open recognition of the inevitability of occasional shortcomings, are required to achieve successful application.

Finally, there is a familiar ring to the critics' charge that many organization members are either unwilling or unable to contribute creatively, or to accept any real measure of responsibility. In fact, this charge brings us back once again to the heart of the conflict in managers' attitudes toward participation—their own view that subordinates are suited only for the *human relations* type of participation, while they themselves are well suited for the full range of participation suggested in the *human resources* model.

28

The Numbers*

HAROLD GENEEN

The drudgery of the numbers will make you free.

Numbers are symbols, very much like words, with their own intrinsic simple meanings when they stand alone, and far more complex and meaningful when in the context of pertinent other numbers. A child learns the alphabet and then how to put letters together to spell words, and words together to make sentences, until he or she grows up to read or to write a book where the real meaning of the words will often be found between the lines. *Cat* can mean a kitten to a child, a Siamese or Persian to a pet owner, or a tiger to a hunter. If I tell you there are five apples in the basket on the table, what does that tell

---

* From Harold Geneen (with Alvin Moscow), *Managing* (New York: Avon Books, 1984), pp. 189–204. Copyright © 1984 by Harold Geneen and Alvin Moscow, Inc.

you? That there are five apples in the basket. Or, if you knew there should be six, that someone had eaten one of your apples.

In business, numbers are the symbols by which you measure the various activities of an individual enterprise or combination of enterprises which make up the parent corporation. When you add and subtract all the numbers, you come up with the well-known "bottom line" on your profit-and-loss statement. That's very simple, like spelling *cat*. In managing the family's finances, such basic arithmetic might be sufficient: Did you take in more than you spent that year? Fine. But if your business shows a profit of $3 million for the year, is that good or not so good? That depends upon the context of that $3 million. Did you earn $2 million or $4 million the year before? Is it $3 million earned on sales of $40 million or $400 million?

The meaning of numbers, like that of words, can only be comprehended in relationship to one another. When I read sets of numbers, either vertically or horizontally, I automatically translate them into meaningful percentage differences. Thus, if $500 million in sales dropped by $50 million, I know that sales dropped 10 percent. If $500,000 in sales of another division decreased by $100,000, my mind's eye tells me the drop was 20 percent. Even though this division lost less money than the first, I suspect immediately that it is probably in deeper trouble than the division that lost $50 million in sales. Actually, those numbers, by way of illustration, tell me a whole lot more. They tell me that I had better look behind those numbers and find out what is happening there.

Too many people mistakenly believe that large American corporations, like ITT, are run (heartlessly) by the numbers. They make that mistake because most people read words better than they do numbers. They may understand the complex novels of Henry James or James Joyce or Marcel Proust, but they read columns of numbers as they would a vocabulary list of strange, esoteric words. As symbols of what is going on in business, numbers represent measurements, not the business activity itself. René Magritte, the surrealist artist, painted a picture of a man's pipe and on the canvas he wrote, "This is not a pipe." It wasn't. It was a picture of a pipe. So I say: The numbers are not the business; they are only pictures of the business.

Nevertheless, no business could run without them. Numbers serve as a sort of thermometer which measures the health and well-being of the enterprise. They serve as the first line of communication which informs management what is going on, and the more precise the numbers are, the more they are based upon "unshakable facts," the clearer the line of communication.

When a manager makes up a budget for the coming year, he is putting down on paper a series of expectations, expressed in numbers.

They include the whole gamut of costs of the product or products—design, engineering, supplies, production, labor, plants, marketing, sales, distribution—and also anticipated income from sales based upon market share, back orders, and what have you. These figures are not pulled out of the air. Nor are they based upon whims or hopes. They are carefully garnered by the people on the firing lines of the company and they are based upon the best facts and figures available. When all the figures are pulled together for one company or one division, you have its budget. As I said, at ITT we had 250 of these profit centers, and their annual budgets, replete with numbers, when lined up side by side, occupied thirty-odd feet of shelf space.

As that budget year proceeds, a similar or parallel set of numbers flows into the company, representing the day-by-day operations, and they are gathered, collated, and reported on a weekly or monthly basis. Thus the actual costs and the actual sales and the actual profit margins and earnings can be compared with the budget forecasts. Does one set of numbers match the other? Is the actuality above or below the company's expectations? If either, what are you going to do about it?

Any significant variation between your expectations and what is actually happening in the marketplace, as expressed in those numbers, is a signal for action. The sooner you see the numbers, the sooner you can take action, if needed. If one of your products is selling above expectations, you may want to increase production immediately. Or you may not. If, as happens more often, one or more of your products are not selling as well as expected, then you may have to find some way to get those sales up or begin to reduce the costs and expenses involved, and the sooner, the better. However—and this is most important—the numbers themselves will not tell you what to do. They are only a signal for action, a trigger to thinking. It is akin to the man with the dividing rod who points to the spot where there is water underground. But to get the water, you have to dig for it. The key issue in business is to find out what is happening behind those numbers.

Once you start digging into the areas which the numbers represent, then you get into the guts of your business. If sales are off, is it because of the design of your product? Its cost? Marketing? Distribution? Financing? What? The search goes on not only at the top of the company but also at the operating levels. Now you get back to the importance of open communications, the honesty and integrity of the men reporting to you. These are the subjects you investigate at your meetings of managers, operating men, and staff. When you find the source of the trouble, then you must put your collective mind—you and your team of managers—to finding the very best answer to your problem. Here at this level is where you insist that management must manage. You don't want to manage the numbers; you don't want to push sales or receivables from one quarter to another, for the truth will always catch up with you. That is like treating the thermometer instead of the patient. If a thermometer registers above 98.6 degrees, it is telling you the patient has a fever; he is sick. It is not telling you *what* is wrong, only that something is wrong, You can put the thermometer in a glass of ice water or dunk the whole patient into a bathtub of cold water, and that will bring the number down. But it won't cure him. In business, you want to manage and control the elements of the business itself, not the numbers on your profit-and-loss statement. The numbers are there to reflect how well or how poorly your business is doing.

There is nothing unique or unusual about this concept. However, the difference between well-managed companies and not-so-well-managed companies is the degree of attention they pay to numbers, the temperature chart of their business. How often are the numbers reported up the chain of command? How accurate are those numbers? How much variation is tolerated between budget forecasts and actual results? How soon is attention directed to and action taken on variations deemed significant? How deep does management dig for its answers?

At ITT, as should be obvious, we took our numbers very seriously indeed. Our budget reviews, which began as early as February and March and continued through the year, were drawn up very carefully. The final budget was considered a solid commitment for performance expected the following year. Our division comptrollers and staff reported weekly; our operating managers reported at least monthly. Our monthly general managers meetings focused upon the variations, if any, between budget forecasts and the results for that given month.

Our entire reporting system was based upon the early-warning system of our numbers. We wanted no "surprises." As soon as we discovered something amiss, or going amiss, we threw every means and every effort into solving our problems, fixing our trouble spots, innovating for a changing marketplace. As a result, we felt that we were in control. The unexpected shocks and surprises that accost everyone in life became for us manageable.

As time went on, we became more and more skilled at interpreting the numbers of our business and projecting into the future what we could do and could not do with the resources at our command. This included investments in plant, new products, increased production, all sorts of things. The skill resided in our ability to control what we were doing at the detail level, even though we were a large, complex company. That is the only way you can run a business. You cannot control an omelet; you control one egg at a time.

Many companies do not take their numbers seriously enough. Divisions may report only quarterly, which hardly provides an early-warning system. Many companies have become accustomed to operating with rather big variations between their budget projections and the actuality of the marketplace. If the numbers are down, they live on hopes and the promises of their sales force. They push harder and sometimes the numbers go back up; sometimes they do not. But oftentimes they never know the real reasons why the numbers went up or down, and when you neglect the signals it may become too late to take effective action. You find that you have lost control and that can spell disaster.

Numbers have an inherent quality to them which is as important as the digits themselves. They can be accurate or not so accurate, precise or rounded off, detailed or averaged and vague. Their quality, as reported, usually depends upon the chief executive of the company and what he expects from the men reporting to him. If he does not give much personal attention to the detailed figures, beyond ascertaining the earnings per share, no one else in his company is going to worry about them. They will round off their figures, averaging the odd numbers, perhaps shaving off a few points from the costs, adding something to boost profit margins. As the practice spreads from division to division, the accumulation of inexact, fuzzy, and then plain incorrect figures can cause havoc with decisions based upon facts which shake and tremble upon the tree of knowledge.

For example, if you are president of a company and your vice president in charge of production reports that "factory costs" for that year are $12 million, what does that tell you? You know that factory costs include payroll, materials, and overhead. But it is still too vague to be meaningful. However, if you trust your vice president, you accept his aggregate figure and go on from there. It may be a relatively small figure in the overall scheme of things and you don't think you have time to delve into such mundane details. But when things go bad and that division starts losing money and other divisions also start losing money, you're fired. A new president comes in and when he looks over those same figures, he calls in that vice president and demands to know: "What do those figures on factory costs mean? What's included there?"

"That's the payroll and overhead at the factory," explains the vice president. "We don't keep it in any more detail than that. Mostly it's payroll, that's all."

"Now wait a minute," says the new president, "that's much too high for the volume you're doing. What goes into that figure, those factory costs; that's what I want to know."

"Well, you can look at the payroll, if you want to."

"No, I don't want to read the payroll. I want to know what those guys are doing there, how much you pay them for the various jobs, how many hours they put in . . ."

"But we don't keep our records like that," says the vice president.

So the new president sets up a time-card system in which each employee category has differently coded time cards, which are punched automatically at the time clock for each shift. Now, when the new president looks over the ingredients of "factory costs," he can readily see that the payroll consists of some three hundred men on the production line, actually making the product, and another hundred are listed as supervisors and inspectors and another hundred as maintenance men.

"That's way out of line," he tells the vice president. "You go look and see what those supervisory men and those maintenance men are doing. We don't need one supervisor for every three men on the line."

That's a very simple example of getting to the facts behind the numbers. The vice president will find all sorts of things that can be corrected. He will find men in the shop sharpening tools that are no longer used, because they have to make work or lose their jobs. He will find boondoggling among the inspectors and supervisors. He will find the causes of those high factory costs and how he solves his newfound problem will reflect upon how good a manager he is.

The new president, meanwhile, will begin to look closely at all the figures that come in from all the divisions of the company, and as he delves into them, things will happen in that company that change it ever so imperceptibly into a well-managed enterprise. He will have to keep at it continually, or else things will begin to slip again. Managing a company is like writing in the snow: You have to go over and over the same words as the snow falls if you want your writing to remain legible. The reward, however, is that you get better and better at it as you repeat the same process.

Most "turnaround" situations in business involve the quality of the numbers reported to the chief executive. One man allows the numbers to slip past him because he does not care enough about financial controls, and then another chief executive comes in and begins to cut costs in order to reestablish the appropriate relationship of costs to sales, which produces that all-important margin of profit.

A new president, to continue the above example, as his first priority will carefully go over the figures of his company, looking not at individual numbers but at the overall numbers in relation to one another. He is searching for trends and currents that tell him what is happening: numbers have a way of synthesizing the mass effects of many, many individual items which make up the whole. Once he has that mainstream in mind, however, he will begin to look into the detailed figures behind the overall averages, and he will focus on the numbers which interest him the most: sales, costs, earnings, margins, marketing, assets investment, debt and interest, whatever.

Suppose he comes up with the number 4 (which can represent $4 million, $40 million, or $400 million) for one element of one division. Breaking down that 4, he may find it does not represent 2 + 2 or 3 + 1. Very frequently in business a total of 4 can mean +12 and −8. Maybe the +12 should be higher, he thinks, but he focuses upon the −8 and he finds that consists of +5 and −13. So he delves into the −13 and perhaps he finds that represents the losses on a series of products that are terribly outmoded and not selling. By stopping production on that one line of products, he saves that loss of 13, and when he applies that saving to the bottom line of that division, the total of +4 rises to +17, a healthy gain for the new regime. Remember, he did not change the numbers; he changed what was behind the numbers.

As he moves on, reading the books of the company, he probably will find gaps in the information he needs and wants. He will then call for figures that had never been collected before and those figures will enable him to maintain a tighter control on the varied operations of the company. Obviously, the head of a company, a division, or a department wants the figures on only the elements in which he has an interest. He may want to know how many tons of coal Plant A is burning every month, but he does not care about the amount of fly ash that is coming out of the chimney. But then one day the Environmental Protection Agency imposes a fine of $1,000 for every day a company's fly ash exceeds 2 percent of the coal burned. When he finds his company is paying $30,000 a month in fines, he becomes interested in a monthly figure on fly ash. Now it is important to him.

Sometimes, however, outside events beyond the control of any individual company overtake the usual early-warning system that even good numbers provide. A sudden rise in the cost of energy, an international event of significant proportions, a plunge into recession of a whole national economy can wreak havoc with the best-laid plans. It has happened to the auto industry, the oil industry, the steel industry, and to segments of ITT.

Consider, for example, one company with $40 million in annual sales and reaping a handsome profit. It expands to $60 million in annual sales, earning even more money. It builds its sales volume to $80 million a year, and profits rise proportionally. Then the cycles change, the economy slumps, customers suddenly stop buying, annual sales slide back down to the old level of $40 million a year. But now the company is losing money on that volume. What happened? What can you do about it? No mere snipping at costs here and there will save the situation. Some men will sit back and say, "We're waiting for the volume to come back. Look, we made lots of money at $80 million and we'll make it again. We just have to wait for the economy to turn around." That's hope. Others might say, "Hell, we're in all kinds of trouble and it's hopeless. Let's sell the thing and get out from under."

At ITT, when outside events overtook us and there was nothing else we could do, we "restructured" the company so that it could cope with its new environment. To sit back and wait for the vicissitudes of the economy to help us was unacceptable as a solution. To sell off a company in times of distress ran against our grain. The numbers, which told us what was going on within that company, played a big part. We went over every relevant figure of every operation and scaled the company back down to the size it was when it was making money on annual sales of $40 million. It is simply amazing how many expenses once deemed necessary become luxuries when your company is operating at a loss. Restructuring also involved cutting back on plant and employees so that the company once again resembled its old $40 million self. At the same time, while restructuring we adopted the practice of putting forth a tremendous effort to try to increase sales a little bit, even 5 or 10 percent. We cut the company back to the $40 million structure and then tried to do $42 and $44 million in business. We called it our "one-two punch." Cannon Electric, which makes heavy-industry electrical connectors, was one ITT subsidiary which went through restructuring during an economic recession and then was built up to a point where it is now three times as big and as successful as it had ever been before. We could not have done it without a firm grasp on its numbers.

In addition to the numbers from daily operations, another complete set of numbers must be monitored carefully and regularly to ensure the well-being of any company. The figures on the "balance sheet" reflect the total assets of the company, its stockholders' investment, and its outstanding debt. These numbers will reveal as well as anything else the basic philosophy of the company, its management, and its board of directors. To the degree that a company carries debt prudently it is trying to maximize the return on its stockholders' investment.

Generally speaking, companies try to operate on as much as 30 or 40 percent debt in relationship to the equity of the company. A 30 percent debt ratio will earn a company, all other things being equal, the highest credit rate of AAA; 40 percent will reduce the rating to AA. The interest one pays on borrowed money is based upon one's credit rating. Some companies choose to operate with less debt than that, or no debt at all, even when interest rates are reasonable. That constitutes a very conservative approach to business. Growth would necessarily be limited. Obviously, the company that borrows money equal to 30 percent of its equity and invests those extra funds properly in expansion should be able to increase its capacity for production and sales 30 percent more than the company of the same size that borrowed no money. The catch is, of course, that you have to increase your earnings enough to pay the interest on your money you borrowed. That will depend upon your increased costs, sales, and earnings, the rate and amount of interest you must pay, the turnover of inventory, the turnover of your receivables, and ultimately the net amount of your cash flow. All these numbers have an intrinsic relationship to one another, and the ratio of one to the other depends upon a manager's philosophy of running his business. Should you, if you could, extend your debt to 30, 40, 50 percent of the value of your net assets to expand your business or to acquire another company? How about 55 percent? Would that be foolhardy? Or courageous? It all depends upon what you are producing and selling, the consumer demand for your products, the marketplace, the general economy, the confidence you have in yourself, in your management team, in your company, in dozens and even hundreds of variables.

No matter what course you choose, you still have to be sure of your company's ability to function in the environment in which you have placed it. You have to be certain your company has enough liquidity to meet all of its normal requirements, including its ability to borrow more and to grow next year and the year after that. The more you borrow in relation to your assets and your cash flow, the higher your expenses will be in doing business; the higher the risk, the lower your credit rating becomes, and then you must pay higher interest rates to borrow in the future or to refinance your present loans. The ability to pay or to refinance your debts as they come due is absolutely essential. The only irreparable mistake in business is to run out of cash. Almost any other mistake in business can be remedied in one way or another. But when you run out of cash, they take you out of the game.

As a concept, all this is child's play to anyone who has graduated from a business school or has run his own business for any length of time. And yet, thousands of businesses go bankrupt every year, hundreds of others merge or are taken over because they are in trouble, and the root of almost all of these troubled situations can be traced back to an inattention to the numbers involved. Someone did not get the message in time. Numbers do not stand alone on the balance sheet or in the budgets or in the weekly or monthly operating reports. They are all interrelated. Obviously, the health of your balance sheet depends upon the profits or losses shown in your operating reports, and the value of those operating reports depends upon the quality of the numbers being reported, and all the numbers are but reflections of what is happening down the line in your factories, in your sales force, in the marketplace . . . and, ultimately, the well-being of your company will depend upon the attention that is paid to all those numbers and the messages they transmit to you.

So the numbers flow in, signaling, sending their messages, and the family checkbook will tell you whether you spent more than you took in that month or vice versa, and your balance sheet will tell you just how solvent you are and will be upon your retirement. Family finances are not too different in concept from those of businesses. The professional manager, however, must cope with reams of figures covering not a single enterprise but a multitude of them, all interrelated. His skill is not just to produce a product that sells in the marketplace and yields a profit. His skill lies in how well he can do it in relation to his competition. Efficiency lies in how well he can cut his costs and maximize his profits across a broad scale of activities involving a multitude of products. That skill, in my estimation, will depend to a great extent upon his ability to understand and act upon the early-warning system provided by the numbers which flow across his desk from sources throughout the company.

The professional's grasp of the numbers is a measure of the control he has over the events that the figures represent. Through his experience, he learns to appreciate the meaning of the variables so that he can act swiftly to amend deviations from the expected; he is going to curtail the number and severity of shocks that any business is heir to; he is not going to run out of cash; he is going to command a tight ship, a well-managed company.

There is a price to pay, too, as there always is: Paying attention to the numbers is a dull, tiresome routine, a drudgery. The more you want to know about your business, the more detail you want to have, the more numbers there will be. They cannot be skimmed. They must be read, understood, and thought about and compared with other sets of numbers which you have read that day, that week, or earlier that year. And you have to do it alone, all by yourself, even when you know that it would be far more stimulating to be doing almost anything else. If you are running a well-managed company, most of the numbers will be those you expect. That makes them even more mundane and dull. But you cannot skip over them; you dare not allow your concentration to flag. Those numbers are your controls, and you read them, on and on, until your mind reels or until you come upon one number or set of numbers which stands out from all the rest, demanding your attention, and getting it.

What you are seeking is *comprehension* of the numbers: what they mean. That will come only with constant exposure, constant repetition, retention of what you read in the past, and a familiarity with the actual activities that the numbers represent. You cannot speed up the process. Comprehension seeps into your brain by a process of osmosis and gradually you find yourself at ease with numbers and what they really represent. Saturating yourself with the numbers and the facts, no matter how remote they may seem at first, brings comprehension; somehow the pieces begin to fit together. It does not mean you are the smartest man in the business world. It is only that repetition is the secret of comprehension. When I read the figures of a given enterprise and ask questions of the manager each month and get answers, each question and answer slightly different from the month before, both the manager and I are adding to our fundamental comprehension of what is going on.

The truth is that the drudgery of the numbers will make you free. The very fact that you go over the progression of those numbers week after week, month after month, means that you have strengthened your memory and familiarity with them so that you retain in your mind a vivid, composite picture of what is going on in your company in relationship to what went on before and, even more important, what might be possible for the future. The self-confidence that you are in control, that you are aware of the significant variations from the expected, gives you the freedom to do things that you would not have been able to do otherwise. You can go ahead and build a new factory plant, finance risk-laden research, or go out and buy a company, and you can do it with assurance because you are able to sit down and figure out what that new venture will do to the total picture on your balance sheet, backed up by the expected performance of your operating divisions. Your experience and skill at working with the numbers, which came from the drudgery of all those long hours at it, will enable you to make projections into the future on paper which can be relied upon as realistic, not only by yourself but also by the banks, the security analysts, and the shareholders. When you have mastered the numbers, you will in fact no longer be reading numbers, any more than you read words when reading a book. You will be reading meanings. Your eyes may be seeing numbers, but your mind will be reading "markets," "costs," "competition," "new products." All the things you are doing and planning will stare out at you, if you will only learn to read *through* the numbers. It is an acquired, special skill perhaps, but it is the key to the mastery of any business.

On a personal note, without any undue feigned modesty, the steady and remarkable growth of ITT over a 20-year period, in which more than 300 companies were acquired and merged into one unified corporation that stretched across the world, was made possible largely because of ITT's earned reputation not for just the tight financial controls over our operations, but for our ability to read "through" them and to think in terms of what those numbers meant and what they called for. Our close scrutiny of the numbers freed us to act with courage. We never encountered trouble borrowing funds for expansion or acquisitions. Banks and financial institutions recognized our adherence to the real meaning of strong financial controls. We were never in danger of running out of cash. ITT grew faster and with more success than other companies of our size during the years of my presidency because we knew our numbers, and we were not afraid to move forward.

In fact, I would argue that anyone in business, if he sets up the proper kinds of controls—controls that tell him when any segment of his company is not doing what he expected, and tell him this promptly enough and in enough detail so that he can go back behind the numbers and analyze precisely where it is that he has to take action—then he (or anyone else not mentally incompetent) could run a progressive, profitable, and growth-oriented company.

That's what a good set of numbers will do for you.

29

In Defense of Enlightened Hardball Management*

JAN P. MUCZYK and ROBERT E. HASTINGS

Few in the United States need reminding that many sectors of the U.S. economy have fared poorly over the past decade. Blame for the plight of these troubled industries has been placed on a host of causes—so many, in fact, that turning troubled companies around appears to be an overwhelming task. Many in top management have not known even where to begin; as a consequence they have done nothing.

Poor management is the most important reason for declining productivity and poor quality, a fact that fortunately is recognized by a sizable portion of American management. Though finger pointing at

---

* From *Business Horizons*, 1985, *28*, 23–29. Copyright © 1985 by Foundation for the School of Business, Indiana University.

this juncture would not be productive, considerable confusion abounds regarding corrective action.

Because the Japanese economy is the envy of the free world while large sectors of the U.S. economy have fallen upon hard times, it is quite natural to emulate Japanese management practices. Given the fundamental cultural differences between the two societies, however, is it practical or even possible to emulate many of the Japanese management practices? Copying management practices, such as consensus decision making, is far more difficult than duplicating physical technology.

We are not suggesting that it is futile to borrow from management styles practiced in other cultures. That is not the case, as just-in-time inventory systems illustrate. Japanese and Europeans have availed themselves of certain American managerial practices and blended them into their own styles without emulating the American system in its entirety. Ironically, they also have adopted management techniques well known in our literature but ignored by our management. However, we believe that the largest and most immediate impact on productivity will be made by focusing on management practices that are compatible with American culture. In many instances, these are practices that have served companies well but were abandoned because the incentive for preserving them, namely competition, was absent. It is time to rediscover the lost lessons of our past successes— matters that are directly under management's control and can be influenced almost immediately.

ESTABLISHING A CONNECTION BETWEEN PERFORMANCE AND REWARDS

The sad truth of the matter is that in many organizations with productivity problems, the below-average, average, and above-average employees at all levels of the organization receive roughly identical rewards—and this applies to nonunionized organizations as well. Therefore, the extrinsic incentives for performing at high levels are absent from the workplace. If executives who lead their firms into bankruptcy are paid hundreds of thousands of dollars, how much would they be worth if their firms made a profit? Incentives must approach a motivational threshold in order to have significant impact on performance. Workers will take their pay in the form of leisure rather than exert maximum effort for an extra 5 or 10 cents an hour.

We have much to learn about motivational thresholds from Lincoln Electric. In 1981, Lincoln Electric employees received, on the average, a $22,000 bonus in addition to their regular compensation. In 1982, the bonus was $15,640, but no one was laid off, although employees worked a shortened work week because sales declined 25 percent. For that kind of incentive, employees will work harder and smarter.

Another excellent example of a company that maintains a strong connection between performance and rewards is Briggs & Stratton Corporation, the world's leading and lowest-cost producer of small engines. Good management is responsible for Briggs & Stratton's success. The firm minimizes the number of managers, and managers communicate with workers constantly. Moreover, quality control is everyone's job. The principal reason for high productivity is that 60 percent of the employees are on either group or individual incentive plans. Some workers earn as much as $30,000 a year. Although Lincoln Electric is not unionized, Briggs & Stratton is. The union has no problems with incentives because the employees prefer them.

Nucor Corp., a Charlotte, North Carolina–based company that operates seven steel-producing minimills, is a third example. Last year the average wage for all Nucor production workers was more than $30,000 because of a work incentive program that its president says is unmatched in the industry. At the same time Nucor maintains its labor costs at $65 per ton, less than half the industry standard. The moral of the Nucor story is how productive the workers are, not how much they earn.

Not only should the compensation of employees be related to their performance, but so should their job security. General Motors officials recently rewarded the Lordstown, Ohio, plant by adding a second shift rather than giving the work to a rival plant. That action put approximately 2,500 people back to work. Why did the Lordstown plant receive the work? Inspections carried out by outside auditors revealed that quality at Lordstown was 8 percent better than at other General Motors plants that could have performed the work.

Not long ago Ford executives proposed to the workers at the Brookpark, Ohio, engine plant the following arrangement: Abandon certain restrictive work rules, and we will produce a V-6 engine at the Brookpark engine plant. The rank and file voted against the work rule change. The V-6 engine was awarded to the Lima, Ohio, plant, where workers were more cooperative. In the meantime, the laid-off employees at Brookpark remained out of work. Their unemployment insurance and supplemental unemployment benefits were exhausted. Moreover, the future of the Brookpark plant was placed under a dark cloud.

Armco, an Ohio steel company, decided not to purchase foreign steel slabs after trying a plan suggested by its workers to boost production at its flat-rolled steel works in Middletown, Ohio. The employees raised production more than 6 percent over the nine-week trial period. If that rate can be maintained, Armco will have no need for foreign steel slabs.

Workers at a Ford Motor Company parts plant in Ypsilanti, Michigan, approved a contract that will ensure them of employment security at least through 1987 in exchange for work-rule concessions.

A single-plant firm may lack the same degree of leverage that a multiplant firm possesses, but outsourcing provides considerable leverage even to a single-plant company. Knowing that a firm is prepared to move to another state or country or simply to close its doors can spur employees to greater cooperation and productivity and more reasonable demands.

If employers are to attempt to exact concessions from employees, they should offer a quid pro quo to employees, such as job security. Otherwise, the employees will perceive the strategy as exploitation, and labor/management relations are likely to deteriorate. Furthermore, executives must share in the pain.

Ford Motor Company has been demanding a variety of concessions from its employees for the past three years—and, in a number of instances, getting them. Yet in 1983 Philip Caldwell, chairman of Ford, received $520,534 in salary, $900,000 in cash bonus, and exercised $5.8 million in accumulated stock options. General Motors paid 5,807 executives $181.7 million in bonuses, not counting salaries and stock options. Ford Motor Company paid 6,035 executives bonuses totalling $80.6 million, while Chrysler Corporation set aside $51.6 million for use as bonuses to 1,400 executives. Who can blame blue-collar operatives, clerical workers, and their unions for resisting concessions when some executives earn as much as $13.2 million per year?[1]

The astronomical compensation packages of top executives are even more difficult to justify when one realizes that executives by and large are interchangeable bureaucrats. One retires, another succeeds him, and nothing of significance changes in the organization. If we exclude entrepreneurs such as Jobs and Wozniak of Apple, there simply aren't many Lee Iacoccas in executive suites.

Creating and maintaining a strong connection between performance and rewards is especially important because the United States is an *instrumental* culture. In other words, American workers will produce at high levels when they are convinced that hard work will obtain for them the goals that they consider important. Japan, on the other hand, is a *normative* culture. That is, Japanese workers are more likely to produce at high levels because of values that they embrace

---

[1] See the latest *Business Week* survey of executive compensation for information regarding current executive remuneration in large firms.

rather than because hard work leads to the attainment of their important goals.

Numerous studies have been conducted over the years comparing the impact on performance of incentive plans versus hourly rates. In most such studies, workers under incentive plans outproduced those under day wages. One survey of 29 studies revealed that incentive plans increased productivity in 26 instances, in 2 cases there was no difference, and in only 1 comparison did productivity decrease. In another survey of 54 cases, incentive strategies increased productivity an average of 22.8 percent. These two surveys are typical of the evidence that indicates that incentive pay systems increase productivity between 15 and 35 percent. According to a 1983 Public Agenda Foundation study, only 22 percent of American workers say there is a direct link between how hard they work and how much they are paid. The same study reveals that 73 percent of American workers attribute their decreased job efforts to a lack of incentive pay. There is even some evidence that the absence of incentive pay is a disincentive or demotivator.

In northeast Ohio a metal stamping plant that employed mostly ethnic women in light assembly and stamping jobs experienced excessive tardiness and absenteeism. The CEO decided to utilize trading stamps, popular in the area, as incentives to reduce tardiness and absenteeism. For example, if a worker showed up for work on time for 15 consecutive work days, she received one book of trading stamps. Astonishingly, tardiness and absenteeism virtually disappeared. (Needless to say, one would not motivate professional employees with trading stamps!)

Individual incentive plans are inappropriate for many of today's jobs because it is difficult to assign to individuals measurable units of output when work assignments are inextricably intertwined. That is why employers are urged to consider group incentive plans and, especially, plant-wide gainsharing plans, such as the Scanlon Plan, the Rucker Share-of-Production Plan, and Improshare.

Why, then, haven't more organizations adopted some sort of incentive scheme? Generally, the reason is that it is more difficult than paying employees on the basis of time, and it is quite natural to follow the path of least resistance. Let's face it! Sloppy management is easy. That's why we have so much of it.

In addition to establishing and maintaining a strong nexus between performance and rewards, organizations should introduce programs designed to change attitudes of all organizational members toward productivity. Too many U.S. workers do not appreciate the relationship between productivity and their self-interest: their job security, the size of their paychecks, their opportunities for promotion. This statement also applies to union leaders, especially at the local level. It is unlikely that programs which appeal to the intellect and focus on economic theory will have much impact on the target groups that are most in need of attitude change. In other words, programs extolling the virtues of free enterprise too often preach only to the converted. Organizations, with union participation where appropriate, would be well advised to design hard-hitting programs based on: (1) examples of companies that went bankrupt because they couldn't compete due to low productivity (there is unfortunately an embarrassment of riches from which to choose); (2) examples of companies (including Japanese companies) that prosper because of high productivity; and (3) the folly of relying on the federal government to enact protective legislation.

At one time Akron, Ohio, was the manufacturing center for U.S. tires. Now only a handful of experimental and racing tires are produced in Akron. Why were the tire workers unaware until the point of no return was reached of the ultimate consequences of their unproductive behavior, which included sabotaging equipment to obtain unscheduled rest breaks?

An excellent example of an attitude change program is the "Hearts and Minds" program initiated at Jaguar. The program began with a series of videotapes describing the history of Jaguar and the efforts to turn around the decline of Jaguar's fortunes. The videotapes present Jaguar's total investment program and illustrate how the firm is pumping in money to support its workers. The videotapes also make it clear that, if the Jaguar employee does not do his job as well as his German counterpart, he will lose his job.

Union leaders, with their own self-interest in mind, must play a leading role in this kind of attitude change program. The reasons are twofold: (1) union leaders have more credibility with rank and file than do supervisors, managers, executives, and consultants; (2) unless productivity is increased in many firms, union leaders, especially at the local level, will be looking for work. If the union leaders prove to be obstructionist, management must talk directly to the workers. To quote John Egan, chairman of Jaguar: "What a lot of British companies have done is rely on the unions to explain things to the workers. You have to tell the worker yourself. Otherwise, the union will tell him all kinds of political claptrap."[2]

Even when individual, group, and plantwide incentive systems are inappropriate, the connection between performance and rewards for all levels of the organization could and should be established through reliable and valid performance appraisals. Unfortunately, perfor-

---

[2] L. Erik Calonius, "Jaguar Climbs Back to Prosperity," *The Wall Street Journal,* July 18, 1984, p. 25.

mance evaluations in many organizations are not worth the paper that they are printed on. This state of affairs is not due to a lack of knowledge but to a dearth of effort. Unless organizations implement performance evaluations capable of identifying high, average, and below-average performers, then these organizations simply cannot differentiate in rewarding performance. Employees who are convinced that rewards do not follow performance will become and remain demotivated. Indeed, improving performance appraisals for everyone should be among the highest priorities of contemporary executives. A good place to start is to develop a consensus by the people doing the evaluating and by those being evaluated regarding performance measurements.[3]

The quality of performance appraisals will improve quite rapidly if those who make thorough performance appraisals are rewarded in a significant manner, and those who fail are sanctioned in a meaningful way, such as being denied promotion or a good salary increase.

TOUGH-MINDED HUMAN RELATIONS

It is essential that employees perceive that they are treated fairly by management and that they are valued by their superiors. Toward that end, employers must experiment with (1) participative decision making, (2) quality circles, (3) job enrichment, (4) participative goal-setting programs, (5) shared ownership (for example, employee stock option plans), and (6) less social distance between workers and management.

Although some aspects of scientific management, such as incentive plans, should be encouraged, the vestiges of other scientific management tenets should be eradicated. Frederick Taylor, the father of scientific management, postulated that the ideal factory worker has the "mentality of an ox." If an employee had a brain, he or she was invited to leave it at home. Contemporary workers possess different values, attitudes, needs, and expectations than their forebears and feel important when provided with opportunities to utilize their brains. The six strategies enumerated above constitute an open invitation to employees to bring their brains to work and to use them.

Worker involvement does not come about automatically or through wishful thinking. The organization must first establish certain preconditions. It is unlikely that the steel workers at Armco's Middletown

---

[3] A well-articulated defense of this position is presented by Andrew S. Grove in *High Output Management* (New York: Random House, 1983). Grove, who is president of Intel Corp., asserts that it takes five to eight hours on each employee's review, about one quarter to one third of 1 percent of the supervisor's work year, in order to execute the performance appraisal task properly.

mill would have suggested productivity improvements had the company not introduced an employee participation program two years before that permitted the employees, their union leaders, and management to appreciate their mutuality of interest and created the instrumentality for presenting ideas and having them evaluated.

In order for employees to perceive a sense of fair treatment, employers should provide a satisfactory judicial system. Organized employees benefit from a grievance procedure negotiated at the collective bargaining table. Unorganized employees frequently have nowhere to turn but the personnel department, hardly a neutral instrumentality, when disputes and grievances occur. In other words, the employees are at the mercy of the hierarchy. Voluntarily installing grievance procedures that are capable of swift resolution of conflict and perceived as being impartial in nonunionized organizations not only will be a step toward obviating a need for a union but should improve morale as well.

It certainly would be desirable if all motivation-related problems could be solved through quality-of-work-life programs, such as job enrichment, quality circles, and participative decision making. However, in numerous organizations with productivity problems, it is because of a general breakdown in discipline that absenteeism is high, coffee breaks excessive, reject levels intolerable, instances of insubordination too frequent, and disregard of rules, policies, and procedures commonplace. Establishing the requisite discipline before it is too late is the logical solution. The Ford Corporation closed its Mahwah, New Jersey plant several years ago because plant management reputedly lost control of the work force to the local union. Because excess capacity existed at the time, it was easier to close the plant than to reestablish control.

RETHINKING THE ROLE AND SIZE OF STAFF DEPARTMENTS

The purpose of staff departments is to serve line departments, not the other way around. Many organizations have bloated staff departments and too many of them. By trying to justify their existence and growth, these staff departments frequently create work for line personnel that is marginally related to the principal mission of the organization, thereby making it more difficult for the line to attain its objectives. For example, the ratio of staff positions to production workers in American manufacturing companies increased from 35 per 100 to 41 per 100 between 1965 and 1975. The increase has been even more dramatic in certain industries. Moreover, there is a direct relationship between size and proportion of staff positions relative to production workers, with the largest companies having the highest ratio of staff employees to production workers.

During the last three years of depressed economic activity, many organizations reduced with impunity the size of their staff departments. When the economy recovers, organizations should remain lean rather than succumb to the temptation of restoring their staff departments to prerecession levels. The same admonition applies to line managers. F. Kenneth Iverson, president and CEO of Nucor Corp., says: "We keep people at our plants where the day-to-day decisions are made. There is no need for a large support staff. Each plant general manager is also a vice president in the company . . . they're the ones who decide the direction their divisions take."[4] The rise and fall of corporate strategic planning departments is an excellent example of rethinking the size and role of staff departments.

C. Northcote Parkinson some years ago formulated the proposition that work expands to fill the time allotted for its completion. Between 1968 and 1977 blue-collar employment rose 9.8 percent while the number of white collar employees increased 27 percent. Since productivity increased at an average annual rate of 1.6 percent during the same period, how much of the increase can be attributed to Parkinson's Law?

Employing industrial engineers to ascertain whether staff departments are too large may be inappropriate, but a comparative analysis should serve the same purpose. For example, a firm can compare its personnel department to personnel departments of companies in the same industry and of similar size. If an organization discovers that its personnel department is substantially larger than some of the companies that are as profitable or more profitable, it may conclude that its personnel function can be trimmed to the level of those in equally or more efficient organizations. Careful comparative analyses of this kind ultimately can produce optimal ratios between the number of line employees and the size of staff departments.

Holding staff departments accountable for tangible accomplishments, as opposed to accepting them on faith, is another way of justifying their existence. The finance department of Bethlehem Steel Corporation has arranged $1.25 billion in special financings since late 1982. In fact, if one accepts dollar volume as a measure of productivity of a finance department, the finance department has accomplished as much in the past two years as it did in the previous 15 years. Furthermore, these transactions were executed with a staff of 93 persons compared with 165 three years ago.

---

[4] Forrest S. Gossett, "Minimill: Steeling for Profits," *The Cleveland Plain Dealer,* April 22, 1984, p. 1-E.

REDUCING THE NUMBER OF LAYERS OF MANAGEMENT

Tall organization structures possess certain advantages, such as more promotional opportunities and more time available to each subordinate from the superior because of narrower spans of control. However, the disadvantages outweigh the advantages. In the typical Japanese factory, foremen report directly to plant managers. The foreman in the typical U.S. factory has three additional layers of management that are expensive and create bureaucratic rigidity. The Lockheed Missiles and Space Company, after a systematic and well-considered analysis, was able to eliminate layers of supervision/management by broadening the span of control. An exercise such as that conducted by Lockheed is recommended for all organizations as a check against unnecessary layers of management/supervision. At Nucor, for instance, there are only five levels of workers—the president, seven vice presidents, department managers, supervisors, and production workers.

CONTINUALLY IMPROVING AND REFINING SPECIFIC MANAGEMENT PRACTICES AND PROCEDURES

A study at a large U.S. firm revealed that 30 percent of the workers' time was wasted because of work scheduling problems alone. No one really knows how much of the workers' time is wasted by the sum total of all inefficient management practices. A senior vice president of a large U.S. firm made the following observations:[5]

- Managers are not sufficiently sensitive to the critical importance of accurate, timely sales forecasts in manufacturing detail. Hence, they don't anticipate well, are unresponsive to customer needs, and miss changes of strategic significance.
- Managers frequently have insufficient data to make the routine but critical decision of what to produce, when, and how many.
- American business systems give insufficient attention to reducing purchase and manufacturing lead times. As a result, American businesses lack flexibility and fail to achieve high levels of service to the customer.
- Many managers do not have a full appreciation of nonfinancial performance standards. As a consequence, they let them slip and deteriorate.

A number of firms in Cleveland are still using standards developed through motion and time studies conducted 25 years ago or longer. In

---

[5] A. William Reynolds, "What Can We Do About Productivity? A Management View," *The Gamut*, Fall 1980, pp. 58–62.

the interim, the jobs have changed to the point that there no longer is a relationship between what people are paid and the value of their work. How can the employees take their jobs seriously when they observe on a daily basis management's indifference to inefficiency?

A CALL TO ACTION

It is imperative that management communicates the importance that it places on productivity to its work force from top to bottom and to the larger community from which it draws employees. There is no better form of communications than through action. By communicating through actions the gospel of efficiency, the organization over time will encourage the departure of individuals who are content simply to put in their time and will attract persons who are committed to productivity and equity.

What is the biggest obstacle to the recommendations in this article? It is managers who are either unwilling or unable to implement them. Executives, managers, and supervisors must be evaluated periodically to see how well they are conforming to these principles; they should be rewarded or sanctioned according to the degree that they comply. Over time the recalcitrant ones need to be replaced with persons committed to lean, performance-based organizations.

Acme-Cleveland Corporation, a machine tool manufacturer faced with intense foreign competition, noncompetitive labor costs, and a rapidly changing marketplace, had to respond quickly or go out of business. Just before assuming the CEO role at Acme-Cleveland, B. Charles Ames met with about 60 of Acme-Cleveland's executives in December 1980 to outline his plans. In April 1984 Ames met again with the management team. This time there were 40 managers; only 6 had been at the previous meeting. Becoming cost-competitive with a radically new product line required a new corporate culture to which most of the old guard could not accommodate themselves. Good effort by well-intentioned people no longer can constitute acceptable performance. Although the agenda we have provided can be acted upon immediately, it is, nonetheless, a challenging one that will take time to complete. Yet, a journey of 10,000 miles begins with a single step.

Enlightened hardball management is not the same thing as sweatshop management or management by coercion, which, in the long run, will backfire. Americans do not tolerate being threatened for very long. Douglas Fraser, the recently retired president of the United Automobile Workers, best summarized the legacy of industrial despotism when he said "Unions don't organize workers. Bosses do." Enlightened hardball management holds all employees—including executives, managers, and staff personnel—to high standards, rewards them in proportion to their contributions, encourages genuine participation, and demands fair treatment. In other words, it is in every sense a two-way street. For those who contend that what we are suggesting is practical only for small- and medium-sized firms, we offer IBM as a rebuttal.

It is paramount to fix what is wrong with U.S. plants, shops, and offices. Relying on the last refuge of the myopic—off-shore production that will be sold in the U.S.—is in the long run suicidal. The American body politic, as it sees more and more jobs exported, will impose import restrictions that will make the Smoot-Hawley Act look like the work of free traders. To whom will the off-shore production be sold then, and what will be the impact on the world economy? Was the Great Depression not lesson enough?

Technology is a force that can increase productivity. Organizations need to adopt, to the extent economically possible, the state-of-the-art technology that applies to their business. Sound management practices coupled with modern technology constitute a winning formula regardless of the source and intensity of foreign competition. Nucor offers a superb example. At a time when the U.S. steel industry was on the ropes and experts were writing its obituary, Nucor grew from $113.2 million sales and $6.1 million profits in 1973 to $482.4 million sales, $45.1 million profits, and Fortune 500 status in 1980. This it accomplished by fusing sound management and the latest continuous casting technology.

Outboard Marine, the world's largest manufacturer of outboard motors, which are sold under the brand names of Evinrude and Johnson, was challenged in the United States and Europe by such redoubtable Japanese firms as Yamaha, Suzuki, and Honda. Initially, the Japanese companies eroded Outboard Marine's European market from 40 percent to 28 percent. Outboard Marine recaptured its former share of the European market, beat back the Japanese challenge in the U.S. market (Outboard Marine commands 50 percent of the U.S. market), and is seriously considering challenging the Japanese on their home ground. To do this, Outboard Marine combined the management practices discussed in this article with the latest technology.

Some people think that our problems are over because the economy is recovering and select groups of workers have granted some concessions. Consider this table, which expresses hourly pay levels abroad as percentages of the U.S. level. The estimates include fringe benefits, and all pay is calculated in U.S. dollars. The data was compiled by the Department of Labor.[6] Some of the gap is due to the

---

[6] Alfred L. Malabre, Jr., "Persistent Pay Gap: U.S. Wage Levels Stay Above Foreign Rivals' Despite Restraint Here," *The Wall Street Journal*, April 18, 1984, p. 1.

strength of the dollar, but most of it is not. If the table is not sufficiently somber, we need only contemplate the record trade deficits and their significance.

	1983	1982	1981
West Germany	84	89	96
Netherlands	78	84	90
Sweden	73	86	108
France	62	67	74
Italy	62	63	67
Britain	53	58	65
Japan	51	49	56
Brazil	14	21	20
Taiwan	13	13	14
Mexico	12	17	33
South Korea	10	10	10

The task of making American organizations productive again has just begun. The solutions lie not in the metaphysics of such recent books as *Theory Z, The Art of Japanese Management, In Search of Excellence,* and *The Next American Frontier,* but in the bread-and-butter issues that were once our strength and could be again.

30

The Ambiguity of Leadership*

JEFFREY PFEFFER

Problems with the concept of leadership are addressed: (a) the ambiguity of its definition and measurement, (b) the issue of whether leadership affects organizational performance, and (c) the process of selecting leaders, which frequently emphasizes organizationally irrelevant criteria. Leadership is a process of attributing causation to individual social actors. Study of leaders as symbols and of the process of attributing leadership might be productive.

Leadership has for some time been a major topic in social and organizational psychology. Underlying much of this research has been

* From *Academy of Management Review* 2, no. 1, (1977), pp. 104–12. An earlier version of this paper was presented at the conference, Leadership: Where Else Can We Go?, Center for Creative Leadership, Greensboro, North Carolina, June 30–July 1, 1975.

the assumption that leadership is causally related to organizational performance. Through an analysis of leadership styles, behaviors, or characteristics (depending on the theoretical perspective chosen), the argument has been made that more effective leaders can be selected or trained or, alternatively, the situation can be configured to provide for enhanced leader and organizational effectiveness.

Three problems with emphasis on leadership as a concept can be posed: (*a*) ambiguity in definition and measurement of the concept itself; (*b*) the question of whether leadership has discernible effects on organizational outcomes; and (*c*) the selection process in succession to leadership positions, which frequently uses organizationally irrelevant criteria and which has implications for normative theories of leadership. The argument here is that leadership is of interest primarily as a phenomenological construct. Leaders serve as symbols for representing personal causation of social events. How and why are such attributions of personal effects made? Instead of focusing on leadership and its effects, how do people make inferences about and react to phenomena labelled as leadership (5)?

THE AMBIGUITY OF THE CONCEPT

While there have been many studies of leadership, the dimensions and definition of the concept remain unclear. To treat leadership as a separate concept, it must be distinguished from other social influence phenomena. Hollander and Julian (24) and Bavelas (2) did not draw distinctions between leadership and other processes of social influence. A major point of the Hollander and Julian review was that leadership research might develop more rapidly if more general theories of social influence were incorporated. Calder (5) also argued that there is no unique content to the construct of leadership that is not subsumed under other, more general models of behavior.

Kochan, Schmidt, and DeCotiis (33) attempted to distinguish leadership from related concepts of authority and social power. In leadership, influence rights are voluntarily conferred. Power does not require goal compatibility—merely dependence—but leadership implies some congruence between the objectives of the leader and the led. These distinctions depend on the ability to distinguish voluntary from involuntary compliance and to assess goal compatibility. Goal statements may be retrospective inferences from action (46, 53) and problems of distinguishing voluntary from involuntary compliance also exist (32). Apparently there are few meaningful distinctions between leadership and other concepts of social influence. Thus, an understanding of the phenomena subsumed under the rubric of leadership may not require the construct of leadership (5).

While there is some agreement that leadership is related to social influence, more disagreement concerns the basic dimensions of leader behavior. Some have argued that there are two tasks to be accomplished in groups—maintenance of the group and performance of some task or activity—and thus leader behavior might be described along these two dimensions (1, 6, 8, 25). The dimensions emerging from the Ohio State leadership studies—consideration and initiating structure—may be seen as similar to the two components of group maintenance and task accomplishment (18).

Other dimensions of leadership behavior have also been proposed (4). Day and Hamblin (10) analyzed leadership in terms of the closeness and punitiveness of the supervision. Several authors have conceptualized leadership behavior in terms of the authority and discretion subordinates are permitted (23, 36, 51). Fiedler (14) analyzed leadership in terms of the least-preferred-co-worker scale (LPC), but the meaning and behavioral attributes of this dimension of leadership behavior remain controversial.

The proliferation of dimensions is partly a function of research strategies frequently employed. Factor analysis on a large number of items describing behavior has frequently been used. This procedure tends to produce as many factors as the analyst decides to find, and permits the development of a large number of possible factor structures. The resultant factors must be named and further imprecision is introduced. Deciding on a summative concept to represent a factor is inevitably a partly subjective process.

Literature assessing the effects of leadership tends to be equivocal. Sales (45) summarized leadership literature employing the authoritarian-democratic typology and concluded that effects on performance were small and inconsistent. Reviewing the literature on consideration and initiating structure dimensions, Korman (34) reported relatively small and inconsistent results, and Kerr and Schriesheim (30) reported more consistent effects of the two dimensions. Better results apparently emerge when moderating factors are taken into account, including subordinate personalities (50), and situational characteristics (23, 51). Kerr et al. (31) list many moderating effects grouped under the headings of subordinate considerations, supervisor considerations, and task considerations. Even if each set of considerations consisted of only one factor (which it does not), an attempt to account for the effects of leader behavior would necessitate considering four-way interactions. While social reality is complex and contingent, it seems desirable to attempt to find more parsimonious explanations for the phenomena under study.

THE EFFECTS OF LEADERS

Hall asked a basic question about leadership: Is there any evidence on the magnitude of the effects of leadership (17, p. 248)? Surprisingly, he could find little evidence. Given the resources that have been spent studying, selecting, and training leaders, one might expect that the question of whether or not leaders matter would have been addressed earlier (12).

There are at least three reasons why it might be argued that the observed effects of leaders on organizational outcomes would be small. First, those obtaining leadership positions are selected, and perhaps only certain, limited styles of behavior may be chosen. Second, once in the leadership position, the discretion and behavior of the leader are constrained. And third, leaders can typically affect only a few of the variables that may impact organizational performance.

Homogeneity of Leaders

Persons are selected to leadership positions. As a consequence of this selection process, the range of behaviors or characteristics exhibited by leaders is reduced, making it more problematic to empirically discover an effect of leadership. There are many types of constraints on the selection process. The attraction literature suggests that there is a tendency for persons to like those they perceive as similar (3). In critical decisions such as the selections of persons for leadership positions, compatible styles of behavior probably will be chosen.

Selection of persons is also constrained by the internal system of influence in the organization. As Zald (56) noted, succession is a critical decision, affected by political influence and by environmental contingencies faced by the organization. As Thompson (49) noted, leaders may be selected for their capacity to deal with various organizational contingencies. In a study of characteristics of hospital administrators, Pfeffer and Salancik (42) found a relationship between the hospital's context and the characteristics and tenure of the administrators. To the extent that the contingencies and power distribution within the organization remain stable, the abilities and behaviors of those selected into leadership positions will also remain stable.

Finally, the selection of persons to leadership positions is affected by a self-selection process. Organizations and roles have images, providing information about their character. Persons are likely to select themselves into organizations and roles based upon their preferences for the dimensions of the organizational and role characteristics as perceived through these images. The self-selection of persons would tend to work along with organizational selection to limit the range of abilities and behaviors in a given organizational role.

Such selection processes would tend to increase homogeneity more within a single organization than across organizations. Yet many studies of leadership effect at the work group level have compared groups within a single organization. If there comes to be a widely shared, socially constructed definition of leadership behaviors or characteristics which guides the selection process, then leadership activity may come to be defined similarly in various organizations, leading to the selection of only those who match the constructed image of a leader.

Constraints on Leader Behavior

Analyses of leadership have frequently presumed that leadership style or leader behavior was an independent variable that could be selected or trained at will to conform to what research would find to be optimal. Even theorists who took a more contingent view of appropriate leadership behavior generally assumed that with proper training, appropriate behavior could be produced (51). Fiedler (13), noting how hard it was to change behavior, suggested changing the situational characteristics rather than the person, but this was an unusual suggestion in the context of prevailing literature which suggested that leadership style was something to be strategically selected according to the variables of the particular leadership theory.

But the leader is embedded in a social system, which constrains behavior. The leader has a role set (27), in which members have expectations for appropriate behavior and persons make efforts to modify the leader's behavior. Pressures to conform to the expectations of peers, subordinates, and superiors are all relevant in determining actual behavior.

Leaders, even in high-level positions, have unilateral control over fewer resources and fewer policies than might be expected. Investment decisions may require approval of others, while hiring and promotion decisions may be accomplished by committees. Leader behavior is constrained by both the demands of others in the role set and by organizationally prescribed limitations on the sphere of activity and influence.

External Factors

Many factors that may affect organizational performance are outside a leader's control, even if he or she were to have complete discretion over major areas of organizational decisions. For example, consider the executive in a construction firm. Costs are largely determined by operation of commodities and labor markets; and demand is largely affected by interest rates, availability of mortgage money, and economic conditions which are affected by governmental policies over which the executive has little control. School superintendents have little control over birth rates and community economic development, both of which profoundly affect school system budgets. While the leader may react to contingencies as they arise, or may be a better or worse forecaster, in accounting for variation in organizational outcomes, he or she may account for relatively little compared to external factors.

Second, the leader's success or failure may be partly due to circumstances unique to the organization but still outside his or her control. Leader positions in organizations vary in terms of the strength and position of the organization. The choice of a new executive does not fundamentally alter a market and financial position that has developed over years and affects the leader's ability to make strategic changes and the likelihood that the organization will do well or poorly. Organizations have relatively enduring strengths and weaknesses. The choice of a particular leader for a particular position has limited impact on these capabilities.

Empirical Evidence

Two studies have assessed the effects of leadership changes in major positions in organizations. Lieberson and O'Connor (35) examined 167 business firms in 13 industries over a 20 year period, allocating variance in sales, profits, and profit margins to one of four sources: year (general economic conditions), industry, company effects, and effects of changes in the top executive position. They concluded that compared to other factors, administration had a limited effect on organizational outcomes.

Using a similar analytical procedure, Salancik and Pfeffer (44) examined the effects of mayors on city budgets for 30 U.S. cities. Data on expenditures by budget category were collected for 1951–1968. Variance in amount and proportion of expenditures was apportioned to the year, the city, or the mayor. The mayoral effect was relatively small, with the city accounting for most of the variance, although the mayor effect was larger for expenditure categories that were not as directly connected to important interest groups. Salancik and Pfeffer argued that the effects of the mayor were limited both by absence of power to control many of the expenditures and tax sources, and by construction of policies in response to demands from interests in the environment.

If leadership is defined as a strictly interpersonal phenomenon, the relevance of these two studies for the issue of leadership effects becomes problematic. But such a conceptualization seems unduly restrictive, and is certainly inconsistent with Selznick's (47) conceptualization of leadership as strategic management and decision making. If one cannot observe differences when leaders change, then what does it matter who occupies the positions or how they behave?

Pfeffer and Salancik (41) investigated the extent to which behaviors selected by first-line supervisors were constrained by expectations of others in their role set. Variance in task and social behaviors could be accounted for by role-set expectations, with adherence to various demands made by role-set participants a function of similarity and relative power. Lowin and Craig (37) experimentally demonstrated that leader behavior was determined by the subordinate's own behavior. Both studies illustrate that leader behaviors are responses to the demands of the social context.

The effect of leadership may vary depending upon level in the organizational hierarchy, while the appropriate activities and behaviors may also vary with organizational level (26, 40). For the most part, empirical studies of leadership have dealt with first-line supervisors or leaders with relatively low organizational status (17). If leadership has any impact, it should be more evident at higher organizational levels or where there is more discretion in decisions and activities.

THE PROCESS OF SELECTING LEADERS

Along with the suggestion that leadership may not account for much variance in organizational outcomes, it can be argued that merit or ability may not account for much variation in hiring and advancement of organizational personnel. These two ideas are related. If competence is hard to judge, or if leadership competence does not greatly affect organizational outcomes, then other, person-dependent criteria may be sufficient. Effective leadership styles may not predict career success when other variables such as social background are controlled.

Belief in the importance of leadership is frequently accompanied by belief that persons occupying leadership positions are selected and trained according to how well they can enhance the organization's performance. Belief in a leadership effect leads to development of a set of activities oriented toward enhancing leadership effectiveness. Simultaneously, persons managing their own careers are likely to place emphasis on activities and developing behaviors that will enhance their own leadership skills, assuming that such a strategy will facilitate advancement.

Research on the bases of hiring and promotion has been concentrated in examination of academic positions (e.g., 7, 19, 20). This is possibly the result of availability of relatively precise and unambiguous measures of performance, such as number of publications or citations. Evidence on criteria used in selecting and advancing personnel in industry is more indirect.

Studies have attempted to predict either the compensation or the attainment of general management positions of MBA students, using personality and other background information (21, 22, 54). There is some evidence that managerial success can be predicted by indicators of ability and motivation such as test scores and grades, but the amount of variance explained is typically quite small.

A second line of research has investigated characteristics and backgrounds of persons attaining leadership positions in major organizations in society. Domhoff (11), Mills (38), and Warner and Abbeglin (52) found a strong preponderance of persons with upper-class backgrounds occupying leadership positions. The implication of these findings is that studies of graduate success, including the success of MBA's, would explain more variance if the family background of the person were included.

A third line of inquiry uses a tracking model. The dynamic model developed is one in which access to elite universities is affected by social status (28) and, in turn, social status and attendance at elite universities affect later career outcomes (9, 43, 48, 55).

Unless one is willing to make the argument that attendance at elite universities or coming from an upper class background is perfectly correlated with merit, the evidence suggests that succession to leadership positions is not strictly based on meritocratic criteria. Such a conclusion is consistent with the inability of studies attempting to predict the success of MBA graduates to account for much variance, even when a variety of personality and ability factors are used.

Beliefs about the bases for social mobility are important for social stability. As long as persons believe that positions are allocated on meritocratic grounds, they are more likely to be satisfied with the social order and with their position in it. This satisfaction derives from the belief that occupational position results from application of fair and reasonable criteria, and that the opportunity exists for mobility if the person improves skills and performance.

If succession to leadership positions is determined by person-based criteria such as social origins or social connections (16), then efforts to enhance managerial effectiveness with the expectation that this will lead to career success divert attention from the processes of stratification actually operating within organizations. Leadership literature has been implicitly aimed at two audiences. Organizations were told how to become more effective, and persons were told what behaviors to acquire in order to become effective, and hence, advance in their careers. The possibility that neither organizational outcomes nor career success are related to leadership behaviors leaves leadership research facing issues of relevance and importance.

THE ATTRIBUTION OF LEADERSHIP

Kelley conceptualized the layman as:

> an applied scientist, that is, as a person concerned about applying his knowledge of causal relationships in order to *exercise control* of his world (29, p. 2).

Reviewing a series of studies dealing with the attributional process, he concluded that persons were not only interested in understanding their world correctly, but also in controlling it.

> The view here proposed is that attribution processes are to be understood not only as a means of providing the individual with a veridical view of his world, but as a means of encouraging and maintaining his effective exercise of control in that world (29, p. 22).

Controllable factors will have high salience as candidates for causal explanation, while a bias toward the more important causes may shift the attributional emphasis toward causes that are not controllable (29, p. 23). The study of attribution is a study of naive psychology—an examination of how persons make sense out of the events taking place around them.

If Kelley is correct that individuals will tend to develop attributions that give them a feeling of control, then emphasis on leadership may derive partially from a desire to believe in the effectiveness and importance of individual action, since individual action is more controllable than contextual variables. Lieberson and O'Connor (35) made essentially the same point in introducing their paper on the effects of top management changes on organizational performance. Given the desire for control and a feeling of personal effectiveness, organizational outcomes are more likely to be attributed to individual actions, regardless of their actual causes.

Leadership is attributed by observers. Social action has meaning only through a phenomenological process (46). The identification of certain organizational roles as leadership positions guides the construction of meaning in the direction of attributing effects to the actions of those positions. While Bavelas (2) argued that the functions of leadership, such as task accomplishment and group maintenance, are shared throughout the group, this fact provides no simple and potentially controllable focus for attributing causality. Rather, the identification of leadership positions provides a simpler and more readily changeable model of reality. When causality is lodged in one or a few persons rather than being a function of a complex set of interactions among all group members, changes can be made by replacing or influencing the occupant of the leadership position. Causes of organizational actions are readily identified in this simple causal structure.

Even if, empirically, leadership has little effect, and even if succession to leadership positions is not predicated on ability or performance, the belief in leadership effects and meritocratic succession provides a simple causal framework and a justification for the structure of the social collectivity. More importantly, the beliefs interpret social actions in terms that indicate potential for effective individual intervention or control. The personification of social causality serves too many uses to be easily overcome. Whether or not leader behavior actually influences performance or effectiveness, it is important because people believe it does.

One consequence of the attribution of causality to leaders and leadership is that leaders come to be symbols. Mintzberg (39), in his discussion of the roles of managers, wrote of the symbolic role, but more in terms of attendance at formal events and formally representing the organization. The symbolic role of leadership is more important than implied in such a description. The leader as a symbol provides a target for action when difficulties occur, serving as a scapegoat when things go wrong. Gamson and Scotch (15) noted that in baseball, the firing of the manager served a scapegoating purpose. One cannot fire the whole team, yet when performance is poor, something must be done. The firing of the manager conveys to the world and to the actors involved that success is the result of personal actions, and that steps can and will be taken to enhance organizational performance.

The attribution of causality to leadership may be reinforced by organizational actions, such as the inauguration process, the choice process, and providing the leader with symbols and ceremony. If leaders are chosen by using a random number table, persons are less likely to believe in their effects than if there is an elaborate search or selection process followed by an elaborate ceremony signifying the changing of control, and if the leader then has a variety of perquisites and symbols that distinguish him or her from the rest of the organization. Construction of the importance of leadership in a given social context is the outcome of various social processes, which can be empirically examined.

Since belief in the leadership effect provides a feeling of personal control, one might argue that efforts to increase the attribution of causality to leaders would occur more when it is more necessary and more problematic to attribute causality to controllable factors. Such an argument would lead to the hypothesis that the more the *context* actually effects organizational outcomes, the more efforts will be made to ensure attribution to *leadership*. When leaders really do have effects, it is less necessary to engage in rituals indicating their effects. Such rituals are more likely when there is uncertainty and unpredictability associated with the organization's operations. This results both from the desire to feel control in uncertain situations and from the fact that in ambiguous contexts, it is easier to attribute consequences to leadership without facing possible disconfirmation.

The leader is, in part, an actor. Through statements and actions, the leader attempts to reinforce the operation of an attribution process which tends to vest causality in that position in the social structure. Successful leaders, as perceived by members of the social system, are those who can separate themselves from organizational failures and associate themselves with organizational successes. Since the meaning of action is socially constructed, this involves manipulation of symbols to reinforce the desired process of attribution. For instance, if a manager knows that business in his or her division is about to improve because of the economic cycle, the leader may, nevertheless, write recommendations and undertake actions and changes that are highly visible and that will tend to identify his or her behavior closely with the division. A manager who perceives impending failure will attempt to associate the division and its policies and decisions with others, particularly persons in higher organizational positions, and to disassociate himself or herself from the division's performance, occasionally even transferring or moving to another organization.

CONCLUSION

The theme of this article has been that analysis of leadership and leadership processes must be contingent on the intent of the researcher. If the interest is in understanding the causality of social phenomena as reliably and accurately as possible, then the concept of leadership may be a poor place to begin. The issue of the effects of leadership is open to question. But examination of situational variables that accompany more or less leadership effect is a worthwhile task.

The more phenomenological analysis of leadership directs attention to the process by which social causality is attributed, and focuses on the distinction between causality as perceived by group members and causality as assessed by an outside observer. Leadership is associated with a set of myths reinforcing a social construction of meaning which legitimates leadership role occupants, provides belief in potential mobility for those not in leadership roles, and attributes social causality to leadership roles, thereby providing a belief in the effectiveness of individual control. In analyzing leadership, this mythology and the process by which such mythology is created and supported should be separated from analysis of leadership as a social influence process, operating within constraints.

REFERENCES

1. Bales, R. F. *Interaction Process Analysis: A Method for the Study of Small Groups* (Reading, Mass.: Addison-Wesley, 1950).
2. Bavelas, Alex. "Leadership: Man and Function," *Administrative Science Quarterly* 4 (1960), pp. 491–98.
3. Berscheid, Ellen, and Elaine Walster. *Interpersonal Attraction* (Reading, Mass.: Addison-Wesley, 1969).
4. Bowers, David G., and Stanley E. Seashore. "Predicting Organizational Effectiveness with a Four-Factor Theory of Leadership," *Administrative Science Quarterly* 11 (1966), pp. 238–63.
5. Calder, Bobby J. "An Attribution Theory of Leadership," in *New Directions in Organizational Behavior*, ed. B. Staw and G. Salancik (Chicago: St. Clair Press, 1976).
6. Cartwright, Dorwin C., and Alvin Zander. *Group Dynamics: Research and Theory*, 3d ed. (Evanston, Ill.: Row, Peterson, 1960).
7. Cole, Jonathan R., and Stephen Cole. *Social Stratification in Science* (Chicago: University of Chicago Press, 1973).
8. Collins, Barry E., and Harold Guetzkow. *A Social Psychology of Group Processes for Decision Making* (New York: Wiley, 1964).
9. Collins, Randall. "Functional and Conflict Theories of Stratification," *American Sociological Review* 36 (1971), pp. 1002–19.
10. Day, R. C., and R. L. Hamblin. "Some Effects of Close and Punitive Styles of Supervision," *American Journal of Sociology* 69 (1964), pp. 499–510.
11. Domhoff, G. William. *Who Rules America?* (Englewood Cliffs, N.J.: Prentice-Hall, 1967).
12. Dubin, Robert. "Supervision and Productivity: Empirical Findings and Theoretical Considerations," in *Leadership and Productivity*, ed. R. Dubin, G. C. Homans, F. C. Mann, and D. C. Miller (San Francisco: Chandler Publishing, 1965), pp. 1–50.
13. Fiedler, Fred E. "Engineering the Job to Fit the Manager," *Harvard Business Review* 43 (1965), pp. 115–22.
14. Fiedler, Fred E. *A Theory of Leadership Effectiveness* (New York: McGraw-Hill, 1967).
15. Gamson, William A., and Norman A. Scotch, "Scapegoating in Baseball," *American Journal of Sociology* 70 (1964), pp. 69–72.
16. Granovetter, Mark. *Getting a Job* (Cambridge, Mass.: Harvard University Press, 1974).
17. Hall, Richard H. *Organizations: Structure and Process* (Englewood Cliffs, N.J.: Prentice-Hall, 1972).
18. Halpin, A. W., and J. Winer. "A Factorial Study of the Leader Behavior Description Questionnaire," in *Leader Behavior: Its Description and Measurement*, ed. R. M. Stogdill and A. E. Coons (Columbus, Ohio: Bureau of Business Research, Ohio State University, 1957), pp. 39–51.
19. Hargens, L. L. "Patterns of Mobility of New Ph.D.'s among American Academic Institutions," *Sociology of Education* 42 (1969), pp. 18–37.

20. Hargens, L. L., and W. O. Hagstrom. "Sponsored and Contest Mobility of American Academic Scientists," *Sociology of Education* 40 (1967), pp. 24–38.

21. Harrell, Thomas W. "High Earning MBA's," *Personnel Psychology* 25 (1972), pp. 523–30.

22. Harrell, Thomas W., and Margaret S. Harrell. "Predictors of Management Success." *Stanford University Graduate School of Business, Technical Report No. 3 to the Office of Naval Research*.

23. Heller, Frank, and Gary Yukl. "Participation, Managerial Decision Making, and Situational Variables," *Organizational Behavior and Human Performance* 4 (1969), pp. 227–41.

24. Hollander, Edwin P., and James W. Julian. "Contemporary Trends in the Analysis of Leadership Processes," *Psychological Bulletin* 71 (1969), pp. 387–97.

25. House, Robert J. "A Path Goal Theory of Leader Effectiveness," *Administrative Science Quarterly* 16 (1971), pp. 321–38.

26. Hunt, J. G. "Leadership-Style Effects at Two Managerial Levels in a Simulated Organization," *Administrative Science Quarterly* 16 (1971), pp. 476–85.

27. Kahn, R. L., D. M. Wolfe, R. P. Quinn, and J. D. Snoek. *Organizational Stress: Studies in Role Conflict and Ambiguity* (New York: Wiley, 1964).

28. Karabel, J., and A. W. Astin. "Social Class, Academic Ability, and College 'Quality'," *Social Forces* 53 (1975), pp. 381–98.

29. Kelley, Harold H. *Attribution in Social Interaction* (Morristown, N.J.: General Learning Press, 1971).

30. Kerr, Steven, and Chester Schriesheim. "Consideration, Initiating Structure and Organizational Criteria—An Update of Korman's 1966 Review," *Personnel Psychology* 27 (1974), pp. 555–68.

31. Kerr, S., C. Schriesheim, C. J. Murphy, and R. M. Stogdill, "Toward a Contingency Theory of Leadership Based Upon the Consideration and Initiating Structure Literature," *Organizational Behavior and Human Performance* 12 (1974), pp. 62–82.

32. Kiesler, C., and S. Kiesler. *Conformity* (Reading, Mass.: Addison-Wesley, 1969).

33. Kochan, T. A., S. M. Schmidt, and T. A. DeCotiis. "Superior-Subordinate Relations: Leadership and Headship," *Human Relations* 28 (1975), pp. 279–94.

34. Korman, A. K. "Consideration, Initiating Structure, and Organizational Criteria—A Review," *Personnel Psychology* 19 (1966), pp. 349–62.

35. Lieberson, Stanley, and James F. O'Connor. "Leadership and Organizational Performance: A Study of Large Corporations," *American Sociological Review* 37 (1972), pp. 117–30.

36. Lippitt, Ronald. "An Experimental Study of the Effect of Democratic and Authoritarian Group Atmospheres," *University of Iowa Studies in Child Welfare* 16 (1940), pp. 43–195.

37. Lowin, A., and J. R. Craig. "The Influence of Level of Performance on Managerial Style: An Experimental Object-Lesson in the Ambiguity of Correlational Data," *Organizational Behavior and Human Performance* 3 (1968), pp. 440–58.

38. Mills, C. Wright. "The American Business Elite: A Collective Portrait," in *Power, Politics, and People*, ed. C. W. Mills (New York: Oxford University Press, 1963), pp. 110–39.
39. Mintzberg, Henry. *The Nature of Managerial Work* (New York: Harper and Row, 1973).
40. Nealey, Stanley M., and Milton R. Blood. "Leadership Performance of Nursing Supervisors at Two Organizational Levels," *Journal of Applied Psychology* 52 (1968), pp. 414–42.
41. Pfeffer, Jeffrey, and Gerald R. Salancik. "Determinants of Supervisory Behavior: A Role Set Analysis," *Human Relations* 28 (1975), pp. 139–54.
42. Pfeffer, Jeffrey, and Gerald R. Salancik. "Organizational Context and the Characteristics and Tenure of Hospital Administrators," *Academy of Management Journal* 20 (1977).
43. Reed, R. H., and H. P. Miller. "Some Determinants of the Variation in Earnings per College Men," *Journal of Human Resources* 5 (1970), 117–90.
44. Salancik, Gerald R., and Jeffrey Pfeffer. "Constraints on Administrator Discretion: The Limited Influence of Mayors on City Budgets," *Urban Affairs Quarterly*, in press.
45. Sales, Stephen M. "Supervisory Style and Productivity: Review and Theory," *Personnel Psychology* 19 (1966), pp. 275–86.
46. Schutz, Alfred. *The Phenomenology of the Social World* (Evanston, Ill.: Northwestern University Press, 1967).
47. Selznick, P. *Leadership in Administration* (Evanston, Ill.: Row, Peterson, 1957).
48. Spaeth, J. L., and A. M. Greeley. *Recent Alumni and Higher Education* (New York: McGraw-Hill, 1970).
49. Thompson, James D. *Organizations in Action* (New York: McGraw-Hill, 1967).
50. Vroom, Victor H. "Some Personality Determinants of the Effects of Participation," *Journal of Abnormal and Social Psychology* 59 (1959), pp. 322–27.
51. Vroom, Victor H., and Phillip W. Yetton. *Leadership and Decision Making* (Pittsburgh: University of Pittsburgh Press, 1973).
52. Warner, W. L., and J. C. Abbeglin. *Big Business Leaders in America* (New York: Harper and Row, 1955).
53. Weick, Karl E. *The Social Psychology of Organizing* (Reading, Mass.: Addison-Wesley, 1969).
54. Weinstein, Alan G., and V. Srinivasan. "Predicting Managerial Success of Master of Business Administration (MBA) Graduates," *Journal of Applied Psychology* 59 (1974), pp. 207–12.
55. Wolfle, Dael. *The Uses of Talent* (Princeton: Princeton University Press, 1971).
56. Zald, Mayer N. "Who Shall Rule? A Political Analysis of Succession in a Large Welfare Organization," *Pacific Sociological Review* 8 (1965), pp. 52–60.

section six

Organizations: Structure, Environment, and Change

Introduction

We concluded the previous section with an article (by Jeffrey Pfeffer) which suggested that leaders—even at the highest levels of rank—receive too much credit and too much blame for what happens in organizations. To begin with, Pfeffer argued that leaders have little latitude for action because of internal constraints; and, furthermore, external forces largely determine the fortunes of organizations. In this section we examine more carefully the "big picture" of the internal structure of organizations, going beyond the level of individual or small group behavior, and we take due account of the external environmental forces that constrain organizational choice.

A selection from the work of Mariann Jelinek describes the various "basic conformations" or types of formal structure that may characterize organizations. To some extent, structure evolves through experience; yet to some extent, structure is also a matter of deliberate choice. In either case, structure depends on the stage of development of the organization, strategies for survival and growth, product line, and technology.

Miles, Snow, Meyer, and Coleman elaborate upon the importance of a proper fit between overall strategy and a corresponding structure. They proceed to identify three types of strategy-structure combinations, each effective in certain environments. A fourth type, the "Reactor," is predicted to fail precisely because of the absence of alignment between distinctive strategy and structure.

Galbraith approaches the issue of structure from the standpoint of the information-processing needs of an organization. These needs depend upon such factors as the diversity of product line, complexity of technology, and market uncertainties.

Not all structure is contained within the formal anatomy of an organization; structure may take the form of a "strong culture." Indeed, Pascale suggests that the perenially excellent companies depend more on culture than bureaucracy to provide structure. He analyzes the process by which new members are socialized into such cultures.

According to Kets de Vries and Miller, organizational cultures can be "neurotic" as well as strong. Drawing from their consulting experience, they sketch the elements of five types of pathological cultures that exhibit symptoms analogous to the behavior of neurotic individuals.

Few citizens today question the imperative that firms have a "social responsibility" to discharge. In the selection concluding this volume, Dalton and Cosier examine four contrasting definitions of this obligation.

31

Organization Structure: The Basic Conformations*

MARIANN JELINEK

A key issue in organization design is the choice of the main structural conformation. There are varieties of each form, and a range of possible styles within the forms. Nevertheless, the choice of one or another of the basic configurations is the selection of certain capabilities and benefits—and certain disadvantages and potential problems as well. The choice implies constraints of a fundamental nature.

What are the main options, and what are their associated constraints? What are the forms' strengths and weaknesses, and the trade-offs involved in choice of one as against another? These topics will be the subject of this paper. In passing, we shall also make reference to various dimensions of structure and other organizational factors, such as strategy and environment, which affect the organization designer's choice. We will deal with the basic organizational configurations as they evolved historically—although clearly no organization is compelled to repeat this historical sequence.

THE SIMPLE ORGANIZATION OR "AGENCY" FORM

The simple organization is one with little or no structure; it typically consists of the boss (owner, leader, or manager) and the employees or workers. An example would be a workshop in which a master craftperson supervised a number of apprentices or helpers. Direction or coordination is provided by personal supervision, and each worker acts as the *agent* or extension of the boss. More extensive examples would include most large organizations before the evolution of formal, bureaucratic means of organizing. For example, kings directed extensive establishments personally, and each subordinate's authority and

---

* This selection was specially written by Mariann Jelinek for inclusion in *Organizations by Design*, ed. Mariann Jelinek, Joseph A. Litterer, and Raymond E. Miles (Plano, Tex.: Business Publications, 1981), where it first appeared. © 1981, Mariann Jelinek.

power derived directly from a relationship with the king, whose agent the subordinate was. More modern examples of the larger sort are difficult to identify, with the possible exception of some religious, cult, or political groups. Here, too, the subordinates' power and authority derive directly from the leader; it is as agents of the leader, doing whatever is required, that the subordinates act. Typically, such a subordinate owes responsibility only to the leader personally, rather than for a position, and duties are defined by the leader's requests.

Many organizations begin as simple organizations. An entrepreneur with an idea hires others to assist in its realization. Typically, each employee does what the entrepreneur directs, and, particularly at initial stages, there is little or no formality. Anyone can be asked to do whatever needs doing, the work is the responsibility of all organization members, under the personal direction of the entrepreneur. As Mintzberg (1979) has pointed out, such organizations are flexible, but decidedly limited in their capacity to cope with complexity. They tend to operate simple technologies in simple environments, in order that needed coordination can take place through the leader—whose capacity to process information is necessarily limited.

DIVIDING THE WORK

Most organizations quickly become more formalized than the simple agency model. As an early step in formalization, work is explicitly divided. Thus the interest of Adam Smith (1776) and Charles Babbage (1832) in the steps or functions that went into pin making: formally dividing the work, and assigning different individuals responsibility for different parts, substitutes this structure for a portion of the control exercised by the leader in the agency or simple form. People no longer must be told what to do; instead they're assigned to do one specific portion of the work regularly. Their responsibility is limited to that portion of the work.

As Smith and Babbage noted, dividing the work permits significant advantages because it facilitates specialization. Among the results are increases in efficiency, speed, and expertise; reduced waste; less time to learn the job (because less must be learned, and more frequent repetition speeds the process); and less time lost in changing from one tool or operation to another. The same advantages accrue whether the work to be subdivided is pin making, assembling an automobile or refrigerator, teaching or engineering: specialization permits development of in-depth knowledge, experience, and facility *within a limited area*. Thus a large and complex task is often better accomplished by dividing it into smaller, more comprehensible pieces. In particular, where the range of skills required in a large task differ markedly, or where the strength or time requirements of different portions of the task differ, division of labor offers advantages.

The consequences of division of work are not wholly positive, however. Once the work is divided, people tend to orient themselves toward their portion of the work, rather than toward other portions, or toward the task as a whole. This orientation colors department members' perceptions, for instance, so that they quite naturally seek to make their own work easier and more meaningful, to acquire a larger share of resources, and to exercise more control over the flow of work to them and from them to others. Essentially, people behave in ways consistent with the structuring of tasks. Division of the work makes one portion of it central to them, and they proceed to behave in just that fashion—as if their portion of the work were central. These tendencies are called "suboptimization," the optimizing of a portion of the work, rather than the whole. They constitute one potentially dysfunctional consequence of dividing the work.

FUNCTIONAL FORM

The systematic division of work, typically reflected in departments, is fairly obvious. Somewhat less obvious is the basis for dividing it. How should the work be divided? There are numerous ways of dividing the work, and, given the potential consequences, the designer should choose knowledgeably from among the options. The basis on which work is divided will implicitly set the various departments' goals, and define members' perceptions. If we note that "function" means "a portion of the tasks or activities necessary" (Litterer, 1973), we will have a starting place. By functional form, we mean an organizational structure that divides the work among departments or units, each responsible for a portion of it. Some common bases for dividing work among functional departments would include (see Figures 1–5):

Business Function: Manufacturing, sales, personnel, R&D departments.

Managerial Function: Controller, planning, operations.

Technical Function or Process: Painting, welding, stamping, assembly.

Similar Tools or Techniques: Typing, operations research, computer center.

Time: Day shift, evening shift.

Shared Product or Purpose: Maintenance, editorial department, police.

Geographic Location: Kalamazoo plant, New England region.

Client Served: Consumer sales, government contracts, industrial equipment.

FIGURE 1
Functional Departments—Manufacturing Firm—Highly Centralized

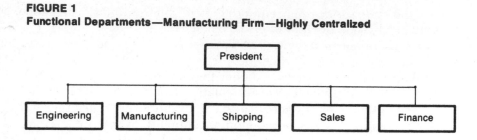

FIGURE 2
Functional Departments—School

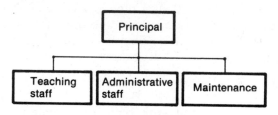

FIGURE 3
Functional Departments—Hospital

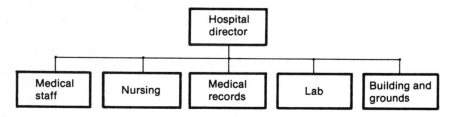

FIGURE 4A
Departments by Managerial Function and Process

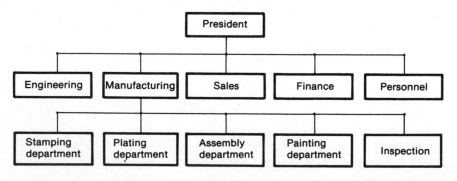

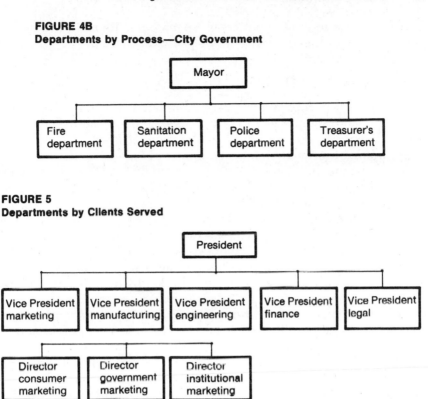

FIGURE 4B
Departments by Process—City Government

FIGURE 5
Departments by Clients Served

Some of these distinctions rest upon the activities of the manufacturing process, others on the output or client, still others on characteristics like time or location. It is important to note that the distinctions are not precise and mutually exclusive. Indeed, they are often used in combinations, particularly in more complex organizational forms. When someone refers to a "functional organization structure," she or he means an organization in which each department performs only a portion of the needed activities of the organization, with coordination occurring at top levels. It is often provided by the president (as in Figures 1, 4A and 4B, for instance)—making the functional form a logical successor to the agency organization, for the top manager still maintains a large amount of control. Functional organization identifies key aspects of the task, and clearly assigns responsibility for them. It permits and encourages specialization around these key tasks. Its disadvantages, beyond suboptimization, include potential difficulties in work flow between and among departments, and information overload as top managers become overwhelmed with too many coordinating decisions. This form of organization *specializes;* its main problem is *reintegration* of the specialized, differentiated activities.

DIVISIONAL STRUCTURE

While product departments were mentioned above, most typically product organization occurs in larger organizations that have evolved several distinctly different products or product lines. It usually implies product coordination at least one level *below* top management. Historically, the divisional structure evolved first at Du Pont and General Motors, to meet a specific set of needs. Du Pont, which was reorganized from a cluster of family-owned predecessor firms in 1902, was soon expanded further by acquisition into the largest explosives manufacturing company in the United States. Du Pont had some 31 factories producing three main product lines—dynamite, black powder, and smokeless military gunpowder. The products were sufficiently different in raw materials, manufacture, and marketing to multiply complexities further. A great many new administrative mechanisms—like uniform and systematic information on costs and revenues, and rational allocation procedures—had to be evolved to make possible the coordination of so many activities.

Because of the differences in the product lines, the basic structure selected was organization into three operating departments, one for each product line. Within each, a functional structure was set up. The operating departments shared a common accounting system, and a common system for evaluating unit performance (return on investment). Resources for investment were allocated from the top. It was clear from the outset, however, that running so large and so complex an organization would require more managerial capacity than just a single chief executive. To coordinate and manage the firm as a whole—in contrast to the individual departments within it—an executive committee made up of the operating department heads was formed. This structure explicitly recognized the need for both product line, or operating responsibilities, and for organizationwide, coordinative responsibilities. It was only thus, by explicitly monitoring and managing relationships among the product lines, that the company as a whole could avoid the inefficiencies that had plagued the predecessor companies. The explicit charge of the executive committee was to coordinate and integrate activities for the firm as a whole. (See Figure 6 for a simplified organization chart.) Over time, the distinction between product line operations and the overall management of the firm was more strongly drawn, and more clearly reflected in structure by ensuring that the operating department heads were not the majority membership of the executive committee. Instead, corporate-level executives were appointed. This separation of tasks allowed the company to concentrate on new products, to allocate investment among the competing activities of the various product lines rationally, and to attend to financing new capital for expansion.

FIGURE 6
Du Pont's Organization Prior to 1911 (much simplified)

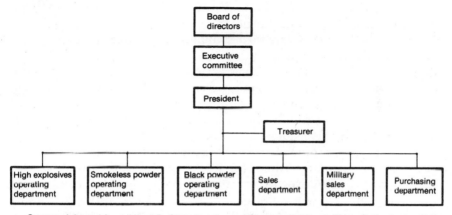

Source: Adapted from Alfred D. Chandler, Jr., and Stephen Salisbury, *Pierre S. Du Pont and the Making of the Modern Corporation* (New York: Harper & Row, 1976).

Du Pont's original structure made use of product-line form (the operating departments), functional departmentalization (within the main operating departments), and of staff as well as line managers. These innovations were essentially structural means to divide the work *of management*, distinguishing various product operations from corporate management, and from the specialized ancillary support functions not concerned directly with operations. By providing structural legitimacy for all of these functions, Du Pont's divisional structure achieved a high order of performance in a vastly more complex business situation than had existed before.

GENERAL MOTORS

General Motors, too, evolved a divisional structure in response to product-line differences. However, the genesis was different from Du Pont's. GM was founded by William C. Durant, who assembled it from widely diverse companies manufacturing everything from entire automobiles—such as Cadillac, Buick, Oakland, and even Cartercar—to components, tractors, an early refrigerator, and other things. Each had originally been an independent firm. There was no overall structure, to begin with, and no communication among different portions of the company. Aside from the name, the various factories shared little. In the absence of controls or coordination, the various lines competed with one another, not only for financial resources within the firm, but outside it, in the marketplace as well.

GM's product line, even after some eliminations, contained 10 car models and seven brands. All but two were losing money in 1921. Since the products competed directly (as smokeless powder and dynamite did not, at Du Pont), coordination was even more essential. The problem at GM was to retain the advantages of decentralized independence—which permitted each division to specialize itself to concentrate on a specific market niche—while coordinating the whole firm. The design problem was to combine centralized control on financial and policy matters (to coordinate among divisions) with decentralized operations (to ensure timely and adequate operating decisions). Under Durant, the executive committee had consisted of the heads of the operating divisions (much like Du Pont's first structure), and had exercised little or no control. After Durant's bankruptcy, the firm was reorganized with a new executive committee. The division heads were retained in an advisory capacity, but were not executive committee members. A central financial staff, answerable to the executive committee, directed accounting and reporting procedures to ensure complete and comparable data. The divisions and their products were reduced, streamlined, and positioned so that each division was responsible for a single product-line and a specific price range designated by the executive committee.

This basic structure reflected the philosophy of the company (see Figure 7): divisions should be autonomous and operate independently within broad policy boundaries laid down by the corporation. Policy should be a corporate responsibility, aimed at corporate coordination. The corporation would direct the reporting and accounting procedures, and would allocate financial resources. This philosophy, and this structure, continues to the present day with relatively little change. GM grew to be the largest producer of automobiles in the world with this structure.

ADMINISTRATIVE STRUCTURES

As organizations grew more complex, greater use was made of formal arrangements, written records and procedures, and explicit assignment of responsibilities. This formality offered many advantages, as Max Weber noted. Weber described a completely specified organization, which he called "bureaucracy" (from the French word for office, *bureau*). Weber's description was "an ideal type," or a model ab-

FIGURE 7
Simplified Organization Chart, General Motors, 1924

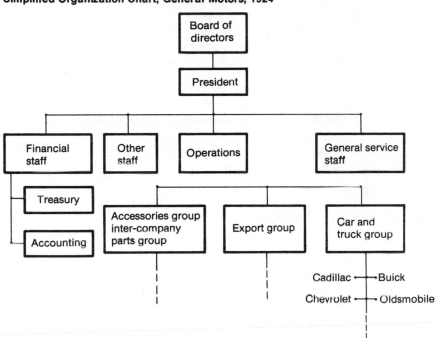

Source: Adapted from Alfred D. Chandler, Jr., and Stephen Salisbury, *Pierre S. Du Pont and the Making of the Modern Corporation* (New York: Harper & Row, 1976).

stracted from the compromises required in the real world. By ignoring such compromises, the ideal type highlights the characteristics of bureaucracy. A bureaucracy, according to Weber, was rules based, in stark contrast to the earlier agency forms based on the leader's preference. As a result, the bureaucratic form provided a notable advance in efficiency, reliability, and predictability. The chief characteristics of the bureaucracy were:

1. Tasks are assigned to specific organization units and members as official duties, attached to *positions* (not individuals).
2. Authority is hierarchical, with higher positions holding greater authority, responsibility, and control. Power is concentrated at the top.
3. Formal rules govern behavior, ensuring uniformity in order to facilitate coordination.
4. Organization membership is a full-time commitment, typically a career for life.

5. Training and expertise are the basis for recruitment. There is a high degree of specialization.
6. Promotion is by seniority and merit.
7. Official activities are carefully segregated from private life; people act in accordance with their roles, not their preferences.
8. Files record and summarize all organizational activities.

Weber was aware of some drawbacks to this sort of organization, but he emphasized the advantages of the form in contrast to earlier methods of organizing. Predictability, reliability, increased output, lessened friction, discretion, and reduced material and personal costs were all advantages he cited as deriving from the technical superiority of the bureaucratic form.

THE DEGREE OF FORMALITY

The advantages of bureaucracy are so great that virtually every modern organization is, to some degree, "bureaucratic." This formality may be limited to an explicit division of labor, allowing and encouraging specialization, for instance. It may even be required by law: for example, hospitals are required to hire only specialists (medical doctors and trained nurses and technicians) to perform medical services. Even in private enterprises manufacturing proprietary materials for profit, such degrees of formality as explicit and accurate records of costs and revenues, payments and taxes, inspections, and injuries are required. These are all examples of formality. Such measures as the number of specialist job categories, differing from one another so that incumbents are not immediately interchangeable, provide one indication of the degree of formality in an organization. Another measure is the degree to which procedures are specified in advance. If most activity within the organization is governed by protocol or procedure, and there is a set response to most situations, we can identify the organization as quite formal. Such organizations typically also have many levels of hierarchy, and require that situations that fall outside the set rules of operation be referred upward, to superiors. So, too, with conflict or differences between different departments or units. Such an organization is often referred to as "mechanistic" (Burns and Stalker, 1961) because it is expected to operate like a machine.

At its extreme, the "machine bureaucracy" centralizes power and decision making, reserving them to the top executive. At the extreme, such an organization is rigid and highly formal—everything is specified, and organization members are allowed virtually no discretion. The underlying assumption is that tasks, environment, and circumstances will always remain the same. Of course the extreme is far more rigid and specific than real-world organization structures would be.

Nevertheless, it is clear that a range of bureaucratization is possible. To the degree that an organization does rely on rules, specify the duties of members, rely on specialists and so on, it is bureaucratic. To the extent that decision making is delegated downward, initiative is permitted or encouraged, and informal arrangements vary the procedures, the organization is less bureaucratic. Virtually every organization of any size, public or private, is to some degree bureaucratic. This ubiquity testifies loudly to the advantages that Weber noted. These benefits are counterbalanced by costs—red tape, alienation, rigidity, inefficiency when rules fail to deal adequately with reality: in short, all that we imply by the stereotype "bureaucratic." The designer must recognize both costs and benefits.

In contrast to the highly bureaucratic, highly formal organization are informal or "organic" organizations (Burns and Stalker, 1961). These organizations rely on expertise and problem solving, rather than "the rules" or hierarchy, to accomplish tasks. People do what must be done, results matter more than rules, and tasks may frequently change, depending on the job at hand. Rather than relying on rules or procedures, such organizations may well rely on external training—as, for instance, when professional engineers, accountants, or architects are hired, then expected to work with relatively few formal rules. Instead, professional training and discretion are invoked. Of course, professional organizations are not the only organic organizations. Any organization that is relatively informal and operates in a flexible fashion may be identified as organic; professional organizations are merely one frequently encountered type of organic organization.

Organic, informal organization is very attractive, to most of us. Many of us like to imagine ourselves operating with few rules or constraints. We see ourselves as capable and responsible organization members, easily able to choose appropriate actions, and always in agreement with organizational goals. The difficulties of organic organizations are the obverse of those of bureaucracy: the informality and lack of rules that allows freedom of action also make for unpredictability; inefficiency, as people may "reinvent the wheel"; inconsistency, as decisions are made one way this week and another next. The lack of structure also fails to provide guidance for some who need direction. In short, organic organizations too have liabilities, and the designer must be aware of these as well as the undeniable advantages in choosing an appropriate degree of formality.

LINE AND STAFF

Bureaucracy, with its carefully delineated hierarchy of authority and control assumes that any higher organization member is more knowledgeable and has more responsibility than any lower member.

Increasing complexity—as at Du Pont and GM—quickly led to the recognition of several sorts of authority, however. While some executives were directly responsible for operations, if the organization as a whole was to be coordinated and run effectively, various administrative mechanisms had to be explicitly managed. Thus, for instance, accounting procedures and reporting systems had to be designed, managed, maintained, and their results interpreted. This was clearly a specialist activity, and just as clearly ancillary to the main activities of the firm. While essential to large-scale, complex operations, it was not part of operations. The solution was to divide the work—to specifically designate responsibility for the new technical requirements to specialists who held no other responsibility, while operating departments and members were designated as "line" activities. Organizationally, since support activity was all-pervasive yet not part of the central activity of manufacturing, these structural units were distinguished as "staff."

Staff units are specialized support activities which are traditionally expected to advise (but not to command) line managers and members. In current organizations, this exclusively "advisory" role frequently breaks down—especially where staff units must approve budgetary expenses, for instance. Nevertheless, the traditional model is still typically invoked. Staff units are usually responsible for the development of specialized expertise and technical data, longer range activities concerning the coordination of the firm as a whole, and the like. The advantages of separating staff activities is akin to that of specialization in general—it encourages the development of greater expertise in the designated area. The disadvantages are also related to specialization. Because the staff unit concentrates only on its specialty, which may be quite arcane and esoteric to other organization members, staff personnel may become cut off from organizational reality and from other organization members. Difficulties include getting staff recommendations accepted by line personnel, ensuring realistic staff recommendations, and resolving jurisdictional disputes between line and staff.

These difficulties, and the need for greater responsiveness to both the needs of external environmental segments and internal coordination led to the next organizational form, simultaneous organization.

SIMULTANEOUS FORMS

The functional and divisional organizational forms were designed with an eye to separating the work into distinct pieces, generally eliminating overlap, and assigning relatively clear responsibility for activities along whatever underlying dimension was selected. In contrast, *simultaneous* organizational forms, of which the most familiar is the matrix, seek to design along multiple dimensions at the same time. The aim is to gain the benefits of several sorts of specialization, several emphases for attention at once. In order to do so, simultaneous organizations arrange people according to two (or occasionally more) basic divisions of work.

Simultaneous organization evolved first under the Defense Department and received major impetus at NASA, the National Aeronautics and Space Administration, and in the aerospace industry. The typical predecessor arrangements were functional departmentalization, with coordination occurring at the top (as in Figure 1). This structure did serve to encourage needed specialization and technical expertise, by grouping technical specialists together. This grouping facilitated their communication with one another around work problems, thus providing a highly experienced technical resource pool. The structure was not adequate for coordinating the highly complex projects of aerospace work, however. The required communications across functional departments and technical specialties were not occurring smoothly, resulting in delays and increased costs. The design solution was to reorganize along both technical specialties and projects, simultaneously. Project teams, drawn from numerous departments as needed, worked together on a given project. Meanwhile, all project members were still members of their functional departments, with access to their resources of technical expertise. (See Figure 8.) Each project member was responsible both to the functional department head, and to the project head; both evaluated the member.

FIGURE 8
Matrix Organization in Manufacturing

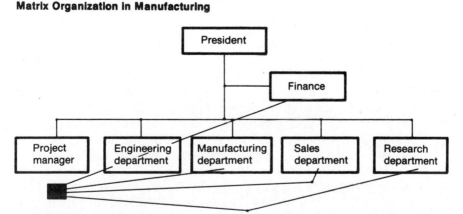

Note: Team members are drawn from various departments as needed, and report to *both* the project manager and their home department head.

Critical characteristics of the matrix form include simultaneous attention to two or more essential organizational tasks (here, the development and maintenance of specialized technical expertise, and the coordination of diverse specialists around a common temporary task). Functional departments are oriented toward the acquisition, maintenance, and development of specialized *resources*—people and equipment, for instance. Project teams are oriented toward the production of *output*. As a result, relationships, authority patterns, and evaluation all become highly complex and usually negotiated—because there are no clear and simple answers. The multiple dimensions of organization foster an ongoing tension—which can be highly creative, if appropriately balanced—between the underlying *resource* orientation and the desired *output* orientation.

The matrix form encourages a far more useful view of organizational realities, because it legitimates the sort of bargaining and negotiation that is essential when many goals—for instance, both output and resource goals—are to be met at once. It also encourages a general managerial viewpoint well down in the organization, where members see these alternate dimensions interacting and begin quite early in their careers to understand the trade-offs required.

Matrix forms, like functional and departmental forms, evolve in response to the problems around them, as managers seek new answers. In the case of the matrix, the first step was temporary teams, and temporary assignments. Later steps simply recognized that the organization faced an ongoing stream of such temporary projects. Thus while any individual project was temporary, another would take its place for firms involved in project work. For such organizations, a permanent project orientation (with projects changing) and a permanent functional organization (with appropriate resources maintained) were needed.

The advantage of simultaneous organizations like the matrix is their ability to maximize along several dimensions. Because project teams can be easily constituted and dissolved, the simultaneous form can be highly responsive to change as well. Because of this responsiveness, and because of the technical support the departmental structure provides, organization members often find they can "have their cake and eat it too," gaining benefits of motivation, involvement, and worthwhile participation. Disadvantages include substantial managerial overhead—particularly in the early stages (which may last for two or three years) while participants learn to negotiate and bargain instead of referring all conflicts up the hierarchy for resolution. The complexity and uncertainty of authority and responsibility lines can trouble some members, as can the need for high order interpersonal skills.

CONCLUSIONS

Choice among organizational forms is contingent upon many factors. No single form—functional, product or geographic division, combination, or simultaneous—is "best" for all circumstances. The best choice is the one that best balances the costs and benefits for maximum gain, in the context of clear thinking about present and future organizational needs. Critical organizational dimensions must be addressed, as must the organization's ability to bear the costs and tolerate the disadvantages of any particular form. Stability is economically efficient, but may impose heavy costs in terms of lost flexibility, creativity, and involvement. Innovative simultaneous organizations emphasize responsiveness, but may impose substantial costs in terms of duplication, inefficiencies, and sheer complexity. Not all people tolerate well an ambiguous structure that requires multiple reporting relationships and bargaining. Each of the major design options—simple organizations, organization by functional components, by product, by division, mixed forms, and simultaneous forms—meets a particular set of needs. Each emphasizes some strengths at the price of some weaknesses. Design is the art of balancing these factors to choose appropriately.

REFERENCES

Babbage, Charles. *On the Economy of Machinery and Manufacturers.* London: Charles Knight, 1832.

Burns, T., and G. M. Stalker. *The Management of Innovation.* London: Tavistock Publications, 1961.

Chandler, Alfred D. *Strategy and Structure.* Cambridge, Mass.: MIT Press, 1962.

Chandler, Alfred D., and Steven Salisbury. *Pierre S. Du Pont and the Making of the Modern Corporation.* New York: Harper & Row, 1977.

Jelinek, Mariann. "Organizational Design." In Don Hellriegel and John W. Slocum, Jr., *Organizational Behavior,* 2d ed. St. Paul: West Publishing Co., 1979, chap. 4.

Litterer, Joseph A. *The Analysis of Organizations,* 2d ed. New York: John Wiley & Sons, 1973.

Mintzberg, Henry. *The Structuring of Organizations.* Englewood Cliffs, N.J.: Prentice-Hall, 1979.

Sloan, Alfred P. *My Years at General Motors,* ed. John McDonald and Catherine Stevens. Garden City, N.Y.: Doubleday Anchor, 1972.

Smith, Adam. *The Wealth of Nations.* London: Straham and Candell, 1776.

32

Organizational Strategy, Structure, and Process*

RAYMOND E. MILES, CHARLES C. SNOW, ALAN D. MEYER, and HENRY J. COLEMAN, JR.

Organizational adaptation is a topic that has received only limited and fragmented theoretical treatment. Any attempt to examine organizational adaptation is difficult, since the process is highly complex and changeable. The proposed theoretical framework deals with alternative ways in which organizations define their product-market domains (strategy) and construct mechanisms (structures and processes) to pursue these strategies. The framework is based on interpretation of existing literature and continuing studies in four industries (college textbook publishing, electronics, food processing, and health care).

An organization is both an articulated purpose and an established mechanism for achieving it. Most organizations engage in an ongoing process of evaluating their purposes—questioning, verifying, and redefining the manner of interaction with their environments. Effective organizations carve out and maintain a viable market for their goods or services. Ineffective organizations fail this market-alignment task. Organizations also constantly modify and refine the mechanism by which they achieve their purposes—rearranging their structure of roles and relationships and their managerial processes. Efficient organizations establish mechanisms that complement their market strategy, but inefficient organizations struggle with these structural and process mechanisms.

For most organizations, the dynamic process of adjusting to environmental change and uncertainty—*of maintaining an effective alignment with the environment while managing internal interdependencies*—is enormously complex, encompassing myriad decisions and

---

* From *Academy of Management Review* 3, no. 3, (1978), pp. 546–62.

behaviors at several organization levels. But the complexity of the adjustment process can be penetrated: by searching for patterns in the behavior of organizations, one can describe and even predict the process of organizational adaptation. This article presents a theoretical framework that managers and students of management can use to analyze an organization as an integrated and dynamic whole—a model that takes into account the interrelationships among strategy, structure, and process. For a complete discussion of the theoretical framework and research studies, see (15). Specifically, the framework has two major elements: (*a*) a general model of the process of adaptation which specifies the major decisions needed by the organization to maintain an effective alignment with its environment and (*b*) an organizational typology which portrays different patterns of adaptive behavior used by organizations within a given industry or other grouping. But as several theorists have pointed out, organizations are limited in their choices of adaptive behavior to those which top management believes will allow the effective direction and control of human resources (4, 5, 6). Thus the theoretical framework to prevailing theories of management is also related. An increased understanding of the adaptive process, of how organizations move through it, and of the managerial requirements of different adjustment patterns can facilitate the difficult process of achieving an effective organization-environment equilibrium.

In the following sections, a typical example of organizational adaptation drawn from one of our empirical research studies is first presented. Second, a model of the adaptive process that arose from this research is described and discussed. In the third section, four alternative forms of adaptation exhibited by the organizations in our studies are described. Finally, the relationship between the organizational forms and currently available theories of management is discussed.

AN EXAMPLE OF ORGANIZATIONAL ADAPTATION

As an example of the problems associated with the adaptive process, consider the experience of a subsidiary of one of the companies in our studies.

> Porter Pump and Valve (PPV) is a semiautonomous division of a medium-sized equipment-manufacturing firm, which is in turn part of a large, highly diversified conglomerate. PPV manufactures a line of heavy-duty pumps and components for fluid-movement systems. The company does most of its own castings, makes many of its own parts, and maintains a complete stock of replacement parts. PPV also does special-order foundry work for other firms as its production schedule allows.

Until recently, Porter Pump and Valve had defined its business as providing quality products and service to a limited set of reliable customers. PPV's general manager, a first-rate engineer who spent much of his time in the machine shop and foundry, personified the company's image of quality and cost efficiency. In the mid-70s corporate management became concerned about both the speed and direction of PPV's growth. The management and staff at corporate headquarters began considering two new product and market opportunities, both in the energy field. Fluid-movement systems required for nuclear power generation provided one of these opportunities, and the development of novel techniques for petroleum exploration, well recovery, and fluid delivery provided the second. PPV had supplied some components to these markets in the past, but it was now clear that opportunities for the sale of entire systems or large-scale subsystems were growing rapidly.

PPV's initial moves toward these new opportunities were tentative. The general manager discovered that contract sales required extensive planning, field-contact work, and careful negotiations—activities not within his primary area of interest or experience. Finally, in an effort to foster more rapid movement into these new markets, executives in the parent organization transferred the general manager to a head-office position and moved into the top spot at PPV a manager with an extensive background in both sales and engineering and who was adept at large-scale contract negotiations.

Within a year of the changeover in general managers, PPV landed several lucrative contracts, and more appeared to be in the offing. The new business created by these contracts, however, placed heavy coordination demands on company management, and while the organization's technology (production and distribution system) has not been drastically revised over the past two years, workflow processes and the operational responsibilities of several managers have changed markedly. Materials control and scheduling, routine tasks in the past, are now complex activities, and managers of these operations meet regularly with the executive planning committee. Moreover, a rudimentary matrix structure has emerged in which various line managers undertake specific project responsibilities in addition to their regular duties. Key personnel additions have been made to the marketing department and more are planned, with particular emphasis on individuals who are capable of performing field planning and supervising and who can quickly bring new fluid systems to full operation. Budgets of some of the older departments are being cut back, and these funds are being diverted to the new areas of activity.

As illustrated, Porter Pump and Value experienced changes in its products and markets, in the technological processes needed to make new products and serve new markets, and in the administrative structure and processes required to plan, coordinate, and control the company's new operations. None of the usual perspectives which might be used to analyze such organizational changes—for example, economics, industrial engineering, marketing, or policy—appears to address all of the problems experienced by Porter Pump and Valve. Therefore, how can the adaptive process which occurred at PPV be described in its entirety?

THE ADAPTIVE CYCLE

We have developed a general model of the adaptive process which we call the *adaptive cycle*. Consistent with the strategic-choice approach to the study of organizations, the model parallels and expands ideas formulated by theorists such as Chandler (9), Child (10), Cyert and March (11), Drucker (12, 13), Thompson (18), and Weick (19, 20). Essentially, proponents of the strategic-choice perspective argue that organizational behavior is only partially preordained by environmental conditions and that the choices which top managers make are the critical determinants of organizational structure and process. Although these choices are numerous and complex, they can be viewed as three broad "problems" of organizational adaptation: the *entrepreneurial problem*, the *engineering problem*, and the *administrative problem*. In mature organizations, management must solve each of these problems simultaneously, but for explanatory purposes, these adaptive problems can be discussed as if they occurred sequentially.

The Entrepreneurial Problem

The adaptive cycle, though evident in all organizations, is perhaps most visible in new or rapidly growing organizations (and in organizations which recently have survived a major crisis). In a new organization, an entrepreneurial insight, perhaps only vaguely defined at first, must be developed into a concrete *definition of an organizational domain: a specific good or service and a target market or market segment*. In an ongoing organization, the entrepreneurial problem has an added dimension. Because the organization has already obtained a set of "solutions" to its engineering and administrative problems, its next attempt at an entrepreneurial "thrust" may be difficult. In the example of Porter Pump and Valve, the company's attempt to modify its products and markets was constrained by its present production process and by the fact that the general manager and his staff did not possess the needed marketing orientation.

In either a new or ongoing organization, the solution to the entrepreneurial problem is marked by management's acceptance of a particular product-market domain, and this acceptance becomes evident when management decides to commit resources to achieve objectives relative to the domain. In many organizations, external and internal commitment to the entrepreneurial solution is sought through the development and projection of an organizational "image" which defines both the organization's market and its orientation toward it (e.g., an emphasis on size, efficiency, or innovation).

Although we are suggesting that the engineering phase begins at this point, the need for further entrepreneurial activities clearly does not disappear. The entrepreneurial function remains a top-management responsibility, although as Bower (7) has described, the identification of a new opportunity and the initial impetus for movement toward it may originate at lower managerial levels.

The Engineering Problem

The engineering problem involves the creation of a system which *operationalizes management's solution to the entrepreneurial problem*. Such a system requires management to select an appropriate technology (input-transformation-output process) for producing and distributing chosen products or services and to form new information, communication, and control linkages (or modify existing linkages) to ensure proper operation of the technology.

As solutions to these problems are reached, initial implementation of the administrative system takes place. There is no assurance that the configuration of the organization, as it begins to emerge during this phase, will remain the same when the engineering problem finally has been solved. The actual form of the organization's structure will be determined during the administrative phase as management solidifies relations with the environment and establishes processes for coordinating and controlling internal operations. Referring again to Porter Pump and Valve, the company's redefinition of its domain required concomitant changes in its technology—from a pure mass-production technology to more of a unit or small-batch technology (21).

The Administrative Problem

The administrative problem, as described by most theories of management, is primarily that of reducing uncertainty within the organizational system, or, in terms of the present model, of rationalizing and stabilizing those activities which successfully solved problems faced by the organization during the entrepreneurial and engineering phases. Solving the administrative problem involves more than simply rationalizing the system already developed (uncertainty reduction); it also involves formulating and implementing those processes which will enable the organization to continue to evolve (innovation). This conception of the administrative problem, as a pivotal factor in the cycle of adaptation, deserves further elaboration.

Rationalization and Articulation. In the ideal organization, management would be equally adept at performing two somewhat conflicting functions: it would be able to create an administrative system (structure and processes) that could smoothly direct and monitor the organization's current activities without, at the same time, allowing the system to become so ingrained that future innovation activities are jeopardized. Such a perspective requires the administrative system to be viewed as both a *lagging* and *leading* variable in the process of adaptation. As a lagging variable, it must rationalize, through the development of appropriate structures and processes, strategic decisions made at previous points in the adjustment process. As a leading variable, the administrative system must facilitate the organization's future capacity to adapt by articulating and reinforcing the paths along which innovative activity can proceed. At Porter Pump and Valve, management modified its planning, coordination, and control processes substantially in order to pursue the company's newly chosen areas of business (the "lagging" aspect of administration). At the same time, key personnel were added to the marketing department; their duties included product development, market research, and technical consulting. These activities were designed to keep PPV at the forefront of new product and market opportunities (the "leading" aspect of administration).

THE STRATEGIC TYPOLOGY

If one accepts the adaptive cycle as valid, the question becomes: How do organizations move through the cycle? That is, using the language of our model, what strategies do organizations employ in solving their entrepreneurial, engineering, and administrative problems? Our research and interpretation of the literature show that there are essentially three *strategic types* of organizations: Defenders, Analyzers, and Prospectors. Each type has its own unique strategy for relating to its chosen market(s), and each has a particular configuration of technology, structure, and process that is consistent with its market strategy. A fourth type of organization encountered in our studies is called the Reactor. The Reactor is a form of strategic "failure" in that inconsistencies exist among its strategy, technology, structure, and process.

Although similar typologies of various aspects of organizational behavior are available (1, 2, 3, 15, 16, 17), our formulation specifies relationships among strategy, technology, structure, and process to the point where entire organizations can be viewed as integrated wholes in dynamic interaction with their environments. Any typology is unlikely to encompass every form of organizational behavior—the world of organizations is much too changeable and complex to permit such a claim. Nevertheless, every organization that we have observed appears, when compared to other organizations in its industry, to fit predominantly into one of the four categories, and its behavior is generally predictable given its typological classification. The "pure" form of each of these organization types is described below.

Defenders

The Defender (i.e., its top management) deliberately enacts and maintains an environment for which a stable form of organization is appropriate. Stability is chiefly achieved by the Defender's definition of, and solution to, its entrepreneurial problem. Defenders define their *entrepreneurial* problem as *how to seal off a portion of the total market in order to create a stable domain,* and they do so by producing only a limited set of products directed at a narrow segment of the total potential market. Within this limited domain, the Defender strives aggressively to prevent competitors from entering its "turf." Such behaviors include standard economic actions like competitive pricing or high-quality products, but Defenders also tend to ignore developments and trends outside of their domains, choosing instead to grow through market penetration and perhaps some limited product development. Over time, a true Defender is able to carve out and maintain a small niche within the industry which is difficult for competitors to penetrate.

Having chosen a narrow product-market domain, the Defender invests a great deal of resources in solving its *engineering* problem: *how to produce and distribute goods or services as efficiently as possible.* Typically, the Defender does so by developing a single core technology that is highly cost-efficient. Technological efficiency is central to the Defender's success since its domain has been deliberately created to absorb outputs on a predictable, continuous basis. Some Defenders extend technological efficiency to its limits through a process of vertical integration—incorporating each stage of production from raw materials supply to distribution of final output into the same organizational system.

Finally, the Defender's solution to its administrative problem is closely aligned with its solutions to the entrepreneurial and engineering problems. The Defender's *administrative* problem—*how to achieve strict control of the organization in order to ensure effi-*

ciency—is solved through a combination of structural and process mechanisms that can be generally described as "mechanistic" (8). These mechanisms include a top-management group heavily dominated by production and cost-control specialists, little or no scanning of the environment for new areas of opportunity, intensive planning oriented toward cost and other efficiency issues, functional structures characterized by extensive division of labor, centralized control, communications through formal hierarchical channels, and so on. Such an administrative system is ideally suited for generating and maintaining efficiency, and the key characteristic of stability is as apparent here as in the solution to the other two adaptive problems.

Pursued vigorously, the Defender strategy can be viable in most industries, although stable industries lend themselves to this type of organization more than turbulent industries (e.g., the relative lack of technological change in the food-processing industry generally favors the Defender strategy compared with the situation in the electronics industry). This particular form of organization is not without its potential risks. The Defender's *primary risk* is that of *ineffectiveness*— being unable to respond to a major shift in its market environment. The Defender relies on the continued viability of its single, narrow domain, and it receives a return on its large technological investment only if the major problems facing the organization continue to be of an engineering nature. If the Defender's market shifts dramatically, this type of organization has little capacity for locating and exploiting new areas of opportunity. In short, the Defender is perfectly capable of responding to today's world. To the extent that tomorrow's world is similar to today's, the Defender is ideally suited for its environment. Table 1 summarizes the Defender's salient characteristics and the major strengths and weaknesses inherent in this pattern of adaptation.

Prospectors

In many ways, Prospectors respond to their chosen environments in a manner that is almost the opposite of the Defender. In one sense, the Prospector is exactly like the Defender: there is a high degree of consistency among its solutions to the three problems of adaptation.

Generally speaking, the Prospector enacts an environment that is more dynamic than those of other types of organizations within the same industry. Unlike the Defender, whose success comes primarily from efficiently serving a stable domain, the Prospector's prime capability is that of finding and exploiting new product and market opportunities. For a Prospector, maintaining a reputation as an innovator in product and market development may be as important as, perhaps even more important than, high profitability. In fact, because of the

TABLE 1
Characteristics of the Defender

Entrepreneurial Problem	Engineering Problem	Administrative Problem
Problem:	*Problem:*	*Problem:*
How to "seal off" a portion of the total market to create a stable set of products and customers.	How to produce and distribute goods or services as efficiently as possible.	How to maintain strict control of the organization in order to ensure efficiency.
Solutions:	*Solutions:*	*Solutions:*
1. Narrow and stable domain.	1. Cost-efficient technology.	1. Financial and production experts most powerful members of the dominant coalition; limited environmental scanning.
2. Aggressive maintenance of domain (e.g., competitive pricing and excellent customer service).	2. Single core technology.	2. Tenure of dominant coalition is lengthy; promotions from within.
3. Tendency to ignore developments outside of domain.	3. Tendency toward vertical integration.	3. Planning is intensive, cost oriented, and completed before action is taken.
4. Cautious and incremental growth primarily through market penetration.	4. Continuous improvements in technology to maintain efficiency.	4. Tendency toward functional structure with extensive division of labor and high degree of formalization.
5. Some product development but closely related to current goods or services.		5. Centralized control and long-looped vertical information systems.
		6. Simple coordination mechanisms and conflict resolved through hierarchical channels.
		7. Organizational performance measured against previous years; reward system favors production and finance.
Costs and Benefits:	*Costs and Benefits:*	*Costs and Benefits:*
It is difficult for competitors to dislodge the organization from its small niche in the industry, but a major shift in the market could threaten survival.	Technological efficiency is central to organizational performance, but heavy investment in this area requires technological problems to remain familiar and predictable for lengthy periods of time.	Administrative system is ideally suited to maintain stability and efficiency but it is not well suited to locating and responding to new product or market opportunities.

Source: Raymond E. Miles and Charles C. Snow, *Organizational Strategy, Structure, and Process* (New York: McGraw-Hill, 1978), Table 3–1.

inevitable "failure rate" associated with sustained product and market innovation, Prospectors may find it difficult consistently to attain the profit levels of the more efficient Defender.

Defining its *entrepreneurial* problem as *how to locate and develop product and market opportunities*, the Prospector's domain is usually broad and in a continuous state of development. The systematic addition of new products or markets, frequently combined with retrenchment in other parts of the domain, gives the Prospector's products and markets an aura of fluidity uncharacteristic of the Defender. To locate new areas of opportunity, the Prospector must develop and maintain the capacity to survey a wide range of environmental conditions, trends, and events. This type of organization invests heavily in individuals and groups who scan the environment for potential opportunities. Because these scanning activities are not limited to the organization's current domain, Prospectors are frequently the creators of change in their respective industries. Change is one of the major tools used by the Prospector to gain an edge over competitors, so Prospector managers typically perceive more environmental change and uncertainty than managers of the Defender (or the other two organization types).

To serve its changing domain properly, the Prospector requires a good deal of flexibility in its technology and administrative system. Unlike the Defender, the Prospector's choice of products and markets is not limited to those which fall within the range of the organization's present technological capability. The Prospector's technology is contingent upon both the organization's current *and* future product mix: entrepreneurial activities always have primacy, and appropriate technologies are not selected or developed until late in the process of product development. Therefore, the Prospector's overall engineering problem is *how to avoid long-term commitments to a single type of technological process*, and the organization usually does so by creating multiple, prototypical technologies which have a low degree of routinization and mechanization.

Finally, the Prospector's *administrative* problem flows from its changing domain and flexible technologies: *how to facilitate rather than control organizational operations*. That is, the Prospector's administrative system must be able to deploy and coordinate resources among numerous decentralized units and projects rather than to plan and control the operations of the entire organization centrally. To accomplish overall facilitation and coordination, the Prospector's structure-process mechanisms must be "organic" (8). These mechanisms include a top-management group dominated by marketing and research and development experts, planning that is broad rather than intensive and oriented toward results not methods, product or project structures characterized by a low degree of formalization, decentralized control, lateral as well as vertical communications, and so on. In contrast to the Defender, the Prospector's descriptive catchword throughout its administrative as well as entrepreneurial and engineering solutions is "flexibility."

Of course, the Prospector strategy also has its costs. Although the Prospector's continuous exploration of change helps to protect it from a changing environment, this type of organization runs the *primary risk* of *low profitability and overextension of resources*. While the Prospector's technological flexibility permits a rapid response to a changing domain, complete efficiency cannot be obtained because of the presence of multiple technologies. Finally, the Prospector's administrative system is well suited to maintain flexibility, but it may, at least temporarily, underutilize or even misutilize physical, financial, and human resources. In short, the Prospector is effective—it can respond to the demands of tomorrow's world. To the extent that the world of tomorrow is similar to that of today, the Prospector cannot maximize profitability because of its inherent inefficiency. Table 2 summarizes the Prospector's salient characteristics and the major strengths and weaknesses associated with this pattern of adaptation.

TABLE 2
Characteristics of the Prospector

Entrepreneurial Problem	Engineering Problem	Administrative Problem

Problem:
  How to locate and exploit new product and market opportunities.
	Problem:
	  How to avoid long-term commitments to a single technological process.
		Problem:
		  How to facilitate and coordinate numerous and diverse operations.

Solutions: 1. Broad and continuously developing domain. 2. Monitors wide range of environmental conditions and events. 3. Creates change in the industry. 4. Growth through product and market development. 5. Growth may occur in spurts.	*Solutions:* 1. Flexible, prototypical technologies. 2. Multiple technologies. 3. Low degree of routinization and mechanization; technology embedded in people.	*Solutions:* 1. Marketing and research and development experts most powerful members of the dominant coalition. 2. Dominant coalition is large, diverse, and transitory; may include an inner circle. 3. Tenure of dominant coalition not always lengthy; key managers may be hired from outside as well as promoted from within. 4. Planning is comprehensive, problem oriented, and cannot be finalized before action is taken.

TABLE 2 *(concluded)*

Entrepreneurial Problem	Engineering Problem	Administrative Problem
		5. Tendency toward product structure with low division of labor and low degree of formalization.
		6. Decentralized control and short-looped horizontal information systems.
		7. Complex coordination mechanisms and conflict resolved through integrators.
		8. Organizational performance measured against important competitors; reward system favors marketing and research and development.
Costs and Benefits:	*Costs and Benefits:*	*Costs and Benefits:*
Product and market Innovation protect the organization from a changing environment, but the organization runs the risk of low profitability and overextension of its resources.	Technological flexibility permits a rapid response to a changing domain, but the organization cannot develop maximum efficiency in its production and distribution system because of multiple technologies.	Administrative system is ideally suited to maintain flexibility and effectiveness but may underutilize and misutilize resources.

Source: Raymond E. Miles and Charles C. Snow, *Organizational Strategy, Structure, and Process* (New York: McGraw-Hill, 1978), Table 4–1.

Analyzers

Based on our research, the Defender and the Prospector seem to reside at opposite ends of a continuum of adjustment strategies. Between these two extremes, a third type of organization is called the Analyzer. The Analyzer is a unique combination of the Prospector and Defender types and represents a viable alternative to these other strategies. A true Analyzer is an organization that attempts to minimize risk while maximizing the opportunity for profit—that is, an experienced Analyzer combines the strengths of both the Prospector and the Defender into a single system. This strategy is difficult to pursue, particularly in industries characterized by rapid market and technological change, and thus the word that best describes the Analyzer's adaptive approach is "balance."

The Analyzer defines its *entrepreneurial* problem in terms similar to both the Prospector and the Defender: *how to locate and exploit new product and market opportunities while simultaneously maintaining a firm core of traditional products and customers.* The Analyzer's solution to the entrepreneurial problem is also a blend of the solutions preferred by the Prospector and the Defender: the Analyzer moves toward new products or new markets but only after their viability has been demonstrated. This periodic transformation of the Analyzer's domain is accomplished through imitation—only the most successful product or market innovations developed by prominent Prospectors are adopted. At the same time, the majority of the Analyzer's revenue is generated by a fairly stable set of products and customer or client groups—a Defender characteristic. Thus, the successful Analyzer must be able to respond quickly when following the lead of key Prospectors while at the same time maintaining operating efficiency in its stable product and market areas. To the extent that it is successful, the Analyzer can grow through market penetration as well as product and market development.

The duality evident in the Analyzer's domain is reflected in its *engineering* problem and solution. This type of organization must learn *how to achieve and protect an equilibrium between conflicting demands for technological flexibility and for technological stability.* This equilibrium is accomplished by partitioning production activities to form a dual technological core. The stable component of the Analyzer's technology bears a strong resemblance to the Defender's technology. It is functionally organized and exhibits high levels of standardization, routinization, and mechanization in an attempt to approach cost efficiency. The Analyzer's flexible technological component resembles the Prospector's technological orientation. In manufacturing organizations, it frequently includes a large group of applications engineers (or their equivalent) who are rotated among teams charged with the task of rapidly adapting new product designs to fit the Analyzer's existing stable technology.

The Analyzer's dual technological core thus reflects the engineering solutions of both the Prospector and the Defender, with the stable and flexible components integrated primarily by an influential applied research group. To the extent that this group is able to develop solutions that match the organization's existing technological capabilities with the new products desired by product managers, the Analyzer can enlarge its product line without incurring the Prospector's extensive research and development expenses.

The Analyzer's administrative problem, as well as its entrepreneurial and engineering problems, contains both Defender and Prospector characteristics. Generally speaking, the *administrative* problem of the Analyzer is *how to differentiate the organization's structure and processes to accommodate both stable and dynamic areas of operation.* The Analyzer typically solves this problem with some version of a matrix organization structure. Heads of key functional units, most notably engineering and production, unite with product managers (usually housed in the marketing department) to form a balanced dominant coalition similar to both the Defender and the Prospector. The product manager's influence is usually greater than the functional manager's since his or her task is to identify promising product-market innovations and to supervise their movement through applied engineering and into production in a smooth and timely manner. The presence of engineering and production in the dominant coalition is to represent the more stable domain and technology which are the foundations of the Analyzer's overall operations. The Analyzer's matrix structure is supported by intensive planning between the functional divisions of marketing and production, broad-gauge planning between the applied research group and the product managers for the development of new products, centralized control mechanisms in the functional divisions and decentralized control techniques in the product groups, and so on. In sum, the key characteristic of the Analyzer's administrative system is the proper differentiation of the organization's structure and processes to achieve a balance between the stable and dynamic areas of operation.

As is true for both the Defender and Prospector, the Analyzer strategy is not without its costs. The duality in the Analyzer's domain forces the organization to establish a dual technological core, and it requires management to operate fundamentally different planning, control, and reward systems simultaneously. Thus, the Analyzer's twin characteristics of stability and flexibility limit the organization's ability to move fully in either direction were the domain to shift dramatically. Consequently, the Analyzer's *primary risks* are both *inefficiency and ineffectiveness* if it does not maintain the necessary balance throughout its strategy-structure relationship. Table 3 summarizes the Analyzer's salient characteristics and the major strengths and weaknesses inherent in this pattern of adaptation.

Reactors

The Defender, the Prospector, and the Analyzer can all be proactive with respect to their environments, though each is proactive in a different way. At the extremes, Defenders continually attempt to develop greater efficiency in existing operations while Prospectors ex-

TABLE 3
Characteristics of the Analyzer

Entrepreneurial Problem	Engineering Problem	Administrative Problem
Problem:	*Problem:*	*Problem:*
How to locate and exploit new product and market opportunities while simultaneously maintaining a firm base of traditional products and customers.	How to be efficient in stable portions of the domain and flexible in changing portions.	How to differentiate the organization's structure and processes to accommodate both stable and dynamic areas of operation.
Solutions:	*Solutions:*	*Solutions:*
1. Hybrid domain that is both stable and changing.	1. Dual technological core (stable and flexible component).	1. Marketing and engineering most influential members of dominant coalition, followed closely by production.
2. Surveillance mechanisms mostly limited to marketing; some research and development.	2. Large and influential applied engineering group.	2. Intensive planning between marketing and production concerning stable portion of domain; comprehensive planning among marketing, engineering, and product managers concerning new products and markets.
3. Steady growth through market penetration and product-market development.	3. Moderate degree of technical rationality.	3. "Loose" matrix structure combining both functional divisions and product groups.
		4. Moderately centralized control system with vertical and horizontal feedback loops.
		5. Extremely complex and expensive coordination mechanisms; some conflict resolution through product managers, some through normal hierarchical channels.
		6. Performance appraisal based on both effectiveness and efficiency measures, most rewards to marketing and engineering.

TABLE 3 (*concluded*)

Entrepreneurial Problem	*Engineering Problem*	*Administrative Problem*
Costs and Benefits:	*Costs and Benefits:*	*Costs and Benefits:*
Low investment in research and development, combined with imitation of demonstrably successful products, minimizes risk, but domain must be optimally balanced at all times between stability and flexibility.	Dual technological core is able to serve a hybrid stable-changing domain, but the technology can never be completely effective or efficient.	Administrative system is ideally suited to balance stability and flexibility, but if this balance is lost, it may be difficult to restore equilibrium.

Source: Raymond E. Miles and Charles C. Snow, *Organizational Strategy, Structure, and Process* (New York: McGraw-Hill, 1978), Table 5–1.

plore environmental change in search of new opportunities. Over time, these action modes stabilize to form a pattern of response to environmental conditions that is both *consistent* and *stable*.

A fourth type of organization, the Reactor, exhibits a pattern of adjustment to its environment that is both *inconsistent* and *unstable;* this type lacks a set of response mechanisms which it can consistently put into effect when faced with a changing environment. As a consequence, Reactors exist in a state of almost perpetual instability. The Reactor's "adaptive" cycle usually consists of responding inappropriately to environmental change and uncertainty, performing poorly as a result, and then being reluctant to act aggressively in the future. Thus, the Reactor is a "residual" strategy, arising when one of the other three strategies is improperly pursued.

Although there are undoubtedly many reasons why organizations become Reactors, we have identified three. First, *top management may not have clearly articulated the organization's strategy.* For example, one company was headed by a one-man Prospector of immense personal skills. A first-rate architect, he led his firm through a rapid and successful growth period during which the company moved from the design and construction of suburban shopping centers, through the construction and management of apartment complexes, and into consulting with municipal agencies concerning urban planning problems. Within 10 years of its inception, the company was a loose but effective collection of semiautonomous units held together by this particular individual. When this individual was suddenly killed in a plane crash, the company was thrown into a strategic void. Because each separate unit of the company was successful, each was able to argue strongly for more emphasis on its particular domain and operations. Consequently, the new chief executive officer, caught between a number of conflicting but legitimate demands for resources, was unable to develop a unified, cohesive statement of the organization's strategy; thus, consistent and aggressive behavior was precluded.

A second and perhaps more common cause of organizational instability is that *management does not fully shape the organization's structure and processes to fit a chosen strategy.* Unless all of the domain, technological, and administrative decisions required to have an operational strategy are properly aligned, strategy is a mere statement, not an effective guide to behavior. One publishing company wished, in effect, to become an Analyzer—management had articulated a direction for the organization which involved operating in both stable and changing domains within the college textbook publishing industry. Although the organization was comprised of several key Defender and Prospector characteristics such as functional structures and decentralized control mechanisms, these structure-process features were not appropriately linked to the company's different domains. In one area where the firm wished to "prospect," for example, the designated unit had a functional structure and shared a large, almost mass-production technology with several other units, thereby making it difficult for the organization to respond to market opportunities quickly. Thus, this particular organization exhibited a weak link between its strategy and its structure-process characteristics.

The third cause of instability—and perhaps ultimate failure—is *a tendency for management to maintain the organization's current strategy-structure relationship despite overwhelming changes in environmental conditions.* Another organization in our studies, a food-processing company, had initially been an industry pioneer in both the processing and marketing of dried fruits and nuts. Gradually, the company settled into a Defender strategy and took vigorous steps to bolster this strategy, including limiting the domain to a narrow line of products, integrating backward into growing and harvesting, and assigning a controller to each of the company's major functional divisions as a means of keeping costs down. Within recent years, the company's market has become saturated, and profit margins have shrunk on most of the firm's products. In spite of its declining market, the organization has consistently clung to a Defender strategy and structure, even to the point of creating ad hoc cross-divisional committees whose sole purpose was to find ways of increasing efficiency further. At the moment, management recognizes that the organization is in trouble, but it is reluctant to make the drastic modifications required to attain a strategy and structure better suited to the changing market conditions.

Unless an organization exists in a "protected" environment such as a monopolistic or highly regulated industry, it cannot continue to behave as a Reactor indefinitely. Sooner or later, it must move toward one of the consistent and stable strategies of Defender, Analyzer, or Prospector.

MANAGEMENT THEORY LINKAGES TO ORGANIZATIONAL STRATEGY AND STRUCTURE

Organizations are limited in their choices of adaptive behavior to those which top management believes will allow the effective direction and control of human resources. Therefore, top executives' theories of management are an important factor in analyzing an organization's ability to adapt to its environment. Although our research is only in its preliminary stage, we have found some patterns in the relationship between management theory and organizational strategy and structure.

A theory of management has three basic components: (*a*) a set of assumptions about human attitudes and behaviors, (*b*) managerial policies and actions consistent with these assumptions, and (*c*) expectations about employee performance if these policies and actions are implemented (see Table 4). Theories of management are discussed in more detail in Miles (14).

During the latter part of the 19th century and the early decades of the 20th, mainstream management theory, as voiced by managers and by management scholars, conformed to what has been termed the *Traditional* model. Essentially, the Traditional model maintained that the capability for effective decision making was narrowly distributed in organizations, and this approach thus legitimized unilateral control of organizational systems by top management. According to this model, a select group of owner-managers was able to direct large numbers of employees by carefully standardizing and routinizing their work and by placing the planning function solely in the hands of top managers. Under this type of management system, employees could be expected to perform up to some minimum standard, but few would be likely to exhibit truly outstanding performance.

Beginning in the 20s, the Traditional model gradually began to give way to the *Human Relations* model. This model accepted the traditional notion that superior decision-making competence was narrowly distributed among the employee population but emphasized the universality of social needs for belonging and recognition. This model argued that impersonal treatment was the source of subordinate resistance to managerial directives, and adherents of this approach urged managers to employ devices to enhance organization members' feel-

TABLE 4
Theories of Management

Traditional Model	Human Relations Model	Human Resources Model
Assumptions	*Assumptions*	*Assumptions*
1. Work is inherently distasteful to most people. 2. What workers do is less important than what they earn for doing it. 3. Few want or can handle work which requires creativity, self-direction, or self-control.	1. People want to feel useful and important. 2. People desire to belong and to be recognized as individuals. 3. These needs are more important than money in motivating people to work.	1. Work is not inherently distasteful. People want to contribute to meaningful goals which they have helped establish. 2. Most people can exercise far more creative, responsible self-direction and self-control than their present jobs demand.
Policies	*Policies*	*Policies*
1. The manager's basic task is to closely supervise and control his (her) subordinates. 2. He (she) must break tasks down into simple, repetitive, easily learned operations. 3. He (she) must establish detailed work routines and procedures and enforce these firmly but fairly.	1. The manager's basic task is to make each worker feel useful and important. 2. He (she) should keep his (her) subordinates informed and listen to their objections to his (her) plans. 3. The manager should allow his (her) subordinate to exercise some self-direction and self-control on routine matters.	1. The manager's basic task is to make use of his (her) "untapped" human resources. 2. He (she) must create an environment in which all members may contribute to the limits of their ability. 3. He (she) must encourage full participation on important matters, continually broadening subordinate self-direction and control.
Expectations	*Expectations*	*Expectations*
1. People can tolerate work if the pay is decent and the boss is fair. 2. If tasks are simple enough and people are closely controlled, they will produce up to standard.	1. Sharing information with subordinates and involving them in routine decisions will satisfy their basic needs to belong and to feel important. 2. Satisfying these needs will improve morale and reduce resistance to formal authority—subordinates will willingly cooperate and produce.	1. Expanding subordinate influence, self-direction, and self-control will lead to direct improvements in organizational performance. 2. Work satisfaction may improve as a "by-product" of subordinates making full use of their resources.

Source: Raymond E. Miles, *Theories of Management* (New York: McGraw-Hill, 1975), Figure 3–1.

ings of involvement and importance in order to improve organizational performance. Suggestion systems, employee counseling, and even company unions had common parentage in this philosophy. The Depression and World War II both acted to delay the development and spread of the Human Relations model, and it was not until the late 40s and early 50s that it became the prime message put forth by managers and management scholars.

Beginning in the mid-50s, a third phase in the evolution of management theory began with the emergence of the *Human Resources* model which argued that the capacity for effective decision making in the pursuit of organizational objectives was widely dispersed and that most organization members represented untapped resources which, if properly managed, could considerably enhance organizational performance. The Human Resources approach viewed management's role not as that of a controller (however benevolent) but as that of a facilitator—removing the constraints that block organization members' search for ways to contribute meaningfully in their work roles. In recent years, some writers have questioned the extent to which the Human Resources model is applicable, arguing for a more "contingent" theory emphasizing variations in member capacity and motivation to contribute and the technological constraints associated with broadened self-direction and self-control. The Human Resources model probably still represents the leading edge of management theory, perhaps awaiting the formulation of a successor model.

Linking the Strategic Typology to Management Theory

Are there identifiable linkages between an organization's strategic type and the management theory of its dominant coalition? For example, do top executives in Defenders profess Traditional beliefs about management and those in Prospectors a Human Resources philosophy? The answer to this question is, in our opinion, a bit more complex than simply yes or no.

One of our studies investigated aspects of the relationship between organizational strategy-structure and management theory. Although the results are only tentative at this point, relatively clear patterns emerged. In general, Traditional and Human Relations managerial beliefs are more likely to be found in Defender and Reactor organizations, while Human Resources beliefs are more often associated with Analyzer and Prospector organizations. But this relationship appears to be *constrained in one direction;* it seems highly unlikely that a Traditional or Human Relations manager can function effectively as the head of a Prospector organization. The prescriptions of the Traditional model simply do not support the degree of decentralized decision making required to create and manage diversified organizations. It is quite possible for a Human Resources manager to lead a Defender organization. Of course, the organization's planning and control processes under such leadership would be less centralized than if the organization were managed according to the Traditional model. Using the Human Resources philosophy, heads of functional divisions might either participate in the planning and budgeting process, or they might simply be delegated considerable autonomy in operating their cost centers. (In Defender organizations operated according to the Human Resources philosophy, human capabilities are aimed primarily at cost efficiency rather than product development.)

The fit between management theory and the strategy, structure, and process characteristics of Analyzers is perhaps more complex than with any of the other types. Analyzers, as previously described, tend to remain cost efficient in the production of a limited line of goods or services while attempting to move as rapidly as possible into promising new areas opened up by Prospectors. Note that the organization structure of the Analyzer does not demand extensive, permanent delegation of decision-making authority to division managers. Most of the Analyzer's products or services can be produced in functionally structured divisions similar to those in Defender organizations. New products or services may be developed in separate divisions or departments created for that purpose and then integrated as quickly as possible into the permanent technology and structure. It seems likely to us, although our evidence is inconclusive, that various members of the dominant coalition in Analyzer organizations hold moderate but different managerial philosophies, that certain key executives believe it is their role to pay fairly close attention to detail while others appear to be more willing to delegate, for short periods, moderate amounts of autonomy necessary to bring new products or services on line rapidly. If these varying managerial philosophies are "mismatched" within the Analyzer's operating units—if, for example, Traditional managers are placed in charge of innovative subunits—then it is unlikely that a successful Analyzer strategy can be pursued.

Holding together a dominant coalition with mixed views concerning strategy and structure is not an easy task. It is difficult, for example, for managers engaged in new product or service development to function within planning, control, and reward systems established for more stable operations, so the Analyzer must be successfully differentiated into its stable and changing areas and managed accordingly. Note that experimentation in the analyzer is usually quite limited. The exploration and risk associated with major product or service breakthroughs are not present (as would be the case in a Prospector), and thus interdependencies within the system may be kept at a manageable level. Such would not be the case if Analyzers attempted to be both cost-efficient producers of stable products or services and active in a major way in new product and market development. Numerous organizations are today being led or forced into such a mixed strategy (multinational companies, certain forms of conglomerates, many organizations in high-technology industries, etc.), and their struggles may well produce a new organization type and demands for a supporting theory of management. Whatever form this new type of organization takes, however, clearly its management-theory requirements will closely parallel or extend those of the Human Resources model (15).

CONCLUSIONS

Our research represents an initial attempt: (*a*) to portray the major elements of organizational adaptation, (*b*) to describe patterns of behavior used by organizations in adjusting to their environments, and (*c*) to provide a language for discussing organizational behavior at the total-system level. Therefore, we have offered a theoretical framework composed of a model of the adaptive process (called the adaptive cycle) and four empirically determined means of moving through this process (the strategic typology). In addition, we have related this theoretical framework to available theories of management (Traditional, Human Relations, Human Resources). Effective organizational adaptation hinges on the ability of managers to not only envision and implement new organizational forms but also to direct and control people within them.

We believe that managers' ability to meet successfully environmental conditions of tomorrow revolves around their understanding of organizations as integrated and dynamic wholes. Hopefully, our framework offers a theory and language for promoting such an understanding.

REFERENCES

1. Anderson, Carl R., and Frank T. Paine. "Managerial Perceptions and Strategic Behavior," *Academy of Management Journal* 18 (1975), pp. 811–23.
2. Ansoff, H. Igor. *Corporate Strategy* (New York: McGraw-Hill, 1965).
3. Ansoff, H. Igor, and Richard Brandenburg, "A Language for Organizational Design," *Management Science* 17(1971), pp. B717–B731.
4. Ansoff, H. Igor, and John M. Stewart. "Strategies for a Technology-Based Business," *Harvard Business Review* 45 (1967), pp. 71–83.

5. Argyris, Chris. "On Organizations of the Future," *Administrative and Policy Study Series* 1, no. 03–006 (Beverly Hills, Calif.: Sage Publications, 1973).
6. Beer, Michael, and Stanley M. Davis. "Creating a Global Organization: Failures along the Way," *Columbia Journal of World Business*, 11 (1976), pp. 72–84.
7. Bower, Joseph L. *Managing the Resource Allocation Process* (Boston: Division of Research, Harvard Business School, 1970).
8. Burns, Tom, and G. M. Stalker. *The Management of Innovation* (London: Tavistock, 1961).
9. Chandler, Alfred D., Jr. *Strategy and Structure* (Garden City, N.Y.: Doubleday, 1962).
10. Child, John. "Organizational Structure, Environment, and Performance—The Role of Strategic Choice," *Sociology* 6 (1972), pp. 1–22.
11. Cyert, Richard, and James G. March. *A Behavioral Theory of the Firm* (Englewood Cliffs, N.J.: Prentice-Hall, 1963).
12. Drucker, Peter F. *The Practice of Management* (New York: Harper & Row, 1954).
13. Drucker, Peter F. *Management: Tasks, Responsibilities, Practices* (New York: Harper & Row, 1974).
14. Miles, Raymond E. *Theories of Management* (New York: McGraw-Hill, 1975).
15. Miles, Raymond E., and Charles C. Snow. *Organizational Strategy, Structure, and Process* (New York: McGraw-Hill, 1978).
16. Rogers, Everett M. *Communication of Innovations: A Cross-Cultural Approach*, 2d ed. (New York: Free Press, 1971).
17. Segal, Morley. "Organization and Environment: A Typology of Adaptability and Structure," *Public Administration Review* 35 (1974), pp. 212–20.
18. Thompson, James D. *Organizations in Action* (New York: McGraw-Hill, 1967).
19. Weick, Karl E. *The Social Psychology of Organizing* (Reading, Mass.: Addison-Wesley, 1969).
20. Weick, Karl E. "Enactment Processes in Organizations," in *New Directions in Organizational Behavior*, ed. Barry M. Staw and Gerald R. Salancik (Chicago: St. Clair, 1977), pp. 267–300.
21. Woodward, Joan. *Industrial Organization: Theory and Practice* (London: Oxford University Press, 1965).

33

Organization Design: An Information Processing View*

JAY R. GALBRAITH

THE INFORMATION PROCESSING MODEL

A basic proposition is that the greater the uncertainty of the task, the greater the amount of information that has to be processed between decision makers during the execution of the task. If the task is well understood prior to performing it, much of the activity can be preplanned. If it is not understood, then during the actual task execution more knowledge is acquired which leads to changes in resource allocations, schedules, and priorities. All these changes require information processing *during* task performance. Therefore *the greater the task uncertainty, the greater the amount of information that must be processed among decision makers during task execution in order to achieve a given level of performance*. The basic effect of uncertainty is to limit the ability of the organization to preplan or to make decisions about activities in advance of their execution. Therefore it is hypothesized that the observed variations in organizational forms are variations in the strategies of organizations (1) to increase their ability to preplan, (2) to increase their flexibility to adapt to their inability to preplan, or (3) to decrease the level of performance required for continued viability. Which strategy is chosen depends on the relative costs of the strategies. The function of the framework is to identify these strategies and their costs.

THE MECHANISTIC MODEL

This framework is best developed by keeping in mind a hypothetical organization. Assume it is large and employs a number of specialist groups and resources in providing the output. After the task has been divided into specialist subtasks, the problem is to integrate the sub-

* Reprinted from *Interfaces* 4, no. 3 (May 1974), pp. 28–36. Copyright © 1974, The Institute of Management Sciences.

tasks around the completion of the global task. This is the problem of organization design. The behaviors that occur in one subtask cannot be judged as good or bad per se. The behaviors are more effective or ineffective depending upon the behaviors of the other subtask performers. There is a design problem because the executors of the behaviors cannot communicate with all the roles with whom they are interdependent. Therefore the design problem is to create mechanisms that permit coordinated action across large numbers of interdependent roles. Each of these mechanisms, however, has a limited range over which it is effective at handling the information requirements necessary to coordinate the interdependent roles. As the amount of uncertainty increases, and therefore information processing increases, the organization must adopt integrating mechanisms which increase its information processing capabilities.

1.   Coordination by Rules or Programs

For routine predictable tasks March and Simon have identified the use of rules or programs to coordinate behavior between interdependent subtasks [March and Simon, 1958, chap. 6]. To the extent that job related situations can be predicted in advance, and behaviors specified for these situations, programs allow an interdependent set of activities to be performed without the need for interunit communication. Each role occupant simply executes the behavior which is appropriate for the task-related situation with which he is faced.

2.   Hierarchy

As the organization faces greater uncertainty its participants face situations for which they have no rules. At this point the hierarchy is employed on an exception basis. The recurring job situations are programmed with rules while infrequent situations are referred to that level in the hierarchy where a global perspective exists for all affected subunits. However, the hierarchy also has a limited range. As uncertainty increases the number of exceptions increases until the hierarchy becomes overloaded.

3.   Coordination by Targets or Goals

As the uncertainty of the organization's task increases, coordination increasingly takes place by specifying outputs, goals or targets [March and Simon, 1958, p. 145]. Instead of specifying specific behaviors to be enacted, the organization undertakes processes to set goals to be achieved and the employees select the behaviors which lead to goal accomplishment. Planning reduces the amount of information process-ing in the hierarchy by increasing the amount of discretion exercised at lower levels. Like the use of rules, planning achieves integrated action and also eliminates the need for continuous communication among interdependent subunits as long as task performance stays within the planned task specifications, budget limits, and targeted completion dates. If it does not, the hierarchy is again employed on an exception basis.

The ability of an organization to coordinate interdependent tasks depends on its ability to compute meaningful subgoals to guide sub-unit action. When uncertainty increases because of introducing new products, entering new markets, or employing new technologies these subgoals are incorrect. The result is more exceptions, more informa-tion processing, and an overloaded hierarchy.

DESIGN STRATEGIES

The ability of an organization to successfully utilize coordination by goal setting, hierarchy, and rules depends on the combination of the frequency of exceptions and the capacity of the hierarchy to handle them. As the task uncertainty increases, the organization must again take organization design action. It can proceed in either of two general ways. First, it can act in two ways to reduce the amount of information that is processed. And second, the organization can act in two ways to increase its capacity to handle more information. The two methods for reducing the need for information and the two methods for increasing processing capacity are shown schematically in Figure 1. The effect of all these actions is to reduce the number of exceptional cases referred upward into the organization through hierarchical channels. The as-sumption is that the critical limiting factor of an organizational form is its ability to handle the nonroutine, consequential events that cannot be anticipated and planned for in advance. The nonprogrammed events place the greatest communication load on the organization.

1.   Creation of Slack Resources

As the number of exceptions begins to overload the hierarchy, one response is to increase the planning targets so that fewer exceptions occur. For example, completion dates can be extended until the num-ber of exceptions that occur are within the existing information pro-cessing capacity of the organization. This has been the practice in solving job shop scheduling problems [Pounds, 1963]. Job shops quote delivery times that are long enough to keep the scheduling

FIGURE 1
Organization Design Strategies

1. Rules and programs

2. Hierarchical referral

3. Goal setting

| 4. Creation of slack resources | 5. Creation of self-contained tasks | 6. Investment in vertical information systems | 7. Creation of lateral relations |

Reduce the need for information processing

Increase the capacity to process information

problem within the computational and information processing limits of the organization. Since every job shop has the same problem standard lead times evolve in the industry. Similarly budget targets could be raised, buffer inventories employed, etc. The greater the uncertainty, the greater the magnitude of the inventory, lead time, or budget needed to reduce an overload.

All of these examples have a similar effect. They represent the use of slack resources to reduce the amount of interdependence between subunits [March and Simon, 1958; Cyert and March, 1963]. This keeps the required amount of information within the capacity of the organization to process it. Information processing is reduced because an exception is less likely to occur and reduced interdependence means that fewer factors need to be considered simultaneously when an exception does occur.

The strategy of using slack resources has its costs. Relaxing budget targets has the obvious cost of requiring more budget. Increasing the time to completion date has the effect of delaying the customer. Inventories require the investment of capital funds which could be used elsewhere. Reduction of design optimization reduces the performance of the article being designed. Whether slack resources are used to reduce information or not depends on the relative cost of the other alternatives.

The design choices are: (1) among which factors to change (lead time, overtime, machine utilization, etc.) to create the slack and (2) by what amount should the factor be changed. Many operations research models are useful in choosing factors and amounts. The time-cost trade-off problem in project networks is a good example.

2. Creation of Self-Contained Tasks

The second method of reducing the amount of information processed is to change the subtask groupings from resource (input) based to output-based categories and give each group the resources it needs to supply the output. For example, the functional organization could be changed to product groups. Each group would have its own product engineers, process engineers, fabricating and assembly operations, and marketing activities. In other situations, groups can be created around product lines, geographical areas, projects, client groups, markets, etc., each of which would contain the input resources necessary for creation of the output.

The strategy of self-containment shifts the basis of the authority structure from one based on input, resource, skill, or occupational categories to one based on output or geographical categories. The shift reduces the amount of information processing through several mechanisms. First, it reduces the amount of output diversity faced by a single collection of resources. For example, a professional organization with multiple skill specialties providing service to three different client groups must schedule the use of these specialties across three demands for their services and determine priorities when conflicts occur. But, if the organization changed to three groups, one for each client category, each with its own full complement of specialists, the schedule conflicts across client groups disappear and there is no need to process information to determine priorities.

The second source of information reduction occurs through a reduced division of labor. The functional or resource specialized structure pools the demand for skills across all output categories. In the example above each client generates approximately one third of the demand for each skill. Since the division of labor is limited by the extent of the market, the division of labor must decrease as the demand decreases. In the professional organization, each client group may have generated a need for one third of a computer programmer. The functional organization would have hired one programmer and shared him across the groups. In the self-contained structure there is insufficient demand in each group for a programmer so the professionals must do their own programming. Specialization is reduced but there is no problem of scheduling the programmer's time across the three possible uses for it.

The cost of the self-containment strategy is the loss of resource specialization. In the example, the organization foregoes the benefit of a specialist in computer programming. If there is physical equipment, there is a loss of economies of scale. The professional organization would require three machines in the self-contained form but only a large time-shared machine in the functional form. But those resources which have large economies of scale or for which specialization is necessary may remain centralized. Thus, it is the degree of self-containment that is the variable. The greater the degree of uncertainty, other things equal, the greater the degree of self-containment.

The design choices are the basis for the self-contained structure and the number of resources to be contained in the groups. No groups are completely self-contained or they would not be part of the same organization. But one product divisionalized firm may have 8 to 15 functions in the division while another may have 12 to 15 in the divisions. Usually accounting, finance, and legal services are centralized and shared. Those functions which have economies of scale, require specialization, or are necessary for control remain centralized and not part of the self-contained group.

The first two strategies reduced the amount of information by lower performance standards and creating small autonomous groups to provide the output. Information is reduced because an exception is less likely to occur and fewer factors need to be considered when an exception does occur. The next two strategies accept the performance standards and division of labor as given and adapt the organization so as to process the new information which is created during task performance.

3. Investment in Vertical Information Systems

The organization can invest in mechanisms which allow it to process information acquired during task performance without overloading the hierarchical communication channels. The investment occurs according to the following logic. After the organization has created its plan or set of targets of inventories, labor utilization, budgets, and schedules, unanticipated events occur which generate exceptions requiring adjustments to the original plan. At some point when the number of exceptions becomes substantial, it is preferable to generate a new plan rather than make incremental changes with each exception. The issue is then how frequently should plans be revised—yearly, quarterly, or monthly? The greater the frequency of replanning the greater the resources, such as clerks, computer time, input-output devices, etc., required to process information about relevant factors.

The cost of information processing resources can be minimized if the language is formalized. Formalization of a decision-making language simply means that more information is transmitted with the same number of symbols. It is assumed that information processing resources are consumed in proportion to the number of symbols transmitted. The accounting system is an example of a formalized language.

Providing more information, more often, may simply overload the decision maker. Investment may be required to increase the capacity of the decision maker by employing computers, various man-machine combinations, assistants-to, etc. The cost of this strategy is the cost of the information processing resources consumed in transmitting and processing the data.

The design variables of this strategy are the decision frequency, the degree of formalization of language, and the type of decision mechanism which will make the choice. This strategy is usually operationalized by creating redundant information channels which transmit data from the point of origination upward in the hierarchy where the point of decision rests. If data are formalized and quantifiable, this strategy is effective. If the relevant data are qualitative and ambiguous, then it may prove easier to bring the decisions down to where the information exists.

4. Creation of Lateral Relationships

The last strategy is to employ selectively joint decision processes which cut across lines of authority. This strategy moves the level of decision making down in the organization to where the information exists but does so without reorganizing around self-contained groups. There are several types of lateral decision processes. Some processes are usually referred to as the informal organization. However, these informal processes do not always arise spontaneously out of the needs of the task. This is particularly true in multinational organizations in which participants are separated by physical barriers, language differences, and cultural differences. Under these circumstances lateral processes need to be designed. The lateral processes evolve as follows with increases in uncertainty.

Direct Contact.   [Direct contact] between managers who share a problem. If a problem arises on the shop floor, the foreman can simply call the design engineer, and they can jointly agree upon a solution. From an information processing view, the joint decision prevents an upward referral and unloads the hierarchy.

Liaison Roles.   When the volume of contacts between any two departments grows, it becomes economical to set up a specialized role to handle this communication. Liaison men are typical examples of specialized roles designed to facilitate communication between two interdependent departments and to bypass the long lines of communication involved in upward referral. Liaison roles arise at lower and middle levels of management.

Task Forces.   Direct contact and liaison roles, like the integration mechanisms before them, have a limited range of usefulness. They work when two managers or functions are involved. When problems arise involving seven or eight departments, the decision-making capacity of direct contacts is exceeded. Then these problems must be referred upward. For uncertain, interdependent tasks such situations arise frequently. Task forces are a form of horizontal contact which is designed for problems of multiple departments.

The task force is made up of representatives from each of the affected departments. Some are full-time members, others may be part-time. The task force is a temporary group. It exists only as long as the problem remains. When a solution is reached, each participant returns to his normal tasks.

To the extent that they are successful, task forces remove problems from higher levels of the hierarchy. The decisions are made at lower levels in the organization. In order to guarantee integration, a group problem-solving approach is taken. Each affected subunit contributes a member and therefore provides the information necessary to judge the impact on all units.

Teams.   The next extension is to incorporate the group decision process into the permanent decision processes. That is, as certain decisions consistently arise, the task forces become permanent. These groups are labeled teams. There are many design issues concerned in team decision making such as at what level do they operate, who participates, etc. [Galbraith, 1973, chaps. 6 and 7]. One design decision is particularly critical. This is the choice of leadership. Sometimes a problem exists largely in one department so that the department manager is the leader. Sometimes the leadership passes from one manager to another. As a new product moves to the marketplace, the leader of the new product team is first the technical manager, followed by the production manager, and then the marketing manager. The result is that if the team cannot reach a consensus decision and the leader decides, the goals of the leader are consistent with the goals of the organization for the decision in question. But quite often obvious leaders cannot be found. Another mechanism must be introduced.

Integrating Roles.   The leadership issue is solved by creating a new role—an integrating role [Lawrence and Lorsch, 1967, chap. 3]. These roles carry the labels of product managers, program managers, project managers, unit managers (hospitals), materials managers, etc. After the role is created, the design problem is to create enough power in the role to influence the decision process. These roles have power even when no one reports directly to them. They have some power because they report to the general manager. But if they are selected so as to be unbiased with respect to the groups they integrate and to have technical competence, they have expert power. They collect information and equalize power differences due to preferential access to knowledge and information. The power equalization increases trust and the quality of the joint decision process. But power equalization occurs only if the integrating role is staffed with someone who can exercise expert power in the form of persuasion and informal influences rather than exert the power of rank or authority.

Managerial Linking Roles. As tasks become more uncertain, it is more difficult to exercise expert power. The role must get more power of the formal authority type in order to be effective at coordinating the joint decisions which occur at lower levels of the organization. This position power changes the nature of the role which for lack of a better name is labeled a managerial linking role. It is not like the integrating role because it possesses formal position power but is different from line managerial roles in that participants do not report to the linking manager. The power is added by the following successive changes:

a.   The integrator receives approval power of budgets formulated in the departments to be integrated.
b.   The planning and budgeting process starts with the integrator making his initiation in budgeting legitimate.
c.   Linking manager receives the budget for the area of responsibility and buys resources from the specialist groups.

These mechanisms permit the manager to exercise influence even though no one works directly for him. The role is concerned with integration but exercises power through the formal power of the position. If this power is insufficient to integrate the subtasks and creation of self-contained groups is not feasible, there is one last step.

Matrix Organization. The last step is to create the dual authority relationship and the matrix organization [Galbraith, 1971]. At some point in the organization some roles have two superiors. The design issue is to select the locus of these roles. The result is a balance of power between the managerial linking roles and the normal line organization roles. Figure 2 depicts the pure matrix design.

The work of Lawrence and Lorsch is highly consistent with the assertions concerning lateral relations [Lawrence and Lorsch, 1967; Lorsch and Lawrence, 1968]. They compared the types of lateral relations undertaken by the most successful firm in three different industries. Their data are summarized in Table 1. The plastics firm has the greatest rate of new product introduction (uncertainty) and the greatest utilization of lateral processes. The container firm was also very successful but utilized only standard practices because its information processing task is much less formidable. Thus, the greater the uncertainty the lower the level of decision making and the integration is maintained by lateral relations.

FIGURE 2
A Pure Matrix Organization

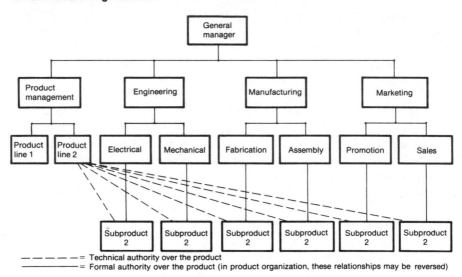

— — — — — = Technical authority over the product
——————— = Formal authority over the product (in product organization, these relationships may be reversed)

Table 1 points out the cost of using lateral relations. The plastics firm has 22 percent of its managers in integration roles. Thus, the greater the use of lateral relations the greater the managerial intensity. This cost must be balanced against the cost of slack resources, self-contained groups and information systems.

TABLE 1

	Plastics	*Food*	*Container*
Percent of new products in last ten years	35%	20%	0%
Integrating devices	Rules	Rules	Rules
	Hierarchy	Hierarchy	Hierarchy
	Planning	Planning	Planning
	Direct contact	Direct contact	Direct contact
	Teams at 3 levels	Task forces	
	Integrating department	Integrators	
Percent of integrators/ managers	22%	17%	0%

Adapted from Paul Lawrence and Jay Lorsch, *Organization and Environment* (Boston: Division of Research, Harvard Business School, 1967), pp. 86–138, and Jay Lorsch and Paul Lawrence, "Environmental Factors and Organization Integration." Paper read at the Annual Meeting of the American Sociological Association, August 27, 1968, Boston, Mass.

CHOICE OF STRATEGY

Each of the four strategies has been briefly presented. The organization can follow one or some combination of several if it chooses. It will choose that strategy which has the least cost in its environmental context. [For an example, see Galbraith, 1970]. However, what may be lost in all of the explanations is that the four strategies are hypothesized to be an exhaustive set of alternatives. That is, if the organization is faced with greater uncertainty due to technological change, higher performance standards due to increased competition, or diversifies its product line to reduce dependence, the amount of information processing is increased. *The organization must adopt at least one of the four strategies when faced with greater uncertainty.* If it does not consciously choose one of the four, then the first, reduced performance standards, will happen automatically. The task information requirements and the capacity of the organization to process information are always matched. If the organization does not consciously match them, reduced performance through budget overruns or schedule overruns will occur in order to bring about equality. Thus the organization should be planned and designed simultaneously with the planning of the strategy and resource allocations. But if the strategy involves introducing new products, entering new markets, etc., then some provision for increased information must be made. Not to decide is to decide, and it is to decide upon slack resources as the strategy to remove hierarchical overload.

There is probably a fifth strategy which is not articulated here. Instead of changing the organization in response to task uncertainty, the organization can operate on its environment to reduce uncertainty. The organization through strategic decisions, long-term contracts, coalitions, etc., can control its environment. But these maneuvers have costs also. They should be compared with costs of the four design strategies presented above.

SUMMARY

The purpose of this paper has been to explain why task uncertainty is related to organizational form. In so doing the cognitive limits theory of Herbert Simon was the guiding influence. As the consequences of cognitive limits were traced through the framework, various organization design strategies were articulated. The framework provides a basis for integrating organizational interventions, such as information systems and group problem solving, which have been treated separately before.

REFERENCES

Cyert, Richard, & James March. *The Behavioral Theory of the Firm.* Englewood Cliffs. N.J.: Prentice-Hall, 1963.

Galbraith, Jay. "Environmental and Technological Determinents of Organization Design: A Case Study." In *Studies in Organization Design,* ed. Paul Lawrence and Jay Lorsch. Homewood, Ill.: Richard D. Irwin, 1970.

Galbraith, Jay. "Designing Matrix Organizations." *Business Horizons,* 1971, pp. 29–40.

Galbraith, Jay. *Organization Design.* Reading, Mass.: Addison-Wesley Publishing, 1973.

Lawrence, Paul, & Jay Lorsch. *Organization and Environment.* Boston, Mass.: Division of Research, Harvard Business School, 1967.

Lorsch, Jay, & Paul Lawrence. "Environmental Factors and Organization Integration." Paper read at the Annual Meeting of the American Sociological Association, August 27, 1968, Boston, Mass.

March, James, & Herbert Simon. *Organizations.* New York: John Wiley & Sons, 1958.

Pounds, William. "The Scheduling Environment." In *Industrial Scheduling,* ed. Muth, John F., and Thompson, Gerald L. Englewood Cliffs, N.J.: Prentice-Hall, 1963.

Simon, Herbert. *Models of Man.* New York: John Wiley & Sons, 1957.

34

Fitting New Employees into the Company Culture*

RICHARD PASCALE

What corporate strategy was in the 1970s, corporate culture is becoming in the 1980s. Companies worry about whether theirs is right for them, consultants hawk advice on the subject, executives wonder if there's anything in it that can help them manage better. A strong culture—a set of shared values, norms, and beliefs that get everybody heading in the same direction—is common to all the companies held up as paragons in the best-seller *In Search of Excellence.*

There is, however, one aspect of culture that nobody seems to want to talk about. This is the process by which newly hired employees are

---

* From *Fortune,* May 28, 1984, pp. 28–42. Copyright © 1984 by Time, Inc.

made part of a company's culture. It may be called learning the ropes, being taught "the way we do things here at XYZ Corp.," or simply training. Almost no one calls it by its precise social science name—socialization.

To American ears, attuned by Constitution and conviction to the full expression of individuality, socialization tends to sound alien and vaguely sinister. Some equate it with the propagation of socialism—which it isn't—but even when it is correctly understood as the development of social conformity, the prospect makes most of us cringe. How many companies caught up in the corporate culture fad will be quite as enthusiastic when they finally grasp that "creating a strong culture" is a nice way of saying that employees have to be more comprehensively socialized?

The tradition at most American corporations is to err in the other direction, to be culturally permissive, to let employees do their own thing to a remarkable degree. We are guided by a philosophy, initially articulated by John Locke, Thomas Hobbes, and Adam Smith, that says that individuals free to choose make the most efficient decisions. The independence of the parts makes for a greater sum. Trendy campaigns to build a strong corporate culture run into trouble when employees are asked to give up some of their individuality for the common good.

The crux of the dilemma is this: We are opposed to the manipulation of individuals for organizational purposes. At the same time we increasingly realize that a degree of social uniformity enables organizations to work better. One need not look to Japan to see the benefits of it. Many of the great American companies that thrive from one generation to the next—IBM, Procter & Gamble, Morgan Guaranty Trust—are organizations that have perfected their processes of socialization. Virtually none talk explicitly about socialization; they may not even be conscious of precisely what they are doing. Moreover, when one examines any particular aspect of their policy toward people—how they recruit or train or compensate—little stands out as unusual. But when the pieces are assembled, what emerges is an awesome internal consistency that powerfully shapes behavior.

It's time to take socialization out of the closet. If some degree of it is necessary for organizations to be effective, then the challenge for managers is to reconcile this necessity with traditional American independence.

Probably the best guide available on how to socialize people properly is what the IBMs and the P&Gs actually do. Looking at the winners company by company, one finds that, with slight variations, they all put new employees through what might be called the seven steps of socialization.

Step One

The company subjects candidates for employment to a selection process so rigorous that it often seems designed to discourage individuals rather than encourage them to take the job. By grilling the applicant, telling him or her the bad side as well as the good, and making sure not to oversell, strong-culture companies prod the job applicant to take himself out of contention if he, who presumably knows more about himself than any recruiter, thinks the organization won't fit his style and values.

Consider the way Procter & Gamble hires people for entry level positions in brand management. The first person who interviews the applicant is drawn not from the human resources department, but from an elite cadre of line managers who have been trained with lectures, videotapes, films, practice interviews, and role-playing. These interviewers use what they've learned to probe each applicant for such qualities as the ability to "turn out high volumes of excellent work," to "identify and understand problems," and to "reach thoroughly substantiated and well-reasoned conclusions that lead to action." Initially, each candidate undergoes at least two interviews and takes a test of his general knowledge. If he passes, he's flown to P&G headquarters in Cincinnati, where he goes through a day of one-on-one interviews and a group interview over lunch.

The New York investment banking house of Morgan Stanley encourages people it is thinking of hiring to discuss the demands of the job with their spouses, girlfriends, or boyfriends—new recruits sometimes work 100 hours a week. The firm's managing directors and their wives take promising candidates and their spouses or companions out to dinner to bring home to them what they will face. The point is to get a person who will not be happy within Morgan's culture because of the way his family feels to eliminate himself from consideration for a job there.

This kind of rigorous screening might seem an invitation to hire only people who fit the mold of present employees. In fact, it often *is* harder for companies with strong cultures to accept individuals different from the prevailing type.

Step Two

The company subjects the newly hired individual to experiences calculated to induce humility and to make him question his prior behavior, beliefs, and values. By lessening the recruit's comfort with himself, the company hopes to promote openness toward its own norms and values.

This may sound like brainwashing or boot camp, but it usually just takes the form of pouring on more work than the newcomer can possibly do. IBM and Morgan Guaranty socialize with training programs in which, to quote one participant, "You work every night until 2 A.M. on your own material, and then help others." Procter & Gamble achieves the same result with what might be called upending experiences— requiring a recent college graduate to color in a map of sales territories, for example. The message is clear: while you may be accomplished in many respects, you are in kindergarten as far as what you know about this organization.

Humility isn't the only feeling brought on by long hours of intense work that carry the individual close to his or her limit. When everybody's vulnerability runs high, one also tends to become close to one's colleagues. Companies sometimes intensify this cohesiveness by not letting trainees out of the pressure cooker for very long—everyone has so much work to do that he doesn't have time to see people outside the company or reestablish a more normal social distance from his co-workers.

Morgan Stanley, for instance, expects newly hired associates to work 12- to 14-hour days and most weekends. Their lunches are not the Lucullan repasts that MBAs fantasize about, but are typically confined to 30 minutes in the unprepossessing cafeteria. One can observe similar patterns—long hours, exhausting travel schedules, and almost total immersion in casework—at law firms and consulting outfits. Do recruits chafe under such discipline? Not that much, apparently. Socialization is a bit like exercise—it's probably easier to reconcile yourself to it while you're young.

Step Three

Companies send the newly humble recruits into the trenches, pushing them to master one of the disciplines at the core of the company's business. The newcomer's promotions are tied to how he does in that discipline.

In the course of the individual's first few months with the company, his universe of experience has increasingly narrowed down to the organization's culture. The company, having got him to open his mind to its way of doing business, now cements that orientation by putting him in the field and giving him lots of carefully monitored experience. It rewards his progress with promotions at predictable intervals.

While IBM hires some MBAs and a few older professionals with prior work experience, almost all of them start at the same level as recruits from college and go through the same training programs. It takes about 15 years, for example, to become a financial controller. At

Morgan Stanley and consulting firms like McKinsey, new associates must similarly work their way up through the ranks. There is almost never a quick way to jump a few rungs on the ladder.

The gains from this approach are cumulative. For starters, when all trainees understand there is just one step-by-step career path, it reduces politicking. Since they are being evaluated on how they do over the long haul, they are less tempted to cut corners or go for short-term victories. By the time they reach senior positions they understand the business not as a financial abstraction, but as a reality of people they know and skills they've learned. They can communicate with people in the lowest ranks in the shorthand of shared experience.

Step Four

At every stage of the new manager's career, the company measures the operating results he has achieved and rewards him accordingly. It does this with systems that are comprehensive and consistent. These systems focus particularly on those aspects of the business that make for competitive success and for the perpetuation of the corporation's values.

Procter & Gamble, for instance, measures managers on three factors it deems critical to a brand's success: building volume, building profit, and conducting planned change—altering a product to make it more effective or more satisfying to the customer in some other way. Information from the outside world—market-share figures, say—is used in the measuring along with financial data. Performance appraisals focus on these criteria as well as on general managerial skill.

IBM uses similar interlocking systems to track adherence to one of its major values, respect for the dignity of the individual. The company monitors this with surveys of employee morale; "Speak Up," a confidential suggestion box; a widely proclaimed policy of having the boss's door open to any subordinates who want to talk; so-called skip-level interviews, in which a subordinate can skip over a couple of organizational levels to discuss a grievance with senior management; and informal social contacts between senior managers and lower level employees. Management moves quickly when any of these systems turns up a problem.

The IBM culture includes a mechanism for disciplining someone who has violated one of the corporate norms—handling his subordinates too harshly, say, or being overzealous against the competition. The malefactor will be assigned to what is called the penalty box—typically, a fairly meaningless job at the same level, sometimes in a less desirable location. A branch manager in Chicago might be moved to a nebulous staff position at headquarters. To the outsider, penalty box assignments look like just another job rotation, but insiders know that the benched manager is out of the game temporarily.

The penalty box provides a place to hold a manager while the mistakes he's made and the hard feelings they've engendered are gradually forgotten. The mechanism lends substance to the belief, widespread among IBM employees, that the company won't fire anybody capriciously. The penalty box's existence says, in effect, that in the career of strong, effective managers there are times when one steps on toes. The penalty box lets someone who has stepped too hard contemplate his error and return to play another day.

Step Five

All along the way, the company promotes adherence to its transcendent values, those overarching purposes that rise way above the day-to-day imperative to make a buck. At the AT&T of yore, for example, the transcendent value was guaranteeing phone service to customers through any emergency. Identification with such a value enables the employee to accept the personal sacrifices the company asks of him.

Placing oneself at the service of an organization entails real costs. There are long hours of work, weekends apart from one's family, bosses one has to endure, criticism that seems unfair, job assignments that are inconvenient or undesirable. The countervailing force making for commitment to the company in these circumstances is the organization's set of transcendent values that connect its purpose to human values of a higher order than just those of the marketplace—values such as serving mankind, providing a first-class product for society, or helping people learn and grow.

Someone going to work for Delta Air Lines will be told again and again about the "Delta family feeling." Everything that's said makes the point that Delta's values sometimes require sacrifices—management takes pay cuts during lean times, senior flight attendants and pilots voluntarily work fewer hours per week so the company won't have to lay off more junior employees. Candidates who accept employment with Delta tend to buy into this quid pro quo, agreeing in effect that keeping the Delta family healthy justifies the sacrifices that the family exacts.

Step Six

The company constantly harps on watershed events in the organization's history that reaffirm the importance of the firm's culture. Folklore reinforces a code of conduct—how we do things around here.

All companies have their stories, but at corporations that socialize well the morals of these stories all tend to point in the same direction. In the old Bell System, story after story extolled Bell employees who made heroic sacrifices to keep the phones working. The Bell folklore was so powerful that when natural disaster struck, all elements of a 1 million-member organization were able to pull together, cut corners, violate normal procedures, even do things that would not look good when measured by usual job performance criteria—all in the interest of restoring phone service. Folklore, when well understood, can legitimize special channels for moving an organization in a hurry.

Step Seven

The company supplies promising individuals with role models. These models are consistent—each exemplary manager displays the same traits.

Nothing communicates more powerfully to younger professionals within an organization than the example of peers or superiors who are recognized as winners and who also share common qualities. The protégé watches the role model make presentations, handle conflict, and write memos, then tries to duplicate the traits that seem to work most effectively.

Strong-culture firms regard role models as constituting the most powerful long-term training program available. Because other elements of the culture are consistent, the people who emerge as role models are consistent. P&G's brand managers, for example, exhibit extraordinary consistency in several traits—they're almost all analytical, energetic, and adept at motivating others. Unfortunately most firms leave the emergence of role models to chance. Some on the fast track seem to be whizzes at analysis, others are skilled at leading people, others seem astute at politics; the result for those below is confusion as to what it *really* takes to succeed. For example, the companies that formerly made up the Bell System have a strong need to become more market oriented and aggressive. Yet the Bell culture continues to discriminate against potential fast-trackers who, judged by the values of the older monopoly culture, are too aggressive.

Many companies can point to certain organizational practices that look like one or two of the seven steps, but rarely are all seven managed in a well-coordinated effort. It is *consistency* across all seven steps of the socialization process that results in a strongly cohesive culture that endures.

When one understands the seven steps, one can better appreciate the case for socialization. All organizations require a degree of order and consistency. They can achieve this through explicit procedures and formal controls or through implicit social controls. American companies, on the whole, tend to rely more on formal controls. The result is that management often appears rigid, bureaucratic, and given to oversteering. A United Technologies executive laments, "I came from the Bell system. Compared with AT&T, this is a weak culture and there is little socialization. But of course there is still need for controls. So they put handcuffs on you, shackle you to every nickel, track every item of inventory, monitor every movement in production and head count. They control you by the balance sheet."

At most American companies, an inordinate amount of energy gets used up in fighting "the system." But when an organization can come up with a strong, consistent set of implicit understandings, it has effectively established for itself a body of common law to supplement its formal rules. This enables it to use formal systems as they are supposed to be used—as tools rather than straitjackets. An IBM manager, conversant with the concept of socialization, puts it this way: "Socialization acts as a fine-tuning device; it helps us make sense out of the procedures and quantitative measures. Any number of times I've been faced with a situation where the right thing for the measurement system was X and the right thing for IBM was Y. I've always been counseled to tilt toward what was right for IBM in the long term and what was right for our people. They pay us a lot to do that. Formal controls, without coherent values and culture, are too crude a compass to steer by."

Organizations that socialize effectively use their cultures to manage ambiguity, ever present in such tricky matters as business politics and personal relationships. This tends to free up time and energy. More goes toward getting the job done and focusing on external considerations like the competition and the customer. "At IBM you spend 50 percent of your time managing the internal context," states a former IBMer, now at ITT. "At most companies it's more like 75 percent." A marketing manager who worked at Atari before it got new management recalls: "You can't imagine how much time and energy around here went into politics. You had to determine who was on first base this month in order to figure out how to obtain what you needed to get the job done. There were no rules. There were no clear values. Two of the men at the top stood for diametrically opposite things. Your bosses were constantly changing. All this meant that you never had time to develop a routine way for getting things done at the interface between your job and the next guy's Without rules for working with one another, a lot of people got hurt, got burned out, and were never taught the 'Atari way' of doing things because there wasn't an Atari way."

The absence of cultural guidelines makes organizational life capricious. This is so because success as a manager requires managing not only the substance of the business but also, increasingly, managing one's role and relationships. When social roles are unclear, no one is speaking the same language; communication and trust break down. A person's power to get things done in a company seldom depends on his title and formal authority alone. In great measure it rests on his track record, reputation, knowledge, and network of relationships. In effect, the power to implement change and execute business strategies depends heavily on what might be called one's social currency— as in money—something a person accumulates over time. Strong-culture firms empower employees, helping them build this currency by supplying continuity and clarity.

Continuity and clarity also help reduce the anxiety people feel about their careers. Mixed signals about rewards, promotions, career paths, criteria for being on the "fast track" or a candidate for termination inevitably generate a lot of gossip, game playing, and unproductive expenditure of energy. Only the naive think that these matters can be entirely resolved by provisions in a policy manual. The reality is that many criteria of success for middle- and senior-level positions can't be articulated in writing. The rules tend to be communicated and enforced via relatively subtle cues. When the socialization process is weak, the cues tend to be poorly or inconsistently communicated.

Look carefully at career patterns in most companies. Ambitious professionals strive to learn the ropes, but there are as many "ropes" as there are individuals who have made their way to the top. So the aspirant picks an approach, and if it happens to coincide with how his superiors do things, he's on the fast track. Commonly, though, the approach that works with one superior is offensive to another. "As a younger manager, I was always taught to touch bases and solicit input before moving ahead," a manager at a Santa Clara, California, electronics firm says, "and it always worked. But at a higher level, with a different boss, my base-touching was equated with being political. The organization doesn't forewarn you when it changes signals. A lot of good people leave owing to misunderstandings of this kind." The human cost of the failure to socialize tends to go largely unrecognized.

What about the cost of conformity? A senior vice president of IBM asserts: "Conformity among IBM employees has often been described as stultifying in terms of dress, behavior, and lifestyle. There is, in fact, strong pressure to adhere to certain norms of superficial behavior, and much more intensely to the three tenets of the company philosophy—respect for the dignity of the individual, first-rate customer service, and excellence. These are the benchmarks. Between them there is wide latitude for divergence in opinions and behavior."

A P&G executive echoes this thought: "There is a great deal of consistency around here in how certain things are done, and these are rather critical to our sustained success. Beyond that, there are very few hard and fast rules. People on the outside might portray our culture as imposing lock-step uniformity. It doesn't feel rigid when you're inside. It feels like it accommodates you. And best of all, you know the game you're in—you know whether you're playing soccer or football; you can find out very clearly what it takes to succeed and you can bank your career on that."

It is useful to distinguish here between norms that are central to the business's success and social conventions that signal commitment and belonging. The former are essential in that they ensure consistency in executing the company's strategy. The latter are the organizational equivalent of shaking hands. They are social conventions that make it easier for people to be comfortable with one another. One need not observe all of them, but one wants to reassure the organization that one is on the team. An important aspect of this second set of social values is that, like a handshake, they are usually not experienced as oppressive. Partly this is because adherence doesn't require much thought or deliberation, just as most people don't worry much about their individuality being compromised by the custom of shaking hands.

The aim of socialization is to establish a base of shared attitudes, habits, and values that foster cooperation, integrity and communication. But without the natural rough-and-tumble friction between competing co-workers, some might argue, there will be little innovation. The record does not bear this out. Consider 3M or Bell Labs. Both are highly innovative institutions—and both remain so by fostering social rules that reward innovation. Socialization does not necessarily discourage competition between employees. Employees compete hard at IBM, P&G, major consulting firms, law firms, and outstanding financial institutions like Morgan Guaranty and Morgan Stanley.

There is, of course, the danger of strong-culture firms becoming incestuous and myopic—what came to be known in the early days of the Japanese auto invasion as the General Motors syndrome. Most opponents of socialization rally around this argument. But what one learns from observing the likes of IBM and P&G is that their cultures keep them constantly facing outward. Most companies like this tend to guard against the danger of complacency by having as one element of their culture an *obsession* with some facet of their performance in the marketplace. For example, McDonald's has an obsessive concern for quality control; IBM, for customer service; 3M, for innovation. These obsessions make for a lot of fire drills. But they also serve as the organizational equivalent of calisthenics, keeping people fit for the day when the emergency is real. When, on the other hand, the central cultural concern points inward rather than outward—as seems to be the case, say, with Delta Air Lines' focus on "family feeling"—the strong-culture company may be riding for a fall.

Revolutions begin with an assault on awareness. It is time to be more candid and clear-minded about socialization. Between our espoused individualism and the reality of most companies lies a zone where organizational and individual interests overlap. If we can manage our ambivalence about socialization, we can make our organizations more effective. Equally important, we can reduce the human costs that arise today as individuals stumble along in careers with companies that fail to articulate ends and means coherently and understandably for all employees.

35

Unstable at the Top*

MANFRED F. R. KETS De VRIES and DANNY MILLER

There are striking similarities between the neurotic behavior of individuals and the practices of failing or borderline businesses. In such neurotic companies, strategy, structure, and organizational climate often reflect the neurotic styles and fantasies of the top echelon of managers. More specifically, the neurotic characteristics of these executives seem to create uniformities of organizational culture, which in turn foster common neurotic organizational styles.

Through our work as organizational researchers, we have identified five such neurotic styles, well established in the psychoanalytic and psychiatric literature: dramatic, depressive, paranoid, compulsive, and schizoid. Each style has its specific characteristics, predominant motivating fantasy and associated dangers (see Table 1). And each has its counterparts in the strategic behavior, climate, and structure of a number of troubled companies. Some of the firms we describe are still in business, but their rigidity seems to contain the seeds of failure.

The Stevens Corporation and Pyrax International exemplify two contrasting neurotic styles. (All names are fictitious, but the situations are

* From *Psychology Today*, October 1984, pp. 27–34. Copyright © 1984 by American Psychological Association.

TABLE 1
Irrational Executives: Making the Diagnosis

	Dramatic	Depressive	Paranoid	Compulsive	Schizoid
Characteristics	Self-dramatization, excessive expression of emotions; incessant drawing of attention to self; craving for activity and excitement; alternating between idealization and devaluation of others; exploitativeness; incapacity to concentrate or focus attention sharply.	Feelings of guilt, worthlessness, self-reproach, inadequacy; sense of helplessness and hopelessness, of being at the mercy of events; diminished ability to think clearly; loss of interest and motivation; inability to experience pleasure.	Suspiciousness and mistrust of others; hypersensitivity and hyperalertness; readiness to counter perceived threats; overconcern with hidden motives and special meanings; intense concentration; cold, rational, unemotional.	Perfectionism; preoccupation with trivial details; insistence that others submit to own way of doing things; relationships seen in terms of dominance and submission; lack of spontaneity; inability to relax; meticulousness, dogmatism, obstinacy.	Detachment, noninvolvement, withdrawal; sense of estrangement; lack of excitement or enthusiasm; indifference to praise or criticism; lack of interest in present or future; cold, unemotional appearance.
Fantasies	I want to get attention from and impress the people who count in my life.	It is hopeless to change the course of events in my life; I am just not good enough.	I cannot really trust anybody; a menacing superior force is out to get me; I had better be on my guard.	I don't want to be at the mercy of events; I have to master and control all the things affecting me.	Reality does not offer satisfaction; interactions with others will fail, so it is safer to remain distant.
Dangers	Superficiality; suggestibility; the risk of operating in an unreal world with action based on hunches; overreaction to minor events; others may feel used and abused.	Overly pessimistic outlook; difficulties in concentration and performance; inhibition of action, indecisiveness.	Distortion of reality due to a preoccupation with confirming suspicions; loss of capacity for spontaneous action because of defensive attitudes.	Inward orientation; indecisiveness due to the fear of making mistakes; inability to deviate from plans; overreliance on regulations; difficulties in seeing the big picture.	Emotional isolation causes frustration of dependency needs of others; bewilderment and aggressiveness may result.

real, taken from our consulting experience.) Pyrax was a rapidly expanding conglomerate making incursions into various industries. The company was run by Alex Herzog, a vain, ambitious, and domineering entrepreneur who was the founder, prime mover and, many thought, the tyrant-in-chief. He drove his employees ruthlessly, seized the lion's share of decision-making power and was noted for his boldness in acquiring firms, some larger than Pyrax itself. A self-made man, Herzog wanted desperately to run a powerful and gigantic enterprise. Through aggressive acquisition, he had gone a long way toward achieving his dream, incurring massive amounts of long-term debt in the process. Mounting interest rates and sinking profits were already starting to threaten Pyrax when it acquired Stevens.

Before the acquisition, Stevens was almost as large as Pyrax. A parts manufacturer in the heavy-equipment field, Stevens was a lively firm whose product innovations had produced a respectable growth rate and whose manufacturing economies had given it the highest rate of return on equity in the industry. The president, David Morse, was devoted to balancing innovation with efficiency and growth with financial strength. Stevens's products were known for their high quality.

Things began to change soon after the acquisition. Herzog disliked having strong managers in charge of his companies. He insisted on making all the major decisions at Stevens even though he knew nothing about the industry. He kept Stevens' top executives busy supplying him with trivial information, and he questioned—even scolded—them when they failed to consult him on decisions. Morse rapidly became disenchanted and finally quit after Herzog insisted on several misplaced cost-cutting measures. It became more and more apparent that Herzog saw Stevens as merely a source of cash to finance his grandiose expansion plans.

The departure of Morse allowed Herzog to install Byron Gorsuch as chief executive at Stevens. Gorsuch, a shy and insecure bureaucrat, knew little about Stevens's markets. His expertise lay in his ability to follow Herzog's directives to the letter. Stevens's managers were forced to play a purely advisory role, and as Herzog and Gorsuch generally failed to heed their advice, the most competent managers left. The remaining executives were passive and fearful; anxious about job security, they slavishly adhered to the rituals laid down by Herzog. Strategic issues were ignored, and as the firm began to stagnate, profitability and sales declined.

The situation at Stevens was not helped by what was happening at Pyrax. The stubborn, grandiose Herzog and his staff had become enmeshed in still more ambitious, and ultimately more disastrous, acquisitions. They were too busy to recognize the danger signs at Stevens, and the depressed, passive managers at Stevens were too insecure to do anything themselves.

In terms of organizational neurosis, Pyrax was dramatic, a company whose bold, grandiose leader caused the firm to overextend its resources. Stevens was a depressive firm; its decline was due to strategic stagnation. In both firms the personalities of the top managers, Herzog and Gorsuch, were strongly reflected in the companies' problematic strategies, structures, and managerial climates.

THE DRAMATIC ORGANIZATION

Let us look at the five types of neurotic organizations in detail, starting with the two we have already discussed. Dramatic firms like Pyrax are hyperactive, impulsive, dramatically venturesome, and dangerously uninhibited. Their decision makers live in a world of hunches and impressions rather than facts as they haphazardly address an array of disparate markets. Their dramatic flair encourages the top people to centralize power, reserving their prerogative to initiate bold ventures.

Audacity, risk taking, and diversification are the corporate themes. Instead of reacting to the business environment, the top decision maker attempts to create his own environment. (We will use male pronouns for convenience; most of the top executives we studied were men.) He enters some markets and leaves others; he constantly is switching to new products while abandoning older ones, placing a sizable proportion of the firm's capital at risk.

Unbridled growth is the goal, reflecting the top manager's considerable narcissistic needs, his desire for attention and visibility. He wants to be at center stage, showing how great an executive he really is.

The structure of the dramatic organization is usually far too primitive for its broad markets. First, too much power is concentrated in the chief executive, who meddles even in routine operating matters because he wants to put his personal stamp on (and take credit for) everything. A second problem follows from this overcentralization—namely, the absence of an effective information system. The top executive does too little scanning of the business environment because he has too little time and prefers to act on intuition rather than facts. Finally, the leader's dominance obstructs effective internal communication, which is mostly from the top down.

THE DEPRESSIVE ORGANIZATION

Depressive firms like Stevens are characterized by inactivity, lack of confidence, extreme conservatism, and insularity. There is an atmosphere of passivity and purposelessness. What gets done is what has been programmed and routinized and requires no special initiative.

Most depressive firms are well established and serve a mature market, one that has had the same technology and competitive patterns for many years. Trade agreements, restrictive trade practices and substantial tariffs are the rule. The primary steel industry and agricultural or industrial chemical businesses are the kinds of markets in which depressive firms are most commonly found. The low level of change, the absence of serious competition and the homogeneity of the customers make the administrative task fairly simple.

Although formal authority is centralized and based on position rather than expertise, the issue of power is not very important. Control is really exercised by formalized programs and policies rather than by managerial initiatives. Suggestions for change are resisted and action is inhibited. It is almost as if the top executives share a sense of impotence and incapacity. They just don't feel they can control events or that they have what it takes to revitalize the firm.

Content with the status quo, these organizations do little to discover the key threats and weaknesses in markets. It is difficult to say whether stagnation causes inattention to information gathering or vice versa. In either event, the two aspects go hand in hand in the depressive firm.

The sense of aimlessness and apathy among top managers precludes any attempt to give the firm clear direction or goals. Strategy is never explicitly considered, so no meaningful change occurs. Yesterday's products and markets become today's, not because of any policy of conservatism, but because of lethargy. Managers spend most of their time working out routine details while procrastinating on major decisions. Where there should be effort to adapt, to grow and to become more effective, there is only inactivity and passivity.

THE PARANOID ORGANIZATION

In this type of company, managerial suspicions translate into a primary emphasis on organizational intelligence and controls. Managers develop sophisticated information systems to identify threats by the government, competitors, and customers, and they develop budgets, cost centers, profit centers, cost-accounting procedures, and similar methods to control internal business. The elaborate information-processing apparatus reflects their desire for perpetual vigilance and preparedness for emergencies.

This paranoia also influences decision making. Frequently, key executives decide that it may be safer to direct their distrust externally rather than withhold information from one another. They share information and make concerted efforts to discover organizational problems and to select alternative solutions for dealing with them. Unfortunately, this type of decision making can become overly consultative, with different people being asked for similar information. Such "institutionalization of suspicion" ensures that accurate information gets to the top of the firm, but it may also lower morale and trust as well as waste valuable time and energy.

Paranoid firms tend to react rather than anticipate. If competitors lower prices, the firm may study the challenge and, eventually, react to it. If other firms introduce a product successfully, the paranoid firm will probably imitate them. But strategic paranoia carries with it a sizable element of conservatism. Fear often entails being afraid to innovate, overextend resources, or take risks. This reactive orientation impedes development of a concerted and consistent strategy. The paranoid firm's direction has too much to do with external forces and not enough with consistent goals, plans, or unifying themes and traditions. Paranoid firms frequently try product diversification to reduce the risk of reliance on any one product, but because diversification requires more elaborate control and information-processing mechanisms, it actually reinforces the firm's paranoia.

Corporate paranoia often stems from a period of traumatic challenge. A strong market dries up, a powerful new competitor enters the market or damaging legislation is passed. The harm done by these forces may cause managers to become very distrustful and fearful, to lose their nerve, to recognize the need for better intelligence.

Paratech, Inc., a semiconductor manufacturer, illustrates how a paranoid organization can develop under those conditions. The organization was run by its two founders, who had earlier worked for a much larger electronics firm that did a good deal of top-secret defense contracting. Three factors contributed to the founders' paranoia. The first was an episode at the large electronics firm in which Soviet spies had stolen valuable designs. Second, a competitor regularly beat Paratech to the marketplace with products that Paratech had conceived. Finally, there was a high rate of bankruptcy in the semiconductor field.

The two founders took all kinds of precautions to prevent their ideas from being stolen. They fragmented jobs and processes so that only a few key people in the company really understood the products. They rarely subcontracted work. And they paid employees very high salaries to give them an incentive to stay with the firm. These three precautions combined to make Paratech's costs among the highest in the industry.

The founders found other ways to create problems for themselves. First, they were financially conservative in an industry known for rewarding risk takers. Paratech spent much less on R&D than the competition did and thus was slow to develop products, making its profit margins among the lowest in the industry. Second, although the founders carefully scanned the environment to see what the competition was up to, they waited too long for the market's reaction before deciding what to imitate. The delay was costly, as markets for high-technology products become saturated very quickly.

Finally, since Paratech did not want to be left out of any segment of the market or be overly dependent on any one sector, it diversified. But the spread was too thin, and the firm was unable to develop any distinctive competence. All these tendencies squeezed Paratech's profit margins and made it one of the least successful firms in a booming industry.

THE COMPULSIVE ORGANIZATION

The compulsive firm is wed to ritual. Every detail of operation is planned carefully in advance and carried out in routinized fashion. Thoroughness, completeness, and conformity to established procedures are emphasized.

Like the paranoid firm, the compulsive firm emphasizes formal controls and information systems. There is a crucial difference, however: In compulsive organizations, controls are really designed to monitor internal operations, production efficiency, costs, and the scheduling and performance of projects, while the paranoid firm is interested chiefly in external conditions.

Operations are standardized as much as possible, and an elaborate set of formal policies and procedures evolves. These include not only production and marketing procedures but dress codes, frequent sales meetings, and even suggested employee attitudes.

The compulsive organization is exceedingly hierarchical, a reflection of the leader's strong concern with control. The compulsive person is always worried about the next move and how he is going to make it. Such preoccupation has often been reinforced by periods when the firm was at the mercy of the other organizations or circumstances. To prevent this from happening again, compulsive executives try to reduce uncertainty and to attain a clearly specified objective in a carefully planned manner. Surprises must be avoided at all costs.

Compulsive firms show the same preoccupation with detail and established procedures in all their business strategies. They generally create a large number of action plans, budgets, and capital expenditure plans. Each project is designed with many checkpoints, exhaustive performance evaluations, and detailed schedules.

Unlike the paranoid company, the compulsive firm has a particular orientation and distinctive competence, and its plans reflect them. This orientation, rather than what is going on in the world, serves as the major guide for the firm's strategy. For example, some organizations take pride in being the leading innovator in the marketplace; they try to be the first out with new products, whether or not these are called for by customers. Innovation may be inappropriate in the light of new market conditions, but the firm's strong inward focus prevents any realization of this fact. Change is difficult.

The Minutiae Corporation was a classically compulsive firm. It was dominated by David Richardson, its founder and chief executive officer for the past 20 years. The firm manufactured roller bearings for railroad cars, costlier than the competitors' but easily the best available. They had been designed by Richardson himself, a mechanical engineer of great ability who made sure that the bearings were manufactured to extremely precise specifications. Minutiae's quality-control procedures were the tightest and most sophisticated in the industry. The machines were always kept in excellent repair. The firm's strategy strongly emphasized selling a very durable, high-quality product, and for many years this strategy paid off, making Minutiae the largest firm in the industry.

In the previous five years, however, smaller firms in the industry had begun to pioneer the use of new materials. Able to produce rather high-quality bearings for a fraction of the cost of the old products, they lowered their prices. Richardson steadfastly refused to adopt the new material and technology because they produced inferior wearing qualities. But Minutiae's product was now twice as expensive as the competition's, and it lost much of its market. Richardson's obsessive attention to product quality focused Minutiae's strategy too narrowly to allow it to survive in a changing environment.

THE SCHIZOID ORGANIZATION

This kind of company, like the depressive type, suffers from a leadership vacuum. Its chief executive, often because of past disappointments, believes most contacts will end painfully and is inclined to daydream to compensate for lack of fulfillment. In some of these organizations, executives on the second level of authority are able to make up for the leader's deficiencies with their own warmth and extroversion. Too often, however, the executives see in the withdrawn nature of the top person an opportunity to pursue their own needs.

The second tier thus becomes a political battlefield for gamesmen who vie to win favor from an unresponsive leader. The combination of leadership vacuum and political infighting produces interesting strategic and structural results. No integrated market strategy develops. The leader—insecure, withdrawn and noncommittal—vacillates between the proposals of one favored subordinate and those of another.

Strategy making resides in a shifting coalition of careerist second-tier managers who try to influence the indecisive leader and simultaneously advance their pet projects and minor empires. The firm muddles through and drifts, making incremental changes in one area and then reversing them whenever a new group of managers wins favor. The initiatives of one group of managers are often neutralized or severely blunted by those of an opposing group.

The divided nature of the organization thwarts effective coordination and communication. Information is used more as a power resource than as a vehicle for effective adaptation; in fact, managers erect barriers to prevent the free flow of information. But this is not the only shortcoming of the information system. Another is the absence of information on the outside business environment. The company's focus is internal—on personal ambitions and catering to the top manager's desires. Second-tier managers find it more useful to ignore real-world events that might reflect poorly on their own behavior or conflict with the wishes of the detached leader.

The Cornish Corporation, a ladies' apparel manufacturer run by Selma Gitnick, was a political battlefield for two of its second-tier managers. Gitnick had once been a very successful manager, but the suicide of her daughter and her recent divorce had turned an already shy woman into a recluse. She rarely left her office or had other managers visit her there. Instead, everything was done through written memos. In a firm that required rapid adaptation to a dynamic and uncertain fashion market, this slowdown in communication caused serious difficulties.

Gitnick reserved the right to make all important final decisions herself, but she was very difficult to reach, and she had been very imprecise in allocating responsibilities and authority to the second-tier managers. Managers were thus required to make most decisions, but because they were unclear about their own and everyone else's authority and responsibilities, each decision inevitably involved a power struggle between them.

The design people believed they could make the final choice of designs. Their boss began to clash frequently with the head of the marketing department, who accused the design people of incompetence and tried to veto their decisions. Each department head wrote to Gitnick, complaining about the other and asking for a final decision. Gitnick was ambiguous in her reply, instructing the managers to give each other full cooperation. The bickering continued, and the consequent delays allowed competitors to purchase the best designs. Moreover, Cornish was two months late with its new line, which proved disastrous for sales.

As organizational researchers, we have wondered why certain decisions are made and particular strategies chosen. Why does an organization end up with a particular kind of structure? Why is a certain individual selected for a particular job? If the observations we have outlined are accurate, the problems of many troubled companies are deeply ingrained, based on the deep-seated neurotic styles and fantasies of top executives.

Since our five common pathologies seem so multifaceted and thematically unified, it is unlikely that they can be adequately addressed by management consultants with a standard bag of tools. New information systems, committees, and quality-of-worklife programs will be of little help as long as executives cling to their dysfunctional fantasies and shared organizational ideologies. The new programs should be complemented either by more realistic views of the business and its environment or by more adaptive executives.

We are not suggesting that neurotic executive styles always require changing. They may sometimes be quite compatible with a firm's environment. But too often they foster a kind of rigidity that inhibits adaptation. In the long run, only a healthy mixture of styles can ensure corporate success.

36

The Four Faces of Social Responsibility*

DAN R. DALTON and RICHARD A. COSIER

Imagine that your company is considering introducing a new plastic container to the market. Your company considers itself to be socially responsible; therefore, an extensive impact assessment program is undertaken. One of your environmentally minded employees suggests that people might light the containers and then cook their meals over the fire. Although the idea sounds bizarre, you don't want to take any chances, so for over a month you cook hamburgers over a fire made from your plastic bottles. Rats are fed this hamburger, then carefully monitored for negative side effects. Tests indicate that these rats suffer no ill effects.

Of course you also perform an extensive series of tests involving energy usage, disposal, and recycling opportunities. Then you invite the public to carefully scheduled hearings across the country in order to encourage consumer inputs. Finally, you market the new product and land a major soft drink company as a customer.

Sound as if your company has fulfilled its responsibilities and forestalled any possible objections? In the mid-1970s Monsanto went through this very process in developing Cycle-Safe bottles and spent more than $47 million to market the product. But in 1977 the FDA banned the bottle because, when stored at 120 degrees for an extended period of time, molecules strayed from the plastic into the contents. Rats, fed with doses that were equivalent to consuming thousands of quarts of soft drink over a human lifetime, developed an above-normal number of tumors.

Monsanto felt that they were providing a product that did something for society—a plastic bottle that could be recycled. But social responsibility is unavoidably a matter of degree and interpretation. Forces outside of the business are liable to interpret a product to be

---

* From *Business Horizons*, 1982, 25, 19–27. Copyright © 1982 by the Foundation for the School of Business, Indiana University.

socially unacceptable, even when the company has undertaken an extensive impact analysis.

A precise evaluation of what is socially responsible is difficult to establish, and of course, many definitions have been suggested. Joseph McGuire, in *Business and Society*, provided a persuasive focus when he stated that the corporation "must act 'justly' as a proper citizen should." Large corporations have not only legal obligations, but also certain responsibilities to society which extend beyond the parameters set by law. As the Monsanto case illustrates, the line between legality and responsibility is sometimes very fine.

Peter Drucker offers a useful way to distinguish between behaviors in organizations; the first is what an organization does *to* society, the other what an organization can do *for* society. This suggests that organizations can be evaluated on at least two dimensions with respect to their performance as "citizens": legality and responsibility. Table 1 illustrates the various combinations of legality and responsibility which may characterize an organization's performance.

TABLE 1
The Four Faces of Social Responsibility

	Illegal	Legal
Irresponsible	A	C
Responsible	B	D

These combinations are the *four faces of social responsibility.* Each cell of the table represents a strategy which could be adopted by an organization. It is unfortunate, but we think true, that no matter which strategy is chosen, the corporation is subject to some criticism.

ILLEGAL AND IRRESPONSIBLE

In modern society, this strategy, if not fatal, is certainly extremely high risk. In an age of social consciousness, it is difficult to imagine an organization that would regularly engage in illegal and irresponsible behavior. What, for example, would be the consequences of an organization's blatantly refusing to employ certain minority groups or deliberately and knowingly using a carcinogenic preservative in foodstuff? Besides the fact that such behavior is patently illegal, it is offensive and irresponsible.

There are, however, instances of illegal and irresponsible corporate conduct which are not so easily condemned.

You Can Hardly Blame Them

Most of us have value systems. They vary, to be sure, from individual to individual and from corporation to corporation. They do, however, have common elements: They are tempered by temptation, consequence, and risk. Sometimes, when faced with high temptation, low consequence, and low risk, our value systems are not the constraining force they could be. This may be the human condition and insufficient justification for the excesses which often accompany individual and corporate decision making. Nonetheless, an appreciation of these factors often makes those decisions entirely understandable.

Suppose that the state in which you live invokes a regulation that all motor vehicles operated on a public thoroughfare must be equipped with an "X" type pollution-control device. This law, for the sake of discussion, is retroactive. All automobiles registered in the state must be refitted with such a device, which costs $500. All automobiles are subject to periodic inspection to assure compliance with the law. Assume that the maximum fine (consequence) for violating this statute is $50. Assume, furthermore, that there is 1 chance in 100 that you will be inspected and found in violation. The analytical question is simply stated: Would you have the device installed? If you do, it will cost $500. If you do not, the cost will be $500 plus a $50 fine, but only *if* you are caught. Many, if not most, of us surely would not install the device. Strictly speaking, our behavior is both illegal and irresponsible. Our failure to comply exacerbates a societal problem—namely, polluting the air. Our reluctance under the described circumstances, however, is understandable: temptation along with low consequence and low risk.

Compare this situation with that of a large organization faced with the decision to install pollution abatement equipment in one of its plants. Suppose, in this case, the total cost of the installation is $500,000; the maximum fine for noncompliance is $10,000; the chance of being caught is one in one hundred. We ask the same question: Would you comply? We have actually been charitable with the balance of costs and probabilities in this example. The Occupational Safety and Health Administration (OSHA), which was given the charter for establishing and enforcing occupational safety and health standards, has a limited number of inspectors and approximately 5 million organizations subject to its mandate. It has been estimated that an organization could plan on being inspected about every 77 years, or approximately as often as you could expect to see Halley's comet.[1] Furthermore, $10,000 is a very large fine by OSHA standards. The fundamental point, of course, is that the temptation to ignore the law ($500,000) is large, the fine ($10,000) low, and the risk (once every 77 years) very small. You cannot be surprised when an organization does not comply any more than you would be surprised that the individual with the polluting car did not comply.

It can be argued that the organization has the greater responsibility. Certainly, a polluting smokestack is more visible, literally and figuratively, than an automobile's exhaust. However, we daresay that the marginal pollution attributable to automobiles far exceeds that of smokestacks in most (if not all) regions. Illegal? Yes. Irresponsible? Yes. Understandable?

Whether or not the behavior is "understandable," the result, at a minimum, is bad publicity. The observation that a corporation is likely to be criticized for operating in that "Illegal/Irresponsible" area is obvious. There has, however, been testimony and documentation that the weight of potential litigations in a classic cost/benefit analysis is far less than the cost of recalling or correcting the alleged deficiencies. While we have suggested that behavior in this area is high risk, there is precious little evidence that it is suicidal.

ILLEGAL/RESPONSIBLE

Being in this cell raises very interesting issues. Monsanto found itself in this cell in the Cycle-Safe incident. The FDA ruled their product illegal, even though Monsanto felt socially responsible. Many times however, organizations find themselves in this area because of jurisdictional disputes. Suppose that prior to the Civil Rights Act of 1964 and attendant legislation, an organization chose to embark on a program to employ women in equal capacities as male employees. At the time, this would have been forward-looking and extremely responsible corporate behavior. Unfortunately, much of the behavior involved in implementing that strategy would have been unquestionably illegal. During that period, "protective legislation" was very common. This legislation, designed to "protect" women, restricted working hours, overtime, the amount of weight that could be lifted, and types of jobs (bartending, for example) available to women. These

---

[1] "Why Nobody Wants to Listen to OSHA," *Business Week*, June 14, 1976, p. 76, from Randall S. Schuler, *Personnel and Human Resource Management* (St. Paul: West Publishing, 1981).

and similar matters were eventually adjudicated largely at the federal court level.

Grover Starling cites an interesting jurisdictional paradox. It seems that the Federal Meat Inspection Service ordered an Armour meat-packing plant to create an aperture in a conveyor line so that inspectors could remove samples for testing. Accordingly, the company did so. The Occupational Safety and Health Administration soon arrived and demanded that the aperture be closed. It seems that an aperture on that line constituted a safety hazard. Predictably, each agency threatened to close down the plant if it refused to comply with its orders.[2] This example demonstrates how an organization could be operating in a fundamentally desirable manner (safely) and yet run afoul of legislation at some level. An organization might adopt a program to train underprivileged children, for example, and find itself in violation of a minimum wage law.

One potential strategy for dealing with problems in this cell is challenging the law. Laws can be, and are regularly, deliberately violated for no other reason than to challenge their application. You cannot get a hearing in a state or federal court on a "what if" basis. In order to get a hearing, someone must be in jeopardy. A classic example is the famous *Gideon* v. *Wainwright* case where the Supreme Court ruled that a suspect has the right to counsel and that the state must provide such counsel if the accused could not afford it. This case could not have been decided without an issue—a man convicted without benefit of counsel. Gideon had to be in jeopardy. Courts do not rule on hypothetical cases.

The public is often critical of the corporate use of the courts. It is true that the courts, aside from their jurisprudential charter, are often used as a delay mechanism. There are, for example, legendary anti-trust cases which have been in the courts for years. The courts have ruled against the acquisition, but organizations, through a series of legal maneuvers, have managed to stall the actual separations. In the meantime, presumably, the benefits of the acquisition continue to accrue. Interestingly, everyone's "pursuit of justice" is someone else's "delay." Even in *Gideon* v. *Wainwright*, we have little doubt that the prosecuting attorney's office saw the several appeals as both a nuisance and a delay.

Again, organizations can find themselves in a dilemma. An organization in the "Illegal/Responsible" cell faces a paradox. It is likely to be criticized whether it lives within the law or, potentially, challenges it.

---

[2] Grover Starling, *The Changing Environment of Business* (Boston: Kent Publishing, 1980).

IRRESPONSIBLE/LEGAL

Historically, there have been astonishing excesses in this area. Some of them would have been laughable if they had not been so serious. For example, prior to the Pure Food and Drug Act, the advertising for a diet pill promised that a person taking this pill could eat virtually anything at any time and still lose weight. Too good to be true? Actually, the claim was quite true; the product lived up to its billing with frightening efficacy. It seems that the primary active ingredient in this "diet supplement" was tapeworm larvae. These larvae would develop in the intestinal tract and, of course, be well fed; the pill taker would in time, quite literally, starve to death.

In another case, which can only be described as amazing, an "anti-alcoholic elixir" was guaranteed to prevent the person who received the "potion" from drinking to excess. It was *very* effective. The product contained such a large dose of codeine that the people taking it became essentially comatose. The good news, of course, is that they certainly did not drink very much. And at the time, this product was not illegal.

There are more current examples with which we are all familiar— black lung disease in miners and asbestos poisoning, among others. Certainly, it was not always illegal to have miners working in mines without sufficient safety equipment to forestall black lung; nor was it illegal to have employees regularly working with asbestos without adequate protection. It can be argued that these consequences were not anticipated and that these situations were not deliberately socially irresponsible. It is, however, less persuasive to make that argument with respect to the ages and extended working hours of children in our industrial past.

But enough of the past. Do major organizations continue to engage in behaviors which, while not illegal, may be completely irresponsible? Among several examples that come to mind, one is, we think, appropriate for discussion but likely to be highly contentious—the manufacture and distribution of cigarettes. Obviously, cigarette manufacturing is not illegal. Is it irresponsible?

We noted earlier that knowledge of the effects of certain drugs may have been lacking in the past. We mentioned codeine-based elixirs. There are others. Some compounds contained as much as three grams of cocaine per base ounce. One asthma reliever was nearly pure cocaine. Even so, perhaps their effects were little understood and little harm was thought to have been done. Can the same be said of the tobacco industry? Is there anyone who is not aware of the harmful effects of smoking? True, there are warning labels which imply that the purchaser knows what he or she is taking. But how many people would endorse the use of codeine or cocaine or any other harmful substance, even with an appropriate warning label? Comparing apples and oranges? Perhaps, but 50 years from now, writers may talk about the manufacture of tobacco products and use terms such as *astonishing, amazing,* and *laughable* as we have to describe other legal, but irresponsible, behaviors.

Certainly, issues other than health are contained in this category. Suppose an organization is faced with more demand for its product than it can meet. Naturally, the organization does not care to encourage competition and would prefer to meet the demand itself if possible. Unfortunately, their plants are already operating 24 hours per day, 7 days a week. There is simply no further capacity. Management decides to build a new plant, which can be completed in no less than four years.

In the meantime, it is discovered that an existing, abandoned plant can be acquired and refitted in six months. Now, this plant will not be efficient, and will be only marginally profitable at best. It will, however, serve to meet the escalating demand until such time as the new plant is ready for full operation, some four years hence.

Jury-rigging this abandoned plant, however, involves several problems. Foremost among them is the fact that the community does not have the infrastructure to serve the plant and the expected influx of employees. School systems will have to be expanded; housing will have to be built; recreational services improved. For the sake of this discussion, suppose that the temporary plant will employ 1,200 persons. It would be reasonable to estimate that this would mean the addition of 3,000 to 3,500 persons in the community. But, remember, this plant will be closed as soon as the new plant in another location is operational.

What is your decision? Do you authorize the refitting of this temporary plant? Certainly, if you notify the community that the plant is temporary, you will pay certain costs. The community would be understandably unlikely to make permanent improvements. Local banks would be somewhat less than enthusiastic about financing building projects, home mortgages, or consumer loans of any description. The simple solution is obvious—don't tell.

The point is that to deliberately use this plant as a stop-gap measure knowing full well that it will be temporary is not illegal. We are aware of no legislation which would prevent this action. There remain, however, some obvious social ramifications of this strategy. The ultimate closing of this plant is likely to reduce this community to a ghost town; there will be widespread unemployment; property values will fall precipitously; the tax base will be destroyed.

Once again, operating in this area is subject to criticism, underscoring our earlier point that being a "law-abiding" corporate citizen is not nearly enough; while organizations may not violate a single law, they may not be socially responsible. What of gambling casinos dealing not only in games of chance, but also offering endless free liquor and decolletage? How about the manufacturers of handguns? Automobiles with questionable, if not lethal, fuel systems? Can a society hold organizations to a standard higher than that demanded by law?

LEGAL/RESPONSIBLE

It would seem that we have finally arrived at a strategy for which an organization cannot be criticized. An organization in this sector is a law-abiding corporate citizen and engages in behaviors which exceed those required by law—voluntary socially oriented action. Alas, even this proactive strategy is subject to four severe criticisms.

- Such behavior amounts to a unilateral, involuntary redistribution of assets.
- These actions lead to inequitable, regressive redistribution of assets.
- An organization engaging in these behaviors clearly exceeds its province.
- Social responsibility is entirely too expensive and rarely subjected to cost/benefit analysis

Involuntary Redistribution

Probably the chief spokesperson of this position is Nobel laureate and economist Milton Friedman. He points out that today, unlike 100 years ago, managers do not "own" the business. They are employees, nothing more and nothing less. As such their primary responsibility is to the owner—the stockholder. Their relationship is essentially a fiduciary one. Friedman argues that the primary charter of the manager, therefore, is to conduct the business in accordance with the wishes of the employer, given that these wishes are within the limits embodied in the law and ethical custom. Any social actions beyond that amount to an involuntary redistribution of assets. To the extent that these actions reduce dividends, stockholders suffer; to the extent that these actions raise prices, consumers suffer; to the extent that such actions reduce potential wages and benefits, employees suffer. Should any or all of these interested parties care to make philanthropic contributions to fund socially desirable projects, they may do so. Without their consent, however, such redistributions are clearly unilateral and involuntary.

Inequitable, Regressive Redistributions

This tendency can be referred to as a reverse Robin Hood effect.[3] Mr. Hood and his band of merry men stole from the rich and gave to the poor, but many programs under the loose rubric of social responsibility have not followed this redistribution pattern. In fact, it can be argued that many programs actually rob the poor to serve the rich. Obviously, the more wealthy persons are, the more regressive this social responsibility "tax."

Many projects which are not commercially feasible are supported by the largest of organizations under the banner of social responsibility. Opera and dance companies, for example, may be subsidized by corporate contributions. Public television is heavily financed by corporate sponsors. The reason that these subsidies are essential to the operation of these programs is that public demand for these products is altogether insufficient to defray their costs. Presumably, the money to finance these ventures comes from somewhere in the organizational coffers. Consumers, employees, and others "contribute," as we previously noted, to the availability of these funds.

Who, however, is the primary beneficiary of these subsidized programs? For the most part, it seems fair to suggest that those who regularly attend ballets, operas, dance companies, live theatre, symphonies, and watch similar programming on public television are relatively more affluent. It would appear that real income is transferred from the poorer to the richer in this exercise of social responsibility.

Exceeding Province

One, if not the foremost, justification for government involvement in private affairs is market failure. When the market cannot provide, for whatever reasons, that which the public demands, then government is (or should be) enfranchised to supply or finance that product or service. National defense, health and safety, and welfare are a few of the services which the private sector is unable to supply. It may be that libraries, museums, parks and recreation, operas, symphonies, and support for other performing arts are in this category as well. The objection which is central here is that it is not the province of private organizations to decide which of these projects should be funded and to what extent. Such support should not be a function of the predilections of corporate officials; this is the charter of government.

The issue clearly goes beyond fighting over who is going to play with what toys. In theory, public officials are subject to review by the

---

[3] Discussion based largely on Dean Carson, "Companies as Heroes?" . . . *New York Times*, 1977.

citizenry. If the public does not approve of the manner in which funds are being prioritized for social concerns, they may petition their various legislatures. Failing in this, they may not support the reelection of the appropriate public officials. The public, on the other hand, does not vote or in any other manner approve or endorse highly ranking officers of corporations. By what right should corporations decide what is "good" and what is "right"? It may well be that a given corporate image of righteousness is somewhat different from your own.

The potential for corporate influence in this public area is enormous. Theodore Levitt, while (we hope) overstating the case somewhat, presents a clear view of the potential of business statesmanship:

> Proliferating employee welfare programs, its serpentine involvement in community, government, charitable, and educational affairs, its prodigious currying of political and public favor through hundreds of peripheral preoccupations, all these well-intended but insidious contrivances are greasing the rails for our collective descent into a social order that would be as repugnant to the corporations themselves as to their critics. The danger is that all things will turn the corporation into a 20th century equivalent of the medieval Church. The corporation would eventually invest itself with all embracing duties, obligations, and finally powers—ministering to the whole man and molding him and society in the image of the corporation's narrow ambitions and its essentially unsocial needs.[4]

A grim scenario, to be sure. The fundamental point remains. Critics argue that any of these voluntary socially responsible behaviors simply exceed the province of the corporation.

Expense of Social Responsibility

A final objection to the general issue of social responsibility, whether mandated by regulation or voluntarily pursued by organizations, is that it is oppressively expensive. The necessity to comply with ever-stricter environmental standards, for example, has literally forced the closing of hundreds of industrial locations across the country. Furthermore, it has been argued that these regulations have seriously affected domestic industry's ability to compete in international markets.

No one would argue that expense alone is sufficient to discard programs of environmental protection, employee safety, consumer protection, or a host of other socially responsive concerns. However, it

---

[4] Theodore Levitt, "The Dangers of Social Responsibility," *Harvard Business Review*, 1958, p. 44.

can be argued that these programs should be subjected to a cost/benefit analysis. Quite often, this is not done. An automobile, for example, could be manufactured so soundly that driver deaths in accidents could be practically eliminated on our highways. But at what cost? We do not intend to address the question of what a human life is worth. Obviously, its value is incalculable. The fact remains that we live in a finite world; resources are limited. When we choose to make expenditures in one area, we necessarily restrict or eliminate expenditures in another. At what point do safety programs become overly paternalistic? At some time, employees, for example, must bear a certain responsibility for their own safety. The same can be said for those who operate motor vehicles on public byways.

While this principle seems clear, it is often not considered. What expense is justifiable to renovate and refit public buildings to render them essentially fireproof? Or, if not fireproof, at least such that the loss of human life by fire is remote? The hard fact is that very few people die each year in fires in multistoried buildings. Who is going to pay for such judicious safety? And for the benefit of how many?

The same approach can be pursued with respect to airliner safety. Fortunately, very few people lose their lives each year in commercial airplanes. There is no doubt that airplanes could be manufactured so that they would be even safer in accidents. Again, at what cost? We do not wish to appear insensitive; the loss of a human life is a tragedy, especially if it could have been prevented. "Safety at any cost," however, is simply not viable in a society restricted by finite resources.

The objection regarding the expense of social responsibility is easily restated. Aside from its absolute expense, which can be formidable, critics argue that social responsibility is often not accompanied by sufficient benefits to justify its cost.

Once again, even while being both legal and responsible, an organization is likely to receive severe criticism.

We have suggested that every cell (Illegal/Irresponsible, Illegal/Responsible, Legal/Irresponsible, Legal/Responsible) is subject to criticism. Furthermore, the cell that your organization occupies may be determined by individuals outside of your firm—federal agencies or consumer groups, to name a few. It may be a classic expression of the aphorism, "You're damned if you do, you're damned if you don't." Inasmuch as all strategies are subject to criticism, where should the organization operate? Which is the optimum strategy?

We think there are three fundamental principles which should be considered by an organization with respect to choosing a strategy for social responsibility; *primum non nocere*, organizational accountability, and the double standard.

Primum Non Nocere

This notion was first explicated over 2,500 years ago in the Hippocratic oath. Freely translated, it means "Above all, knowingly do no harm." This would seem to be a sound principle for both legality and responsibility. Organizations should not engage in any behavior if they know that harm will be done as a result. This is not meant to be literally interpreted. Certainly, knowing that some individuals will injure themselves is insufficient to bar the manufacture and distribution of, for example, steak knives. This, like any principle, should be tempered with good sense.

Organizational Accountability

An organization should be responsible for its impacts, *to* or *for* society, whether they are intended or not. Ordinarily, in the course of providing a good or a service, costs are incurred. Presumably, the price of the product or service is, at least in part, a function of the costs of its manufacture or delivery. The difference between the cost and the price is profit—the *sine qua non* of private enterprise. This would be acceptable, except for one oversight—very often society underwrites portions of the cost. Historically, given that the production of energy through sulphurous coal leads to higher levels of air pollution, the costs of producing electricity have been artificially low. That pollution is a cost. Sooner or later, someone has to pay to clean it up. But who? The consumer did not have to pay a premium for the electricity to enter a "clean-up" fund. The power company made no such contribution.

Today, we could argue that cigarette manufacturing enterprises enjoy a certain cost reduction. The manufacturer and the smoker can be thought of as enjoying a subsidy. Arguably, the retail price of cigarettes does not approach that necessary to cover its total costs. Where, for instance, is the fund that will eventually be called upon to pay for the medical costs allegedly associated with smoking? The point is that someone should be accountable for these behaviors.

Double Standard

Traditionally, the concept of a double standard has had a negative connotation. In the area of social corporate responsibility, we think it is reasonable, even commendable. As we have continuously noted, there are no rules that apply to organizations about what, where, when, how much, and how often they can engage in behaviors *for* society, but a certain power-responsibility equation has been suggested.[5] Essentially, this equation argues that the social responsibility expected of an organization should be commensurate with the size of the social power it exercises. Large companies—AT&T, General Motors, Exxon, IBM, General Electric, Du Pont—whose operations can literally dominate entire regions of the country have a greater responsibility than smaller organizations with less influence.

The larger an organization becomes, the more actual and potential influence it commands over society. Society, necessarily, takes a greater interest in the affairs of such organizations. Society has correspondingly less expectation of social responsibility from smaller organizations.

This is the nature of the double standard to which we have referred. While any double standard is somewhat unfair, it highlights an observation made by Drucker. He argues that the quest for social responsibility is not a result of hostility towards the business community. Rather the demand for social responsibility is, in large measure, the price of success. Success and influence may well lead to a greater responsibility to society. A double standard, to be sure, but perhaps a reasonable one.

SO WHICH STRATEGY?

We believe that organizations should adopt a strategy reflected in cell D—legal and responsible. Remember, however, that the classification of cell D will be determined by the public (or government acting "for" the public). Organizations have to anticipate, and in some cases, influence the public reaction—be proactive. However, a proactive stance involves some risk. As we noted earlier, critics abound regardless of the cell in the table occupied by the organization. A certain risk, nevertheless, is necessary for any business to succeed. Drucker rightly states that to try to eliminate risk in business is futile. Risk is inherent in the commitment of present resources to future expectations. The attempt to eliminate risk may result in the greatest risk of all—rigidity.

We would argue that merely being a law-abiding corporate citizen is something less than social responsibility. It may be that large organizations must "do something." Affirmative action is a compelling analogy. It is not enough not to discriminate. Organizations must do something proactively to further the goals of equal employment opportunity. Perhaps this is true for other issues of corporate social re-

---

[5] Y. N. Chang and Filemon Campo-Flores, *Business Policy and Strategy* (Santa Monica, Calif.: Goodyear Publishing, 1980).

sponsibility as well. There may be an expectation that organizations must do something to further benefit society beyond following its formal laws.

Basically, some action is better than no action. Throughout the course of history, inaction has never advanced mankind. In our view, errors of commission are far better than those of omission. If our ancestors had heeded the critics who were opposed to doing something, we might all still be drawing on cave walls. This issue is not entirely philosophical; there are important pragmatic considerations as well, as evidenced in the remarks of Du Pont chairperson Irving S. Shapiro:

> I think we're a means to an end, and while producing goods and providing jobs is our primary function, we can't live successfully in a society if the hearts of its cities are decaying and its people can't make the whole system work. . . . It means that, just as you want libraries, and you want schools, and you want fire departments and police departments, you also want businesses to help do something about unsolved social problems.[6]

Occasionally, it is argued that true social responsibility does not exist. Organizations do not operate out of social responsibility—but good business. Many instances of activities which could be referred to as "responsible" are public relations strategies which are sound business; it pays to advertise. Truly philanthropic efforts occur without fanfare. Some argue that only when organizations anonymously contribute their executives and other resources to socially responsible programs do you have true responsiveness. Perhaps. But we choose not to define social responsibility as philanthropy. We have no objection to enlightened self-interest.

Assuming that society is not totally victimized by actions justified under the banner of social responsibility, then corporations, even pursuing their interests, present a win-win situation. If restoring land to its natural state after mining is *only* done because it is good business, fine. Society benefits. The same can be said for many, if not most, socially responsible behaviors by organizations. We are less concerned with *why* it is done than with the fact that it *is* done. We think it can be best done legally and responsibly.

---

[6] Irving S. Shapiro, "Today's Executive: Private Steward and Public Servant," *Harvard Business Review*, 1978, p. 101.